Python Cookbook

Python Cookbook

Edited by Alex Martelli and David Ascher

O'REILLY®

Beijing · Cambridge · Farnham · Köln · Paris · Sebastopol · Taipei · Tokyo

Python Cookbook
Edited by Alex Martelli and David Ascher

Compilation copyright © 2002 O'Reilly & Associates, Inc. All rights reserved.
Printed in the United States of America.

Copyright of original recipes is retained by the individual authors.

Published by O'Reilly & Associates, Inc., 1005 Gravenstein Highway North, Sebastopol, CA 95472.

Editors:	Paula Ferguson and Laura Lewin
Production Editor:	Matt Hutchinson
Cover Designer:	Pam Spremulli
Interior Designer:	David Futato

Printing History:

July 2002:	First Edition.

ISBN: 0-596-00167-3   [10/02]
[M]

Table of Contents

Foreword

Forget the jokes about tasty snake dishes, here's the Python Cookbook! Python's famous comedian namesakes would have known exactly what to do with this title: recipes for crunchy frog, spring surprise, and, of course, blancmange (or was that a tennis-playing alien?). The not-quite-so-famous-yet Python programming community has filled in the details a little differently: we like to have fun here as much as the next person, but we're not into killing halibuts, especially not if their first name is Eric.

So what exactly is a Python cookbook? It's a collection of recipes for Python programmers, contributed by Python community members. The original contributions were made through a web site set up by ActiveState, from which a selection was made by editors Alex Martelli and David Ascher. Other Python luminaries such as Fredrik Lundh, Paul Dubois, and Tim Peters were asked to write chapter introductions.

Few cookbooks teach how to cook, and this one is no exception: we assume that you're familiar with programming in Python. But most of these recipes don't require that you be an expert programmer, either, nor an expert in Python (though we've sprinkled a few hard ones throughout just to give the gurus something to watch for). And while these recipes don't teach Python programming basics, most were selected because they teach something—for example, performance tips, advanced techniques, explanations of dark corners of the language, warnings about common pitfalls, and even suggestions that seem to go against accepted wisdom.

Most recipes are short enough for the attention span of the average Python programmer. For easy access, they are grouped into chapters, which contain either recipes for a specific application area, such as network programming or XML, or are about specific programming techniques, such as searching and sorting or object-oriented programming. While there's some logical progression among the chapters and among the recipes in a chapter, we expect that most readers will sample the recipes at random or based on the job at hand (just as you would choose a food recipe based upon your appetite or the contents of your refrigerator).

All in all, the breadth and depth of this collection are impressive. This is a testimony to Python's wide range of application areas, but also to its user community. When I created the first version of Python, more than 12 years ago now, all I wanted was a language that would let me write system-administration scripts in less time. (Oh, and I wanted it to be elegant, too.) I never could have guessed most of the application areas where Python is currently the language of choice for many—and that's not just because the World Wide Web hadn't been invented yet. In many areas, code written by generous Python users is as important as Python's standard library: think of numeric algorithms, databases, and user interfaces, in which the number of third-party choices dwarfs Python's standard-library offerings, despite the language's reputation that it comes with "batteries included."

Python is an evolving language. This cookbook offers some recipes that work only with the latest Python version, and a few that have been made obsolete by recent Python versions. Don't think this means that Python has built-in obsolescence! Usually, these obsolete recipes work fine, and the code that uses them will continue to work in future Python versions. It's just that when you're irked by a roundabout way of expressing a particular idea in code, there's often a better way available in a newer Python version, and we'd like you to know about it. On the other hand, it's sometimes useful to know how to write code that works for several Python versions at once, without explicitly checking version numbers all the time. Some recipes touch upon this topic, as well.

The increase in size of the community has caused some growing pains. Now that the early adopters are already using Python, growth must come from luring more conservative users to the language. This is easy enough, as Python is a very friendly language, but it does present new challenges. For example, as a special case of Murphy's law, anything that can go wrong during the installation process will go wrong for someone, somewhere, and they won't be pleased. The new Python users are often not savvy enough to diagnose and correct problems themselves, so our solution has been to make the installer even more bulletproof than it already was.

The same holds for almost all aspects of the language: from the documentation and the error messages to the runtime's behavior in long-running servers, Python gets more user-testing than I ever bargained for. Of course, we also get more offers to help, so all in all, things are working out very nicely. What this means is that we've had to change some of our habits. You could say that the Python developer community is losing some of its innocence: we're no longer improving Python just for our own sake. Many hundreds of thousands of individual Python users are affected, and an ever-growing number of companies are using or selling software based on Python. For their benefit, we now issue strictly backward-compatible bug-fix releases for Python versions up to 2 years old, which are distinct from the feature-introducing major releases every 6 to 12 months.

Let me end on a different aspect of the community: the Python Software Foundation. After the failed experiments of the Python Software Activity and the Python Consortium, I believe we have finally found the proper legal form for a nonprofit organization focused on Python. Keeping a fairly low profile, the PSF is quietly becoming a safe haven for Python software, where no single individual or organization can hold a monopoly on Python, and where everybody benefits. The PSF, in turn, benefits from the sales of this book: a portion of the royalties goes to the PSF, representing the many Python programmers who contributed one or more recipes to the cookbook project. Long live the Python community!

—Guido van Rossum
Reston, Virginia
April 2002

Preface

This book is not a typical O'Reilly book, written as a cohesive manuscript by one or two authors. Instead, it is a new kind of book—a first, bold attempt at applying some principles of open source development to book authoring. About 200 members of the Python community contributed recipes to this book. In this Preface, we, the editors, want to give you, the reader, some background regarding how this book came about and the processes and people involved, and some thoughts about the implications of this new form.

The Design of the Book

In early 2000, Frank Willison, then Editor-in-Chief of O'Reilly & Associates, Inc., contacted me (David Ascher) to find out if I wanted to write a book. Frank had been the editor for *Learning Python*, which I cowrote with Mark Lutz. Since I had just taken a job at what was then considered a Perl shop (ActiveState), I didn't have the bandwidth necessary to write another book, and plans for the project were gently shelved. Periodically, however, Frank would send me an email or chat with me at a conference regarding some of the book topics we'd discussed. One of Frank's ideas was to create a *Python Cookbook*, based on the concept first used by Tom Christiansen and Nathan Torkington with the *Perl Cookbook*. Frank wanted to replicate the success of the *Perl Cookbook*, but he wanted a broader set of people to provide input. He thought that, much as in a real cookbook, a larger set of authors would provide for a greater range of tastes. The quality, in his vision, would be ensured by the oversight of a technical editor, combined with O'Reilly's editorial review process.

Frank and Dick Hardt, ActiveState's CEO, realized that Frank's goal could be combined with ActiveState's goal of creating a community site for open source programmers, called the ActiveState Programmer's Network (ASPN). ActiveState had a popular web site, with the infrastructure required to host a wide variety of content, but it wasn't in the business of creating original content. ActiveState always felt that the open source communities were the best sources of accurate and up-to-date content, even if sometimes that content was hard to find.

The O'Reilly and ActiveState teams quickly realized that the two goals were aligned and that a joint venture would be the best way to achieve the following key objectives:

- Creating an online repository of Python recipes by Python programmers for Python programmers
- Publishing a book containing the best of those recipes, accompanied by overviews and background material written by key Python figures
- Learning what it would take to create a book with a different authoring model

At the same time, two other activities were happening. First, I and others at ActiveState, including Paul Prescod, were actively looking for "stars" to join ActiveState's development team. One of the candidates being recruited was the famous (but unknown) Alex Martelli. Alex was famous because of his numerous and exhaustive postings on the Python mailing list, where he exhibited an unending patience for explaining Python's subtleties and joys to the increasing audience of Python programmers. He was unknown because he lived in Italy and, since he was a relative newcomer to the Python community, none of the old Python hands had ever met him—their paths had not happened to cross back when Alex lived in the U.S., when he was working for IBM Research and enthusiastically using and promoting other high-level languages.

ActiveState wooed Alex, trying to convince him to move to Vancouver. We came quite close, but his employer put some golden handcuffs on him, and somehow Vancouver's weather couldn't compete with Italy's. Alex stayed in Italy, much to my disappointment. As it happened, Alex was also at that time negotiating with O'Reilly about writing a book. Alex wanted to write a cookbook, but O'Reilly explained that the cookbook was already signed. Later, Alex and O'Reilly signed a contract for *Python in a Nutshell*.

The second ongoing activity was the creation of the Python Software Foundation. For a variety of reasons, best left to discussion over beers at a conference, everyone in the Python community wanted to create a non-profit organization that would be the holder of Python's intellectual property, to ensure that Python would be on a legally strong footing. However, such an organization needed both financial support and buy-in from the Python community to be successful.

Given all these parameters, the various parties agreed to the following plan:

- ActiveState would build an online cookbook, a mechanism by which anyone could submit a recipe (i.e., a snippet of Python code addressing a particular problem, accompanied by a discussion of the recipe, much like a description of why one should use cream of tartar when whipping egg whites). To foster a community of authors and encourage peer review, the web site would also let readers of the recipes suggest changes, ask questions, and so on.

- As part of my ActiveState job, I would edit and ensure the quality of the recipes. (Alex Martelli joined the project as a co-editor as the material was being prepared for publication.)
- O'Reilly would publish the best recipes as the *Python Cookbook*.
- In lieu of author royalties for the recipes, a portion of the proceeds from the book sales would be donated to the Python Software Foundation.

The Implementation of the Book

The online cookbook (at *http://aspn.activestate.com/ASPN/Cookbook/Python/*) was the entry point for the recipes. Users got free accounts, filled in a form, and presto, their recipes became part of the cookbook. Thousands of people read the recipes, and some added comments, and so, in the publishing equivalent of peer review, the recipes matured and grew. (The online cookbook is still very much active and growing.)

Going from the online version to the version you have in front of you was a fairly complex process. The data was first extracted from Zope and converted into XML. We then categorized the recipes and selected those recipes that seemed most valuable, distinctive, and original. Then, it was just a matter of editing the recipes to fit the format of the cookbook, checking the code for correctness (the PyChecker tool deserves special thanks, as it was quite useful in this regard), adding a few recipes here and there for completeness of coverage in some areas, and doing a final copy-editing pass.

It sounds simple when you write it down in one paragraph. Somehow, we don't remember it as quite as being simple as that!

A Note About Licenses

Software licenses are both the curse and the foundation of the open source movement. Every software project needs to make careful, deliberate decisions about what kind of license should be used for the code—who is allowed to use the code, under what conditions, and so on. Given the nature of the cookbook, we wanted the recipes to be usable under any circumstances where Python could be used. In other words, we wanted to ensure completely unfettered use, in the same spirit as the Python license. Unfortunately, the Python license cannot really be used to refer to anything other than Python itself. As a compromise, we chose to use the modified Berkeley license, which is considered among the most liberal of licenses. We contacted each of the recipe authors and confirmed that they agreed to publish these recipes under said license. The license template reads (substitute `<OWNER>` and `<ORGANIZATION>` with the author of each recipe):

```
Copyright (c) 2001, <OWNER>
All rights reserved.
Redistribution and use in source and binary forms, with or without
modification, are permitted provided that the following conditions
are met:
    * Redistributions of source code must retain the above copyright
      notice, this list of conditions and the following disclaimer.
    * Redistributions in binary form must reproduce the above
      copyright notice, this list of conditions and the following
      disclaimer in the documentation and/or other materials provided
      with the distribution.
    * Neither the name of the <ORGANIZATION> nor the names of its
      contributors may be used to endorse or promote products derived
      from this software without specific prior written permission.
THIS SOFTWARE IS PROVIDED BY THE COPYRIGHT HOLDERS AND CONTRIBUTORS
"AS IS" AND ANY EXPRESS OR IMPLIED WARRANTIES, INCLUDING, BUT NOT
LIMITED TO, THE IMPLIED WARRANTIES OF MERCHANTABILITY AND FITNESS
FOR A PARTICULAR PURPOSE ARE DISCLAIMED. IN NO EVENT SHALL THE REGENTS
OR CONTRIBUTORS BE LIABLE FOR ANY DIRECT, INDIRECT, INCIDENTAL, SPECIAL,
EXEMPLARY, OR CONSEQUENTIAL DAMAGES (INCLUDING, BUT NOT LIMITED TO,
PROCUREMENT OF SUBSTITUTE GOODS OR SERVICES; LOSS OF USE, DATA, OR PROFITS;
OR BUSINESS INTERRUPTION) HOWEVER CAUSED AND ON ANY THEORY OF LIABILITY,
WHETHER IN CONTRACT, STRICT LIABILITY, OR TORT (INCLUDING NEGLIGENCE OR
OTHERWISE) ARISING IN ANY WAY OUT OF THE USE OF THIS SOFTWARE, EVEN IF
ADVISED OF THE POSSIBILITY OF SUCH DAMAGE.
```

Audience

We expect that you know at least some Python. This book does not attempt to teach Python as a whole; rather, it presents some specific techniques (or tricks) for dealing with particular tasks. If you are looking for an introduction to Python, consider some of the books described in the "Further Reading" section of this Preface. However, you don't need to know a lot of Python to find this book helpful. Furthermore, somewhat to the editors' surprise, even if you do know a lot about Python, you might very well learn a few things—we did!

Organization

This book has 17 chapters, each of which is devoted to a particular kind of recipe, such as algorithms, text processing, or databases. Each chapter contains an introduction, written by an expert in the field, followed by recipes selected from the online cookbook (or, in some cases, specially added) and edited to fit the book's formatting and style requirements. Alex Martelli did the vast majority of the editing, with some help from David Ascher. This editing proved to be quite a challenge, as the original recipes varied widely in their organization and level of sophistication. Also, with about 200 authors involved, there were about 200 different "voices" in the text. We tried to maintain this variety of styles, given the collaborative nature of this book. However, each recipe was edited, sometimes considerably, to make it as accessible and useful as possible, with enough uniformity in structure and presention to maximize the usability of the book as a whole.

Chapter 1, Python Shortcuts, introduction by David Ascher

This chapter includes recipes for many common techniques that don't really fit into any of the other, more specific recipe categories.

David Ascher is a co-editor of this volume. David's background spans physics, vision research, scientific visualization, computer graphics, a variety of programming languages, co-authoring *Learning Python* (O'Reilly), teaching Python, and, these days, a slew of technical and nontechnical tasks such as architecting developer tools and managing a team of programmers. David also gets roped into organizing Python conferences on a regular basis.

Chapter 2, Searching and Sorting, introduction by Tim Peters

This chapter covers techniques for searching and sorting in Python. Many of the recipes explore creative uses of list.sort in conjunction with the decorate-sort-undecorate (DSU) pattern.

Tim Peters, also known as *the tim-bot*, is one of the mythological figures of the Python world. He is the oracle, channeling Guido van Rossum when Guido is busy, channeling the IEEE-754 floating-point committee when anyone asks anything remotely relevant, and appearing conservative while pushing for a constant evolution in the language. Tim is a member of the PythonLabs team led by Guido.

Chapter 3, Text, introduction by Fred L. Drake, Jr.

This chapter contains recipes for manipulating text in a variety of ways, including combining, filtering, and validating strings, as well as evaluating Python code inside textual data.

Fred Drake is yet another member of the PythonLabs group, working with Guido daily on Python development. A father of three, Fred is best known in the Python community for single-handedly maintaining the official documentation. Fred is a co-author of *Python & XML* (O'Reilly).

Chapter 4, Files, introduction by Mark Lutz

This chapter presents techniques for working with data in files and for manipulating files and directories within the filesystem.

Mark Lutz is well known to most Python users as the most prolific author of Python books, including *Programming Python*, *Python Pocket Reference*, and *Learning Python*, which he co-authored with David Ascher (all from O'Reilly).

Mark is also a leading Python trainer, spreading the Python gospel throughout the world.

Chapter 5, Object-Oriented Programming, introduction by Alex Martelli

This chapter offers a wide range of recipes that demonstrate the power of object-oriented programming with Python, from basic techniques such as overriding methods to advanced implementations of various design patterns.

Alex Martelli, also known as *the martelli-bot*, is a co-editor of this volume. After almost a decade with IBM Research, then a bit more than that with think3, Alex now works for AB Strakt, a Swedish Python-centered firm that develops exciting new technologies for real-time workflow and groupware applications. He also edits and writes Python articles and books, including the forthcoming *Python in a Nutshell* (O'Reilly) and, occasionally, research works on the game of contract bridge.

Chapter 6, Threads, Processes, and Synchronization, introduction by Greg Wilson

This chapter covers a variety of techniques for working with threads in Python.

Dr. Greg Wilson is an author of children's books. Oh, he's also an author of books on parallel programming, a contributing editor with *Doctor Dobb's Journal*, an expert on scientific computing, and a Canadian. Greg provided a significant boost to the Python community as coordinator of the Software Carpentry project, and he currently works for Baltimore Technologies.

Chapter 7, System Administration, introduction by Donn Cave

This chapter includes recipes for a number of common system administration tasks, such as generating passwords and interacting with the Windows registry.

Donn Cave is a Software Engineer at the University of Washington's central computer site. Over the years, Donn has proven to be a fount of information on *comp.lang.python* on all matters related to system calls, Unix, system administration, files, signals, and the like.

Chapter 8, Databases and Persistence, introduction by Aaron Watters

This chapter presents techniques for interacting with databases and maintaining persistence in Python.

Aaron Watters was one of the earliest advocates of Python and is an expert in databases. He's known for having been the lead author on the first book on Python (*Internet Programming with Python* (M&T Books), now out of print), and he has authored many widely used Python extensions, such as kjBuckets and kwParsing. Aaron currently works for ReportLab, a Python-based startup based in England and the U.S.

Chapter 9, User Interfaces, introduction by Fredrik Lundh

This chapter contains recipes for common GUI tasks and includes techniques for working with Tkinter, wxPython, GTk, and Qt.

Fredrik Lundh, also known as the *eff-bot*, is the CTO of Secret Labs AB, a Swedish Python-focused company providing a variety of products and technologies, including the PythonWorks Pro IDE. Fredrik is the world's leading expert on Tkinter, the most popular GUI toolkit for Python, as well as the main author of the Python Imaging Library (PIL). He is also the author of *Python Standard Library* (O'Reilly) (a good complement to this volume), which focuses on the modules in the standard Python library. Finally, he is a prolific contributor to *comp.lang.python*, helping novices and experts alike.

Chapter 10, Network Programming, introduction by Guido van Rossum

This chapter covers a variety of network programming techniques, from writing basic TCP clients and servers to manipulating MIME messages.

Guido created Python, nurtured it throughout its infancy, and is shepherding its growth. Need we say more?

Chapter 11, Web Programming, introduction by Andy McKay

This chapter presents a variety of web-related recipes, including ones for CGI scripting, running a Java servlet with Jython, and accessing the content of web pages.

Andy McKay was ActiveState's web guru and is currently employed by Merlin Technologies. In the last two years, Andy went from being a happy Perl user to a fanatical Python and Zope expert. He is professionally responsible for several very complex and high-bandwidth Zope sites, and he runs the popular Zope discussion site, *http://www.zopezen.org*.

Chapter 12, Processing XML, introduction by Paul Prescod

This chapter offers techniques for parsing, processing, and generating XML using a variety of Python tools.

Paul Prescod is an expert in three technologies: Python, which he need not justify; XML, which makes sense in a pragmatic world (Paul is co-author of the *XML Handbook*, with Charles Goldfarb, published by Prentice Hall); and Unicode, which somehow must address some deep-seated desire for pain and confusion that neither of the other two technologies satisfies. Paul is currently an independent consultant and trainer, although some Perl folks would challenge his independence based on his track record as, shall we say, a fairly vocal Python advocate.

Chapter 13, Distributed Programming, introduction by Jeremy Hylton

This chapter provides recipes for using Python in simple distributed systems, including XML-RPC, SOAP, and CORBA.

Jeremy Hylton works for Zope Corporation as a member of the PythonLabs group. In addition to his new twins, Jeremy's interests including programming-language theory, parsers, and the like. As part of his work for CNRI, Jeremy worked on a variety of distributed systems.

Chapter 14, Debugging and Testing, introduction by Mark Hammond

This chapter includes a collection of recipes that assist with the debugging and testing process, from customized error logging to traceback information to debugging the garbage collection process.

Mark Hammond is best known for his work supporting Python on the Windows platform. With Greg Stein, he built an incredible library of modules interfacing Python to a wide variety of APIs, libraries, and component models such as COM. He is also an expert designer and builder of developer tools, most notably Pythonwin and Komodo. Finally, Mark is an expert at debugging even the most messy systems—during Komodo development, for example, Mark was often called upon to debug problems that spanned three languages (Python, C++, JavaScript), multiple threads, and multiple processes. Mark is also co-author of *Python Programming on Win32* (O'Reilly), with Andy Robinson.

Chapter 15, Programs About Programs, introduction by Paul F. Dubois

This chapter contains Python techniques that involve parsing, lexing, program introspection, and other program-related tasks.

Paul Dubois has been working at the Lawrence Livermore National Laboratory for many years, building software systems for scientists working on everything from nuclear simulations to climate modeling. He has considerable experience with a wide range of scientific computing problems, as well as experience with language design and advanced object-oriented programming techniques.

Chapter 16, Extending and Embedding, introduction by David Beazley

This chapter offers techniques for extending Python and recipes that assist in the development of extensions.

David Beazley's chief claim to fame is SWIG, an amazingly powerful hack that lets one quickly wrap C and other libraries and use them from Python, Tcl, Perl, and myriad other languages. Behind this seemingly language-neutral tool lies a Python supporter of the first order, as evidenced by his book, *Python Essential Reference* (New Riders). David Beazley is a fairly sick man (in a good way), leading us to believe that more scarily useful tools are likely to emerge from his brain. He's currently inflicting his sense of humor on computer science students at the University of Chicago.

Chapter 17, Algorithms, introduction by Tim Peters

This chapter provides a collection of useful algorithms implemented in Python.

See the discussion of Chapter 2 for information about Tim Peters.

Further Reading

There are many texts available to help you learn Python or refine your Python knowledge, from introductory texts all the way to quite formal language descriptions.

We recommend the following books for general information about Python:

- *Learning Python*, by Mark Lutz and David Ascher (O'Reilly), is a thorough introduction to the fundamentals of the Python language.
- *Python Standard Library*, by Fredrik Lundh (O'Reilly), provides a use case for each module in the rich library that comes with every standard Python distribution.
- *Programming Python*, by Mark Lutz (O'Reilly), is a thorough rundown of Python programming techniques.
- The forthcoming *Python in a Nutshell*, by Alex Martelli (O'Reilly), is a comprehensive quick reference to the Python language and the key libraries used by most Python programmers.
- *Python Essential Reference*, by David Beazley (New Riders), is a quick reference that focuses on the Python language and the core Python libraries.

In addition, there are a few more special-purpose books that help you explore particular aspects of Python programming:

- *Python & XML*, by Christopher A. Jones and Fred L. Drake, Jr. (O'Reilly), covers everything there is to know about how to use Python to read, process, and transform XML.
- *Jython Essentials*, by Samuele Pedroni and Noel Rappin (O'Reilly), is the authoritative book on Jython, the port of Python to the Java Virtual Machine (JVM).
- *Python Web Programming*, by Steve Holden (New Riders), covers building networked systems using Python.

In addition to these books, there are other important sources of information that can help explain some of the code in the recipes in this book. We've pointed out the information that seemed particularly relevant in the "See Also" sections of each recipe. In these sections, we often refer to the standard Python documentation: the *Library Reference*, the *Reference Manual*, and occasionally the *Tutorial*. This documentation is available in a variety of media:

- On the *python.org* web site (at *http://www.python.org/doc/*), which always contains the most up-to-date, if sometimes dry, description of the language.
- In Python itself. Recent versions of Python boast a nice online help system, which is worth exploring if you've never used it. Just type help( ) at the interactive prompt to start exploring.
- As part of the online help in your Python installation. ActivePython's installer, for example, includes a searchable Windows Help file. The standard Python distribution currently includes HTML pages, but there are plans to include a similar Windows Help file in future releases.

Note that we have not included section numbers in our references to the standard Python documentation, since the organization of these manuals can change from release to release. You should be able to use the table of contents and indexes to find the relevant material.

Conventions Used in This Book

The following typographical conventions are used throughout this book:

Italic

Used for commands, URLs, filenames, file extensions, directory or folder names, emphasis, and new terms where they are defined.

`Constant width`

Used for all code listings and to designate anything that would appear literally in a Python or C program. This includes module names, method names, class names, function names, statements, and HTML tags.

`Constant width italic`

Used for general placeholders that indicate that an item should be replaced by some actual value in your own program.

`Constant width bold`

Used to emphasize particular lines within code listings and show output that is produced.

How to Contact Us

We have tested and verified all the information in this book to the best of our abilities, but you may find that features have changed or that we have let errors slip through the production of the book. Please let us know of any errors that you find, as well as suggestions for future editions, by writing to:

> O'Reilly & Associates, Inc.
> 1005 Gravenstein Highway North
> Sebastopol, CA 95472
> (800) 998-9938 (in the United States or Canada)
> (707) 829-0515 (international/local)
> (707) 829-0104 (fax)

We have a web site for the book, where we'll list examples, errata, and any plans for future editions. You can access this page at:

> *http://www.oreilly.com/catalog/python_cookbook/*

To ask technical questions or comment on the book, send email to:

> *bookquestions@oreilly.com*

For more information about our books, conferences, Resource Centers, and the O'Reilly Network, see our web site at:

http://www.oreilly.com/

The online cookbook from which most of the recipes for this book were taken is available at:

http://aspn.activestate.com/ASPN/Cookbook/Python

Acknowledgments

Most publications, from mysteries to scientific papers to computer books, claim that the work being published would not have been possible without the collaboration of many others, typically including local forensic scientists, colleagues, and children, respectively. This book makes this claim to an extreme degree. Most of the words, code, and ideas in this volume were contributed by people not listed on the front cover. The original recipe authors, readers who submitted comments to the web site, and the authors of the chapter introductions are the true authors of the book, and they deserve the credit.

David Ascher

The online cookbook was the product of Andy McKay's constant and diligent effort. Andy was ActiveState's key Zope developer during the online data-collection phase of this project, and one of the key developers behind ASPN (*http://aspn.activestate. com*), ActiveState's content site, which serves a wide variety of information for and by programmers of open source languages such as Python, Perl, PHP, Tcl, and XSLT. Andy McKay used to be a Perl developer, by the way. At about the same time that I started at ActiveState, the company decided to use Zope to build what would become ASPN. In the years that followed, Andy has become a Zope master and somewhat of a Python fanatic (without any advocacy from me!). Based on an original design by myself and Diane Mueller, also of ActiveState, Andy single-handedly implemented ASPN in record time, then proceeded to adjust it to ever-changing requirements for new features that we hadn't anticipated in the early design phase, staying cheerful and professional throughout. It's a pleasure to have him as the author of the introduction to the chapter on web recipes.

Paul Prescod, then also of ActiveState, was a kindred spirit throughout the project, helping with the online editorial process, suggesting changes, and encouraging readers of *comp.lang.python* to visit the web site and submit recipes. Paul also helped with some of his considerable XML knowledge when it came to figuring out how to take the data out of Zope and get it ready for the publication process.

The last activator I'd like to thank, for two different reasons, is Dick Hardt, founder and CEO of ActiveState. The first is that Dick agreed to let me work on the cookbook as part of my job. Had he not, I wouldn't have been able to participate in it. The second reason I'd like to thank Dick is for suggesting at the outset that a share of the book royalties go to the Python Software Foundation. This decision not only made it easier to enlist Python users into becoming contributors but will also hopefully result in at least some long-term revenue to an organization that I believe needs and deserves financial support. All Python users will benefit.

Translating the original recipes into the versions you will see here was a more complex process than any of us understood at the onset. First, the whole community of readers of the online cookbook reviewed and submitted comments on recipes, which in some cases helped turn rough recipes into useful and polished code samples. Even with those comments, however, a great deal of editing had to be done to turn the raw data into publishable material. While this was originally my assignment, my work schedule made that process painfully slow. Luckily, a secret weapon was waiting in the wings. My opinion of Alex Martelli had only gone up since the beginning of the project, as Alex's numerous submissions to the online cookbook were always among the most complete, thorough, and well-liked recipes. At that point, I felt as editor that I owed Alex dinner. So, naturally, when help was needed to edit the recipes into a book, I called upon Alex. Alex not only agreed to help, but did so heroically. He categorized, filtered, edited, and corrected all of the material, incorporating the substance of the comments from readers into coherent recipes and discussions, and he added a few recipes where they were needed for completeness. What is more, he did all of this cheerfully and enthusiastically. At this point, I feel I owe Alex breakfast, lunch, and dinner for a week.

Finally, I'd like to thank the O'Reilly editors who have had a big hand in shaping the cookbook. Laura Lewin was the original editor, and she helped make sure that the project moved along, securing and coordinating the contributions of the introduction authors. Paula Ferguson then took the baton, provided a huge amount of precious feedback, and copyedited the final manuscript, ensuring that the prose was as readable as possible given the multiplicity of voices in the book. Laura's, and then Paula's, constant presence was essential to keeping me on the ball, even though I suspect it was sometimes like dentistry. As we come to the end of the project, I can't help but remember Laura's mentor, O'Reilly's Editor-in-Chief, Frank Willison. Frank died suddenly on a black day, July 30, 2001. He was the person who most wanted to see this book happen, for the simple reason that he believed the Python community deserved it. Frank was always willing to explore new ideas, and he was generous to a fault. The idea of a book with over a hundred authors would have terrified most editors. Frank saw it as a challenge and an experiment. I miss Frank.

Alex Martelli

I first met Python thanks to the gentle insistence of a former colleague, Alessandro Bottoni. He kept courteously repeating that I really should give Python a try, in spite of my claims that I already knew more programming languages than I knew what to do with. If I hadn't trusted his technical and aesthetic judgment enough to invest the needed time and energy on his suggestion, I most definitely wouldn't be writing and editing Python books today. Thanks for your well-placed stubbornness, Alessandro!

Of course, once I tasted Python, I was irretrievably hooked—my lifelong taste for high-level ("scripting") languages at last congealed into one superb synthesis. Here, at long last, was a language with the syntactic ease of Rexx (and then some), the semantic simplicity of Tcl (and then some), and the awesome power of Perl (and then some). How could I resist? Still, I do owe a debt to Mike Cowlishaw (inventor of Rexx), who I had the pleasure of having as a colleague when I worked for IBM, for first getting me hooked on scripting. I must also thank John Ousterhout and Larry Wall, the inventors of Tcl and Perl, respectively, for later reinforcing my addiction through their brainchildren.

Greg Wilson first introduced me to O'Reilly, so he must get his share of thanks, too—and I'm overjoyed at having him as one of the introduction authors. I am also grateful to David Ascher and Laura Lewin, for signing me up as co-editor of this book (which of course delayed *Python in a Nutshell*, which I'm also writing—double thanks to Laura for agreeing to let the nutshell's schedule slip!). Finally, Paula Ferguson's copious and excellent feedback steered the final stages of editing in a superb way—more thanks!

And so, thanks to the good offices of all these people, I was at last faced with the task of editing this book, to O'Reilly levels of quality, and *fast*. Could I do it? Not without an impressive array of technology. I don't know the names of all the people I should thank for the Internet, ADSL, the Google search engine, and the Opera browser, which, together, let me look things up so easily—or for many of the other hardware and software technologies cooperating to amplify my productivity. But, I do know I couldn't have made it without Theo de Raadt's OpenBSD operating system, Bram Moolenar's VIM editor, and, of course, Guido van Rossum's Python language... so, I'll single out Theo, Bram, and Guido for special thanks!

But equally, I couldn't have made it without the patience and support of all my friends and family, who for so long saw me only rarely, and then with bleary eyes, muttering about recipes and cookbooks. Special thanks and love for this to my girl-friend Marina, my children Lucio and Flavia, and my sister Elisabetta. But my father Lanfranco deserves a super-special mention, because, in addition to all this, he was also always around to brew excellent espresso, indispensable for keeping me awake and alert. Besides, how else did I learn to work hard and relentlessly, never sparing either energy or effort, except from his lifelong example? So, *thanks*, Dad!

## CHAPTER 1

Python Shortcuts

1.0   Introduction

Credit: David Ascher, ActiveState, co-author of Learning Python (O'Reilly)

Programming languages are like natural languages. Each has a set of qualities that polyglots generally agree on as characteristics of the language. Russian and French are often admired for their lyricism, while English is more often cited for its precision and dynamism: unlike the Académie-defined French language, the English language routinely grows words to suit its speakers' needs, such as "carjacking," "earwitness," "snail mail," "email," "googlewhacking," and "blogging." In the world of computer languages, Perl is well known for its many degrees of freedom: TMTOWTDI (There's More Than One Way To Do It) is one of the mantras of the Perl programmer. Conciseness is also seen as a strong virtue in the Perl and APL communities. In contrast, as you'll see in many of the discussions of recipes throughout this volume, Python programmers often express their belief in the value of clarity and elegance. As a well-known Perl hacker once said, Python's prettier, but Perl is more fun. I agree with him that Python does have a strong (as in well-defined) aesthetic, while Perl has more of a sense of humor. I still have more fun coding in Python, though.

The reason I bring up these seemingly irrelevant bits at the beginning of this book is that the recipes you see in this first chapter are directly related to Python's aesthetic and social dynamics. In most of the recipes in this chapter, the author presents a single elegant language feature, but one that he feels is underappreciated. Much like I, a proud resident of Vancouver, will go out of my way to show tourists the really neat things about the city, from the parks to the beaches to the mountains, a Python user will seek out friends and colleagues and say, "You gotta see this!" Programming in Python, in my mind, is a shared social pleasure, not all that competitive. There's great pleasure in learning a new feature and appreciating its design, elegance, and judicious use, and there's a twin pleasure in teaching another or another thousand about that feature.

When we identified the recipe categories for this collection, our driving notion was that there would be recipes of various kinds, each aiming to achieve something specific—a souffle recipe, a tart recipe, an osso buco recipe. Those would naturally bunch into fairly typical categories, such as desserts, appetizers, and meat dishes, or their perhaps less appetizing, nonmetaphorical equivalents, such as files, algorithms, and so on. So we picked a list of categories, added the categories to the Zope site used to collect recipes, and opened the floodgates.

Pretty soon, it became clear that some submissions were really hard to fit into the predetermined categories. These recipes are the Pythonic equivalent of making a roux (melted butter or fat combined with flour, used in sauce-making, for those of you without an Italian sauce background), kneading dough, flouring, flipping a pan's contents, blanching, and the myriad other tricks that any accomplished cook knows, but that you won't find in any "straight" recipe book. Many of these tricks and techniques are used in preparing various kinds of meals, but it's hard to pigeonhole them as relevant for a given type of dish. And if you're a novice cook looking up a fancy recipe, you're likely to get frustrated quickly, as these techniques are typically found only in books like *Cooking for Divorced Middle-Aged Men*. We didn't want to exclude this precious category from this book, so a new category was born. That explains why this chapter exists.

This chapter is pretty flimsy, though, in that while the title refers to shortcuts, there is nothing here like what one could have expected had the language in question been Python's venerable cousin, Perl. If this had been a community-authored Perl cookbook, entries in this category would probably have outnumbered those in most other chapters. That is because Perl's syntax provides, proudly, many ways to do pretty much anything. Furthermore, each way is "tricky" in a good way: the writer gets a little thrill out of exploiting an odd corner of the language. That chapter would be impressive, and competitive, and fun. Python programmers just don't get to have that kind of fun on that kind of scale (by which I mean the scale of syntactic shortcuts and semantic-edge cases). No one gives multi-hour talks about tricks of the Python grand masters... Python grand masters simply don't have that many frequently used tricks up their sleeves!

I believe that the recipes in this chapter are among the most time-sensitive of the recipes in this volume. That's because the aspects of the language that people consider shortcuts or noteworthy techniques seem to be relatively straightforward, idiomatic applications of recent language features. List comprehensions, `zip`, and dictionary methods such as `setdefault` are all relatively recent additions to the language, dating from Python 2.0 or later. In fact, many of these newish language features were added to Python to eliminate the need for what used to be fancy recipes.

My favorite recent language features are list comprehensions and the new applicability of the * and ** tokens to function calls as well as to function definitions. List comprehensions have clearly become wildly successful, if the authors of this volume are representative of the Python community at large, and have largely demoted the `map` and `filter` built-in functions. Less powerful, but equally elegant, are * and **. Since Python 2.0, the oft-quoted recipe:

```python
def method(self, argument, *args, **kw):
    # Do something with argument
    apply(callable, args, kw)
```

can now be done much more elegantly as:

```python
def method(self, argument, *args, **kw):
    # Do something with argument
    callable(*args, **kw)
```

The apply built-in function is still somewhat useful, at least occasionally, but these new syntactic forms are elegant and provably Pythonic. This leads me to my closing comment on language shortcuts: the best source of shortcuts and language tricks is probably the list of language changes that comes with each Python release. Special thanks should be extended to Andrew Kuchling for publishing a list of "What's new with Python 2.x," available at *http://amk.ca/python/*, for each major release since 2.0. It's the place I head for when I want a clear and concise view of Python's recent evolution.

1.1 Swapping Values Without Using a Temporary Variable

Credit: Hamish Lawson

Problem

You want to swap the values of some variables, but you don't want to use a temporary variable.

Solution

Python's automatic tuple packing and unpacking make this a snap:

```python
a, b, c = b, c, a
```

Discussion

Most programming languages make you use temporary intermediate variables to swap variable values:

```python
temp = a
a = b
b = c
c = temp
```

But Python lets you use tuple packing and unpacking to do a direct assignment:

```python
a, b, c = b, c, a
```

In an assignment, Python requires an expression on the righthand side of the =. What we wrote there—b, c, a—is indeed an expression. Specifically, it is a *tuple*, which is an immutable sequence of three values. Tuples are often surrounded with parentheses, as in (b, c, a), but the parentheses are not necessary, except where the commas would otherwise have some other meaning (e.g., in a function call). The commas are what create a tuple, by *packing* the values that are the tuple's items.

On the lefthand side of the = in an assignment statement, you normally use a single *target*. The target can be a simple identifier (also known as a variable), an indexing (such as alist[i] or adict['freep']), an attribute reference (such as anobject.someattribute), and so on. However, Python also lets you use several targets (variables, indexings, etc.), separated by commas, on an assignment's lefthand side. Such a multiple assignment is also called an *unpacking* assignment. When there are two or more comma-separated targets on the lefthand side of an assignment, the value of the righthand side must be a sequence of as many items as there are comma-separated targets on the lefthand side. Each item of the sequence is assigned to the corresponding target, in order, from left to right.

In this recipe, we have three comma-separated targets on the lefthand side, so we need a three-item sequence on the righthand side, the three-item tuple that the packing built. The first target (variable a) gets the value of the first item (which used to be the value of variable b), the second target (b) gets the value of the second item (which used to be the value of c), and the third and last target (c) gets the value of the third and last item (which used to be the value of a). The net result is a swapping of values between the variables (equivalently, you could visualize this particular example as a rotation).

Tuple packing, done using commas, and sequence unpacking, done by placing several comma-separated targets on the lefthand side of a statement, are both useful, simple, general mechanisms. By combining them, you can simply, elegantly, and naturally express any permutation of values among a set of variables.

See Also

The *Reference Manual* section on assignment statements.

1.2 Constructing a Dictionary Without Excessive Quoting

Credit: Brent Burley

Problem

You'd like to construct a dictionary without having to quote the keys.

Solution

Once you get into the swing of Python, you may find yourself constructing a lot of dictionaries. However, the standard way, also known as a *dictionary display*, is just a smidgeon more cluttered than you might like, due to the need to quote the keys. For example:

```
data = { 'red' : 1, 'green' : 2, 'blue' : 3 }
```

When the keys are identifiers, there's a cleaner way:

```
def makedict(**kwargs):
    return kwargs
data = makedict(red=1, green=2, blue=3)
```

You might also choose to forego some simplicity to gain more power. For example:

```
def dodict(*args, **kwds):
    d = {}
    for k, v in args: d[k] = v
    d.update(kwds)
    return d
tada = dodict(*data.items( ), yellow=2, green=4)
```

Discussion

The syntax for constructing a dictionary can be slightly tedious, due to the amount of quoting required. This recipe presents a technique that avoids having to quote the keys, when they are identifiers that you already know at the time you write the code.

I've often found myself missing Perl's => operator, which is well suited to building hashes (Perl-speak for dictionaries) from a literal list:

```
%data = (red => 1, green => 2, blue => 3);
```

The => operator in Perl is equivalent to Perl's own ,, except that it implicitly quotes the word to its left.

Perl's syntax is very similar to Python's function-calling syntax for passing keyword arguments. And the fact that Python collects the keyword arguments into a dictionary turned on a light bulb in my head.

When you declare a function in Python, you may optionally conclude the list of formal arguments with *args* or **kwds* (if you want to use both, the one with ** must be last). If you have *args*, your function can be called with any number of extra actual arguments of the positional, or plain, kind. Python collects all the extra positional arguments into a tuple and binds that tuple to the identifier *args*. Similarly, if you have **kwds*, your function can be called with any number of extra actual arguments of the named, or keyword, kind. Python collects all the extra named arguments into a dictionary (with the names as the keys and the values as the values) and binds that dictionary to the identifier *kwds*. This recipe exploits the way that Python knows how to perform the latter task.

The makedict function should be very efficient, since the compiler is doing work equivalent to that done with a dictionary literal. It is admittedly idiomatic, but it can make large dictionary literals a lot cleaner and a lot less painful to type. When you need to construct dictionaries from a list of key/item pairs, possibly with explicit override of, or addition to, some specifically named key, the dodict function (although less crystal-clear and speedy) can be just as handy. In Python 2.2, the first two lines of dodict can be replaced with the more concise and faster equivalent:

```
d = dict(args)
```

See Also

The *Library Reference* section on mapping types.

1.3   Getting a Value from a Dictionary

Credit: Andy McKay

Problem

You need to obtain a value from a dictionary, without having to handle an exception if the key you seek is not in the dictionary.

Solution

That's what the get method of dictionaries is for. Say you have a dictionary:

```
d = {'key':'value'}
```

You can write a test to pull out the value of 'key' from d in an exception-safe way:

```
if d.has_key('key'):       # or, in Python 2.2 or later: if 'key' in d:
  print d['key']
else:
  print 'not found'
```

However, there is a much simpler syntax:

```
print d.get('key', 'not found')
```

Discussion

Want to get a value from a dictionary but first make sure that the value exists in the dictionary? Use the simple and useful get method.

If you try to get a value with a syntax such as d[x], and the value of x is not a key in dictionary d, your attempt raises a KeyError exception. This is often okay. If you expected the value of x to be a key in d, an exception is just the right way to inform you that you're wrong (i.e., that you need to debug your program).

However, you often need to be more tentative about it: as far as you know, the value of x may or may not be a key in d. In this case, don't start messing with the has_key method or with try/except statements. Instead, use the get method. If you call d.get(x), no exception is thrown: you get d[x] if x is a key in d, and if it's not, you get None (which you can check for or propagate). If None is not what you want to get when x is not a key of d, call d.get(x, *somethingelse*) instead. In this case, if x is not a key, you will get the value of *somethingelse*.

get is a simple, useful mechanism that is well explained in the Python documentation, but a surprising number of people don't know about it. This idiom is also quite common in Zope, for example, when pulling variables out of the REQUEST dictionary.

See Also

The *Library Reference* section on mapping types.

1.4   Adding an Entry to a Dictionary

Credit: Alex Martelli

Problem

Working with a dictionary D, you need to use the entry D[k] if it's already present, or add a new D[k] if k isn't yet a key in D.

Solution

This is what the setdefault method of dictionary objects is for. Say we're building a word-to-page numbers index. A key piece of code might be:

```
theIndex = {}
def addword(word, pagenumber):
    if theIndex.has_key(word):
        theIndex[word].append(pagenumber)
    else:
        theIndex[word] = [pagenumber]
```

Good Pythonic instincts suggest substituting this "look before you leap" pattern with an "easier to get permission" pattern (see Recipe 5.3 for a detailed discussion of these phrases):

```
def addword(word, pagenumber):
    try: theIndex[word].append(pagenumber)
    except AttributeError: theIndex[word] = [pagenumber]
```

This is just a minor simplification, but it satisfies the pattern of "use the entry if it is already present; otherwise, add a new entry." Here's how using setdefault simplifies this further:

```
def addword(word, pagenumber):
    theIndex.setdefault(word, []).append(pagenumber)
```

Discussion

The setdefault method of a dictionary is a handy shortcut for this task that is especially useful when the new entry you want to add is mutable. Basically, dict.setdefault(k, v) is much like dict.get(k, v), except that if k is not a key in the dictionary, the setdefault method assigns dict[k]=v as a side effect, in addition to returning v. (get would just return v, without affecting dict in any way.) Therefore, setdefault is appropriate any time you have get-like needs but also want to produce this specific side effect on the dictionary.

setdefault is particularly useful in a dictionary with values that are lists, as detailed in Recipe 1.5. The single most typical usage form for setdefault is:

```
somedict.setdefault(somekey, []).append(somevalue)
```

Note that setdefault is normally not very useful if the values are immutable. If you just want to count words, for example, something like the following is no use:

```
theIndex.setdefault(word, 1)
```

In this case, you want:

```
theIndex[word] = 1 + theIndex.get(word, 0)
```

since you will be rebinding the dictionary entry at theIndex[word] anyway (because numbers are immutable).

See Also

Recipe 5.3; the *Library Reference* section on mapping types.

1.5 Associating Multiple Values with Each Key in a Dictionary

Credit: Michael Chermside

Problem

You need a dictionary that maps each key to multiple values.

Solution

By nature, a dictionary is a one-to-one mapping, but it's not hard to make it one-to-many—in other words, to make one key map to multiple values. There are two possible approaches, depending on how you want to treat duplications in the set of values for a key. The following approach allows such duplications:

```
d1 = {}
d1.setdefault(key, []).append(value)
```

while this approach automatically eliminates duplications:

```
d2 = {}
d2.setdefault(key, {})[value] = 1
```

Discussion

A normal dictionary performs a simple mapping of a key to a value. This recipe shows two easy, efficient ways to achieve a mapping of each key to multiple values. The semantics of the two approaches differ slightly but importantly in how they deal with duplication. Each approach relies on the setdefault method of a dictionary to initialize the entry for a key in the dictionary, if needed, and in any case to return said entry.

Of course, you need to be able to do more than just add values for a key. With the first approach, which allows duplications, here's how to retrieve the list of values for a key:

```
list_of_values = d1[key]
```

Here's how to remove one value for a key, if you don't mind leaving empty lists as items of d1 when the last value for a key is removed:

```
d1[key].remove(value)
```

Despite the empty lists, it's still easy to test for the existence of a key with at least one value:

```
def has_key_with_some_values(d, key):
    return d.has_key(key) and d[key]
```

This returns either 0 or a list, which may be empty. In most cases, it is easier to use a function that always returns a list (maybe an empty one), such as:

```
def get_values_if_any(d, key):
    return d.get(key, [])
```

You can use either of these functions in a statement. For example:

```
if get_values_if_any(d1, somekey):
if has_key_with_some_values(d1, somekey):
```

However, get_values_if_any is generally handier. For example, you can use it to check if 'freep' is among the values for somekey:

```
if 'freep' in get_values_if_any(d1, somekey):
```

This extra handiness comes from get_values_if_any always returning a list, rather than sometimes a list and sometimes 0.

The first approach allows each value to be present multiple times for each given key. For example:

```
example = {}
example.setdefault('a', []).append('apple')
example.setdefault('b', []).append('boots')
example.setdefault('c', []).append('cat')
example.setdefault('a', []).append('ant')
example.setdefault('a', []).append('apple')
```

Now example['a'] is ['apple', 'ant', 'apple']. If we now execute:

```
example['a'].remove('apple')
```

the following test is still satisfied:

```
if 'apple' in example['a']
```

'apple' was present twice, and we removed it only once. (Testing for 'apple' with get_values_if_any(example, 'a') would be more general, although equivalent in this case.)

The second approach, which eliminates duplications, requires rather similar idioms. Here's how to retrieve the list of the values for a key:

```
list_of_values = d2[key].keys()
```

Here's how to remove a key/value pair, leaving empty dictionaries as items of d2 when the last value for a key is removed:

```
del d2[key][value]
```

The has_key_with_some_values function shown earlier also works for the second approach, and you also have analogous alternatives, such as:

```
def get_values_if_any(d, key):
    return d.get(key, {}).keys()
```

The second approach doesn't allow duplication. For example:

```
example = {}
example.setdefault('a', {})['apple']=1
example.setdefault('b', {})['boots']=1
example.setdefault('c', {})['cat']=1
example.setdefault('a', {})['ant']=1
example.setdefault('a', {})['apple']=1
```

Now example['a'] is {'apple':1, 'ant':1}. Now, if we execute:

```
del example['a']['apple']
```

the following test is not satisfied:

```
if 'apple' in example['a']
```

'apple' was present, but we just removed it.

This recipe focuses on how to code the raw functionality, but if you want to use this functionality in a systematic way, you'll want to wrap it up in a class. For that purpose, you need to make some of the design decisions that the recipe highlights. Do you want a value to be in the entry for a key multiple times? (Is the entry a bag rather than a set, in mathematical terms?) If so, should remove just reduce the number of occurrences by 1, or should it wipe out all of them? This is just the beginning of the choices you have to make, and the right choices depend on the specifics of your application.

See Also

The *Library Reference* section on mapping types.

1.6   Dispatching Using a Dictionary

Credit: Dick Wall

Problem

You need to execute appropriate pieces of code in correspondence with the value of some control variable—the kind of problem that in some other languages you might approach with a case, switch, or select statement.

Solution

Object-oriented programming, thanks to its elegant concept of dispatching, does away with many (but not all) such needs. But dictionaries, and the fact that in Python functions are first-class values (in particular, they can be values in a dictionary), conspire to make the problem quite easy to solve:

```
animals = []
number_of_felines = 0

def deal_with_a_cat():
    global number_of_felines
    print "meow"
    animals.append('feline')
    number_of_felines += 1
```

```
def deal_with_a_dog():
    print "bark"
    animals.append('canine')

def deal_with_a_bear():
    print "watch out for the *HUG*!"
    animals.append('ursine')

tokenDict = {
    "cat": deal_with_a_cat,
    "dog": deal_with_a_dog,
    "bear": deal_with_a_bear,
    }

# Simulate, say, some words read from a file
words = ["cat", "bear", "cat", "dog"]

for word in words:
    # Look up the function to call for each word, then call it
    functionToCall = tokenDict[word]
    functionToCall()
    # You could also do it in one step, tokenDict[word]()
```

Discussion

The basic idea behind this recipe is to construct a dictionary with string (or other) keys and with bound methods, functions, or other callables as values. During execution, at each step, use the string keys to select which method or function to execute. This can be used, for example, for simple parsing of tokens from a file through a kind of generalized case statement.

It's embarrassingly simple, but I use this technique often. Instead of functions, you can also use bound methods (such as self.method1) or other callables. If you use unbound methods (such as class.method), you need to pass an appropriate object as the first actual argument when you do call them. More generally, you can also store tuples, including both callables and arguments, as the dictionary's values, with diverse possibilities.

I primarily use this in places where in other languages I might want a case, switch, or select statement. I also use it to provide a poor man's way to parse command files (e.g., an X10 macro control file).

See Also

The *Library Reference* section on mapping types; the *Reference Manual* section on bound and unbound methods.

1.7 Collecting a Bunch of Named Items

Credit: Alex Martelli

Problem

You want to collect a bunch of items together, naming each item of the bunch, and you find dictionary syntax a bit heavyweight for the purpose.

Solution

Any (classic) class inherently wraps a dictionary, and we take advantage of this:

```
class Bunch:
    def __init__(self, **kwds):
        self.__dict__.update(kwds)
```

Now, to group a few variables, create a Bunch instance:

```
point = Bunch(datum=y, squared=y*y, coord=x)
```

You can access and rebind the named attributes just created, add others, remove some, and so on. For example:

```
if point.squared > threshold:
    point.isok = 1
```

Discussion

Often, we just want to collect a bunch of stuff together, naming each item of the bunch; a dictionary's okay for that, but a small do-nothing class is even handier and is prettier to use.

A dictionary is fine for collecting a few items in which each item has a name (the item's key in the dictionary can be thought of as the item's name, in this context). However, when all names are identifiers, to be used just like variables, the dictionary-access syntax is not maximally clear:

```
if point['squared'] > threshold
```

It takes minimal effort to build a little class, as in this recipe, to ease the initialization task and provide elegant attribute-access syntax:

```
if bunch.squared > threshold
```

An equally attractive alternative implementation to the one used in the solution is:

```
class EvenSimplerBunch:
    def __init__(self, **kwds): self.__dict__ = kwds
```

The alternative presented in the Bunch class has the advantage of not rebinding self.__dict__ (it uses the dictionary's update method to modify it instead), so it will keep working even if, in some hypothetical far-future dialect of Python, this specific dictionary became nonrebindable (as long, of course, as it remains mutable). But this EvenSimplerBunch is indeed even simpler, and marginally speedier, as it just rebinds the dictionary.

It is not difficult to add special methods to allow attributes to be accessed as bunch['squared'] and so on. In Python 2.1 or earlier, for example, the simplest way is:

```
import operator

class MurkierBunch:
    def __init__(self, **kwds):
        self.__dict__ = kwds
    def __getitem__(self, key):
        return operator.getitem(self.__dict__, key)
    def __setitem__(self, key, value):
        return operator.setitem(self.__dict__, key, value)
    def __delitem__(self, key):
        return operator.delitem(self.__dict__, key)
```

In Python 2.2, we can get the same effect by inheriting from the dict built-in type and delegating the other way around:

```
class MurkierBunch22(dict):
    def __init__(self, **kwds): dict.__init__(self, kwds)
    __getattr__ = dict.__getitem__
    __setattr__ = dict.__setitem__
    __delattr__ = dict.__delitem__
```

Neither approach makes these Bunch variants into fully fledged dictionaries. There are problems with each—for example, what is someBunch.keys supposed to mean? Does it refer to the method returning the list of keys, or is it just the same thing as someBunch['keys']? It's definitely better to avoid such confusion: Python distinguishes between attributes and items for clarity and simplicity. However, many newcomers to Python do believe they desire such confusion, generally because of previous experience with JavaScript, in which attributes and items are regularly confused. Such idioms, however, seem to have little usefulness in Python. For occasional access to an attribute whose name is held in a variable (or otherwise runtime-computed), the built-in functions getattr, setattr, and delattr are quite adequate, and they are definitely preferable to complicating the delightfully simple little Bunch class with the semantically murky approaches shown in the previous paragraph.

See Also

The *Tutorial* section on classes.

1.8 Finding the Intersection of Two Dictionaries

Credit: Andy McKay, Chris Perkins, Sami Hangaslammi

Problem

Given two dictionaries, you need to find the set of keys that are in both dictionaries.

Solution

Dictionaries are a good concrete representation for sets in Python, so operations such as intersections are common. Say you have two dictionaries (but pretend that they each contain thousands of items):

```python
some_dict = { 'zope':'zzz', 'python':'rocks' }
another_dict = { 'python':'rocks', 'perl':'$' }
```

Here's a bad way to find their intersection that is very slow:

```python
intersect = []
for item in some_dict.keys():
    if item in another_dict.keys():
        intersect.append(item)
print "Intersects:", intersect
```

And here's a good way that is simple and fast:

```python
intersect = []
for item in some_dict.keys():
    if another_dict.has_key(item):
        intersect.append(item)
print "Intersects:", intersect
```

In Python 2.2, the following is elegant and even faster:

```python
print "Intersects:", [k for k in some_dict if k in another_dict]
```

And here's an alternate approach that wins hands down in speed, for Python 1.5.2 and later:

```python
print "Intersects:", filter(another_dict.has_key, some_dict.keys())
```

Discussion

The keys method produces a list of all the keys of a dictionary. It can be pretty tempting to fall into the trap of just using `in`, with this list as the righthand side, to test for membership. However, in the first example, you're looping through all of `some_dict`, then each time looping through all of `another_dict`. If `some_dict` has $N1$ items, and `another_dict` has $N2$ items, your intersection operation will have a compute time proportional to the product of $N1 \times N2$. ($O(N1 \times N2)$ is the common computer-science notation to indicate this.)

By using the has_key method, you are not looping on another_dict any more, but rather checking the key in the dictionary's hash table. The processing time for has_key is basically independent of dictionary size, so the second approach is $O(N1)$. The difference is quite substantial for large dictionaries! If the two dictionaries are very different in size, it becomes important to use the smaller one in the role of some_dict, while the larger one takes on the role of another_dict (i.e., loop on the keys of the smaller dictionary, thus picking the smaller $N1$).

Python 2.2 lets you iterate on a dictionary's keys directly, with the statement:

```
for key in dict
```

You can test membership with the equally elegant:

```
if key in dict
```

rather than the equivalent but syntactically less nice dict.has_key(key). Combining these two small but nice innovations of Python 2.2 with the list-comprehension notation introduced in Python 2.0, we end up with a very elegant approach, which is at the same time concise, clear, and quite speedy.

However, the fastest approach is the one that uses filter with the bound method another_dict.has_key on the list some_dict.keys. A typical intersection of two 500-item dictionaries with 50% overlap, on a typical cheap machine of today (AMD Athlon 1.4GHz, DDR2100 RAM, Mandrake Linux 8.1), took 710 microseconds using has_key, 450 microseconds using the Python 2.2 technique, and 280 microseconds using the filter-based way. While these speed differences are almost substantial, they pale in comparison with the timing of the bad way, for which a typical intersection took 22,600 microseconds—30 times longer than the simple way and 80 times longer than the filter-based way! Here's the timing code, which shows a typical example of how one goes about measuring relative speeds of equivalent Python constructs:

```
import time

def timeo(fun, n=1000):
    def void( ): pass
    start = time.clock( )
    for i in range(n): void( )
    stend = time.clock( )
    overhead = stend - start
    start = time.clock( )
    for i in range(n): fun( )
    stend = time.clock( )
    thetime = stend-start
    return fun.__name__, thetime-overhead

to500 = {}
for i in range(500): to500[i] = 1
evens = {}
for i in range(0, 1000, 2): evens[i] = 1
```

```
def simpleway():
    result = []
    for k in to500.keys():
        if evens.has_key(k):
            result.append(k)
    return result

def pyth22way():
    return [k for k in to500 if k in evens]

def filterway():
    return filter(evens.has_key, to500.keys())

def badsloway():
    result = []
    for k in to500.keys():
        if k in evens.keys():
            result.append(k)
    return result

for f in simpleway, pyth22way, filterway, badsloway:
    print "%s: %.2f"%timeo(f)
```

You can save this code into a *.py* file and run it (a few times, on an otherwise quiescent machine, of course) with python -O to check how the timings of the various constructs compare on any specific machine in which you're interested. (Note that this script requires Python 2.2 or later.) Timing different code snippets to find out how their relative speeds compare is an important Python technique, since intuition is a notoriously unreliable guide to such relative-speed comparisons. For detailed and general instruction on how to time things, see the introduction to Chapter 17.

When applicable without having to use a lambda form or a specially written function, filter, map, and reduce often offer the fastest solution to any given problem. Of course, a clever Pythonista cares about speed only for those very, very few operations where speed really matters more than clarity, simplicity, and elegance! But these built-ins are pretty elegant in their own way, too.

We don't have a separate recipe for the union of the keys of two dictionaries, but that's because the task is even easier, thanks to a dictionary's update method:

```
def union_keys(some_dict, another_dict):
    temp_dict = some_dict.copy()
    temp_dict.update(another_dict)
    return temp_dict.keys()
```

See Also

The *Library Reference* section on mapping types.

1.9 Assigning and Testing with One Statement

Credit: Alex Martelli

Problem

You are transliterating C or Perl code to Python, and, to keep close to the original's structure, you need an expression's result to be both assigned and tested (as in `if((x=foo( ))` or `while((x=foo( ))` in such other languages).

Solution

In Python, you can't code:

```
if x=foo( ):
```

Assignment is a statement, so it cannot fit into an expression, which is necessary for conditions of `if` and `while` statements. Normally this isn't a problem, as you can just structure your code around it. For example, this is quite Pythonic:

```
while 1:
    line = file.readline( )
    if not line: break
    process(line)
```

In modern Python, this is far better, but it's even farther from C-like idioms:

```
for line in file.xreadlines( ):
    process(line)
```

In Python 2.2, you can be even simpler and more elegant:

```
for line in file:
    process(line)
```

But sometimes you're transliterating C, Perl, or some other language, and you'd like your transliteration to be structurally close to the original.

One simple utility class makes this easy:

```
class DataHolder:
    def __init__(self, value=None):
        self.value = value
    def set(self, value):
        self.value = value
        return value
    def get(self):
        return self.value
# optional and strongly discouraged, but handy at times:
import __builtin__
__builtin__.DataHolder = DataHolder
__builtin__.data = DataHolder( )
```

With the help of the `DataHolder` class and its `data` instance, you can keep your C-like code structure intact in transliteration:

```
while data.set(file.readline()):
    process(data.get())
```

Discussion

In Python, assignment is not an expression. Thus, you cannot assign the result that you are testing in, for example, an `if`, `elif`, or `while` statement. This is usually okay: you just structure your code to avoid the need to assign while testing (in fact, your code will often become clearer as a result). However, sometimes you may be writing Python code that is the transliteration of code originally written in C, Perl, or another language that supports assignment-as-expression. For example, such transliteration often occurs in the first Python version of an algorithm for which a reference implementation is supplied, an algorithm taken from a book, and so on. In such cases, having the structure of your initial transliteration be close to that of the code you're transcribing is often preferable. Fortunately, Python offers enough power to make it pretty trivial to satisfy this requirement.

We can't redefine assignment, but we can have a method (or function) that saves its argument somewhere and returns that argument so it can be tested. That "somewhere" is most naturally an attribute of an object, so a method is a more natural choice than a function. Of course, we could just retrieve the attribute directly (i.e., the get method is redundant), but it looks nicer to have symmetry between `data.set` and `data.get`.

Special-purpose solutions, such as the `xreadlines` method of file objects, the similar decorator function in the `xreadlines` module, and (not so special-purpose) Python 2.2 iterators, are obviously preferable for the purposes for which they've been designed. However, such constructs can imply even wider deviation from the structure of the algorithm being transliterated. Thus, while they're great in themselves, they don't really address the problem presented here.

`data.set(whatever)` can be seen as little more than syntactic sugar for `data.value=whatever`, with the added value of being acceptable as an expression. Therefore, it's the one obviously right way to satisfy the requirement for a reasonably faithful transliteration. The only difference is the syntactic sugar variation needed, and that's a minor issue.

Importing `__builtin__` and assigning to its attributes is a trick that basically defines a new built-in object at runtime. All other modules will automatically be able to access these new built-ins without having to do an import. It's not good practice, though, since readers of those modules should not need to know about the strange side effects of other modules in the application. Nevertheless, it's a trick worth knowing about in case you encounter it.

Not recommended, in any case, is the following abuse of list format as comprehension syntax:

```
while [line for line in (file.readline(),) if line]:
    process(line)
```

It works, but it is unreadable and error-prone.

See Also

The *Tutorial* section on classes; the documentation for the `builtin` module in the *Library Reference*.

1.10   Using List Comprehensions Instead of map and filter

Credit: Luther Blissett

Problem

You want to perform an operation on all the elements of a list, but you'd like to avoid using `map` and `filter` because they can be hard to read and understand, particularly when they need `lambda`.

Solution

Say you want to create a new list by adding 23 to each item of some other list. In Python 1.5.2, the solution is:

```
thenewlist = map(lambda x: x + 23, theoldlist)
```

This is hardly the clearest code. Fortunately, since Python 2.0, we can use a list comprehension instead:

```
thenewlist = [x + 23 for x in theoldlist]
```

This is much clearer and more elegant.

Similarly, say you want the new list to comprise all items in the other list that are larger than 5. In Python 1.5.2, the solution is:

```
thenewlist = filter(lambda x: x > 5, theoldlist)
```

But in modern Python, we can use the following list comprehension:

```
thenewlist = [x for x in theoldlist if x > 5]
```

Now say you want to combine both list operations. In Python 1.5.2, the solution is quite complex:

```
thenewlist = map(lambda x: x+23, filter(lambda x: x>5, theoldlist))
```

A list comprehension affords far greater clarity, as we can both perform selection with the `if` clause and use some expression, such as adding 23, on the selected items:

```
thenewlist = [x + 23 for x in theoldlist if x > 5]
```

Discussion

Elegance and clarity, within a generally pragmatic attitude, are Python's core values. List comprehensions, added in Python 2.0, delightfully display how pragmatism can enhance both clarity and elegance. The built-in `map` and `filter` functions still have their uses, since they're arguably of equal elegance and clarity as list comprehensions when the `lambda` construct is not necessary. In fact, when their first argument is another built-in function (i.e., when `lambda` is not involved and there is no need to write a function just for the purpose of using it within a `map` or `filter`), they can be even faster than list comprehensions.

All in all, Python programs optimally written for 2.0 or later use far fewer `map` and `filter` calls than similar programs written for 1.5.2. Most of the `map` and `filter` calls (and quite a few explicit loops) are replaced with list comprehensions (which Python borrowed, after some prettying of the syntax, from Haskell, described at *http://www.haskell.org*). It's not an issue of wanting to play with a shiny new toy (although that desire, too, has its place in a programmer's heart)—the point is that the toy, when used well, is a wonderfully useful instrument, further enhancing your Python programs' clarity, simplicity, and elegance.

See Also

The *Reference Manual* section on list displays (the other name for list comprehensions).

1.11 Unzipping Simple List-Like Objects

Credit: gyro funch

Problem

You have a sequence and need to pull it apart into a number of pieces.

Solution

There's no built-in `unzip` counterpart to `zip`, but it's not hard to code our own:

```
def unzip(p, n):
    """ Split a sequence p into a list of n tuples, repeatedly taking the
```

```
next unused element of p and adding it to the next tuple.  Each of the
resulting tuples is of the same length; if p%n != 0, the shorter tuples
are padded with None (closer to the behavior of map than to that of zip).
    Example:
    >>> unzip(['a','b','c','d','e'], 3)
    [('a', 'd'), ('b', 'e'), ('c', None)]
"""
# First, find the length for the longest sublist
mlen, lft = divmod(len(p), n)
if lft != 0: mlen += 1

# Then, initialize a list of lists with suitable lengths
lst = [[None]*mlen for i in range(n)]

# Loop over all items of the input sequence (index-wise), and
# Copy a reference to each into the appropriate place
for i in range(len(p)):
    j, k = divmod(i, n)      # Find sublist-index and index-within-sublist
    lst[k][j] = p[i]         # Copy a reference appropriately

# Finally, turn each sublist into a tuple, since the unzip function
# is specified to return a list of tuples, not a list of lists
return map(tuple, lst)
```

Discussion

The function in this recipe takes a list and pulls it apart into a user-defined number
of pieces. It acts like a sort of reverse zip function (although it deals with only the
very simplest cases). This recipe was useful to me recently when I had to take a
Python list and break it down into a number of different pieces, putting each consecutive item of the list into a separate sublist.

Preallocating the result as a list of lists of None is generally more efficient than building up each sublist by repeated calls to append. Also, in this case, it already ensures
the padding with None that we would need anyway (unless length(p) just happens to
be a multiple of n).

The algorithm that unzip uses is quite simple: a reference to each item of the input
sequence is placed into the appropriate item of the appropriate sublist. The built-in
function divmod computes the quotient and remainder of a division, which just happen to be the indexes we need for the appropriate sublist and item in it.

Although we specified that unzip must return a list of tuples, we actually build a list
of sublists, and we turn each sublist into a tuple as late in the process as possible by
applying the built-in function tuple over each sublist with a single call to map. It is
much simpler to build sublists first. Lists are mutable, so we can bind specific items
separately; tuples are immutable, so we would have a harder time working with them
in our unzip function's main loop.

See Also

Documentation for the zip and divmod built-ins in the *Library Reference*.

1.12 Flattening a Nested Sequence

Credit: Luther Blissett

Problem

You have a sequence, such as a list, some of whose items may in turn be lists, and so on. You need to flatten it out into a sequence of its scalar items (the leaves, if you think of the nested sequence as a tree).

Solution

Of course, we need to be able to tell which of the elements we're handling are to be deemed scalar. For generality, say we're passed as an argument a predicate that defines what is scalar—a function that we can call on any element and that returns 1 if the element is scalar or 0 otherwise. Given this, one approach is:

```
def flatten(sequence, scalarp, result=None):
    if result is None: result = []
    for item in sequence:
        if scalarp(item): result.append(item)
        else: flatten(item, scalarp, result)
    return result
```

In Python 2.2, a simple generator is an interesting alternative, and, if all the caller needs to do is loop over the flattened sequence, may save the memory needed for the result list:

```
from __future__ import generators
def flatten22(sequence, scalarp):
    for item in sequence:
        if scalarp(item):
            yield item
        else:
            for subitem in flatten22(item, scalarp):
                yield subitem
```

Discussion

The only problem with this recipe is that determining what is a scalar is not as obvious as it might seem, which is why I delegated that decision to a callable predicate argument that the caller is supposed to pass to flatten. Of course, we must be able to loop over the items of any non-scalar with a for statement, or flatten will raise an exception (since it does, via a recursive call, attempt a `for` statement over any non-scalar item). In Python 2.2, that's easy to check:

```
def canLoopOver(maybeIterable):
    try: iter(maybeIterable)
    except: return 0
    else: return 1
```

The built-in function `iter`, new in Python 2.2, returns an iterator, if possible. `for x in s` implicitly calls the `iter` function, so the `canLoopOver` function can easily check if `for` is applicable by calling `iter` explicitly and seeing if that raises an exception.

In Python 2.1 and earlier, there is no `iter` function, so we have to try more directly:

```
def canLoopOver(maybeIterable):
    try:
        for x in maybeIterable:
            return 1
        else:
            return 1
    except:
        return 0
```

Here we have to rely on the `for` statement itself raising an exception if `maybeIterable` is not iterable after all. Note that this approach is not fully suitable for Python 2.2: if `maybeIterable` is an iterator object, the `for` in this approach consumes its first item.

Neither of these implementations of `canLoopOver` is entirely satisfactory, by itself, as our scalar-testing predicate. The problem is with strings, Unicode strings, and other string-like objects. These objects are perfectly good sequences, and we could loop on them with a `for` statement, but we typically want to treat them as scalars. And even if we didn't, we would at least have to treat any string-like objects with a length of 1 as scalars. Otherwise, since such strings are iterable and yield themselves as their only items, our `flatten` function would not cease recursion until it exhausted the call stack and raised a `RuntimeError` due to "maximum recursion depth exceeded."

Fortunately, we can easily distinguish string-like objects by attempting a typical string operation on them:

```
def isStringLike(obj):
    try: obj+''
    except TypeError: return 0
    else: return 1
```

Now, we finally have a good implementation for the scalar-checking predicate:

```
def isScalar(obj):
    return isStringLike(obj) or not canLoopOver(obj)
```

By simply placing this `isScalar` function and the appropriate implementation of `canLoopOver` in our module, before the recipe's functions, we can change the signatures of these functions to make them easier to call in most cases. For example:

```
def flatten22(sequence, scalarp=isScalar):
```

Now the caller needs to pass the scalarp argument only in those (hopefully rare) cases where our definition of what is scalar does not quite meet the caller's application-specific needs.

See Also

The *Library Reference* section on sequence types.

1.13 Looping in Parallel over Index and Sequence Items

Credit: Alex Martelli

Problem

You need to loop on a sequence, but at each step you also need to know what index into the sequence you have reached.

Solution

Together, the built-in functions xrange and zip make this easy. You need only this one instance of xrange, as it is fully reusable:

```
indices = xrange(sys.maxint)
```

Here's how you use the indices instance:

```
for item, index in zip(sequence, indices):
    something(item, index)
```

This gives the same semantics as:

```
for index in range(len(sequence)):
    something(sequence[index], index)
```

but the change of emphasis allows greater clarity in many usage contexts.

Another alternative is to use class wrappers:

```
class Indexed:
    def __init__(self, seq):
        self.seq = seq
    def __getitem__(self, i):
        return self.seq[i], i
```

For example:

```
for item, index in Indexed(sequence):
    something(item, index)
```

In Python 2.2, with from __future__ import generators, you can also use:

```
def Indexed(sequence):
    iterator = iter(sequence)
```

```
for index in indices:
    yield iterator.next( ), index
# Note that we exit by propagating StopIteration when .next raises it!
```

However, the simplest roughly equivalent way remains the good old:

```
def Indexed(sequence):
    return zip(sequence, indices)
```

Discussion

We often want to loop on a sequence but also need the current index in the loop body. The canonical Pydiom for this is:

```
for i in range(len(sequence)):
```

using sequence[i] as the item reference in the loop's body. However, in many contexts, it is clearer to emphasize the loop on the sequence items rather than on the indexes. zip provides an easy alternative, looping on indexes and items in parallel, since it truncates at the shortest of its arguments. Thus, it's okay for some arguments to be unbounded sequences, as long as not all the arguments are unbounded. An unbounded sequence of indexes is trivial to write (xrange is handy for this), and a reusable instance of that sequence can be passed to zip, in parallel to the sequence being indexed.

The same zip usage also affords a client code–transparent alternative to the use of a wrapper class Indexed, as demonstrated by the Indexed class, generator, and function shown in the solution. Of these, when applicable, zip is simplest.

The performance of each of these solutions is roughly equivalent. They're all $O(N)$ (i.e., they execute in time proportional to the number of elements in the sequence), they all take $O(1)$ extra memory, and none is anything close to twice as fast or as slow as another.

Note that zip is not lazy (i.e., it cannot accept all argument sequences being unbounded). Therefore, in certain cases in which zip cannot be used (albeit not the typical one in which range(len(sequence)) is the alternative), other kinds of loop might be usable. See Recipe 17.12 for lazy, iterator-based alternatives, including an xzip function (Python 2.2 only).

See Also

Recipe 17.12; the *Library Reference* section on sequence types.

1.14   Looping Through Multiple Lists

Credit: Andy McKay

Problem

You need to loop through every item of multiple lists.

Solution

There are basically three approaches. Say you have:

```
a = ['a1', 'a2', 'a3']
b = ['b1', 'b2']
```

Using the built-in function map, with a first argument of None, you can iterate on both lists in parallel:

```
print "Map:"
for x, y in map(None, a, b):
    print x, y
```

The loop runs three times. On the last iteration, y will be None.

Using the built-in function zip also lets you iterate in parallel:

```
print "Zip:"
for x, y in zip(a, b):
    print x, y
```

The loop runs two times; the third iteration simply is not done.

A list comprehension affords a very different iteration:

```
print "List comprehension:"
for x, y in [(x,y) for x in a for y in b]:
    print x, y
```

The loop runs six times, over each item of b for each item of a.

Discussion

Using map with None as the first argument is a subtle variation of the standard map call, which typically takes a function as the first argument. As the documentation indicates, if the first argument is None, the identity function is used as the function through which the arguments are mapped. If there are multiple list arguments, map returns a list consisting of tuples that contain the corresponding items from all lists (in other words, it's a kind of transpose operation). The list arguments may be any kind of sequence, and the result is always a list.

Note that the first technique returns None for sequences in which there are no more elements. Therefore, the output of the first loop is:

```
Map:
a1 b1
a2 b2
a3 None
```

zip lets you iterate over the lists in a similar way, but only up to the number of elements of the smallest list. Therefore, the output of the second technique is:

```
Zip:
a1 b1
a2 b2
```

Python 2.0 introduced list comprehensions, with a syntax that some found a bit strange:

```
[(x,y) for x in a for y in b]
```

This iterates over list b for every element in a. These elements are put into a tuple (x, y). We then iterate through the resulting list of tuples in the outermost for loop. The output of the third technique, therefore, is quite different:

```
List comprehension:
a1 b1
a1 b2
a2 b1
a2 b2
a3 b1
a3 b2
```

See Also

The *Library Reference* section on sequence types; documentation for the zip and map built-ins in the *Library Reference*.

1.15 Spanning a Range Defined by Floats

Credit: Dinu C. Gherman, Paul M. Winkler

Problem

You need an arithmetic progression, just like the built-in function range, but with float values (range works only on integers).

Solution

Although this functionality is not available as a built-in, it's not hard to code it with a loop:

```
def frange(start, end=None, inc=1.0):
    "A range-like function that does accept float increments..."
```

```
    if end == None:
        end = start + 0.0      # Ensure a float value for 'end'
        start = 0.0
    assert inc                 # sanity check

    L = []
    while 1:
        next = start + len(L) * inc
        if inc > 0 and next >= end:
            break
        elif inc < 0 and next <= end:
            break
        L.append(next)

    return L
```

Discussion

Sadly missing in the Python standard library, the function in this recipe lets you use ranges, just as with the built-in function range, but with float arguments.

Many theoretical restrictions apply, but this function is more useful in practice than in theory. People who work with floating-point numbers all the time have many war stories about billion-dollar projects that failed because someone did not take into consideration the strange things that modern hardware does when comparing floating-point numbers. But for pedestrian cases, simple approaches like this recipe generally work.

You can get a substantial speed boost by preallocating the list instead of calling append repeatedly. This also allows you to get rid of the conditionals in the inner loop. For one element, this version is barely faster, but with more than 10 elements it's consistently about 5 times faster—the kind of performance ratio that is worth caring about. I get identical output for every test case I can think of:

```
def frange2(start, end=None, inc=1.0):
    "A faster range-like function that does accept float increments..."
    if end == None:
        end = start + 0.0
        start = 0.0
    else: start += 0.0 # force it to be a float

    count = int((end - start) / inc)
    if start + count * inc != end:
        # Need to adjust the count. AFAICT, it always comes up one short.
        count += 1

    L = [start] * count
    for i in xrange(1, count):
        L[i] = start + i * inc

    return L
```

Both versions rely on a single multiplication and one addition to compute each item, to avoid accumulating error by repeated additions. This is why, for example, the body of the for loop in frange2 is not:

```
L[i] = L[i-1] + inc
```

In Python 2.2, if all you need to do is loop on the result of frange, you can save some memory by turning this function into a simple generator, yielding an iterator when you call it:

```
from __future__ import generators

def frangei(start, end=None, inc=1.0):
    "An xrange-like simple generator that does accept float increments..."

    if end == None:
        end = start + 0.0
        start = 0.0
    assert inc                  # sanity check

    i = 0
    while 1:
        next = start + i * inc
        if inc > 0 and next >= end:
            break
        elif inc < 0 and next <= end:
            break
        yield next
        i += 1
```

If you use this recipe a lot, you should probably take a look at Numeric Python and other third-party packages that take computing with floating-point numbers seriously. This recipe, for example, will not scale well to very large ranges, while those defined in Numeric Python will.

See Also

Documentation for the range built-in function in the *Library Reference*; Numeric Python (*http://www.pfdubois.com/numpy/*).

1.16 Transposing Two-Dimensional Arrays
Credit: Steve Holden

Problem

You need to transpose a list of lists, turning rows into columns and vice versa.

Solution

You must start with a list whose items are lists all of the same length:

```
arr = [[1,2,3], [4,5,6], [7,8,9], [10,11,12]]
```

A list comprehension offers a simple, handy way to transpose it:

```
print [[r[col] for r in arr] for col in range(len(arr[0]))]
[[1, 4, 7, 10], [2, 5, 8, 11], [3, 6, 9, 12]]
```

Discussion

This recipe shows a concise way (although not necessarily the fastest way) to turn rows into columns. List comprehensions are known for being concise.

Sometimes data just comes at you the wrong way. For instance, if you use Microsoft's ADO database interface, due to array element ordering differences between Python and Microsoft's preferred implementation language (Visual Basic), the GetRows method actually appears to return database columns in Python, despite its name. This recipe's solution to this common problem was chosen to demonstrate nested list comprehensions.

Notice that the inner comprehension varies what is selected from (the row), while the outer comprehension varies the selector (the column). This process achieves the required transposition.

If you're transposing large arrays of numbers, consider Numeric Python and other third-party packages. Numeric Python defines transposition and other axis-swinging routines that will make your head spin.

See Also

The *Reference Manual* section on list displays (the other name for list comprehensions); Numeric Python (*http://www.pfdubois.com/numpy/*).

1.17 Creating Lists of Lists Without Sharing References

Credit: David Ascher

Problem

You want to create a multidimensional list, but the apparently simplest solution is fraught with surprises.

Solution

Use list comprehensions (also known as list displays) to avoid implicit reference sharing:

```
multilist = [[0 for col in range(5)] for row in range(10)]
```

Discussion

When a newcomer to Python is shown the power of the multiplication operation on lists, he often gets quite excited about it, since it is such an elegant notation. For example:

```
>>> [0] * 5
[0, 0, 0, 0, 0]
```

The problem is that one-dimensional problems often grow a second dimension, so there is a natural progression to:

```
>>> multi = [[0] * 5] * 3
>>> print multi
[[0, 0, 0, 0, 0], [0, 0, 0, 0, 0], [0, 0, 0, 0, 0]]
```

This appears to have worked, but the same newcomer is then often puzzled by bugs, which typically can be boiled down to the following test:

```
>>> multi[0][0] = 'Changed!'
>>> print multi
[['Changed!', 0, 0, 0, 0], ['Changed!', 0, 0, 0, 0], ['Changed!', 0, 0, 0, 0]]
```

This problem definitely confuses most programmers at least once, if not a few times (see the FAQ entry at *http://www.python.org/doc/FAQ.html#4.50*). To understand it, it helps to decompose the creation of the multidimensional list into two steps:

```
>>> row = [0] * 5      # a list with five references to 0
>>> multi = [row] * 3  # a list with three references to the row object
```

The problem still exists in this version (Python is not that magical). The comments are key to understanding the source of the confusion. The process of multiplying a sequence by a number creates a new sequence with the specified number of new references to the original contents. In the case of the creation of row, it doesn't matter whether references are being duplicated or not, since the referent (the object being referred to) is immutable. In other words, there is no difference between an object and a reference to an object if that object is immutable. In the second line, however, what is created is a new list containing three references to the contents of the [row] list, which is a single reference to a list. Thus, multi contains three references to a single object. So when the first element of the first element of multi is changed, you are actually modifying the first element of the shared list. Hence the surprise.

List comprehensions, added in Python 2.2, provide a nice syntax that avoids the problem, as illustrated in the solution. With list comprehensions, there is no sharing of references—it's a truly nested computation. Note that the performance characteristics of the solution are $O(M \times N)$, meaning that it will scale with each dimension. The list-multiplication idiom, however, is an $O(M)$ computation, as it doesn't really do duplications.

See Also

Documentation for the range built-in function in the *Library Reference*.

CHAPTER 2
Searching and Sorting

2.0   Introduction

Credit: Tim Peters, PythonLabs

Computer manufacturers of the 1960s estimated that more than 25 percent of the running time on their computers was spent on sorting, when all their customers were taken into account. In fact, there were many installations in which the task of sorting was responsible for more than half of the computing time. From these statistics we may conclude that either (i) there are many important applications of sorting, or (ii) many people sort when they shouldn't, or (iii) inefficient sorting algorithms have been in common use.

—Donald Knuth
"The Art of Computer Programming",
Volume 3, Sorting and Searching, page 3

Professor Knuth's masterful work on the topics of sorting and searching spans nearly 800 pages of sophisticated technical text. In Python practice, we reduce it to two imperatives (we read Knuth so you don't have to):

- When you need to sort, find a way to use the built-in `sort` method of Python lists.

- When you need to search, find a way to use built-in dictionaries.

Many recipes in this chapter illustrate these principles. The most common theme is using the *decorate-sort-undecorate* (DSU) pattern, a general approach to transforming a sorting problem by creating an auxiliary that we can then sort with the default, speedy `sort` method. This is the single most useful technique to take from this chapter. It relies on an unusual feature of Python's built-in comparisons: sequences are compared lexicographically. Lexicographical order is a generalization to tuples and lists of the everyday rules used to compare strings (i.e., alphabetical order). The built-in `cmp(s1, s2)`, when s1 and s2 are sequences, is equivalent to this Python code:

```
def lexcmp(s1, s2):
    # Find leftmost nonequal pair
    i = 0
    while i < len(s1) and i < len(s2):
        outcome = cmp(s1[i], s2[i])
        if outcome:
            return outcome
        i += 1
    # All equal, until at least one sequence was exhausted
    return cmp(len(s1), len(s2))
```

This code looks for the first nonequal corresponding elements. If such a nonequal pair is found, that pair determines the outcome. Otherwise, if one sequence is a proper prefix of the other, the prefix is considered to be the smaller sequence. Finally, if these cases don't apply, the sequences are identical and are considered equal. Here are some examples:

```
>>> cmp((1, 2, 3), (1, 2, 3))   # identical
0
>>> cmp((1, 2, 3), (1, 2))      # first larger because second is a prefix
1
>>> cmp((1, 100), (2, 1))       # first smaller because 1<2
-1
>>> cmp((1, 2), (1, 3))         # first smaller because 1==1, then 2<3
-1
```

An immediate consequence of lexicographical comparisons is that if you want to sort a list of objects by a primary key, breaking ties by comparing a secondary key, you can simply build a list of tuples, in which each tuple contains the primary key, secondary key, and original object, in that order. Because tuples are compared lexicographically, this automatically does the right thing. When comparing tuples, the primary keys are compared first, and if (and only if) the primary keys are equal, the secondary keys are compared.

The examples of the DSU pattern in this chapter show many applications of this idea; perhaps the cutest is Recipe 2.3, which ensures a stable sort by using each object's list index as a secondary key. Of course, the DSU technique applies to any number of keys. You can add as many keys to the tuples as you like, in the order in which you want the keys compared.

A definitive generalization is provided by Recipe 2.7, which provides a general routine to sort lists of objects by user-specified index position or attribute name. This is fine code, and you are free to use it for your own purposes. It suffers from a problem common to many frameworks in Python, though: once you get the hang of it, using the DSU pattern is so easy that you'll find it's quicker to do it from scratch than to remember how to use the framework. I haven't yet decided whether this is a strength or weakness of Python, but it's definitely a real phenomenon.

Searching and Sorting FAQ

To help you further understand searching and sorting in Python, I thought I'd answer some frequently asked questions about the topic:

What algorithm does Python's list.sort use?

In early releases of Python, list.sort used the qsort routine from the underlying platform's C library. This didn't work out for several reasons, but primarily because the quality of qsort varied widely across machines. Some versions were extremely slow when given a list with many equal values or in reverse-sorted order. Some even dumped core because they weren't reentrant. A user-defined __cmp__ function can also invoke list.sort, so that one list.sort can invoke others as a side effect of comparing. Some platform qsort routines couldn't handle that. A user-defined __cmp__ function can also (if it's insane or malicious) mutate the list while it's being sorted, and many platform qsort routines dumped core when that happened.

Python then grew its own implementation of the quicksort algorithm. This was rewritten with every release, as real-life cases of unacceptable slowness were discovered. Quicksort is a delicate algorithm!

In Python 1.5.2 the quicksort algorithm was replaced by a hybrid of samplesort and binary insertion sort, and that hasn't changed again to date. Samplesort can be viewed as a variant of quicksort that uses a very large sample size to pick the partitioning element, also known as the pivot (it recursively samplesorts a large random subset of the elements and picks the median of those). This variant makes quadratic-time behavior almost impossible and brings the number of comparisons in the average case much closer to the theoretical minimum.

However, because samplesort is a complicated algorithm, it has too much administrative overhead for small lists. Therefore, small lists (and small slices resulting from samplesort partitioning) are handled by a separate binary insertion sort. This is an ordinary insertion sort, except that it uses binary search to determine where each new element belongs. Most sorting texts say this isn't worth the bother, but that's because most texts assume that comparing two elements is as cheap as or cheaper than swapping them in memory. This isn't true for Python's sort! Moving an object is very cheap, since what is copied is just a reference to the object. Comparing two objects is expensive, though, because all of the object-oriented machinery for finding the appropriate code to compare two objects and for coercion gets reinvoked each time. This makes binary search a major win for Python's sort.

On top of this hybrid approach, a few common special cases are exploited for speed. First, already-sorted or reverse-sorted lists are detected and handled in linear time. For some applications, these kinds of lists are very common. Second, if an array is mostly sorted, with just a few out-of-place elements at the end, the binary insertion sort handles the whole job. This is much faster than letting samplesort have at it and is common in applications that repeatedly sort a list, append a few new elements, then sort it again. Finally, special code in the samplesort looks for stretches of equal elements, so that the slice they occupy can be marked as done early.

In the end, all of this yields an in-place sort with excellent performance in all known real cases and supernaturally good performance in common special cases. It spans about 500 lines of complicated C code, which gives special poignancy to Recipe 2.11.

Is Python's sort stable?

No, samplesort is not stable, and it cannot be made stable efficiently. See Recipe 2.3 if you need stability.

But I've tried many examples, and they're all stable!

You tried small examples. The binary insertion sort is stable, and, as I explained earlier, samplesort doesn't kick in until the list gets larger.

How large?

It's an implementation detail you can't rely on across releases. Today, the answer is 100 items.

But Recipe 2.11 shows a stable sort. Why not use that?

It's a cute example, but it does twice as many comparisons as a real quicksort. As I explained earlier, the cost of comparisons dominates sorting time, so it would take at least twice as long as Python's sort even if it was coded in C. Even if it didn't take twice as long, samplesort is quicker than quicksort.

Mergesort does few comparisons and can be made stable easily. Why doesn't Python use that?

Mergesort requires extra memory, and it does much more data movement than Python's current sort. Despite the fact that comparison time dominates, samplesort does few enough comparisons that the extra data movement done by mergesort is significant. I implemented three mergesorts while investigating quicksort alternatives for Python 1.5.2, and they were all significantly slower than the approach Python uses.

Why is passing a comparison function so much slower than using the DSU pattern?

In search performance, comparison time dominates, and an explicit comparison function written in Python adds the substantial overhead of a Python-level function call to each comparison. The built-in comparisons are all coded in C, so they don't incur the overhead of Python-level function calls.

So I should never pass an explicit comparison function, right?

Speed isn't always everything. If you can afford the speed hit, and you find it more convenient and clearer in a given case to pass a comparison function, go ahead. I do.

Why does Python use the three-outcome cmp *for sorting? Why doesn't it use a simple less-than comparison instead?*

This is a historical consequence of Python initially using the C qsort function, since qsort requires a three-outcome comparison function. Like many people, I wish it used a simple less-than comparison, but it's too late now. When rich comparisons were introduced, Python's list.sort was reworked a little, so that although it uses a three-outcome comparison function at the user level, internally it also works fine with objects that implement only __lt__ comparison.

What's the best way to sort a list in reverse order?

Reversing the sense of the comparison works fine:

```
list.sort(lambda a, b: cmp(b, a))
```

Here's another technique that is faster and more obvious but that is often avoided by those who mistakenly believe that writing two lines of code where one might do is somehow sinful:

```
list.sort( )
list.reverse( )
```

What kind of hash table does Python's dictionary type use?

The dictionary type uses contiguous tables with power-of-two sizes. Collisions are handled within the table, and the table is kept at most two-thirds full, so that collision handling is very unlikely to degenerate. When a table gets too full, the table size is doubled and all the elements are reinserted. For more detail, read the source code in *dictobject.c* and *dictobject.h*. As of Python 2.2, the source code is extensively commented.

I've heard that Python's dictionary implementation is very fast. Is that true?

Yes. Because Python uses dictionaries to implement module and object namespaces, dictionary performance is crucial. For the past decade, smart people in the Python community have helped optimize it—the result is open source at its best.

2.1 Sorting a Dictionary

Credit: Alex Martelli, Raymond Hettinger

Problem

You want to sort a dictionary. Because sorting is a concept that only makes sense for sequences, this presumably means that you want a sequence of the values of the dictionary in the order obtained by sorting the keys.

Solution

The simplest approach is to sort the items (i.e., key/value pairs), then pick just the values:

```
def sortedDictValues1(adict):
    items = adict.items()
    items.sort()
    return [value for key, value in items]
```

However, an alternative implementation that sorts just the keys, then uses them to index into the dictionary to build the result, happens to run more than twice as fast (for a dictionary of a few thousand entries) on my system:

```
def sortedDictValues2(adict):
    keys = adict.keys()
    keys.sort()
    return [adict[key] for key in keys]
```

A further small speed-up (15% on my system) is to perform the last step by mapping a bound method. map is often marginally faster than a list comprehension when no lambda is involved:

```
def sortedDictValues3(adict):
    keys = adict.keys()
    keys.sort()
    return map(adict.get, keys)
```

A really tiny extra speed-up (about 3% on my system) is available in Python 2.2 by using adict.__getitem__ rather than adict.get in this latest, bound-method version.

Discussion

The concept of sorting applies only to a collection that has order—in other words, a sequence. A mapping, such as a dictionary, has no order, so it cannot be sorted. And yet, "How do I sort a dictionary?" is a frequent question on the Python lists. More often than not, the question is about sorting some sequence of keys and/or values from the dictionary.

A dictionary's keys can be extracted as a list, which can then be sorted. The functions in this recipe return the values in order of sorted keys, which corresponds to the most frequent actual need when it comes to sorting a dictionary. Another frequent need is sorting by the values in the dictionary, for which you should see Recipe 17.6.

The implementation choices are interesting. Because we are sorting key/value pairs by the key field and returning only the list of value fields, it seems conceptually simplest to use the first solution, which gets a list of the key/value pairs, sorts them, and then uses a list comprehension to pick the values. However, this is not the fastest solution. Instead, with Python 2.2, on dictionaries of a few thousand items, extracting just the keys, sorting them, and then accessing the dictionary for each key in the resulting list comprehension—the second solution—appears to be over twice as fast.

This faster approach can be further optimized by extracting the bound method adict.get, which turns each key into its corresponding value, and then using the built-in function `map` to build the list by applying this callable to each item in the sorted list of keys. In Python 2.2, using `adict.__getitem__` rather than `adict.get` is even a little bit better (probably not enough to justify making your program version-dependent, but if you're already dependent on Python 2.2 for other reasons, you may as well use this approach).

Simplicity is one the greatest virtues for any program, but the second and third solutions aren't really more complicated than the first; they are just, perhaps, a little bit more subtle. Those solutions are probably worth using to sort any dictionary, even though their performance advantages are really measurable only for very large ones.

See Also

Recipe 17.6 for another application of sorting on dictionaries.

2.2 Processing Selected Pairs of Structured Data Efficiently

Credit: Alex Martelli, David Ascher

Problem

You need to efficiently process pairs of data from two large and related data sets.

Solution

Use an auxiliary dictionary to do preprocessing of the data, thereby reducing the need for iteration over mostly irrelevant data. For instance, if xs and ys are the two data sets, with matching keys as the first item in each entry, so that `x[0]  ==  y[0]` defines an "interesting" pair:

```
auxdict = {}
for y in ys: auxdict.setdefault(y[0], []).append(y)
result = [ process(x, y) for x in xs for y in auxdict[x[0]] ]
```

Discussion

To make the problem more concrete, let's look at an example. Say you need to analyze data about visitors to a web site who have purchased something online. This means you need to perform some computation based on data from two log files—one from the web server and one from the credit-card processing framework. Each log file is huge, but only a small number of the web server log entries correspond to credit-card log entries. Let's assume that `cclog` is a sequence of records, one for each credit-card transaction, and that `weblog` is a sequence of records describing each web site hit. Let's further assume that each record uses the attribute `ipaddress` to refer to the IP address involved in each event. In this case, a reasonable first approach would be to do something like:

```
results = [ process(webhit, ccinfo) for webhit in weblog for ccinfo in cclog \
                if ccinfo.ipaddress==webhit.ipaddress ]
```

The problem with this approach is that the nested list comprehension will iterate over each entry in the web server log, and, for each entry in the web server log, it will also iterate over each entry in the credit-card log. This means that the algorithm has $O(M \times N)$ performance characteristics—in other words, the time it takes to compute will be proportional to the product of the size of both logs. As the web site becomes more popular and as data accumulates, the performance of the algorithm will rapidly deteriorate.

The key to optimizing this algorithm is to recognize that the computation (process) needs to happen for only a small subset of all of the possible combinations of the two variables (in this case, webhit and ccinfo). If we could search for only the right pairs, we might be able to speed up the process. As Tim Peters says in the introduction to this chapter, if you need to search, use an auxiliary dictionary. The solution described earlier, rewritten to use our variables, yields:

```
ipdict = {}
for webhit in weblog: ipdict.setdefault(webhit.ipaddress, []).append(webhit)
results = [ process(webhit, ccinfo) for ccinfo in cclog \
                                for webhit in ipdict[ccinfo.ipaddress] ]
```

The highlighted line creates a dictionary mapping IP addresses to lists containing the data for each web hit. Because we're indexing the dictionary by IP address, we are optimizing the data structures for a particular query: "give me all of the web records for a particular IP address." The list comprehension now iterates over only the data we require—for each credit-card transaction, we iterate over all of the web hits corresponding to the IP address used in that transaction. Not only did the algorithm go from $O(M \times N)$ to $O(M+N)$ from a theoretical point of view, but, because we chose to hold in the auxiliary dictionary data that is sparser from the point of view of the task at hand, we've made the solution faster than the alternative (which would also be $O(M+N)$).

Note that the test used to determine whether two records correspond to a pair of interest can be arbitrary. The generic description of the solution uses indexing, while the web example uses attribute-getting. The test you use will depend on your application and your data structures.

See Also

Recipe 1.5 for more details on the setdefault method of dictionaries; the introduction to Chapter 2.

2.3 Sorting While Guaranteeing Sort Stability

Credit: Alex Martelli, David Goodger

Problem

You need to sort a Python list in a guaranteed-stable way (i.e., with no alteration in the relative ordering of items that compare equal).

Solution

In addition to speed, decorate-sort-undecorate (DSU) offers flexibility that sort with a comparison function argument just can't match. For example, you can ensure the sort's stability, as follows:

```
def stable_sorted_copy(alist, _indices=xrange(sys.maxint)):
    # Decorate: prepare a suitable auxiliary list
    decorated = zip(alist, _indices)

    # Sort: do a plain built-in sort on the auxiliary list
    decorated.sort( )

    # Undecorate: extract the list from the sorted auxiliary list
    return [ item for item, index in decorated ]

def stable_sort_inplace(alist):
    # To sort in place: assign sorted result to all-list slice of original list
    alist[:] = stable_sorted_copy(alist)
```

Discussion

The notion of a stable sort is typically not relevant if the sequences you are sorting contain objects that are uniform in type and are simple, such as a list of integers. In such cases, objects that compare equal are equal in all measurable ways. However, in cases where equality for the sake of ordering doesn't correspond to "deep" equality—such as tuples containing floating-point and integer numbers, or, more commonly, rich objects with arbitrary internal structure—it may matter that the elements that start off earlier in the list than their "equal" counterparts remain earlier after the sort.

Python lists' sort method is not guaranteed to be stable: items that compare equal may or may not be in unchanged order (they often are, but you cannot be sure). Ensuring stability is easy, as one of the many applications of the common DSU idiom. For another specific example of DSU usage, see Recipe 2.6.

First, you build an auxiliary list (the decorate step), where each item is a tuple made up of all sort keys, in descending order of significance, of the corresponding item of the input sequence. You must include in each tuple of the auxiliary list all of the information in the corresponding item, and/or an index to it, so that you can fetch the item back, or reconstruct it, in the third step.

In the second step, you sort the auxiliary list by its built-in sort method, without arguments (this is crucial for performance).

Finally, you reconstruct the desired sorted list by undecorating the now-sorted auxiliary list. Steps 1 and 3 can be performed in several ways: with map, zip, list comprehensions, or explicit loops. List comprehensions and zip are generally simpler, although they require Python 2.0 or later. If you need to be compatible with Python 1.5.2, you will have to use map, which unfortunately is often less clear and readable.

This idiom is also known as the "Schwartzian transform," by analogy with a related Perl idiom. However, that term implies using Perl's map and grep functions and performing the whole idiom inside of a single statement.

DSU inherently supplies a sorted copy, but if the input sequence is a list, we can just assign to its include-everything slice to get an in-place effect instead.

This recipe specifically demonstrates using DSU to achieve a stable sort (i.e., a sort where items that compare equal keep the same relative order in the result list as they had in the input sequence). For this specific task, passing an argument to the built-in sort method is of no use. More generally, the DSU idiom can sometimes be replaced by passing a comparison function argument to sort, but DSU tends to be much faster, and speed often matters when you are sorting sequences that aren't tiny.

The speed comes from maximally accelerating (by not using a Python-coded function as an argument to sort) the $O(N \log N)$ part, which dominates sorting time for sequences of substantial length N. The decoration and undecoration steps are both $O(N)$, and thus they contribute negligible time if N is large enough and reasonably little time even for many practical values of N.

Note the named argument _indices. This ensures that a single copy of the necessary xrange object is generated at function-definition time. It can then be reused to decorate any argument sequence with indexes, by exploiting zip's truncation behavior on unequal-length arguments (see Recipe 1.13).

See Also

Recipes 1.13 and 2.6.

2.4   Sorting by One Field, Then by Another

Credit: José Sebrosa

Problem

You need to sort a list by more than one field of each item.

Solution

Passing a comparison function to a list's sort method is slow for lists of substantial size, but it can still be quite handy when you need to sort lists that are reasonably small. In particular, it offers a rather natural idiom to sort by more than one field:

```
import string

star_list = ['Elizabeth Taylor', 'Bette Davis', 'Hugh Grant', 'C. Grant']

star_list.sort(lambda x,y: (
    cmp(string.split(x)[-1], string.split(y)[-1]) or  # Sort by last name...
    cmp(x, y)))                                        # ...then by first name

print "Sorted list of stars:"
for name in star_list:
    print name
```

Discussion

This recipe uses the properties of the cmp built-in function and the or operator to produce a compact idiom for sorting a list over more than one field of each item.

cmp(X, Y) returns false (0) when X and Y compare equal, so only in these cases does or let the next call to cmp happen. To reverse the sorting order, simply swap X and Y as arguments to cmp.

The fundamental idea of this recipe can also be used if another sorting criterion is associated with the elements of the list. We simply build an auxiliary list of tuples to pack the sorting criterion together with the main elements, then sort and unpack the result. This is more akin to the DSU idiom:

```
def sorting_criterion_1(data):
    return string.split(data)[-1]   # This is again the last name

def sorting_criterion_2(data):
    return len(data)                # This is some fancy sorting criterion

# Pack an auxiliary list:
aux_list = map(lambda x: (x,
                          sorting_criterion_1(x),
                          sorting_criterion_2(x)),
               star_list)

# Sort:
aux_list.sort(lambda x,y: (
    cmp(x[1], y[1])  or     # Sort by criteria 1 (last name)...
    cmp(y[2], x[2])  or     # ...then by criteria 2 (in reverse order)...
    cmp(x, y)))             # ...then by the value in the main list

# Unpack the resulting list:
star_list = map(lambda x: x[0], aux_list)
```

```
print "Another sorted list of stars:"
for name in star_list:
    print name
```

Of course, once we're doing decorating, sorting, and undecorating, it may be worth taking a little extra trouble to be able to call the sort step without a comparison function (the DSU idiom), which will speed up the whole thing quite a bit for lists of substantial size. After all, packing the fields to be compared in the right order in each decorated tuple and plucking out the right field again in the undecorate step is pretty simple:

```
# Pack a better-ordered auxiliary list:
aux_list = map(lambda x: (sorting_criterion_1(x),
                          sorting_criterion_2(x),
                          x),
               star_list)

# Sort in a much simpler and faster way:
aux_list.sort( )

# Unpack the resulting list:
star_list = map(lambda x: x[-1], aux_list)
```

However, this doesn't deal with the reverse order, which you can easily obtain when passing a comparison function to sort by just switching arguments to cmp. To use DSU instead, you need to pack a suitably altered value of the criterion field. For a numeric field, changing the sign is fine. In this example, the sorting_criterion_2 that needs reverse sorting is indeed a number, so our task is easy:

```
# Pack a better-ordered auxiliary list yielding the desired order:
aux_list = map(lambda x: (sorting_criterion_1(x),
                          -sorting_criterion_2(x),
                          x),
               star_list)
```

For reverse sorting on a string field with DSU, you need a string-translation operation that maps each chr(x) into chr(255-x)—or an even wider translation table for Unicode strings. It is a bit of a bother, but you only have to write it once. For example, for plain old strings:

```
import string
all_characters = string.maketrans('','')
all_characters_list = list(all_characters)
all_characters_list.reverse( )
rev_characters = ''.join(all_characters_list)
rev_trans = string.maketrans(all_characters, rev_characters)
```

Now, if we want to reverse the first sorting criterion:

```
# Pack a better-ordered and corrected auxiliary list:
aux_list = map(lambda x: (string.translate(sorting_criterion_1(x), rev_trans),
                          sorting_criterion_2(x),
                          x),
               star_list)
```

```
# Sort in a much simpler and faster way AND get just the desired result:
aux_list.sort()

# Unpack the resulting list:
star_list = map(lambda x: x[-1], aux_list)
```

See Also

The *Reference Manual* section on sequences, and the subsection on mutable sequences (such as lists).

2.5 Looking for Items in a Sorted Sequence Using Binary Search

Credit: Noah Spurrier, Alex Martelli

Problem

You need to look for a lot of items in a sequence.

Solution

Binary search is a basic algorithm provided by bisect in Python. How to perform a binary search to check if a value is present in a list can be summarized in three lines of code:

```
thelist.sort()
item_insert_point = bisect.bisect(thelist, theitem)
is_present = thelist[item_insert_point-1:item_insert_point] == [theitem]
```

Discussion

A friend of mine was searching a large file for missing lines. A linear search was taking forever, so a binary search was needed. The name of the bisect module misled him into believing that Python did not have a binary search algorithm. I created an example to show how bisect is used to perform a binary search.

The third line in the recipe may not be immediately obvious. If we know that thelist is not empty, this is much simpler and more obvious:

```
is_present = thelist[item_insert_point-1] == theitem
```

However, this simpler approach raises an exception for an empty thelist, since indexing must check for a valid index (the only way to return an indicator of "no such index" is by raising IndexError). Slicing is more relaxed than indexing, since it results in an empty slice for invalid slice-boundary indexes. Therefore, in general:

```
somelist[x:x+1]
```

yields the same one-item list as:

```
[somelist[x]]
```

when x is a valid index in somelist. However, it results in an empty list ([ ]) when the indexing would raise an IndexError. The third line in the recipe uses this idea to avoid having to deal with exceptions, thereby handling empty and nonempty cases for thelist in a perfectly uniform way. Another approach is:

```
is_present = thelist and thelist[item_insert_point-1] == theitem
```

This exploits and's short-circuiting behavior to guard the indexing, instead of using slicing. Both approaches are worth keeping in mind, since their areas of applicability overlap but do not coincide.

In my friend's case, of course, an auxiliary dictionary was also a possibility, because strings are hashable. However, the approach based on a sorted list may be the only way out in a few other cases, with items that are not hashable (but only if they are comparable, of course, since otherwise the list cannot be sorted). Also, if the list is already sorted, and the number of items you need to look up in it is not extremely large, it may be faster to use bisect rather than to build an auxiliary dictionary, since the investment of time in the latter operation might not be fully amortized.

See Also

Documentation for the bisect module in the *Library Reference*.

2.6 Sorting a List of Objects by an Attribute of the Objects

Credit: Yakov Markovitch, Nick Perkins

Problem

You have a list of objects that you need to sort according to one attribute of each object, as rapidly and portably as possible.

Solution

In this case, the obvious approach is concise, but quite slow:

```
def sort_by_attr_slow(seq, attr):
    def cmp_by_attr(x, y, attr=attr):
        return cmp(getattr(x, attr), getattr(y, attr))
    seq.sort(cmp_by_attr)
```

There is a faster way, with DSU:

```
def sort_by_attr(seq, attr):
    import operator
```

```
    intermed = map(None, map(getattr, seq, (attr,)*len(seq)),
        xrange(len(seq)), seq)
    intermed.sort()
    return map(operator.getitem, intermed, (-1,)*len(intermed))

def sort_by_attr_inplace(lst, attr):
    lst[:] = sort_by_attr(lst, attr)
```

Discussion

Sorting a list of objects by an attribute of each object is best done using the DSU idiom. Since this recipe uses only built-ins and doesn't use explicit looping, it is quite fast. Moreover, the recipe doesn't use any Python 2.0–specific features (such as zip or list comprehensions), so it can be used for Python 1.5.2 as well.

List comprehensions are neater, but this recipe demonstrates that you can do without them, if and when you desperately need portability to stone-age Python installations. Of course, the correct use of map can be tricky. Here, for example, when we build the auxiliary list intermed, we need to call the built-in function getattr on each item of sequence seq using the same string, attr, as the second argument in each case. To do this, in the inner call to map, we need a tuple in which attr is repeated as many times as there are items in seq. We build that tuple by the not immediately obvious expression:

    (attr,)*len(seq)

which is len(seq) repetitions of the one-item tuple (attr,), whose only item is exactly attr.

If you do want to use list comprehensions, that's easy, too. Just substitute the sort_by_attr of the recipe with the following alternative version:

```
def sort_by_attr2(seq, attr):
    intermed = [(getattr(seq[i], attr), i, seq[i]) for i in xrange(len(seq))]
    intermed.sort()
    return [ tup[-1] for tup in intermed ]
```

However, if this piece of code is run in a speed-critical bottleneck of your program, you should carefully measure performance. map is often surprisingly fast when compared to list comprehensions, at least when no lambda is involved in the map. The difference in performance is not huge either way, so it's worth exploring only if this code is run in a speed-critical bottleneck.

Whether you use map or list comprehensions, the point of the DSU idiom is to gain both speed and flexibility (for example, making the sort a stable one, as we did here) when compared to passing a comparison function to the sort method. For a simpler application and a somewhat wider discussion of DSU, see Recipe 2.3.

Note that in addition to making the sort stable, putting the index i as the second item of each tuple in the auxiliary list intermed (through the insertion of xrange in the call to map or, more simply, that of i in the list-comprehension version sort_by_attr2) also serves a potentially crucial role here. It ensures that two objects (two items of seq) will never be compared, even if their values are the same for the attribute named attr, because even in that case their indexes will surely differ, and thus the lexicographic comparison of the tuples will never get all the way to comparing the tuples' last items (the objects). Avoiding object comparison may save us from extremely slow operations or even from attempting forbidden ones. For example, when we sort a list of complex numbers by their real attributes, in Python 2.0 or later, we will get an exception if we try to compare two complex numbers directly, as no ordering is defined on complex numbers.

See Also

Recipe 2.3.

2.7   Sorting by Item or by Attribute

Credit: Matthew Wood

Problem

You need to sort a list of (x, y) coordinates by item y, or, more generally, sort a list of objects by any attribute or item.

Solution

You might first think of something like the following class, based on the simple but slow approach of passing a comparison function to the sort method:

```
class Sorter:
    # Notice how __compare is dependent on self.__whichindex
    def __compare(self, x, y):
        return cmp(x[self.__whichindex], y[self.__whichindex])

    # Pass the sort function the __compare function defined above
    def __call__(self, data, whichindex = None):
        if whichindex is None :
            data.sort()
        else :
            self.__whichindex = whichindex
            data.sort(self.__compare)
        return data                    # handy for inlining, and low-cost
```

The trick is to use a bound method that accesses instance state as the comparison function to determine which item (or attribute, but this version deals only with items) to fetch. Unfortunately, this makes the approach nonreentrant and not thread-safe.

Thanks to the faster, more robust, and more flexible DSU idiom, it's not hard to make a more general version that allows attributes as well as items, guarantees a stable sort, is both reentrant and thread-safe, and is speedier to boot:

```
class Sorter:
    def _helper(self, data, aux, inplace):
        aux.sort()
        result = [data[i] for junk, i in aux]
        if inplace: data[:] = result
        return result

    def byItem(self, data, itemindex=None, inplace=1):
        if itemindex is None:
            if inplace:
                data.sort()
                result = data
            else:
                result = data[:]
                result.sort()
            return result
        else:
            aux = [(d[i][itemindex], i) for i in range(len(data))]
            return self._helper(data, aux, inplace)

    # a couple of handy synonyms
    sort = byItem
    __call__ = byItem

    def byAttribute(self, data, attributename, inplace=1):
        aux = [(getattr(d[i],attributename),i) for i in range(len(data))]
        return self._helper(data, aux, inplace)
```

Of course, since the second version doesn't use its "classhood" in any way, making it a class is somewhat peculiar. It would be far more Pythonic, and clearer, to use a module with free-standing functions, rather than an artificial class with instances that have no state.

Discussion

How do you efficiently sort a list of (x, y) coordinates by y? More generally, how do you sort a list of dictionaries, lists, or class instances by a particular item or attribute? I *hate* not being able to sort by any item or attribute, so I wrote an auxiliary class to do it for me.

The DSU idiom is much faster than passing sort a comparison function, as discussed in other recipes. The second version of Sorter in this recipe uses DSU because of this, as well as auxiliary flexibility advantages. This second version gets no benefit from being a class rather than just a couple of functions, but casting it as a class makes it drop-in compatible with the first, inferior version, which did use some state as a trick (losing reentrancy and thread-safety in the process).

Here is some example code (note that it instantiates the Sorter class only once, another hint that it is not at all an optimal architecture to wrap this functionality as a class):

```
sort = Sorter( )

if __name__ == '__main__' :
    list = [(1, 2), (4, 8), (0, 3)]
    dict = [{'a': 3, 'b': 4}, {'a': 5, 'b': 2}, {'a': 0, 'b': 0},
        {'a': 9, 'b': 9}]
    dumb = [1, 4, 6, 7, 2, 5, 9, 2, 4, 6]

    print 'list normal:', list
    sort(list, 0)
    print 'sort by [0]:', list
    sort(list, 1)
    print 'sort by [1]:', list

    print

    print "dict normal:", dict
    sort(dict, 'a')
    print "sort by 'a':",  dict
    sort(dict, 'b')
    print "sort by 'b':",  dict

    print

    print 'dumb normal:', dumb
    sort(dumb)
    print 'normal sort:', dumb
```

Returning the sorted list is cheap (it's just an extra reference, since Python, fortunately, never does any copying of data unless you specifically request it) and offers uniform behavior between in-place and non-in-place cases. Often, we only want to do:

```
for x in sort(something, inplace=0):
```

Returning a reference to the sorted data gives us just the right amount of flexibility for this.

See Also

Recipes 2.3 and 4.9.

2.8 Selecting Random Elements from a List Without Repetition

Credit: Iuri Wickert, Duncan Grisby, Steve Holden, Alex Martelli

Problem

You need to consume, in random order, the items of a rather long list, and the most direct approach is painfully slow.

Solution

While it's a common mistake to be overly concerned with speed, you should not ignore the different performances of various algorithms. Suppose we must process all of the items in a long list in random order, without repetition. For example:

```
import random

# an example of a processing function
def process(datum): print datum
# an example of a set of data to process
data = range(10000)
```

The simplest version is very slow:

```
def simple():
    while data:
        # returns element, not index (doesn't help)
        elem = random.choice(data)
        # needs to search for the element throughout the list!
        data.remove(elem)
        process(elem)
```

Here is a faster version:

```
def faster():
    while data:
        index = random.randrange(len(data))
        elem = data[index]
        # direct deletion, no search needed
        del data[index]
        process(elem)

# the same, but preserving the data list
def faster_preserve():
    aux = range(len(data))
    while aux:
        posit = random.randrange(len(aux))
        index = aux[posit]
        elem = data[index]
        # alters the auxiliary list only
        del aux[posit]
        process(elem)
```

However, the key improvement is to switch to an $O(N)$ algorithm:

```
def improved():
    size = len(data)
    while size:
        index = random.randrange(size)
        elem = data[index]
        data[index] = data[size-1]
        size = size - 1
        process(elem)
```

Of course, you can also implement a version of this that preserves the data list.

But the winner is the version that appears to be the simplest:

```
def best():
    random.shuffle(data)
    for elem in data: process(elem)

# or, if you need to preserve the data list's original ordering:
def best_preserve():
    aux = list(data)
    random.shuffle(aux)
    for elem in aux: process(elem)
```

Discussion

The simplest, most direct way of consuming a list in a random fashion is painfully slow for lists with a few hundred elements. While it is tempting to use the simple, clear choice/remove combination, as in the simple function, this is a bad choice, because remove must linearly search through the list to find the element to delete. In other words, the overall performance is $O(N^2)$, with a large multiplicative constant.

Fortunately, there are equally simple (or simpler), but much faster, ways to do this. The faster function, using randrange/del to generate the random indexes for the list, can skip the costly search for the deletion. If it's important to preserve the input list, you can use a disposable auxiliary list to generate the data list indexes, as in the faster_preserve function.

However, del anylist[x] for a random x is still $O(N)$, so overall performance is still $O(N^2)$, albeit with a much smaller multiplicative constant. Incidentally, the pseudo-random order in which items are processed is not the same with the various approaches, even if random is seeded in the same way. All of the orderings are equally pseudorandom, though.

Pursuing $O(N)$ performance, one possibility is not to delete an item from a list at all, but rather to overwrite it with the last item and decrease at each step the number of items from which we're choosing. The improved function takes this tack and benefits greatly from it, in terms of performance.

The fastest approach, however, is to shuffle the data (or an auxiliary copy of it) once, at the start, then just process the items sequentially in the resulting pseudorandom order. The nice thing about this approach, shown in the best and best_preserve functions, is that it's actually the simplest of all.

On lists of 10,000 items, as shown in this recipe, the overhead (meaning pure overhead, using a do-nothing processing function) of simple is about 13 or 14 times more than that of faster and faster_preserve. Those functions, in turn, have over twice as much overhead as improved, best, and best_preserve. On lists of 100,000 items, faster and faster_preserve become about 15 times slower than improved, best, and best_preserve. The latter two have, for every list size, about 20%–30% less overhead than improved—a very minor issue, although their utter simplicity clearly *does* make them deserve their names.

While an improvement of 25%, or even a factor of 2, may be neglected without substantial cost for the performance of your program as a whole, the same does not apply to an algorithm that is 10 or more times as slow as it could be. Such terrible performance is likely to make that program fragment a bottleneck, all by itself, particularly when we're talking about $O(N^2)$ versus $O(N)$ behavior.

See Also

The documentation for the random module in the *Library Reference*.

2.9 Performing Frequent Membership Tests on a Sequence

Credit: Alex Martelli

Problem

You need to perform frequent tests for membership in a sequence. The $O(N)$ behavior of repeated in operators hurts performance, but you can't switch to using just a dictionary, as you also need the sequence's order.

Solution

Say you need to append items to a list only if they're not already in the list. The simple, naive solution is excellent but may be slow:

```
def addUnique1(baseList, otherList):
    for item in otherList:
        if item not in baseList:
            baseList.append(item)
```

If otherList is large, it may be faster to build an auxiliary dictionary:

```
def addUnique2(baseList, otherList):
    auxDict = {}
    for item in baseList:
        auxDict[item] = None
    for item in otherList:
        if not auxDict.has_key(item):
            baseList.append(item)
            auxDict[item] = None
```

For a list on which you must often perform membership tests, it may be best to wrap the list, together with its auxiliary dictionary, into a class. You can then define a special `__contains__` method to speed the `in` operator. The dictionary must be carefully maintained to stay in sync with the sequence. Here's a version that does the syncing just in time, when a membership test is required and the dictionary is out of sync, and works with Python 2.1 or later:

```
from __future__ import nested_scopes
import UserList
try: list.__getitem__
except: Base = UserList.UserList
else: Base = list

class FunkyList(Base):
    def __init__(self, initlist=None):
        Base.__init__(self, initlist)
        self._dict_ok = 0
    def __contains__(self, item):
        if not self._dict_ok:
            self._dict = {}
            for item in self:
                self._dict[item] = 1
            self._dict_ok = 1
        return self._dict.has_key(item)

def _wrapMethod(methname):
    _method = getattr(Base, methname)
    def wrapper(self, *args):
        # Reset 'dictionary OK' flag, then delegate
        self._dict_ok = 0
        return _method(self, *args)
    setattr(FunkyList, methname, wrapper)
for meth in 'setitem delitem setslice delslice iadd'.split():
    _wrapMethod('__%s__'%meth)
for meth in 'append insert pop remove extend'.split():
    _wrapMethod(meth)
del _wrapMethod
```

Discussion

Python's `in` operator is extremely handy, but it's $O(N)$ when applied to an N-item sequence. If a sequence is subject to frequent `in` tests, and the items are hashable, an auxiliary dictionary at the sequence's side can provide a signficant performance boost. A membership check (using the in operator) on a sequence of N items is $O(N)$; if M such tests are performed, the overall time is $O(M \times N)$. Preparing an auxiliary dictionary whose keys are the sequence's items is also roughly $O(N)$, but the M tests are roughly $O(M)$, so overall we have roughly $O(N+M)$. This is rather less than $O(N \times M)$ and can thus offer a very substantial performance boost when M and N are large.

Even better overall performance can often be obtained by permanently placing the auxiliary dictionary alongside the sequence, encapsulating both into one object. However, in this case, the dictionary must be maintained as the sequence is modified, so that it stays in sync with the actual membership of the sequence.

The FunkyList class in this recipe, for example, extends list (UserList in Python 2.1) and delegates every method to it. However, each method that can modify list membership is wrapped in a closure that resets a flag asserting that the auxiliary dictionary is in sync. The in operator calls the __contains__ method when it is applied to an instance that has such a method. The __contains__ method rebuilds the auxiliary dictionary, unless the flag is set, proving that the rebuilding is unnecessary.

If our program needs to run only on Python 2.2 and later versions, we can rewrite the __contains__ method in a much better way:

```
def __contains__(self, item):
    if not self.dict_ok:
        self._dict = dict(zip(self,self))
        self.dict_ok = 1
    return item in self._dict
```

The built-in type dict, new in Python 2.2, lets us build the auxiliary dictionary faster and more concisely. Furthermore, the ability to test for membership in a dictionary directly with the in operator, also new in Python 2.2, has similar advantages in speed, clarity, and conciseness.

Instead of building and installing the wrapping closures for all the mutating methods of the list into the FunkyList class with the auxiliary function _wrapMethod, we could simply write all the needed defs for the wrapper methods in the body of FunkyList, with the advantage of extending backward portability to Python versions even older than 2.1. Indeed, this is how I tackled the problem in the first version of this recipe that I posted to the online Python cookbook. However, the current version of the recipe has the important advantage of minimizing boilerplate (repetitious plumbing code that is boring and voluminous and thus a likely home for bugs). Python's advanced abilities for introspection and dynamic modification give you a choice: you can build method wrappers, as this recipe does, in a smart and concise way, or you can choose to use the boilerplate approach anyway, if you don't mind repetitious code and prefer to avoid what some would call the "black magic" of advanced introspection and dynamic modification of class objects.

Performance characteristics depend on the actual pattern of membership tests versus membership modifications, and some careful profiling may be required to find the right approach for a given use. This recipe, however, caters well to a rather common pattern of use, where sequence-modifying operations tend to happen in bunches, followed by a period in which no sequence modification is performed, but several membership tests may be performed.

Rebuilding the dictionary when needed is far simpler than incrementally maintaining it at each sequence-modifying step. Incremental maintenance requires careful analysis of what is being removed and of what is inserted, particularly upon such operations as slice assignment. If that strategy is desired, the values in the dictionary should probably be a count of the number of occurrences of each key's value in the sequence. A list of the indexes in which the value is present is another possibility, but that takes even more work to maintain. Depending on usage patterns, the strategy of incremental maintenance can be substantially faster or slower.

Of course, all of this is necessary only if the sequence itself is needed (i.e., if the order of items in the sequence is significant). Otherwise, keeping just the dictionary is obviously simpler and more effective. Again, the dictionary can map values to counts, if you the need the data structure to be, in mathematical terms, a bag rather than a set.

An important requisite for any of these membership-test optimizations is that the values in the sequence must be hashable (otherwise, of course, they cannot be keys in a dictionary). For example, a list of tuples might be subjected to this recipe's treatment, but for a list of lists the recipe as it stands is not applicable. You can sometimes use cPickle.dumps to create dictionary keys—or, for somewhat different application needs, the object's id—but neither workaround is always fully applicable. In the case of cPickle.dumps, even when it is applicable, the overhead may negate some or most of the optimization.

See Also

The *Library Reference* sections on sequences types and mapping types.

2.10 Finding the Deep Index of an Item in an Embedded Sequence

Credit: Brett Cannon

Problem

You need to find the deep index of an item in an embedded sequence (i.e., the sequence of indexes that will reach the item when applied one after the other to peel off successive layers of nesting). For example, the 6 in [[1,2],[3,[4,[5,6]]],7,[8,9]] has the deep index of [1,1,1,1].

Solution

Lists can be nested (i.e., items of lists can, in turn, be lists), but it takes some care to unnest them when we need to reach for an item:

```
import sys, types

class Found(Exception): pass

_indices = xrange(sys.maxint)

def _is_sequence(obj):
    return isinstance(obj, types.ListType) or isinstance(obj, types.TupleType)

def deepindex(sequence, goal, is_subsequence=_is_sequence):
    """ deepindex(sequence, goal) -> index list """
    def helper(sequence, index_list, goal=goal):
        for item, index in zip(sequence, _indices):
            if item==goal:
                raise Found, index_list+[index]
            elif is_subsequence(item):
                helper(item, index_list+[index])

    try: helper(sequence, [])
    except Found, index_list: return index_list
    else: return -1

if __name__=='__main__':
    print deepindex([[1,2],[3,[4,[5,6]]],7,[8,9]], 6)
    print deepindex([[1,2],[3,[4,[5,6]]],7,[8,9]], 66)
```

Discussion

This recipe is handy when you have deeply nested sequences and thus need something better than somelist.index(item) to get the index with which an item can be retrieved from the list. It also works as a way to determine if an item is in a deep sequence, regardless of the item's location within the nested sequence. The recipe is coded to work with Python 2.0 or later.

The nested helper function is recursive. helper iterates on its argument sequence, examining each item. When the current item equals goal, the search is finished, and helper breaks out of whatever number of levels of recursion it's in, using the following statement:

```
raise Found, index_list+[index]
```

When the current item is a nested sequence, `helper` calls itself recursively on the subsequence, with an updated `index_list`. If the recursive call returns normally, that branch of the search has proved fruitless (successful searches don't return normally, but rather raise a `Found` exception), so `helper` keeps looking. Note that `helper` checks for nested sequences via type tests for tuples and lists specifically; see Recipe 1.12 for alternative ways to perform this check.

This recipe is an interesting, although controversial, show-off for the concept of raising an exception as a way to return a value from deeply nested recursive calls. If using exceptions as building blocks for alternative control structures is ever appropriate, this case for their application surely would be. We avoid having to arrange some artificial means of signaling "found" versus "not found," and, even better, we avoid having to arrange for the complexity of returning from a deep stack of calls when the item has been found. In any case, this usage surely underscores how, in Python, exceptions can be used for conditions that are not errors, and indeed not even truly exceptional.

See Also

Recipe 1.12; documentation for the `range` built-in function in the *Library Reference*.

2.11 Showing Off Quicksort in Three Lines

Credit: Nathaniel Gray

Problem

You need to show that Python's support for the functional programming paradigm is quite a bit better than it might seem at first sight.

Solution

Functional programming languages, of which Haskell is a great example, are splendid animals, but Python can hold its own in such company:

```
def qsort(L):
    if len(L) <= 1: return L
    return qsort([lt for lt in L[1:] if lt < L[0]]) + L[0:1] + \
           qsort([ge for ge in L[1:] if ge >= L[0]])
```

In my humble opinion, this is almost as pretty as the Haskell version from *http://www.haskell.org*:

```
qsort [] = []
qsort (x:xs) = qsort elts_lt_x ++ [x] ++ qsort elts_ge_x
                 where
                     elts_lt_x = [y | y <- xs, y < x]
                     elts_ge_x = [y | y <- xs, y >= x]
```

Here's a test function for the Python version:

```
def qs_test(length):
    import random
    joe = range(length)
    random.shuffle(joe)
    qsJoe = qsort(joe)
    for i in range(len(qsJoe)):
        assert qsJoe[i] == i, 'qsort is broken at %d!'%i
```

Discussion

This is a rather naive implementation of quicksort that illustrates the expressive power of list comprehensions. Do not use this in real code! Python's own built-in sort is of course much faster and should always be preferred. The only proper use of this recipe is for impressing friends, particularly ones who (quite understandably) are enthusiastic about functional programming, and particularly about the Haskell language.

I cooked up this function after finding the wonderful Haskell quicksort (which I've reproduced above) at *http://www.haskell.org/aboutHaskell.html*. After marveling at the elegance of this code for a while, I realized that list comprehensions made the same thing possible in Python. Not for nothing did we steal list comprehensions right out of Haskell, just Pythonizing them a bit by using keywords rather than punctuation!

Both implementations pivot on the first element of the list and thus have worst-case $O(N^2)$ performance for the very common case of sorting an already-sorted list, so you would never want to do this in production code. Because this is just a propaganda thing, though, it doesn't really matter.

List comprehensions were introduced in Python 2.0, so this recipe's code will not work on any earlier version. But then, you wouldn't be trying to impress a friend with a many-years-old version of Python, right?

A less compact version with the same architecture can easily be written to use named local variables and functions for enhanced clarity:

```
def qsort(L):
    if not L: return L
    pivot = L[0]
    def lt(x, pivot=pivot): return x<pivot
    def ge(x, pivot=pivot): return x>=pivot
    return qsort(filter(lt, L[1:]))+[pivot]+qsort(filter(ge, L[1:]))
```

This one works on old and crusty Python versions, but in Python 2.1 (with a `from __future__ import nested_scopes`) and later, you can do without the `pivot=pivot` trick in the formal argument lists of `lt` and `ge`.

See Also

The Haskell web site (*http://www.haskell.org*).

2.12 Sorting Objects Using SQL's ORDER BY Syntax

Credit: Andrew M. Henshaw

Problem

You need to sort by multiple keys, with each key independently ascending or descending, mimicking the functionality of the SQL ORDER BY clause.

Solution

Sometimes you get data from a database and need the data ordered in several ways in succession. Rather than doing multiple SELECT queries on the database with different ORDER BY clauses, you can emulate the sorting flexibility of ORDER BY in your Python code and get the data just once:

```
class sqlSortable:
    def __init__(self, **args):
        self.__dict__.update(args)

    def setSort(self, sortOrder):
        self.sortFields = []
        for text in sortOrder:
            sortBy, direction = (text+' ').split(' ', 1)
            self.sortFields.append((sortBy, direction[0:4].lower() == 'desc'))

    def __repr__(self):
        return repr([getattr(self, x) for x, reverse in self.sortFields])

    def __cmp__(self, other):
        myFields    = []
        otherFields = []
        for sortBy, reverse in self.sortFields:
            myField, otherField = getattr(self, sortBy), getattr(other, sortBy)
            if reverse:
                myField, otherField = otherField, myField
            myFields.append(myField)
            otherFields.append(otherField)
        return cmp(myFields, otherFields)
```

Discussion

Occasionally, I need to do database processing that is more complex than the SQL framework can handle. With this class, I can extract the database rows and instantiate the class object for each row. After massaging the objects, I apply a list of sort conditions and sort. For example, this search description, when supplied as the argument to the recipe's setSort method:

```
['name', 'value DESC']
```

is equivalent to the SQL clause:

```
ORDER BY name, value DESC
```

The class handles multiple-key, multiple-direction sorts in the __cmp__ method. A list of attributes is built for each key, and individual items are swapped between the two objects if that particular key has a reversed sort order. Performance may not be great, but the idea is both simple and useful.

Here is the self-test code that would normally be placed at the end of the module, both to test functionality and to provide an example of use:

```python
def testSqlSortable():
    data = [('Premier', 'Stealth U-11'), ('Premier', 'Stealth U-10'),
            ('Premier', 'Stealth U-12'),
            ('Co-ed',   'Cyclones'),     ('Co-ed',   'Lightning'),
            ('Co-ed',   'Dolphins'),
            ('Girls',   'Dynamos'),      ('Girls',   'Tigers'),
            ('Girls',   'Dolphins')]

    testList = [sqlSortable(program=program, name=name)
                for program, name in data]

    tests = [['program DESC', 'name'],
             ['name desc', 'program asc']]

    for sortBy in tests:
        print '#### Test basic sorting ###', sortBy
        for sortable in testList:
            sortable.setSort(sortBy)
        testList.sort()
        for item in testList:
            print item

    print '#### Test modification of attributes ###', sortBy
    assert testList[4].name == 'Lightning'
    testList[4].name = 'ZZ 1st name'
    testList.sort()
    for item in testList:
        print item

if __name__ == '__main__':
    testSqlSortable()
```

See Also

The O'Reilly Network, for an article about SQL ORDER BY (*http://linux.oreillynet.com/pub/a/linux/2001/02/13/aboutSQL.html*); your database's reference for SQL.

## CHAPTER 3

Text

3.0 Introduction

Credit: Fred L. Drake, Jr., PythonLabs

Text-processing applications form a substantial part of the application space for any scripting language, if only because everyone can agree that text processing is useful. Everyone has bits of text that need to be reformatted or transformed in various ways. The catch, of course, is that every application is just a little bit different from every other application, so it can be difficult to find just the right reusable code to work with different file formats, no matter how similar they are.

What Is Text?

Sounds like an easy question, doesn't it? After all, we know it when we see it, don't we? Text is a sequence of characters, and it is distinguished from binary data by that very fact. Binary data, after all, is a sequence of bytes.

Unfortunately, all data enters our applications as a sequence of bytes. There's no library function we can call that will tell us whether a particular sequence of bytes represents text, although we can create some useful heuristics that tell us whether data can safely (not necessarily correctly) be handled as text.

Python strings are immutable sequences of bytes or characters. Most of the ways we create and process strings treat them as sequences of characters, but many are just as applicable to sequences of bytes. Unicode strings are immutable sequences of Unicode characters: transformations of Unicode strings into and from plain strings use codecs (coder-decoder) objects that embody knowledge about the many standard ways in which sequences of characters can be represented by sequences of bytes (also known as *encodings* and *character sets*). Note that Unicode strings do not serve double duty as sequences of bytes.

Okay, let's assume that our application knows from the context that it's looking at text. That's usually the best approach, because that's where external input comes into play. We're either looking at a file because it has a well-known name and defined format (common in the Unix world) or because it has a well-known file-name extension that indicates the format of the contents (common on Windows). But now we have a problem: we had to use the word "format" to make the previous paragraph meaningful. Wasn't text supposed to be simple?

Let's face it: there's no such thing as "pure" text, and if there were, we probably wouldn't care about it (with the possible exception of applications in the field of computational linguistics, where pure text may indeed be studied for its own sake). What we want to deal with in our applications is information content contained in text. The text we care about may contain configuration data, commands to control or define processes, documents for human consumption, or even tabular data. Text that contains configuration data or a series of commands usually can be expected to conform to a fairly strict syntax that can be checked before relying on the information in the text. Informing the user of an error in the input text is typically sufficient to deal with things that aren't what we were expecting.

Documents intended for humans tend to be simple, but they vary widely in detail. Since they are usually written in a natural language, their syntax and grammar can be difficult to check, at best. Different texts may use different character sets or encodings, and it can be difficult or even impossible to tell what character set or encoding was used to create a text if that information is not available in addition to the text itself. It is, however, necessary to support proper representation of natural-language documents. Natural-language text has structure as well, but the structures are often less explicit in the text and require at least some understanding of the language in which the text was written. Characters make up words, which make up sentences, which make up paragraphs, and still larger structures may be present as well. Paragraphs alone can be particularly difficult to locate unless you know what typographical conventions were used for a document: is each line a paragraph, or can multiple lines make up a paragraph? If the latter, how do we tell which lines are grouped together to make a paragraph? Paragraphs may be separated by blank lines, indentation, or some other special mark. See Recipes 4.8 and 12.7 for examples of processing and inputting paragraphs separated by blank lines.

Tabular data has many issues that are similar to the problems associated with natural-language text, but it adds a second dimension to the input format: the text is no longer linear—it is no longer a sequence of characters, but rather a matrix of characters from which individual blocks of text must be identified and organized.

Basic Textual Operations

As with any other data format, we need to do different things with text at different times. However, there are still three basic operations:

- Parsing the data into a structure internal to our application
- Transforming the input into something similar in some way, but with changes of some kind
- Generating completely new data

Parsing can be performed in a variety of ways, and many formats can be suitably handled by ad hoc parsers that deal effectively with a very constrained format. Examples of this approach include parsers for RFC 2822–style email headers (see the rfc822 module in Python's standard library) and the configuration files handled by the ConfigParser module. The netrc module offers another example of a parser for an application-specific file format, this one based on the shlex module. shlex offers a fairly typical tokenizer for basic languages, useful in creating readable configuration files or allowing users to enter commands to an interactive prompt. These sorts of ad hoc parsers are abundant in Python's standard library, and recipes using them can be found in Chapter 4 and Chapter 10. More formal parsing tools are also available for Python; they depend on larger add-on packages and are surveyed in the introduction to Chapter 15.

Transforming text from one format to another is more interesting when viewed as text processing, which is what we usually think of first when we talk about text. In this chapter, we'll take a look at some ways to approach transformations that can be applied for different purposes, including three different recipes that deal with replacing embedded Python expressions with their evaluations. Sometimes we'll work with text stored in external files, and other times we'll simply work with it as strings in memory.

The generation of textual data from application-specific data structures is most easily performed using Python's print statement or the write method of a file or file-like object. This is often done using a method of the application object or a function, which takes the output file as a parameter. The function can then use statements such as these:

```
print >>file, sometext
file.write(sometext)
```

which generate output to the appropriate file. However, this isn't generally thought of as text processing, as here there is no input text to be processed. Examples of using both print and write can be found throughout this book.

Sources of Text

Working with text stored as a string in memory can be easy when the text is not too large. Operations that search the text can operate over multiple lines very easily and quickly, and there's no need to worry about searching for something that might cross a buffer boundary. Being able to keep the text in memory as a simple string makes it very easy to take advantage of the built-in string operations available as methods of the string object.

File-based transformations deserve special treatment, because there can be substantial overhead related to I/O performance and the amount of data that must actually be stored in memory. When working with data stored on disk, we often want to avoid loading entire files into memory, due to the size of the data: loading an 80-MB file into memory should not be done too casually! When our application needs only part of the data at a time, working on smaller segments of the data can yield substantial performance improvements, simply because we've allowed enough space for our program to run. If we are careful about buffer management, we can still maintain the performance advantage of using a small number of relatively large disk read and write operations by working on large chunks of data at a time. File-related recipes are found in Chapter 4.

Another interesting source for textual data comes to light when we consider the network. Text is often retrieved from the network using a socket. While we can always view a socket as a file (using the makefile method of the socket object), the data that is retrieved over a socket may come in chunks, or we may have to wait for more data to arrive. The textual data may also not consist of all data until the end of the data stream, so a file object created with makefile may not be entirely appropriate to pass to text-processing code. When working with text from a network connection, we often need to read the data from the connection before passing it along for further processing. If the data is large, it can be handled by saving it to a file as it arrives and then using that file when performing text-processing operations. More elaborate solutions can be built when the text processing needs to be started before all the data is available. Examples of the parsers that are useful in such situations may be found in the htmilib and HTMLParser modules in the standard library.

String Basics

The main tool Python gives us to process text is strings—immutable sequences of characters. There are actually two kinds of strings: plain strings, which contain eight-bit (ASCII) characters; and Unicode strings, which contain Unicode characters. We won't deal much with Unicode strings here: their functionality is similar to that of plain strings, except that each character takes up 2 (or 4) bytes, so that the number of different characters is in the tens of thousands (or even billions), as opposed to the 256 different characters that comprise plain strings. Unicode strings are important if you must deal with text in many different alphabets, particularly Asian ideographs. Plain strings are sufficient to deal with English or any of a limited set of non-Asian languages. For example, all Western European alphabets can be encoded in plain strings, typically using the international standard encoding known as ISO-8859-1 (or ISO-8859-15, if you need the Euro currency symbol as well).

In Python, you express a literal string as:

```
'this is a literal string'
"this is another string"
```

String values can be enclosed in either single or double quotes. The two different kinds of quotes work the same way, but having both allows you to include one kind of quotes inside of a string specified with the other kind of quotes, without needing to escape them with the backslash character:

```
'isn\'t that grand'
"isn't that grand"
```

To have a string span multiple lines, you can use a backslash as the last character on the line, which indicates that the next line is a continuation:

```
big = "This is a long string\
that spans two lines."
```

You must embed newlines in the string if you want the string to output on two lines:

```
big = "This is a long string\n\
that prints on two lines."
```

Another approach is to enclose the string in a pair of matching triple quotes (either single or double):

```
bigger = """
This is an even
bigger string that
spans three lines.
"""
```

In this case, you don't need to use the continuation character, and line breaks in the string literal are preserved as newline characters in the resulting Python string object. You can also make a string a "raw" string by preceding it with an r or R:

```
big = r"This is a long string\
with a backslash and a newline in it"
```

With a raw string, backslash escape sequences are left alone, rather than being interpreted. Finally, you can precede a string with a u or U to make it a Unicode string:

```
hello = u'Hello\u0020World'
```

Strings are immutable, which means that no matter what operation you do on a string, you will always produce a new string object, rather than mutating the existing string. A string is a sequence of characters, which means that you can access a single character:

```
mystr = "my string"
mystr[0]        # 'm'
mystr[-2]       # 'n'
```

You can also access a portion of the string with a slice:

```
mystr[1:4]      # 'y s'
mystr[3:]       # 'string'
mystr[-3:]      # 'ing'
```

You can loop on a string's characters:

```
for c in mystr:
```

This will bind c to each of the characters in mystr. You can form another sequence:

```
list(mystr)      # returns ['m','y',' ','s','t','r','i','n','g']
```

You can concatenate strings by addition:

```
mystr+'oid'      # 'my stringoid'
```

You can also repeat strings by multiplication:

```
'xo'*3           # 'xoxoxo'
```

In general, you can do anything to a string that you can do to a sequence, as long as it doesn't require changing the sequence, since strings are immutable.

String objects have many useful methods. For example, you can test a string's contents with s.isdigit, which returns true if s is not empty and all of the characters in s are digits (otherwise, it returns false). You can produce a new modified string with a method such as s.toupper, which returns a new string that is like s, but with every letter changed into its uppercase equivalent. You can search for a string inside another with haystack.count("needle"), which returns the number of times the substring "needle" appears in the string haystack. When you have a large string that spans multiple lines, you can split it into a list of single-line strings with splitlines:

```
list_of_lines = one_large_string.splitlines()
```

And you can produce the single large string again with join:

```
one_large_string = '\n'.join(list_of_lines)
```

The recipes in this chapter show off many methods of the string object. You can find complete documentation in Python's *Library Reference*.

Strings in Python can also be manipulated with regular expressions, via the re module. Regular expressions are a powerful (but complicated) set of tools that you may already be familiar with from another language (such as Perl), or from the use of tools such as the *vi* editor and text-mode commands such as *grep*. You'll find a number of uses of regular expressions in recipes in the second half of this chapter. For complete documentation, see the *Library Reference*. *Mastering Regular Expressions*, by J. E. F. Friedl (O'Reilly), is also recommended if you do need to master this subject—Python's regular expressions are basically the same as Perl's, which Friedl covers thoroughly.

Python's standard module string offers much of the same functionality that is available from string methods, packaged up as functions instead of methods. The string module also offers additional functions, such as the useful string.maketrans function that is demonstrated in a few recipes in this chapter, and helpful string constants (string.digits, for example, is '0123456789'). The string-formatting operator, %, provides a handy way to put strings together and to obtain precisely formatted strings from such objects as floating-point numbers. Again, you'll find recipes in this chapter that show how to use % for your purposes. Python also has lots of standard and extension modules that perform special processing on strings of many kinds, although this chapter doesn't cover such specialized resources.

3.1 Processing a String One Character at a Time

Credit: Luther Blissett

Problem

You want to process a string one character at a time.

Solution

You can use list with the string as its argument to build a list of characters (i.e., strings each of length one):

```
thelist = list(thestring)
```

You can loop over the string in a for statement:

```
for c in thestring:
    do_something_with(c)
```

You can apply a function to each character with map:

```
map(do_something_with, thestring)
```

This is similar to the for loop, but it produces a list of results of the function do_something_with called with each character in the string as its argument.

Discussion

In Python, characters are just strings of length one. You can loop over a string to access each of its characters, one by one. You can use map for much the same purpose, as long as what you need to do with each character is call a function on it. Finally, you can call the built-in type list to obtain a list of the length-one substrings of the string (i.e., the string's characters).

See Also

The *Library Reference* section on sequences; *Perl Cookbook* Recipe 1.5.

3.2   Testing if an Object Is String-Like

Credit: Luther Blissett

Problem

You need to test if an object, typically an argument to a function or method you're writing, is a string (or more precisely, whether the object is string-like).

Solution

The first thing that comes to mind is type-testing:

```
def isAString(anobj): return type(anobj) is type('')
```

However, this approach is not appropriate, as it wilfully destroys one of Python's greatest strengths—smooth, signature-based polymorphism. Using the isinstance built-in function, which can accept a type argument in Python 2.0 or later, is only marginally better:

```
def isAString(anobj): return isinstance(anobj, type(''))
```

This does accept instances of subclasses of type str (in Python 2.2 or better), but it still miserably fails to accept such clearly string-like objects as instances of UserString.UserString and Unicode strings. What you really want is a way to check if some object is string-like (i.e., whether it behaves like a string):

```
def isStringLike(anobj):
    try: anobj + ''
    except: return 0
    else: return 1
```

Discussion

If it walks like a duck, and quacks like a duck, it's duck-like enough for our purposes. The isStringLike function in this recipe goes only as far as the "quacks like" part, but that's still far better than the disastrous attempts at rigorous duckhood-checking in the two unacceptable functions named isAString in the solution. It's easy to test a few more properties by using a richer expression in the try clause, if and when you need to check for more string-like features of the object anobj. For example:

```
try: anobj.lower( ) + anobj + ''
```

But in my experience, the simple test shown in the solution usually does exactly what I need.

The most Pythonic approach to type validation (or any validation task, really) is to try to perform whatever task you need to do, detecting and handling any errors or exceptions that might result if the situation is somehow invalid. try/except works very well for this. Sometimes, as in this recipe, you may choose some simple task, such as concatenating to the empty string, as a stand-in for a much richer set of properties (such as all the various operations and methods available on string objects).

See Also

Documentation for the built-in functions isinstance, type, and issubclass in the *Library Reference*.

3.3 Aligning Strings

Credit: Luther Blissett

Problem

You want to align strings left, right, or center.

Solution

That's what the ljust, rjust, and center methods of string objects are for. Each takes a single argument, the width of the string you want as a result, and returns the starting string with spaces on either or both sides:

```
>>> print '|', 'hej'.ljust(20), '|', 'hej'.rjust(20), '|', 'hej'.center(20), '|'
| hej                |                  hej |        hej         |.
```

Discussion

Centering, left-justifying, or right-justifying text comes up surprisingly often—for example, when you want to print a simple report with centered page numbers. Because of this, Python string objects supply this functionality through their methods.

See Also

The *Library Reference* section on string methods; *Java Cookbook* Recipe 3.5.

3.4 Trimming Space from the Ends of a String

Credit: Luther Blissett

Problem

You need to work on a string without regard for any extra leading or trailing spaces a user may have typed.

Solution

That's what the lstrip, rstrip, and strip methods of string objects are for. Each takes no argument and returns the starting string, shorn of whitespace on either or both sides:

```
>>> x = '    hej    '
>>> print '|', x.lstrip(), '|', x.rstrip(), '|', x.strip(), '|'
| hej    |    hej | hej |
```

Discussion

Just as you may need to add space to either end of a string to align that string left, right, or center in a field of fixed width, so may you need to remove all whitespace (blanks, tabs, newlines, etc.) from either or both ends. Because this is a frequent need, Python string objects supply this functionality through their methods.

See Also

The *Library Reference* section on string methods; *Java Cookbook* Recipe 3.12.

3.5   Combining Strings

Credit: Luther Blissett

Problem

You have several small strings that you need to combine into one larger string.

Solution

The + operator concatenates strings and therefore offers seemingly obvious solutions for putting small strings together into a larger one. For example, when you have all the pieces at once, in a few variables:

```
largeString = small1 + small2 + ' something ' + small3 + ' yet more'
```

Or when you have a sequence of small string pieces:

```
largeString = ''
for piece in pieces:
    largeString += piece
```

Or, equivalently, but a bit more compactly:

```
import operator
largeString = reduce(operator.add, pieces, '')
```

However, none of these solutions is generally optimal. To put together pieces stored in a few variables, the string-formatting operator % is often best:

```
largeString = '%s%s something %s yet more' % (small1, small2, small3)
```

To join a sequence of small strings into one large string, the string operator `join` is invariably best:

```
largeString = ''.join(pieces)
```

Discussion

In Python, string objects are immutable. Therefore, any operation on a string, including string concatenation, produces a new string object, rather than modifying an existing one. Concatenating N strings thus involves building and then immediately throwing away each of $N-1$ intermediate results. Performance is therefore quite a bit better for operations that build no intermediate results, but rather produce the desired end result at once. The string-formatting operator % is one such operation, particularly suitable when you have a few pieces (for example, each bound to a different variable) that you want to put together, perhaps with some constant text in addition. In addition to performance, which is never a major issue for this kind of task, the % operator has several potential advantages when compared to an expression that uses multiple + operations on strings, including readability, once you get used to it. Also, you don't have to call str on pieces that aren't already strings (e.g., numbers) because the format specifier %s does so implicitly. Another advantage is that you can use format specifiers other than %s, so that, for example, you can control how many significant digits the string form of a floating-point number should display.

When you have many small string pieces in a sequence, performance can become a truly important issue. The time needed for a loop using + or += (or a fancier but equivalent approach using the built-in function reduce) tends to grow with the square of the number of characters you are accumulating, since the time to allocate and fill a large string is roughly proportional to the length of that string. Fortunately, Python offers an excellent alternative. The join method of a string object s takes as its only argument a sequence of strings and produces a string result obtained by joining all items in the sequence, with a copy of s separating each item from its neighbors. For example, `''.join(pieces)` concatenates all the items of pieces in a single gulp, without interposing anything between them. It's the fastest, neatest, and most elegant and readable way to put a large string together.

Even when your pieces come in sequentially from input or computation, and are not already available as a sequence, you should use a list to hold the pieces. You can prepare that list with a list comprehension or by calling the append or extend methods. At the end, when the list of pieces is complete, you can build the string you want, typically with `''.join(pieces)`. Of all the handy tips and tricks I could give you about Python strings, I would call this one the most significant.

See Also

The *Library Reference* sections on string methods, string-formatting operations, and the operator module.

3.6 Checking Whether a String Contains a Set of Characters

Credit: Jürgen Hermann, Horst Hansen

Problem

You need to check for the occurrence of any of a set of characters in a string.

Solution

The solution generalizes to any sequence (not just a string), and any set (any object in which membership can be tested with the in operator, not just one of characters):

```
def containsAny(str, set):
    """ Check whether sequence str contains ANY of the items in set. """
    return 1 in [c in str for c in set]

def containsAll(str, set):
    """ Check whether sequence str contains ALL of the items in set. """
    return 0 not in [c in str for c in set]
```

Discussion

While the find and count string methods can check for substring occurrences, there is no ready-made function to check for the occurrence in a string of a set of characters.

While working on a condition to check whether a string contained the special characters used in the glob.glob standard library function, I came up with the above code (with help from the OpenProjects IRC channel #python). Written this way, it really is compatible with human thinking, even though you might not come up with such code intuitively. That is often the case with list comprehensions.

The following code creates a list of 1/0 values, one for each item in the set:

```
[c in str for c in set]
```

Then this code checks whether there is at least one true value in that list:

```
1 in [c in str for c in set]
```

Similarly, this checks that no false values are in the list:

```
0 not in [c in str for c in set]
```

Usage examples are best cast in the form of unit tests to be appended to the *.py* source file of this module, with the usual idiom to ensure that the tests execute if the module runs as a main script:

```
if __name__ == "__main__":
    # unit tests, must print "OK!" when run
    assert containsAny('*.py', '*?[]')
    assert not containsAny('file.txt', '*?[]')
    assert containsAll('43221', '123')
    assert not containsAll('134', '123')
    print "OK!"
```

Of course, while the previous idioms are neat, there are alternatives (aren't there always?). Here are the most elementary—and thus, in a sense, the most Pythonic—alternatives:

```
def containsAny(str, set):
    for c in set:
        if c in str: return 1
    return 0

def containsAll(str, set):
    for c in set:
        if c not in str: return 0
    return 1
```

Here are some alternatives that ensure minimal looping (earliest possible return). These are the most concise and thus, in a sense, the most powerful:

```
from operator import and_, or_, contains

def containsAny(str, set):
    return reduce(or_, map(contains, len(set)*[str], set))

def containsAll(str, set):
    return reduce(and_, map(contains, len(set)*[str], set))
```

Here are some even slimmer variants of the latter that rely on a special method that string objects supply only in Python 2.2 and later:

```
from operator import and_, or_

def containsAny(str, set):
    return reduce(or_, map(str.__contains__, set))

def containsAll(str, set):
    return reduce(and_, map(str.__contains__, set))
```

And here is a tricky variant that relies on functionality also available in 2.0:

```
def containsAll(str, set):
    try: map(str.index, set)
    except ValueError: return 0
    else: return 1
```

Fortunately, this rather tricky approach lacks an immediately obvious variant applicable to implement containsAny. However, one last tricky scheme, based on string. translate's ability to delete all characters in a set, does apply to both functions:

```
import string
notrans = string.maketrans('', '')  # identity "translation"

def containsAny(str, set):
    return len(set)!=len(set.translate(notrans, str))

def containsAll(str, set):
    return 0==len(set.translate(notrans, str))
```

This trick at least has some depth—it relies on set.translate(notrans, str) being the subsequence of set that is made of characters not in str. If that subsequence has the same length as set, no characters have been removed by set.translate, so no characters of set are in str. Conversely, if that subsequence has length 0, all characters have been removed, so all characters of set are in str. The translate method of string objects keeps coming up naturally when one wants to treat strings as sets of characters, partly because it's so speedy and partly because it's so handy and flexible. See Recipe 3.7 for another similar application.

One last observation is that these different ways to approach the task have very different levels of generality. At one extreme, the earliest approaches, relying only on in (for looping on str and for membership in set) are the most general; they are not at all limited to string processing, and they make truly minimal demands on the representations of str and set. At the other extreme, the last approach, relying on the translate method, works only when both str and set are strings or closely mimic string objects' functionality.

See Also

Recipe 3.7; documentation for the translate and maketrans functions in the string module in the *Library Reference*.

3.7   Filtering a String for a Set of Characters

Credit: Jürgen Hermann, Nick Perkins

Problem

Given a set of characters to keep, you need to build a filtering *functor* (a function-like, callable object). The specific functor you need to build is one that, applied to any string s, returns a copy of s that contains only characters in the set.

Solution

The string.maketrans function and translate method of string objects are fast and handy for all tasks of this ilk:

```
import string

# Make a reusable string of all characters
_allchars = string.maketrans('', '')

def makefilter(keep):
    """ Return a functor that takes a string and returns a partial copy of that
        string consisting of only the characters in 'keep'.
    """
    # Make a string of all characters that are not in 'keep'
    delchars = _allchars.translate(_allchars, keep)

    # Return the functor, binding the two strings as default args
    return lambda s, a=_allchars, d=delchars: s.translate(a, d)

def canonicform(keep):
    """ Given a string, considered as a set of characters, return the
        string's characters as a canonic-form string: alphabetized
        and without duplicates.
    """
    return makefilter(keep)(_allchars)

if __name__ == '__main__':
    identifier = makefilter(string.letters + string.digits + '_')
    print identifier(_allchars)
```

Discussion

The key to understanding this recipe lies in the definitions of the translate and maketrans functions in the string module. translate takes a string and replaces each character in it with the corresponding character in the translation table passed in as the second argument, deleting the characters specified in the third argument. maketrans is a utility routine that helps create the translation tables.

Efficiency is vastly improved by splitting the filtering task into preparation and execution phases. The string of all characters is clearly reusable, so we build it once and for all when this module is imported. That way, we ensure that each filtering functor has a reference to the same string of all characters, not wasting any memory. The string of characters to delete depends on the set of characters to keep, so we build it in the makefilter factory function. This is done quite rapidly using the translate method to delete the characters to keep from the string of all characters. The translate method is very fast, as are the construction and execution of these useful little functors. The solution also supplies an extremely simple function to put any set of characters, originally an arbitrary string, into canonic-string form (alphabetically sorted, without duplicates). The same trick encapsulated in the `canonicform` function is also explicitly used in the test code that is executed when this runs as a script.

Of course, you don't have to use `lambda` (here or anywhere else). A named function local to the factory function will do just as well. In other words, this recipe works fine if you change `makefilter`'s `return` statement into the following two statements:

```
def filter(s, a=_allchars, d=delchars): return s.translate(a, d)
return filter
```

Many Pythonistas would consider this clearer and more readable.

This isn't a big issue, but remember that `lambda` is never necessary. In any case in which you find yourself straining to fit code into a `lambda`'s limitations (i.e., just an expression, with no statements allowed), you can and should always use a local named function instead, to avoid all the limitations and problems.

With Python 2.2, or Python 2.1 and a `from __future__ import nested_scopes`, you get lexically nested scopes, so that if you want to, you can avoid binding `_allchars` and `delchars` as default values for arguments in the returned functor. However, it is (marginally) faster to use this binding anyway: local variables are the fastest kind to access, and arguments are nothing but prebound local variables. Globals and names from nested scopes require a little more effort from the interpreter (and sometimes, perhaps more significantly, from a human being who is reading the code). This is why we bind `_allchars` as argument a here despite the fact that, in any release of Python, we could have just accessed it as a global variable.

See Also

Documentation for the `maketrans` function in the `string` module in the *Library Reference*.

3.8   Controlling Case

Credit: Luther Blissett

Problem

You need to convert a string from uppercase to lowercase, or vice versa.

Solution

That's what the `upper` and `lower` methods of string objects are for. Each takes no arguments and returns a copy of the string in which each letter has been changed to upper- or lowercase, respectively.

```
big = little.upper( )
little = big.lower( )
```

s.capitalize is similar to s[:1].upper()+s[1:].lower(). The first character is changed to uppercase, and all others are changed to lowercase. s.title is similar, but it uppercases the first letter of each word:

```
>>> print 'one two three'.capitalize()
One two three
>>> print 'one two three'.title()
One Two Three
```

Discussion

Case manipulation of strings is a very frequent need. Because of this, several string methods let you produce case-altered copies of strings. Moreover, you can also check if a string object is already in a given case form with the methods isupper, islower, and istitle, which all return 1 if the string is nonempty and already meets the uppercase, lowercase, or titlecase constraints. There is no iscapitalized method, but we can code it as a function:

```
def iscapitalized(s):
    return s[:1].isupper() and s[1:].islower()
```

This may not be exactly what you want, because each of the is methods returns 0 for an empty string, and the three case-checking ones also return 0 for strings that, while not empty, contain no letters at all. This iscapitalized function does not quite match these semantics; rather, it accepts a string s only if s starts with an uppercase letter, followed by at least one more character, including at least one more letter somewhere, and all letters except the first one are lowercase. Here's an alternative whose semantics may be easier to understand:

```
def iscapitalized(s):
    return s == s.capitalize()
```

However, this version deviates from the boundary-case semantics of the methods by accepting strings that are empty or contain no letters. Depending on your exact needs for boundary cases, you may of course implement precisely those checks you want to perform.

See Also

The *Library Reference* section on string methods; *Perl Cookbook* Recipe 1.9.

3.9   Reversing a String by Words or Characters

Credit: Alex Martelli

Problem

You want to reverse the characters or words in a string.

Solution

Strings are immutable, so we need to make a copy. A list is the right intermediate data structure, since it has a reverse method that does just what we want and works in place:

```
revchars = list(astring)      # string -> list of chars
revchars.reverse( )           # reverse the list in place
revchars = ''.join(revchars)  # list of strings -> string
```

To flip words, we just work with a list of words instead of a list of characters:

```
revwords = astring.split( )    # string -> list of words
revwords.reverse( )            # reverse the list in place
revwords = ' '.join(revwords)  # list of strings -> string
```

Note that we use a ' ' (space) joiner for the list of words, but a '' (empty string) joiner for the list of characters.

If you need to reverse by words while preserving untouched the intermediate whitespace, regular-expression splitting can be useful:

```
import re
revwords = re.split(r'(\s+)', astring)  # separators too since '(...)'
revwords.reverse( )                     # reverse the list in place
revwords = ''.join(revwords)            # list of strings -> string
```

Note that the joiner becomes the empty string again in this case, because the whitespace separators are kept in the revwords list by using re.split with a regular expression that includes a parenthesized group.

Discussion

The snippets in this recipe are fast, readable, and Pythonic. However, some people have an inexplicable fetish for one-liners. If you are one of those people, you need an auxiliary function (you can stick it in your built-ins from *sitecustomize.py*) like this:

```
def reverse(alist):
    temp = alist[:]
    temp.reverse( )
    return temp
```

or maybe this, which is messier and slower:

```
def reverse_alternative(alist):
    return [alist[i-1] for i in range(len(alist), 0, -1)]
```

This is, indeed, in-lineable, but not worth it in my opinion.

Anyway, armed with such an almost-built-in, you can now do brave new one-liners, such as:

```
revchars = ''.join(reverse(list(astring)))
revwords = ' '.join(reverse(astring.split( )))
```

In the end, Python does not twist your arm to make you choose the obviously right approach: Python gives you the right tools, but it's up to you to use them.

See Also

The *Library Reference* section on sequence types; *Perl Cookbook* Recipe 1.6.

3.10 Accessing Substrings

Credit: Alex Martelli

Problem

You want to access portions of a string. For example, you've read a fixed-width record and want to extract the record's fields.

Solution

Slicing is great, of course, but it only does one field at a time:

```
afield = theline[3:8]
```

If you need to think in terms of field length, struct.unpack may be appropriate. Here's an example of getting a five-byte string, skipping three bytes, getting two eight-byte strings, and then getting the rest:

```
import struct

# Get a 5-byte string, skip 3, get two 8-byte strings, then all the rest:
baseformat = "5s 3x 8s 8s"
numremain = len(theline)-struct.calcsize(baseformat)
format = "%s %ds" % (baseformat, numremain)
leading, s1, s2, trailing = struct.unpack(format, theline)
```

If you need to split at five-byte boundaries, here's how you could do it:

```
numfives, therest = divmod(len(theline), 5)
form5 = "%s %dx" % ("5s "*numfives, therest)
fivers = struct.unpack(form5, theline)
```

Chopping a string into individual characters is of course easier:

```
chars = list(theline)
```

If you prefer to think of your data as being cut up at specific columns, slicing within list comprehensions may be handier:

```
cuts = [8,14,20,26,30]
pieces = [ theline[i:j] for i, j in zip([0]+cuts, cuts+[sys.maxint]) ]
```

Discussion

This recipe was inspired by Recipe 1.1 in the *Perl Cookbook*. Python's slicing takes the place of Perl's substr. Perl's built-in unpack and Python's struct.unpack are similar. Perl's is slightly handier, as it accepts a field length of * for the last field to mean all the rest. In Python, we have to compute and insert the exact length for either extraction or skipping. This isn't a major issue, because such extraction tasks will usually be encapsulated into small, probably local functions. *Memoizing*, or automatic caching, may help with performance if the function is called repeatedly, since it allows you to avoid redoing the preparation of the format for the struct unpacking. See also Recipe 17.7.

In a purely Python context, the point of this recipe is to remind you that struct.unpack is often viable, and sometimes preferable, as an alternative to string slicing (not quite as often as unpack versus substr in Perl, given the lack of a *-valued field length, but often enough to be worth keeping in mind).

Each of these snippets is, of course, best encapsulated in a function. Among other advantages, encapsulation ensures we don't have to work out the computation of the last field's length on each and every use. This function is the equivalent of the first snippet in the solution:

```
def fields(baseformat, theline, lastfield=None):
    numremain = len(theline)-struct.calcsize(baseformat)
    format = "%s %d%s" % (baseformat, numremain, lastfield and "s" or "x")
    return struct.unpack(format, theline)
```

If this function is called in a loop, caching with a key of (baseformat, len(theline), lastfield) may be useful here because it can offer an easy speed-up.

The function equivalent of the second snippet in the solution is:

```
def split_by(theline, n, lastfield=None):
    numblocks, therest = divmod(len(theline), n)
    baseblock = "%d%s"%(n, lastfield and "s" or "x")
    format = "%s %dx"%(baseblock*numblocks, therest)
```

And for the third snippet:

```
def split_at(theline, cuts, lastfield=None):
    pieces = [ theline[i:j] for i, j in zip([0]+cuts, cuts) ]
    if lastfield:
        pieces.append(theline(cuts[-1:]))
    return pieces
```

In each of these functions, a decision worth noticing (and, perhaps, worth criticizing) is that of having a lastfield=None optional parameter. This reflects the observation that while we often want to skip the last, unknown-length subfield, sometimes we want to retain it instead. The use of lastfield in the expression lastfield and "s" or "x" (equivalent to C's lastfield?'s':'c') saves an if/else, but it's unclear whether the saving is worth it. "sx"[not lastfield] and other similar alternatives are roughly equivalent in this respect; see Recipe 17.5. When `lastfield` is false, applying `struct.unpack` to just a prefix of `theline` (specifically, `theline[:struct.calcsize(format)]`) is an alternative, but it's not easy to merge with the case of `lastfield` being true, when the format does need a supplementary field for `len(theline)-struct.calcsize(format)`.

See Also

Recipes 17.5 and 17.7; *Perl Cookbook* Recipe 1.1.

3.11 Changing the Indentation of a Multiline String

Credit: Tom Good

Problem

You have a string made up of multiple lines, and you need to build another string from it, adding or removing leading spaces on each line so that the indentation of each line is some absolute number of spaces.

Solution

We don't need re for this. The `string` module (or string methods, in Python 2.0 and later) is quite sufficient:

```
import string
def reindent(s, numSpaces):
    s = string.split(s, '\n')
    s = [(numSpaces * ' ') + string.lstrip(line) for line in s]
    s = string.join(s, '\n')
    return s
```

Discussion

When working with text, it may be necessary to change the indentation level of a block. This recipe's code takes a multiline string and adds or removes leading spaces on each line so that the indentation level of each line of the block matches some absolute number of spaces. For example:

```
>>> x = """line one
... line two
... and line three
... """
>>> print x
line one
line two
and line three
```

```
>>> print reindent(x, 8)
        line one
        line two
        and line three
```

Even if the lines in s are initially indented differently, this recipe makes their indentation homogeneous. This is sometimes what we want, and sometimes not. A frequent need is to adjust the amount of leading spaces in each line, so that the relative indentation of each line in the block is preserved. This is not hard either, for either positive or negative values of the adjustment. However, negative values need a check to ensure that no nonspaces are snipped from the start of the lines. Thus, we may as well split the functionality into two functions to perform the transformations, plus one to measure the number of leading spaces of each line and return the result as a list:

```
def addSpaces(s, numAdd):
    white = " "*numAdd
    return white + white.join(s.splitlines(1))

def delSpaces(s, numDel):
    def aux(line, numDel=numDel, white=" "*numDel):
        if line[:numDel] != white:
            raise ValueError, "removing more spaces than there are!"
        return line[numDel:]
    return ''.join(map(aux, s.splitlines(1)))

def numSpaces(s):
    return [len(line)-len(line.lstrip()) for line in s.splitlines()]
```

This alternative approach relies on the string method splitlines (and so requires Python 2.0 or later, like any other recipe using string methods and/or list comprehensions), which is similar to a split on '\n', with the extra ability to leave the trailing newline on each line when called with a true argument. This is not often crucial (the last statement in delSpaces, for example, might just as easily return '\n'. join(map(aux, s.split('\n')))), but sometimes it turns out to be (addSpaces could not be quite as short and sweet without this ability of the splitlines string method).

For example, here's how we can combine these functions to build another function that deletes enough leading spaces from each line to ensure that the least-indented line of the block becomes flush-left, while preserving the relative indentations of all the other lines:

```
def unIndentBlock(s):
    return delSpaces(s, min(numSpaces(s)))
```

See Also

The *Library Reference* section on sequence types.

3.12 Testing Whether a String Represents an Integer

Credit: Robin Parmar

Problem

You want to know whether the contents of a string represent an integer (which is not quite the same thing as checking whether the string contains only digits).

Solution

try/except is almost invariably the best approach to such validation problems:

```
def isInt(astring):
    """ Is the given string an integer? """
    try: int(astring)
    except ValueError: return 0
    else: return 1
```

Testing if a string contains only digits is a different problem:

```
def isAllDigits(astring):
    """ Is the given string composed entirely of digits? """
    # In Python 2.0 and later, "astring.isdigit() or not astring" is faster
    import string
    acceptable_characters = string.digits
    for acharacter in astring:
        if acharacter not in acceptable_characters:
            return 0
    return 1
```

Discussion

It's always a good idea to make a Python source file runnable as a script, as well as usable via import. When run as a script, some kind of unit test or demo code executes. In this case, for example, we can finish up the little module containing this recipe's functions with:

```
if __name__ == '__main__':
    print isInt('23')
    print isInt('sd')
    print isInt('233835859285')
    print isAllDigits('233835859285')
```

Running the module as a script will now confirm that 23 represents an integer, sd does not, and neither does 233835859285 (because it's too large—it would need an integer greater than sys.maxint, which is impossible by definition). However, as the fourth and last print statement shows, even the latter string is indeed made up entirely of digits.

Exceptions provide a handy way of performing simple tests. For example, if you want to know whether the contents of a string represent an integer, why not just try to convert it? That's what isInt does. The try/except mechanism catches the exception raised when the string cannot be converted to an integer and, in the exception handler thus established, turns the exception into a harmless return 0. The else clause runs only when no exception is raised in the try clause, and in this case, we use it to perform a return 1 when the string is okay.

You can write similar tests for types other than integer. Indeed, tests in the try/except style are even more useful for types with string representation that can be more complicated, such as floats. More generally, exceptions can provide a simple, direct way of performing many tests that could otherwise be quite laborious. Don't be misled by the word "exception" or by what is considered good style in other programming languages. In Python, exceptions are useful for many nonexceptional cases, too. Relying on exceptions and try/except for validation tasks is a highly Pythonic, pragmatic, and useful idiom. It even has its own name, "It's Easier to Ask Forgiveness Than Permission", and acronym, EAFTP.

This type-like test is quite different from the pure-syntax testing of whether a string contains only digits. isAllDigits will help you there, in the relatively rare cases in which you care only about such purely syntactical aspects and not about the actual semantics at all. This style of validation is also known as "Look Before You Leap" (LBYL), and, while it has many pitfalls, in some rare cases it is indeed exactly what you need. In Python 2.0 and later, the isdigit method of string objects performs substantially the same test as the isAllDigits function shown in this recipe, but faster. One peculiarity is that ''.isdigit() is 0, while IsAllDigits('') is 1. It is of course easy to compensate for this, either way, by inserting a suitable check for not astring in the code (strings, like other sequences, are false if and only if they're empty).

See Also

Documentation for the built-in function int in the *Library Reference*.

3.13 Expanding and Compressing Tabs

Credit: Alex Martelli

Problem

You want to convert tabs in a string to the appropriate number of spaces, or vice versa.

Solution

Changing tabs to the appropriate number of spaces is a reasonably frequent task, easily accomplished with Python strings' built-in expandtabs method. Because strings are immutable, the method returns a new string object (a modified copy of the original one). However, it's easy to rebind a string variable name from the original to the modified-copy value:

```
mystring = mystring.expandtabs( )
```

This doesn't change the string object to which mystring originally referred, but it does rebind the name mystring to a newly created string object in which tabs are expanded into runs of spaces.

Changing spaces into tabs is a rare and peculiar need. Compression, if that's what you're after, is far better performed in other ways, so Python doesn't offer a built-in way to unexpand spaces into tabs. We can, of course, write one. String processing tends to be fastest in a split/process/rejoin approach, rather than with repeated overall string transformations:

```python
def unexpand(astring, tablen=8):
    import re
    pieces = re.split(r'( +)', astring.expandtabs(tablen))
    lensofar = 0
    for i in range(len(pieces)):
        thislen = len(pieces[i])
        lensofar += thislen
        if pieces[i][0]==' ':
            numblanks = lensofar % tablen
            numtabs = (thislen-numblanks+tablen-1)/tablen
            pieces[i] = '\t'*numtabs + ' '*numblanks
    return ''.join(pieces)
```

Discussion

If expandtabs didn't exist, we could write it up as a function. Here is a regular expression–based approach, similar to the one used in the recipe's unexpand function:

```python
def expand_with_re(astring, tablen=8):
    import re
    pieces = re.split(r'(\t)', astring)
    lensofar = 0
    for i in range(len(pieces)):
        if pieces[i]=='\t':
            pieces[i] = ' '*(tablen-lensofar%tablen)
        lensofar += len(pieces[i])
    return ''.join(pieces)
```

When the regular expression contains a (parenthesized) group, re.split gives us the splitters too. This is useful here for massaging the pieces list into the form we want for the final `''.join`. However, a string split by `'\t'`, followed by interleaving the spaces joiners of suitable lengths, looks a bit better in this case:

```
def expand(astring, tablen=8):
    result = []
    for piece in astring.split('\t'):
        result.append(piece)
        result.append(' '*(tablen-len(piece)%tablen))
    return ''.join(result[:-1])
```

See Also

Documentation for the expandtabs function in the `string` module in the *Library Reference*; *Perl Cookbook* Recipe 1.7.

3.14 Replacing Multiple Patterns in a Single Pass

Credit: Xavier Defrang

Problem

You need to perform several string substitutions on a string.

Solution

Sometimes regular expressions afford the fastest solution even in cases where their applicability is anything but obvious. In particular, the `sub` method of `re` objects makes regular expressions a good way to perform string substitutions. Here is how you can produce a result string from an input string where each occurrence of any key in a given dictionary is replaced by the corresponding value in the dictionary:

```
# requires Python 2.1 or later
from __future__ import nested_scopes

import re

# the simplest, lambda-based implementation
def multiple_replace(adict, text):
    # Create a regular expression from all of the dictionary keys
    regex = re.compile("|".join(map(re.escape, adict.keys())))

    # For each match, look up the corresponding value in the dictionary
    return regex.sub(lambda match: adict[match.group(0)], text)
```

A more powerful and flexible approach is to wrap the dictionary into a callable object that directly supports the lookup and replacement idea, which you can use directly as the callback in the `sub` method. This object-oriented approach is more flexible because the callable object can keep its own state and therefore is easily extensible to other tasks. In Python 2.2 and later, you can create a class for this object by extending the `dict` built-in type, while in older Python versions you must fall back on `UserDict.UserDict` (built-in types were not subclassable in older versions). A try/except lets us easily write code that works optimally on both old and new versions of Python:

```
try: dict
except: from UserDict import UserDict as dict

class Xlator(dict):
    """ All-in-one multiple-string-substitution class """
    def _make_regex(self):
        """ Build re object based on the keys of the current dictionary """
        return re.compile("|".join(map(re.escape, self.keys())))

    def __call__(self, match):
        """ Handler invoked for each regex match """
        return self[match.group(0)]

    def xlat(self, text):
        """ Translate text, returns the modified text. """
        return self._make_regex().sub(self, text)
```

Discussion

This recipe shows how to use the Python standard re module to perform single-pass multiple-string substitution using a dictionary. Let's say you have a dictionary-based, one-to-one mapping between strings. The keys are the set of strings (or regular-expression patterns) you want to replace, and the corresponding values are the strings with which to replace them. You can perform the substitution by calling `re.sub` for each key/value pair in the dictionary, thus processing and creating a new copy of the whole text several times, but it is clearly better to do all the changes in a single pass, processing and creating a copy of the text only once. Fortunately, `re.sub`'s callback facility makes this better approach quite easy.

First, we have to build a regular expression from the set of keys we want to match. Such a regular expression is a pattern of the form "a1|a2|...|an" and can easily be generated using a one-liner, as shown in the recipe. Then, instead of giving `re.sub` a replacement string, we call it with a callback argument. `re.sub` calls this object for each match, with a `re.MatchObject` as its only argument, and expects the replacement string as the call's result. In our case, the callback just has to look up the matched text in the dictionary and return the corresponding value.

The recipe has two implementations: one is `lambda`-based, and the other uses a callable, dictionary-like object. The second option is better if you want to perform additional processing on each match (e.g., build a histogram of the number of times each possible substitution is actually performed) or if you just dislike `lambda`. Another potential advantage of the class-based approach is performance. If you know that the translation dictionary is static, and you must apply the same translation to several input strings, you can move the _make_regex call from the xlat method, where it's currently done, to an `__init__` method, to avoid repeatedly preparing and compiling the regular expression.

Here's a usage example for each half of this recipe. We would normally have it as a part of the same *.py* source file as the function and class shown in the recipe, so it is guarded by the traditional Python idiom that runs it if and only if the module is called as a main script:

```python
if __name__ == "__main__":
    text = "Larry Wall is the creator of Perl"
    adict = {
      "Larry Wall" : "Guido van Rossum",
      "creator" : "Benevolent Dictator for Life",
      "Perl" : "Python",
    }

    print multiple_replace(adict, text)

    xlat = Xlator(adict)
    print xlat.xlat(text)
```

Substitutions such as those performed by this recipe are often intended to operate on entire words, rather than on arbitrary substrings. Regular expressions are good at picking up the beginnings and endings of words, thanks to the special sequence `r'\b'`. Thus, we can easily make a version of the Xlator class that is constrained to substitute only entire words:

```python
class WordXlator(Xlator):
    """ An Xlator version to substitute only entire words """
    def _make_regex(self):
        return re.compile(
            r'\b'+r'\b|\b'.join(map(re.escape, self.keys()))+r'\b')
```

Note how much easier it is to customize Xlator than it would be to customize the `multiple_replace` function. Ease of customization by subclassing and overriding helps you avoid copy-and-paste coding, and this is another excellent reason to prefer object-oriented structures over simpler procedural ones. Of course, just because some functionality is packaged up as a class doesn't magically make it customizable in just the way you want. Customizability also takes some foresight in dividing the functionality into separately overridable methods that correspond to the right pieces of overall functionality. Fortunately, you don't have to get it right the first time; when code does not have the optimal internal structure for the task at hand (e.g., reuse by subclassing and selective overriding), you can and should refactor the code so that its internal structure serves your needs. Just make sure you have a suitable battery of tests ready to run to ensure that your refactoring hasn't broken anything, and then you can refactor to your heart's content. See *http://www.refactoring.com* for more information on the important art and practice of refactoring.

See Also

Documentation for the re module in the *Library Reference*; the Refactoring home page (*http://www.refactoring.com*).

3.15 Converting Between Different Naming Conventions

Credit: Sami Hangaslammi

Problem

You have a body of code whose identifiers use one of the common naming conventions to represent multiple words in a single identifier (CapitalizedWords, mixedCase, or under_scores), and you need to convert the code to another naming convention in order to merge it smoothly with other code.

Solution

re.sub covers the two hard cases, converting underscore to and from the others:

```
import re

def cw2us(x): # capwords to underscore notation
    return re.sub(r'(?<=[a-z])[A-Z]|(?<!^)[A-Z](?=[a-z])',
        r"_\g<0>", x).lower( )

def us2mc(x): # underscore to mixed-case notation
    return re.sub(r'_([a-z])', lambda m: (m.group(1).upper( )), x)
```

Mixed-case to underscore is just like capwords to underscore (the case-lowering of the first character becomes redundant, but it does no harm):

```
def mc2us(x): # mixed-case to underscore notation
    return cw2us(x)
```

Underscore to capwords can similarly exploit the underscore to mixed-case conversion, but it needs an extra twist to uppercase the start:

```
def us2cw(x): # underscore to capwords notation
    s = us2mc(x)
    return s[0].upper( )+s[1:]
```

Conversion between mixed-case and capwords is, of course, just an issue of lower-casing or uppercasing the first character, as appropriate:

```
def mc2cw(x): # mixed-case to capwords
    return s[0].lower( )+s[1:]

def cw2mc(x): # capwords to mixed-case
    return s[0].upper( )+s[1:]
```

Discussion

Here are some usage examples:

```
>>> cw2us("PrintHTML")
'print_html'
>>> cw2us("IOError")
'io_error'
>>> cw2us("SetXYPosition")
'set_xy_position'
>>> cw2us("GetX")
'get_x'
```

The set of functions in this recipe is useful, and very practical, if you need to homogenize naming styles in a bunch of code, but the approach may be a bit obscure. In the interest of clarity, you might want to adopt a conceptual stance that is general and fruitful. In other words, to convert a bunch of formats into each other, find a neutral format and write conversions from each of the N formats into the neutral one and back again. This means having $2N$ conversion functions rather than $N \times (N–1)$—a big win for large N—but the point here (in which N is only three) is really one of clarity.

Clearly, the underlying neutral format that each identifier style is encoding is a list of words. Let's say, for definiteness and without loss of generality, that they are lower-case words:

```
import string, re
def anytolw(x):  # any format of identifier to list of lowercased words

    # First, see if there are underscores:
    lw = string.split(x,'_')
    if len(lw)>1: return map(string.lower, lw)

    # No. Then uppercase letters are the splitters:
    pieces = re.split('([A-Z])', x)

    # Ensure first word follows the same rules as the others:
    if pieces[0]: pieces = [''] + pieces
    else: pieces = pieces[1:]

    # Join two by two, lowercasing the splitters as you go
    return [pieces[i].lower()+pieces[i+1] for i in range(0,len(pieces),2)]
```

There's no need to specify the format, since it's self-describing. Conversely, when translating from our internal form to an output format, we do need to specify the format we want, but on the other hand, the functions are very simple:

```
def lwtous(x): return '_'.join(x)
def lwtocw(x): return ''.join(map(string.capitalize,x))
def lwtomc(x): return x[0]+''.join(map(string.capitalize,x[1:]))
```

Any other combination is a simple issue of functional composition:

```
def anytous(x): return lwtous(anytolw(x))
cwtous = mctous = anytous
def anytocw(x): return lwtocw(anytolw(x))
ustocw = mctocw = anytocw
def anytomc(x): return lwtomc(anytolw(x))
cwtomc = ustomc = anytomc
```

The specialized approach is slimmer and faster, but this generalized stance may ease understanding as well as offering wider application.

See Also

The *Library Reference* sections on the re and string modules.

3.16 Converting Between Characters and Values

Credit: Luther Blissett

Problem

You need to turn a character into its numeric ASCII (ISO) or Unicode code, and vice versa.

Solution

That's what the built-in functions ord and chr are for:

```
>>> print ord('a')
97
>>> print chr(97)
a
```

The built-in function ord also accepts as an argument a Unicode string of length one, in which case it returns a Unicode code, up to 65536. To make a Unicode string of length one from a numeric Unicode code, use the built-in function unichr:

```
>>> print ord(u'u2020')
8224
>>> print unichr(8224)
u' '
```

Discussion

It's a mundane task, to be sure, but it is sometimes useful to turn a character (which in Python just means a string of length one) into its ASCII (ISO) or Unicode code, and vice versa. The built-in functions ord, chr, and unichr cover all the related needs. Of course, they're quite suitable with the built-in function map:

```
>>> print map(ord, 'ciao')
[99, 105, 97, 111]
```

To build a string from a list of character codes, you must use both map and ''.join:

```
>>> print ''.join(map(chr, range(97, 100)))
abc
```

See Also

Documentation for the built-in functions chr, ord, and unichr in the *Library Reference*.

3.17 Converting Between Unicode and Plain Strings

Credit: David Ascher, Paul Prescod

Problem

You need to deal with data that doesn't fit in the ASCII character set.

Solution

Unicode strings can be encoded in plain strings in a variety of ways, according to whichever encoding you choose:

```
# Convert Unicode to plain Python string: "encode"
unicodestring = u"Hello world"
utf8string = unicodestring.encode("utf-8")
asciistring = unicodestring.encode("ascii")
isostring = unicodestring.encode("ISO-8859-1")
utf16string = unicodestring.encode("utf-16")

# Convert plain Python string to Unicode: "decode"
plainstring1 = unicode(utf8string, "utf-8")
plainstring2 = unicode(asciistring, "ascii")
plainstring3 = unicode(isostring, "ISO-8859-1")
plainstring4 = unicode(utf16string, "utf-16")

assert plainstring1==plainstring2==plainstring3==plainstring4
```

Discussion

If you find yourself dealing with text that contains non-ASCII characters, you have to learn about Unicode—what it is, how it works, and how Python uses it.

Unicode is a big topic. Luckily, you don't need to know everything about Unicode to be able to solve real-world problems with it: a few basic bits of knowledge are enough. First, you must understand the difference between bytes and characters. In older, ASCII-centric languages and environments, bytes and characters are treated as the same thing. Since a byte can hold up to 256 values, these environments are limited to 256 characters. Unicode, on the other hand, has tens of thousands of characters. That means that each Unicode character takes more than one byte, so you need to make the distinction between characters and bytes.

Standard Python strings are really byte strings, and a Python character is really a byte. Other terms for the standard Python type are "8-bit string" and "plain string." In this recipe we will call them byte strings, to remind you of their byte-orientedness.

Conversely, a Python Unicode character is an abstract object big enough to hold the character, analogous to Python's long integers. You don't have to worry about the internal representation; the representation of Unicode characters becomes an issue only when you are trying to send them to some byte-oriented function, such as the `write` method for files or the `send` method for network sockets. At that point, you must choose how to represent the characters as bytes. Converting from Unicode to a byte string is called *encoding* the string. Similarly, when you load Unicode strings from a file, socket, or other byte-oriented object, you need to *decode* the strings from bytes to characters.

There are many ways of converting Unicode objects to byte strings, each of which is called an *encoding*. For a variety of historical, political, and technical reasons, there is no one "right" encoding. Every encoding has a case-insensitive name, and that name is passed to the decode method as a parameter. Here are a few you should know about:

- The *UTF-8* encoding can handle any Unicode character. It is also backward compatible with ASCII, so a pure ASCII file can also be considered a UTF-8 file, and a UTF-8 file that happens to use only ASCII characters is identical to an ASCII file with the same characters. This property makes UTF-8 very backward-compatible, especially with older Unix tools. UTF-8 is far and away the dominant encoding on Unix. It's primary weakness is that it is fairly inefficient for Eastern texts.

- The *UTF-16* encoding is favored by Microsoft operating systems and the Java environment. It is less efficient for Western languages but more efficient for Eastern ones. A variant of UTF-16 is sometimes known as UCS-2.

- The *ISO-8859* series of encodings are 256-character ASCII supersets. They cannot support all of the Unicode characters; they can support only some particular language or family of languages. ISO-8859-1, also known as *Latin-1*, covers most Western European and African languages, but not Arabic. ISO-8859-2, also known as *Latin-2*, covers many Eastern European languages such as Hungarian and Polish.

If you want to be able to encode all Unicode characters, you probably want to use UTF-8. You will probably need to deal with the other encodings only when you are handed data in those encodings created by some other application.

See Also

Unicode is a huge topic, but a recommended book is *Unicode: A Primer*, by Tony Graham (Hungry Minds, Inc.)—details are available at *http://www.menteith.com/unicode/primer/*.

3.18 Printing Unicode Characters to Standard Output

Credit: David Ascher

Problem

You want to print Unicode strings to standard output (e.g., for debugging), but they don't fit in the default encoding.

Solution

Wrap the stdout stream with a converter, using the codecs module:

```
import codecs, sys
sys.stdout = codecs.lookup('iso8859-1')[-1](sys.stdout)
```

Discussion

Unicode strings live in a large space, big enough for all of the characters in every language worldwide, but thankfully the internal representation of Unicode strings is irrelevant for users of Unicode. Alas, a file stream, such as sys.stdout, deals with bytes and has an encoding associated with it. You can change the default encoding that is used for new files by modifying the site module. That, however, requires changing your entire Python installation, which is likely to confuse other applications that may expect the encoding you originally configured Python to use (typically ASCII). This recipe rebinds sys.stdout to be a stream that expects Unicode input and outputs it in ISO8859-1 (also known as Latin-1). This doesn't change the encoding of any previous references to sys.stdout, as illustrated here. First, we keep a reference to the original, ASCII-encoded stdout:

```
>>> old = sys.stdout
```

Then we create a Unicode string that wouldn't go through stdout normally:

```
>>> char = u"\N{GREEK CAPITAL LETTER GAMMA}"  # a character that doesn't fit in ASCII
>>> print char
Traceback (most recent call last):
  File "<stdin>", line 1, in ?
UnicodeError: ASCII encoding error: ordinal not in range(128)
```

Now we wrap `stdout` in the codecs stream writer for UTF-8, a much richer encoding, rebind `sys.stdout` to it, and try again:

```
>>> sys.stdout = codecs.lookup('utf-8')[-1](sys.stdout)
>>> print char
Γ
```

See Also

Documentation for the `codecs` and `site` modules and `setdefaultencoding` in `sys` in the *Library Reference*.

3.19 Dispatching Based on Pattern Matches

Credit: Michael Robin

Problem

You need to use regular expressions to match strings and then automatically call functions with arguments based on the matched strings.

Solution

Once again, a class offers a good way to package together some state and some behavior:

```python
import re

class Dispatcher:

    def _dispatch(self, cmdList, str):
        """ Find a match for str in the cmdList and call the associated
            method with arguments that are the matching grouped subexpressions
            from the regex.
        """
        for comment, pattern, command in cmdList:
            found = pattern.match(str)    # or, use .search()
            if found: return command(self, *found.groups())

    def runCommand(self, cmd):
        self._dispatch(Commands, cmd)

    # example methods

    def cmd1(self, num, name):
        print "The number for %s is %d" % (name, int(num))
        return 42

    def cmd2(self, partnum):
        print "Widget serial #: %d" % int(partnum)
```

```
    Commands = [
        [ 'Number-to-name correspondence',
                r'X (?P<num>\d),(?P<name>.*)$',
                Dispatcher.cmd1],
        [ 'Extract Widget part-number',
                r'Widget (?P<partnum>.*)$',
                Dispatcher.cmd2],
    ]

    # Prepare the Commands list for execution by compiling each re for cmd in Commands:
    try:
        cmd[1] = re.compile( cmd[1] )
    except:
        print "Bad pattern for %s: %s" % ( cmd[0], cmd[1] )
```

Discussion

In Python, it's generally best to compile regular expressions into re objects. The re module does some caching of string-form regular expressions that you use directly, but it's still better to make sure that regular expressions are not needlessly recompiled. The string form is still available as r.pattern for any compiled re object r, anyway, should you need it (e.g., for debugging/logging purposes).

You can use regular expressions to match strings (or search into strings) and automatically call appropriate functions, passing as arguments substrings of the matched string that correspond to the groups of the regular expression.

This recipe exemplifies one approach to this solution. The idea is that:

```
    r = self.runCommand("X 36,Mike")
```

automatically calls:

```
    cmd1(self, "36", "Mike")
```

and binds the variable r to 42, the result of cmd1.

This specific example might be best approached with direct string manipulation (testing str[0], then using the split method of strings), but regular expressions let you handle much more complicated cases with nearly equal ease.

An idiomatic Pythonic approach is to put each pattern to be compiled directly in the structure to be created at load-time. For example:

```
    Cmds = ( (re.compile(r"^pa(t)t1$"), fn), ... )
```

This is simple, if you don't require any special processing, but I think it's a little prettier to avoid including code in data-structure initializers.

See Also

Documentation for the re module and regular-expression objects in the *Library Reference*.

3.20 Evaluating Code Inside Strings

Credit: Joonas Paalasmaa

Problem

You have a string that contains embedded Python expressions, and you need to copy the string while evaluating those expressions.

Solution

This recipe's trick is to use the % string-formatting operator's named-values variant. That variant normally takes a dictionary as the righthand operand, but in fact it can take any mapping, so we just prepare a rather special mapping for the recipe's purpose:

```python
class Eval:
    """ mapping that does expression evaluation when asked to fetch an item """
    def __getitem__(self, key):
        return eval(key)
```

Now we can perform feats such as:

```python
>>> number = 20
>>> text = "python"
>>> print "%(text.capitalize())s %(number/9.0).1f rules!" % Eval()
Python 2.2 rules!
```

Discussion

This recipe can be seen as a templating task, akin to Recipes 3.21 and 3.22, but it is substantially simpler, because it needs to handle only embedded expressions, not statements. However, because the solution is so much simpler and faster than the general templating ones, it's better to think of this as a totally separate task.

In Python, the % operator of strings is typically used for normal formatting. The values to be interpolated in the string are the items of the righthand side, which is either a tuple, for unnamed-value formatting, or a mapping, for named-value formatting (where format items have forms such as %(name)s). The mapping is often obtained by functions such as the built-in vars, which returns a dictionary that represents the current status of local variables.

Named-value formatting is actually much more flexible. For each name string in the format, which is enclosed in parentheses after the % character that denotes the start of a format item in the format string, Python calls the get-item method of the righthand-side mapping (e.g., the special method __getitem__, when the righthand side is an instance object). That method can perform the necessary computation. The recipe shows off this possibility by simply delegating item-fetching to the built-in function eval, which evaluates the name as an expression. This can be very useful in practice, but as presented in the solution, it's limited to accessing global variables of the module in which the Eval class is itself defined. That makes it unwieldy for most practical purposes.

This problem is easily fixed, of course, because the sys._getframe function (in Python 2.1 and later) makes it easy to learn about your caller's local and global variables. So, you can tailor the evaluation environment:

```
import sys
class Evalx:
    def __init__(self, locals=None, globals=None):
        if locals is None: self.locals = sys._getframe(1).f_locals
        else: self.locals = locals
        if globals is None: self.globals = sys._getframe(1).f_globals
        else: self.globals = globals
    def __getitem__(self, name):
        return eval(name, self.globals, self.locals)
```

See Recipe 14.8 for a way to get the same functionality in other, older versions of Python.

Any instance of the Evalx class can now be used for expression evaluation, either with explicitly specified namespaces or, by default, with the local and global namespaces of the function that instantiated it.

See Also

Recipes 3.21, 3.22, and 14.8.

3.21 Replacing Python Code with the Results of Executing That Code

Credit: Joel Gould

Problem

You have a template string that may include embedded Python code, and you need a copy of the template in which any embedded Python code is replaced by the results of executing that code.

Solution

This recipe exploits the ability of the standard function re.sub to call a user-supplied replacement function for each match and to substitute the matched substring with the replacement function's result:

```
import re
import sys
import string
```

```python
def runPythonCode(data, global_dict={}, local_dict=None, errorLogger=None):
    """ Main entry point to the replcode module """

    # Encapsulate evaluation state and error logging into an instance:
    eval_state = EvalState(global_dict, local_dict, errorLogger)

    # Execute statements enclosed in [!! .. !!]; statements may be nested by
    # enclosing them in [1!! .. !!1], [2!! .. !!2], and so on:
    data = re.sub(r'(?s)\[(?P<num>\d?)!!(?P<code>.+?)!!(?P=num)\]',
        eval_state.exec_python, data)

    # Evaluate expressions enclosed in [?? .. ??]:
    data = re.sub(r'(?s)\[\?\?(?P<code>.+?)\?\?\]',
        eval_state.eval_python, data)

    return data

class EvalState:
    """ Encapsulate evaluation state, expose methods to execute/evaluate """

    def __init__(self, global_dict, local_dict, errorLogger):
        self.global_dict = global_dict
        self.local_dict = local_dict
        if errorLogger:
            self.errorLogger = errorLogger
        else:
            # Default error "logging" writes error messages to sys.stdout
            self.errorLogger = sys.stdout.write

        # Prime the global dictionary with a few needed entries:
        self.global_dict['OUTPUT'] = OUTPUT
        self.global_dict['sys'] = sys
        self.global_dict['string'] = string
        self.global_dict['__builtins__'] = __builtins__

    def exec_python(self, result):
        """ Called from the 1st re.sub in runPythonCode for each block of
        embedded statements. Method's result is OUTPUT_TEXT (see also the OUTPUT
        function later in the recipe). """

        # Replace tabs with four spaces; remove first line's indent from all lines
        code = result.group('code')
        code = string.replace(code, '\t', '    ')
        result2 = re.search(r'(?P<prefix>\n[ ]*)[#a-zA-Z0-9''"]', code)
        if not result2:
            raise ParsingError, 'Invalid template code expression: ' + code
        code = string.replace(code, result2.group('prefix'), '\n')
        code = code + '\n'

        try:
            self.global_dict['OUTPUT_TEXT'] = ''
            if self.local_dict:
                exec code in self.global_dict, self.local_dict
            else:
```

```
            exec code in self.global_dict
            return self.global_dict['OUTPUT_TEXT']
        except:
            self.errorLogger('\n---- Error parsing statements: ----\n')
            self.errorLogger(code)
            self.errorLogger('\n----------------------\n')
            raise

    def eval_python(self, result):
        """ Called from the 2nd re.sub in runPythonCode for each embedded
        expression. The method's result is the expr's value as a string. """
        code = result.group('code')
        code = string.replace(code, '\t', '    ')

        try:
            if self.local_dict:
                result = eval(code, self.global_dict, self.local_dict)
            else:
                result = eval(code, self.global_dict)
            return str(result)
        except:
            self.errorLogger('\n---- Error parsing expression: ----\n')
            self.errorLogger(code)
            self.errorLogger('\n----------------------\n')
            raise

def OUTPUT(data):
    """ May be called from embedded statements: evaluates argument 'data' as
    a template string, appends the result to the global variable OUTPUT_TEXT """

    # a trick that's equivalent to sys._getframe in Python 2.0 and later but
    # also works on older versions of Python...:
    try: raise ZeroDivisionError
    except ZeroDivisionError:
        local_dict  = sys.exc_info()[2].tb_frame.f_back.f_locals
        global_dict = sys.exc_info()[2].tb_frame.f_back.f_globals

    global_dict['OUTPUT_TEXT'] = global_dict['OUTPUT_TEXT'] + runPythonCode(
        data, global_dict, local_dict)
```

Discussion

This recipe was originally designed for dynamically creating HTML. It takes a template, which is a string that may include embedded Python statements and expressions, and returns another string, in which any embedded Python is replaced with the results of executing that code. I originally designed this code to build my home page. Since then, I have used the same code for a CGI-based web site and for a documentation-generation program.

Templating, which is what this recipe does, is a very popular task in Python, for which you can find any number of existing Pythonic solutions. Many templating approaches aim specifically at the task of generating HTML (or, occasionally, other forms of structured text). Others, such as this recipe, are less specialized, and thus can be simultaneously wider in applicability and simpler in structure. However, they do not offer HTML-specific conveniences. See Recipe 3.22 for another small-scale approach to templating with general goals that are close to this one's but are executed in a rather different style.

Usually, the input template string is taken directly from a file, and the output expanded string is written to another file. When using CGI, the output string can be written directly to sys.stdout, which becomes the HTML displayed in the user's browser when it visits the script.

By passing in a dictionary, you control the global namespace in which the embedded Python code is run. If you want to share variables with the embedded Python code, insert the names and values of those variables into the global dictionary before calling runPythonCode. When an uncaught exception is raised in the embedded code, a dump of the code being evaluated is first written to stdout (or through the errorLogger function argument, if specified) before the exception is propagated to the routine that called runPythonCode.

This recipe handles two different types of embedded code blocks in template strings. Code inside [?? ??] is evaluated. Such code should be an expression and should return a string, which will be used to replace the embedded Python code. Code inside [!! !!] is executed. That code is a suite of statements, and it is not expected to return anything. However, you can call OUTPUT from inside embedded code, to specify text that should replace the executed Python code. This makes it possible, for example, to use loops to generate multiple blocks of output text.

Here is an interactive-interpreter example of using this *replcode.py* module:

```
>>> import replcode
>>> input_text = """
...     Normal line.
...     Expression [?? 1+2 ??].
...     Global variable [?? variable ??].
...     [!!
...         def foo(x):
...             return x+x !!].
...     Function [?? foo('abc') ??].
...     [!!
...         OUTPUT('Nested call [?? variable ??]') !!].
...     [!!
...         OUTPUT('''Double nested [1!!
...             myVariable = '456' !!1][?? myVariable ??]''') !!].
...     """
>>> global_dict = { 'variable': '123' }
>>> output_text = replcode.runPythonCode(input_text, global_dict)
>>> print output_text

    Normal line.
    Expression 3.
```

```
Global variable 123.
.
Function abcabc.
Nested call 123.
Double nested 456.
```

See Also

Recipe 3.22.

3.22 Module: Yet Another Python Templating Utility (YAPTU)

Credit: Alex Martelli

Templating is the process of defining a block of text that contains embedded variables, code, and other markup. This text block is then automatically processed to yield another text block, in which the variables and code have been evaluated and the results have been substituted into the text. Most dynamic web sites are generated with the help of templating mechanisms.

Example 3-1 contains Yet Another Python Templating Utility (YAPTU), a small but complete Python module for this purpose. YAPTU uses the sub method of regular expressions to evaluate embedded Python expressions but handles nested statements via recursion and line-oriented statement markers. YAPTU is suitable for processing almost any kind of structured-text input, since it lets client code specify which regular expressions denote embedded Python expressions and/or statements. Such regular expressions can then be selected to avoid conflict with whatever syntax is needed by the specific kind of structured text that is being processed (HTML, a programming language, RTF, TeX, etc.) See Recipe 3.21 for another approach, in a very different Python style, with very similar design goals.

YAPTU uses a compiled re object, if specified, to identify expressions, calling sub on each line of the input. For each match that results, YAPTU evaluates match.group(1) as a Python expression and substitutes in place the result, transformed into a string. You can also pass a dictionary to YAPTU to use as the global namespace for the evaluation. Many such nonoverlapping matches per line are possible, but YAPTU does not rescan the resulting text for further embedded expressions or statements.

YAPTU also supports embedded Python statements. This line-based feature is primarily intended to be used with if/elif/else, for, and while statements. YAPTU recognizes statement-related lines through three more re objects that you pass it: one each for statement, continuation, and finish lines. Each of these arguments can be None if no such statements are to be embedded. Note that YAPTU relies on explicit block-end marks rather than indentation (leading whitespace) to determine statement nesting. This is because some structured-text languages that you might want to process with

YAPTU have their own interpretations of the meaning of leading whitespace. The statement and continuation markers are followed by the corresponding statement lines (i.e., beginning statement and continuation clause, respectively, where the latter normally makes sense only if it's an else or elif). Statements can nest without limits, and normal Pythonic indentation requirements do not apply.

If you embed a statement that does not end with a colon (e.g., an assignment statement), a Python comment must terminate its line. Conversely, such comments are not allowed on the kind of statements that you may want to embed most often (e.g., if, else, for, and while). The lines of such statements must terminate with their :, optionally followed by whitespace. This line-termination peculiarity is due to a slightly tricky technique used in YAPTU's implementation, whereby embedded statements (with their continuations) are processed by exec, with recursive calls to YAPTU's copyblock function substituted in place of the blocks of template text they contain. This approach takes advantage of the fact that a single, controlled, simple statement can be placed on the same line as the controlling statement, right after the colon, avoiding any whitespace issues. As already explained, YAPTU does not rely on whitespace to discern embedded-statement structure; rather, it relies on explicit markers for statement start, statement continuation, and statement end.

Example 3-1. Yet Another Python Templating Utility

```
"Yet Another Python Templating Utility, Version 1.3"

import sys

# utility stuff to avoid tests in the mainline code
class _nevermatch:
    "Polymorphic with a regex that never matches"
    def match(self, line): return None
    def sub(self, repl, line): return line
_never = _nevermatch()      # one reusable instance of it suffices

def identity(string, why):
    "A do-nothing-special-to-the-input, just-return-it function"
    return string

def nohandle(string, kind):
    "A do-nothing handler that just reraises the exception"
    sys.stderr.write("*** Exception raised in %s {%s}\n"%(kind, string))
    raise


# and now, the real thing:
class copier:
    "Smart-copier (YAPTU) class"

    def copyblock(self, i=0, last=None):
        "Main copy method: process lines [i,last) of block"
```

Example 3-1. Yet Another Python Templating Utility (continued)

```python
        def repl(match, self=self):
            "return the eval of a found expression, for replacement"
            # uncomment for debug: print '!!! replacing', match.group(1)
            expr = self.preproc(match.group(1), 'eval')
            try: return str(eval(expr, self.globals, self.locals))
            except: return str(self.handle(expr, 'eval'))

    block = self.locals['_bl']
    if last is None: last = len(block)
    while i<last:
        line = block[i]
        match = self.restat.match(line)
        if match:   # a statement starts "here" (at line block[i])
            # i is the last line NOT to process
            stat = match.string[match.end(0):].strip()
            j = i+1   # Look for 'finish' from here onwards
            nest = 1  # Count nesting levels of statements
            while j<last:
                line = block[j]
                # First look for nested statements or 'finish' lines
                if self.restend.match(line):    # found a statement-end
                    nest = nest - 1     # Update (decrease) nesting
                    if nest==0: break   # j is first line NOT to process
                elif self.restat.match(line):   # found a nested statement
                    nest = nest + 1     # Update (increase) nesting
                elif nest==1:   # Look for continuation at this nesting
                    match = self.recont.match(line)
                    if match:             # found a continued statement
                        nestat = match.string[match.end(0):].strip()
                        # key "trick": cumulative recursive copyblock call
                        stat = '%s _cb(%s,%s)\n%s' % (stat,i+1,j,nestat)
                        i = j   # i is the last line NOT to process
                j += 1
            stat = self.preproc(stat, 'exec')
            # second half of key "trick": do the recursive copyblock call
            stat = '%s _cb(%s,%s)' % (stat, i+1, j)
            # uncomment for debug: print "-> Executing: {"+stat+"}"
            try: exec stat in self.globals, self.locals
            except: return str(self.handle(expr, 'exec'))
            i=j+1
        else:        # normal line, just copy with substitutions
            self.oufun(self.regex.sub(repl, line))
            i=i+1

def __init__(self, regex=_never, globals={},
        restat=_never, restend=_never, recont=_never,
        preproc=identity, handle=nohandle, oufun=sys.stdout.write):
    "Initialize self's attributes"
    def self_set(**kwds): self.__dict__.update(kwds)
    self_set(locals={'_cb': self.copyblock}, **vars())

def copy(self, block=None, inf=sys.stdin):
    "Entry point: copy-with-processing a file, or a block of lines"
```

Example 3-1. Yet Another Python Templating Utility (continued)

```
        if block is None: block = inf.readlines()
        self.locals['_bl'] = block
        self.copyblock()

if __name__=='__main__':
    "Test: copy a block of lines to stdout, with full processing"
    import re
    rex=re.compile('@([^@]+)@')
    rbe=re.compile('\+')
    ren=re.compile('-')
    rco=re.compile('= ')
    x=23 # just a variable to try substitution
    cop = copier(rex, globals(), rbe, ren, rco)  # Instantiate smart copier
    lines_block = """
A first, plain line -- it just gets copied.
A second line, with @x@ substitutions.
+ x+=1   # Nonblock statements (nonblock ones ONLY!) must end with comments
-
Now the substitutions are @x@.
+ if x>23:
After all, @x@ is rather large!
= else:
After all, @x@ is rather small!
-
+ for i in range(3):
  Also, @i@ times @x@ is @i*x@.
-
One last, plain line at the end.""".splitlines(1)
    print "*** input:"
    print ''.join(lines_block)
    print "*** output:"
    cop.copy(lines_block)
```

Not counting comments, whitespace, and docstrings, YAPTU is just 50 lines of
source code, but rather a lot happens within that code. An instance of the auxiliary
class _nevermatch is used for all default placeholder values for optional regular-
expression arguments. This instance is polymorphic with compiled re objects for the
two methods of the latter that YAPTU uses (sub and match), which simplifies the
main body of code and saves quite a few tests. This is a good general idiom to keep
in mind for generality and concise code (and often speed as well). See Recipe 5.23 for
a more systematic and complete development of this idiom into the full-fledged Null
Object design pattern.

An instance of the copier class has a certain amount of state, in addition to the relevant compiled re objects (or _nevermatch instance) and the output function to use
(normally a write bound method for some file or file-like object). This state is held in
two dictionary attributes: self.globals, the dictionary that was originally passed in
for expression substitution; and self.locals, another dictionary that is used as the
local namespace for all of YAPTU's exec and eval calls. Note that while self.globals

is available to YAPTU, YAPTU does not change anything in it, as that dictionary is owned by YAPTU's caller.

There are two internal-use-only items in self.locals. The value at key '_bl' indicates the block of template text being copied (a sequence of lines, each ending with \n), while the value at key '_cb', self.copyblock, is the bound method that performs the copying. Holding these two pieces of state as items in self.locals is key to YAPTU's workings, since self.locals is what is guaranteed to be available to the code that YAPTU processes with exec. copyblock must be recursive, as this is the simplest way to ensure there are no nesting limitations. Thus, it is important to ensure that nested recursive calls are always able to further recurse, if needed, through their exec statements. Access to _bl is similarly necessary, since copyblock takes as arguments only the line indexes inside _bl that a given recursive call is processing (in the usual Python form, with the lower bound included and the upper bound excluded).

copyblock is the heart of YAPTU. The repl nested function is the one that is passed to the sub method of compiled re objects to get the text to be used for each expression substitution. repl uses eval on the expression string and str on the result, to ensure that the returned value is also a string.

Most of copyblock is a while loop that examines each line of text. When a line doesn't match a statement-start marker, the loop performs substitutions and then calls the output function. When a line does match a statement-start marker, the loop enters a smaller nested loop, looking for statement-continuation and statement-end markers (with proper accounting for nesting levels, of course). The nested loop builds up, in the local variable stat, a string containing the original statement and its continuations at the same nesting level (if any) followed by a recursive call to _cb(i,j) after each clause-delimiting colon, with newlines as separators between any continuations. Finally, stat is passed to the exec statement, the nested loop terminates, and the main loop resumes from a position immediately following the embedded statement just processed. Thanks to perfectly normal recursive-invocation mechanisms, although the exec statement inevitably invokes copyblock recursively, this does not disturb the loop's state (which is based on local variables unoriginally named i and j because they are loop counters and indexes on the _bl list).

YAPTU supports optional preprocessing for all expressions and statements by passing an optional callable preproc when creating the copier. The default, however, is no preprocessing. Exceptions may be handled by passing an optional callable handle. The default behavior is for YAPTU to reraise the exception, which terminates YAPTU's processing and propagates the exception outward to YAPTU's caller. You should also note that the __init__ method avoids the usual block of boilerplate self.spam = spam statements that you typically see in __init__. Instead, it uses a "self-set" idiom to achieve exactly the same result without repetitious, verbose, and error-prone boilerplate code.

Recipes 3.21, 5.23, and 17.7.

3.23 Module: Roman Numerals

Credit: Paul M. Winkler

There are many algorithms for creating Roman numerals. Example 3-2 presents the easiest-to-read algorithm that I've been able to find for this purpose: it establishes a mapping between integer values and Roman numerals, then counts how many of each value can fit into the input integer. The code uses two tuples for the mapping, instead of a dictionary, because it needs to go through them sequentially and doesn't care about random access. Thus, a dictionary would be more hindrance than help.

Example 3-2. Roman numerals

```
def int_to_roman(input):
    """ Convert an integer to a Roman numeral. """

    if not isinstance(input, type(1)):
        raise TypeError, "expected integer, got %s" % type(input)
    if not 0 < input < 4000:
        raise ValueError, "Argument must be between 1 and 3999"
    ints = (1000, 900,  500, 400, 100,  90, 50,  40, 10,  9,   5,  4,   1)
    nums = ('M',  'CM', 'D', 'CD','C', 'XC','L','XL','X','IX','V','IV','I')
    result = []
    for i in range(len(ints)):
        count = int(input / ints[i])
        result.append(nums[i] * count)
        input -= ints[i] * count
    return ''.join(result)

def roman_to_int(input):
    """ Convert a Roman numeral to an integer. """

    """
    if not isinstance(input, type("")):
        raise TypeError, "expected string, got %s" % type(input)
    input = input.upper()
    nums = {'M':1000, 'D':500, 'C':100, 'L':50, 'X':10, 'V':5, 'I':1}
    sum = 0
    for i in range(len(input)):
        try:
            value = nums[input[i]]
            # If the next place holds a larger number, this value is negative
            if i+1 < len(input) and nums[input[i+1]] > value:
                sum -= value
            else: sum += value
        except KeyError:
            raise ValueError, 'input is not a valid Roman numeral: %s' % input
    # easiest test for validity...
```

Example 3-2. Roman numerals (continued)

```
    if int_to_roman(sum) == input:
        return sum
    else:
        raise ValueError, 'input is not a valid Roman numeral: %s' % input
```

Here are some usage examples of converting integers to Roman numerals and vice versa:

```
>>> print int_to_roman(2002)
MMII
>>> print int_to_roman(1999)
MCMXCIX
>>> roman_to_int('XLII')
42
>>> roman_to_int('VVVIV')
Traceback (most recent call last):
  ...
ValueError: input is not a valid Roman numeral: VVVIV
```

The rules for Roman numerals are as follows:

1. I = 1, V = 5, X = 10, L = 50, C = 100, D = 500, M = 1000.
2. Zero is not represented.
3. Numbers greater than 3,999 are not represented.
4. Roman numerals are repeated to add value: III is equivalent to 1 +1 +1 = 3.
5. Only powers of 10 may be repeated in this way. Thus, VV is invalid; 5 + 5 would instead be expressed as X.
6. No more than three repetitions of a numeral can be used. Five repetitions can be represented with a single, larger numeral; to represent four, use the next larger numeral, but precede it with a numeral to subtract from it. Thus, IIII is invalid and would instead be written as IV (one less than five). Likewise, XC represents 90 (10 less than 100), and XL represents 40 (10 less than 50).
7. A numeral used for subtraction in this way must be the largest power of 10 that is less than the numeral it precedes. Thus, XC is valid but IC is invalid.

In my first attempt at int_to_roman, my approach was simply to follow, as closely as I could, the plain English description of these rules. I rejected that version, because it ended up being longer and more complicated than the version given here. It's actually easier to forcibly assign values to IV and its friends than it is to implement the rule that determines the values.

A different approach to a Roman-numeral-to-integer converter can be found in Mark Pilgrim's *Dive Into Python* (*http://diveintopython.org/roman_divein.html*), an online book containing lots of useful information, all free for use under the Python license. Mark relies on a regular expression to validate the input. This is a fine idea that makes his function nice and short, but it puts a lot of the logic in the regular expression, which may be easier to misunderstand than the slightly longer function in this recipe.

Here is another approach, based on Mark's, but with an additional field in each tuple to enforce the maximum number of repetitions allowed for a numeral. It relies on the ordering of the tuple to enforce the correct ordering of numerals, so it doesn't need a regular expression (or any double-checking in the end through int_to_roman, as in Example 3-2):

```
def roman_to_int(input):
    try: input = input.upper()
    except AttributeError:
        raise TypeError, 'expected string, got %s' % type(input)
    # map of (numeral, value, maxcount) tuples
    roman_numeral_map = (('M', 1000, 3), ('CM', 900, 1),
        ('D', 500, 1), ('CD', 400, 1),
        ('C', 100, 3), ('XC', 90, 1),
        ('L', 50, 1), ('XL', 40, 1),
        ('X', 10, 3), ('IX', 9, 1),
        ('V', 5, 1), ('IV', 4, 1), ('I', 1, 3))
    result, index = 0, 0
    for numeral, value, maxcount in roman_numeral_map:
        count = 0
        while input[index: index+len(numeral)] == numeral:
            count += 1 # how many of this numeral we have
            if count > maxcount:
                raise ValueError, \
                    'input is not a valid roman numeral: %s' % input
            result += value
            index += len(numeral)
    if index < len(input): # There are characters unaccounted for
        raise ValueError, 'input is not a valid roman numeral: %s'%input
    return result
```

However, this version is not quite rigid enough in diagnosing malformed Roman numerals. For example, this version accepts XCXL, translating it into 130, while the version in Example 3-2 properly rejects it. The canonical way to represent 130 as a Roman numeral is CXXX, but it's not easy to capture the fact that XCXL is invalid (indeed, although it should be forbidden, none of the rules appears to forbid it). The version in Example 3-2, by checking that the string it has just parsed is indeed the canonical (and thus, the only allowed) representation for the resulting integer, gains a substantial measure of solidity in rejecting plausible but noncanonical strings.

This leads to a general idea that you should keep in mind whenever you are coding bidirectional transformation functions between two formats, where the functions are inverses of each other. When one of the directions has a more clearly specified transformation algorithm, you can verify the function that implements the more loosely specified transformation by checking that the other function does indeed result in the original input value when applied to the candidate result. If only the canonical form is to be accepted, this pattern lets you easily reject plausible but noncanonical inputs that it might otherwise be difficult to detect.

See Also

Mark Pilgrim's *Dive Into Python* (*http://diveintopython.org*).

## CHAPTER 4

Files

4.0   Introduction

Credit: Mark Lutz, author of Programming Python, co-author of Learning Python

Behold the file—one of the first things that any reasonably pragmatic programmer reaches for in a programming language's toolbox. Because processing external files is a very real, tangible task, the quality of file-processing interfaces is a good way to assess the practicality of a programming tool.

As the examples in this chapter attest, Python shines here too. In fact, files in Python are supported in a variety of layers: from the built-in open function's standard file object, to specialized tools in standard library modules such as os, to third-party utilities available on the Web. All told, Python's arsenal of file tools provides several powerful ways to access files in your scripts.

File Basics

In Python, a file object is an instance of a built-in type. The built-in function open creates and returns a file object. The first argument, a string, specifies the file's path (i.e., the filename preceded by an optional directory path). The second argument to open, also a string, specifies the mode in which to open the file. For example:

```
input = open('data', 'r')
output = open('/tmp/spam', 'w')
```

open accepts a file path in which directories and files are separated by slash characters (/), regardless of the proclivities of the underlying operating system. On systems that don't use slashes, you can use a backslash character (\) instead, but there's no real reason to do so. Backslashes are harder to fit nicely in string literals, since you have to double them up or use "raw" strings. If the file path argument does not include the file's directory name, the file is assumed to reside in the current working directory (which is a disjoint concept from the Python module search path).

For the mode argument, use `'r'` to read the file in text mode; this is the default value and is commonly omitted, so that open is called with just one argument. Other common modes are `'rb'` to read the file in binary mode, `'w'` to create and write to the file in text mode, and `'wb'` to create and write to the file in binary mode.

The distinction between text mode and binary mode is important on non-Unix-like platforms, because of the line-termination characters used on these systems. When you open a file in binary mode, Python knows that it doesn't need to worry about line-termination characters; it just moves bytes between the file and in-memory strings without any kind of translation. When you open a file in text mode on a non-Unix-like system, however, Python knows it must translate between the `'\n'` line-termination characters used in strings and whatever the current platform uses in the file itself. All of your Python code can always rely on `'\n'` as the line-termination character, as long as you properly indicate text or binary mode when you open the file.

Once you have a file object, you perform all file I/O by calling methods of this object, as we'll discuss in a moment. When you're done with the file, you should finish by calling the close method on the object, to close the connection to the file:

```
input.close()
```

In short scripts, people often omit this step, as Python automatically closes the file when a file object is reclaimed during garbage collection. However, it is good programming practice to close your files, and it is especially a good idea in larger programs. Note that try/finally is particularly well suited to ensuring that a file gets closed, even when the program terminates by raising an uncaught exception.

To write to a file, use the write method:

```
output.write(s)
```

where s is a string. Think of s as a string of characters if output is open for text-mode writing and as a string of bytes if output is open for binary-mode writing. There are other writing-related methods, such as flush, which sends any data that is being buffered, and writelines, which writes a list of strings in a single call. However, none of these other methods appear in the recipes in this chapter, as write is by far the most commonly used method.

Reading from a file is more common than writing to a file, and there are more issues involved, so file objects have more reading methods than writing ones. The readline method reads and returns the next line from a text file:

```
while 1:
    line = input.readline()
    if not line: break
    process(line)
```

This was idiomatic Python, but it is no longer the best way to read lines from a file. Another alternative is to use the `readlines` method, which reads the whole file and returns a list of lines:

```
for line in input.readlines():
    process(line)
```

However, this is useful only for files that fit comfortably in physical memory. If the file is truly huge, `readlines` can fail or at least slow things down quite drastically as virtual memory fills up and the operating system has to start copying parts of physical memory to disk. Python 2.1 introduced the `xreadlines` method, which works just like `readlines` in a `for` loop but consumes a bounded amount of memory regardless of the size of the file:

```
for line in input.xreadlines():
    process(line)
```

Python 2.2 introduced the ideal solution, whereby you can loop on the file object itself, implicitly getting a line at a time with the same memory and performance characteristics of `xreadlines`:

```
for line in input:
    process(line)
```

Of course, you don't always want to read a file line by line. You may instead want to read some or all of the bytes in the file, particularly if you've opened the file for binary-mode reading, where lines are unlikely to be an applicable concept. In this case, you can use the `read` method. When called without arguments, `read` reads and returns all the remaining bytes from the file. When `read` is called with an integer argument N, it reads and returns the next N bytes (or all the remaining bytes, if less than N bytes remain). Other methods worth mentioning are `seek` and `tell`, which support random access to files. These are normally used with binary files made up of fixed-length records.

Portability and Flexibility

On the surface, Python's file support is straightforward. However, there are two aspects of Python's file support that I want to underscore up-front, before you peruse the code in this chapter: script portability and interface flexibility.

Keep in mind that most file interfaces in Python are fully portable across platform boundaries. It would be difficult to overstate the importance of this feature. A Python script that searches all files in a directory tree for a bit of text, for example, can be freely moved from platform to platform without source-code changes: just copy the script's source file to the new target machine. I do it all the time—so much so that I can happily stay out of operating-system wars. With Python's portability, the underlying platform is largely irrelevant.

Also, it has always struck me that Python's file-processing interfaces are not restricted to real, physical files. In fact, most file tools work with any kind of object that exposes the same interface as a real file object. Thus, a file reader cares only about read methods, and a file writer cares only about write methods. As long as the target object implements the expected protocol, all goes well.

For example, suppose you have written a general file-processing function such as the following, intending to apply a passed-in function to each line in an input file:

```
def scanner(fileobject, linehandler):
    for line in fileobject.readlines():
        linehandler(line)
```

If you code this function in a module file and drop that file in a directory listed on your Python search path, you can use it anytime you need to scan a text file, now or in the future. To illustrate, here is a client script that simply prints the first word of each line:

```
from myutils import scanner
def firstword(line): print line.split()[0]
file = open('data')
scanner(file, firstword)
```

So far, so good; we've just coded a reusable software component. But notice that there are no type declarations in the scanner function, only an interface constraint— any object with a readlines method will do. For instance, suppose you later want to provide canned test input from a string object, instead of from a real, physical file. The standard StringIO module, and the equivalent but faster cStringIO, provide the appropriate wrapping and interface forgery:

```
from cStringIO import StringIO
from myutils import scanner
def firstword(line): print line.split()[0]
string = StringIO('one\ntwo xxx\nthree\n')
scanner(string, firstword)
```

Here, StringIO objects are plug-and-play compatible with file objects, so scanner takes its three lines of text from an in-memory string object, rather than a true external file. You don't need to change the scanner to make this work—just send it the right kind of object. For more generality, use a class to implement the expected interface instead:

```
class MyStream:
    def readlines(self):
        # Grab and return text from a source here
        return ['a\n', 'b c d\n']

from myutils import scanner
def firstword(line): print line.split()[0]
object = MyStream()
scanner(object, firstword)
```

This time, as scanner attempts to read the file, it really calls out to the readlines method you've coded in your class. In practice, such a method might use other Python standard tools to grab text from a variety of sources: an interactive user, a pop-up GUI input box, a shelve object, an SQL database, an XML or HTML page, a network socket, and so on. The point is that scanner doesn't know or care what kind of object is implementing the interface it expects, or what that interface actually does.

Object-oriented programmers know this deliberate naiveté as polymorphism. The type of the object being processed determines what an operation, such as the readlines method call in scanner, actually does. Everywhere in Python, object interfaces, rather than specific data types, are the unit of coupling. The practical effect is that functions are often applicable to a much broader range of problems than you might expect. This is especially true if you have a background in strongly typed languages such as C or C++. It is almost as if we get C++ templates for free in Python. Code has an innate flexibility that is a byproduct of Python's dynamic typing.

Of course, code portability and flexibility run rampant in Python development and are not really confined to file interfaces. Both are features of the language that are simply inherited by file-processing scripts. Other Python benefits, such as its easy scriptability and code readability, are also key assets when it comes time to change file-processing programs. But, rather than extolling all of Python's virtues here, I'll simply defer to the wonderful example programs in this chapter and this text at large for more details. Enjoy!

4.1   Reading from a File

Credit: Luther Blissett

Problem

You want to read text or data from a file.

Solution

Here's the most convenient way to read all of the file's contents at once into one big string:

```
all_the_text = open('thefile.txt').read()    # all text from a text file
all_the_data = open('abinfile', 'rb').read() # all data from a binary file
```

However, it is better to bind the file object to a variable so that you can call close on it as soon as you're done. For example, for a text file:

```
file_object = open('thefile.txt')
all_the_text = file_object.read()
file_object.close()
```

There are four ways to read a text file's contents at once as a list of strings, one per line:

```
list_of_all_the_lines = file_object.readlines( )
list_of_all_the_lines = file_object.read( ).splitlines(1)
list_of_all_the_lines = file_object.read().splitlines( )
list_of_all_the_lines = file_object.read( ).split('\n')
```

The first two ways leave a '\n' at the end of each line (i.e., in each string item in the result list), while the other two ways remove all trailing '\n' characters. The first of these four ways is the fastest and most Pythonic. In Python 2.2 and later, there is a fifth way that is equivalent to the first one:

```
list_of_all_the_lines = list(file_object)
```

Discussion

Unless the file you're reading is truly huge, slurping it all into memory in one gulp is fastest and generally most convenient for any further processing. The built-in function open creates a Python file object. With that object, you call the read method to get all of the contents (whether text or binary) as a single large string. If the contents are text, you may choose to immediately split that string into a list of lines, with the split method or with the specialized splitlines method. Since such splitting is a frequent need, you may also call readlines directly on the file object, for slightly faster and more convenient operation. In Python 2.2, you can also pass the file object directly as the only argument to the built-in type list.

On Unix and Unix-like systems, such as Linux and BSD variants, there is no real distinction between text files and binary data files. On Windows and Macintosh systems, however, line terminators in text files are encoded not with the standard '\n' separator, but with '\r\n' and '\r', respectively. Python translates the line-termination characters into '\n' on your behalf, but this means that you need to tell Python when you open a binary file, so that it won't perform the translation. To do that, use 'rb' as the second argument to open. This is innocuous even on Unix-like platforms, and it's a good habit to distinguish binary files from text files even there, although it's not mandatory in that case. Such a good habit will make your programs more directly understandable, as well as letting you move them between platforms more easily.

You can call methods such as read directly on the file object produced by the open function, as shown in the first snippet of the solution. When you do this, as soon as the reading operation finishes, you no longer have a reference to the file object. In practice, Python notices the lack of a reference at once and immediately closes the file. However, it is better to bind a name to the result of open, so that you can call close yourself explicitly when you are done with the file. This ensures that the file stays open for as short a time as possible, even on platforms such as Jython and hypothetical future versions of Python on which more advanced garbage-collection mechanisms might delay the automatic closing that Python performs.

If you choose to read the file a little at a time, rather than all at once, the idioms are different. Here's how to read a binary file 100 bytes at a time, until you reach the end of the file:

```
file_object = open('abinfile', 'rb')
while 1:
    chunk = file_object.read(100)
    if not chunk: break
    do_something_with(chunk)
file_object.close( )
```

Passing an argument N to the read method ensures that read will read only the next N bytes (or fewer, if the file is closer to the end). read returns the empty string when it reaches the end of the file.

Reading a text file one line at a time is a frequent task. In Python 2.2 and later, this is the easiest, clearest, and fastest approach:

```
for line in open('thefile.txt'):
    do_something_with(line)
```

Several idioms were common in older versions of Python. The one idiom you can be sure will work even on extremely old versions of Python, such as 1.5.2, is quite similar to the idiom for reading a binary file a chunk at a time:

```
file_object = open('thefile.txt')
while 1:
    line = file_object.readline( )
    if not line: break
    do_something_with(line)
file_object.close( )
```

readline, like read, returns the empty string when it reaches the end of the file. Note that the end of the file is easily distinguished from an empty line because the latter is returned by readline as '\n', which is not an empty string but rather a string with a length of 1.

See Also

Recipe 4.2; documentation for the open built-in function and file objects in the *Library Reference*.

4.2   Writing to a File

Credit: Luther Blissett

Problem

You want to write text or data to a file.

Solution

Here is the most convenient way to write one big string to a file:

```
open('thefile.txt', 'w').write(all_the_text)   # text to a text file
open('abinfile', 'wb').write(all_the_data)     # data to a binary file
```

However, it is better to bind the file object to a variable so that you can call close on it as soon as you're done. For example, for a text file:

```
file_object = open('thefile.txt', 'w')
file_object.write(all_the_text)
file_object.close( )
```

More often, the data you want to write is not in one big string but in a list (or other sequence) of strings. In this case, you should use the writelines method (which, despite its name, is not limited to lines and works just as well with binary data as with text files):

```
file_object.writelines(list_of_text_strings)
open('abinfile', 'wb').writelines(list_of_data_strings)
```

Calling writelines is much faster than either joining the strings into one big string (e.g., with ''.join) and then calling write, or calling write repeatedly in a loop.

Discussion

To create a file object for writing, you must always pass a second argument to open—either 'w' to write textual data, or 'wb' to write binary data. The same considerations illustrated in Recipe 4.1 also apply here, except that calling close explicitly is even more advisable when you're writing to a file rather than reading from it. Only by closing the file can you be reasonably sure that the data is actually on the disk and not in some temporary buffer in memory.

Writing a file a little at a time is more common and less of a problem than reading a file a little at a time. You can just call write and/or writelines repeatedly, as each string or sequence of strings to write becomes ready. Each write operation appends data at the end of the file, after all the previously written data. When you're done, call the close method on the file object. If you have all the data available at once, a single writelines call is faster and simpler. However, if the data becomes available a little at a time, it's at least as easy and fast to call write as it comes as it would be to build up a temporary list of pieces (e.g., with append) to be able to write it all at once in the end with writelines. Reading and writing are quite different from each other, with respect to the performance implications of operating in bulk versus operating a little at a time.

See Also

Recipe 4.1; documentation for the open built-in function and file objects in the *Library Reference*.

4.3 Searching and Replacing Text in a File

Credit: Jeff Bauer

Problem

You need to change one string into another throughout a file.

Solution

String substitution is most simply performed by the replace method of string objects. The work here is to support reading from the specified file (or standard input) and writing to the specified file (or standard output):

```python
#!/usr/bin/env python
import os, sys

nargs = len(sys.argv)

if not 3 <= nargs <= 5:
    print "usage: %s search_text replace_text [infile [outfile]]" % \
        os.path.basename(sys.argv[0])
else:
    stext = sys.argv[1]
    rtext = sys.argv[2]
    input = sys.stdin
    output = sys.stdout
    if nargs > 3:
        input = open(sys.argv[3])
    if nargs > 4:
        output = open(sys.argv[4], 'w')
    for s in input.xreadlines():
        output.write(s.replace(stext, rtext))
    output.close()
    input.close()
```

Discussion

This recipe is really simple, but that's what beautiful about it—why do complicated stuff when simple stuff suffices? The recipe is a simple main script, as indicated by the leading "shebang" line. The script looks at its arguments to determine the search text, the replacement text, the input file (defaulting to standard input), and the output file (defaulting to standard output). Then, it loops over each line of the input file, writing to the output file a copy of the line with the substitution performed on it. That's all! For accuracy, it closes both files at the end.

As long as it fits comfortably in memory in two copies (one before and one after the replacement, since strings are immutable), we could, with some speed gain, operate on the whole input file's contents at once instead of looping. With today's PCs typically coming with 256 MB of memory, handling files of up to about 100 MB should not be a problem. It suffices to replace the for loop with one single statement:

```
output.write(input.read( ).replace(stext, rtext))
```

As you can see, that's even simpler than the loop used in the recipe.

If you're stuck with an older version of Python, such as 1.5.2, you may still be able to use this recipe. Change the import statement to:

```
import os, sys, string
```

and change the last two lines of the recipe into:

```
for s in input.readlines( ):
    output.write(string.replace(s, stext, rtext))
```

The xreadlines method used in the recipe was introduced with Python 2.1. It takes precautions not to read all of the file into memory at once, while readlines must do so, and thus may have problems with truly huge files.

In Python 2.2, the for loop can also be written more directly as:

```
for s in input:
    output.write(s.replace(stext, rtext))
```

This offers the fastest and simplest approach.

See Also

Documentation for the open built-in function and file objects in the *Library Reference*.

4.4   Reading a Particular Line from a File

Credit: Luther Blissett

Problem

You want to extract a single line from a file.

Solution

The standard linecache module makes this a snap:

```
import linecache
theline = linecache.getline(thefilepath, desired_line_number)
```

Discussion

The standard `linecache` module is usually the optimal Python solution for this task, particularly if you have to do this repeatedly for several of a file's lines, as it caches the information it needs to avoid uselessly repeating work. Just remember to use the module's `clearcache` function to free up the memory used for the cache, if you won't be getting any more lines from the cache for a while but your program keeps running. You can also use `checkcache` if the file may have changed on disk and you require the updated version.

`linecache` reads and caches all of the text file whose name you pass to it, so if it's a very large file and you need only one of its lines, `linecache` may be doing more work than is strictly necessary. Should this happen to be a bottleneck for your program, you may get some speed-up by coding an explicit loop, encapsulated within a function. Here's how to do this in Python 2.2:

```
def getline(thefilepath, desired_line_number):
    if desired_line_number < 1: return ''
    current_line_number = 0
    for line in open(thefilepath):
        current_line_number += 1
        if current_line_number == desired_line_number: return line
    return ''
```

It's not much worse in Python 2.1—you just need to change the for statement into this slightly slower and less concise form:

```
for line in open(thefilepath).xreadlines( ):
```

Python 2.0 and earlier had no such facilities for speedy reading of huge text files, line by line, consuming bounded amounts of memory. Should you be stuck with one of these older versions of Python, `linecache` will probably be the preferable solution under most circumstances.

See Also

Documentation for the `linecache` module in the *Library Reference*; *Perl Cookbook* Recipe 8.8.

4.5 Retrieving a Line at Random from a File of Unknown Size

Credit: Richard Papworth

Problem

You have a file of unknown (but potentially very large) size, and you need to select one line at random from it, with a single pass on the file.

Solution

We do need to read the whole file, but we don't have to read it all at once:

```
import random

def randomLine(file_object):
    "Retrieve a random line from a file, reading through the file once"
    lineNum = 0
    selected_line = ''

    while 1:
        aLine = file_object.readline()
        if not aLine: break
        lineNum = lineNum + 1
        # How likely is it that this is the last line of the file?
        if random.uniform(0,lineNum)<1:
            selected_line = aLine
    file_object.close()
    return selected_line
```

Discussion

Of course, a more obvious approach would be:

```
random.choice(file_object.readlines())
```

But that requires reading the whole file into memory at once, which can be a problem for truly enormous files.

This recipe works thanks to an unobvious but not terribly deep theorem: when we have seen the first N lines in the file, there is a probability of exactly $1/N$ that each of them is the one selected so far (i.e., the one to which the selected_line variable refers at this point). This is easy to see for the last line (the one just read into the aLine variable), because we explicitly choose it with a probability of 1.0/lineNum. The general validity of the theorem follows by induction. If it was true after the first $N-1$ lines were read, it's clearly still true after the Nth one is read. As we select the very first line with probability 1, the limit case of the theorem clearly does hold when $N=1$.

Of course, the same technique holds for a uniform-probability selection from any finite sequence that, for whatever reason, is made available only one item at a time. But, apart from, for example, selecting a random word from *usr/dict/words*, there aren't all that many practical applications of this pretty theorem.

See Also

Documentation for the random module in the *Library Reference*.

4.6 Counting Lines in a File

Credit: Luther Blissett

Problem

You need to compute the number of lines in a file.

Solution

The simplest approach, for reasonably sized files, is to read the file as a list of lines so that the count of lines is the length of the list. If the file's path is in a string bound to the thefilepath variable, that's just:

```
count = len(open(thefilepath).readlines( ))
```

For a truly huge file, this may be very slow or even fail to work. If you have to worry about humongous files, a loop using the xreadlines method always works:

```
count = 0
for line in open(thefilepath).xreadlines( ): count += 1
```

Here's a slightly tricky alternative, if the line terminator is '\n' (or has '\n' as a substring, as happens on Windows):

```
count = 0
thefile = open(thefilepath, 'rb')
while 1:
    buffer = thefile.read(8192*1024)
    if not buffer: break
    count += buffer.count('\n')
thefile.close( )
```

Without the 'rb' argument to open, this will work anywhere, but performance may suffer greatly on Windows or Macintosh platforms.

Discussion

If you have an external program that counts a file's lines, such as wc -l on Unix-like platforms, you can of course choose to use that (e.g., via os.popen( )). However, it's generally simpler, faster, and more portable to do the line-counting in your program. You can rely on almost all text files having a reasonable size, so that reading the whole file into memory at once is feasible. For all such normal files, the len of the result of readlines gives you the count of lines in the simplest way.

If the file is larger than available memory (say, a few hundred of megabytes on a typical PC today), the simplest solution can become slow, as the operating system struggles to fit the file's contents into virtual memory. It may even fail, when swap space is exhausted and virtual memory can't help any more. On a typical PC, with 256 MB of RAM and virtually unlimited disk space, you should still expect serious problems when you try to read into memory files of, say, 1 or 2 GB, depending on your operating system (some operating systems are much more fragile than others in handling virtual-memory issues under such overstressed load conditions). In this case, the xreadlines method of file objects, introduced in Python 2.1, is generally a good way to process text files line by line. In Python 2.2, you can do even better, in terms of both clarity and speed, by looping directly on the file object:

```
for line in open(thefilepath): count += 1
```

However, xreadlines does not return a sequence, and neither does a loop directly on the file object, so you can't just use len in these cases to get the number of lines. Rather, you have to loop and count line by line, as shown in the solution.

Counting line-terminator characters while reading the file by bytes, in reasonably sized chunks, is the key idea in the third approach. It's probably the least immediately intuitive, and it's not perfectly cross-platform, but you might hope that it's fastest (for example, by analogy with Recipe 8.2 in the *Perl Cookbook*).

However, remember that, in most cases, performance doesn't really matter all that much. When it does matter, the time sink might not be what your intuition tells you it is, so you should never trust your intuition in this matter—instead, always benchmark and measure. For example, I took a typical Unix syslog file of middling size, a bit over 18 MB of text in 230,000 lines:

```
[situ@tioni nuc]$ wc nuc
 231581 2312730 18508908 nuc
```

and I set up the following benchmark framework script, *bench.py*:

```
import time

def timeo(fun, n=10):
    start = time.clock( )
    for i in range(n): fun( )
    stend = time.clock( )
    thetime = stend-start
    return fun.__name__, thetime

import os

def linecount_wc( ):
    return int(os.popen('wc -l nuc').read().split( )[0])

def linecount_1( ):
    return len(open('nuc').readlines( ))

def linecount_2( ):
    count = 0
    for line in open('nuc').xreadlines( ): count += 1
    return count

def linecount_3( ):
    count = 0
    thefile = open('nuc')
```

```
        while 1:
            buffer = thefile.read(65536)
            if not buffer: break
            count += buffer.count('\n')
        return count

    for f in linecount_wc, linecount_1, linecount_2, linecount_3:
        print f.__name__, f()

    for f in linecount_1, linecount_2, linecount_3:
        print "%s: %.2f"%timeo(f)
```

First, I print the line counts obtained by all methods, thus ensuring that there is no anomaly or error (counting tasks are notoriously prone to off-by-one errors). Then, I run each alternative 10 times, under the control of the timing function timeo, and look at the results. Here they are:

```
[situ@tioni nuc]$ python -O bench.py
linecount_wc 231581
linecount_1 231581
linecount_2 231581
linecount_3 231581
linecount_1: 4.84
linecount_2: 4.54
linecount_3: 5.02
```

As you can see, the performance differences hardly matter: a difference of 10% or so in one auxiliary task is something that your users will never even notice. However, the fastest approach (for my particular circumstances, a cheap but very recent PC running a popular Linux distribution, as well as this specific benchmark) is the humble loop-on-every-line technique, while the slowest one is the ambitious technique that counts line terminators by chunks. In practice, unless I had to worry about files of many hundreds of megabytes, I'd always use the simplest approach (i.e., the first one presented in this recipe).

See Also

The *Library Reference* section on file objects and the time module; *Perl Cookbook* Recipe 8.2.

4.7 Processing Every Word in a File

Credit: Luther Blissett

Problem

You need to do something to every word in a file, similar to the foreach function of *csh*.

Solution

This is best handled by two nested loops, one on lines and one on the words in each line:

```
for line in open(thefilepath).xreadlines():
    for word in line.split():
        dosomethingwith(word)
```

This implicitly defines words as sequences of nonspaces separated by sequences of spaces (just as the Unix program wc does). For other definitions of words, you can use regular expressions. For example:

```
import re
re_word = re.compile(r'[\w-]+')

for line in open(thefilepath).xreadlines():
    for word in re_word.findall(line):
        dosomethingwith(word)
```

In this case, a word is defined as a maximal sequence of alphanumerics and hyphens.

Discussion

For other definitions of words you will obviously need different regular expressions. The outer loop, on all lines in the file, can of course be done in many ways. The xreadlines method is good, but you can also use the list obtained by the readlines method, the standard library module fileinput, or, in Python 2.2, even just:

```
for line in open(thefilepath):
```

which is simplest and fastest.

In Python 2.2, it's often a good idea to wrap iterations as iterator objects, most commonly by simple generators:

```
from __future__ import generators

def words_of_file(thefilepath):
    for line in open(thefilepath):
        for word in line.split():
            yield word

for word in words_of_file(thefilepath):
    dosomethingwith(word)
```

This approach lets you separate, cleanly and effectively, two different concerns: how to iterate over all items (in this case, words in a file) and what to do with each item in the iteration. Once you have cleanly encapsulated iteration concerns in an iterator object (often, as here, a generator), most of your uses of iteration become simple for statements. You can often reuse the iterator in many spots in your program, and if maintenance is ever needed, you can then perform it in just one place—the definition of the iterator—rather than having to hunt for all uses. The advantages are thus very similar to those you obtain, in any programming language, by appropriately defining and using functions rather than copying and pasting pieces of code all over the place. With Python 2.2's iterators, you can get these advantages for looping control structures, too.

See Also

Documentation for the `fileinput` module in the *Library Reference*; PEP 255 on simple generators (*http://www.python.org/peps/pep-0255.html*); *Perl Cookbook* Recipe 8.3.

4.8   Reading a Text File by Paragraphs

Credit: Alex Martelli, Magnus Lie Hetland

Problem

You need to read a file paragraph by paragraph, in which a paragraph is defined as a sequence of nonempty lines (in other words, paragraphs are separated by empty lines).

Solution

A wrapper class is, as usual, the right Pythonic architecture for this (in Python 2.1 and earlier):

```
class Paragraphs:

    def __init__(self, fileobj, separator='\n'):

        # Ensure that we get a line-reading sequence in the best way possible:
        import xreadlines
        try:
            # Check if the file-like object has an xreadlines method
            self.seq = fileobj.xreadlines()
        except AttributeError:
            # No, so fall back to the xreadlines module's implementation
            self.seq = xreadlines.xreadlines(fileobj)

        self.line_num = 0    # current index into self.seq (line number)
        self.para_num = 0    # current index into self (paragraph number)

        # Ensure that separator string includes a line-end character at the end
        if separator[-1:] != '\n': separator += '\n'
        self.separator = separator


    def __getitem__(self, index):
        if index != self.para_num:
            raise TypeError, "Only sequential access supported"
        self.para_num += 1
```

```
        # Start where we left off and skip 0+ separator lines
        while 1:
        # Propagate IndexError, if any, since we're finished if it occurs
            line = self.seq[self.line_num]
            self.line_num += 1
            if line != self.separator: break
        # Accumulate 1+ nonempty lines into result
        result = [line]
        while 1:
        # Intercept IndexError, since we have one last paragraph to return
            try:
                # Let's check if there's at least one more line in self.seq
                line = self.seq[self.line_num]
            except IndexError:
                # self.seq is finished, so we exit the loop
                break
            # Increment index into self.seq for next time
            self.line_num += 1
            if line == self.separator: break
            result.append(line)
        return ''.join(result)

# Here's an example function, showing how to use class Paragraphs:
def show_paragraphs(filename, numpars=5):
    pp = Paragraphs(open(filename))
    for p in pp:
        print "Par#%d, line# %d: %s" % (
            pp.para_num, pp.line_num, repr(p))
        if pp.para_num>numpars: break
```

Discussion

Python doesn't directly support paragraph-oriented file reading, but, as usual, it's
not hard to add such functionality. We define a paragraph as a string formed by joining a nonempty sequence of nonseparator lines, separated from any adjoining paragraphs by nonempty sequences of separator lines. By default, a separator line is one
that equals '\n' (empty line), although this concept is easy to generalize. We let the
client code determine what a separator is when instantiating this class. Any string is
acceptable, but we append a '\n' to it, if it doesn't already end with '\n' (since we
read the underlying file line by line, a separator not ending with '\n' would never
match).

We can get even more generality by having the client code pass us a callable that
looks at any line and tells us whether that line is a separator or not. In fact, this is
how I originally architected this recipe, but then I decided that such an architecture
represented a typical, avoidable case of overgeneralization (also known as overengi-
neering and "Big Design Up Front"; see *http://xp.c2.com/BigDesignUpFront.html*), so
I backtracked to the current, more reasonable amount of generality. Indeed, another

reasonable design choice for this recipe's class would be to completely forego the customizability of what lines are to be considered separators and just test for separator lines with `line.isspace( )`, so that stray blanks on an empty-looking line wouldn't misleadingly transform it into a nonseparator line.

This recipe's adapter class is a special case of sequence adaptation by bunching. An underlying sequence (here, a sequence of lines, provided by xreadlines on a file or file-like object) is bunched up into another sequence of larger units (here, a sequence of paragraph strings). The pattern is easy to generalize to other sequence-bunching needs. Of course, it's even easier with iterators and generators in Python 2.2, but even Python 2.1 is pretty good at this already. Sequence adaptation is an important general issue that arises particularly often when you are sequentially reading and/or writing files; see Recipe 4.9 for another example.

For Python 2.1, we need an index of the underlying sequence of lines and a way to check that our __getitem__ method is being called with properly sequential indexes (as the for statement does), so we expose the line_num and para_num indexes as useful attributes of our object. Thus, client code can determine our position during a sequential scan, in regard to the indexing on the underlying line sequence, the paragraph sequence, or both, without needing to track it itself.

The code uses two separate loops, each in a typical pattern:

```
while 1:
    ...
    if xxx: break
```

The first loop skips over zero or more separators that may occur between arbitrary paragraphs. Then, a separate loop accumulates nonseparators into a result list, until the underlying file finishes or a separator is encountered.

It's an elementary issue, but quite important to performance, to build up the result as a list of strings and combine them with `''.join` at the end. Building up a large string as a string, by repeated application of += in a loop, is never the right approach—it's slow and clumsy. Good Pythonic style demands using a list as the intermediate accumulator when building up a string.

The show_paragraphs function demonstrates all the simple features of the Paragraphs class and can be used to unit-test the latter by feeding it a known text file.

Python 2.2 makes it very easy to build iterators and generators. This, in turn, makes it very tempting to build a more lightweight version of the by-paragraph buncher as a generator function, with no classes involved:

```
from __future__ import generators

def paragraphs(fileobj, separator='\n'):
    if separator[-1:] != '\n': separator += '\n'
    paragraph = []
```

```
        for line in fileobj:
            if line == separator:
                if paragraph:
                    yield ''.join(paragraph)
                    paragraph = []
            else:
                paragraph.append(line)
        if paragraph: yield ''.join(paragraph)
```

We don't get the line and paragraph numbers, but the approach is much more lightweight, and it works polymorphically on any fileobj that can be iterated on to yield
a sequence of lines, not just a file or file-like object. Such useful polymorphism is
always a nice plus, particularly considering that it's basically free. Here, we have
merged the loops into one, and we use the intermediate list paragraph itself as the
state indicator. If the list is empty, we're skipping separators; otherwise, we're accumulating nonseparators.

See Also

Recipe 4.9; documentation on the xreadlines module in the *Library Reference*; the
Big Design Up Front Wiki page (*http://xp.c2.com/BigDesignUpFront.html*).

4.9   Reading Lines with Continuation Characters

Credit: Alex Martelli

Problem

You have a file that includes long logical lines split over two or more physical lines,
with backslashes to indicate that a continuation line follows. You want to process a
sequence of logical lines, rejoining those split lines.

Solution

As usual, a class is the right way to wrap this functionality in Python 2.1:

```
class LogicalLines:

    def __init__(self, fileobj):

        # Ensure that we get a line-reading sequence in the best way possible:
        import xreadlines
        try:
            # Check if the file-like object has an xreadlines method
            self.seq = fileobj.xreadlines( )
        except AttributeError:
            # No, so fall back to the xreadlines module's implementation
            self.seq = xreadlines.xreadlines(fileobj)
```

```python
        self.phys_num = 0  # current index into self.seq (physical line number)
        self.logi_num = 0  # current index into self (logical line number)

    def __getitem__(self, index):
        if index != self.logi_num:
            raise TypeError, "Only sequential access supported"
        self.logi_num += 1
        result = []
        while 1:
            # Intercept IndexError, since we may have a last line to return
            try:
                # Let's see if there's at least one more line in self.seq
                line = self.seq[self.phys_num]
            except IndexError:
                # self.seq is finished, so break the loop if we have any
                # more data to return; else, reraise the exception, because
                # if we have no further data to return, we're finished too
                if result: break
                else: raise
            self.phys_num += 1
            if line.endswith('\\\n'):
                result.append(line[:-2])
            else:
                result.append(line)
                break
        return ''.join(result)

# Here's an example function, showing off usage:
def show_logicals(fileob, numlines=5):
    ll = LogicalLines(fileob)
    for l in ll:
        print "Log#%d, phys# %d: %s" % (
            ll.logi_num, ll.phys_num, repr(l))
        if ll.logi_num>numlines: break

if __name__=='__main__':
    from cStringIO import StringIO
    ff = StringIO(
r"""prima \
seconda \
terza
quarta \
quinta
sesta
settima \
ottava
""")
    show_logicals( ff )
```

Discussion

This is another sequence-bunching problem, like Recipe 4.8. In Python 2.1, a class wrapper is the most natural approach to getting reusable code for sequence-bunching tasks. We need to support the sequence protocol ourselves and handle the sequence protocol in the sequence we wrap. In Python 2.1 and earlier, the sequence protocol is as follows: a sequence must be indexable by successively larger integers (0, 1, 2, ...), and it must raise an IndexError as soon as an integer that is too large is used as its index. So, if we need to work with Python 2.1 and earlier, we must behave this way ourselves and be prepared for just such behavior from the sequence we are wrapping.

In Python 2.2, thanks to iterators, the sequence protocol is much simpler. A call to the next method of an iterator yields its next item, and the iterator raises a StopIteration when it's done. Combined with a simple generator function that returns an iterator, this makes sequence bunching and similar tasks far easier:

```
from __future__ import generators

def logical_lines(fileobj):
    logical_line = []
    for physical_line in fileobj:
        if physical_line.ends_with('\\\n'):
            logical_line.append(physical_line[:-2])
        else:
            yield ''.join(logical_line)+physical_line
            logical_line = []
    if logical_line: yield ''.join(logical_line)
```

See Also

Recipe 4.8; *Perl Cookbook* Recipe 8.1.

4.10   Reading Data from ZIP Files

Credit: Paul Prescod

Problem

You have an archive in ZIP format, and you want to examine some or all of the files it contains directly, without expanding them on disk.

Solution

ZIP files are a popular, cross-platform way of archiving files. Python's standard library comes with a zipfile module to access them easily:

```
import zipfile

z = zipfile.ZipFile("zipfile.zip", "r")

for filename in z.namelist( ):
    print 'File:', filename,
    bytes = z.read(filename)
    print 'has',len(bytes),'bytes'
```

Discussion

Python can work directly with data in ZIP files. You can look at the list of items in the directory and work with the data files themselves. This recipe is a snippet that lists all of the names and content lengths of the files included in the ZIP archive *zipfile.zip*.

The zipfile module does not currently handle multidisk ZIP files or ZIP files that have appended comments. Take care to use 'r' as the flag argument, not 'rb', which might seem more natural (e.g., on Windows). With ZipFile, the flag is not used the same way as for opening a file, and 'rb' is not recognized. The 'r' flag takes care of the inherently binary nature of the ZIP file on all platforms.

See Also

Documentation for the zipfile module in the *Library Reference*.

4.11   Reading INI Configuration Files

Credit: Dirk Holtwick

Problem

You want to load a configuration file for your program, but you don't want to use a Python module for this purpose, as that might expose you to security risks or troublesome syntax and other errors in the module.

Solution

The standard ConfigParser library module gives us almost all we need to use INI files for configuration:

```
import ConfigParser
import string

_ConfigDefault = {
    "database.dbms":            "mysql",
```

```
    "database.name":            "",
    "database.user":            "root",
    "database.password":        "",
    "database.host":            "127.0.0.1"
    }

def LoadConfig(file, config={}):
    """
    returns a dictionary with keys of the form
    <section>.<option> and the corresponding values
    """
    config = config.copy()
    cp = ConfigParser.ConfigParser()
    cp.read(file)
    for sec in cp.sections():
        name = string.lower(sec)
        for opt in cp.options(sec):
            config[name + "." + string.lower(opt)] = string.strip(
                cp.get(sec, opt))
    return config

if __name__=="__main__":
    print LoadConfig("some.ini", _ConfigDefault)
```

Discussion

Many people use Python modules as configuration files, but this may allow your program to be manipulated or let a syntax error come into that file. To use INI-style configuration files, which are known from Windows (but can also be used under Unix-like systems, since they're just text files with some structure), try the small script here.

The code in the recipe is just for reading configuration files, but writing them is also easy to implement. An INI file looks like this:

```
[database]
user = dummy
password = tosca123
```

You can set the defaults in advance. Note that the keys of the dictionary are always lowercase.

See Also

Documentation for the ConfigParser module in the *Library Reference*.

4.12 Sending Binary Data to Standard Output Under Windows

Credit: Hamish Lawson

Problem

You want to send binary data (e.g., an image) to `stdout`, under Windows.

Solution

That's what the `setmode` function, in the platform-dependent `msvcrt` module in Python's standard library, is for:

```
import sys

if sys.platform == "win32":
    import os, msvcrt
    msvcrt.setmode(sys.stdout.fileno( ), os.O_BINARY)
```

Discussion

If you are reading or writing binary data, such as an image, under Windows, the file must be opened in binary mode (Unix doesn't make a distinction between text and binary modes). However, this is a problem for programs that write binary data to standard output (as a CGI program could be expected to do), because Python opens the `sys.stdout` file object on your behalf, normally in text mode.

You can have `stdout` opened in binary mode instead by supplying the `-u` command-line option to the Python interpreter. However, if you want to control this mode from within a program, you can use the `setmode` function provided by the Windows-specific `msvcrt` module to change the mode of `stdout`'s underlying file descriptor, as shown in the recipe.

See Also

Documentation for the `msvcrt` module in the *Library Reference*.

4.13 Using Random-Access Input/Output

Credit: Luther Blissett

Problem

You want to read a binary record from somewhere inside a large file of fixed-length records, without reading a record at a time to get there.

Solution

The byte offset of the start of a record in the file is the record size multiplied by the record number (counting from 0). So just seek, then read:

```
thefile = open('somebinfile', 'rb')
thefile.seek(record_size * record_number)
buffer = thefile.read(record_size)
```

Discussion

This approach works only on files (generally binary ones) defined in terms of records that are all the same, fixed size; it doesn't on normal text files. For clarity, the recipe shows the file being opened for reading as a binary file, by passing 'rb' as the second argument to open. Of course, you don't need to open the file just before performing the first seek on it. As long as the file object is open for reading as a binary file, you can perform as many seek and read operations as you want before eventually closing the file again.

See Also

The section of the *Library Reference* on file objects; *Perl Cookbook* Recipe 8.12.

4.14 Updating a Random-Access File

Credit: Luther Blissett

Problem

You want to read a binary record from somewhere inside a large file of fixed-length records, change the values, and write the record back.

Solution

Read the record, unpack it, perform whatever computations you need for the update, pack the fields back into the record, seek to the start of the record again, and write it back. Phew. Faster to code than to say:

```
import struct

thefile = open('somebinfile', 'r+b')
record_size = struct.calcsize(format_string)

thefile.seek(record_size * record_number)
buffer = thefile.read(record_size)
fields = list(struct.unpack(format_string, buffer))

# Perform computations, suitably modifying fields, then:
```

```
buffer = struct.pack(format_string, *fields)
thefile.seek(record_size * record_number)
thefile.write(buffer)

thefile.close( )
```

Discussion

This approach works only on files (generally binary ones) defined in terms of records that are all the same, fixed size; it doesn't work on normal text files. Furthermore, the size of each record must be that defined by a struct's format string, as shown in the recipe's code. A typical format string, for example, might be "8l", to specify that each record is made up of eight four-byte integers, each to be interpreted as a signed value and unpacked into a Python int. In this case, the fields variable in the recipe would be bound to a list of eight ints. Note that struct.unpack returns a tuple. Because tuples are immutable, the computation would have to rebind the entire fields variable. A list is not immutable, so each field can be rebound as needed. Thus, for convenience, we explicitly ask for a list when we bind fields. Make sure, however, not to alter the length of the list. In this case, it needs to remain composed of exactly eight integers, or the struct.pack call will raise an exception when we call it with a format_string that is still "8l". Also note that this recipe is not suitable for working with records that are not all of the same, unchanging length.

To seek back to the start of the record, instead of using the record_size*record_number offset again, you may choose to do a relative seek:

```
thefile.seek(-record_size, 1)
```

The second argument to the seek method (1) tells the file object to seek relative to the current position (here, so many bytes back, because we used a negative number as the first argument). seek's default is to seek to an absolute offset within the file (i.e., from the start of the file). You can also explicitly request this default behavior by calling seek with a second argument of 0.

Of course, you don't need to open the file just before you do the first seek or close it right after the write. Once you have a file object that is correctly opened (i.e., for update, and as a binary rather than a text file), you can perform as many updates on the file as you want before closing the file again. These calls are shown here to emphasize the proper technique for opening a file for random-access updates and the importance of closing a file when you are done with it.

The file needs to be opened for updating (i.e., to allow both reading and writing). That's what the 'r+b' argument to open means: open for reading and writing, but do not implicitly perform any transformations on the file's contents, because the file is a binary one (the 'b' part is unnecessary but still recommended for clarity on Unix and Unix-like systems—however, it's absolutely crucial on other platforms, such as Macintosh and Windows). If you're creating the binary file from scratch but you still want to be able to reread and update some records without closing and reopening the file, you can use a second argument of 'w+b' instead. However, I have never witnessed this strange combination of requirements; binary files are normally first created (by opening them with 'wb', writing data, and closing the file) and later opened for update with 'r+b'.

See Also

The sections of the *Library Reference* on file objects and the `struct` module; *Perl Cookbook* Recipe 8.13.

4.15   Splitting a Path into All of Its Parts

Credit: Trent Mick

Problem

You want to process subparts of a file or directory path.

Solution

We can define a function that uses `os.path.split` to break out all of the parts of a file or directory path:

```
import os, sys
def splitall(path):
    allparts = []
    while 1:
        parts = os.path.split(path)
        if parts[0] == path:  # sentinel for absolute paths
            allparts.insert(0, parts[0])
            break
        elif parts[1] == path: # sentinel for relative paths
            allparts.insert(0, parts[1])
            break
        else:
            path = parts[0]
            allparts.insert(0, parts[1])
    return allparts
```

Discussion

The `os.path.split` function splits a path into two parts: everything before the final slash and everything after it. For example:

```
>>> os.path.split('c:\\foo\\bar\\baz.txt')
('c:\\foo\\bar', 'baz.txt')
```

Often, it's useful to process parts of a path more generically; for example, if you want to walk up a directory. This recipe splits a path into each piece that corresponds to a mount point, directory name, or file. A few test cases make it clear:

```
>>> splitall('a/b/c')
['a', 'b', 'c']
>>> splitall('/a/b/c/')
['/', 'a', 'b', 'c', '']
>>> splitall('/')
['/']
>>> splitall('C:')
['C:']
>>> splitall('C:\\')
['C:\\']
>>> splitall('C:\\a')
['C:\\', 'a']
>>> splitall('C:\\a\\')
['C:\\', 'a', '']
>>> splitall('C:\\a\\b')
['C:\\', 'a', 'b']
>>> splitall('a\\b')
['a', 'b']
```

See Also

Recipe 4.16; documentation on the os.path module in the *Library Reference*.

4.16   Treating Pathnames as Objects

Credit: David Ascher

Problem

You want to manipulate path objects as if they were sequences of path parts.

Solution

Although it is only available this elegantly in Python 2.2 and later, you can create a subclass of the string type that knows about pathnames:

```
_translate = { '..': os.pardir }
class path(str):
    def __str__(self):
        return os.path.normpath(self)
    def __div__(self, other):
        other = _translate.get(other, other)
        return path(os.path.join(str(self), str(other)))
    def __len__(self):
        return len(splitall(str(self)))
    def __getslice__(self, start, stop):
        parts = splitall(str(self))[start:stop]
```

```
        return path(os.path.join(*parts))
    def __getitem__(self, i):
        return path(splitall(str(self))[i])
```

Note that this solution relies on Recipe 4.15.

Discussion

I designed this class after I had to do a lot of path manipulations. These are typically done with a function such as os.path.join, which does the job well enough, but is somewhat cumbersome to use:

```
root = sys.prefix
sitepkgs = os.path.join(root, 'lib', 'python', 'site-packages')
```

To use this recipe, the first path must be created with the path function. After that, divisions are all that we need to append to the path:

```
root = path(sys.prefix)
sitepkgs = root / 'lib' / 'python' / 'site-packages'
```

As an additional bonus, you can treat the path as a sequence of path parts:

```
>>> print sitepkgs
C:\Apps\Python22\lib\python\site-packages
>>> print len(sitepkgs)
6
>>> sitepkgs[0], sitepkgs[1], sitepkgs[-1]
('C:\\', 'Apps', 'site-packages')
```

This class could be made richer by, for example, adding method wrappers for many of the functions that are defined in the os.path module (isdir, exists, etc.).

The code is fairly straightforward, thanks to the ease with which one can subclass strings in Python 2.2 and later. The call to os.path.normpath is important, since it ensures that casual use of . and .. do not wreak havoc:

```
>>> root / '..' / 'foo' / "."
'C:\\Apps\\foo\\.'
```

The overriding of the division operator uses a little trick that is overkill for this recipe but can come in handy in other contexts. The following line:

```
other = _translate.get(other, other)
```

does a simple lookup for other in the _translate dictionary and leaves it alone if that key isn't found in the dictionary.

See Also

Recipe 4.15; documentation for the os.path module in the *Library Reference*.

4.17 Creating Directories Including Necessary Parent Directories

Credit: Trent Mick, Alex Martelli

Problem

You want a way to make a directory that is more convenient than Python's standard os.mkdir.

Solution

A good make-directory function should, first of all, make the necessary parent directories, which os.makedirs does quite nicely. We also want our function to complete silently if the directory already exists but to fail if the needed directory exists as a plain file. To get that behavior, we need to write some code:

```
import os, errno
def mkdirs(newdir, mode=0777):
    try: os.makedirs(newdir, mode)
    except OSError, err:
        # Reraise the error unless it's about an already existing directory
        if err.errno != errno.EEXIST or not os.path.isdir(newdir):
            raise
```

Discussion

Python's standard os.mkdir works much like the underlying *mkdir* system call (i.e., in a pretty spare and rigorous way). For example, it raises an exception when the directory you're trying to make already exists. You almost always have to handle that exception, because it's not generally an error if the directory already exists as a directory, while it is indeed an error if a file of that name is in the way. Further, all the parent directories of the one you're trying to make must already exist, as os.mkdir itself only makes the leaf directory out of the whole path.

There used to be a time when *mkdir*, as used in Unix shell scripts, worked the same way, but we're spoiled now. For example, the --parents switch in the GNU version of *mkdir* implicitly creates all intermediate directories, and gives no error if the target directory already exists as a directory. Well, why not have the same convenience in Python? This recipe shows it takes very little to achieve this—the little function mkdirs can easily become part of your standard bag of tricks. Of course, Python's standard os.makedirs is doing most of the job. However, mkdirs adds the important convenience of not propagating an exception when the requested directory already exists and is indeed a directory. However, if the requested directory exists as a file or if the operating system diagnoses any other kind of trouble, function mkdirs does explicitly re-raise the exception, to ensure it propagates further.

See Also

Documentation for the os module in the *Library Reference*.

4.18 Walking Directory Trees

Credit: Robin Parmar, Alex Martelli

Problem

You need to examine a directory, or an entire directory tree rooted in a certain directory, and obtain a list of all the files (and optionally folders) that match a certain pattern.

Solution

os.path.walk is sufficient for this purpose, but we can pretty it up quite at bit:

```python
import os.path, fnmatch

def listFiles(root, patterns='*', recurse=1, return_folders=0):

    # Expand patterns from semicolon-separated string to list
    pattern_list = patterns.split(';')
    # Collect input and output arguments into one bunch
    class Bunch:
        def __init__(self, **kwds): self.__dict__.update(kwds)
    arg = Bunch(recurse=recurse, pattern_list=pattern_list,
        return_folders=return_folders, results=[])

    def visit(arg, dirname, files):
        # Append to arg.results all relevant files (and perhaps folders)
        for name in files:
            fullname = os.path.normpath(os.path.join(dirname, name))
            if arg.return_folders or os.path.isfile(fullname):
                for pattern in arg.pattern_list:
                    if fnmatch.fnmatch(name, pattern):
                        arg.results.append(fullname)
                        break
        # Block recursion if recursion was disallowed
        if not arg.recurse: files[:]=[]

    os.path.walk(root, visit, arg)

    return arg.results
```

Discussion

The standard directory-tree function os.path.walk is powerful and flexible, but it can be confusing to beginners. This recipe dresses it up in a listFiles function that lets

---

you choose the root folder, whether to recurse down through subfolders, the file patterns to match, and whether to include folder names in the result list.

The file patterns are case-insensitive but otherwise Unix-style, as supplied by the standard fnmatch module, which this recipe uses. To specify multiple patterns, join them with a semicolon. Note that this means that semicolons themselves can't be part of a pattern.

For example, you can easily get a list of all Python and HTML files in directory */tmp* or any subdirectory thereof:

```
thefiles = listFiles('/tmp', '*.py;*.htm;*.html')
```

See Also

Documentation for the os.path module in the *Library Reference*.

4.19   Swapping One File Extension for Another Throughout a Directory Tree

Credit: Julius Welby

Problem

You need to rename files throughout a subtree of directories, specifically changing the names of all files with a given extension so that they end in another extension.

Solution

Operating throughout a subtree of directories is easy enough, with the os.path.walk function from Python's standard library:

```
import os, string

def swapextensions(dir, before, after):
    if before[:1]!='.': before = '.'+before
    if after[:1]!='.': after = '.'+after
    os.path.walk(dir, callback, (before, -len(before), after))

def callback((before, thelen, after), dir, files):
    for oldname in files:
        if oldname[thelen:]==before:
            oldfile = os.path.join(dir, oldname)
            newfile = oldfile[:thelen] + after
            os.rename(oldfile, newfile)

if __name__=='__main__':
    import sys
    if len(sys.argv) != 4:
        print "Usage: swapext rootdir before after"
```

```
        sys.exit(100)
    swapextensions(sys.argv[1], sys.argv[2], sys.argv[3])
```

Discussion

This recipe shows how to change the file extensions of (i.e., rename) all files in a specified directory, all of its subdirectories, all of their subdirectories, and so on. This technique is useful for changing the extensions of a whole batch of files in a folder structure, such as a web site. You can also use it to correct errors made when saving a batch of files programmatically.

The recipe is usable either as a module, to be imported from any other, or as a script to run from the command line, and it is carefully coded to be platform-independent and compatible with old versions of Python as well as newer ones. You can pass in the extensions either with or without the leading dot (.), since the code in this recipe will insert that dot if necessary.

See Also

The author's web page at *http://www.outwardlynormal.com/python/swapextensions.htm*.

4.20   Finding a File Given an Arbitrary Search Path

Credit: Chui Tey

Problem

Given a search path (a string of directories with a separator in between), you need to find the first file along the path whose name is as requested.

Solution

Basically, you need to loop over the directories in the given search path:

```
import os, string

def search_file(filename, search_path, pathsep=os.pathsep):
    """ Given a search path, find file with requested name """
    for path in string.split(search_path, pathsep):
        candidate = os.path.join(path, filename)
        if os.path.exists(candidate): return os.path.abspath(candidate)
    return None

if __name__ == '__main__':
    search_path = '/bin' + os.pathsep + '/usr/bin'  # ; on Windows, : on Unix
    find_file = search_file('ls',search_path)
    if find_file:
```

```
        print "File found at %s" % find_file
    else:
        print "File not found"
```

Discussion

This is a reasonably frequent task, and Python makes it extremely easy. The search loop can be coded in many ways, but returning the normalized path as soon as a hit is found is simplest as well as fast. The explicit return None after the loop is not strictly needed, since None is what Python returns when a function falls off the end, but having the return explicit in this case makes the functionality of search_file much clearer at first sight.

To find files specifically on Python's own search path, see Recipe 4.21.

See Also

Recipe 4.21; documentation for the module os in the *Library Reference*.

4.21 Finding a File on the Python Search Path

Credit: Mitch Chapman

Problem

A large Python application includes resource files (e.g., Glade project files, SQL templates, and images) as well as Python packages. You want to store these associated files together with the Python packages that use them.

Solution

You need to be able to look for either files or directories along Python's sys.path:

```
import sys, os

class Error(Exception): pass

def _find(pathname, matchFunc=os.path.isfile):
    for dirname in sys.path:
        candidate = os.path.join(dirname, pathname)
        if matchFunc(candidate):
            return candidate
    raise Error("Can't find file %s" % pathname)

def findFile(pathname):
    return _find(pathname)

def findDir(path):
    return _find(path, matchFunc=os.path.isdir)
```

Discussion

Larger Python applications consist of sets of Python packages and associated sets of resource files. It's convenient to store these associated files together with the Python packages that use them, and it's easy to do so if you use this variation on Recipe 4.20 to find files or directories with pathnames relative to the Python search path.

See Also

Recipe 4.20; documentation for the os module in the *Library Reference*.

4.22 Dynamically Changing the Python Search Path

Credit: Robin Parmar

Problem

Modules must be on the Python search path before they can be imported, but you don't want a huge permanent path, because that slows things down—you want to change the path dynamically.

Solution

We just conditionally add a directory to Python's sys.path, carefully checking to avoid duplication:

```
def AddSysPath(new_path):
    """ AddSysPath(new_path): adds a directory to Python's sys.path

    Does not add the directory if it does not exist or if it's already on
    sys.path. Returns 1 if OK, -1 if new_path does not exist, 0 if it was
    already on sys.path.
    """
    import sys, os

    # Avoid adding nonexistent paths
    if not os.path.exists(new_path): return -1

    # Standardize the path. Windows is case-insensitive, so lowercase
    # for definiteness.
    new_path = os.path.abspath(new_path)
    if sys.platform == 'win32':
        new_path = new_path.lower( )

    # Check against all currently available paths
    for x in sys.path:
        x = os.path.abspath(x)
        if sys.platform == 'win32':
```

```
                x = x.lower( )
            if new_path in (x, x + os.sep):
                return 0
        sys.path.append(new_path)
        return 1

    if __name__ == '__main__':
        # Test and show usage
        import sys

        print 'Before:'
        for x in sys.path: print x

        if sys.platform == 'win32':
            print AddSysPath('c:\\Temp')
            print AddSysPath('c:\\temp')
        else:
            print AddSysPath('usr/lib/my_modules')

        print 'After:'
        for x in sys.path: print x
```

Discussion

Modules must be on the Python search path before they can be imported, but we don't want to have a huge permanent path, because that would slow down every import performed by every Python script and application. This simple recipe dynamically adds a directory to the path, but only if that directory exists and was not already on sys.path.

sys.path is a list, so it's easy to add directories to its end, using sys.path.append. Every import performed after such an append will automatically look in the newly added directory, if it cannot be satisfied from earlier ones.

It's no big problem if sys.path ends up with some duplicates or if some nonexistent directory is accidentally appended to it; Python's import statement is clever enough to shield itself against such issues. However, each time such a problem occurs at import time (from duplicate unsuccessful searches, errors from the operating system that need to be handled gracefully, etc.), there is a price to pay in terms of performance. To avoid the risk of these performance issues, this recipe does a conditional addition to sys.path, never appending any dictionary that doesn't exist or is already in sys.path.

See Also

Documentation for the sys module in the *Library Reference*.

4.23   Computing Directory Sizes in a Cross-Platform Way

Credit: Frank Fejes

Problem

You need to compute the total size of a directory (or set of directories) in a way that works under both Windows and Unix-like platforms.

Solution

There are easier platform-dependent solutions, such as Unix's *du*, but Python also makes it quite feasible to have a cross-platform solution:

```
import os
from os.path import *

class DirSizeError(Exception): pass

def dir_size(start, follow_links=0, start_depth=0, max_depth=0, skip_errs=0):

    # Get a list of all names of files and subdirectories in directory start
    try: dir_list = os.listdir(start)
    except:
        # If start is a directory, we probably have permission problems
        if os.path.isdir(start):
            raise DirSizeError('Cannot list directory %s'%start)
        else:  # otherwise, just re-raise the error so that it propagates
            raise

    total = 0L
    for item in dir_list:
        # Get statistics on each item--file and subdirectory--of start
        path = join(start, item)
        try: stats = os.stat(path)
        except:
            if not skip_errs:
                raise DirSizeError('Cannot stat %s'%path)
        # The size in bytes is in the seventh item of the stats tuple, so:
        total += stats[6]
        # recursive descent if warranted
        if isdir(path) and (follow_links or not islink(path)):
            bytes = dir_size(path, follow_links, start_depth+1, max_depth)
            total += bytes
            if max_depth and (start_depth < max_depth):
                print_path(path, bytes)
    return total

def print_path(path, bytes, units='b'):
    if units == 'k':
        print '%-8ld%s' % (bytes / 1024, path)
```

```python
        elif units == 'm':
            print '%-5ld%s' % (bytes / 1024 / 1024, path)
        else:
            print '%-11ld%s' % (bytes, path)

    def usage (name):
        print "usage: %s [-bkLm] [-d depth] directory [directory...]" % name
        print '\t-b\t\tDisplay in Bytes (default)'
        print '\t-k\t\tDisplay in Kilobytes'
        print '\t-m\t\tDisplay in Megabytes'
        print '\t-L\t\tFollow symbolic links (meaningful on Unix only)'
        print '\t-d, --depth\t# of directories down to print (default = 0)'


    if __name__=='__main__':
        # When used as a script:
        import string, sys, getopt

        units = 'b'
        follow_links = 0
        depth = 0

        try:
            opts, args = getopt.getopt(sys.argv[1:], "bkLmd:", ["depth="])
        except getopt.GetoptError:
            usage(sys.argv[0])
            sys.exit(1)

        for o, a in opts:
            if o == '-b': units = 'b'
            elif o == '-k': units = 'k'
            elif o == '-L': follow_links = 1
            elif o == '-m': units = 'm'
            elif o in ('-d', '--depth'):
                try: depth = int(a)
                except:
                    print "Not a valid integer: (%s)" % a
                    usage(sys.argv[0])
                    sys.exit(1)

        if len(args) < 1:
            print "No directories specified"
            usage(sys.argv[0])
            sys.exit(1)
        else:
            paths = args

        for path in paths:
            try: bytes = dir_size(path, follow_links, 0, depth)
            except DirSizeError, x: print "Error:", x
            else: print_path(path, bytes)
```

Discussion

Unix-like platforms have the *du* command, but that doesn't help when you need to get information about disk-space usage in a cross-platform way. This recipe has been tested under both Windows and Unix, although it is most useful under Windows, where the normal way of getting this information requires using a GUI. In any case, the recipe's code can be used both as a module (in which case you'll normally call only the dir_size function) or as a command-line script. Typical use as a script is:

```
C:\> python dir_size.py "c:\Program Files"
```

This will give you some idea of where all your disk space has gone. To help you narrow the search, you can, for example, display each subdirectory:

```
C:\> python dir_size.py --depth=1 "c:\Program Files"
```

The recipe's operation is based on recursive descent. os.listdir provides a list of names of all the files and subdirectories of a given directory. If dir_size finds a subdirectory, it calls itself recursively. An alternative architecture might be based on os.path.walk, which handles the recursion on our behalf and just does callbacks to a function we specify, for each subdirectory it visits. However, here we need to be able to control the depth of descent (e.g., to allow the useful --depth command-line option, which turns into the max_depth argument of the dir_size function). This control is easier to attain when we administer the recursion directly, rather than letting os.path.walk handle it on our behalf.

See Also

Documentation for the os.path and getopt modules in the *Library Reference*.

4.24 File Locking Using a Cross-Platform API

Credit: Jonathan Feinberg, John Nielsen

Problem

You need to lock files in a cross-platform way between NT and Posix, but the Python standard library offers only platform-specific ways to lock files.

Solution

When the Python standard library itself doesn't offer a cross-platform solution, it's often possible to implement one ourselves:

```
import os

# needs win32all to work on Windows
if os.name == 'nt':
```

```
        import win32con, win32file, pywintypes
        LOCK_EX = win32con.LOCKFILE_EXCLUSIVE_LOCK
        LOCK_SH = 0 # the default
        LOCK_NB = win32con.LOCKFILE_FAIL_IMMEDIATELY
        __overlapped = pywintypes.OVERLAPPED( )

        def lock(file, flags):
            hfile = win32file._get_osfhandle(file.fileno( ))
            win32file.LockFileEx(hfile, flags, 0, 0xffff0000, __overlapped)

        def unlock(file):
            hfile = win32file._get_osfhandle(file.fileno( ))
            win32file.UnlockFileEx(hfile, 0, 0xffff0000, __overlapped)
    elif os.name == 'posix':
        from fcntl import LOCK_EX, LOCK_SH, LOCK_NB

        def lock(file, flags):
            fcntl.flock(file.fileno( ), flags)

        def unlock(file):
            fcntl.flock(file.fileno( ), fcntl.LOCK_UN)
    else:
        raise RuntimeError("PortaLocker only defined for nt and posix platforms")
```

Discussion

If you have multiple programs or threads that may want to access a shared file, it's wise to ensure that accesses are synchronized, so that two processes don't try to modify the file contents at the same time. Failure to do so could corrupt the entire file in some cases.

This recipe supplies two functions, lock and unlock, that request and release locks on a file, respectively. Using the *portalocker.py* module is a simple matter of calling the lock function and passing in the file and an argument specifying the kind of lock that is desired:

LOCK_SH

> A shared lock (the default value). This denies all processes write access to the file, including the process that first locks the file. All processes can read the locked file.

LOCK_EX

> An exclusive lock. This denies all other processes both read and write access to the file.

LOCK_NB

> A nonblocking lock. If this value is specified, the function returns immediately if it is unable to acquire the requested lock. Otherwise, it waits. LOCK_NB can be ORed with either LOCK_SH or LOCK_EX.

For example:

```
import portalocker
file = open("somefile", "r+")
portalocker.lock(file, portalocker.LOCK_EX)
```

The implementation of the lock and unlock functions is entirely different on Unix-like systems (where they can rely on functionality made available by the standard fcntl module) and on Windows systems (where they must use the win32file module, part of the very popular win32all package of Windows-specific extensions to Python, authored by Mark Hammond). But the important thing is that, despite the differences in implementation, the functions (and the flags you can pass to the lock function) behave in the same way across platforms. Such cross-platform packaging of differently implemented but equivalent functionality is what lets you write cross-platform applications, which is one of Python's strengths.

When you write a cross-platform program, it's nice if the functionality that your program uses is, in turn, encapsulated in a cross-platform way. For file locking in particular, this is helpful to Perl users, who are used to an essentially transparent lock system call across platforms. More generally, if os.name== just does not belong in application-level code. It should ideally always be in the standard library or an application-independent module, as it is here.

See Also

Documentation on the fcntl module in the *Library Reference*; documentation on the win32file module at *http://ASPN.ActiveState.com/ASPN/Python/Reference/Products/ ActivePython/PythonWin32Extensions/win32file.html*; Jonathan Feinberg's web site (*http://MrFeinberg.com*).

4.25 Versioning Filenames

Credit: Robin Parmar

Problem

You want make a backup copy of a file, before you overwrite it, with the standard protocol of appending a three-digit version number to the name of the old file.

Solution

This simple approach to file versioning uses a function, rather than wrapping file objects into a class:

```
def VersionFile(file_spec, vtype='copy'):
    import os, shutil

    if os.path.isfile(file_spec):
```

```
    # or, do other error checking:
    if vtype not in 'copy', 'rename':
        vtype = 'copy'

    # Determine root filename so the extension doesn't get longer
    n, e = os.path.splitext(file_spec)

    # Is e an integer?
    try:
        num = int(e)
        root = n
    except ValueError:
        root = file_spec

    # Find next available file version
    for i in xrange(1000):
        new_file = '%s.%03d' % (root, i)
        if not os.path.isfile(new_file):
            if vtype == 'copy':
                shutil.copy(file_spec, new_file)
            else:
                os.rename(file_spec, new_file)
            return 1

    return 0

if __name__ == '__main__':
    # test code (you will need a file named test.txt)
    print VersionFile('test.txt')
    print VersionFile('test.txt')
    print VersionFile('test.txt')
```

Discussion

The purpose of the VersionFile function is to ensure that an existing file is copied (or renamed, as indicated by the optional second parameter) before you open it for writing or updating and therefore modify it. It is polite to make such backups of files before you mangle them. The actual copy or renaming is performed by shutil.copy and os.rename, respectively, so the only issue is what name to use as the target.

A popular way to determine backups' names is versioning (i.e., appending to the filename a gradually incrementing number). This recipe determines the new_name by first extracting the filename's root (just in case you call it with an already-versioned filename) and then successively appending to that root the further extensions .000, .001, and so on, until a name built in this manner does not correspond to any existing file. Then, and only then, is the name used as the target of a copy or renaming. Note that VersionFile is limited to 1,000 versions, so you should have an archive plan after that. You also need the file to exist before it is first versioned—you cannot back up what does not yet exist.

This is a lightweight implementation of file versioning. For a richer, heavier, and more complete one, see Recipe 4.26.

See Also

Recipe 4.26; documentation for the os and shutil modules in the *Library Reference*.

4.26 Module: Versioned Backups

Credit: Mitch Chapman

Before overwriting an existing file, it is often desirable to make a backup. Example 4-1 emulates the behavior of Emacs by saving versioned backups. It's also compatible with the marshal module, so you can use versioned output files for output in marshal format. If you find other file-writing modules that, like marshal, type-test rather than using file-like objects polymorphically, the class supplied here will stand you in good stead.

When Emacs saves a file *foo.txt*, it first checks to see if *foo.txt* already exists. If it does, the current file contents are backed up. Emacs can be configured to use versioned backup files, so, for example, *foo.txt* might be backed up to *foo.txt.~1~*. If other versioned backups of the file already exist, Emacs saves to the next available version. For example, if the largest existing version number is 19, Emacs will save the new version to *foo.txt.~20~*. Emacs can also prompt you to delete old versions of your files. For example, if you save a file that has six backups, Emacs can be configured to delete all but the three newest backups.

Example 4-1 emulates the versioning backup behavior of Emacs. It saves backups with version numbers (e.g., backing up *foo.txt* to *foo.txt.~n~* when the largest existing backup number is $n-1$. It also lets you specify how many old versions of a file to save. A value that is less than zero means not to delete any old versions.

The marshal module lets you marshal an object to a file by way of the dump function, but dump insists that the file object you provide actually be a Python file object, rather than any arbitrary object that conforms to the file-object interface. The versioned output file shown in this recipe provides an asFile method for compatibility with marshal.dump. In many (but, alas, far from all) cases, you can use this approach to use wrapped objects when a module type-tests and thus needs the unwrapped object, solving (or at least ameliorating) the type-testing issue mentioned in Recipe 5.8. Note that Example 4-1 can be seen as one of many uses of the automatic-delegation idiom mentioned there.

The only true solution to the problem of modules using type tests rather than Python's smooth, seamless polymorphism is to change those errant modules, but this can be hard in the case of errant modules that you did not write (particularly ones in Python's standard library).

Example 4-1. Saving backups when writing files

```python
""" This module provides versioned output files. When you write to such
a file, it saves a versioned backup of any existing file contents. """

import sys, os, glob, string, marshal

class VersionedOutputFile:
    """ Like a file object opened for output, but with versioned backups
    of anything it might otherwise overwrite """

    def __init__(self, pathname, numSavedVersions=3):
        """ Create a new output file. pathname is the name of the file to
        [over]write. numSavedVersions tells how many of the most recent
        versions of pathname to save. """
        self._pathname = pathname
        self._tmpPathname = "%s.~new~" % self._pathname
        self._numSavedVersions = numSavedVersions
        self._outf = open(self._tmpPathname, "wb")

    def __del__(self):
        self.close()

    def close(self):
        if self._outf:
            self._outf.close()
            self._replaceCurrentFile()
            self._outf = None

    def asFile(self):
        """ Return self's shadowed file object, since marshal is
        pretty insistent on working with real file objects. """
        return self._outf

    def __getattr__(self, attr):
        """ Delegate most operations to self's open file object. """
        return getattr(self._outf, attr)

    def _replaceCurrentFile(self):
        """ Replace the current contents of self's named file. """
        self._backupCurrentFile()
        os.rename(self._tmpPathname, self._pathname)

    def _backupCurrentFile(self):
        """ Save a numbered backup of self's named file. """
        # If the file doesn't already exist, there's nothing to do
        if os.path.isfile(self._pathname):
            newName = self._versionedName(self._currentRevision() + 1)
            os.rename(self._pathname, newName)

            # Maybe get rid of old versions
            if ((self._numSavedVersions is not None) and
                (self._numSavedVersions > 0)):
                self._deleteOldRevisions()
```

Example 4-1. Saving backups when writing files (continued)

```python
    def _versionedName(self, revision):
        """ Get self's pathname with a revision number appended. """
        return "%s.~%s~" % (self._pathname, revision)

    def _currentRevision(self):
        """ Get the revision number of self's largest existing backup. """
        revisions = [0] + self._revisions()
        return max(revisions)

    def _revisions(self):
        """ Get the revision numbers of all of self's backups. """
        revisions = []
        backupNames = glob.glob("%s.~[0-9]*~" % (self._pathname))
        for name in backupNames:
            try:
                revision = int(string.split(name, "~")[-2])
                revisions.append(revision)
            except ValueError:
                # Some ~[0-9]*~ extensions may not be wholly numeric
                pass
        revisions.sort()
        return revisions

    def _deleteOldRevisions(self):
        """ Delete old versions of self's file, so that at most
        self._numSavedVersions versions are retained. """
        revisions = self._revisions()
        revisionsToDelete = revisions[:-self._numSavedVersions]
        for revision in revisionsToDelete:
            pathname = self._versionedName(revision)
            if os.path.isfile(pathname):
                os.remove(pathname)

def main():
    """ mainline module (for isolation testing) """
    basename = "TestFile.txt"
    if os.path.exists(basename):
        os.remove(basename)
    for i in range(10):
        outf = VersionedOutputFile(basename)
        outf.write("This is version %s.\n" % i)
        outf.close()

    # Now there should be just four versions of TestFile.txt:
    expectedSuffixes = ["", ".~7~", ".~8~", ".~9~"]
    expectedVersions = []
    for suffix in expectedSuffixes:
        expectedVersions.append("%s%s" % (basename, suffix))
    expectedVersions.sort()
    matchingFiles = glob.glob("%s*" % basename)
    matchingFiles.sort()
    for filename in matchingFiles:
```

Example 4-1. Saving backups when writing files (continued)

```
        if filename not in expectedVersions:
            sys.stderr.write("Found unexpected file %s.\n" % filename)
        else:
            # Unit tests should clean up after themselves:
            os.remove(filename)
            expectedVersions.remove(filename)
    if expectedVersions:
        sys.stderr.write("Not found expected file")
        for ev in expectedVersions:
            sys.sdterr.write(' '+ev)
        sys.stderr.write('\n')

    # Finally, here's an example of how to use versioned
    # output files in concert with marshal:
    import marshal

    outf = VersionedOutputFile("marshal.dat")
    # Marshal out a sequence:
    marshal.dump([1, 2, 3], outf.asFile())
    outf.close()
    os.remove("marshal.dat")

if __name__ == "__main__":
    main()
```

For a more lightweight, simpler approach to file versioning, see Recipe 4.25.

See Also

Recipes 4.25 and 5.8; documentation for the marshal module in the *Library Reference*.

## CHAPTER 5

Object-Oriented Programming

5.0   Introduction

Credit: Alex Martelli, AB Strakt, author of forthcoming Python in a Nutshell

Object-oriented programming (OOP) is among Python's greatest strengths. Python's OOP features keep improving steadily and gradually, just like Python in general. You could write object-oriented programs better in Python 1.5.2 (the ancient, long-stable version that was new when I first began to work with Python) than in any other popular language (excluding, of course, Lisp and its variants—I doubt there's anything you can't do well in Lisp-like languages, as long as you can stomach the parentheses-heavy concrete syntax). Now, with Python 2.2, OOP is substantially better than with 1.5.2. I am constantly amazed at the systematic progress Python achieves without sacrificing solidity, stability, and backward compatibility.

To get the most out of Python's OOP features, you should use them "the Python way," rather than trying to mimic C++, Java, Smalltalk, or other languages you may be familiar with. You can do a lot of mimicry, but you'll get better mileage if you invest in understanding the Python way. Most of the investment is in increasing your understanding of OOP itself: what does OOP buy you, and which underlying mechanisms can your object-oriented programs use? The rest of the investment is in understanding the specific mechanisms that Python itself offers.

One caveat is in order. For such a high-level language, Python is quite explicit about the OOP mechanisms it uses behind the curtains: they're exposed and available for your exploration and tinkering. Exploration and understanding are good, but beware the temptation to tinker. In other words, don't use unnecessary black magic just because you can. Specifically, don't use it in production code (code that you and others must maintain). If you can meet your goals with simplicity (and most often, in Python, you can), then keep your code simple.

So what is OOP all about? First of all, it's about keeping some *state* (data) and some *behavior* (code) together in handy packets. "Handy packets" is the key here. Every program has state and behavior—programming paradigms differ only in how you view, organize, and package them. If the packaging is in terms of objects that typically comprise state and behavior, you're using OOP. Some object-oriented languages force you to use OOP for everything, so you end up with many objects that lack either state or behavior. Python, however, supports multiple paradigms. While everything in Python is an object, you package things up as OOP objects only when you want to. Other languages try to force your programming style into a predefined mold for your own good, while Python empowers you to make and express your own design choices.

With OOP, once you have specified how an object is composed, you can instantiate as many objects of that kind as you need. When you don't want to create multiple objects, consider using other Python constructs, such as modules. In this chapter, you'll find recipes for Singleton, an object-oriented design pattern that takes away the multiplicity of instantiation. But if you want only one instance, in Python it's often best to use a module, not an OOP object.

To describe how an object is made up, use the `class` statement:

```
class SomeName:
    """ You usually define data and code here (in the class body). """
```

SomeName is a *class object*. It's a first-class object like every Python object, so you can reference it in lists and dictionaries, pass it as an argument to a function, and so on.

When you want a new instance of a class, call the class object as if it was a function. Each call returns a new instance object:

```
anInstance = SomeName()
another = SomeName()
```

anInstance and another are two distinct *instance objects*, both belonging to the SomeName class. (See Recipe 1.7 for a class that does little more than this but is quite useful.) You can bind and access *attributes* (state) of an instance object:

```
anInstance.someNumber = 23 * 45
print anInstance.someNumber          # 1035
```

Instances of an "empty" class like this have no behavior, but they may have state. Most often, however, you want instances to have behavior. Specify this behavior by defining *methods* in the class body:

```
class Behave:
    def __init__(self, name):
        self.name = name
    def once(self):
        print "Hello, ", self.name
    def rename(self, newName)
        self.name = newName
    def repeat(self, N):
        for i in range(N): self.once()
```

Define methods with the same def statement Python uses to define functions, since methods are basically functions. However, a method is an attribute of a class object, and its first formal argument is (by universal convention) named self. self always refers to the instance on which you call the method.

The method with the special name __init__ is known as the *constructor* for the class. Python calls it to initialize each newly created instance, with the arguments that you passed when calling the class (except for self, which you do not pass explicitly, as Python supplies it automatically). The body of __init__ typically binds attributes on the newly created self instance to initialize the instance's state appropriately.

Other methods implement the behavior of instances of the class. Typically, they do so by accessing instance attributes. Also, methods often rebind instance attributes, and they may call other methods. Within a class definition, these actions are always done with the self.something syntax. Once you instantiate the class, however, you call methods on the instance, access the instance's attributes, and even rebind them using the theobject.something syntax:

```
beehive = Behave("Queen Bee")
beehive.repeat(3)
beehive.rename("Stinger")
beehive.once( )
print beehive.name
beehive.name = 'See, you can rebind it "from the outside" too, if you want'
beehive.repeat(2)
```

If you're new to OOP in Python, try implementing these things in an interactive Python environment, such as the GUI shell supplied by the free IDLE development environment that comes with Python.

In addition to the constructor (__init__), your class may have other special methods, which are methods with names that start and end with two underscores. Python calls the special methods of a class when instances of the class are used in various operations and built-in functions. For example, len(x) returns x.__len__( ), a+b returns a.__add__(b), and a[b] returns a.__getitem__(b). Therefore, by defining special methods in a class, you can make instances of that class interchangeable with objects of built-in types, such as numbers, lists, dictionaries, and so on.

The ability to handle different objects in similar ways, called *polymorphism*, is a major advantage of OOP. With polymorphism, you can call the same method on each object and let each object implement the method appropriately. For example, in addition to the Behave class, you might have another class that implements a repeat method, with a rather different behavior:

```
class Repeater:
    def repeat(self, N): print N*"*-*"
```

You can mix instances of Behave and Repeater at will, as long as the only method you call on them is repeat:

```
aMix = beehive, Behave('John'), Repeater(), Behave('world')
for whatever in aMix: whatever.repeat(3)
```

Other languages require inheritance or the formal definition and implementation of interfaces for polymorphism to work. In Python, all you need is methods with the same signature (i.e., methods that are callable with the same arguments).

Python also has *inheritance*, which is a handy way to reuse code. You can define a class by inheriting from another and then adding or redefining (known as *overriding*) some of its methods:

```
class Subclass(Behave):
    def once(self): print '(%s)' % self.name
subInstance = Subclass("Queen Bee")
subInstance.repeat(3)
```

The Subclass class overrides only the once method, but you can also call the repeat method on subInstance, as it inherits that method from the Behave superclass. The body of the repeat method calls once N times on the specific instance, using whatever version of the once method the instance has. In this case, it uses the method from the Subclass class, which prints the name in parentheses, not the version from the Behave class, which prints it after a greeting. The idea of a method calling other methods on the same instance and getting the appropriately overridden version of each is important in every object-oriented language, including Python. This is known as the Template-Method design pattern.

Often, the method of a subclass overrides a method from the superclass, but needs to call the method of the superclass as a part of its own operation. You do this in Python by explicitly getting the method as a class attribute and passing the instance as the first argument:

```
class OneMore(Behave):
    def repeat(self, N): Behave.repeat(self, N+1)
zealant = OneMore("Worker Bee")
zealant.repeat(3)
```

The OneMore class implements its own repeat method in terms of the method with the same name in its superclass, Behave, with a slight change. This approach, known as *delegation*, is pervasive in all programming. Delegation involves implementing some functionality by letting another existing piece of code do most of the work, often with some slight variation. Often, an overriding method is best implemented by delegating some of the work to the same method in the superclass. In Python, the syntax Classname.method(self, ...) delegates to Classname's version of the method.

Python actually supports multiple inheritance: one class can inherit from several others. In terms of coding, this is a minor issue that lets you use the mix-in class idiom, a convenient way to supply some functionality across a broad range of classes. (See Recipe 5.13 for an unusual variant of this.) However, multiple inheritance is important because of its implications for object-oriented analysis—how you conceptualize your problem and your solution in the first place. Single inheritance pushes you to frame your problem space via taxonomy (i.e., mutually exclusive classification). The real world doesn't work like that. Rather, it resembles Jorge Luis Borges's explanation in "The Analytical Language of John Wilkins", from a purported Chinese Encyclopedia, *The Celestial Emporium of Benevolent Knowledge*. Borges explains that all animals are divided into:

- Those that belong to the Emperor
- Embalmed ones
- Those that are trained
- Suckling pigs
- Mermaids
- Fabulous ones
- Stray dogs
- Those included in the present classification
- Those that tremble as if they were mad
- Innumerable ones
- Those drawn with a very fine camelhair brush
- Others
- Those that have just broken a flower vase
- Those that from a long way off look like flies

You get the point: taxonomy forces you to pigeonhole, fitting everything into categories that aren't truly mutually exclusive. Modeling aspects of the real world in your programs is hard enough without buying into artificial constraints such as taxonomy. Multiple inheritance frees you from these constraints.

Python 2.2 has introduced an important innovation in Python's object model. Classic classes, such as those mentioned in this introduction, still work as they always did. In addition, you can use new-style classes, which are classes that subclass a built-in type, such as list, dict, or file. If you want a new-style class and do not need to inherit from any specific built-in type, you can subclass the new type object, which is the root of the whole inheritance hierarchy.

New-style classes work like existing ones, with some specific changes and several additional options. The recipes in this book were written and collected before the release of Python 2.2, and therefore use mostly classic classes. However this chapter specifies if a recipe might be inapplicable to a new-style class (a rare issue) or if new-style classes might offer alternative (and often preferable) ways to accomplish the same tasks (which is most often the case). The information you find in this chapter is therefore just as useful whether you use Python 2.1, 2.2, or even the still-experimental 2.3 (being designed as we write), which won't change any of Python's OOP features.

5.1   Overriding a Built-In Method

Credit: Dave Haynes

Problem

You need to wrap (or, in Python 2.2, inherit from) a list or tuple, delegating several operations to it, and want to provide proper slicing (i.e., through the special method __getitem__).

Solution

In most cases, overriding special methods of built-in objects when you inherit from those objects (or wrap them with automatic delegation, which is not technically an override) poses no special challenge. When inheriting in Python 2.2, you can call the special method of the superclass with the usual unbound-method syntax. When wrapping, use the syntax that is specific to the operation, such as self.data[someindex] for indexing.

Slicing is harder, because while slicing should go through the same special method __getitem__ as indexing (since Python 2.0), lists and tuples still implement an older approach: the more limited special method __getslice__ (and similarly for __setitem__ versus __setslice__ and __delitem__ versus __delslice__). So, you must provide a remedy, normally with a try/except:

```
class SliceTester:
    def __init__(self):
        self.data = ['zero', 'one', 'two', 'three', 'four']

    def __getitem__(self, indexOrSlice):
        try:
            return self.data[indexOrSlice]
        except TypeError:
            return self.data[indexOrSlice.start:indexOrSlice.stop]
```

Discussion

When a user-defined class wraps (or, in Python 2.2, inherits from) a list or tuple, it often needs to define the __set*__ and __get*__ special methods and delegate part or all of their operation to the wrapped (or inherited) built-in object to provide the correct access to the data.

The documentation for Python 2.0 and later deprecates the use of __getslice__ and __setslice__. Instead, it suggests providing suitably extended versions of __getitem__ and __setitem__. This is a truly excellent idea because it enables the use of the extended-form slicing approaches (including step, ellipsis, and so on) that Numeric Python has made so deservedly popular among its regular users. Unfortunately, if you try to pass a slice object to the item-oriented special methods of a list or tuple object, you get a TypeError; the underlying C API still insists on receiving integer parameters, not slice objects in all their glory, whatever the documentation may say.

Fortunately, working around this problem isn't as dramatic as all that. You just need to trap the TypeError you get from trying to index an old-fashioned sequence with a slice, and remedy it suitably. Here's the typical self-test code that you can append to the recipe's module and execute when it is run as a main script:

```
if __name__ == "__main__":
    theSlice = SliceTester( )
    a = theSlice[2]
    b = theSlice[:3]
    print a
    print b
```

In the recipe's SliceTester example class, the remedy is pretty minimal; it's just an attempt to use start and stop attributes of the noninteger index (presumably an instance of the slice built-in type). You may want to do a lot more (implement step, ellipsis, and so on).

Note that this recipe doesn't cover all of the cases in which slices can be used. There is a third argument to the slice operator that defines the step, or stride, of the slicing. For example, if data is a Numeric Python array (the only widely used software that supports slicing in all its glory), data[0:101:10] returns the sequence data[0], data[10], data[20]—up to data[100]. Similarly, data[::-1] returns a sequence containing the contents of data reversed. The third argument to the slice operator is stored in the step attribute of slice objects and is set to None if a step isn't specified (as in list[start:end]). Given this, it shouldn't be a surprise that the recipe shown earlier will not magically add support for steps to objects that don't support new-style slices.

The point of this recipe is that you must be aware of these limitations and take precautionary measures. Also, don't type-test for an index of type slice. If normal indexing refuses the index, you are better off catching the TypeError in an except clause and entering another try/except in which you try to use the index as the slice you now expect it to be. This lets client code pass you objects that are polymorphic to slice objects.

See Also

The section of the *Language Reference* on slicing; the description of the slice built-in function in the *Library Reference*.

5.2 Getting All Members of a Class Hierarchy

Credit: Jürgen Hermann, Alex Martelli

Problem

You need to map all members of a class, including inherited members, into a dictionary of class attribute names.

Solution

Here is a solution that works portably and transparently on both new-style (Python 2.2) and classic classes with any Python version:

```
def all_members(aClass):
    try:
        # Try getting all relevant classes in method-resolution order
        mro = list(aClass.__mro__)
    except AttributeError:
        # If a class has no __mro__, then it's a classic class
        def getmro(aClass, recurse):
            mro = [aClass]
            for base in aClass.__bases__: mro.extend(recurse(base, recurse))
            return mro
        mro = getmro(aClass, getmro)
    mro.reverse( )
    members = {}
    for someClass in mro: members.update(vars(someClass))
    return members
```

Discussion

The `all_members` function in this recipe creates a dictionary that includes each member (such as methods and data attributes) of a class with the name as the key and the class attribute value as the corresponding value. Here's a usage example:

```
class Eggs:
    eggs = 'eggs'
    spam = None

class Spam:
    spam = 'spam'

class Breakfast(Spam, Eggs):
    eggs = 'scrambled'

print all_members(Eggs)
print all_members(Spam)
print all_members(Breakfast)
```

And here's the output of this example (note that the order in which each dictionary's items are printed is arbitrary and may vary between Python interpreters):

```
{'spam': None, '__doc__': None, 'eggs': 'eggs', '__module__': '__main__'}
{'spam': 'spam', '__doc__': None, '__module__': '__main__'}
{'__doc__': None, 'eggs': 'scrambled', 'spam': 'spam', '__module__': '__main__'}
```

After constructing the dictionary d with d=all_members(c), you can use d for repeated introspection about class c. d.has_key(x) is the same as hasattr(c,x), and d.get(x) is the same as getattr(c,x,None), but it doesn't repeat the dynamic search procedure each time. Apart from the order of its items, d.keys is like dir(c) if c is a new-style class (for which dir also returns the names of inherited attributes) but is richer and potentially more useful than dir(c) if c is a classic class (for which dir does not list inherited attributes, only attributes defined or overridden directly in class c itself).

The all_members function starts by getting a list of all relevant classes (the class itself and all of its bases, direct and indirect), in the order in which attributes are looked up, in the mro variable (MRO stands for method-resolution order). This happens immediately for a new-style class, since it exposes this information with its __mro__ attribute—we just need to build a list from it, since it is a tuple. If accessing __mro__ fails, we're dealing with a classic class and must build mro up in a recursive way. We do that in the nested function getmro in the except clause. Note that we give getmro itself as an argument to facilitate recursion in older Python versions that did not support lexically nested scopes.

Once we have mro, we need to reverse it, because we build up our dictionary with the update method. When we call adict.update(anotherdict), the entries in the two dictionaries adict and anotherdict are merged as the new contents of adict. In case of conflict (i.e., a key k is present in both dictionaries), the value used is anotherdict[k], which overrides the previous value of adict[k]. Therefore, we must build our dictionary starting with the classes that are looked up last when Python is looking for an attribute. We move towards the classes that are looked up earlier to reproduce how overriding works with inheritance. The dictionaries we merge in this way are those given sequentially by the built-in function vars on each class. vars takes any object as its argument and returns a dictionary of the object's attributes. Note that even for new-style classes in Python 2.2, vars does not consider inherited attributes, just the attributes defined or overridden directly in the object itself, as dir does only for classic classes.

See Also

Understanding method resolution order is a new challenge even for old Python hands. The best description is in Guido's essay describing the unification of types and classes (*http://www.python.org/2.2/descrintro.html#mro*), which was refined somewhat in PEP 253 (*http://www.python.org/peps/pep-0253.html*).

5.3 Calling a Superclass __init__ Method if It Exists

Credit: Alex Martelli

Problem

You want to ensure that __init__ is called for all superclasses that define it, and Python does not do this automatically.

Solution

There are several ways to perform this task. In a Python 2.2 new-style class, the built-in super function makes it easy (as long as all superclass __init__ methods also use super similarly):

```
class NewStyleOnly(A, B, C):
    def __init__(self):
        super(NewStyleOnly, self).__init__()
        # Subclass-specific initialization follows
```

For classic classes, we need an explicit loop over the superclasses, but we can still choose different ways to handle the possibility that each superclass may or may not have an __init__ method. The most intuitive approach is to "Look Before You Leap" (LBYL), i.e., check for existence before calling. While in many other cases LBYL has problems, in this specific case it doesn't, so we use it because it is the simplest approach:

```
class LookBeforeYouLeap(X, Y, Z):
    def __init__(self):
        for base in self__class__.__bases__:
            if hasattr(base, '__init__'):
                base.__init__(self)
        # Subclass-specific initialization follows
```

Discussion

Often, we want to call a method on an instance (or class) if and only if that method exists. Otherwise, we do nothing or default to another action. For example, this often applies to the __init__ method of superclasses, since Python does not automatically call this method if it exists. A direct call of X.__init__(self) (including approaches such as those in Recipe 5.4) works only if base class X defines an __init__ method. We may, however, want to make our subclass independent from such a superclass implementation detail. Typically, the coupling of a subclass to its base classes is pretty tight; loosening it is not a bad idea, if it is feasible and inexpensive.

In Python 2.2's new-style object model, the built-in super function provides the simplest, fastest, and most direct solution, as long as all superclasses are also new-style and use super similarly. Note that all new-style classes have an __init__ method because they all subclass object, and object defines __init__ as a do-nothing function that accepts and ignores its arguments. Therefore, all new-style classes have an __init__ method, either by inheritance or by override.

More generally, however, we may want to hand-craft another solution, which will help us for classic classes, mixtures of new-style and classic classes, and other methods that may or may not be present in each given superclass. Even though this recipe is about __init__, its ideas can clearly apply to other cases in which we want to call all the superclass implementations of any other given method. We then have a choice of three general categories of approaches:

1. Check for attribute existence with hasattr before the otherwise normal call.
2. Try the call (or the attribute fetching with getattr) and catch the error, if any.
3. Use getattr to return the desired attribute, or else a do-nothing function (more generally, a callable object with suitable default functionality) if the attribute does not exist, then proceed by calling whatever callable is returned.

The solution shows the first approach, which is the simplest and most appropriate for the common case of __init__ in a multiple, classic-class inheritance. (The recipe's code works just as well with single inheritance, of course. Indeed, as a special case, it works fine even when used in a class without any bases.) Using the LBYL approach here has the great advantage of being obvious. Note that the built-in hasattr function implements proper lookup in the bases of our bases, so we need not worry about that. As a general idiom, LBYL often has serious issues, but they don't apply in this specific case. For example, LBYL can interrupt an otherwise linear control flow with readability-damaging checks for rare circumstances. With LBYL, we also run the risk that the condition we're checking might change between the moment when we look and the moment when we leap (e.g., in a multithreaded scenario). If you ever have to put locks and safeguards bracketing the look and the leap, it's best to choose another approach. But this recipe's specific case is one of the few in which LBYL is okay.

The second approach is known as "Easier to Ask Forgiveness than Permission" (EAFP). The following naive variant of it is somewhat fragile:

```
class EasierToAskForgiveness_Naive(X, Y, Z):
    def __init__(self):
        for base in self.__class__.__bases__:
            try: base.__init__(self)
            except AttributeError: pass
        # Subclass-specific initialization follows
```

While EAFP is a good general approach and very Pythonic, we still need to be careful to catch only the specific exception we're expecting from exactly where we're expecting it. The previous code is not accurate and careful enough. If base.__init__ exists but fails, and an AttributeError is raised because of an internal logic problem, typo, etc., __init__ will mask it. It's not hard to fashion a much more robust version of EAFP:

```
class EasierToAskForgiveness_Robust(X, Y, Z):
    def __init__(self):
        for base in self__class__.__bases__:
            try: fun = base.__init__
            except AttributeError: pass
            else: fun(self)
        # Subclass-specific initialization follows
```

The _Robust variant is vastly superior, since it separates the subtask of accessing the base.__init__ callable object (unbound method object) from the task of calling it. Only the access to the callable object is protected in the try/except. The call happens only when no exception was seen (which is what the else clause is for in the try/except statement), and if executing the call raises any exceptions, they are correctly propagated.

Separating the acquisition of the callable from calling it leads us to the third approach, known as "Homogenize Different Cases" (HDC). It's best implemented with a small do-nothing local function:

```
class HomogenizeDifferentCases1(X, Y, Z):
    def __init__(self):
        def doNothing(obj): pass
        for base in self__class__.__bases__:
            fun = getattr(base, '__init__', doNothing)
            fun(self)
        # Subclass-specific initialization follows
```

For lambda fanatics, here is an alternative implementation:

```
class HomogenizeDifferentCases2(X, Y, Z):
    def __init__(self):
        for base in self__class__.__bases__:
            fun = getattr(base, '__init__', lambda x: None)
            fun(self)
        # Subclass-specific initialization follows
```

Again, this is a good general approach (in Python and more generally in programming) that often leads to simpler, more linear code (and sometimes to better speed). Instead of checking for possible special cases, we do some preprocessing that ensures we are in regular cases, then we proceed under full assumption of regularity. The sentinel idiom in searches is a good example of HDC in a completely different context, as is the Null Object design pattern (see Recipe 5.23). The only difference between the two HDC examples described here is how the do-nothing callable is built: the first uses a simple nested function with names that make its role (or, perhaps, nonrole) totally obvious, while the other uses a lambda form. The choice between them is strictly a style issue.

See Also

Recipes 5.4 and 5.23.

5.4 Calling a Superclass Implementation of a Method

Credit: Alex Martelli

Problem

You need functionality equivalent to Java's super keyword to delegate part of a method to a superclass.

Solution

When you override the method of a superclass, you often want to call the super-class's version of a method as part of your override. In a Python 2.2 new-style class, the new built-in super function helps a lot:

```
class A(B, C):
    def amethod(self):
        # First, call the superclass's version
        super(A, self).amethod( )
        # Continue with A-specific implementation
        ...
```

With super, you transparently call amethod in the B or C superclass, or in both, if both classes define it, and B also uses super in the same way.

This doesn't work for classic classes (or in Python 2.1 and earlier), but we can arrange for a slightly weaker version:

```
def super(class_, inst):
    # First, try the real thing, if available and applicable
    try: return __builtins__.super(class_, inst)
    except (TypeError, AttributeError): pass
    # Otherwise, arrange for a weaker substitute
    class Super:
        def __init__(self, class_, inst):
            # Just remember the bases and instance
            self.bases = class_.__bases__
            self.inst = inst
        def __getattr__(self, name):
            # Seek the bases for an unbound method; break when found
            for base in self.bases:
                method = getattr(name, method, None)
                if method is not None: break
            else: raise AttributeError, name   # No base has it, so raise
            # Found, so create and return the bound-method version
            import new
            return new.instancemethod(method, self.inst, method.im_class)
```

Used in a classic class, this super calls a method only in the base where it first finds it. In classic-class settings, to call a method in all superclasses that have it, use the approaches shown in Recipe 5.3.

Discussion

When you override a method, it is quite common to want to delegate part of its execution to a superclass. In other words, even though you are overriding the method to provide extra features, you still need to use the superclass's implementation as part of your own. If there is just a single superclass, or if you know which superclass implementation you need to call, it is easy to do this with the normal Python idiom `Superclass.themethod(self, ...)`. However, with multiple inheritance, you may not know which superclass you want. If you refactor your code, you may move methods between superclasses, so you shouldn't depend on a method's exact location in the subclass you're writing. Often, you may want to call all implementations of a method in all superclasses, particularly for special methods, such as `__init__` or `__del__`.

Python 2.2's new-style object model offers a direct solution for this task: the new super built-in function. You call `super` with two arguments: the class in which you're overriding the method and `self`. Looking up any method on super's return value returns the appropriate superclass implementation to call as a bound method (i.e., you don't explicitly pass it `self` again). If you use this technique systematically in all the classes that override this method, you end up calling every superclass implementation (in the new-style model's canonical method resolution order, so you don't have to worry about diamond-shaped inheritance graphs).

In the classic object model, `super` doesn't work (and in Python 2.1 and earlier, it doesn't even exist). In this recipe, we simulate it in a slightly weaker but still useful way. The recipe defines a factory function (i.e., a function that builds and returns a suitable object) also called `super`, so that it shadows the built-in super from normal use. You use it as you use the built-in super, except that you can use it in classic or new-style classes interchangeably. The recipe's function first tries to use the built-in super. If that's not found or not applicable, the function falls back to the slightly weaker but useful equivalent, the Super class.

The Super class does not let you transparently call a method in several superclasses, nor does it apply the new-style method resolution order. However, it does work for simple cases. `__init__` simply stashes away the instance and the list of bases. `__getattr__` loops on all bases; if the loop does not find the method, and thus never breaks, the `else` clause is entered, which raises `AttributeError`. If the method is found, `__getattr__` wraps it into a bound method (the better to simulate the built-in super's workings) and returns it. The wrapping is performed via the `instancemethod` function in the new module using the `im_class` attribute of the unbound method, which records the class that supplied the method.

See Also

Recipes 5.3, 14.7, and 14.8.

5.5 Implementing Properties

Credit: Luther Blissett

Problem

You want client code to use normal attribute-access syntax for using, binding, or deleting instance attributes, but you want the semantics of these actions to be determined by method calls (e.g., to compute an attribute's value on the fly).

Solution

With Python 2.2 new-style classes, the new built-in property function lets you do this directly:

```
class Rectangle(object):
    def __init__(self, width, height):
        self.width = width
        self.height = height
    def getArea(self): return self.width * self.height
    def setArea(self, value): raise AttributeError, "Can't set 'area' attribute"
    area = property(getArea, setArea)
```

With classic classes, you must implement properties yourself with the special methods __getattr__ and __setattr__:

```
class Rectangle:
    def __init__(self, width, height):
        self.width = width
        self.height = height
    def getArea(self): return self.width * self.height
    def setArea(self, value): raise AttributeError, "Can't set 'area' attribute"
    def __getattr__(self, name):
        if name=='area': return self.getArea( )
        raise AttributeError, name
    def __setattr__(self, name, value):
        if name=='area': return self.setArea(value)
        self.__dict__[name] = value
```

Discussion

Properties are an important object-oriented concept. Instances of a class often need to expose two different kinds of attributes: those that hold data and those that are computed on the fly with a suitable method, whenever their values are required. If you expose the real attributes directly and the computed attributes via methods, such as getArea, current implementation issues will appear in the interface for your class and throughout the client code, which should really be independent from such issues. And if you ever change the implementation, you are in serious trouble.

The alternative of exposing everything via so-called accessor methods is also far from satisfactory. In this case, the code for your class fills up with highly repetitive boiler-plate code such as:

```
def getWidth(self): return self.width
```

Even worse, your client code is cluttered with more verbose and less-readable statements such as:

```
r.setHeight(r.getHeight()+1)
```

rather than more concise and readable statements such as:

```
r.height += 1
```

Moreover, the unnecessary calls to the accessor methods slow your code's operation.

Properties let you have your cake and eat it too. Client code accesses all attributes uniformly (e.g., r.width, r.area) without caring or needing to know which are real and which are computed on the fly. Your class just needs a way to ensure that when client code accesses a computed attribute, the right method is called, and its return value is taken as the attribute's value. For example:

```
>>> r = Rectangle(10, 20)
>>> print r.area
200
```

When client code accesses a real attribute, nothing special is needed.

With Python 2.2's new-style classes, you can use the built-in property function to define properties. You pass it the accessor functions for get and set operations, optionally followed by one to use for deletions (an optional fourth argument is the attribute's documentation string). You bind the return value to the name, in class scope, that you want the client code to use when accessing the property on class instances.

In classic classes, you can still have properties, but you need to implement them yourself. When any code accesses an attribute that doesn't exist for an object, Python calls the __getattr__ method for the class (if it exists) with the attribute's name as the argument. You just need to test for the names of the properties that you are implementing and delegate to the appropriate method, as shown in the second solution. Whenever an attribute is set on your object (whether the attribute exists or not), Python calls the __setattr__ method for the class (if it exists) with the attribute's name and the new value assigned to it as arguments. Since __setattr__ is called for all attribute settings, it must also deal with setting real attributes in the normal ways (as items in self.__dict__). Also, other methods in classes that implement __setattr__ often set items in self.__dict__ directly to avoid triggering __setattr__ needlessly.

See Also

Properties are currently underdocumented. There is a minimal description in Guido's essay describing the unification of types and classes (*http://www.python.org/ 2.2/descrintro.html#property*); additional minimal information is available from the online help system (help(property)). However, by the time you read this, the *Language Reference* will likely have been updated.

5.6   Implementing Static Methods

Credit: Alex Martelli, Carel Fellinger

Problem

You want to call methods directly on a class without supplying an instance of the class as the first argument, or on any instance without having the instance implicitly become the first argument.

Solution

In Python 2.2 (on either classic or new-style classes), the new built-in staticmethod function wraps any callable into a static method, and we just bind the same name to the staticmethod object in class scope:

```
class Greeter:
    def greet(name): print "Hello", name
    greet = staticmethod(greet)
```

In Python 2.1 and earlier, we can easily simulate the same construct:

```
class staticmethod:
    def __init__(self, anycallable): self.__call__ = anycallable
```

Now, with any release of Python, we can say:

```
>>> greeting = Greeter( )
>>> greeting.greet("Peter")
Hello Peter
>>> Greeter.greet("Paul")
Hello Paul
```

You can get a static method as a class attribute or as the attribute of any instance of the class. It does not matter which, because when you call the static method, it calls the underlying callable anyway.

Discussion

In Python, when you want to make a function available for calling, you normally expose it as an attribute of a module, not of a class. An attribute of a class object that starts out as a Python function implicitly mutates into an unbound method (see Recipe

5.12 for a way to exploit this). Thus, if you want to make the function available as a class attribute, without mutation, you need to wrap the function into a callable of another type and bind that wrapper callable as the class attribute. Python 2.2 offers a new built-in staticmethod type that performs just such a wrapping. This recipe shows how to use it and how to emulate it easily in earlier Python versions with a tiny auxiliary class of the same name.

As the recipe shows, you normally define the function that will become a static method with a def statement in the class body, and then immediately rebind the same name to the staticmethod object. You don't have to do it this way, though. You could simply write the following code outside of the class body:

```
def anotherfunction( ): print "Yes, you CAN do that"
Greeter.peculiarmethodname = staticmethod(anotherfunction)
```

Unless you have a good reason to proceed in this way, such a noncustomary way of doing things will just confuse future readers of your code.

In some languages (such as C++ or Java), static methods are also sometimes called class methods. However, the term class methods should be reserved for methods that belong to the class, in the same way that normal methods belong to the instance (i.e., for methods that receive the class object as their first implicit argument). Static methods in Python, as in C++, are little more than bland syntactical sugar for free-standing functions. See Recipe 5.7 for how to make real class methods (a la Smalltalk) in Python.

See Also

Recipes 5.7 and 5.12.

5.7   Implementing Class Methods

Credit: Thomas Heller

Problem

You want to call methods directly on a class without having to supply an instance, and with the class itself as the implied first argument.

Solution

In Python 2.2 (on either classic or new-style classes), the new built-in classmethod function wraps any callable into a class method, and we just bind the same name to the classmethod object in class scope:

```
class Greeter:
    def greet(cls, name): print "Hello from %s"%cls.__name__, name
    greet = classmethod(greet)
```

In Python 2.1 or earlier, we need a wrapper that is slightly richer than the one used for static methods in Recipe 5.6:

```
class classmethod:
    def __init__(self, func, klass=None):
        self.func = func
        self.klass = klass
    def __call__(self, *args, **kw):
        return self.func(self.klass, *args, **kw)
```

Furthermore, with this solution, the following rebinding is not sufficient:

```
greet = classmethod(greet)
```

This leaves greet.klass set to None, and if the class inherited any class methods from its bases, their klass attributes would also be set incorrectly. It's possible to fix this by defining a function to finish preparing a class object and always explicitly calling it right after every class statement. For example:

```
def arrangeclassmethods(cls):
    for attribute_name in dir(cls):
        attribute_value = getattr(cls, attribute_name)
        if not isinstance(attribute_value, classmethod): continue
        setattr(cls, classmethod(attribute_value.func, cls))
```

However, this isn't completely sufficient in Python versions before 2.2, since, in those versions, dir ignored inherited attributes. We need a recursive walk up the bases for the class, as in Recipe 5.2. But a worse problem is that we might forget to call the arrangeclassmethods function on a class object right after its class statement.

For older Python versions, a better solution is possible if you have Jim Fulton's ExtensionClass class. This class is the heart of Zope, so you have it if Zope is installed with Python 2.1 or earlier. If you inherit from ExtensionClass.Base and define a method called __class_init__, the method is called with the class object as its argument after the class object is built. Therefore:

```
import ExtensionClass

class ClassWithClassMethods(ExtensionClass.Base):
    def __class_init__(cls): arrangeclassmethods(cls)
```

Inherit from ClassWithClassMethods directly or indirectly, and arrangeclassmethods is called automatically on your class when it's built. You still have to write a recursive version of arrangeclassmethods for generality, but at least the problem of forgetting to call it is solved.

Now, with any of these solutions, we can say:

```
>>> greeting = Greeter( )
>>> greeting.greet("Peter")
Hello from Greeter Peter
>>> Greeter.greet("Paul")
Hello from Greeter Paul
```

Discussion

Real class methods, like those in Smalltalk, implicitly receive the actual class as the first parameter and are inherited by subclasses, which can override them. While they can return anything, they are particularly useful as factory methods (i.e., methods that create and return instances of their classes). Python 2.2 supports class methods directly. In earlier releases, you need a wrapper, such as the classmethod class shown in this recipe, and, more problematically, you need to arrange the wrapper objects right after you create a class, so that the objects refer to the actual class when you call them later.

Zope's ExtensionClass helps with the latter part. Metaclasses should also help you achieve the same effect, but, since they were hard to use before Python 2.2, and the likeliest reason to still use Python 2.1 is that you use a version of Zope that requires Python 2.1, this should be avoided. The point is that statements in the class body execute before the class object is created, while our arranging needs to take place after that. Classes that inherit from ExtensionClass.Base solve this problem for us, since their __class_init__ method automatically executes just after the class object is created, with the class object itself as the only argument. This is an ideal situation for us to delegate to our arrangeclassmethods function.

In Python 2.2, the wrapping inside the class body suffices because the new built-in type classmethod does not need to access the class object at the point of creation, so it's not an issue if the class object does not yet exist when the class methods are wrapped. However, notice that you have to perform the wrapping again if a subclass overrides particular class methods (not, however, if they inherit them).

See Also

Recipe 5.6; ExtensionClass is not available as a standalone class, but is part of Zope (*http://www.zope.org*).

5.8 Delegating Automatically as an Alternative to Inheritance

Credit: Alex Martelli

Problem

You'd like to inherit from a built-in type, but you are using Python 2.1 (or earlier), or need a semantic detail of classic classes that would be lost by inheriting from a built-in type in Python 2.2.

Solution

With Python 2.2, we can inherit directly from a built-in type. For example, we can subclass file with our own new-style class and override some methods:

```
class UppercaseFile(file):
    def write(self, astring):
        return file.write(self, astring.upper())
    def writelines(self, strings):
        return file.writelines(self, map(string.upper,strings))
upperOpen = UppercaseFile
```

To open such a file, we can call upperOpen just like a function, with the same arguments as the built-in open function. Because we don't override __init__, we inherit file's arguments, which are the same as open's.

If we are using Python 2.1 or earlier, or if we need a classic class for whatever purpose, we can use automatic delegation:

```
class UppercaseFile:
    # Initialization needs to be explicit
    def __init__(self, file):
        # NOT self.file=file, to avoid triggering __setattr__
        self.__dict__['file'] = file

    # Overrides aren't very different from the inheritance case:
    def write(self, astring):
        return self.file.write(astring.upper())
    def writelines(self, strings):
        return self.file.writelines(map(string.upper,strings))

    # Automatic delegation is a simple and short boilerplate:
    def __getattr__(self, attr):
        return getattr(self.file, attr)
    def __setattr__(self, attr, value):
        return setattr(self.file, attr, value)

def upperOpen(*args, **kwds):
    return UppercaseFile(open(*args, **kwds))
```

In this variant, upperOpen is called just as before but it separates the generation of the file object internally (done via the built-in open function) and its wrapping into the automatically delegating class (UppercaseFile).

Discussion

Automatic delegation, which the special methods __getattr and __setattr__ let us perform so smoothly, is a powerful and general technique. In this recipe, we show how to use it to get an effect that is almost indistinguishable from subclassing a built-in type, but in a way that also works with Python 2.1 and earlier. This technique also produces a classic class, just in case we want the classic object model's semantics even in newer versions of Python. Performance isn't quite as good as with real inheritance, but we get better flexibility and finer-grained control as compensation.

The fundamental idea is that each instance of our class holds an instance of the type we are wrapping (i.e., extending and/or tweaking). Whenever client code tries to get an attribute from an instance of our class, unless the attribute is specifically defined there (e.g., the write and writelines methods in this recipe), __getattr__ transparently shunts the request to the wrapped instance. In Python, methods are also attributes, accessed in just the same way, so we don't need to do anything more to access methods—the approach used to access data attributes works for methods just as well. __setattr__ plays a similar role when client code sets an attribute. Remember that to avoid triggering __setattr__ from inside the methods you code, you must set values in self.__dict__ explicitly. While Python calls __getattr__ only for attributes it does not find in the usual way, it calls __setattr__ for every attribute that is set (except for a few special ones such as __dict__ and __class__, held in the object itself and not in its dictionary).

Note that wrapping by automatic delegation does not work well with client or framework code that, one way or another, does type-testing. In such cases, it is the client or framework code that is breaking polymorphism and should be rewritten. Remember not to use type-tests in your own client code, as you probably do not need them anyway. See Recipe 5.10 for better alternatives.

In Python 2.2, you'll use automatic delegation less often, since you don't need it for the specific purpose of subclassing built-ins. However, delegation still has its place—it is just a bit farther from the spotlight than in 2.1 and earlier. Although the new-style object model (which you get by subclassing built-ins) is almost always preferable, there are a few cases in which you should use classic classes because they are even more dynamic than new-style classes. For example, if your program needs to change an instance's __class__ on the fly, this is always allowed for instances of classic classes, but subject to constraints for instances of new-style classes. More importantly, delegation is generally more flexible than inheritance, and sometimes such flexibility is invaluable. For example, an object can delegate to different subobjects over time or even all at once (see Recipe 5.20), and inheritance doesn't offer anything comparable.

See Also

Recipes 5.10 and 5.20; PEP 253 (*http://www.python.org/peps/pep-0253.html*) describes in detail what there is to know about subtyping built-in types.

5.9 Decorating an Object with Print-Like Methods

Credit: Jürgen Hermann

Problem

You want functionality similar to that of the print statement on a file object that is not necessarily standard output, and you want to access this functionality in an object-oriented manner.

Solution

Statement print is quite handy, but we can emulate (and optionally tweak) its semantics with nicer, object-oriented syntax by writing a suitable class:

```python
class PrintDecorator:
    """ Add print-like methods to any writable file-like object. """

    def __init__(self, stream, do_softspace=1):
        """ Store away the stream for later use. """
        self.stream = stream
        self.do_softspace = do_softspace
        self.softspace = 0

    def Print(self, *args, **kw):
        """ Print all arguments as strings, separated by spaces.

            Take an optional "delim" keyword parameter to change the
            delimiting character and an optional "linend" keyword
            parameter to insert a line-termination string. Ignores
            unknown keyword parameters for simplicity.
        """
        delim = kw.get('delim', ' ')
        linend = kw.get('linend', '')
        if self.do_softspace and self.softspace and args: start = delim
        else: start = ''
        self.stream.write(start + delim.join(map(str, args)) + linend)
        self.softspace = not linend

    def PrintLn(self, *args, **kw):
        """ Just like self.Print(), but linend defaults to line-feed.
        """
        kw.setdefault('linend','\n')
        self.Print(*args, **kw)

if __name__ == '__main__':
    # Here's how you use this:
    import sys
    out = PrintDecorator(sys.stdout)
    out.PrintLn(1, "+", 1, "is", 1+1)
```

```
out.Print("Words", "Smashed", "Together", delim='')
out.PrintLn()
```

Discussion

This recipe shows how to decorate objects with new functions, specifically by decorating an arbitrary writable stream (file-like object opened for writing) with two methods that work like the built-in print statement.

The Print method takes any number of positional arguments, converts them to strings (via the map and str built-ins), joins these strings with the given delim, then finally writes the resulting string to the stream. An optional linend, the empty string by default, allows line termination.

The PrintLn method delegates to Print, changing the default for the linend argument to '\n'. Other ways of sharing common code between Print and PrintLn run into difficulties—for example, when delim is nonwhitespace or on multitasking environments where printing operations need to be atomic (a single call to the stream's method write per call to the decorator's Print or PrintLn methods).

Softspace functionality is also provided to emulate the print statement's ability to avoid inserting a useless trailing space if a newline should immediately follow. This seems simple, and it's definitely useful, but it can be tricky to implement. Furthermore, this wrapper supports softspace functionality independently of the decorated stream's support for setting and getting the softspace attribute. Softspace behavior can, however, appear somewhat strange if successive Print calls use different delim strings. The softspace functionality can be turned off at instantiation time.

The code uses Python 2.x syntax (string methods, new-style argument passing), but it can be easily ported to Python 1.5.2 (if necessary) by using apply for function calling and the string module instead of string methods.

See Also

The documentation for the string built-in module and built-in file objects in the *Library Reference*.

5.10 Checking if an Object Has Necessary Attributes

Credit: Alex Martelli

Problem

You need to check if an object has certain necessary attributes, before performing state-altering operations, but you want to avoid type-testing because you know it reduces polymorphism.

Solution

In Python, you normally try whatever operations you need to perform. For example, here's the simplest, no-checks code for manipulations of a list:

```
def munge1(alist):
    alist.append(23)
    alist.extend(range(5))
    alist.append(42)
    alist[4] = alist[3]
    alist.extend(range(2))
```

While this is usually adequate, there may be occasional problems. For example, if the alist object has an append method but not an extend method, the munge1 function will partially alter alist before an exception is raised. Such partial alterations are generally not cleanly undoable, and, depending on your application, they can be quite a bother.

To avoid partial alteration, you might want to check the type. A naive Look Before You Leap (LBYL) approach looks safer, but it has a serious defect: it loses polymorphism. The worst approach of all is checking for equality of types:

```
def munge2(alist):
    if type(alist)==type([]):
        munge1(alist)
    else: raise TypeError, "expected list, got %s"%type(alist)
```

A better, but still unfavorable, approach (which at least works for list subclasses in 2.2) is using isinstance:

```
def munge3(alist):
    if isinstance(alist, type[]):
        munge1(alist)
    else: raise TypeError, "expected list, got %s"%type(alist)
```

The proper solution is accurate LBYL, which is safer and fully polymorphic:

```
def munge4(alist):
    # Extract all bound methods you need (immediate exception
    # if any needed method is missing)
    append = alist.append
    extend = alist.extend

    # Check operations, such as indexing, to raise
    # exceptions ASAP if signature compatibility is missing
    try: a[0]=a[0]
    except IndexError: pass    # An empty alist is okay

    # Operate -- no exceptions expected at this point
    append(23)
    extend(range(5))
    append(42)
```

```
alist[4] = alist[3]
extend(range(2))
```

Discussion

Python functions are naturally polymorphic on their arguments, and checking argument types loses polymorphism. However, we may still get early checks and some extra safety without any substantial cost.

The Easier to Ask Forgiveness than Permission (EAFP) approach, in which we try operations and handle any resulting exceptions, is the normal Pythonic way of life and usually works great. Explicit checking of types severely restricts Python's normal signature-based polymorphism and should be avoided in most cases. However, if we need to perform several operations on an object, trying to do them all could result in some of them succeeding and partially altering the object before an exception is raised.

For example, suppose that munge1, in the recipe's code, is called with an actual argument value for alist that has an append method but lacks extend. In this case, alist will be altered by the first call to append, and the attempt to call extend will raise an exception, leaving alist's state partially altered in a way that may be hard to recover from. Sometimes, a sequence of operations should be atomic: either all of the alterations happen or none of them do.

We can get closer to that by switching to LBYL, but in an accurate, careful way. Typically, we extract all bound methods we'll need, then noninvasively test the necessary operations (such as indexing on both sides of the assignment operator). We move on to actually changing the object state only if all of this succeeds. From there, it's far less likely (though not impossible) that exceptions will occur in midstream, with state partially altered.

This extra complication is pretty modest, and the slowdown due to the checks is typically more or less compensated by the extra speed of using bound methods versus explicit attribute access (at least if the operations include loops, which is often the case). It's important to avoid overdoing the checks, and assert can help with that. For example, you can add assert callable(append) to munge4( ). In this case, the compiler will remove the assert entirely when the program is run with optimization (i.e., with flags -O or -OO), while performing the checks when the program is run for testing and debugging (i.e., without the optimization flags).

See Also

assert and the meaning of the -O and -OO command-line arguments are defined in all Python reference texts; the *Library Reference* section on sequence types.

5.11 Making a Fast Copy of an Object

Credit: Alex Martelli

Problem

You need to implement the special method __copy__ so your class can cooperate with the copy.copy function. If the __init__ method of your class is slow, you need to bypass it and get an empty object of the class.

Solution

Here's a solution that works for both new-style and classic classes:

```
def empty_copy(obj):
    class Empty(obj.__class__):
        def __init__(self): pass
    newcopy = Empty( )
    newcopy.__class__ = obj.__class__
    return newcopy
```

Your classes can use this function to implement __copy__ as follows:

```
class YourClass:
    def __init__(self):
        print "assume there's a lot of work here"
    def __copy__(self):
        newcopy = empty_copy(self)
        print "now copy some relevant subset of self's attributes to newcopy"
        return newcopy
```

Here's a usage example:

```
if __name__ == '__main__':
    import copy
    y = YourClass( )      # This, of course, does run __init__
    print y
    z = copy.copy(y)      # ...but this doesn't
    print z
```

Discussion

Python doesn't implicitly copy your objects when you assign them. This is a great thing, because it gives fast, flexible, and uniform semantics. When you need a copy, you explicitly ask for it, ideally with the copy.copy function, which knows how to copy built-in types, has reasonable defaults for your own objects, and lets you customize the copying process by defining a special method __copy__ in your own classes. If you want instances of a class to be noncopyable, you can define __copy__ and raise a TypeError there. In most cases, you can let copy.copy's default mechanism work, and you get free clonability for most of your classes. This is quite a bit nicer than languages that force you to implement a specific clone method for every class whose instances you want to be clonable.

__copy__ often needs to start with an empty instance of the class in question (e.g., self), bypassing __init__ when that is a costly operation. The simplest way to do this is to use the ability that Python gives you to change an instance's class on the fly by creating a new object in a local empty class, then setting its __class__ attribute, as the recipe's code shows. Note that inheriting class Empty from obj.__class__ is redundant (but quite innocuous) for old Python versions (up to Python 2.1), but in Python 2.2 it becomes necessary to make the empty_copy function compatible with all kinds of objects of classic or new-style classes (including built-in and extension types). Once you choose to inherit from obj's class, you must override __init__ in class Empty, or else the whole purpose of the recipe is lost.

Once you have an empty object of the required class, you typically need to copy a subset of self's attributes. If you need all of the attributes, you're better off not defining __copy__ explicitly, since copying all instance attributes is copy.copy's default. Unless, of course, you should need to do a little bit more than copying instance attributes. If you do need to copy all of self's attributes into newcopy, here are two techniques:

```
newcopy.__dict__.update(self.__dict__)
newcopy.__dict__ = self.__dict__.copy()
```

An instance of a new-style class doesn't necessarily keep all of its state in __dict__, so you may need to do some class-specific state copying.

Alternatives based on the new standard module can't be made transparent across classic and new-style classes in Python 2.2 (at least, I've been unable to do this). Besides, the new module is often thought of as dangerous black magic (rather exaggerating its dangers). Anyway, this recipe lets you avoid using the new module for this specific purpose.

Note that so far we have been talking about shallow copies, which is what you want most of the time. With a shallow copy, your object is copied, but objects it refers to (attributes or items) are not, so the new copied object and the original object refer to the same items or attributes objects. A deep copy is a heavyweight operation, potentially duplicating a large graph of objects that refer to each other. You get a deep copy by calling copy.deepcopy on an object. If you need to customize how instances of your class are deep-copied, you can define the special method __deepcopy__ and follow its somewhat complicated memoization protocol. The technique shown in this recipe—getting empty copies of objects by bypassing their __init__ methods—can sometimes still come in handy, but there is a lot of other work you need to do.

See Also

The *Library Reference* section on the copy module.

5.12 Adding Methods to a Class at Runtime

Credit: Brett Cannon

Problem

You want to add a method to a class at an arbitrary point in your code for highly dynamic customization.

Solution

The best way to perform this task works for both classic and new-style classes:

```
def funcToMethod(func, clas, method_name=None):
    setattr(clas, method_name or func.__name__, func)
```

If a method of the specified name already exists in the class, funcToMethod replaces it with the new implementation.

Discussion

Ruby can add a method to a class at an arbitrary point in your code. I figured Python must have a way for allowing this to happen, and it turned out it did. There are several minor possible variations, but this recipe is very direct and compact, and works for both classic and new-style classes. The method just added is available instantly to all existing instances and to those not yet created. If you specify method_name, that name is used as the method name; otherwise, the method name is the same as the name of the function.

You can use this recipe for highly dynamic customization of a running program. On command, you can load a function from a module and install it as a method of a class (even in place of another previous implementation), thus instantly changing the behavior of all existing and new instances of the class.

One thing to make sure of is that the function has a first argument for the instance that will be passed to it (which is, conventionally, always named self). Also, this approach works only if func is a Python function, not a built-in or callable. For example, a built-in such as math.sin can be installed with this recipe's funcToMethod function. However, it doesn't turn into a method; it remains exactly the same, regardless of whether you access it as an attribute of a class or of an instance. Only true Python functions implicitly mutate into methods (bound or unbound as appropriate) when installed and accessed this way.

For classic classes, you can use a different approach for installing a callable as a method of a class:

```
def callableToMethod(func, clas, method_name=None):
    import new
    method = new.instancemethod(func, None, clas)
    setattr(clas, method_name or func.__name__, method)
```

Now func can be any callable, such as an instance of any class that supplies a __call__ special method, a built-in, or a bound method.

The name of the instancemethod function of the new module may be slightly misleading. The function generates both bound and unbound methods, depending on whether the second argument is None (unbound) or an instance of the class that is the third argument. This function, however, works only with classic classes, not with new-style classes. See *http://www.python.org/doc/current/lib/module-new.html* for all the details (there's not much more to it than this, though).

See Also

The *Library Reference* section on the new module.

5.13 Modifying the Class Hierarchy of an Instance

Credit: Ken Seehof

Problem

You need to modify the class hierarchy of an instance object that has already been instantiated.

Solution

A rather unusual application of the mix-in concept lets us perform this task in Python 2.0 or later (with some limitations in Python 2.2):

```
def adopt_class(klass, obj, *args, **kwds):
    're-class obj to inherit klass; call __init__ with *args, **kwds'
    # In Python 2.2, klass and obj.__class__ must be compatible,
    # e.g., it's okay if they're both classic, as in the 'demo' function
    classname = '%s_%s' % (klass.__name__, obj.__class__.__name__)
    obj.__class__ = new.classobj(classname, (klass, obj.__class__), {})
    klass.__init__(obj, *args, **kwds)

def demo():
    class Sandwich:
        def __init__(self, ingredients):
            self.ingredients = ingredients
        def __repr__(self):
            return ' and '.join(self.ingredients)

    class WithSpam:
        def __init__(self, spam_count):
            self.spam_count = spam_count
        def __repr__(self):
            return Sandwich.__repr__(self) + self.spam_count * ' and spam'
```

```
pbs = Sandwich(['peanut butter', 'jelly'])
adopt_class(WithSpam, pbs, 2)
print pbs
```

Discussion

Sometimes class adoption, as illustrated by this recipe, is the cleanest way out of class hierarchy problems that arise when you wish to avoid module interdependencies (e.g., within a layered architecture). It's more often useful if you want to add functionality to objects created by third-party modules, since modifying those modules' source code is undesirable.

In the following example, the programmer has these constraints:

- There are several classes in *objects.py*, and more will be added in the future.

- *objects.py* must not import or know about *graphics.py*, since the latter is not available in all configurations. Therefore, class G cannot be a base class for the *objects.py* classes.

- *graphics.py* should not require modification to support additional classes that may be added to *objects.py*.

```
######################
# objects.py
class A(Base):
...
class B(Base):
...
def factory(...):
... returns an instance of A or B or ...

######################
# graphics.py
from oop_recipes import adopt_class
import objects

class G:
... provides graphical capabilities

def gfactory(...):
    obj = objects.factory(...)
    adopt_class(G, obj, ...)
    return obj
```

Given the constraints, the adopt_class function provides a viable solution.

In Python 2.2, there are compatibility limitations on which classes can be used to multiply inherit from (otherwise, you get a "metatype conflict among bases" TypeError exception). These limitations affect multiple inheritance performed dynamically by means of the new.classobj function (as in this recipe) in the same way as they affect multiple inheritance expressed in the more usual way.

Classic classes (classes with no built-in type among their ancestors, not even the new built-in type object) can still be multiply inherited from quite peaceably, so the example in this recipe keeps working. The example given in the discussion will also keep working the same way, since class G is classic. Only two new-style classes with different built-in type ancestors would conflict.

See Also

The *Library Reference* section on built-in types, especially the subsections on special attributes and functions.

5.14 Keeping References to Bound Methods Without Inhibiting Garbage Collection

Credit: Joseph A. Knapka

Problem

You want to hold bound methods, while still allowing the associated object to be garbage-collected.

Solution

Weak references were an important addition to Python 2.1, but they're not directly usable for bound methods, unless you take some precautions. To allow an object to be garbage-collected despite outstanding references to its bound methods, you need some wrappers. Put the following in the *weakmethod.py* file:

```python
import weakref

class _weak_callable:
    def __init__(self, obj, func):
        self.im_self = obj
        self.im_func = func

    def __call__(self, *args, **kws):
        if self.im_self is None:
            return self.im_func(*args, **kws)
        else:
            return self.im_func(self.im_self, *args, **kws)

class WeakMethod:
    """ Wraps a function or, more importantly, a bound method in
    a way that allows a bound method's object to be GCed, while
    providing the same interface as a normal weak reference. """

    def __init__(self, fn):
        try:
```

```
                self._obj = weakref.ref(fn.im_self)
                self._meth = fn.im_func
            except AttributeError:
                # It's not a bound method
                self._obj = None
                self._meth = fn

    def __call__(self):
        if self._dead(): return None
        return _weak_callable(self._getobj(), self._meth)

    def _dead(self):
        return self._obj is not None and self._obj() is None

    def _getobj(self):
        if self._obj is None: return None
        return self._obj()
```

Discussion

A normal bound method holds a strong reference to the bound method's object. That means that the object can't be garbage-collected until the bound method is disposed of:

```
>>> class C:
...     def f(self):
...         print "Hello"
...     def __del__(self):
...         print "C dying"
...
>>> c = C()
>>> cf = c.f
>>> del c  # c continues to wander about with glazed eyes...
>>> del cf # ...until we stake its bound method, only then it goes away:
C dying
```

Sometimes that isn't what you want. For example, if you're implementing an event-dispatch system, it might not be desirable for the mere presence of an event handler (a bound method) to prevent the associated object from being reclaimed. A normal weakref.ref to a bound method doesn't quite work the way one might expect, because bound methods are first-class objects. Weak references to bound methods are dead-on-arrival, i.e., they always return None when dereferenced, unless another strong reference to the same bound method exists. The following code, for example, doesn't print "Hello" but instead raises an exception:

```
>>> from weakref import *
>>> c = C()
>>> cf = ref(c.f)
>>> cf  # Oops, better try the lightning again, Igor...
<weakref at 80ce394; dead>
>>> cf()()
Traceback (most recent call last):
```

```
File "", line 1, in ?
TypeError: object of type 'None' is not callable
```

WeakMethod allows you to have weak references to bound methods in a useful way:

```
>>> from weakmethod import *
>>> cf = WeakMethod(c.f)
>>> cf()() # It LIVES! Bwahahahaha!
Hello
>>> del c # ...and it dies
C dying
>>> print cf()
None
```

A known problem is that _weak_callable and WeakMethod don't provide exactly the same interface as normal callables and weak references. To return a normal bound method, we can use new.instancemethod (from the standard module new), but for that purpose, WeakMethod should also find out and memorize the class in which the weakly held bound method is defined.

See Also

The *Library Reference* section on the weakref module.

5.15 Defining Constants

Credit: Alex Martelli

Problem

You need to define module-level variables that client code cannot accidentally rebind (i.e., named constants).

Solution

In Python 2.1 and later, you can install any instance as if it was a module. Just put the following in *const.py*:

```
class _const:

    class ConstError(TypeError): pass

    def __setattr__(self, name, value):
        if self.__dict__.has_key(name):
            raise self.ConstError, "Can't rebind const(%s)"%name
        self.__dict__[name] = value

    def __delattr__(self, name):
        if self.__dict__.has_key(name):
            raise self.ConstError, "Can't unbind const(%s)"%name
        raise NameError, name
```

```
import sys
sys.modules[__name__] = _const()
```

Now any client code can import const, then bind an attribute on the const module just once, as follows:

```
const.magic = 23
```

Once the attribute is bound, the program cannot accidentally rebind or unbind it:

```
const.magic = 88        # would raise const.ConstError
del const.magic         # would raise const.ConstError
```

Discussion

In Python, variables can be rebound at will, and modules don't let you define special methods such as an instance's __setattr__ to stop rebinding. An easy solution (in Python 2.1 and later) is to set up an instance as if it was a module.

In Python 2.1 and later, no check is made to force entries in sys.modules to be actual module objects. You can install an instance object there and take advantage of attribute-access special methods (e.g., to prevent rebinding, to synthesize attributes on the fly in __getattr__, and so on), while still allowing client code to access it with import somename. You may even see this as a more Pythonic Singleton-style idiom (but see Recipe 5.22).

Note that this recipe ensures a constant binding for a given name, not an object's immutability, which is quite a different issue. Numbers, strings, and tuples are immutable: if you bind a name in const to such an object, not only will the name always be bound to that object, but the object's contents will also always be the same, since the object is immutable. However, other objects, such as lists and dictionaries, are mutable: if you bind a name in const to, for example, a list object, the name will always remain bound to that list object, but the contents of the list may change (items in it may be rebound or unbound, more items can be added with the object's append method, and so on).

See Also

Recipes 5.22 and 15.5; the description of the modules attribute of the sys built-in module in the *Library Reference*.

5.16 Managing Options

Credit: Sébastien Keim

Problem

You have classes that need vast numbers of options to be passed to their constructors for configuration purposes. This often happens with GUI toolkits in particular.

Solution

We can model the options with a suitable class:

```
class Options:
    def __init__(self, **kw):
        self.__dict__.update(kw)

    def __lshift__(self, other):
        """ overloading operator << """
        s = self.__copy__()
        s.__dict__.update(other.__dict__)
        return s

    def __copy__(self):
        return self.__class__(**self.__dict__)
```

and then have all classes using options inherit from the following class:

```
class OptionsUser:
    """ Base class for classes that need to use options """

    class OptionError(AttributeError): pass

    def initOptions(self, option, kw):
        """ To be called from the derived class constructor.
        Puts the options into object scope. """
        for k, v in option.__dict__.items() + kw.items():
            if not hasattr(self.__class__, k):
                raise self.OptionError, "invalid option " + k
            setattr(self, k, v)

    def reconfigure(self, option=Options(), **kw):
        """ used to change options during object life """
        self.initOptions(option, kw)
        self.onReconfigure(self)

    def onReconfigure(self):
        """ To be overloaded by derived classes. Called by the reconfigure
        method or from outside after direct changes to option attributes. """
        pass
```

Discussion

To explain why you need this recipe, let's start with an example:

```
class TextBlock:
    def __init__ (self, font='Times', size=14, color=(0,0,0), height=0,
        width=0, align='LEFT', lmargin=1, rmargin=1)
        ...
```

If you have to instantiate several objects with the same parameter values, your first action might be to repeat these values each time:

```
block1 = TextBlock(font='Arial', size=10, color=(1,0,0), height=20, width=200)
block2 = TextBlock(font='Arial', size=10, color=(1,0,0), height=80, width=100)
block3 = TextBlock(font='Courier', size=12, height=80, width=100)
```

This isn't a particularly good solution, though, as you are duplicating code with all the usual problems. For example, when any change is necessary, you must hunt down all the places where it's needed, and it's easy to go wrong. The frequent mistake of duplicating code is also known as the antipattern named "copy-and-paste coding."

A much better solution is to reuse code by inheritance rather than by copy and paste. With this Options recipe, you can easily avoid copy-and-paste:

```
stdBlockOptions = Options(font='Arial', size=10, color=(1,0,0),
    height=80, width=100)
block1 = TextBlock(stdBlockOptions, height=20, width=200)
block2 = TextBlock(stdBlockOptions)
block3 = TextBlock(stdBlockOptions, font='Courier', size=12)
```

This feels a lot like using a stylesheet in a text processor. You can change one characteristic for all of your objects without having to copy this change in all of your declarations. The recipe also lets you specialize options. For example, if you have many TextBlocks to instantiate in Courier size 12, you can create:

```
courierBlockOptions = stdBlockOptions << Options(font='Courier', size=12)
```

Then any changes you make to the definition of stdBlockOptions change courierBlockOptions, except for size and font, which are specialized in the courierBlockOptions instance.

To create a class that accepts Options objects, your class should inherit from the OptionsUser class. You should define default values of options as static members, that is, attributes of the class object itself. And finally, the constructor of your class should call the initOptions method. For example:

```
class MyClass(OptionsUser):
    # options specification (default values)
    length = 10
    width = 20
    color = (0,0,0)
    xmargin = 1
    ymargin = 1

    def __init__ (self, opt=Options(), **kw):
        """ instance-constructor """
        self.initOptions(opt, kw)
```

The constructor idiom is intended to provide backward compatibility and ease of use for your class, as the specification of an Options object is optional, and the user can specify options in the constructor even if an Options object is specified. In other words, explicitly specified options override the content of the Options object.

You can, of course, adapt this recipe if your constructor needs parameters that can't be sent as options. For example, for a class related to the Tkinter GUI, you would probably have a constructor signature such as:

```
def __init__(self, parentFrame, opt=Options(), **kw):
```

If you have many classes with the same default options, you should still use derivation (inheritance) for optimal reuse:

```
class MyDefaultOptions(OptionsUser):
    # options specification (default values)
    length=10
    width=20
    color=(0,0,0)

class MyClass(MyDefaultOptions):
    # options specification (specific options or additional default values)
    color=(1,0,0)
    xmargin = 1
    ymargin = 1

    def __init__(self, opt=Options(), **kw):
        """ instance-constructor """
        self.initOptions(opt,kw)
```

To change an instance object's options at runtime, you can use either direct access to the options (object.option = value) or the reconfigure method (object.reconfigure(option=value)). The reconfigure method is defined in the OptionsUser class and accepts both an Options object and/or named parameters. To detect the change of an option at runtime, the reconfigure method calls the onReconfigure method. You should override it in your classes to do whatever is appropriate for your application's specific needs. Direct access, however, cannot be handled automatically in a totally general and safe way, so you should ask your user to call the onReconfigure method to signal option changes.

There are several design choices in this recipe that deserve specific discussion. I used the << operator for overloading options because I wanted to avoid the problems caused by collision between a method name and an option in the Options class. So normal identifiers were not appropriate as method names. This left two possible solutions: using an operator or using an external function. I decided to use an operator. My first idea was to use the + operator, but when I started to deal with it, I discovered that it was a mistake, because overloading options isn't a commutative operation. So I decided to use the << operator; because it is mostly unused in Python, its standard meaning isn't commutative, and I found that its picture fit quite well with the overloading-option notion.

I put options in the class scope because this practice has the great benefit of improving default-options specification. I haven't found a nonugly implementation for this, except for putting options in class scope, which allows direct access to options.

I used setattr in the initOptions method, even though a direct copy of __dict__ would substantially improve performance. But a class can emulate an option with the class's __getattr__ and __setattr__ methods. And in Python 2.2, we now have getter and setter methods for specific data attributes. These all work with the setattr approach, but they would not work right if I used __dict__.update( ) instead. So my approach is more general and also fully compatible with Python 2.2's new-style classes.

Finally, I chose to raise an exception when an option has no default value. When I first started to test the Options module, I once used size instead of length as the name of an option. Of course, everything worked well, except that my length option wasn't initialized. It took me quite a long time to find the mistake, and I wonder what could happen if the same mistake happened in a large hierarchy of options with much overloading. So I do think that it is important to check for this.

See Also

The section on emulating numeric types in the *Reference Manual*.

5.17   Implementing a Set Class

Credit: Thomas Heller

Problem

You need to model a set (i.e., a collection of items, with no particular ordering and no duplicates).

Solution

A Python dictionary is a good representation for a set abstract data type, but by wrapping it into a class, we can use it more naturally:

```python
class Set:
    def __init__(self, *args):
        self._dict = {}
        for arg in args:
            self.add(arg)
```

```python
    def __repr__(self):
        import string
        elems = map(repr, self._dict.keys())
        elems.sort()
        return "%s(%s)" % (self.__class__.__name__, string.join(elems, ', '))

    def extend(self, args):
        """ Add several items at once. """
        for arg in args:
            self.add(arg)

    def add(self, item):
        """ Add one item to the set. """
        self._dict[item] = item

    def remove(self, item):
        """ Remove an item from the set. """
        del self._dict[item]

    def contains(self, item):
        """ Check whether the set contains a certain item. """
        return self._dict.has_key(item)

    # High-performance membership test for Python 2.0 and later
    __contains__ = contains

    def __getitem__(self, index):
        """ Support the 'for item in set:' protocol. """
        return self._dict.keys()[index]

    def __iter__(self):
        """ Better support of 'for item in set:' via Python 2.2 iterators """
        return iter(self._dict.copy())

    def __len__(self):
        """ Return the number of items in the set """
        return len(self._dict)

    def items(self):
        """ Return a list containing all items in sorted order, if possible """
        result = self._dict.keys()
        try: result.sort()
        except: pass
        return result
```

Discussion

Sets are such fundamental constructs that you often find yourself needing one. Python dictionaries model them well, and the Set class in this recipe is basically a thin veneer of nice-looking syntactic sugar over a dictionary.

Of course, an important limitation (both of bare dictionaries and of this Set class) is that the items must be hashable (which typically means immutable). As with other recipes involving dictionaries, to work around this one can sometimes use cPickle.dumps(item) as the dictionary key corresponding to item, but this may be inapplicable or too heavyweight in some cases.

It's not hard to make this Set into a Bag, if that's what you need. A Bag differs from a Set in that each item is in a Bag a certain number of times (i.e., duplications are counted rather than ignored or disallowed).

For Bag-modeling purposes, rather than keeping the item as both key and value, use the item's membership count as the value. Adding an item becomes:

```
self._dict[item]=1+self.get(item,0)
```

and so on. You probably need both a .remove method (decrements the count by one) and a .wipeout method (removes the entry totally, no matter what). Similar duplications (and hard choices about which version to use as the basic special-method) loom for other functionality (e.g., what's __len__, the number of different items or the total?). Python gives you all the bricks, but it's still up to you to put them together to form the right shape.

Another extension worth considering is the possibility of adding set operations. Rather than overloading operators, which might lead to confusion, it's probably best to define union, intersection, and so on as either methods or standalone functions. Both choices are quite defensible. Functions have the advantage of being able to coerce both arguments more naturally. Of course, apart from performance issues, set operations can be implemented in terms of the abstract primitives supplied by the Set class, another consideration that argues for using free-standing functions rather than methods. For example:

```
def union(s1, s2):
    import copy
    result = copy.copy(s1)
    for item in s2:
        result.add(item)
    return result
```

This allows highly polymorphic use of such operations and amounts to a decisive advantage for free-standing functions over methods in most cases. It is for similar reasons that many of Python's most fundamental built-ins, such as len, are free-standing functions (which may call a special method if present but still afford polymorphic use on many objects that lack the special method).

See Also

The *Library Reference* section on sequence types.

5.18   Implementing a Ring Buffer

Credit: Sébastien Keim

Problem

You want to define a buffer with a fixed size, so that when it fills up, adding another element must overwrite the first (oldest) one. This kind of data structure is particularly useful for storing log and history information.

Solution

This recipe changes the buffer object's class on the fly, from a non-full buffer class to a full-buffer class, when it fills up:

```
class RingBuffer:
    """ class that implements a not-yet-full buffer """
    def __init__(self,size_max):
        self.max = size_max
        self.data = []

    class __Full:
        """ class that implements a full buffer """
        def append(self, x):
            """ Append an element overwriting the oldest one. """
            self.data[self.cur] = x
            self.cur = (self.cur+1) % self.max
        def get(self):
            """ return list of elements in correct order """
            return self.data[self.cur:]+self.data[:self.cur]

    def append(self,x):
        """append an element at the end of the buffer"""
        self.data.append(x)
        if len(self.data) == self.max:
            self.cur = 0
            # Permanently change self's class from non-full to full
            self.__class__ = __Full

    def get(self):
        """ Return a list of elements from the oldest to the newest. """
        return self.data

# sample usage
if __name__=='__main__':
    x=RingBuffer(5)
    x.append(1); x.append(2); x.append(3); x.append(4)
    print x.__class__, x.get()
    x.append(5)
    print x.__class__, x.get()
    x.append(6)
    print x.data, x.get()
```

```
x.append(7); x.append(8); x.append(9); x.append(10)
print x.data, x.get( )
```

Discussion

A ring buffer is a buffer with a fixed size. When it fills up, adding another element overwrites the oldest one that was still being kept. It's particularly useful for the storage of log information and history. There is no direct support in Python for this kind of structure, but it's easy to construct one. The implementation in this recipe is optimized for element insertion.

The notable design choice in the implementation is that, since these objects undergo a nonreversible state transition at some point in their lifetimes—from non-full buffer to full-buffer (and behavior changes at that point)—I modeled that by changing self.__class__. This works even in Python 2.2, as long as both classes have the same slots (for example, it works fine for two classic classes, such as RingBuffer and __Full in this recipe).

Changing the class of an instance may be strange in many languages, but it is a Pythonic alternative to other ways of representing occasional, massive, irreversible, and discrete changes of state that vastly affect behavior, as in this recipe. Good thing that Python supports it for all kinds of classes.

See Also

The *Reference Manual* section on the standard type hierarchy.

5.19 Implementing a Collection

Credit: Skip Montanaro

Problem

You have a bunch of objects and want to make method calls and implement attribute lookups that operate on each object in the bunch.

Solution

I'm used to thinking of a proxy that forwards attribute lookups to a bunch of objects as a collection. Here's how to make one in Python 2.2:

```
class Collection(list):
    def get(self, attr):
        """ Return a collection of same-named attributes from our items. """
        return Collection([getattr(x, attr) for x in self if hasattr(x, attr)])
    def call(self, attr, *args, **kwds):
        """ Return the result of calling 'attr' for each of our elements. """
        attrs = self.get(attr)
        return Collection([x(*args, **kwds) for x in attrs if callable(x)])
```

If you need to be portable to Python 2.0 or 2.1, you can get a similar effect by subclassing UserList.UserList instead of list (this means you have to import UserList first).

Using this recipe is fairly simple:

```
>>> import sys
>>> streams = Collection([sys.stdout, sys.stderr, sys.stdin])
>>> streams.call('fileno')
[1, 2, 0]
>>> streams.get('name')
['<stdout>', '<stderr>', '<stdin>']
```

Discussion

In some object-oriented environments, such Collection classes are heavily used. This recipe implements a Python class that defines methods named get (for retrieving attribute values) and call (for calling attributes).

In this recipe's class, it's not an error to try to fetch attributes or call methods that not all items in the collection implement. The resulting collection just skips any unsuitable item, so the length of results (which are different from those of the map built-in function) may be different from the length of the collection. You can easily change this behavior in a couple of different ways. For example, you can remove the hasattr check to make it an error to try to fetch an attribute unless all items have it. Or you could add a third argument to getattr, such as None or a null object (see Recipe 5.23), to stand in for missing results.

One of the interesting aspects of this recipe is that it highlights how Python makes it possible but not necessary to make classes for encapsulating fairly sophisticated behavior such as method and attribute proxying. Doing this is valuable in two respects. First, centralizing the code reduces the risk of errors creeping in duplicate copies throughout a code base. Second, naming the behavior (in this case based on prior art from another language) enriches the programmer's lexicon, thereby making it more likely that the concept will be reused in the future.

See Also

Recipes 5.20 and 5.23.

5.20 Delegating Messages to Multiple Objects

Credit: Eduard Hiti

Problem

You need to multiplex messages (attribute requests) to several objects that share the same interface.

Solution

As usual, this task is best wrapped in a class:

```
import operator

# faster in Python 2.2, but we also handle any release from 2.0 and later
try: dict
except: from UserDict import UserDict as dict

class Multiplex(dict):
    """ Multiplex messages to registered objects """
    def __init__(self, objs=[]):
        dict.__init__(self)
        for alias, obj in objs: self[alias] = obj

    def __call__(self, *args, **kwargs):
        """ Call registered objects and return results through another
        Multiplex. """
        return self.__class__( [ (alias, obj(*args, **kwargs))
            for alias, obj in self.items() ] )

    def __nonzero__(self):
        """ A Multiplex is true if all registered objects are true. """
        return reduce(operator.and_, self.values(), 1)

    def __getattr__(self, name):
        """ Wrap requested attributes for further processing. """
        try: return dict.__getattr__(self, name)
        except:
            # Return another Multiplex of the requested attributes
            return self.__class__( [ (alias, getattr(obj, name) )
                for alias, obj in self.items() ] )
```

As usual, this module is also invokable as a script, and, when run that way, supplies a self-test (or, here, a demo/example):

```
if __name__ == "__main__":
    import StringIO

    file1 = StringIO.StringIO( )
    file2 = StringIO.StringIO( )

    delegate = Multiplex( )
    delegate[id(file1)] = file1
    delegate[id(file2)] = file2

    assert not delegate.closed

    delegate.write("Testing")
    assert file1.getvalue() == file2.getvalue() == "Testing"
```

```
delegate.close( )
assert delegate.closed

print "Test complete"
```

Discussion

A `Multiplex` object exposes the same interface as the multiplexed registered object targets. Multiplexing doesn't work for the dictionary interface, since that is used by the `Multiplex` class itself. We take care to ensure that all attributes of a dictionary object are indeed accessed in the way one deals with dictionaries. Note that this interferes with delegating such attribute names as `'items'`, `'keys'`, `'values'`, and `'get'`. If this is a problem for your application, you can avoid inheriting `Multiplex` from `dict`, have `Multiplex` use a `dict` by containment instead, and give it another interface. However, whatever names you do decide to put on the public interface will still not be subject to multiplexed delegation.

Attributes of individual registered objects can be accessed by the alias used to register them for multiplexed delegation:

```
delegate["test"] = aClass( )
print delegate.aClassAttribute["test"]
```

Message chains are also possible:

```
print delegate.aClassAttribute.aMethod( )
```

This calls `aMethod` on `aClassAttribute` from all multiplex targets.

Behind the scenes, as a result of how `Multiplex.__getattr__` is coded, `delegate.aClassAttribute` returns another `Multiplex` object, as does the `.aMethod` (which collects bound methods into the other anonymous `Multiplex`). Finally, the special method `Multiplex.__call__` enters the scene, and `Multiplex` delegates the call operation to each of the bound methods, collecting their results into yet another `Multiplex`.

The design choice for `Multiplex.__nonzero__` is, of course, quite debatable. As coded in the recipe, it makes a `Multiplex` true if all the registered objects are true, including when there are no registered objects at all, which may be a bit counterintuitive. Depending on your application, you might therefore want to code this quite differently. Be sure to look at Recipe 5.8 for a different approach to a similar problem.

See Also

Recipes 5.7 and 5.8; documentation for the `operator` built-in module in the *Library Reference*.

5.21 Implementing the Singleton Design Pattern

Credit: Jürgen Hermann

Problem

You want to make sure that only one instance of a class is ever created.

Solution

One way to make a Singleton is to use a private inner class and delegate all operations to a single instance of that class:

```
class Singleton:
    """ A Pythonic Singleton """

    class __impl:
        """ Implementation of the Singleton class """
        def spam(self):
            """ Just an example method that returns Singleton instance's ID """
            return id(self)

    # The private class attribute holding the "one and only instance"
    __instance = __impl( )

    def __getattr__(self, attr):
        return getattr(self.__instance, attr)

    def __setattr__(self, attr, value):
        return setattr(self.__instance, attr, value)
```

Discussion

This recipe shows one way to implement the Singleton design pattern in Python (see *Design Patterns: Elements of Reusable Object-Oriented Software*, Addison-Wesley). A Singleton is a class that makes sure only one instance of it is ever created. Typically, such a class is used to manage resources that by their nature can exist only once. This recipe proposes an alternate approach to accessing such a single instance, which is arguably more Pythonic and more useful than the traditional implementation by a factory function.

This recipe uses the Singleton.__impl inner class as the class that is created only once. Note that inner classes are nothing special nor magical in Python, which is quite different from Java, and similar, instead, to C++. They are just classes that happen to have their class statement in the body of another class.

The outer class, `Singleton`, ensures that exactly one instance of the inner class, `Singleton.__impl`, is created on demand (i.e., the first time an instance of `Singleton` is created). Each instance of `Singleton` is a proxy to the one instance of `Singleton.__impl`, using automatic delegation (see Recipe 5.8) to delegate to it all state and behavior. (Note that this idiom has also been called Letter/Envelope by other authors, such as Coplien; in that naming, `Singleton` would be the Envelope, and `Singleton.__impl` the Letter.) While the `id` of each handle object is different, the `id` of the instance of the inner class that implements the Singleton behavior is constant.

We can complete the module with the usual self-test idiom and show this `id` behavior:

```
if __name__ == '__main__':

    s1 = Singleton( )
    print id(s1), s1.spam( )

    s2 = Singleton( )
    print id(s2), s2.spam( )
```

When we run this module as a script, we get the following output; note that the second (inner) `id` is constant:

```
8172684 8176268
8168588 8176268
```

Of course, the inner class isn't really hidden, as with almost everything else in Python. If you need to protect against malicious attempts to access it, you need to use the rexec and `Bastion` standard modules and rely on a restricted execution sandbox (but this is really necessary only when you must run code that you do not trust, such as code you received from an unknown source).

In addition to the secondary issue of using `id` for `Singleton`'s instances, there is a concrete issue in terms of subclassability. It's not really feasible for client code to subclass the real class (`Singleton.__impl`) in the recipe as presented. Subclassing the wrapper class (`Singleton`) is not the same thing, since other clients will still get a non-subclassed version. As the ability to subclass is high on the list of problems that the Singleton design pattern is supposed to resolve, this is a significant weakness. See Recipe 5.22 for a Pythonic solution to this problem.

See Also

Recipes 5.8 and 5.22; *Design Patterns: Elements of Reusable Object-Oriented Software*, by E. Gamma, R. Helm, R. Johnson, and J. Vlissides (Addison-Wesley, 1995).

5.22 Avoiding the Singleton Design Pattern with the Borg Idiom

Credit: Alex Martelli

Problem

You want to make sure that only one instance of a class is ever created, but you don't care about the id of the resulting instances, just about their state and behavior.

Solution

Just about every application need related to Singleton is met by ensuring that all instances share state and behavior, which is easier and more flexible than fiddling with instance creation. Just subclass the following Borg class:

```
class Borg:
    _shared_state = {}
    def __init__(self):
        self.__dict__ = self._shared_state
```

Ensure that Borg.__init__ is called, just as you always do for every base class's constructor, and you're home free.

Discussion

Here's a typical example of Borg use:

```
if __name__ == '__main__':
    class Example(Borg):
        def __init__(self, name=None):
            Borg.__init__(self)
            if name is not None: self.name = name
        def __str__(self): return 'Example(%s)' % self.name
    a = Example('Lara')
    b = Example()
    print a, b
    c = Example('Boris')
    print a, b, c
    b.name = 'Marcel'
    print a, b, c
```

When running this module as a main script, the output is:

```
Example(Lara) Example(Lara)
Example(Boris) Example(Boris) Example(Boris)
Example(Marcel) Example(Marcel) Example(Marcel)
```

All instances of Example share state, so any setting of the name attribute of any instance, either in __init__ or directly, affects all instances equally. However, note that their id differs, so since we have not defined __eq__ and __hash__, they are distinct keys in a dictionary. Thus, if we continued our sample code as follows:

```
adict = {}
j = 0
for i in a, b, c:
    adict[i] = j
    j = j + 1

for i in a, b, c:
    print i, adict[i]
```

the output would be:

```
Example(Marcel) 0
Example(Marcel) 1
Example(Marcel) 2
```

If that's not what you want, you can add __eq__ and __hash__ to the Example class or the Borg class. For example, here are these special methods added to Borg:

```
class Borg:
    _shared_state = {}
    def __init__(self): self.__dict__ = self._shared_state
    def __hash__(self): return 1
    def __eq__(self, other):
        try: return self.__dict__ is other.__dict__
        except: return 0
```

Now the example's output concludes with:

```
Example(Marcel) 2
Example(Marcel) 2
Example(Marcel) 2
```

You might want to do this to simulate the existence of only one instance.

The Singleton design pattern has a catchy name, but the wrong focus for most purposes: on object identity, rather than on state. The Borg design nonpattern makes all instances share state instead, and Python makes this a snap.

In most cases in which you might think of using Singleton or Borg, you don't really need either of them. Simply define a Python module, with functions and module-global variables, instead of defining a class, with methods and per-instance attributes. You need to use a class only if you must be able to inherit from it or if you need to take advantage of the class's ability to define special methods (for this issue, see Recipe 5.15)

The Singleton design pattern is all about ensuring that just one instance of a certain class is ever created. In my experience, it is usually not a good solution to the problems it tries to solve, displaying different kinds of problems in different object models. Typically, what we really want is to let as many instances be created as necessary, but all with shared state. Who cares about identity? It's state (and behavior) we care about. This alternate pattern to solve roughly the same problems has also been called Monostate. Incidentally, I like to call Singleton "Highlander", since there can be only one.

In Python, you can implement Monostate in many ways, but the Borg design nonpattern is often best. Simplicity is its greatest strength. Since the __dict__ of any instance can be re-bound, Borg rebinds it in its __init__ to a class-attribute dictionary. Now, any reference or binding of an instance attribute will actually affect all instances equally. I thank David Ascher for suggesting the appropriate name "Borg" for this nonpattern. It's a nonpattern because it had no known uses at the time of publication: two or more known uses are part of the prerequisites for being a design pattern. See the detailed discussion at *http://www.aleax.it/Python/5ep.html*.

The __getattr__ and __setattr__ special methods are not involved. You can define them independently for whatever other purposes you want, or leave them undefined. There is no problem either way, since Python does not call __setattr__ for the rebinding of __dict__ itself.

Also, if you want instances of your class to share state among themselves but not with instances of other subclasses of Borg, make sure that your class has the statement:

```
_shared_state = {}
```

in class scope so that it doesn't inherit the _shared_state attribute from Borg but rather overrides it. It's to enable this usage that Borg's __init__ method refers to self._shared_state instead of Borg._shared_state.

Borg also works for the new-style classes of Python 2.2, as long as they don't choose to keep state somewhere other than in the instance's __dict__. For example, Borg cannot support the __slots__ optimization. However, Borg saves as least as much memory per instance as __slots__ (the few tens of bytes normally taken up by the instance's nonshared __dict__), so this isn't really an issue. To Borg-ize a new-style class that inherits from list or dict and keeps state in the items of its built-in base class, you can use automatic delegation, as shown in Recipe 5.8. This technique involves wrapping a classic class around the new-style one and Borg-izing the classic class; I call this idea DeleBorg on *http://www.aleax.it/Python/5ep.html*.

Calling this recipe a Singleton would be as silly as calling an arcade an umbrella. Both may serve similar purposes (letting you walk in the rain without getting wet)— or solve similar forces, in design patterns parlance—but since they do so in utterly different ways, they're not instances of the same pattern. If anything (as already mentioned), Borg has similarities to the Monostate alternative design pattern to Singleton. (But Monostate is a design pattern, while Borg is not. And a Python Monostate can exist perfectly well without being a Borg.)

For reasons mysterious to me, people often conflate issues germane to Borg and Highlander with others that are really independent, such as access control and, particularly, access from multiple threads. If you need to control access to an object, that need is exactly the same whether there is 1 instance of that object's class or 23, and whether those multiple instances share state or not. A fruitful approach to problem-solving is known as "divide and conquer," or making problems easier by splitting their different aspects apart. Making problems harder by joining several aspects together must be an example of an approach known as "unite and suffer!"

See Also

Recipes 5.8 and 5.21; the article "Five Easy Pieces: Simple Python Non-Patterns" by Alex Martelli (*http://www.aleax.it/5ep.html*).

5.23   Implementing the Null Object Design Pattern

Credit: Dinu C. Gherman

Problem

You want to reduce the need for conditional statements in your code, particularly the need to keep checking for special cases.

Solution

The usual marker for "there's nothing here" is None, but we may be able to do better than that:

```
class Null:
    """ Null objects always and reliably "do nothing." """

    def __init__(self, *args, **kwargs): pass
    def __call__(self, *args, **kwargs): return self
    def __repr__(self): return "Null()"
    def __nonzero__(self): return 0

    def __getattr__(self, name): return self
    def __setattr__(self, name, value): return self
    def __delattr__(self, name): return self
```

Discussion

An instance of the Null class can replace the primitive value None. Using this class, you can avoid many conditional statements in your code and can often express algorithms with little or no checking for special values. This recipe is a sample implementation of the Null Object design pattern (see "The Null Object Pattern", B. Woolf, *Pattern Languages of Programming*, PLoP 96, September 1996).

This recipe's Null class ignores all parameters passed when constructing or calling instances and any attempt to set or delete attributes. Any call or attempt to access an attribute (or a method, since Python does not distinguish between the two and calls __getattr__ either way) returns the same Null instance (i.e., self, since there's no reason to create a new one). For example, if you have a computation such as:

```
def compute(x, y):
    try: "lots of computation here to return some appropriate object"
    except SomeError: return None
```

and you use it like this:

```
for x in xs:
    for y in ys:
        obj = compute(x, y)
        if obj is not None:
            obj.somemethod(y, x)
```

you can usefully change the computation to:

```
def compute(x, y):
    try: "lots of computation here to return some appropriate object"
    except SomeError: return Null( )
```

and thus simplify it as:

```
for x in xs:
    for y in ys:
        compute(x, y).somemethod(y, x)
```

Thus, you don't need to check whether compute has returned a real result or an instance of Null. Even in the latter case, you can safely and innocuously call on it whatever method you want.

Python calls __getattr__ for special methods as well. This means that you may have to take some care and customize Null to your application's needs, either directly in the class's sources or by subclassing it appropriately. For example, with this recipe's Null, any comparison between Null instances, even a==a, returns a Null instance and evaluates as false. (Note that we've had to explicitly define __nonzero__ for this purpose, since __nonzero__ must return an int.) If this is a problem for your purposes, you must define __eq__ (in Null itself or in an appropriate subclass) and implement it appropriately. Similar delicate considerations apply to several other special methods.

The goal of Null objects is to provide an intelligent replacement for the often-used primitive value None in Python (Null or null pointers in other languages). These "nobody lives here" markers are used for many purposes, including the important case in which one member of a group of otherwise similar elements is special. Usually, this usage results in conditional statements to distinguish between ordinary elements and the primitive null (e.g., None) value, but Null objects help you avoid that.

Among the advantages of using `Null` objects are the following:

- Superfluous conditional statements can be avoided by providing a first-class object alternative for the primitive value `None`, thereby improving code readability.
- They can act as a placeholder for objects whose behavior is not yet implemented.
- They can be used polymorphically with instances of any other class.
- They are very predictable.

To cope with the disadvantage of creating large numbers of passive objects that do nothing but occupy memory space, the Null Object pattern is often combined with the Singleton pattern (see Recipe 5.21), but this recipe does not explore that combination.

See Also

"The Null Object Pattern", B. Woolf, *Pattern Languages of Programming*, PLoP 96, September 1996, *http://www.cs.wustl.edu/~schmidt/PLoP-96/woolf1.ps.gz*.

## CHAPTER 6

Threads, Processes, and Synchronization

6.0 Introduction

Credit: Greg Wilson, Baltimore Technologies

Thirty years ago, in his classic *The Mythical Man-Month: Essays on Software Engineering* (Addison-Wesley), Fred Brooks drew a distinction between accidental and intrinsic complexity. Languages such as English and C++, with their inconsistent rules, exceptions, and special cases, are examples of the former: they make communication and programming harder than they need to be. Concurrency, on the other hand, is a prime example of the latter. Most people have to struggle to keep one chain of events straight in their minds. Keeping track of two, three, or a dozen, plus all of their possible interactions, is just plain hard.

Computer scientists began studying ways of running multiple processes safely and efficiently in a single physical address space in the mid-1960s. Since then, a rich theory has been developed in which assertions about the behavior of interacting processes can be formalized and proved, and entire languages devoted to concurrent and parallel programming have been created. *Foundations of Multithreaded, Parallel, and Distributed Programming*, by Gregory R. Andrews (Addison-Wesley), is not only an excellent introduction to this theory, but also contains a great deal of historical information tracing the development of major ideas.

Over the past 20 years, opportunity and necessity have conspired to make concurrency a part of programmers' everyday lives. The opportunity is for greater speed, which comes from the growing availability of multiprocessor machines. In the early 1980s, these were expensive curiosities; today, many programmers have dual-processor workstations on their desks and four-way or eight-way servers in the back room. If a calculation can be broken down into independent (or nearly independent) pieces, such machines can potentially solve them two, four, or eight times faster than their uniprocessor equivalents. While there are limits to the potential gains from this approach, it works well for problems as diverse as image processing, serving HTTP requests, and recompiling multiple source files.

In today's terminology, *processes* run in separate logical address spaces that are protected from each other. Using concurrent processing for performance purposes, particularly in multiprocessor machines, is more attractive with *threads*, which execute simultaneously within the same program, in the same address space, without being protected from each other. The lack of mutual protection allows lower overhead and easier and faster communication, particularly because of the shared address space. Since all threads run code from the same program, there are no special security risks caused by a lack of mutual protection, any more than there are in a single-threaded program. Thus, concurrency used for performance purposes is most often focused on adding threads to a single program.

However, adding threads to a Python program to speed it up is often not a successful strategy. The reason for this is the Global Interpreter Lock (GIL), which protects Python's internal data structures. This lock *must* be held by a thread before it can safely access Python objects. Without the lock, even simple operations (such as incrementing an integer) could fail.

Therefore, only the thread with the GIL can manipulate Python objects or call Python/C API functions. To make life easier for programmers, the interpreter releases and reacquires the lock every 10 bytecode instructions (a value that can be changed using sys.setcheckinterval). The lock is also released and reacquired around I/O operations, such as reading or writing a file, so that other threads can run while the thread that requests the I/O is waiting for the I/O operation to complete. However, effective performance-boosting exploitation of multiple processors from multiple pure-Python threads of the same process is just not in the cards. Unless the CPU performance bottlenecks in your Python application are in C-coded extensions that release the GIL, you will not observe substantial performance increases by moving your multithreaded application to a multiprocessor machine.

The necessity for concurrent programming is largely because of the ever-growing importance of GUIs and network applications. Graphical interfaces often need to appear to be doing several things at once, such as displaying images while scrolling ads across the bottom of the screen. While it is possible to do the necessary interleaving manually, it is much simpler to code each operation on its own and let the underlying operating system decide on a concrete order of operations. Similarly, network applications often have to listen on several sockets at once or send data on one channel while receiving data on another.

Uniting these two types of applications is the fact that a GUI can't know when the user will press a key or move the mouse, and an HTTP server can't know which datagram will arrive next. Handling each stream of events with a separate control thread is often the simplest way to cope with this unpredictability, even on single-processor machines, and when high throughput is not an overriding concern. Event-driven programming can often be used in these kinds of applications as well, and Python frameworks such as Medusa and asyncore are proof that this approach often delivers excellent performance with complexity that, while different from that inherent in multithreading, is not necessarily larger.

The standard Python library allows programmers to approach multithreaded programming at two different levels. The core module, thread, is a thin wrapper around the basic primitives that any threading library must provide. Three of these primitives are used to create, identify, and end threads; others are used to create, test, acquire, and release simple mutual-exclusion locks (or binary semaphores). In general, programmers should avoid using these primitives directly, and should instead use the tools included in the higher-level threading module, which is substantially more programmer-friendly and has similar performance characteristics.

The most important elements of the threading module are classes that represent threads and various high-level synchronization constructs. The Thread class represents a separate control thread; it can be told what to do by passing a callable object to its constructor or by overriding its run method. One thread can start another by calling its start method or wait for it to complete by calling join. Python also supports daemon threads, which do background processing until all of the nondaemon threads in the program exit and shut themselves down automatically.

The synchronization constructs in the threading module include locks, reentrant locks (which a single thread can safely relock many times without deadlocking), counting semaphores, conditions, and events. Events can be used by one thread to signal others that something interesting has happened (e.g., that a new item has been added to a queue, or that it is now safe for the next thread to modify a shared data structure). The documentation that comes with Python describes each of these classes.

The relatively low number of recipes in this chapter, compared to others in this cookbook, reflects both Python's focus on programmer productivity (rather than absolute performance) and the degree to which other packages (such as httplib and wxWindows) hide the unpleasant details of concurrency in important application areas. This also reflects many Python programmers' tendencies to look for the simplest way to solve any particular problem, which complex threading rarely is.

However, this chapter's brevity may also reflect the Python community's underappreciation of the potential that simple threading has, when used appropriately, to simplify a programmer's life. The Queue module in particular supplies a delightfully self-contained synchronization and cooperation structure that can provide all the interthread supervision services you need. Consider a typical program, which accepts requests from a GUI (or from the network) and, as a result of such requests, will often find itself faced with a substantial chunk of work that might take so long to perform all at once that the program may appear unresponsive to the GUI (or network).

In a purely event-driven architecture, it may take considerable effort on the programmer's part to slice up the chunk into slices of work thin enough so each can be performed in idle time, without ever giving the appearance of unresponsiveness. Then, just a dash of multithreading can help considerably. The main thread pushes the substantial chunk of background work onto a dedicated Queue, then goes back to its task of making the program's interface appear responsive at all times.

At the other end of the Queue, a pool of daemonic worker threads await, each ready to peel a work request off the Queue and run it straight through. This kind of overall architecture combines event-driven and multithreaded approaches in the overarching ideal of simplicity, and is thus maximally Pythonic, even though you may need just a little bit more work if the result of a worker thread's efforts must be presented again to the main thread (via another Queue, of course), which is normally the case with GUIs. If you're willing to cheat just a little and use polling for the mostly event-driven main thread to access the result Queue back from the daemonic worker threads, see Recipe 9.6 to get an idea of how simple that little bit of work can be.

6.1 Storing Per-Thread Information

Credit: John E. Barham

Problem

You need to allocate storage to each thread for objects that only that thread can use.

Solution

Thread-specific storage is a useful pattern, and Python does not support it directly. A simple dictionary, protected by a lock, makes it pretty easy to program. For once, it's slightly more general, and not significantly harder, to program to the lower-level thread module, rather than to the more common, higher-level threading module that Python also offers on top of it:

```
try:
    import thread
except:
    """ We're running on a single-threaded OS (or the Python interpreter has
    not been compiled to support threads), so return a standard dictionary. """
    _tss = {}
    def get_thread_storage():
        return _tss
else:
    """ We do have threads; so, to work: """
    _tss = {}
    _tss_lock = thread.allocate_lock()
    def get_thread_storage():
        """ Return a thread-specific storage dictionary. """
        thread_id = thread.get_ident()  # Identify the calling thread
        tss = _tss.get(thread_id)
        if tss is None:  # First time being called by this thread
            try:  # Entering critical section
```

```
                _tss_lock.acquire( )
                _tss[thread_id] = tss = {} # Create thread-specific dictionary
            finally:
                _tss_lock.release( )
        return tss
```

Discussion

The get_thread_storage function in this recipe returns a thread-specific storage dictionary. It is a generalization of the get_transaction function from ZODB, the object database underlying Zope. The returned dictionary can be used to store data that is private to the thread.

One benefit of multithreaded programs is that all of the threads can share global objects. Often, however, each thread needs some storage of its own—for example, to store a network or database connection unique to itself. Indeed, such externally oriented objects are best kept under the control of a single thread to avoid multiple possibilities of highly peculiar behavior, race conditions, and so on.

The get_thread_storage function returns a dictionary object that is unique to each thread. For an exhaustive treatment of thread-specific storage (albeit aimed at C++ programmers), see *http://www.cs.wustl.edu/~schmidt/PDF/TSS-pattern.pdf*.

A useful extension would be to add a delete_thread_storage function, particularly if a way could be found to automate its being called upon thread termination. Python's threading architecture does not make this task particularly easy. You could spawn a watcher thread to do the deletion after a join with the calling thread, but that might be rather heavyweight. The recipe as presented, without deletion, is quite appropriate for the common architecture in which you have a pool of (typically daemonic) worker threads that are spawned at the start and do not go away until the end of the whole process.

See Also

"Thread-specific Storage: an Object Behavioral Pattern for Efficiently Accessing per-Thread State", by Douglas Schmidt, Timothy Harrisson, and Nat Pryce (*http://www.cs.wustl.edu/~schmidt/PDF/TSS-pattern.pdf*).

6.2   Terminating a Thread

Credit: Doug Fort

Problem

You must terminate a thread from the outside, but Python doesn't let one thread brutally kill another, so you need a controlled-termination idiom.

Solution

A frequently asked question is: How do I kill a thread? The answer is: You don't. Instead, you kindly ask it to go away. The thread must periodically check if it's been asked to go away and then comply (typically after some kind of clean-up):

```python
import threading

class TestThread(threading.Thread):

    def __init__(self, name='TestThread'):
        """ constructor, setting initial variables """
        self._stopevent = threading.Event()
        self._sleepperiod = 1.0

        threading.Thread.__init__(self, name=name)

    def run(self):
        """ main control loop """
        print "%s starts" % (self.getName(),)

        count = 0
        while not self._stopevent.isSet():
            count += 1
            print "loop %d" % (count,)
            self._stopevent.wait(self._sleepperiod)

        print "%s ends" % (self.getName(),)

    def join(self, timeout=None):
        """ Stop the thread. """
        self._stopevent.set()
        threading.Thread.join(self, timeout)

if __name__ == "__main__":
    testthread = TestThread()
    testthread.start()

    import time
    time.sleep(10.0)

    testthread.join()
```

Discussion

Often, you will want to control a thread from the outside, but the ability to kill it is, well, overkill. Python doesn't give you this ability, and thus forces you to design your thread systems more carefully. This recipe is based on the idea of a thread whose main function uses a loop. Periodically, the loop checks if a threading.Event object has been set. If so, the thread terminates; otherwise, it waits for the object.

The TestThread class in this recipe also overrides threading.Thread's join method. Normally, join waits only for a certain thread to terminate (for a specified amount of time, if any) without doing anything to cause that termination. In this recipe, however, join sets the stop event object before delegating the rest of its operation to the normal (base class) join method. Therefore, in this recipe, the join call is guaranteed to terminate the target thread in a short amount of time.

You can use the recipe's central idea (a loop periodically checking a threading.Event to see if it must terminate) in several other, slightly different ways. The Event's wait method can let you pause the target thread. You can also expose the Event, letting controller code set it and then go on its merry way without bothering to join the thread, knowing the thread will terminate in a short amount of time. I have found that the simplicity of this recipe gives me the modest amount of control I need, with no headaches—so I haven't pursued the more sophisticated (and complicated) ideas.

See Also

Documentation of the standard library module threading in the *Library Reference*.

6.3 Allowing Multithreaded Read Access While Maintaining a Write Lock

Credit: Sami Hangaslammi

Problem

You need to allow unlimited read access to a resource when it is not being modified while keeping write access exclusive.

Solution

"One-writer, many-readers" locks are a frequent necessity, and Python does not supply them directly. As usual, they're not hard to program yourself, in terms of other synchronization primitives that Python does supply:

```
import threading

class ReadWriteLock:
    """ A lock object that allows many simultaneous "read locks", but
    only one "write lock." """

    def __init__(self):
        self._read_ready = threading.Condition(threading.Lock())
        self._readers = 0
```

```
def acquire_read(self):
    """ Acquire a read lock. Blocks only if a thread has
    acquired the write lock. """
    self._read_ready.acquire()
    try:
        self._readers += 1
    finally:
        self._read_ready.release()

def release_read(self):
    """ Release a read lock. """
    self._read_ready.acquire()
    try:
        self._readers -= 1
        if not self._readers:
            self._read_ready.notifyAll()
    finally:
        self._read_ready.release()

def acquire_write(self):
    """ Acquire a write lock. Blocks until there are no
    acquired read or write locks. """
    self._read_ready.acquire()
    while self._readers > 0:
        self._read_ready.wait()

def release_write(self):
    """ Release a write lock. """
    self._read_ready.release()
```

Discussion

It is often convenient to allow unlimited read access to a resource when it is not being modified and still keep write access exclusive. While the threading module does not contain a specific class for the job, the idiom is easy to implement using a Condition object, and this recipe shows how you can do that.

An instance of the ReadWriteLock class is initialized without arguments, as in:

```
rw = ReadWriteLock()
```

Internally, rw._readers counts the number of readers who are currently in the read-write lock (initially zero). The actual synchronization is performed by a threading.Condition object (created at __init__ around a new Lock object and held in rw._read_ready).

The acquire_read and release_read methods increment and decrement the number of active readers. Of course, this happens between acquire and release calls to _read_ready—such bracketing is obviously necessary even to avoid race conditions between different threads wanting to acquire or release a read lock. But we also exploit _read_ready for another purpose, which is why release_read also does a notifyAll on it, if and when it notices it has removed the last read lock.

The notifyAll method of a Condition object wakes up all threads (if any) that are on a wait condition on the object. In this recipe, the only way a thread can get into such a wait is via the acquire_write method, when it finds there are readers active after acquiring _read_ready. The wait call on the Condition object releases the underlying lock, so release_read methods can execute, but reacquires it again before waking up, so acquire_write can safely keep checking whenever it wakes up, if it's finally in a no-readers-active situation. When that happens, acquire_write returns to its caller, but keeps the lock, so no other writer or reader can enter again, until the writer calls release_write, which lets the lock go again.

Note that this recipe offers no guarantee against what is technically known as a starvation situation. In other words, there is no guarantee that a writer won't be kept waiting indefinitely by a steady stream of readers arriving, even if no reader keeps its read lock for very long. If this is a problem in your specific application, you can avoid starvation by adding complications to ensure that new readers don't enter their lock if they notice that a writer is waiting. However, in many cases, you can count on situations in which no readers are holding read locks, without special precautions to ensure that such situations occur. In such cases, this recipe is directly applicable, and besides eschewing complications, it avoids potentially penalizing reader performance by making several readers wait for one pending writer.

See Also

Documentation of the standard library module threading in the *Library Reference*.

6.4 Running Functions in the Future

Credit: David Perry

Problem

You want to run a time-consuming function in a separate thread while allowing the main thread to continue uninterrupted.

Solution

The Future class sometimes allows you to hide the fact that you're using threading while still taking advantage of threading's potential performance advantages:

```
from threading import *
import copy

class Future:
```

```python
    def __init__(self, func, *param):
        # constructor
        self.__done = 0
        self.__result = None
        self.__status = 'working'

        self.__C = Condition()  # Notify on this Condition when result is ready

        # Run the actual function in a separate thread
        self.__T = Thread(target=self.Wrapper, args=(func, param))
        self.__T.setName("FutureThread")
        self.__T.start()

    def __repr__(self):
        return '<Future at '+hex(id(self))+':'+self.__status+'>'

    def __call__(self):
        self.__C.acquire()
        while self.__done==0:
            self.__C.wait()
        self.__C.release()
        # Deepcopy __result to prevent accidental tampering with it
        result = copy.deepcopy(self.__result)
        return result

    def isDone(self):
        return self.__done

    def Wrapper(self, func, param):
        # Run the actual function and housekeep around it
        self.__C.acquire()
        self.__result = func(*param)
        self.__done=1
        self.__status=`self.__result`
        self.__C.notify()
        self.__C.release()
```

Discussion

Although Python's thread syntax is nicer than the syntax in many languages, it can
still be a pain if all you want to do is run a time-consuming function in a separate
thread while allowing the main thread to continue uninterrupted. A Future object
provides a legible and intuitive way to achieve such an end.

To run a function in a separate thread, simply put it in a Future object:

```
>>> A=Future(longRunningFunction, arg1, arg2 ...)
```

Both the calling thread and the execution of the function will continue on their
merry ways until the caller needs the function's result. When it does, the caller can
read the result by calling Future like a function. For example:

```
>>> print A()
```

If the Future object has completed executing, the call returns immediately. If it is still running, the call (and the calling thread in it) blocks until the function completes. The result of the function is stored in an attribute of the Future instance, so subsequent calls to it return immediately.

Since you wouldn't expect to be able to change the result of a function, Future objects are not meant to be mutable. This is enforced by requiring Future to be called, rather than directly reading __result. If desired, stronger enforcement of this rule can be achieved by playing with __getattr__ and __setattr__ or, in Python 2.2, by using property.

Future runs its function only once, no matter how many times you read it. Thus, you will have to recreate Future if you want to rerun your function (e.g., if the function is sensitive to the time of day).

For example, suppose you have a function named muchComputation that can take a rather long time (tens of seconds or more) to compute its results, because it churns along in your CPU or it must read data from the network or from a slow database. You are writing a GUI, and a button on that GUI needs to start a call to muchComputation with suitable arguments, displaying the results somewhere on the GUI when done. You can't afford to run the function itself as the command associated with the button, since if you did, the whole GUI would appear to freeze until the computation is finished, and that is unacceptable. Future offers one easy approach to handling this situation. First, you need to add a list of pending Future instances that are initially empty to your application object called, for example, app.futures. When the button is clicked, execute something like this:

```
app.futures.append(Future(muchComputation, with, its, args, here))
```

and then return, so the GUI keeps being serviced (Future is now running the function, but in another thread). Finally, in some periodically executed poll in your main thread, do something like this:

```
for future in app.futures[:]:    # Copy list and alter it in loop
    if future.isDone( ):
        appropriately_display_result(future( ))
        app.futures.remove(future)
```

See Also

Documentation of the standard library modules threading and copy in the *Library Reference*; *Practical Parallel Programming*, by Gregory V. Wilson (MIT Press, 1995).

6.5   Synchronizing All Methods in an Object

Credit: André Bjärby

Problem

You want to share an object among multiple threads, but to avoid conflicts you need to ensure that only one thread at a time is inside the object, possibly excepting some methods for which you want to hand-tune locking behavior.

Solution

Java offers such synchronization as a built-in feature, while in Python you have to program it explicitly using reentrant locks, but this is not all that hard:

```python
import types

def _get_method_names(obj):
    """ Get all methods of a class or instance, inherited or otherwise. """
    if type(obj) == types.InstanceType:
        return _get_method_names(obj.__class__)
    elif type(obj) == types.ClassType:
        result = []
        for name, func in obj.__dict__.items():
            if type(func) == types.FunctionType:
                result.append((name, func))
        for base in obj.__bases__:
            result.extend(_get_method_names(base))
        return result


class _SynchronizedMethod:
    """ Wrap lock and release operations around a method call. """

    def __init__(self, method, obj, lock):
        self.__method = method
        self.__obj = obj
        self.__lock = lock

    def __call__(self, *args, **kwargs):
        self.__lock.acquire()
        try:
            return self.__method(self.__obj, *args, **kwargs)
        finally:
            self.__lock.release()


class SynchronizedObject:
    """ Wrap all methods of an object into _SynchronizedMethod instances. """
```

```
def __init__(self, obj, ignore=[], lock=None):
    import threading

    # You must access __dict__ directly to avoid tickling __setattr__
    self.__dict__['_SynchronizedObject__methods'] = {}
    self.__dict__['_SynchronizedObject__obj'] = obj
    if not lock: lock = threading.RLock()
    for name, method in _get_method_names(obj):
        if not name in ignore and not self.__methods.has_key(name):
            self.__methods[name] = _SynchronizedMethod(method, obj, lock)

def __getattr__(self, name):
    try:
        return self.__methods[name]
    except KeyError:
        return getattr(self.__obj, name)

def __setattr__(self, name, value):
    setattr(self.__obj, name, value)
```

Discussion

As usual, we complete this module with a small self test, executed only when the module is run as main script. This also serves to show how the module's functionality can be used:

```
if __name__ == '__main__':
    import threading
    import time

    class Dummy:

        def foo (self):
            print 'hello from foo'
            time.sleep(1)

        def bar (self):
            print 'hello from bar'

        def baaz (self):
            print 'hello from baaz'

    tw = SynchronizedObject(Dummy(), ignore=['baaz'])
    threading.Thread(target=tw.foo).start()
    time.sleep(.1)
    threading.Thread(target=tw.bar).start()
    time.sleep(.1)
    threading.Thread(target=tw.baaz).start()
```

Thanks to the synchronization, the call to bar runs only when the call to foo has completed. However, because of the ignore= keyword argument, the call to baaz bypasses synchronization and thus completes earlier. So the output is:

```
hello from foo
hello from baaz
hello from bar
```

When you find yourself using the same single-lock locking code in almost every method of an object, use this recipe to refactor the locking away from the object's application-specific logic. The key code idiom is:

```
self.lock.acquire()
try:
    # The "real" application code for the method
finally:
    self.lock.release()
```

To some extent, this recipe can also be handy when you want to postpone worrying about a class's locking behavior. Note, however, that if you intend to use this code for production purposes, you should understand all of it. In particular, this recipe is not wrapping direct accesses, be they get or set, to the object's attributes. If you also want them to respect the object's lock, you'll need the object you're wrapping to define, in turn, its own __getattr__ and __setattr__ special methods.

This recipe is carefully coded to work with every version of Python, including old ones such as 1.5.2, as long as you're wrapping classic classes (i.e., classes that don't subclass built-in types). Issues, as usual, are subtly different for Python 2.2 new-style classes (which subclass built-in types or the new built-in type object that is now the root class). Metaprogramming (e.g., the tasks performed in this recipe) sometimes requires a subtly different approach when you're dealing with the new-style classes of Python 2.2 and later.

See Also

Documentation of the standard library modules threading and types in the *Library Reference*.

6.6 Capturing the Output and Error Streams from a Unix Shell Command

Credit: Brent Burley

Problem

You need to run an external process in a Unix-like environment and capture both the output and error streams from the external process.

Solution

The popen2 module lets you capture both streams, but you also need help from fcntl to make the streams nonblocking and thus avoid deadlocks:

```
import os, popen2, fcntl, FCNTL, select

def makeNonBlocking(fd):
    fl = fcntl.fcntl(fd, FCNTL.F_GETFL)
    try:
        fcntl.fcntl(fd, FCNTL.F_SETFL, fl | FCNTL.O_NDELAY)
    except AttributeError:
        fcntl.fcntl(fd, FCNTL.F_SETFL, fl | FCNTL.FNDELAY)

def getCommandOutput(command):
    child = popen2.Popen3(command, 1) # Capture stdout and stderr from command
    child.tochild.close()            # don't need to write to child's stdin
    outfile = child.fromchild
    outfd = outfile.fileno()
    errfile = child.childerr
    errfd = errfile.fileno()
    makeNonBlocking(outfd)           # Don't deadlock! Make fd's nonblocking.
    makeNonBlocking(errfd)
    outdata = errdata = ''
    outeof = erreof = 0
    while 1:
        ready = select.select([outfd,errfd],[],[]) # Wait for input
        if outfd in ready[0]:
            outchunk = outfile.read()
            if outchunk == '': outeof = 1
            outdata = outdata + outchunk
        if errfd in ready[0]:
            errchunk = errfile.read()
            if errchunk == '': erreof = 1
            errdata = errdata + errchunk
        if outeof and erreof: break
        select.select([],[],[],.1) # Allow a little time for buffers to fill
    err = child.wait()
    if err != 0:
        raise RuntimeError, '%s failed with exit code %d\n%s' % (
            command, err, errdata)
    return outdata

def getCommandOutput2(command):
    child = os.popen(command)
    data = child.read()
    err = child.close()
    if err:
        raise RuntimeError, '%s failed with exit code %d' % (command, err)
    return data
```

Discussion

This recipe shows how to execute a Unix shell command and capture the output and error streams in Python. By contrast, os.system sends both streams directly to the terminal. The presented getCommandOutput(command) function executes a command and returns the command's output. If the command fails, an exception is raised, using the text captured from the command's stderr as part of the exception's arguments.

Most of complexity of this code is due to the difficulty of capturing both the output and error streams of the child process at the same time. Normal (blocking) read calls may deadlock if the child is trying to write to one stream, and the parent is waiting for data on the other stream, so the streams must be set to nonblocking, and select must be used to wait for data on the streams.

Note that the second select call adds a 0.1-second sleep after each read. Counterintuitively, this allows the code to run much faster, since it gives the child time to put more data in the buffer. Without this, the parent may try to read only a few bytes at a time, which can be very expensive.

If you want to capture only the output, and don't mind the error stream going to the terminal, you can use the much simpler code presented in getCommandOutput2. If you want to suppress the error stream altogether, that's easy, too. You can append 2>/dev/null to the command. For example:

```
ls -1 2>/dev/null
```

Since Version 2.0, Python includes the os.popen4 function, which combines the output and error streams of the child process. However, the streams are combined in a potentially messy way, depending on how they are buffered in the child process, so this recipe can still help.

See Also

Documentation of the standard library modules os, popen2, fcntl, and select in the *Library Reference*.

6.7   Forking a Daemon Process on Unix

Credit: Jürgen Hermann

Problem

You need to fork a daemon process on a Unix or Unix-like system, and this, in turn, requires a certain precise sequence of system calls.

Solution

Daemon processes must detach from their controlling terminal and process group. This is not hard, but it does take some care:

```python
import sys, os

def main():
    """ An example daemon main routine; writes a datestamp to file
        /tmp/daemon-log every 10 seconds.
    """
    import time

    f = open("/tmp/daemon-log", "w")
    while 1:
        f.write('%s\n' % time.ctime(time.time()))
        f.flush()
        time.sleep(10)

if __name__ == "__main__":
    # Do the Unix double-fork magic; see Stevens's book "Advanced
    # Programming in the UNIX Environment" (Addison-Wesley) for details
    try:
        pid = os.fork()
        if pid > 0:
            # Exit first parent
            sys.exit(0)
    except OSError, e:
        print >>sys.stderr, "fork #1 failed: %d (%s)" % (
            e.errno, e.strerror)
        sys.exit(1)

    # Decouple from parent environment
    os.chdir("/")
    os.setsid()
    os.umask(0)

    # Do second fork
    try:
        pid = os.fork()
        if pid > 0:
            # Exit from second parent; print eventual PID before exiting
            print "Daemon PID %d" % pid
            sys.exit(0)
    except OSError, e:
        print >>sys.stderr, "fork #2 failed: %d (%s)" % (
            e.errno, e.strerror)
        sys.exit(1)

    # Start the daemon main loop
    main()
```

Discussion

Forking a daemon on Unix requires a certain specific sequence of system calls, which is explained in W. Richard Steven's seminal book, *Advanced Programming in the Unix Environment* (Addison-Wesley). We need to fork twice, terminating each parent process and letting only the grandchild of the original process run the daemon's code. This allows us to decouple the daemon process from the calling terminal, so that the daemon process can keep running (typically as a server process without further user interaction, like a web server, for example) even after the calling terminal is closed. The only visible effect of this is that when you run this script as a main script, you get your shell prompt back immediately.

For all of the details about how and why this works in Unix and Unix-like systems, see Stevens's book. Stevens gives his examples in the C programming language, but since Python's standard library exposes a full POSIX interface, this can also be done in Python. Typical C code for a daemon fork translates almost literally to Python; the only difference you have to care about—a minor detail—is that Python's os.fork does not return –1 on errors but throws an OSError exception. Therefore, rather than testing for a less-than-zero return code from fork, as we would in C, we run the fork in the try clause of a try/except statement, so that we can catch the exception, should it happen, and print appropriate diagnostics to standard error.

See Also

Documentation of the standard library module os in the *Library Reference*; Unix manpages for the fork, umask, and setsid system calls; *Advanced Programming in the Unix Environment*, by W. Richard Stevens (Addison-Wesley, 1992).

6.8 Determining if Another Instance of a Script Is Already Running in Windows

Credit: Bill Bell

Problem

In a Win32 environment, you want to ensure that only one instance of a script is running at any given time.

Solution

Many tricks can be used to avoid starting multiple copies of an application, but they're all quite fragile—except those based on a mutual-exclusion (mutex) kernel object, such as this one. Mark Hammond's precious `win32all` package supplies all the needed hooks into the Windows APIs to let us exploit a mutex for this purpose:

```
from win32event import CreateMutex
from win32api import GetLastError
from winerror import ERROR_ALREADY_EXISTS
from sys import exit

handle = CreateMutex(None, 1, 'A unique mutex name')

if GetLastError() == ERROR_ALREADY_EXISTS:
    # Take appropriate action, as this is the second
    # instance of this script; for example:
    print 'Oh! dear, I exist already.'
    exit(1)
else:
    # This is the only instance of the script; let
    # it do its normal work. For example:
    from time import sleep
    for i in range(10):
        print "I'm running",i
        sleep(1)
    print "I'm done"
```

Discussion

The string `'A unique mutex name'` must be chosen to be unique to this script, but it should not be dynamically generated, as it must be the same for all potential simultaneous instances of the same script. A fresh, globally unique ID generated at script-authoring time would be a good choice. According to the Windows documentation, the string can contain any characters except backslashes (\\). On Windows platforms that implement Terminal Services, you can have a prefix of `Global\` or `Local\`, but such prefixes would make the string invalid for Windows NT, 95, 98, and ME.

The Win32 API call `CreateMutex` creates a Windows kernel object of the mutual-exclusion (mutex) kind and returns a handle to it. Note that we do not close this handle; it needs to exist throughout the time this process is running. The Windows kernel takes care of removing the handle (and the object it indicates, if the handle being removed is the only handle to that kernel object) when our process terminates.

The only thing we really care about is the return code from the API call, which we obtain by calling the `GetLastError` API right after it. That code is `ERROR_ALREADY_EXISTS` if and only if the mutual-exclusion object we tried to create already exists (i.e., if another instance of this script is already running).

Note that this approach is perfectly safe and not subject to race conditions and similar anomalies if two instances of the script are trying to start at the same time (a reasonably frequent occurrence, for example, if the user erroneously double-clicks in an Active Desktop setting where a single click already starts the application). The

Windows specifications guarantee that only one of the instances will create the mutex, while the other will be informed that the mutex already exists. Mutual exclusion is therefore guaranteed by the Windows kernel itself, and the recipe is entirely solid.

See Also

Documentation for the Win32 API in `win32all` (*http://starship.python.net/crew/ mhammond/win32/Downloads.html*) or ActivePython (*http://www.activestate.com/ ActivePython/*); Windows API documentation available from Microsoft (*http:// msdn.microsoft.com*); *Python Programming on Win32*, by Mark Hammond and Andy Robinson (O'Reilly, 2000).

6.9 Processing Windows Messages Using MsgWaitForMultipleObjects

Credit: Michael Robin

Problem

In a Win32 application, you need to process messages, but you also want to wait for kernel-level waitable objects and coordinate several activities.

Solution

A Windows application message loop, also known as its message pump, is at the heart of Windows. It's worth some effort to ensure that the heart beats properly and regularly:

```
import win32event
import pythoncom

TIMEOUT = 200 # ms

StopEvent = win32event.CreateEvent(None, 0, 0, None)
OtherEvent = win32event.CreateEvent(None, 0, 0, None)

class myCoolApp:
    def OnQuit(self):
            if areYouSure( ):
                win32event.SetEvent(StopEvent) # Exit msg pump

def _MessagePump( ):
    waitables = StopEvent, OtherEvent
    while 1:
        rc = win32event.MsgWaitForMultipleObjects(
            waitables,
            0, # Wait for all = false, so it waits for anyone
```

```
            TIMEOUT, # (or win32event.INFINITE)
            win32event.QS_ALLEVENTS) # Accepts all input

    # You can call a function here, if it doesn't take too long. It will
    # be executed at least every 200ms -- possibly a lot more often,
    # depending on the number of Windows messages received.

    if rc == win32event.WAIT_OBJECT_0:
        # Our first event listed, the StopEvent, was triggered, so we must exit
        break
    elif rc == win32event.WAIT_OBJECT_0+1:
        # Our second event listed, "OtherEvent", was set. Do whatever needs
        # to be done -- you can wait on as many kernel-waitable objects as
        # needed (events, locks, processes, threads, notifications, and so on).
        pass
    elif rc == win32event.WAIT_OBJECT_0+len(waitables):
        # A windows message is waiting - take care of it. (Don't ask me
        # why a WAIT_OBJECT_MSG isn't defined < WAIT_OBJECT_0...!).
        # This message-serving MUST be done for COM, DDE, and other
        # Windowsy things to work properly!
        if pythoncom.PumpWaitingMessages():
            break # we received a wm_quit message
    elif rc == win32event.WAIT_TIMEOUT:
        # Our timeout has elapsed.
        # Do some work here (e.g, poll something you can't thread)
        # or just feel good to be alive.
        pass
    else:
        raise RuntimeError("unexpected win32wait return value")
```

Discussion

Most Win32 applications must process messages, but often you want to wait on kernel waitables and coordinate a lot of things going on at the same time. A good message pump structure is the key to this, and this recipe exemplifies a reasonably simple but effective one.

Messages and other events will be dispatched as soon as they are posted, and a timeout allows you to poll other components. You may need to poll if the proper calls or event objects are not exposed in your Win32 event loop, as many components insist on running on the application's main thread and cannot run on spawned threads.

You can add many other refinements, just as you can to any other Win32 message-pump approach. Python lets you do this with as much precision as C does. But the relatively simple message pump in the recipe is already a big step up from the typical naive application that can either serve its message loop or wait on kernel waitables, but not both.

The key to this recipe is the Windows API call MsgWaitForMultipleObjects, which takes several parameters. The first is a tuple of kernel objects you want to wait for. The second parameter is a flag that is normally 0; 1 indicates that you should wait until all the kernel objects in the first parameter are signaled, although you almost invariably want to stop waiting when any one of these objects is signaled. The third is a flag that specifies which Windows messages you want to interrupt the wait; always pass win32event.QS_ALLEVENTS here to make sure any Windows message interrupts the wait. The fourth parameter is a timeout period (in milliseconds), or win32event.INFINITE if you are sure you do not need to do any periodic polling.

This function is a polling loop and, sure enough, it loops (with a while 1:, which is terminated only by a break within it). At each leg of the loop, it calls the API that waits for multiple objects. When that API stops waiting, it returns a code that explains why it stopped waiting. A value of win32event.WAIT_OBJECT_0 to win32event.WAIT_OBJECT_0+N-1 (in which N is the number of waitable kernel objects in the tuple you passed as the first parameter) means that the wait finished because one of those objects was signaled (which means different things for each kind of waitable kernel object). The return's code difference from win32event.WAIT_OBJECT_0 is the index of the relevant object in the tuple. win32event.WAIT_OBJECT_0+N means that the wait finished because a message was pending, and in this case our recipe processes all pending Windows messages via a call to pythoncom.PumpWaitingMessages. This function returns true if a WM_QUIT message was received, so in this case we break out of the whole while loop. A code of win32event. WAIT_TIMEOUT means the wait finished because of a timeout, so we can do our polling there. In this case, no message is waiting, and none of our kernel objects of interest were signaled.

Basically, the way to tune this recipe for yourself is by using the right kernel objects as waitables (with an appropriate response to each) and by doing whatever you need to do periodically in the polling case. While this means you must have some detailed understanding of Win32, of course, it's still quite a bit easier than designing your own special-purpose, message-loop function from scratch.

See Also

Documentation for the Win32 API in win32all (*http://starship.python.net/crew/ mhammond/win32/Downloads.html*) or ActivePython (*http://www.activestate.com/ ActivePython/*); Windows API documentation available from Microsoft (*http:// msdn.microsoft.com*); *Python Programming on Win32*, by Mark Hammond and Andy Robinson (O'Reilly, 2000).

CHAPTER 7
System Administration

7.0   Introduction

Credit: Donn Cave, University of Washington

In this chapter, we consider a class of programmer—the humble system administrator—in contrast to every other chapter's focus on a functional domain. As a programmer, the system administrator faces most of the same problems that other programmers face, and should find the rest of this book of at least equal interest.

Python's advantages in this domain are also quite familiar to any other Python programmer, but its competition is different. On Unix platforms, at any rate, the landscape is dominated by a handful of lightweight languages such as the Bourne shell and awk that aren't exactly made obsolete by Python. These little languages can often support a simpler, clearer, and more efficient solution than Python. But Python can do things these languages can't, and it's often more robust in the face of things such as unusually large data inputs. Of course, another notable competitor, especially on Unix systems, is Perl (which isn't really a little language).

One thing that stands out in this chapter's solutions is the wrapper: the alternative, programmed interface to a software system. On Unix, this is usually a fairly prosaic matter of diversion and analysis of text I/O. Python has recently improved its support in this area with the addition of C-level pseudotty functions, and it would be interesting to see more programmers experiment with them (see the pty module). The pseudotty device is like a bidirectional pipe with tty driver support, so it's essential for things such as password prompts that insist on a tty. And because it appears to be a tty, applications writing to a pseudotty normally use line buffering instead of the block buffering that can be a problem with pipes. Pipes are more portable and less trouble to work with, but they don't work for every application.

On Windows, the situation is often not as prosaic as on Unix-like platforms, as information may be somewhere in the registry, available via APIs, or available via COM. The standard Python _winreg module and Mark Hammond's win32all package give the Windows administrator access to all of these sources, and you'll see more Windows administration recipes here than you will for Unix. The competition for Python as a system administration language on Windows is feeble compared to that on Unix, so this is another reason for the platform's prominence here. The win32all extensions are available for download from Mark Hammond's web page at *http://starship.python.net/crew/mhammond/win32/Downloads.html*. win32all also comes with ActiveState's ActivePython (*http://www.activestate.com/ActivePython/*). To use this extremely useful package most effectively, you also need *Python Programming on Win32*, by Mark Hammond and Andy Robinson (O'Reilly, 2000).

While it may be hard to see what brought all the recipes together in this chapter, it isn't hard to see why system administrators deserve their own chapter: Python would be nowhere without them! Who else can bring an obscure, fledgling language into an organization and almost covertly infiltrate it into the working environment? If it weren't for the offices of these benevolent anarchists, Python would surely have languished in obscurity despite its merits.

7.1 Running a Command Repeatedly

Credit: Philip Nunez

Problem

You need to run a command repeatedly, with arbitrary periodicity.

Solution

The time.sleep function offers a simple approach to this task:

```
import time, os, sys, string

def main(cmd, inc=60):
    while 1:
        os.system(cmd)
        time.sleep(inc)

if __name__ == '__main__' :
    if len(sys.argv) < 2 or len(sys.argv) > 3:
        print "usage: " + sys.argv[0] + " command [seconds_delay]"
        sys.exit(1)

    cmd = sys.argv[1]
    if len(sys.argv) < 3:
        main(cmd)
    else:
        inc = string.atoi(sys.argv[2])
        main(cmd, inc)
```

Discussion

You can use this recipe with a command that periodically checks for something (e.g., polling) or performs an endlessly-repeating action, such as telling a browser to reload a URL whose contents change often, so you always have a recent version of that URL up for viewing. The recipe is structured into a function called main and a body that is preceded by the usual if __name__=='__main__': idiom, which ensures that the body executes only if the script runs as a main script. The body examines the command-line arguments you used with the script and calls main appropriately (or gives a usage message if there are too many or too few arguments). This is always the best way to structure a script, so its key functionality is also available to other scripts that may import it as a module.

The main function accepts a cmd string, which is a command you should pass periodically to the operating system's shell, and, optionally, a period of time in seconds, with a default value of 60 (one minute). main loops forever, alternating between executing the command with os.system and waiting (without consuming resources) with time.sleep.

The script's body looks at the command-line arguments you used with the script, which are found in sys.argv. The first, sys.argv[0], is the name of the script, often useful when the script identifies itself as it prints out messages. The body checks that there are one or two other arguments in addition to this name. The first (mandatory) is the command to be run. The second (optional) is the delay in seconds between two runs of the command. If the second argument is missing, the body calls main just with the command argument, accepting the default delay (of 60 seconds). Note that if there is a second argument, the body must transform it from a string (all items in sys.argv are always strings) into an integer. In modern Python, you would do this with the int built-in function:

```
inc = int(sys.argv[2])
```

But the recipe is coded in such a way as to work even with old versions of Python that did not allow you to use int in this way.

See Also

Documentation of the standard library modules os and time in the *Library Reference*.

7.2 Generating Random Passwords

Credit: Devin Leung

Problem

You need to create new passwords randomly—for example, to assign them automatically to new user accounts.

Solution

One of the chores of system administration is installing a lot of new user accounts. Assigning each new user a different, totally random password is a good idea in such cases. Save the following as *makepass.py*:

```
from random import choice
import string

# Python 1.5.2 style
def GenPasswd(length=8, chars=string.letters+string.digits):
    newpasswd = []
    for i in range(length):
        newpasswd.append(choice(chars))
    return string.join(newpasswd,'')

# Python 2.0 and later style
def GenPasswd2(length=8, chars=string.letters+string.digits):
    return ''.join([choice(chars) for i in range(length)])
```

Discussion

This recipe is useful when creating new user accounts and assigning each of them a different, totally random password. The GenPasswd2 version shows how to use some features that are new in Python 2.0 (e.g., list comprehensions and string methods).

Here's how to print out 6 passwords (letters only, of length 12):

```
>>> import makepass, string
>>> for i in range(6):
...     print makepass.GenPasswd2(12, string.letters)
...
uiZWGSJLWjOI
FVrychdGsAaT
CGCXZAFGjsYI
TPpQwpWjQEIi
HMBwIvRMoIvh
otBPtnIYWXGq
```

Of course, such totally random passwords, while providing an excellent theoretical basis for security, are impossibly hard to remember for most users. If you require users to stick with them, many users will probably write down their passwords somewhere. The best you can hope for is that new users will set their own passwords at their first login, assuming, of course, that the system you're administering lets each user change their own password (most operating systems do, but you might be assigning passwords for other kinds of services without such facilities).

A password that is written down anywhere is a serious security risk, since pieces of paper get lost, misplaced, and peeked at. Therefore, from a pragmatic point of view, you might be better off assigning passwords that are not totally random; the users are more likely to remember these and less likely to write them down (see Recipe 7.3).

This may violate the theory of password security, but, as all practicing system administrators know, pragmatism trumps theory.

See Also

Recipe 7.3; documentation of the standard library module random in the *Library Reference*.

7.3   Generating Non-Totally Random Passwords

Credit: Luther Blissett

Problem

You need to create new passwords randomly—for example, to assign them automatically to new user accounts—and want the passwords to be somewhat feasible to remember for typical users, so they won't be written down.

Solution

We can use a pastiche approach for this, mimicking letter n-grams in actual English words. A grander way to look at the same approach is to call it a Markov Chain simulation of English:

```python
import random, string

class password:
    # Any substantial file of English words will do just as well
    data = open("/usr/share/dict/words").read().lower()
    def renew(self, n, maxmem=3):
        self.chars = []
        for i in range(n):
            # Randomly "rotate" self.data
            randspot = random.randrange(len(self.data))
            self.data = self.data[randspot:] + self.data[:randspot]
            where = -1
            # Get the n-gram
            locate = ''.join(self.chars[-maxmem:])
            while where<0 and locate:
                # Locate the n-gram in the data
                where = self.data.find(locate)
                # Back off to a shorter n-gram if necessary
                locate = locate[1:]
            c = self.data[where+len(locate)+1]
            if not c.islower(): c = random.choice(string.lowercase)
            self.chars.append(c)
    def __str__(self):
        return ''.join(self.chars)

if __name__ == '__main__':
    "Usage: pastiche [passwords [length [memory]]]"
```

```
import sys
if len(sys.argv)>1: dopass = int(sys.argv[1])
else: dopass = 8
if len(sys.argv)>2: length = int(sys.argv[2])
else: length = 10
if len(sys.argv)>3: memory = int(sys.argv[3])
else: memory = 3
onepass = password( )
for i in range(dopass):
    onepass.renew(length, memory)
    print onepass
```

Discussion

This recipe is useful when creating new user accounts and assigning each user a different, random password, using passwords that a typical user will find feasible to remember, so that the passwords will not be written down. See Recipe 7.2 if you prefer totally-random passwords.

The recipe's idea is based on the good old pastiche concept. Each letter (always lowercase) in the password is chosen pseudo-randomly from data that is a collection of words in a natural language familiar to the users. This recipe uses */usr/share/dict/ words* as supplied with Linux systems (on my machine, a file of over 45,000 words), but any large document in plain text will do just as well. The trick that makes the passwords sort of memorable, and not fully random, is that each letter is chosen based on the last few letters already picked for the password as it stands so far, so that letter transitions will tend to be repetitive. There is a break when the normal choice procedure would have chosen a nonalphabetic character, in which case a random letter is chosen instead.

Here are a couple of typical sample runs of this *pastiche.py* password-generation script:

```
[situ@tioni cooker]$ python pastiche.py
yjackjaceh
ackjavagef
aldsstordb
dingtonous
stictlyoke
cvaiwandga
lidmanneck
olexnarinl
[situ@tioni cooker]$ python pastiche.py
ptiontingt
punchankin
cypresneyf
sennemedwa
iningrated
fancejacev
sroofcased
```

```
nryjackman
[situ@tioni cooker]$
```

As you can see, some of these are definitely wordlike, others less so, but for a typical human being, none are more problematic to remember than a sequence of even fewer totally random, uncorrelated letters. No doubt some theoretician will complain (justifiably, in a way) that these aren't as random as all that. Well, tough. My point is that they had better not be if some poor fellow is going to have to remember them! You can compensate for this by making them a bit longer. If said theoretician shows us how to compute the entropy per character of this method of password generation (versus the obvious 4.7 bits/character of passwords made up of totally random lowercase letters, for example), now that would be a useful contribution indeed. Meanwhile, I'll keep generating passwords this way, rather than in a totally random way, whenever I'm asked to do so. If nothing else, it's the closest thing to a useful application for the pastiche concept that I've found.

See Also

Recipe 7.2; documentation of the standard library module random in the *Library Reference*.

7.4 Checking the Status of a Unix Network Interface

Credit: Jürgen Hermann

Problem

You need to check the status of a network interface on a Linux or other Unix-compatible platform.

Solution

One approach to system-administration scripts is to dig down into system internals, and Python supports this approach:

```
#! /usr/bin/env python
import fcntl, struct, sys
from socket import *

# Set some symbolic constants
SIOCGIFFLAGS = 0x8913
null256 = '\0'*256

# Get the interface name from the command line
ifname = sys.argv[1]
```

```
# Create a socket so we have a handle to query
s = socket(AF_INET, SOCK_DGRAM)

# Call ioctl( ) to get the flags for the given interface
result = fcntl.ioctl(s.fileno( ), SIOCGIFFLAGS, ifname + null256)

# Extract the interface's flags from the return value
flags, = struct.unpack('H', result[16:18])

# Check "UP" bit and print a message
up = flags & 1
print ('DOWN', 'UP')[up]

# Return a value suitable for shell's "if"
sys.exit(not up)
```

Discussion

This recipe shows how to call some of the low-level modules of Python's standard library, handling their results with the struct module. To really understand how this recipe works, you need to take a look at the system includes. On Linux, the necessary definitions are located in */usr/include/linux/if.h*.

Though this code is certainly more complex than the traditional scripting approach (i.e., running */sbin/ifconfig* and parsing its output), you get two positive effects in return. Directly using the system calls avoids the overhead (albeit modest) of spawning a new process for such a simple query, and you are not dependent on the output format of *ifconfig*, which might change over time (or from system to system) and break your code. On the other hand, of course, you are dependent on the format of the structure returned by ioctl, which may be a bit more stable than *ifconfig*'s text output but no more widespread. Win some, lose some. It is nice (and crucial) that Python gives you a choice!

See Also

Documentation of the standard library modules fcntl and socket in the *Library Reference*; Unix manpages for the details of the network interfaces, such as ioctl and fcntl.

7.5 Calculating Apache Hits per IP Address

Credit: Mark Nenadov

Problem

You need to examine a log file from Apache to know the number of hits recorded from each individual IP address that accessed it.

Solution

Many of the chores of administering a web server have to do with analyzing Apache logs, which Python makes easy:

```
def CalculateApacheIpHits(logfile_pathname):
    # Make a dictionary to store IP addresses and their hit counts
    # and read the contents of the log file line by line
    IpHitListing = {}
    Contents = open(logfile_pathname, "r").xreadlines()
    # You can use .readlines in old Python, but if the log is huge...

    # Go through each line of the logfile
    for line in Contents:
        # Split the string to isolate the IP address
        Ip = line.split(" ")[0]

        # Ensure length of the IP address is proper (see discussion)
        if 6 < len(Ip) <= 15:
            # Increase by 1 if IP exists; else set hit count = 1
            IpHitListing[Ip] = IpHitListing.get(Ip, 0) + 1

    return IpHitListing
```

Discussion

This recipe shows a function that returns a dictionary containing the hit counts for each individual IP address that has accessed your Apache web server, as recorded in an Apache log file. For example, a typical use would be:

```
HitsDictionary = CalculateApacheIpHits("/usr/local/nusphere/apache/logs/access_log")
print HitsDictionary["127.0.0.1"]
```

This function is quite useful for many things. For example, I often use it in my code to determine the number of hits that are actually originating from locations other than my local host. This function is also used to chart which IP addresses are most actively viewing pages that are served by a particular installation of Apache.

This function performs a modest validation of each IP address, which is really just a length check:

- An IP address will never be longer than 15 characters (4 sets of triplets and 3 periods).

- An IP address will never be shorter than 7 characters (4 sets of single digits and 3 periods).

The purpose of this check is not to enforce any stringent validation (for that, we could use a regular expression), but rather to reduce, at extremely low runtime cost, the probability of data that is obviously garbage getting into the dictionary. As a general technique, performing low-cost, highly approximate sanity checks for data that is expected to be okay (but one never knows for sure) is worth considering.

See Also

The Apache web server is available and documented at *http://httpd.apache.org*.

7.6   Calculating the Rate of Client Cache Hits on Apache

Credit: Mark Nenadov

Problem

You need to monitor how often client requests are refused by your Apache web server because the client's cache of the page is up to date.

Solution

When a browser queries a server for a page that the browser has in its cache, the browser lets the server know about the cached data, and the server returns an error code (rather than serving the page again) if the client's cache is up to date. Here's how to find the statistics for such occurrences in your server's logs:

```
def ClientCachePercentage(logfile_pathname):
    Contents = open(logfile_pathname, "r").xreadlines( )
    TotalRequests = 0
    CachedRequests = 0

    for line in Contents:
        TotalRequests += 1
        if line.split(" ")[8] == "304":  # if server returned "not modified"
            CachedRequests += 1

    return (100*CachedRequests)/TotalRequests
```

Discussion

The percentage of requests to your Apache server that are met by the client's own cache is an important factor in the perceived performance of your server. The code in this recipe helps you get this information from the server's log. Typical use would be:

```
log_path = "/usr/local/nusphere/apache/logs/access_log"
print "Percentage of requests that are client-cached: " + str(
    ClientCachePercentage(log_path)) + "%"
```

The recipe reads the log file via the special method xreadlines, introduced in Python 2.1, rather than via the more normal readlines. readlines must read the whole file into memory, since it returns a list of all lines, making it unsuitable for very large files, which server log files can certainly be. Therefore, trying to read the whole log file into memory at once might not work (or work too slowly due to virtual-memory thrashing effects). xreadlines returns a special object, meant to be used only in a for statement (somewhat like an iterator in Python 2.2; Python 2.1 did not have a formal concept of iterators), which can save a lot of memory. In Python 2.2, it would be simplest to iterate on the file object directly, with a for statement such as:

```
for line in open(logfile_pathname):
```

This is the simplest and fastest approach, but it does require Python 2.2 or later to work.

The body of the for loop calls the split method on each line string, with a string of a single space as the argument, to split the line into a tuple of its space-separated fields. Then it uses indexing ([8]) to get the ninth such field. Apache puts the error code into the ninth field of each line in the log. Code "304" means "not modified" (i.e., the client's cache was already correctly updated). We count those cases in the CachedRequests variable and all lines in the log in the TotalRequests variable, so that, in the end, we can return the percentage of cache hits. Note that in the expression used with the return statement, it's important to multiply by 100 before we divide, since up to Python 2.1 (and even in 2.2, by default), division between integers truncates (i.e., ignores the remainder). If we divided first, that would truncate to 0; so multiplying by 100 would still give 0, which is not a very useful result!

See Also

The Apache web server is available and documented at *http://httpd.apache.org*.

7.7   Manipulating the Environment on Windows NT/2000/XP

Credit: Wolfgang Strobl

Problem

You need to check and/or set system-environment variables on Windows NT (or 2000 or XP) via the registry, not in the transient way supported by os.environ.

Solution

Many Windows system-administration tasks boil down to working with the Windows registry, so the _winreg module, part of the Python core, often plays a crucial role in such scripts. This recipe reads all the system-environment variables, then modifies one of them, accessing the registry for both tasks:

```
import _winreg

x = _winreg.ConnectRegistry(None, _winreg.HKEY_LOCAL_MACHINE)
y = _winreg.OpenKey(x,
```

```
            r"SYSTEM\CurrentControlSet\Control\Session Manager\Environment")
    print "System Environment variables are:"
    print "#", "name", "value", "type"
    for i in range(1000):
        try:
            n, v, t = _winreg.EnumValue(y, i)
            print i, n, v, t
        except EnvironmentError:
            print "You have", i, "System Environment variables"
            break

    path = _winreg.QueryValueEx(y, "path")[0]
    print "Your PATH was:", path
    _winreg.CloseKey(y)

    # Reopen Environment key for writing
    y = _winreg.OpenKey(x,
        r"SYSTEM\CurrentControlSet\Control\Session Manager\Environment",
        0, _winreg.KEY_ALL_ACCESS)
    # Now append C:\ to the path as an example of environment change
    _winreg.SetValueEx(y, "path", 0, _winreg.REG_EXPAND_SZ, path+";C:\\")
    _winreg.CloseKey(y)
    _winreg.CloseKey(x)
```

Discussion

Python's normal access to the environment, via os.environ, is transient: it deals with only the environment of this process, and any change affects only processes spawned by the original process after the change. This is true on all platforms.

In system administration, program installation, and other such uses, you may prefer to check and change the system-level environment variables, which are automatically set for each process started normally at process startup time. On Unix-like platforms, and on Windows 95/98/ME, such system-level environment variables are set by startup scripts, so your task is to parse and/or change those scripts in appropriate ways.

On Windows NT/2000/XP, however, system-level environment variables are stored in the system registry, which makes this task substantially easier. The Python standard library, in the Python distribution for Windows, comes with a _winreg module that lets scripts read and write the registry on any kind of Windows machine. This recipe shows how to use _winreg to read the system-environment variables and, as a further example, how to modify the PATH environment variable.

The ConnectRegistry function of the _winreg module returns a registry object. The module's other functions take that object, or another registry key object, as their first argument. When you are done with a key or a whole registry, you pass it to the CloseKey function.

The `OpenKey` function returns a registry key object: its first argument is a registry object, and the second is a path in it. The path needs backslashes, so we use the Python raw-string syntax (`r'...'`) to avoid having to double up each backslash. The `EnumValue` function takes a key and an index and returns a triple of name, value, and type for that entry in the key, or raises `EnvironmentError` if there aren't that many entries in the key. In this recipe, we call it with progressively larger indices, from 0 and up, and catch the exception to learn the exact number of entries in the environment key.

`QueryValueEx` takes the key and an entry name and returns the value for that entry. `SetValueEx` also takes flags (normally 0), a type code (many constants for which are found in `_winreg`), and finally a value, and sets the given value and type for the entry of that name.

The script in this recipe can be run only by a user with suitable administrative privileges, of course, as it changes a protected part of the registry. This doesn't matter under versions of Windows that don't enforce protection, such as Windows 95, but it does for versions that do enforce protection, such as Windows 2000.

See Also

Documentation for the standard module `_winreg` in the *Library Reference*; Windows API documentation available from Microsoft (*http://msdn.microsoft.com*).

7.8 Checking and Modifying the Set of Tasks Windows Automatically Runs at Logon

Credit: Daniel Kinnaer

Problem

You need to check which tasks Windows is set to automatically run at logon and possibly change these tasks.

Solution

When administering Windows machines, it's crucial to keep track of the tasks each machine runs at logon. Like so many Windows tasks, this requires working with the registry, and standard Python module `_winreg` enables this:

```
from _winreg import *

aReg = ConnectRegistry(None, HKEY_LOCAL_MACHINE)

try:
    targ = r'SOFTWARE\Microsoft\Windows\CurrentVersion\Run'
    print "*** Reading from", targ, "***"
```

```
        aKey = OpenKey(aReg, targ)
        try:
            for i in range(1024):
                try:
                    n, v, t = EnumValue(aKey, i)
                    print i, n, v, t
                except EnvironmentError:
                    print "You have", i, "tasks starting at logon"
                    break
        finally:
            CloseKey(aKey)

        print "*** Writing to", targ, "***"
        aKey = OpenKey(aReg, targ, 0, KEY_WRITE)
        try:
            try:
                SetValueEx(aKey, "MyNewKey", 0, REG_SZ, r"c:\winnt\explorer.exe")
            except EnvironmentError:
                print "Encountered problems writing into the Registry..."
                raise
        finally:
            CloseKey(aKey)
finally:
    CloseKey(aReg)
```

Discussion

The Windows registry holds a wealth of crucial system-administration data, and the Python standard module _winreg makes it feasible to read and alter data held in the registry. One of the items held in the Windows registry is a list of tasks to be run at logon. This recipe shows how to examine this list and how to add a task to the list so it is run at logon.

If you want to remove the specific key added by this recipe, you can use the following simple script:

```
from _winreg import *
aReg = ConnectRegistry(None, HKEY_LOCAL_MACHINE)
targ = r'SOFTWARE\Microsoft\Windows\CurrentVersion\Run'
aKey = OpenKey(aReg, targ, 0, KEY_WRITE)
DeleteValue(aKey, "MyNewKey")
CloseKey(aKey)
CloseKey(aReg)
```

The try/finally constructs used in the recipe are far more robust than this simple sequence of function calls, since they ensure everything is closed correctly regardless of whether the intervening calls succeed or fail. This is strongly advisable for scripts that will be run in production, particularly for system-administration scripts that will generally run with administrator privileges and therefore might potentially harm a system's setup if they don't clean up after themselves properly. However, you can omit the try/finally when you know the calls will succeed or don't care what happens if they fail. In this case, if you have successfully added a task with the recipe's script, the calls in this simple cleanup script should work.

See Also

Documentation for the standard module _winreg in the *Library Reference*; Windows API documentation available from Microsoft (*http://msdn.microsoft.com*); information on what is where in the registry tends to be spread among many sources, but for some collections of such information, see *http://www.winguides.com/registry* and *http://www.activewin.com/tips/reg/index.shtml*.

7.9 Examining the Microsoft Windows Registry for a List of Name Server Addresses

Credit: Wolfgang Strobl

Problem

You need to find out which DNS name servers are being used, but you're on Microsoft Windows, so you can't just parse the *resolv.conf* file, as you might do on Unix and Unix-like platforms.

Solution

On Windows, DNS servers (like much other information) can be found in the registry, which can be accessed with the standard module _winreg:

```
import string
import _winreg

def binipdisplay(s):
    "convert a binary array of ip addresses to a python list"
    if len(s)%4!= 0:
        raise EnvironmentError # well ...
    ol=[]
    for i in range(len(s)/4):
        s1=s[:4]
        s=s[4:]
        ip=[]
        for j in s1:
            ip.append(str(ord(j)))
        ol.append(string.join(ip,'.'))
    return ol

def stringdisplay(s):
    'convert "d.d.d.d,d.d.d.d" to ["d.d.d.d","d.d.d.d"]'
    return string.split(s,",")
```

```
def RegistryResolve():
    """ Return the list of dotted-quads addresses of name servers found in
    the registry -- tested on NT4 Server SP6a, Win/2000 Pro SP2, XP, ME
    (each of which has a different registry layout for nameservers!) """

    nameservers=[]
    x=_winreg.ConnectRegistry(None,_winreg.HKEY_LOCAL_MACHINE)
    try:
        y= _winreg.OpenKey(x,
          r"SYSTEM\CurrentControlSet\Services\Tcpip\Parameters")
    except EnvironmentError: # so it isn't NT/2000/XP
        # Windows ME, perhaps?
        try: # for Windows ME
            y = _winreg.OpenKey(x,
              r"SYSTEM\CurrentControlSet\Services\VxD\MSTCP")
            nameserver, dummytype = _winreg.QueryValueEx(y,'NameServer')
            if nameserver and not (nameserver in nameservers):
                nameservers.extend(stringdisplay(nameserver))
        except EnvironmentError:
            pass # Must be another Windows dialect, so who knows?
        return nameservers

    nameserver = _winreg.QueryValueEx(y,"NameServer")[0]
    if nameserver:
        nameservers = [nameserver]
    _winreg.CloseKey(y)
    try: # for win2000
        y = _winreg.OpenKey(x, r"SYSTEM\CurrentControlSet\Services\Tcpip"
                               r"\Parameters\DNSRegisteredAdapters")
        for i in range(1000):
            try:
                n = _winreg.EnumKey(y,i)
                z = _winreg.OpenKey(y,n)
                dnscount,dnscounttype = _winreg.QueryValueEx(z,
                    'DNSServerAddressCount')
                dnsvalues,dnsvaluestype = _winreg.QueryValueEx(z,
                    'DNSServerAddresses')
                nameservers.extend(binipdisplay(dnsvalues))
                _winreg.CloseKey(z)
            except EnvironmentError:
                break
        _winreg.CloseKey(y)
    except EnvironmentError:
        pass

    try: # for XP
        y = _winreg.OpenKey(x,
          r"SYSTEM\CurrentControlSet\Services\Tcpip\Parameters\Interfaces")
        for i in range(1000):
            try:
                n = _winreg.EnumKey(y,i)
                z = _winreg.OpenKey(y,n)
                try:
                    nameserver,dummytype = _winreg.QueryValueEx(z,'NameServer')
```

```
                if nameserver and not (nameserver in nameservers):
                        nameservers.extend(stringdisplay(nameserver))
                except EnvironmentError:
                    pass
                _winreg.CloseKey(z)
            except EnvironmentError:
                break
        _winreg.CloseKey(y)
    except EnvironmentError:
        # Print "Key Interfaces not found, just do nothing"
        pass

    _winreg.CloseKey(x)
    return nameservers

if __name__=="__main__":
    print "Name servers:",RegistryResolve()
```

Discussion

RegistryResolve returns a list of IP addresses (dotted quads) by scanning the registry
for interfaces with name server entries. This is useful when porting utilities that scan
resolv.conf from Unix-based systems to Microsoft Windows. As shown, the code
handles differences between NT, 2000, XP, and ME (I haven't tried it on Windows
95/98, but it should work), and is thus a good example of the many huge differences
under the cover that the system administrator must handle for systems that may
appear to end users to be reasonably close to each other.

Checking which name servers each given machine is using is quite useful when
administering that machine, or a whole network. Basically, all user access to the network is mediated by DNS. Since no user wants to work with dotted quads, almost all
URLs use hostnames and not IP addresses. From the user's viewpoint, if a DNS
server is down, or if name service is misconfigured for a given machine, it's almost as
bad as if there is no network access at all. This recipe makes it feasible for you to
keep an eye on this crucial aspect of networking service, available from Python
scripts, for client machines running Windows (client machines running Unix or
Unix-like systems are easy to use from this point of view, since */etc/resolv.conf* is a
text file, and a pretty easy one to parse).

See Also

Documentation for the standard module _winreg in the *Library Reference*; Windows
API documentation available from Microsoft (*http://msdn.microsoft.com*).

7.10 Getting Information About the Current User on Windows NT/2000

Credit: Wolfgang Strobl

Problem

You need information about the user who is currently logged into a Windows NT/2000 system, and the user may have domain validation rather than being a local-machine user.

Solution

If the user is validated on the domain rather than locally, it's not all that hard to get information from the domain controller:

```
import win32api, win32net, win32netcon
def UserGetInfo(user=None):
    if user is None: user=win32api.GetUserName()
    dc=win32net.NetServerEnum(None, 100, win32netcon.SV_TYPE_DOMAIN_CTRL)
    if dc[0]:  # We have a domain controller; query it
        dcname=dc[0][0]['name']
        return win32net.NetUserGetInfo("\\\\"+dcname, user, 1)
    else:      # No domain controller; try getting info locally
        return win32net.NetUserGetInfo(None, user, 1)

if __name__=="__main__":
    print UserGetInfo()
```

Discussion

The following call:

```
win32net.NetUserGetInfo(None, win32api.GetUserName(), 1)
```

works only for users logged into the local machine but fails for domain users. This recipe shows how to find the domain controller (if it exists) and query it about the user.

Obviously, this recipe works only on Windows NT/2000. In addition, it needs Mark Hammond's Win32 extensions, which goes almost without saying, since you can hardly do effective system-administration work with Python on Windows without those extensions (or a distribution that already includes them).

See Also

Documentation for win32api, win32net, and win32netcon in win32all (*http://starship. python.net/crew/mhammond/win32/Downloads.html*) or ActivePython (*http://www. activestate.com/ActivePython/*); Windows API documentation available from

Microsoft (*http://msdn.microsoft.com*); *Python Programming on Win32*, by Mark Hammond and Andy Robinson (O'Reilly).

7.11 Getting the Windows Service Name from Its Long Name

Credit: Andy McKay

Problem

You need to find the actual name of a Windows service from the longer display name, which is all that many programs show you.

Solution

Unfortunately, a Windows service has two names: a real one (to be used in many operations) and a display name (meant for human display). Fortunately, Python helps you translate between them:

```python
import win32api
import win32con

def GetShortName(longName):
    # Looks up a service's real name from its display name
    hkey = win32api.RegOpenKey(win32con.HKEY_LOCAL_MACHINE,
        "SYSTEM\\CurrentControlSet\\Services", 0, win32con.KEY_ALL_ACCESS)
    num = win32api.RegQueryInfoKey(hkey)[0]

    # Loop through the given number of subkeys
    for x in range(0, num):
        # Find service name; open subkey
        svc = win32api.RegEnumKey(hkey, x)
        skey = win32api.RegOpenKey(win32con.HKEY_LOCAL_MACHINE,
            "SYSTEM\\CurrentControlSet\\Services\\%s" % svc,
            0, win32con.KEY_ALL_ACCESS)
        try:
            # Find short name
            shortName = str(win32api.RegQueryValueEx(skey, "DisplayName")[0])
            if shortName == longName:
                return svc
        except win32api.error:
            # in case there is no key called DisplayName
            pass
    return None

if __name__=='__main__':
    assert(GetShortName('Windows Time') == 'W32Time')
    assert(GetShortName('FoobarService') == None)
```

Discussion

Many programs show only the long description (display name) of a Windows Service, such as Windows Time, but you need the actual service name to operate on the service itself (to restart it, for example). This recipe's function loops through the services on a Windows system (2000/NT) as recorded in the registry. For each service, the code opens the registry key and looks inside the key for the DisplayName value. The service's real name is the key name for which the given long-name argument matches the DisplayName value, if any.

This recipe also shows how to access the Windows registry from Python as an alternative to the _winreg module in Python's standard library. Mark Hammond's win32all extensions include registry access APIs in the win32api module, and the functionality they expose is richer and more complete than _winreg's. If you have win32all installed (and you should if you use Python for system-administration tasks on Windows machines), you should use it instead of the standard _winreg module to access and modify the Windows registry.

See Also

Documentation for win32api and win32con in win32all (*http://starship.python.net/crew/mhammond/win32/Downloads.html*) or ActivePython (*http://www.activestate.com/ActivePython/*); Windows API documentation available from Microsoft (*http://msdn.microsoft.com*); *Python Programming on Win32*, by Mark Hammond and Andy Robinson (O'Reilly).

7.12 Manipulating Windows Services

Credit: Andy McKay

Problem

You need to control Windows services on any local machine.

Solution

The win32all package includes a win32serviceutil module that is specifically designed to handle Windows services:

```
# needs win32all, or ActiveState's ActivePython distribution
import win32serviceutil

def service_running(service, machine):
    return win32serviceutil.QueryServiceStatus(service, machine)[1] == 4

def service_info(action, machine, service):
    running = service_running(service, machine)
```

```
        servnam = 'service (%s) on machine(%s)'%(service, machine)
        action = action.lower( )
        if action == 'stop':
            if not running:
                print "Can't stop, %s not running"%servnam
                return 0
            win32serviceutil.StopService(service, machine)
            running = service_running(service, machine)
            if running:
                print "Can't stop %s (???)"%servnam
                return 0
            print '%s stopped successfully' % servnam
        elif action == 'start':
            if running:
                print "Can't start, %s already running"%servnam
                return 0
            win32serviceutil.StartService(service, machine)
            running = service_running(service, machine)
            if not running:
                print "Can't start %s (???)"%servnam
                return 0
            print '%s started successfully' % servnam
        elif action == 'restart':
            if not running:
                print "Can't restart, %s not running"%servnam
                return 0
            win32serviceutil.RestartService(service, machine)
            running = service_running(service, machine)
            if not running:
                print "Can't restart %s (???)"%servnam
                return 0
            print '%s restarted successfully' % servnam
        elif action == 'status':
            if running:
                print "%s is running" % servnam
            else:
                print "%s is not running" % servnam
        else:
            print "Unknown action (%s) requested on %s"%(action, servnam)

if __name__ == '__main__':
    # Just some test code; change at will!
    machine = 'cr582427-a'
    service = 'Zope23'
    action = 'start'
    service_info(action, machine, service)
```

Discussion

Mark Hammond's `win32all` package makes it child's play to code Python scripts for
a huge variety of Windows system-administration tasks. For example, controlling
Windows services becomes a snap. In addition to the few features exemplified in this

---

recipe, which are similar to those provided by Windows' own net command, win32all also gives you options such as installing and removing services.

The functions this recipe uses from the win32serviceutil module are StartService, StopService, RestartService, and QueryServiceStatus. Each takes two arguments: the name of the service and the name of the machine. The first three perform the start, stop, and restart as requested. The fourth returns a structured code describing whether and how the given service is running on the given machine, but in this recipe we exploit only the fact, encapsulated in the recipe's service_running function, that the second item of the return value is the integer 4 if and only if the service is running successfully.

See Also

Documentation for win32serviceutil in win32all (*http://starship.python.net/crew/ mhammond/win32/Downloads.html*) or ActivePython (*http://www.activestate.com/ ActivePython/*); Windows API documentation available from Microsoft (*http:// msdn.microsoft.com*); *Python Programming on Win32*, by Mark Hammond and Andy Robinson (O'Reilly).

7.13 Impersonating Principals on Windows

Credit: John Nielsen

Problem

You need to authenticate a thread temporarily as another principal on a Windows machine—for example, to make something run with the appropriate administrative rights.

Solution

On Unix, you can call setuid. On Windows, the impersonation task is slightly more involved, but not terribly so:

```
import win32security, win32con

class Impersonate:
    def __init__(self, login, password):
        self.domain = 'bedrock'
        self.login = login
        self.password = password

    def logon(self):
        self.handle = win32security.LogonUser(self.login, self.domain,
            self.password, win32con.LOGON32_LOGON_INTERACTIVE,
            win32con.LOGON32_PROVIDER_DEFAULT)
        win32security.ImpersonateLoggedOnUser(self.handle)
```

```
        def logoff(self):
            win32security.RevertToSelf() # terminates impersonation
            self.handle.Close() # guarantees cleanup

    if __name__=='__main__':
        a = Impersonate('barney', 'bambam')

        try:
            a.logon() # become the user
            try:
                # Do whatever you need to do, e.g.,:
                print win32api.GetUserName() # show you're someone else
            finally:
                a.logoff() # Ensure return-to-normal no matter what
        except:
            print 'Exception:', sys.exc_type, sys.exc_value
```

Discussion

Sometimes it is convenient to authenticate a thread as another principal. For example, perhaps something should run temporarily with administrative rights. This is especially useful if you do not want the hassle of making a COM object or a service (which are other ways to solve the problem or, rather, work around it). On Windows, processes run with a specific security token. By default, all threads use that token. You can, however, easily attach another token to the thread, thanks to Mark Hammond's win32all package.

The way to do this is with the Win32 calls LogonUser and ImpersonateLoggedOnUser. LogonUser gives you a handle that ImpersonateLoggedOnUser can then use to become the user. To do this, the thread calling LogonUser needs the SE_TCB_NAME, SE_CHANGE_NOTIFY_NAME, and SE_ASSIGNPRIMARYTOKEN_NAME privileges.

See Also

Documentation for the win32security and win32con in win32all (*http://starship. python.net/crew/mhammond/win32/Downloads.html*) or ActivePython (*http://www. activestate.com/ActivePython/*); Windows API documentation available from Microsoft (*http://msdn.microsoft.com*); *Python Programming on Win32*, by Mark Hammond and Andy Robinson (O'Reilly).

7.14 Changing a Windows NT Password Using ADSI

Credit: Devin Leung

Problem

You need to change a user's password on Windows NT.

Solution

The simplest approach is to access the Active Directory Services Interface (ADSI) via COM automation:

```
import pythoncom
import win32com.client

class NTUser:
    # Uses ADSI to change password under user privileges
    def __init__(self, userid):
        self.adsiNS = win32com.client.Dispatch('ADsNameSpaces')
        Userpath = "WinNT://DOMAIN/" + userid + ",user"
        self.adsNTUser = self.adsiNS.GetObject("", Userpath)

    def reset(self, OldPasswd, NewPasswd):
        self.adsNTUser.ChangePassword(OldPasswd, NewPasswd)

        # If you're running under admin privileges, you might use:
        self.adsNTUser.SetPassword(NewPasswd)

def changepass(account, OldPassword, NewPassword):
    try:
        nt = NTUser(account)
        nt.reset(OldPassword, NewPassword)
        print "NT Password change was successful."
        return 1
    except pythoncom.com_error, (hr, msg, exc, arg):
        # Give clearer error messages; avoid stack traces
        scode = exc[5]
        print "NT Password change has failed."

        if scode == 0x8007005:
            print "Your NT Account (%s) is locked out."%account
        elif scode == 0x80070056:
            print "Invalid Old NT Password."
        elif scode == 0x800708ad:
            print "The specified NT Account (%s) does not exist."%account
        elif scode == 0x800708c5:
            print "Your new password cannot be the same as any of your"
            print "previous passwords, and must satisfy the domain's"
            print "password-uniqueness policies."
        else:
            print "ADSI Error - %x: %s, %x\n" % (hr, msg, scode)
        return 0
```

Discussion

This recipe gives an example of how to use Python COM to instantiate an ADSI object and change an NT user's password. ADSI, Microsoft's Active Directory Services Interface, is documented at *http://www.microsoft.com/windows2000/techinfo/ howitworks/activedirectory/adsilinks.asp*.

Python's COM access is perhaps the most important single feature of Mark Hammond's win32all extensions. You call win32com.client.Dispatch with the COM automation ProgID string as its single argument and get as a result a Python object on which you can call methods and get and set properties to access all of the functionality of the COM server named by ProgId. The set of methods and properties available is different for every COM server, and you need to find and study the documentation for the specific object model of each server to use it most fruitfully. For example, the methods we call here on COM objects that model active-directory namespaces and NT users are documented in the ADSI documentation.

This recipe can be used to roll your own password-change program. I am currently using it as part of a multiplatform password-changing utility, which helps users keep their passwords in sync on many machines that run different operating systems, both Windows and non-Windows.

See Also

Documentation for pythoncom and win32com.client in win32all (*http://starship. python.net/crew/mhammond/win32/Downloads.html*) or ActivePython (*http://www. activestate.com/ActivePython/*); Windows API documentation available from Microsoft (*http://msdn.microsoft.com*); *Python Programming on Win32*, by Mark Hammond and Andy Robinson (O'Reilly).

7.15 Working with Windows Scripting Host (WSH) from Python

Credit: Kevin Altis

Problem

You need to use the Windows Scripting Host (WSH) to perform the same tasks as in the classic WSH examples, but you must do so by driving the WSH from within a normal Python script.

Solution

Python's abilities on Windows are greatly enhanced by win32all's ability to access COM automation servers, such as the WSH. First, we connect to the Windows shell's COM automation interface:

```
import sys, win32com.client
shell = win32com.client.Dispatch("WScript.Shell")
```

Then, we launch Notepad to edit this script in the simplest way (basically, with the same functionality as os.system). This script's name is, of course, sys.argv[0], since we're driving from Python:

```
shell.Run("notepad " + sys.argv[0])
```

For a *.pys* script driven from WSH, it would be WScript.ScriptFullName instead. shell.Run has greater functionality than the more portable os.system. To show it off, we can set the window type, wait until Notepad is shut down by the user, and get the code returned from Notepad when it is shut down before proceeding:

```
ret = shell.Run("notepad " + sys.argv[0], 1, 1)
print "Notepad return code:", ret
```

Now, we open a command window, change the path to *C:*, and execute a dir:

```
shell.Run("cmd /K CD C:\ & Dir")
```

Note that cmd works only on Windows NT/2000/XP; on Windows 98/ME, you need to run Command instead, and this does not support the & joiner to execute two consecutive commands. The shell object has many more methods besides the Run method used throughout this recipe. For example, we can get any environment string (similar to accessing os.environ):

```
print shell.ExpandEnvironmentStrings("%windir%")
```

Discussion

This recipe shows three Windows Scripting Host (WSH) examples converted to Python. WSH documentation can be found at *http://msdn.microsoft.com/library/en-us/ script56/html/wsoriWindowsScriptHost.asp*.

Note that this recipe shows a Python program driving WSH, so save the code to a file with extension *.py* rather than *.pys*. Extension *.pys* would be used if WSH was driving (i.e., via *cscript.exe*)—and, thus, if Python was being used via the ActiveScripting protocol. But the point of the recipe is that you don't need to rely on ActiveScripting: you can use WSH system-specific functionality, such as SendKeys and ExpandEnvironmentStrings, from within a regular Python program, further enhancing the use of Python for system administration and automating tasks in a Windows environment.

Note that you do not need to worry about closing the COM objects you create. Python's garbage collection takes care of them quite transparently. For example, if and when you want to explicitly close (release) a COM object, you can use a del statement (in this case, you need to ensure that you remove or rebind all references to the COM object that you want to release).

See Also

Documentation for `pythoncom` and `win32com.client` in win32all (*http://starship.python. net/crew/mhammond/win32/Downloads.html*) or ActivePython (*http://www.activestate. com/ActivePython/*); Windows API documentation available from Microsoft (*http:// msdn.microsoft.com*); *Python Programming on Win32*, by Mark Hammond and Andy Robinson (O'Reilly).

7.16   Displaying Decoded Hotkeys for Shortcuts in Windows

Credit: Bill Bell

Problem

You need to display the hotkeys associated with Windows shortcuts as readable key-combination names, such as Alt-Ctrl-Z or Shift-Ctrl-B.

Solution

Key combinations are returned as binary-coded numbers, but it's not hard to decode them into human-readable combinations:

```
import sys
# Append to sys.path the complete path to the folder that contains
# 'link.py' (the demo use of pythoncom.CoCreateInstance with
# shell.CLSID_ShellLink in the ActiveState distribution of Python)
# so that link can be imported as a module
sys.path.append('C:/Python21/win32comext/shell/test')
import link
import commctrl
class PyShortcut_II(link.PyShortcut):
    def decode_hotkey(self):
        hk = self.GetHotkey( )
        result = ''
        if hk:
            mod = hk >> 8
            if mod & commctrl.HOTKEYF_SHIFT: result += 'Shift-'
            if mod & commctrl.HOTKEYF_CONTROL: result += 'Control-'
            if mod & commctrl.HOTKEYF_ALT: result += 'Alt-'
            result += chr ( hk % 256 )
        return result
```

Here's a typical usage pattern:

```
>>> shortcut = PyShortcut_II( )
>>> shortcut.load(r'C:\WINDOWS\DESKTOP\Pygris.lnk' )
>>> shortcut.decode_hotkey( )
'Control-Alt-T'
```

Discussion

The ActiveState Python distribution includes an example that shows how to get and set Win32 shortcuts. This recipe shows how to extend the example to decode the hotkeys (such as Alt-Ctrl-Z and Shift-Ctrl-B) that can be associated with shortcuts.

On Win32, each shortcut can have an associated hotkey. In the *link.py* that is distributed as a demo with ActiveState's ActivePython, the hotkey is returned as a 16-bit code: the lower 8 bits encode the hotkey's characters, and the upper 8 bits encode modifiers, such as Shift, Control, and Alt. This recipe shows how to decode such a 16-bit code in terms of a printable key name for a shortcut's hotkey. Of course, this idea can also be useful for other similar needs, whenever key modifiers encoded as a bitmask using the bits named in the commctrl module need to be displayed readably.

See Also

Windows API documentation available from Microsoft (*http://msdn.microsoft.com*); the commctrl module is derived from the *commctrl.h* standard Windows include file.

## CHAPTER 8

Databases and Persistence

8.0 Introduction

Credit: Aaron Watters, CTO, ReportLab

There are three kinds of people in this world: those who can count and those who can't.

However, there are only two kinds of computer programs: toy programs and programs that interact with persistent databases of some kind. That is to say, most real computer programs must retrieve stored information and record information for future use. These days, this is true of almost every computer game, which can typically save and restore the state of the game at any time. So when I refer to toy programs, I mean programs written as exercises, or for the fun of programming. Nearly all real programs (such as programs that people get paid to write) have some persistent database storage/retrieval component.

When I was a Fortran programmer in the 1980s I noticed that although almost every program had to retrieve and store information, they almost always did it using homegrown methods. Furthermore, since the storage and retrieval part of the program was the least interesting component from the programmer's point of view, these parts of the program were frequently implemented very sloppily and were hideous sources of intractable bugs. This repeated observation convinced me that the study and implementation of database systems sat at the core of programming pragmatics, and that the state of the art as I saw it then required much improvement.

Later, in graduate school, I was delighted to find that there was an impressive and sophisticated body of work relating to the implementation of database systems. The literature of database systems covered issues of concurrency, fault tolerance, distribution, query optimization, database design, and transaction semantics, among others. In typical academic fashion, many of the concepts had been elaborated to the point of absurdity (such as the silly notion of conditional multivalued dependencies), but much of the work was directly related to the practical implementation of reliable and efficient storage and retrieval systems. The starting point for much of this work was

E. F. Codd's seminal work "A Relational Model of Data for Large Shared Data Banks" from *Communications of the ACM*, Vol. 13, No. 6, June 1970, pp. 377-387, *http://www.acm.org/classics/nov95/toc.html*.

I also found that among my fellow graduate students, and even among most of the faculty, the same body of knowledge was either disregarded or regarded with some scorn. Everyone recognized that knowledge of conventional relational technology could be lucrative, but they generally considered such knowledge to be on the same level as knowing how to write (or more importantly, maintain) COBOL programs. This was not helped by the fact that the emerging database interface standard, SQL (which is now very well established), looked like an extension of COBOL and bore little obvious relationship to any modern programming language.

Those who were interested in database systems were generally drawn to alternatives to the relational model, such as functional or object-oriented database system implementations. There was also a small group of people interested in logic databases. Logic databases were largely an interesting footnote to the study of logic programming and prolog-like programming languages, but the underlying concepts also resonated strongly with Codd's original vision for relational databases. The general feeling was that relational-database technology, at least at the level of SQL, was a mistake and that something better would soon overtake it.

Now it is more than a decade later, and there is little sign that anything will soon overtake SQL-based relational technology for the majority of data-based applications. In fact, relational-database technology seems more pervasive than ever. The largest software vendors—IBM, Microsoft, and Oracle—all provide various relational-database implementations as crucial components of their core offerings. Other large software firms, such as SAP and PeopleSoft, essentially provide layers of software built on top of a relational-database core.

Generally, relational databases have been augmented rather than replaced. Enterprise software-engineering dogma frequently espouses three-tier systems, in which the bottom tier is a carefully designed relational database, the middle tier defines a view of the database as business objects, and the top tier consists of applications or transactions that manipulate the business objects, with effects that ultimately translate to changes in the underlying relational tables.

Microsoft's Open Database Connectivity (ODBC) standard provides a common programming API for SQL-based relational databases that permits programs to interact with many different database engines with no, or few, changes. For example, a Python program can be implemented using Microsoft Access as a backend database for testing and debugging purposes. Once the program is stable, it can be put into production use, remotely accessing a backend DB2 database on an IBM mainframe residing on another continent, by changing (at most) one line of code.

This is not to say that relational databases are appropriate for all applications. In particular, a computer game or engineering design tool that must save and restore sessions should probably use a more direct method of persisting the logical objects of the program than the flat tabular representation encouraged in relational-database design. However, even in domains such as engineering or scientific information, I must caution that a hybrid approach that uses some relational methods is often advisable. For example, I have seen a complex relational-database schema for archiving genetic-sequencing information—in which the sequences show up as binary large objects (BLOBs)—but a tremendous amount of important ancillary information can fit nicely into relational tables. But as the reader has probably surmised, I fear, I speak as a relational bigot.

Within the Python world there are many ways of providing persistence and database functionality. My favorite is Gadfly, a simple and minimal SQL implementation that works primarily with in-memory databases. It is my favorite for no other reason than because it is mine, and it's biggest advantage is that if it becomes unworkable for you, it is easy to switch over to another, industrial-strength SQL engine. Many Gadfly users have started an application with Gadfly (because it was easy to use) and switched later (because they needed more).

However, many people may prefer to start by using other SQL implementations such as mySQL, MS-Access, Oracle, Sybase, MS SQL server, or others that provide the advantages of an ODBC interface (which Gadfly does not do).

Python provides a standard interface for accessing relational databases: the Python DB Application Programming Interface (Py-DBAPI), originally designed by Greg Stein. Each underlying database API requires a wrapper implementation of the Py-DBAPI, and implementations are available for many underlying database interfaces, notably Oracle and ODBC.

When the relational approach is overkill, Python provides built-in facilities for storing and retrieving data. At the most basic level, the programmer can manipulate files directly, as covered in Chapter 4. A step up from files, the marshal module allows programs to serialize data structures constructed from simple Python types (not including, for example, classes or class instances). marshal has the advantage in that it can retrieve large data structures with blinding speed. The pickle and cPickle modules allow general storage of objects, including classes, class instances, and circular structures. cPickle is so named because it is implemented in C and is consequently quite fast, but it remains noticeably slower than marshal.

While marshal and pickle provide basic serialization and deserialization of structures, the application programmer will frequently desire more functionality, such as transaction support and concurrency control. In this case, if the relational model doesn't fit the application, a direct object database implementation such as the Z-Object Database (ZODB) might be appropriate (*http://www.amk.ca/zodb/*).

I must conclude with a plea to those who are dismissive of relational-database technology. Please remember that it is successful for some good reasons, and it might be worth considering. To paraphrase Churchill:

```
text = """ Indeed, it has been said that democracy is the worst form of
    government, except for all those others that have been tried
    from time to time. """
import string
for a, b in [("democracy", "SQL"), ("government", "database")]:
    text = string.replace(text, a, b)
print text
```

8.1   Serializing Data Using the marshal Module

Credit: Luther Blissett

Problem

You have a Python data structure composed of only fundamental Python objects (e.g., lists, tuples, numbers, and strings, but no classes, instances, etc.), and you want to serialize it and reconstruct it later as fast as possible.

Solution

If you know that your data is composed entirely of fundamental Python objects, the lowest-level, fastest approach to serializing it (i.e., turning it into a string of bytes and later reconstructing it from such a string) is via the marshal module. Suppose that data is composed of only elementary Python data types. For example:

```
data = {12:'twelve', 'feep':list('ciao'), 1.23:4+5j, (1,2,3):u'wer'}
```

You can serialize data to a byte string at top speed as follows:

```
import marshal
bytes = marshal.dumps(data)
```

You can now sling bytes around as you wish (e.g., send it across a network, put it as a BLOB in a database, etc.), as long as you keep its arbitrary binary bytes intact. Then you can reconstruct the data any time you'd like:

```
redata = marshal.loads(bytes)
```

This reconstructs a data structure that compares equal (==) to data. In other words, the order of keys in dictionaries is arbitrary in both the original and reconstructed data structures, but order in any kind of sequence is meaningful, and thus it is preserved. Note that loads works independently of machine architecture, but you must guarantee that it is used by the same release of Python under which bytes was originally generated via dumps.

When you specifically want to write the data to a disk file, as long as the latter is open for binary (not the default text mode) input/output, you can also use the dump function of the `marshal` module, which lets you dump several data structures one after the other:

```
ouf = open('datafile.dat', 'wb')
marshal.dump(data, ouf)
marshal.dump('some string', ouf)
marshal.dump(range(19), ouf)
ouf.close( )
```

When you have done this, you can recover from *datafile.dat* the same data structures you dumped into it, in the same sequence:

```
inf = open('datafile.dat', 'rb')
a = marshal.load(inf)
b = marshal.load(inf)
c = marshal.load(inf)
inf.close( )
```

Discussion

Python offers several ways to serialize data (i.e., make the data into a string of bytes that you can save on disk, in a database, send across the network, and so on) and corresponding ways to reconstruct the data from such serialized forms. The lowest-level approach is to use the `marshal` module, which Python uses to write its bytecode files. `marshal` supports only elementary data types (e.g., dictionaries, lists, tuples, numbers, and strings) and combinations thereof. `marshal` does not guarantee compatibility from one Python release to another, so data serialized with `marshal` may not be readable if you upgrade your Python release. However, it does guarantee independence from a specific machine's architecture, so it is guaranteed to work if you're sending serialized data between different machines, as long as they are all running the same version of Python—similar to how you can share compiled Python byte-code files in such a distributed setting.

`marshal`'s `dumps` function accepts any Python data structure and returns a byte string representing it. You can pass that byte string to the `loads` function, which will return another Python data structure that compares equal (`==`) to the one you originally dumped. In between the `dumps` and `loads` calls, you can subject the byte string to any procedure you wish, such as sending it over the network, storing it into a database and retrieving it, or encrypting it and decrypting it. As long as the string's binary structure is correctly restored, `loads` will work fine on it (again, as long as it is under the same Python release with which you originally executed `dumps`).

When you specifically need to save the data to a file, you can also use `marshal`'s `dump` function, which takes two arguments: the data structure you're dumping and the open file object. Note that the file must be opened for binary I/O (not the default, which is text I/O) and can't be a file-like object, as `marshal` is quite picky about it being a true file. The advantage of `dump` is that you can perform several calls to `dump` with various data structures and the same open file object: each data structure is then dumped together with information about how long the dumped byte string is. As a consequence, when you later open the file for binary reading and then call `marshal.load`, passing the file as the argument, each previously dumped data structure is reloaded sequentially. The return value of `load`, like that of `loads`, is a new data structure that compares equal to the one you originally dumped.

See Also

Recipe 4.26; Recipe 8.2 for `cPickle`, the big brother of `marshal`; documentation on the `marshal` standard library module in the *Library Reference*.

8.2 Serializing Data Using the pickle and cPickle Modules

Credit: Luther Blissett

Problem

You have a Python data structure, which may include fundamental Python objects, and possibly classes and instances, and you want to serialize it and reconstruct it at a reasonable speed.

Solution

If you don't want to assume that your data is composed of only fundamental Python objects, or you need portability across versions of Python, or you need to transmit the serialized form as text, the best way of serializing your data is with the `cPickle` module (the `pickle` module is a pure-Python equivalent, but it's far slower and not worth using except if you're missing `cPickle`). For example:

```
data = {12:'twelve', 'feep':list('ciao'), 1.23:4+5j, (1,2,3):u'wer'}
```

You can serialize data to a text string:

```
import cPickle
text = cPickle.dumps(data)
```

or to a binary string, which is faster and takes up less space:

```
bytes = cPickle.dumps(data, 1)
```

You can now sling `text` or `bytes` around as you wish (e.g., send it across a network, put it as a BLOB in a database, etc.), as long as you keep it intact. In the case of `bytes`, this means keeping its arbitrary binary bytes intact. In the case of `text`, this means keeping its textual structure intact, including newline characters. Then you can reconstruct the data at any time, regardless of machine architecture or Python release:

```
redata1 = cPickle.loads(text)
redata2 = cPickle.loads(bytes)
```

Either call reconstructs a data structure that compares equal to data. In other words, the order of keys in dictionaries is arbitrary in both the original and reconstructed data structures, but order in any kind of sequence is meaningful, and thus it is preserved. You don't need to tell cPickle.loads whether the original dumps used text mode (the default) or binary (faster and more compact)—loads figures it out by examining its argument's contents.

When you specifically want to write the data to a file, you can also use the dump function of the cPickle module, which lets you dump several data structures one after the other:

```
ouf = open('datafile.txt', 'w')
cPickle.dump(data, ouf)
cPickle.dump('some string', ouf)
cPickle.dump(range(19), ouf)
ouf.close( )
```

Once you have done this, you can recover from *datafile.txt* the same data structures you dumped into it, in the same sequence:

```
inf = open('datafile.txt')
a = cPickle.load(inf)
b = cPickle.load(inf)
c = cPickle.load(inf)
inf.close( )
```

You can also pass cPickle.dump a third argument of 1 to tell it to serialize the data in binary form (faster and more compact), but the datafile must be opened for binary I/O, not in the default text mode, when you originally dump to it and when you later load from it.

Discussion

Python offers several ways to serialize data (i.e., make the data into a string of bytes that you can save on disk, in a database, send across the network, and so on) and corresponding ways to reconstruct the data from such serialized forms. Typically, the best approach is to use the cPickle module. There is also a pure-Python equivalent, called pickle (the cPickle module is coded in C as a Python extension), but pickle is substantially slower, and the only reason to use it is if you don't have cPickle (e.g., a Python port onto a handheld computer with tiny storage space, where you saved every byte you possibly could by installing only an indispensable subset of Python's large standard library).

cPickle supports most elementary data types (e.g., dictionaries, lists, tuples, numbers, strings) and combinations thereof, as well as classes and instances. Pickling classes and instances saves only the data involved, not the code. (Code objects are not even among the types that cPickle knows how to serialize, basically because there would be no way to guarantee their portability across disparate versions of Python). See Recipe 8.3 for more about pickling classes and instances.

cPickle guarantees compatibility from one Python release to another and independence from a specific machine's architecture. Data serialized with cPickle will still be readable if you upgrade your Python release, and pickling is guaranteed to work if you're sending serialized data between different machines.

The dumps function of cPickle accepts any Python data structure and returns a text string representing it. Or, if you call dumps with a second argument of 1, it returns an arbitrary byte string instead, which is faster and takes up less space. You can pass either the text or the byte string to the loads function, which will return another Python data structure that compares equal (==) to the one you originally dumped. In between the dumps and loads calls, you can subject the byte string to any procedure you wish, such as sending it over the network, storing it in a database and retrieving it, or encrypting it and decrypting it. As long as the string's textual or binary structure is correctly restored, loads will work fine on it (even across platforms and releases).

When you specifically need to save the data into a file, you can also use cPickle's dump function, which takes two arguments: the data structure you're dumping and the open file object. If the file is opened for binary I/O, rather than the default (text I/O), by giving dump a third argument of 1, you can ask for binary format, which is faster and takes up less space. The advantage of dump over dumps is that, with dump, you can perform several calls, one after the other, with various data structures and the same open file object. Each data structure is then dumped with information about how long the dumped string is. Consequently, when you later open the file for reading (binary reading, if you asked for binary format), and then repeatedly call cPickle.load, passing the file as the argument, each data structure previously dumped is reloaded sequentially, one after the other. The return value of load, as that of loads, is a new data structure that compares equal to the one you originally dumped.

See Also

Recipes 8.1 and 8.3; documentation for the standard library module cPickle in the *Library Reference*.

8.3 Using the cPickle Module on Classes and Instances

Credit: Luther Blissett

Problem

You want to save and restore class and instance objects using the cPickle module.

Solution

Often, you need no special precautions to use cPickle on your classes and their instances. For example, the following works fine:

```
import cPickle

class ForExample:
    def __init__(self, *stuff): self.stuff = stuff
anInstance = ForExample('one', 2, 3)
saved = cPickle.dumps(anInstance)
reloaded = cPickle.loads(save)
assert saved.stuff == reloaded.stuff
```

However, sometimes there are problems:

```
anotherInstance = ForExample(1, 2, open('three', 'w'))
wontWork = cPickle.dumps(anotherInstance)
```

This causes a TypeError: "can't pickle file objects exception", because the state of anotherInstance includes a file object, and file objects cannot be pickled. You would get exactly the same exception if you tried to pickle any other container that includes a file object among its items.

However, in some cases, you may be able to do something about it:

```
import types
class PrettyClever:
    def __init__(self, *stuff): self.stuff = stuff
    def __getstate__(self):
        def normalize(x):
            if type(x) == types.FileType:
                return 1, (x.name, x.mode, x.tell())
            return 0, x
        return [ normalize(x) for x in self.stuff ]
    def __setstate__(self, stuff):
        def reconstruct(x):
            if x[0] == 0:
                return x[1]
            name, mode, offs = x[1]
            openfile = open(name, mode)
```

```
            openfile.seek(offs)
            return openfile
        self.stuff = tuple([reconstruct(x) for x in stuff])
```

By defining the __getstate__ and __setstate__ special methods in your class, you gain fine-grained control about what, exactly, your class's instances consider to be their state. As long as you can define such "state" in picklable terms, and reconstruct your instances from the unpickled state sufficiently for your application, you can make your instances themselves picklable and unpicklable in this way.

Discussion

cPickle dumps class and function objects by name (i.e., through their module's name and their name within the module). Thus, you can dump only classes defined at module level (not inside other classes and functions). Reloading such objects requires the respective modules to be available for import. Instances can be saved and reloaded only if they belong to such classes. In addition, the instance's state must also be picklable.

By default, an instance's state is the contents of its __dict__ plus, in Python 2.2, whatever state it may get from the built-in type it inherits from. (For example, an instance of a new-style class that subclasses list includes the list items as part of the instance's state. Also, in Python 2.2, cPickle supports __slots__ if an object and/or its bases define them, instead of using __dict__, the default way, to hold per-instance state). This default approach is often quite sufficient and satisfactory.

Sometimes, however, you may have nonpicklable attributes or items as part of your instance's state (as cPickle defines it by default). In this recipe, for example, I show a class whose instances hold arbitrary stuff, which may include open file objects. To handle this case, your class can define the special method __getstate__. cPickle calls that method on your object, if your object's class defines it or inherits it, instead of going directly for the object's __dict__ (or possibly __slots__ and/or built-in type bases in Python 2.2).

Normally, when you define the __getstate__ method, you define the __setstate__ method as well, as shown in the solution. __getstate__ can return any picklable object, and that same object would then be passed as __setstate__'s argument. In the solution, __getstate__ returns a list that's similar to the instance's default state self.stuff, except that each item is turned into a tuple of two items. The first item in the pair can be set to 0 to indicate that the second one will be taken verbatim, or 1 to indicate that the second item will be used to reconstruct an open file. (Of course, the reconstruction may fail or be unsatisfactory in several ways. There is no general way to save an open file's state, which is why cPickle itself doesn't even try. But suppose that in the context of our application we know the given approach will work.) When reloading the instance from pickled form, cPickle will call __setstate__ with the list of pairs, and __setstate__ can reconstruct self.stuff by processing each pair appropriately in its nested reconstruct function. This scheme clearly generalizes to getting and restoring state that may contain various kinds of normally unpicklable objects—just be sure to use different numbers to tag various kinds of nonverbatim pairs.

In a particular case, you can define __getstate__ without defining __setstate__. __getstate__ must return a dictionary, and reloading the instance from pickled form uses that dictionary just as the instance's __dict__ would normally be used. Not running your own code at reloading time is a serious hindrance, but it may come in handy when you want to use __getstate__, not to save otherwise unpicklable state, but rather as an optimization. Typically, this happens when your instance caches results that it may recompute if they're absent, and you decide it's best not to store the cache as a part of the instance's state. In this case, you should define __getstate__ to return a dictionary that's the indispensable subset of the instance's __dict__.

With either the default pickling/unpickling approach or your own __getstate__ and __setstate__, the instance's special method __init__ is not called. If the most convenient way for you to reconstruct an instance is to call the __init__ method with appropriate parameters, then instead of __getstate__, you may want to define the special method __getinitargs__. In this case, cPickle calls this method without arguments: the method must return a tuple, and cPickle calls __init__ at reloading time with the arguments that are that tuple's items.

The *Library Reference* for the pickle and copy_reg modules details even subtler things you can do when pickling and unpickling, as well as security issues that come from unpickling data from untrusted sources. However, the techniques I've discussed here should suffice in almost all practical cases, as long as the security aspects of unpickling are not a problem. As a further practical advantage, if you define __getstate__ (and then, typically, __setstate__) or __getinitargs__, in addition to being used for pickling and unpickling your class's instances, they'll be used by the functions in the copy module that perform shallow and deep copies of your objects (the copy and deepcopy functions, respectively). The issues of extracting and restoring instance state are almost the same when copying the instance directly, as when serializing (saving) it to a string (or file, e.g.) and then restoring it, which can be seen as just one way to copy it at a later time and/or in another machine.

See Also

Recipe 8.2; documentation for the standard library module cPickle in the *Library Reference*.

8.4 Mutating Objects with shelve

Credit: Luther Blissett

Problem

You are using the standard module shelve, some of the values you have shelved are mutable objects, and you need to mutate these objects.

Solution

The shelve module, which offers a kind of persistent dictionary, occupies an important niche between the power of relational-database engines and the simplicity of marshal, pickle, dbm, and similar file formats. However, there's a typical trap that you need to avoid when using shelve. Consider the following:

```
>>> import shelve
>>> # Build a simple sample shelf
>>> she=shelve.open('try.she', 'c')
>>> for c in 'spam': she[c]={c:23}
...
>>> for c in she.keys(): print c, she[c]
...
p {'p': 23}
s {'s': 23}
a {'a': 23}
m {'m': 23}
>>> she.close()
```

We've created the shelve object, added some data to it, and closed it. Now we can reopen it and work with it:

```
>>> she=shelve.open('try.she','c')
>>> she['p']
{'p': 23}
>>> she['p']['p'] = 42
>>> she['p']
{'p': 23}
```

What's going on here? We just set the value to 42, but it didn't take in the shelve object. The problem is that we were working with a temporary object that shelve gave us, but shelve doesn't track changes to the temporary object. The solution is to bind a name to this temporary object, do our mutation, and then assign the mutated object back to the appropriate item of shelve:

```
>>> a = she['p']
>>> a['p'] = 42
>>> she['p'] = a
>>> she['p']
{'p': 42}
>>> she.close()
```

We can even verify the change:

```
>>> she=shelve.open('try.she','c')
>>> for c in she.keys( ): print c,she[c]
...
p {'p': 42}
s {'s': 23}
a {'a': 23}
m {'m': 23}
```

Discussion

The standard Python module shelve can be quite convenient in many cases, but it hides a potentially nasty trap, which I could not find documented anywhere. Suppose you're shelving mutable objects, such as dictionaries or lists. Naturally, you will want to mutate some of those objects—for example, by calling mutating methods (append on a list, update on a dictionary, and so on), or by assigning a new value to an item or attribute of the object. However, when you do this, the change doesn't occur in the shelve object. This is because we are actually mutating a temporary object that the shelve object has given us as the result of its __getitem__ method, but the shelve object does not keep track of that temporary object, nor does it care about it once it returns it.

As shown in the recipe, the solution is to bind a name to the temporary object obtained by keying into the shelf, do whatever mutations are needed to the object via the name, then assign the newly mutated object back to the appropriate item of the shelve object. When you assign to a shelve item, the __setitem__ method is invoked, and it appropriately updates the shelve object itself, so that the change does occur.

See Also

Recipes 8.1 and Recipe 8.2 for alternative serialization approaches; documentation for the shelve standard library module in the *Library Reference*.

8.5 Accesssing a MySQL Database

Credit: Mark Nenadov

Problem

You need to access a MySQL database.

Solution

The MySQLdb module makes this task extremely easy:

```
import MySQLdb

# Create a connection object, then use it to create a cursor
Con = MySQLdb.connect(host="127.0.0.1", port=3306,
    user="joe", passwd="egf42", db="tst")
Cursor = Con.cursor( )

# Execute an SQL string
sql = "SELECT * FROM Users"
Cursor.execute(sql)

# Fetch all results from the cursor into a sequence and close the connection
Results = Cursor.fetchall( )
Con.close( )
```

Discussion

You can get the MySQLdb module from *http://sourceforge.net/projects/mysql-python*. It is a plain and simple implementation of the Python DB API 2.0 that is suitable for all Python versions from 1.5.2 to 2.2.1 and MySQL Versions 3.22 to 4.0.

As with all other Python DB API implementations, you start by importing the module and calling the connect function with suitable parameters. The keyword parameters you can pass when calling connect depend on the database involved: host (defaulting to the local host), user, passwd (password), and db (name of the database) are typical. In the recipe, I explicitly pass the default local host's IP address and the default MySQL port (3306) to show that you can specify parameters explicitly even when you're passing their default values (e.g., to make your source code clearer and more readable and maintainable).

The connect function returns a connection object, and you can proceed to call methods on this object until, when you are done, you call the close method. The method you most often call on a connection object is cursor, which returns a cursor object, which is what you use to send SQL commands to the database and fetch the commands' results. The underlying MySQL database engine does not in fact support SQL cursors, but that's no problem—the MySQLdb module emulates them on your behalf quite transparently. Once you have a cursor object in hand, you can call methods on it. The recipe uses the execute method to execute an SQL statement and the fetchall method to obtain all results as a sequence of tuples—one tuple per row in the result. There are many refinements you can use, but these basic elements of the Python DB API's functionality already suffice for many tasks.

See Also

The Python/MySQL interface module (*http://sourceforge.net/projects/mysql-python*); the Python DB API (*http://www.python.org/topics/database/DatabaseAPI-2.0.html*).

8.6   Storing a BLOB in a MySQL Database

Credit: Luther Blissett

Problem

You need to store a binary large object (BLOB) in a MySQL database.

Solution

The `MySQLdb` module does not support full-fledged placeholders, but you can make do with its escape_string function:

```
import MySQLdb, cPickle

# Connect to a DB, e.g., the test DB on your localhost, and get a cursor
connection = MySQLdb.connect(db="test")
cursor = connection.cursor()

# Make a new table for experimentation
cursor.execute("CREATE TABLE justatest (name TEXT, ablob BLOB)")

try:
    # Prepare some BLOBs to insert in the table
    names = 'aramis', 'athos', 'porthos'
    data = {}
    for name in names:
        datum = list(name)
        datum.sort()
        data[name] = cPickle.dumps(datum, 1)

    # Perform the insertions
    sql = "INSERT INTO justatest VALUES(%s, %s)"
    for name in names:
        cursor.execute(sql, (name, MySQLdb.escape_string(data[name])) )

    # Recover the data so you can check back
    sql = "SELECT name, ablob FROM justatest ORDER BY name"
    cursor.execute(sql)
    for name, blob in cursor.fetchall():
        print name, cPickle.loads(blob), cPickle.loads(data[name])
finally:
    # Done. Remove the table and close the connection.
    cursor.execute("DROP TABLE justatest")
    connection.close()
```

Discussion

MySQL supports binary data (BLOBs and variations thereof), but you need to be careful when communicating such data via SQL. Specifically, when you use a normal INSERT SQL statement and need to have binary strings among the VALUES you're inserting, you need to escape some characters in the binary string according to MySQL's own rules. Fortunately, you don't have to figure out those rules for yourself: MySQL supplies a function that does all the needed escaping, and `MySQLdb` exposes it to your Python programs as the `escape_string` function. This recipe shows a typical case: the BLOBs you're inserting come from `cPickle.dumps`, and so they may represent almost arbitrary Python objects (although, in this case, we're just using them for a few lists of characters). The recipe is purely demonstrative and works by creating a table and dropping it at the end (using a `try/finally` statement to ensure that finalization is performed even if the program terminates because of an uncaught exception). With recent versions of MySQL and MySQLdb, you don't need to call the `escape_string` function anymore, so you can change the relevant statement to the simpler:

```
cursor.execute(sql, (name, data [name]))
```

An alternative is to save your binary data to a temporary file and use MySQL's own server-side `LOAD_FILE` SQL function. However, this works only when your program is running on the same machine as the MySQL database server, or the two machines at least share a filesystem on which you can write and from which the server can read. The user that runs the SQL including the `LOAD_FILE` function must also have the `FILE` privilege in MySQL's grant tables. If all conditions are met, here's how we can instead perform the insertions in the database:

```
import tempfile
tempname = tempfile.mktemp('.blob')
sql = "INSERT INTO justatest VALUES(%%s, LOAD_FILE('%s'))"%tempname
for name in names:
    fileobject = open(tempname,'wb')
    fileobject.write(data[name])
    fileobject.close()
    cursor.execute(sql, (name,))
import os
os.remove(tempname)
```

This is clearly too much of a hassle (particularly considering the many conditions you must meet, as well as the code bloat) for BLOBs of small to medium sizes, but it may be worthwhile if your BLOBs are quite large. Most often, however, `LOAD_FILE` comes in handy only if you already have the BLOB data in a file, or if you want to put the data into a file anyway for another reason.

See Also

Recipe 8.7 for a PostgreSQL-oriented solution to the same problem; the MySQL home page (*http://www.mysql.org*); the Python/MySQL interface module (*http://sourceforge.net/projects/mysql-python*).

8.7 Storing a BLOB in a PostgreSQL Database

Credit: Luther Blissett

Problem

You need to store a binary large object (BLOB) in a PostgreSQL database.

Solution

PostgreSQL 7.2 supports large objects, and the psycopg module supplies a Binary escaping function:

```
import psycopg, cPickle

# Connect to a DB, e.g., the test DB on your localhost, and get a cursor
connection = psycopg.connect("dbname=test")
cursor = connection.cursor( )

# Make a new table for experimentation
cursor.execute("CREATE TABLE justatest (name TEXT, ablob BYTEA)")

try:
    # Prepare some BLOBs to insert in the table
    names = 'aramis', 'athos', 'porthos'
    data = {}
    for name in names:
        datum = list(name)
        datum.sort( )
        data[name] = cPickle.dumps(datum, 1)

    # Perform the insertions
    sql = "INSERT INTO justatest VALUES(%s, %s)"
    for name in names:
        cursor.execute(sql, (name, psycopg.Binary(data[name])) )

    # Recover the data so you can check back
    sql = "SELECT name, ablob FROM justatest ORDER BY name"
    cursor.execute(sql)
    for name, blob in cursor.fetchall( ):
        print name, cPickle.loads(blob), cPickle.loads(data[name])
finally:
    # Done. Remove the table and close the connection.
    cursor.execute("DROP TABLE justatest")
    connection.close( )
```

Discussion

PostgreSQL supports binary data (BYTEA and variations thereof), but you need to be careful when communicating such data via SQL. Specifically, when you use a normal INSERT SQL statement and need to have binary strings among the VALUES you're inserting, you need to escape some characters in the binary string according to PostgreSQL's own rules. Fortunately, you don't have to figure out those rules for yourself: PostgreSQL supplies functions that do all the needed escaping, and psycopg exposes such a function to your Python programs as the Binary function. This recipe shows a typical case: the BYTEAs you're inserting come from cPickle.dumps, so they may represent almost arbitrary Python objects (although, in this case, we're just using them for a few lists of characters). The recipe is purely demonstrative and works by creating a table and dropping it at the end (using a try/finally statement to ensure finalization is performed even if the program terminates because of an uncaught exception).

Earlier PostgreSQL releases put limits of a few KB on the amount of data you could store in a normal field of the database. To store really large objects, you needed to use roundabout techniques to load the data into the database (such as PostgreSQL's nonstandard SQL function LO_IMPORT to load a datafile as an object, which requires superuser privileges and datafiles that reside on the machine running the PostgreSQL server) and store a field of type OID in the table to be used later for indirect recovery of the data. Fortunately, none of these techniques are necessary anymore: since Release 7.1 (the current release at the time of writing is 7.2.1), PostgreSQL embodies the results of project TOAST, which removes the limitations on field-storage size and therefore the need for peculiar indirection. psycopg supplies the handy Binary function to let you escape any binary string of bytes into a form acceptable for placeholder substitution in INSERT and UPDATE SQL statements.

See Also

Recipe 8.6 for a MySQL-oriented solution to the same problem; PostgresSQL's home page (*http://www.postgresql.org/*); the Python/PostgreSQL module (*http://initd.org/software/psycopg*).

8.8   Generating a Dictionary Mapping from Field Names to Column Numbers

Credit: Tom Jenkins

Problem

You want to access data fetched from a DB API cursor object, but you want to access the columns by field name, not by number.

Solution

Accessing columns within a set of database-fetched rows by column index is neither readable nor robust if columns are ever reordered. This recipe exploits the description attribute of Python DB API's cursor objects to build a dictionary that maps column names to index values, so you can use cursor_row[field_dict[fieldname]] to get the value of a named column:

```
def fields(cursor):
    """ Given a DB API 2.0 cursor object that has been executed, returns
    a dictionary that maps each field name to a column index; 0 and up. """
    results = {}
    column = 0
    for d in cursor.description:
        results[d[0]] = column
        column = column + 1

    return results
```

Discussion

When you get a set of rows from a call to:

```
cursor.fetch{one, many, all}
```

it is often helpful to be able to access a specific column in a row by the field name and not by the column number. This recipe shows a function that takes a DB API 2.0 cursor object and returns a dictionary with column numbers keyed to field names.

Here's a usage example (assuming you put this recipe's code in a module that you call *dbutils.py* somewhere on your sys.path):

```
>>> c = conn.cursor( )
>>> c.execute('''select * from country_region_goal where
crg_region_code is null''')
>>> import pprint
>>> pp = pprint.pprint
>>> pp(c.description)
(('CRG_ID', 4, None, None, 10, 0, 0),
 ('CRG_PROGRAM_ID', 4, None, None, 10, 0, 1),
 ('CRG_FISCAL_YEAR', 12, None, None, 4, 0, 1),
 ('CRG_REGION_CODE', 12, None, None, 3, 0, 1),
 ('CRG_COUNTRY_CODE', 12, None, None, 2, 0, 1),
 ('CRG_GOAL_CODE', 12, None, None, 2, 0, 1),
 ('CRG_FUNDING_AMOUNT', 8, None, None, 15, 0, 1))
>>> import dbutils
>>> field_dict = dbutils.fields(c)
>>> pp(field_dict)
{'CRG_COUNTRY_CODE': 4,
 'CRG_FISCAL_YEAR': 2,
 'CRG_FUNDING_AMOUNT': 6,
 'CRG_GOAL_CODE': 5,
 'CRG_ID': 0,
 'CRG_PROGRAM_ID': 1,
 'CRG_REGION_CODE': 3}
>>> row = c.fetchone( )
```

```
>>> pp(row)
(45, 3, '2000', None, 'HR', '26', 48509.0)
>>> ctry_code = row[field_dict['CRG_COUNTRY_CODE']]
>>> print ctry_code
HR
>>> fund = row[field_dict['CRG_FUNDING_AMOUNT']]
>>> print fund
48509.0
```

See Also

Recipe 8.9 for a slicker and more elaborate approach to the same task.

8.9 Using dtuple for Flexible Access to Query Results

Credit: Steve Holden

Problem

You want flexible access to sequences, such as the rows in a database query, by either name or column number.

Solution

Rather than coding your own solution, it's often more clever to reuse a good existing one. For this recipe's task, a good existing solution is packaged in Greg Stein's dtuple module:

```
import dtuple
import mx.ODBC.Windows as odbc

flist = ["Name", "Num", "LinkText"]

descr = dtuple.TupleDescriptor([[n] for n in flist])

conn = odbc.connect("HoldenWebSQL") # Connect to a database
curs = conn.cursor()                # Create a cursor

sql = """SELECT %s FROM StdPage
         WHERE PageSet='Std' AND Num<25
         ORDER BY PageSet, Num""" % ", ".join(flist)
print sql
curs.execute(sql)
rows = curs.fetchall()

for row in rows:
    row = dtuple.DatabaseTuple(descr, row)
    print "Attribute: Name: %s Number: %d" % (row.Name, row.Num or 0)
```

```
        print "Subscript: Name: %s Number: %d" % (row[0], row[1] or 0)
        print "Mapping:    Name: %s Number: %d" % (row["Name"], row["Num"] or 0)

    conn.close( )
```

Discussion

Novice Python programmers are often deterred from using databases because query results are presented by DB API–compliant modules as a list of tuples. Since these can only be numerically subscripted, code that uses the query results becomes opaque and difficult to maintain. Greg Stein's dtuple module, available from *http://www.lyra.org/greg/python/dtuple.py*, helps by defining two useful classes: TupleDescriptor and DatabaseTuple.

The TupleDescriptor class creates a description of tuples from a list of sequences, the first element of which is a column name. It is often convenient to describe data with such sequences. For example, in an interactive, or forms-based application, each column name might be followed by validation parameters such as data type and allowable length. TupleDescriptor's purpose is to allow the creation of DatabaseTuple objects. In this particular application, no other information about the columns is needed beyond the names, so the required list of sequences is constructed from a list of field names using a list comprehension.

Created from TupleDescriptor and a tuple such as a database row, DatabaseTuple is an object whose elements can be accessed by numeric subscript (like a tuple) or column-name subscript (like a dictionary). If column names are legal Python names, you can also access the columns in your DatabaseTuple as attributes. A purist might object to this crossover between items and attributes, but it's a highly pragmatic choice in this case, and Python is nothing if not a highly pragmatic language, so I see nothing wrong with this convenience.

To demonstrate the utility of DatabaseTuple, the simple test program in this recipe creates a TupleDescriptor and uses it to convert each row retrieved from a SQL query into DatabaseTuple. Because the sample uses the same field list to build both TupleDescriptor and the SQL SELECT statement, it demonstrates how database code can be parameterized relatively easily.

See Also

See Recipe 8.8 for a simple way to convert field names to column numbers; the dtuple module (*http://www.lyra.org/greg/python/dtuple.py*).

8.10 Pretty-Printing the Contents of Database Cursors

Credit: Steve Holden

Problem

You want to present a query's result with appropriate column headers and widths (optional), but you do not want to hardcode this information, which you may not even know when you're writing the code, in your program.

Solution

Discovering the column headers and widths dynamically is the most flexible approach, and it gives you code that's highly reusable over many such presentation tasks:

```
def pp(cursor, data=None, rowlens=0):
    d = cursor.description
    if not d:
        return "#### NO RESULTS ###"
    names = []
    lengths = []
    rules = []
    if not data:
        data = cursor.fetchall( )
    for dd in d:        # iterate over description
        l = dd[1]
        if not l:
            l = 12              # or default arg ...
        l = max(l, len(dd[0])) # Handle long names
        names.append(dd[0])
        lengths.append(l)
    for col in range(len(lengths)):
        if rowlens:
            rls = [len(row[col]) for row in data if row[col]]
            lengths[col] = max([lengths[col]]+rls)
        rules.append("-"*lengths[col])
    format = " ".join(["%%-%ss" % l for l in lengths])
    result = [format % tuple(names)]
    result.append(format % tuple(rules))
    for row in data:
        result.append(format % row)
    return "\n".join(result)
```

Discussion

Relational databases are often perceived as difficult to use. The Python DB API can make them much easier, but if your programs work with several different DB engines, it's sometimes tedious to reconcile the implementation differences between the various modules and the engines they connect to. One of the problems of dealing with databases is presenting the result of a query when you may not know much about the data. This recipe uses the cursor's description attribute to try and provide appropriate headings and optionally examines each output row to ensure column widths are adequate.

In some cases, a cursor can yield a solid description of the data it returns, but not all database modules are kind enough to supply cursors that do so. The pretty printer takes as an argument a cursor, on which you have just executed a retrieval operation (such as the execute of an SQL SELECT statement). It also takes an optional argument for the returned data; to use the data for other purposes, retrieve it from the cursor, typically with fetchall, and pass it in. The second optional argument tells the pretty printer to determine the column lengths from the data rather than from the cursor's description, which is helpful with some RDBMS engines and DB API module combinations.

A simple test program shows the value of the second optional argument when a Microsoft Jet database is used through the mxODBC module:

```
import mx.ODBC.Windows as odbc
import dbcp # contains pp function
conn = odbc.connect("MyDSN")
curs = conn.cursor( )
curs.execute("""SELECT Name, LinkText, Pageset FROM StdPage
ORDER BY PageSet, Name""")
rows = curs.fetchall( )
print "\n\nWithout rowlens:"
print dbcp.pp(curs, rows)
print "\n\nWith rowlens:"
print dbcp.pp(curs, rows, rowlens=1)
conn.close( )
```

In this case, the description does not include column lengths. The first output shows that the default column length of 12 is too short. The second output corrects this by examining the data:

```
Without rowlens:

Name         LinkText     Pageset
------------ ------------ ------------
ERROR        ERROR: Cannot Locate Page None
home         Home None
consult      Consulting Activity Std
contact      Contact Us    Std
expertise    Areas of Expertise Std
ffx          FactFaxer     Std
hardware     Hardware Platforms Std
ltree        Learning Tree Std
python       Python        Std
rates        Rates         Std
technol      Technologies Std
wcb          WebCallback   Std
```

With rowlens:

```
Name          LinkText                  Pageset
------------  ------------------------  ------------
ERROR         ERROR: Cannot Locate Page None
home          Home                      None
consult       Consulting Activity       Std
contact       Contact Us                Std
expertise     Areas of Expertise        Std
ffx           FactFaxer                 Std
hardware      Hardware Platforms        Std
ltree         Learning Tree             Std
python        Python                    Std
rates         Rates                     Std
technol       Technologies              Std
wcb           WebCallback               Std
```

This function is useful during testing, as it lets you easily verify that you are indeed retrieving what you expect from the database. The output is pretty enough to display ad hoc query outputs to users. The function currently makes no attempt to represent null values other than the None the DB API returns, though it could easily be modified to show a null string or some other significant value.

See Also

The mxODBC package, a DB API–compatible interface to ODBC (*http://www. egenix.com/files/python/mxODBC.html*).

8.11   Establishing Database Connections Lazily

Credit: John B. Dell'Aquila

Problem

You want to access a relational database via lazy connections (i.e., connections that are only established just in time) and access query results by column name rather than number.

Solution

Lazy (just-in-time) operation is sometimes very handy. This recipe transparently wraps any DB API–compliant interface (DCOracle, odbc, cx_oracle, etc.) and provides lazy evaluation and caching of database connections and a one-step query facility with data access by column name. As usual, a class is the right way to package this wrapper:

```
class Connection:
    """ Lazy proxy for database connection """
```

```python
    def __init__(self, factory, *args, **keywords):
        """ Initialize with factory method to generate DB connection
        (e.g., odbc.odbc, cx_Oracle.connect) plus any positional and/or
        keyword arguments required when factory is called. """
        self.__cxn = None
        self.__factory = factory
        self.__args = args
        self.__keywords = keywords

    def __getattr__(self, name):
        if self.__cxn is None:
            self.__cxn = self.__factory(*self.__args, **self.__keywords)
        return getattr(self.__cxn, name)

    def close(self):
        if self.__cxn is not None:
            self.__cxn.close()
            self.__cxn = None

    def __call__(self, sql, **keywords):
        """ Execute SQL query and return results. Optional keyword
        args are '%' substituted into query beforehand. """
        cursor = self.cursor()
        cursor.execute(sql % keywords)
        return RecordSet(
            [list(x) for x in cursor.fetchall()],
            [x[0].lower() for x in cursor.description]
            )


class RecordSet:
    """ Wrapper for tabular data """

    def __init__(self, tableData, columnNames):
        self.data = tableData
        self.columns = columnNames
        self.columnMap = {}
        for name,n in zip(columnNames, xrange(10000)):
            self.columnMap[name] = n

    def __getitem__(self, n):
        return Record(self.data[n], self.columnMap)

    def __setitem__(self, n, value):
        self.data[n] = value

    def __delitem__(self, n):
        del self.data[n]

    def __len__(self):
        return len(self.data)

    def __str__(self):
        return '%s: %s' % (self.__class__, self.columns)
```

```
class Record:
    """ Wrapper for data row. Provides access by
    column name as well as position. """

    def __init__(self, rowData, columnMap):
        self.__dict__['_data_'] = rowData
        self.__dict__['_map_'] = columnMap

    def __getattr__(self, name):
        return self._data_[self._map_[name]]

    def __setattr__(self, name, value):
        try:
            n = self._map_[name]
        except KeyError:
            self.__dict__[name] = value
        else:
            self._data_[n] = value

    def __getitem__(self, n):
        return self._data_[n]

    def __setitem__(self, n, value):
        self._data_[n] = value

    def __getslice__(self, i, j):
        return self._data_[i:j]

    def __setslice__(self, i, j, slice):
        self._data_[i:j] = slice

    def __len__(self):
        return len(self._data_)

    def __str__(self):
        return '%s: %s' % (self.__class__, repr(self._data_))
```

Discussion

The module implemented by this recipe, LazyDB, extends the DB API to provide lazy
connections (established only when needed) and access to query results by column
name. A LazyDB connection can transparently replace any normal DB API connection but is significantly more convenient, making SQL queries feel almost like a built-
in Python feature.

Here is a simple usage example:

```
import LazyDB, cx_Oracle
myDB = LazyDB.Connection(cx_Oracle.connect, 'user/passwd@server')
pctSQL = 'SELECT * FROM all_tables WHERE pct_used >= %(pct)s'
hogs = [(r.table_name, r.pct_used) for r in myDB(pctSQL, pct=90)]
```

You can wrap all your standard database connections with LazyDB and place them in a single module that you can import whenever you need a database. This keeps all your passwords in a single place and costs almost nothing, since connections aren't opened until you actually use them.

The one-step query facility cannot be used for extremely large result sets because fetchall will fail. It also shouldn't be used to run the same query multiple times with different parameters. For optimal performance, use the native DB API parameter substitution, so the SQL won't be reparsed each time.

Capitalization conventions vary among databases. LazyDB arbitrarily forces column names to lowercase to provide consistent Python attribute names and thus ease portability of your code among several databases.

See Also

The Python DB API (*http://www.python.org/topics/database/DatabaseAPI-2.0.html*).

8.12 Accessing a JDBC Database from a Jython Servlet

Credit: Brian Zhou

Problem

You're writing a servlet in Jython, and you need to connect to a database server (e.g., Oracle, Sybase, MS SQL Server, MySQL) via JDBC.

Solution

The technique is basically the same for any kind of database, give or take a couple of statements. Here's the code for when your database is Oracle:

```
import java, javax
class emp(javax.servlet.http.HttpServlet):
  def doGet(self, request, response):
    response.setContentType("text/plain")
    out = response.getOutputStream( )
    self.dbQuery(out)
    out.close( )
  def dbQuery(self, out):
    driver = "oracle.jdbc.driver.OracleDriver"
    java.lang.Class.forName(driver).newInstance( )
    server, db = "server", "ORCL"
    url = "jdbc:oracle:thin:@" + server + ":" + db
    usr, passwd = "scott", "tiger"
    conn = java.sql.DriverManager.getConnection(url, usr, passwd)
    query = "SELECT EMPNO, ENAME, JOB FROM EMP"
    stmt = conn.createStatement( )
```

```
        if stmt.execute(query):
            rs = stmt.getResultSet()
            while rs and rs.next():
                out.println(rs.getString("EMPNO"))
                out.println(rs.getString("ENAME"))
                out.println(rs.getString("JOB"))
                out.println()
        stmt.close()
        conn.close()
```

When your database is Sybase or Microsoft SQL Server, use the following:

```
import java, javax
class titles(javax.servlet.http.HttpServlet):
    def doGet(self, request, response):
        response.setContentType("text/plain")
        out = response.getOutputStream()
        self.dbQuery(out)
        out.close()
    def dbQuery(self, out):
        driver = "sun.jdbc.odbc.JdbcOdbcDriver"
        java.lang.Class.forName(driver).newInstance()
        # Use "pubs" DB for mssql and "pubs2" for Sybase
        url = "jdbc:odbc:myDataSource"
        usr, passwd = "sa", "password"
        conn = java.sql.DriverManager.getConnection(url, usr, passwd)
        query = "select title, price, ytd_sales, pubdate from titles"
        stmt = conn.createStatement()
        if stmt.execute(query):
            rs = stmt.getResultSet()
            while rs and rs.next():
                out.println(rs.getString("title"))
                if rs.getObject("price"):
                    out.println("%2.2f" % rs.getFloat("price"))
                else:
                    out.println("null")
                if rs.getObject("ytd_sales"):
                    out.println(rs.getInt("ytd_sales"))
                else:
                    out.println("null")
                out.println(rs.getTimestamp("pubdate").toString())
                out.println()
        stmt.close()
        conn.close()
```

And here's the code for when your database is MySQL:

```
import java, javax
class goosebumps(javax.servlet.http.HttpServlet):
    def doGet(self, request, response):
        response.setContentType("text/plain")
        out = response.getOutputStream()
        self.dbQuery(out)
```

```
        out.close( )
    def dbQuery(self, out):
        driver = "org.gjt.mm.mysql.Driver"
        java.lang.Class.forName(driver).newInstance( )
        server, db = "server", "test"
        usr, passwd = "root", "password"
        url = "jdbc:mysql://%s/%s?user=%s&password=%s" % (
            server, db, usr, passwd)
        conn = java.sql.DriverManager.getConnection(url)
        query = "select country, monster from goosebumps"
        stmt = conn.createStatement( )
        if stmt.execute(query):
            rs = stmt.getResultSet( )
            while rs and rs.next( ):
                out.println(rs.getString("country"))
                out.println(rs.getString("monster"))
                out.println( )
        stmt.close( )
```

Discussion

You might want to use different JDBC drivers and URLs, but you can see that the basic technique is quite simple and straightforward. This recipe's code uses a content type of text/plain because the recipe is about accessing the database, not about formatting the data you get from it. Obviously, you can change this to whatever content type is appropriate for your application.

In each case, the basic technique is first to instantiate the needed driver (whose package name, as a string, we place in variable driver) via the Java dynamic loading facility. The forName method of the java.lang.Class class loads and gives us the relevant Java class, and that class's newInstance method ensures that the driver we need is instantiated. Then, we can call the getConnection method of java.sql.DriverManager with the appropriate URL (or username and password, where needed) and thus obtain a connection object to place in the conn variable. From the connection object, we can create a statement object with the createStatement method and use it to execute a query that we have in the query string variable with the execute method. If the query succeeds, we can obtain the results with the getResultSet method. Finally, Oracle and MySQL allow easy sequential navigation of the result set to present all results, while Sybase and Microsoft SQL Server need a bit more care, but overall, the procedure is similar in all cases.

See Also

The Jython site (*http://www.jython.org*); JDBC's home page (*http://java.sun.com/products/jdbc*).

8.13 Module: jet2sql—Creating a SQL DDL from an Access Database

Credit: Matt Keranen

If you need to migrate a Jet (Microsoft Access *.mdb*) database to another DBMS system, or need to understand the Jet database structure in detail, you must reverse engineer from the database a standard ANSI SQL DDL description of its schema.

Example 8-1 reads the structure of a Jet database file using Microsoft's DAO services via Python COM and creates the SQL DDL necessary to recreate the same structure (schema). Microsoft DAO has long been stable (which in the programming world is almost a synonym for dead) and will never be upgraded, but that's not really a problem for us here, given the specific context of this recipe's use case. Additionally, the Jet database itself is almost stable, after all. You could, of course, recode this recipe to use the more actively maintained ADO services instead of DAO (or even the ADOX extensions), but my existing DAO-based solution seems to do all I require, so I was never motivated to do so, despite the fact that ADO and DAO are really close in programming terms.

This code was originally written to aid in migrating Jet databases to larger RDBMS systems through E/R design tools when the supplied import routines of said tools missed objects such as indexes and FKs. A first experiment in Python, it became a common tool.

Note that for most uses of COM from Python, for best results, you need to ensure that Python has read and cached the type library. Otherwise, for example, constant names cannot be used, since only type libraries hold those names. You would have to use numeric literals instead, seriously hampering readability and usability (not to mention the bother of finding out which numeric literals you should use, when all available documentation is written in terms of symbolic constants).

In recent releases of `win32all`, the simplest way to make sure that the type library has indeed been cached is to substitute, in lieu of the statement in the recipe:

```
daoEngine = win32com.client.Dispatch('DAO.DBEngine.36')
```

the equivalent statement:

```
daoEngine = win32com.client.gencache.EnsureDispatch('DAO.DBEngine.36')
```

`EnsureDispatch` ensures the relevant type library is cached, instantiates the requested COM server, and returns a reference just like `Dispatch` would.

Alternatively, you can use *makepy.py*, either by hand or through the Tools menu of PythonWin (in this case, from the COM Makepy Utility, select an entry such as Microsoft DAO 3.6 Library). Yet another possibility is calling `win32com.client.gencache.EnsureModule`, but this is inelegant and unwieldy, because you need to find out the UUID and version numbers for the (registered) type library you want to ensure is cached. The newer `EnsureDispatch` is far handier, since it takes a good old `ProgID` string, which is easier to find out, more readable, and more compact.

Microsoft's widespread Jet (a.k.a. Access) database engine isn't quite SQL-compliant, but it comes close. Using this engine, all you need to migrate a database to a standard SQL relational database is a little help in reverse engineering the details of the structure, as shown in Example 8-1.

Example 8-1. Creating a SQL DDL from an Access database

```
# jet2sql.py - Matthew C Keranen <mck@mpinet.net> [07/12/2000]
# ----------------------------------------------------------------------
# Creates ANSI SQL DDL from a MS Jet database file.  Useful to reverse
# engineer a database's design in various E/R tools.
#
# Requires DAO 3.6 library.
# ----------------------------------------------------------------------
# Usage: python jet2sql.py infile.MDB outfile.SQL

import sys, string, pythoncom, win32com.client

const = win32com.client.constants
daoEngine = win32com.client.Dispatch('DAO.DBEngine.36')

quot = chr(34)
class jetReverse:
    def __init__(self, infile):
        self.jetfilename=infile
        self.dtbs = daoEngine.OpenDatabase(infile)

    def terminate(self):
        pass

    def writeTable(self, currTabl):
        self.writeLine('\ncreate table '
            + quot + currTabl.Name + quot, "", 1)
        self.writeLine('(', "", 1)

        # Write columns
        cn=0
        for col in currTabl.Fields:
            cn = cn + 1
            self.writeColumn(col.Name, col.Type, col.Size,
                col.Required, col.Attributes, col.DefaultValue,
                col.ValidationRule, currTabl.Fields.Count-cn)

        # Validation rule
        tablRule = currTabl.ValidationRule
        if tablRule != "":
            tablRule = "    check(" + tablRule + ") "
            self.writeLine("", ",", 1) # add a comma and CR
            self.writeLine(tablRule, "", 0)
```

Example 8-1. Creating a SQL DDL from an Access database (continued)

```
        # Primary key
        pk=self.getPrimaryKey(currTabl)
        if pk <> "":
            self.writeLine("", ",", 1) # add a comma and CR
            self.writeLine(pk, "", 0)

        # End of table
        self.writeLine("", "", 1) # terminate previous line
        self.writeLine(');', "", 1)

        # Write table comment
        try: sql = currTabl.Properties("Description").Value
        except pythoncom.com_error: sql = ""
        if sql != "":
            sql = ("comment on table " + quot + currTabl.Name + quot +
                " is " + quot + sql + quot + ";")
            self.writeLine(sql, "", 1)

        # Write column comments
        for col in currTabl.Fields:
            try: sql = col.Properties("Description").Value
            except pythoncom.com_error: sql = ""
            if sql != "":
                sql = ("comment on column " + quot + currTabl.Name
                    + quot + "." + quot + col.Name + quot +
                    " is " + quot + sql + quot + ";")
                self.writeLine(sql,"",1)

        # Write indexes
        self.writeIndexes(currTabl)

    def writeColumn(self, colName, colType, length, requird,
        attributes, default, check, colRix):
        # colRix: 0-based index of column from right side
        # 0 indicates rightmost column
        if colType == const.dbByte: dataType = "Byte"
        elif colType == const.dbInteger: dataType = "Integer"
        elif colType == const.dbSingle: dataType = "Single"
        elif colType == const.dbDouble: dataType = "Double"
        elif colType == const.dbDate: dataType = "DateTime"
        elif colType == const.dbLongBinary: dataType = "OLE"
        elif colType == const.dbMemo: dataType = "Memo"
        elif colType == const.dbCurrency: dataType = "Currency"
        elif colType == const.dbLong:
            if attributes & const.dbAutoIncrField:
                dataType = "Counter"
            else:
                dataType = "LongInteger"
        elif colType == const.dbText:
            if length == 0: dataType = "Text"
            else: dataType = "char("+str(length)+")"
        elif colType == const.dbBoolean:
```

Example 8-1. Creating a SQL DDL from an Access database (continued)

```
                    dataType = "Bit"
                    if default == "Yes": default = "1"
                    else: default = "0"
                else:
                    if length == 0: dataType = "Text"
                    else: dataType = "Text("+str(length)+")"

                if default != "":
                    defaultStr = "default " + default + " "
                else: defaultStr = ""

                if check != "":
                    checkStr = "check(" + check + ") "
                else:
                    checkStr = ""

                if requird or (attributes & const.dbAutoIncrField):
                    mandatory = "not null "
                else:
                    mandatory = ""

                sql = ("     " + quot + colName + quot + " " + dataType
                    + " " + defaultStr + checkStr + mandatory)
                if colRix > 0:
                    self.writeLine(sql, ",", 1)
                else:
                    self.writeLine(sql, "", 0)

        def getPrimaryKey(self, currTabl):
            # Get primary key fields
            sql = ""
            for idx in currTabl.Indexes:
                if idx.Primary:
                    idxName = idx.Name
                    sql = "    primary key "
                    cn = 0
                    for col in idx.Fields:
                        cn = cn+1
                        sql = sql + quot + col.Name + quot
                        if idx.Fields.Count > cn: sql = sql + ","
            return sql

        def writeIndexes(self, currTabl):
            # Write index definition
            nIdx = -1
            for idx in currTabl.Indexes:
                nIdx = nIdx + 1
                idxName = idx.Name
                tablName = currTabl.Name
                if idx.Primary:
                    idxName = tablName + "_PK"
                elif idxName[:9] == "REFERENCE":
```

Example 8-1. Creating a SQL DDL from an Access database (continued)

```
            idxName = tablName + "_FK" + idxName[10:]
        else:
            idxName = tablName + "_IX" + str(nIdx)

        sql = "create "
        if idx.Unique: sql = sql + "unique "
        if idx.Clustered: sql = sql + "clustered "
        sql = sql + "index " + quot + idxName + quot
        sql = sql + " on " + quot + tablName + quot + " ("

        # Write index columns
        cn = 0
        for col in idx.Fields:
            cn = cn + 1
            sql = sql + quot + col.Name + quot
            if col.Attributes & const.dbDescending:
                sql = sql + " desc"
            else:
                sql = sql + " asc"
            if idx.Fields.Count > cn: sql = sql + ","

        sql = sql + " );"

        self.writeLine(sql,"",1)

    def writeForeignKey(self, currRefr):
        # Export foreign key
        sql = "\nalter table " + quot + currRefr.ForeignTable + quot
        self.writeLine(sql, "", 1)

        sql = "    add foreign key ("
        cn = 0
        for col in currRefr.Fields:
            cn = cn + 1
            sql = sql + quot + col.ForeignName + quot
            if currRefr.Fields.Count > cn: sql = sql + ","

        sql = sql + ")"
        self.writeLine(sql, "", 1)

        sql = "    references " + quot + currRefr.Table + quot + " ("
        cn = 0
        for col in currRefr.Fields:
            cn = cn + 1
            sql = sql + quot + col.Name + quot
            if currRefr.Fields.Count > cn: sql = sql + ","

        sql = sql + ")"
        if currRefr.Attributes & const.dbRelationUpdateCascade:
            sql = sql + " on update cascade"
        if currRefr.Attributes & const.dbRelationDeleteCascade:
            sql = sql + " on delete cascade"
```

Example 8-1. Creating a SQL DDL from an Access database (continued)

```
        sql = sql + ";"
        self.writeLine(sql, "", 1)

    def writeQuery(self, currQry):
        sql = "\ncreate view " + quot + currQry.Name + quot + " as"
        self.writeLine(sql, "", 1)

        # Write query text
        sql = string.replace(currQry.SQL, chr(13), "") # Remove extra \ns
        self.writeLine(sql, "", 1)

        # Write query comment
        try: sql = currQry.Properties("Description").Value
        except pythoncom.com_error: sql = ""
        if sql <> "":
            sql = ("comment on table " + quot + currQry.Name +
                quot + " is " + quot + sql + quot)
            self.writeLine(sql,"",1)

    def writeLine(self, strLine, delimit, newline):
        # Used for controlling where lines terminate with a comma
        # or other continuation mark
        sqlfile.write(strLine)
        if delimit: sqlfile.write(delimit)
        if newline: sqlfile.write('\n')

if __name__ == '__main__':
    if len(sys.argv) != 3:
        print "Usage: jet2sql.py infile.mdb outfile.sql"
    else:
        jetEng = jetReverse(sys.argv[1])
        outfile = sys.argv[2]
        sqlfile = open(outfile,'w')
        print "\nReverse engineering %s to %s" % (
            jetEng.jetfilename, outfile)

        # Tables
        sys.stdout.write("\n   Tables")
        for tabl in jetEng.dtbs.TableDefs:
            if tabl.Name[:4] != "MSys" and tabl.Name[:4] != "~TMP":
                sys.stdout.write(".")
                jetEng.writeTable(tabl)
            else:
                sys.stdout.write(",")

        # Relations/FKs
        sys.stdout.write("\n   Relations")
        for fk in jetEng.dtbs.Relations:
            sys.stdout.write(".")
            jetEng.writeForeignKey(fk)

        # Queries
        sys.stdout.write("\n   Queries")
```

Example 8-1. Creating a SQL DDL from an Access database (continued)

```
        for qry in jetEng.dtbs.QueryDefs:
            sys.stdout.write(".")
            jetEng.writeQuery(qry)

    print "\n   Done\n"

    # Done
    sqlfile.close( )
    jetEng.terminate( )
```

## CHAPTER 9

User Interfaces

9.0 Introduction

Credit: Fredrik Lundh, SecretLabs AB (PythonWare), author of Python Standard Library

Back in the early days of interactive computing, most computers offered terminals that looked and behaved pretty much like clunky typewriters. The main difference from an ordinary typewriter was that the computer was in the loop. It could read what the user typed and print hardcopy output on a roll of paper.

So when you found yourself in front of a 1960s Teletype ASR-33, the only reasonable way to communicate with the computer was to type a line of text, press the send key, hope that the computer would manage to figure out what you meant, and wait for the response to appear on the paper roll. This line-oriented way of communicating with your computer is known as a *command-line interface* (CLI).

Some 40 years later, the paper roll has been replaced with high-resolution video displays, which can display text in multiple typefaces, color photographs, and even animated 3D graphics. The keyboard is still around, but we also have pointing devices such as the mouse, trackballs, game controls, touchpads, and other input devices.

The combination of a graphics display and the mouse made it possible to create a new kind of user interface: the *graphical user interface* (GUI). When done right, a GUI can give the user a better overview of what a program can do (and what it is doing), and make it easier to carry out many kinds of tasks.

However, most programming languages, including Python, make it easy to write programs using teletype-style output and input. In Python, you use the `print` statement to print text to the display and the `input` and `raw_input` functions to read expressions and text strings from the keyboard.

Creating graphical user interfaces takes more work. You need access to functions to draw text and graphics on the screen, select typefaces and styles, and read information from the keyboard and other input devices. You need to write code to interact with other applications (via a window manager), keep your windows updated when the user moves them around, and respond to key presses and mouse actions.

To make this a bit easier, programmers have developed *graphical user interface toolkits*, which provide standard solutions to these problems. A typical GUI toolkit provides a number of ready-made GUI building blocks, usually called *widgets*. Common standard widgets include text and image labels, buttons, and text-entry fields. Many toolkits also provide more advanced widgets, such as Tkinter's Text widget, which is a rather competent text editor/display component.

All major toolkits are *event-based*. This means that your program hands control over to the toolkit (usually by calling a main loop function or method). The toolkit then calls back into your application when certain events occur—for example, when the user clicks OK in a dialog, when a window needs to be redrawn, and so on. Most toolkits also provide ways to position widgets on the screen automatically (e.g., in tables, rows, or columns) and to modify widget behavior and appearance.

Tkinter is the de-facto standard toolkit for Python and comes with most Python distributions. Tkinter provides an object-oriented layer on top of the Tcl/Tk GUI library and runs on Windows, Unix, and Macintosh systems. Tkinter is easy to use but provides a relatively small number of standard widgets. Tkinter extension libraries, such as Pmw and Tix, supply many components missing from plain Tkinter, and you can use Tkinter's advanced Text and Canvas widgets to create custom widgets. The Widget Construction Kit lets you write all sorts of new widgets in pure Python and is available as part of the uiToolkit product (*http://www.pythonware.com/products/uitoolkit/*) and also as part of Tkinter 3000 (*http://effbot.org/tkinter/*), which is currently in the alpha stage.

wxPython (*http://www.wxPython.org*) is another popular toolkit; it is based on the wxWindows C++ library (*http://www.wxWindows.org*). wxPython is modeled somewhat after the Windows MFC library but is available for multiple platforms. wxPython provides a rich set of widgets, and it's relatively easy to create custom widgets.

PyGTK (*http://www.daa.com.au/~james/pygtk*) is an object-oriented Python interface to the GTK toolkit, used in projects such as Gnome and the Gimp. This is a good choice for Linux applications, especially if you want them to run in the Gnome environment.

PyQt (*http://www.riverbankcomputing.co.uk/pyqt/index.php*) is a Python wrapper for TrollTech's Qt library (*http://www.trolltech.com*), which is the basis of the popular KDE environment, as well as the Qtopia environment for handheld computers; it also runs on Windows and Mac OS/X. Qt requires license fees for commercial (non-free software) use but is free for free software development; PyQt itself is always free.

You can also use many other toolkits from Python. Mark Hammond's PythonWin gives access to Windows MFC. There are also interfaces to Motif/X11 and MacIntosh native toolboxes, and many other toolkits. Cameron Laird maintains a list of toolkits at *http://starbase.neosoft.com/~claird/comp.lang.python/python_GUI.html*. It currently lists about 20 toolkits.

Finally, the anygui project (*www.anygui.org*) is working on a unified Python API for the above toolkits (and others, including Java's Swing toolkit, which is used with the Jython version of Python, and text screens driven with, or even without, the curses library). The new unified API is implemented by a shared front-end layer and small, specific backends sitting on top of the many existing libraries.

9.1   Avoiding lambda in Writing Callback Functions

Credit: Danny Yoo

Problem

You need to use many callbacks without arguments, typically while writing a Tkinter-based GUI, and would rather avoid using `lambda`.

Solution

Between the classic `lambda` approach and a powerful general-purpose currying mechanism, there's a third, extremely simple way that can come in handy in many practical cases:

```
class Command:
    def __init__(self, callback, *args, **kwargs):
        self.callback = callback
        self.args = args
        self.kwargs = kwargs

    def __call__(self):
        return apply(self.callback, self.args, self.kwargs)
```

Discussion

I remember seeing this utility class a while back, but don't remember who to attribute it to. Perhaps I saw this in John E. Grayson's book, *Python and Tkinter Programming* (Manning).

Writing a lot of callbacks that give customized arguments can look a little awkward with `lambda`, so this `Command` class gives an alternative syntax that looks nicer. For example:

```
import Tkinter
def hello(name): print "Hello", name
root = Tk( )
```

```
# the lambda way of doing it:
Button(root, text="Guido", command=lambda name="Guido": hello(name)).pack( )

# using the Command class:
Button(root, text="Guido", command=Command(hello, "Guido")).pack( )
```

Of course, you can also use a more general currying approach, which lets you fix some of the arguments when you bind the callback, while others may be given at call time (see Recipe 15.7). However, "doing the simplest thing that can possibly work" is a good programming principle. If your application needs some callbacks that fix all arguments at currying time and others that leave some arguments to be determined at callback time, it's probably simpler to use the more general currying approach for all the callbacks. But if all the callbacks you need must fix all arguments at currying time, it may be simpler to forego unneeded generality and use the simpler, less-general approach in this recipe exclusively. You can always refactor later if it turns out you need the generality.

See Also

Recipe 15.7; information about Tkinter can be obtained from a variety of sources, such as Pythonware's *An Introduction to Tkinter*, by Fredrik Lundh (*http://www.pythonware.com/library*), New Mexico Tech's *Tkinter reference* (*http://www.nmt.edu/tcc/help/lang/python/docs.html*), and various books.

9.2   Creating Menus with Tkinter

Credit: Luther Blissett

Problem

You want to create a window that has a menu bar at the top.

Solution

Use the Tkinter Menu widget:

```
import sys
from Tkinter import *

root = Tk( )

# Insert a menu bar on the main window
menubar = Menu(root)
root.config(menu=menubar)

# Create a menu button labeled "File" that brings up a menu
filemenu = Menu(menubar)
menubar.add_cascade(label='File', menu=filemenu)
```

```
# Create entries in the "File" menu
# simulated command functions that we want to invoke from our menus
def doPrint(): print 'doPrint'
def doSave(): print 'doSave'
filemenu.add_command(label='Print', command=doPrint)
filemenu.add_command(label='Save', command=doSave)
filemenu.add_separator()
filemenu.add_command(label='Quit', command=sys.exit)

root.mainloop()
```

Discussion

Menus in Tkinter applications are handled entirely by the Menu widget. As shown in the recipe, you use Menu both for the top-level menu bar (which you add to a top-level window as its menu configuration setting) and for cascading menus (which you add to the menu bar, or to other menus, with the add_cascade method).

A menu can have several kinds of entries. A cascade entry pops up a submenu when the user selects it, and is added with add_cascade. A command entry calls a function when the user selects it, and is added with add_command. A separator visually separates other entries, and is added with add_separator.

A checkbutton entry is added with add_checkbutton and has an associated Tkinter IntVar, with an on value and an off value. If the associated variable has the on value, the entry displays a check besides its value; if it has the off value, it doesn't. When the user selects the entry, this toggles the state of the variable:

```
vdebug = IntVar()
filemenu.add_checkbutton(label='Debug', var=vdebug)
```

You can access the value of vdebug by calling vdebug.get and set it to any integer value n by calling vdebug.set(n). A checkbutton entry can also optionally have a command to call a function when the user selects it.

A group of radiobutton entries is associated with a single IntVar instance. Only one radiobutton associated with that variable can be on at any time. Selecting a radiobutton gives the variable the value associated with it:

```
vlevel = IntVar()
filemenu.add_radiobutton(label='Level 1', var=vlevel, value=1)
filemenu.add_radiobutton(label='Level 2', var=vlevel, value=2)
filemenu.add_radiobutton(label='Level 3', var=vlevel, value=3)
```

A radiobutton entry can also optionally have a command to call a function when the user selects it.

See Also

Information about Tkinter can be obtained from a variety of sources, such as Pythonware's *An Introduction to Tkinter*, by Fredrik Lundh (*http://www.pythonware. com/library*), New Mexico Tech's *Tkinter reference* (*http://www.nmt.edu/tcc/help/ lang/python/docs.html*), and various books.

9.3   Creating Dialog Boxes with Tkinter

Credit:Luther Blissett

Problem

You want to create a dialog box (i.e., a new top-level window with buttons to make the window go away).

Solution

For the simplest jobs, you can use the Tkinter Dialog widget:

```
import Dialog

def ask(title, text, strings=('Yes', 'No'), bitmap='questhead', default=0):
    d = Dialog.Dialog(
            title=title, text=text, bitmap=bitmap, default=default, strings=strings)
    return strings[d.num]
```

This function shows a modal dialog with the given title and text and as many buttons as there are items in strings. The function doesn't return until the user clicks a button, at which point it returns the string that labels the button.

Discussion

Dialog is simplest when all you want is a dialog box with some text, a title, a bitmap, and all the buttons you want, each with a string label of your choice.

On the other hand, when you're happy with the standard OK and Cancel buttons, you may want to import the tkSimpleDialog module instead. It offers the askinteger, askfloat, and askstring functions, each of which accepts title and prompt arguments, as well as, optionally, initialvalue, minvalue, and maxvalue:

```
import tkSimpleDialog
x = tkSimpleDialog.askinteger("Choose an integer", "Between 1 and 6 please:",
    initialvalue=1, minvalue=1, maxvalue=6)
print x
```

Each function pops up a suitable, simple modal dialog and returns either a value entered by the user that meets the constraints you gave, or None if the user clicks Cancel.

See Also

Information about Tkinter can be obtained from a variety of sources, such as Pythonware's *An Introduction to Tkinter*, by Fredrik Lundh (*http://www.pythonware. com/library*), New Mexico Tech's *Tkinter reference* (*http://www.nmt.edu/tcc/help/ lang/python/docs.html*), and various books.

9.4 Supporting Multiple Values per Row in a Tkinter Listbox

Credit: Brent Burley

Problem

You need a Tkinter widget that works just like a normal Listbox but with multiple values per row.

Solution

When you find a functional limitation in Tkinter, most often the best solution is to build your own widget as a Python class, subclassing an appropriate existing Tkinter widget (often Frame, so you can easily aggregate several native Tkinter widgets into your own compound widget) and extending and tweaking its functionality when necessary. Rather than solving the problems of just one application, this gives you a reusable component that you can reuse in many applications. For example, here's a way to make a multicolumn equivalent of a Tkinter Listbox:

```python
from Tkinter import *

class MultiListbox(Frame):
    def __init__(self, master, lists):
        Frame.__init__(self, master)
        self.lists = []
        for l,w in lists:
            frame = Frame(self); frame.pack(side=LEFT, expand=YES, fill=BOTH)
            Label(frame, text=l, borderwidth=1, relief=RAISED).pack(fill=X)
            lb = Listbox(frame, width=w, borderwidth=0, selectborderwidth=0,
                         relief=FLAT, exportselection=FALSE)
            lb.pack(expand=YES, fill=BOTH)
            self.lists.append(lb)
            lb.bind('<B1-Motion>', lambda e, s=self: s._select(e.y))
            lb.bind('<Button-1>', lambda e, s=self: s._select(e.y))
            lb.bind('<Leave>', lambda e: 'break')
            lb.bind('<B2-Motion>', lambda e, s=self: s._b2motion(e.x, e.y))
            lb.bind('<Button-2>', lambda e, s=self: s._button2(e.x, e.y))
        frame = Frame(self); frame.pack(side=LEFT, fill=Y)
        Label(frame, borderwidth=1, relief=RAISED).pack(fill=X)
        sb = Scrollbar(frame, orient=VERTICAL, command=self._scroll)
```

```
        sb.pack(expand=YES, fill=Y)
        self.lists[0]['yscrollcommand']=sb.set

    def _select(self, y):
        row = self.lists[0].nearest(y)
        self.selection_clear(0, END)
        self.selection_set(row)
        return 'break'

    def _button2(self, x, y):
        for l in self.lists: l.scan_mark(x, y)
        return 'break'

    def _b2motion(self, x, y):
        for l in self.lists: l.scan_dragto(x, y)
        return 'break'

    def _scroll(self, *args):
        for l in self.lists:
            apply(l.yview, args)

    def curselection(self):
        return self.lists[0].curselection()

    def delete(self, first, last=None):
        for l in self.lists:
            l.delete(first, last)

    def get(self, first, last=None):
        result = []
        for l in self.lists:
            result.append(l.get(first,last))
        if last: return apply(map, [None] + result)
        return result

    def index(self, index):
        self.lists[0].index(index)

    def insert(self, index, *elements):
        for e in elements:
            i = 0
            for l in self.lists:
                l.insert(index, e[i])
                i = i + 1

    def size(self):
        return self.lists[0].size()

    def see(self, index):
        for l in self.lists:
            l.see(index)
```

```
        def selection_anchor(self, index):
            for l in self.lists:
                l.selection_anchor(index)

        def selection_clear(self, first, last=None):
            for l in self.lists:
                l.selection_clear(first, last)

        def selection_includes(self, index):
            return self.lists[0].selection_includes(index)

        def selection_set(self, first, last=None):
            for l in self.lists:
                l.selection_set(first, last)

    if __name__ == '__main__':
        tk = Tk()
        Label(tk, text='MultiListbox').pack()
        mlb = MultiListbox(tk, (('Subject', 40), ('Sender', 20), ('Date', 10)))
        for i in range(1000):
          mlb.insert(END,
                ('Important Message: %d' % i, 'John Doe', '10/10/%04d' % (1900+i)))
        mlb.pack(expand=YES,fill=BOTH)
        tk.mainloop()
```

Discussion

This recipe shows a compound widget that gangs multiple Tk Listbox widgets to a single scrollbar to achieve a simple multicolumn scrolled listbox. Most of the Listbox API is mirrored to make the widget act like the normal Listbox, but with multiple values per row. The resulting widget is lightweight, fast, and easy to use. The main drawback is that only text is supported, which is a fundamental limitation of the underlying Listbox widget.

In this implementation, only single-selection is allowed, but it could be extended to multiple selection. User-resizable columns and auto-sorting by clicking on the column label should also be possible. Auto-scrolling while dragging Button-1 was disabled because it broke the synchronization between the lists. However, scrolling with Button-2 works fine.

One note about the implementation: in the MultiListbox.__init__ method, several lambda forms are used as the callable second arguments (callbacks) of the bind method calls on the contained Listbox widgets. This is traditional, but if you share in the widespread dislike for lambda, note that lambda is never truly necessary. In this case, the easiest way to avoid the lambdas is to redefine all the relevant methods (_select, _button2, etc.) as taking two formal arguments (self, e) and extract the data they need from argument e. Then in the bind calls you can simply pass the bound self._select method, and so on.

See Also

Information about Tkinter can be obtained from a variety of sources, such as Pythonware's *An Introduction to Tkinter*, by Fredrik Lundh (*http://www.pythonware. com/library*), New Mexico Tech's *Tkinter reference* (*http://www.nmt.edu/tcc/help/ lang/python/docs.html*), and various books.

9.5 Embedding Inline GIFs Using Tkinter

Credit: Brent Burley

Problem

You need to embed GIF images inside your source code—for use in Tkinter buttons, labels, etc.—to make toolbars and the like without worrying about installing the right icon files.

Solution

A lively Tkinter GUI can include many small images. However, you probably shouldn't require that a small GIF file be present for each of these; ensuring the presence of many small files is a bother, and if they're missing, your GUI may be unusable or look wrong. Fortunately, you can construct Tkinter `PhotoImage` objects with inline data. It's easy to convert a GIF to inline form as Python source code:

```
import base64
print "icon='''\\n" + base64.encodestring(open("icon.gif").read()) + "'''"
```

You can then split the result into lines of reasonable length:

```
icon='''R0lGODdhFQAVAPMAAAAQ2PESapISCBASCBMTCxPxmNCQiJJya/ISChGRmzPz+/PxmzDQyZ
DQyZDQyZDQyZCwAAAAAFQAVAAAElJDISau9Vh2WMDOgqHHelJwnsXVloqDd2hrMm8pYYiSHYfMMRm
53ULlQHGFFx1MZCciUiVOsPmEkKNVp3UBhJ40hy1UxerSgJGZMMBbcBACQlVhRiHvaUsXHgywTdyc
LdxyB gm1vcTyIZW4MeU6NgQEBXEGRcQcI1wQIAwEHoioCAgWmCZ0Iq5+hA6wIpqislgGhthEAOw==
'''
```

and use it in Tkinter:

```
import Tkinter
root = Tkinter.Tk( )
iconImage = Tkinter.PhotoImage(master=root, data=icon)
Tkinter.Button(image=iconImage).pack( )
```

Discussion

The basic technique is to encode the GIF with the standard Python module `base64` and store the results as a string literal in the Python code, which will be passed to Tkinter's `PhotoImage`. The current release of `PhotoImage` supports GIF and PPM, but inline data is supported only for GIF. You can use `file='filename'`, instead of `data=string`, for either GIF or PPM.

You must keep a reference to the PhotoImage object yourself; it is not kept by the Tkinter widget. If you pass it to Button and forget it, you will become very frustrated! Here's an easy workaround for this minor annoyance:

```
def makeImageWidget(icondata, *args, **kwds):
    if args: klass = args.pop(0)
    else: klass = Tkinter.Button
    class Widget(klass):
        def __init__(self, image, *args, **kwds):
            kwds['image']=image
            klass.__init__(self, args, kwds)
            self.__image = image
    return Widget(Tkinter.PhotoImage(data=icondata), *args, **kwds)
```

Using this, the equivalent of the example in the recipe becomes:

```
makeImageWidget(icon).pack( )
```

The master argument on PhotoImage is optional; it defaults to the default application window. If you create a new application window (by calling Tk again), you will need to create your images in that context and supply the master argument, so the makeImageWidget function would need to be updated to let you optionally pass the master argument to the PhotoImage constructor. However, most applications do not require this.

See Also

Information about Tkinter can be obtained from a variety of sources, such as Pythonware's *An Introduction to Tkinter*, by Fredrik Lundh (*http://www.pythonware. com/library*), New Mexico Tech's *Tkinter reference* (*http://www.nmt.edu/tcc/help/ lang/python/docs.html*), and various books.

9.6   Combining Tkinter and Asynchronous I/O with Threads

Credit: Jacob Hallén

Problem

You need to access sockets, serial ports, and do other asynchronous (but blocking) I/O while running a Tkinter-based GUI.

Solution

The solution is to handle a Tkinter interface on one thread and communicate to it (via Queue objects) the events on I/O channels handled by other threads:

```
import Tkinter
import time
```

```
import threading
import random
import Queue

class GuiPart:
    def __init__(self, master, queue, endCommand):
        self.queue = queue
        # Set up the GUI
        console = Tkinter.Button(master, text='Done', command=endCommand)
        console.pack()
        # Add more GUI stuff here depending on your specific needs

    def processIncoming(self):
        """Handle all messages currently in the queue, if any."""
        while self.queue.qsize():
            try:
                msg = self.queue.get(0)
                # Check contents of message and do whatever is needed. As a
                # simple test, print it (in real life, you would
                # suitably update the GUI's display in a richer fashion).
                print msg
            except Queue.Empty:
                # just on general principles, although we don't
                # expect this branch to be taken in this case
                pass

class ThreadedClient:
    """
    Launch the main part of the GUI and the worker thread. periodicCall and
    endApplication could reside in the GUI part, but putting them here
    means that you have all the thread controls in a single place.
    """
    def __init__(self, master):
        """
        Start the GUI and the asynchronous threads. We are in the main
        (original) thread of the application, which will later be used by
        the GUI as well. We spawn a new thread for the worker (I/O).
        """
        self.master = master

        # Create the queue
        self.queue = Queue.Queue()

        # Set up the GUI part
        self.gui = GuiPart(master, self.queue, self.endApplication)

        # Set up the thread to do asynchronous I/O
        # More threads can also be created and used, if necessary
        self.running = 1
        self.thread1 = threading.Thread(target=self.workerThread1)
        self.thread1.start()
```

```
        # Start the periodic call in the GUI to check if the queue contains
        # anything
        self.periodicCall( )

    def periodicCall(self):
        """
        Check every 200 ms if there is something new in the queue.
        """
        self.gui.processIncoming( )
        if not self.running:
            # This is the brutal stop of the system. You may want to do
            # some cleanup before actually shutting it down.
            import sys
            sys.exit(1)
        self.master.after(200, self.periodicCall)

    def workerThread1(self):
        """
        This is where we handle the asynchronous I/O. For example, it may be
        a 'select( )'. One important thing to remember is that the thread has
        to yield control pretty regularly, by select or otherwise.
        """
        while self.running:
            # To simulate asynchronous I/O, we create a random number at
            # random intervals. Replace the following two lines with the real
            # thing.
            time.sleep(rand.random( ) * 1.5)
            msg = rand.random( )
            self.queue.put(msg)

    def endApplication(self):
        self.running = 0

rand = random.Random( )
root = Tkinter.Tk( )

client = ThreadedClient(root)
root.mainloop( )
```

Discussion

This recipe shows the easiest way of handling access to sockets, serial ports, and
other asynchronous I/O ports while running a Tkinter-based GUI. Note that the recipe's principles generalize to other GUI toolkits, since most of them make it preferable to access the GUI itself from a single thread, and all offer a toolkit-dependent way
to set up periodic polling as this recipe does.

Tkinter, like most other GUIs, is best used with all graphic commands in a single
thread. On the other hand, it's far more efficient to make I/O channels block, then
wait for something to happen, rather than using nonblocking I/O and having to poll
at regular intervals. The latter approach may not even be available in some cases,

since not all data sources support nonblocking I/O. Therefore, for generality as well as for efficiency, we should handle I/O with a separate thread, or more than one. The I/O threads can communicate in a safe way with the main, GUI-handling thread through one or more Queues. In this recipe, the GUI thread still has to do some polling (on the Queues), to check if something in the Queue needs to be processed. Other architectures are possible, but they are much more complex than the one in this recipe. My advice is to start with this recipe, which will handle your needs over 90% of the time, and explore the much more complex alternatives only if it turns out that this approach cannot meet your performance requirements.

This recipe lets a worker thread block in a select (simulated by random sleeps in the recipe's example worker thread). Whenever something arrives, it is received and inserted in a Queue. The main (GUI) thread polls the Queue five times per second (often enough that the end user will not notice any significant delay, but rarely enough that the computational load on the computer will be negligible—you may want to fine-tune this, depending on your exact needs) and processes all messages that have arrived since it last checked.

This recipe seems to solve a common problem, since there is a question about how to do it a few times a month in *comp.lang.python*. There are other solutions, involving synchronization between threads, that let you solve such problems without polling (the root.after call in the recipe). Unfortunately, such solutions are generally complicated and messy, since you tend to raise and wait for semaphores throughout your code. In any case, a GUI already has several polling mechanisms built into it (the main event loop), so adding one more won't make much difference, especially since it seldom runs. The code has been tested only under Linux, but it should work on any platform with working threads, including Windows.

See Also

Documentation of the standard library modules threading and Queue in the *Library Reference*; information about Tkinter can be obtained from a variety of sources, such as Pythonware's *An Introduction to Tkinter*, by Fredrik Lundh (*http://www.pythonware.com/library*), New Mexico Tech's *Tkinter reference* (*http://www.nmt.edu/tcc/help/lang/python/docs.html*), and various books.

9.7   Using a wxPython Notebook with Panels
Credit: Mark Nenadov

Problem

You want to design a wxPython GUI comprised of multiple panels—each driven by a separate Python script running in the background—that let the user switch back and forth (i.e., a wxPython Notebook).

Solution

Notebooks are a powerful GUI approach, as they let the user select the desired view from several options at any time with an instinctive button click. wxPython supports this by supplying a wxNotebook widget:

```
from wxPython.wx import *

class MainFrame(wxFrame):
    #
    # snipped: mainframe class attributes
    #
    def __init__(self, parent, id, title):
        #
        # snipped: frame-specific initialization
        #

        # Create the notebook
        self.nb = wxNotebook(self, -1,
            wxPoint(0,0), wxSize(0,0), wxNB_FIXEDWIDTH)

        # Populate the notebook with pages (panels)
        panel_names = "First Panel", "Second Panel", "The Third One"
        panel_scripts = "panel1", "panel2", "panel3"
        for name, script in zip(panel_names, panel_scripts):
            # Make panel named 'name' (driven by script 'script'.py)
            self.module = __import__(script, globals())
            self.window = self.module.runPanel(self, self.nb)
            if self.window: self.nb.AddPage(self.window, name)

        #
        # snipped: rest of frame initialization
        #
```

Discussion

wxPython provides a powerful notebook user-interface object, with multiple panels, each of which is built and driven by a separate Python script. Each panel's script runs in the background, even when the panel is not selected, and maintains state as the user switches back and forth.

Of course, this recipe isn't a fully functional wxPython application, but it demonstrates how to use notebooks and panels (which it loads by importing files) adequately. Of course, this recipe assumes that you have files named *panel1.py*, *panel2.py*, and *panel3.py*, each of which contains a runPanel function that returns a wxPanel object. The specific notebook functionality is easy: the notebook object is created by the wxNotebook function, and an instance of this recipe's MainFrame class saves its notebook object as the self.nb instance attribute. Then, each page (a wxPanel object) is added to the notebook by calling the notebook's AddPage method, with the page object as the first argument and a name string as the second. Your code only needs to make the notebook and its panels usable; the wxWindows framework, as wrapped by the wxPython package, handles all the rest on your behalf.

See Also

wxPython, and the wxWindows toolkit it depends on, are described in detail at *http://www.wxPython.org* and *http://www.wxWindows.org*.

9.8   Giving the User Unobtrusive Feedback During Data Entry with Qt

Credit: Alex Martelli

Problem

You want to validate the contents of a line-entry widget on the fly while the user is entering data and give unobtrusive feedback about whether the current contents are valid, incomplete, or invalid.

Solution

Changing the widget's background color to different shades is an excellent way to provide unobtrusive feedback during data entry. As usual, it's best to package the solution as a reusable widget:

```
from qt import *

class ValidatingLineEdit(QLineEdit):

    colors = Qt.red, Qt.yellow, Qt.green

    def __init__(self, validate, parent=None, name=None):
        QLineEdit.__init__(self, parent, name)
        self.validate = validate
        self.connect(self, SIGNAL("textChanged(const QString &)"), self.changed)
        self.color = None
        self.changed('')

    def changed(self, newText):
        colorIndex = self.validate(unicode(newText))
        if colorIndex is None: return
        color = self.colors[colorIndex].light(196)
        if color != self.color:
            self.setPaletteBackgroundColor(color)
            self.color = color
```

The function passed as the validate argument must accept a Unicode string and return either None, meaning no color change, or an index into the widget's colors attribute. By default, 0 indicates red (an incorrect entry), 1 indicates yellow (an incomplete entry), and 2 indicates green (an entry that is already acceptable).

Discussion

When the user is entering data in a line-entry field, it can be helpful to validate the field's contents on the fly, at every change, and give unobtrusive feedback about whether the current content is valid, incomplete, or invalid. One way to do this is by setting the field's background color accordingly (using light pastel shades, not strong contrast colors, so the feedback is unobtrusive).

Qt has a reputation for being cranky about color control, but Qt 3 now supplies the setPaletteBackgroundColor method on all widgets, which is effective for our specific purpose. This recipe packages a LineEdit widget with the minimal amount of infrastructure to ensure that the background color is changed appropriately, based on a validation function that you pass when you instantiate the widget.

Here is a simple validation function, suitable for instantiating a ValidatingLineEdit widget. As an example criterion, this function assumes that a valid entry is one containing 4, 5, or 6 digits, and no character that is not a digit:

```python
def validate(text):
    if not text: return 1            # empty -> "incomplete"
    if not text.isdigit(): return 0  # nondigits -> "invalid"
    if len(text) < 4: return 1       # too short -> "incomplete"
    if len(text) > 6: return 0       # too long -> "invalid"
    return 2                         # otherwise -> "acceptable"
```

Note that you can also customize the widget's colors attribute by assigning to it a tuple of QColor instances of your choice at any time. The validation function must always return either None, meaning no color change, or a valid index into the widget's current colors attribute.

If content-validation takes a long time, you should delay validating the field and wait until the user is done with it. Often, a good time for relatively lengthy validation is when the entry widget loses focus, although it may be simplest (but maybe not as effective, ergonomically) to validate all fields only when the user clicks an OK button (the latter strategy is surely preferable when complex validation criteria depend on the contents of several widgets).

This widget's architecture is simpler, and a bit less flexible, than the usual, recommended Qt approach. To be Qt-canonical, you should emit signals and expose slots, leaving it up to containers and applications to connect them appropriately. This is an excellent approach, and a flexible one, but simplicity also has its appeal. You should be aware of the vast potential of the signals/slots approach, but—unless you're writing widgets for mass distribution—you can wait to architect this approach into a specific customized widget until you need it in your application.

See Also

Information about Qt is available at *http://www.trolltech.com*; PyQt is available and
described at *http://www.riverbankcomputing.co.uk/pyqt/index.php*.

9.9 Building GUI Solutions Independent of the Specific GUI Toolkit

Credit: Magnus Lie Hetland, Alex Martelli

Problem

You want to write a simple GUI that can be deployed on just about any toolkit the
end user prefers, including Tkinter, wxPython, Swing with Jython, curses-based text
I/O, and many others.

Solution

The anygui package lets you do this. For example, here's an anygui-based GUI implementation of *chmod*:

```
import sys, os
from anygui import *

filename = sys.argv[1]  # file whose permissions we study and modify

# main-level stuff
app = Application( )
win = Window(title='chmod '+filename, size=(280,175))

# headers for CheckBoxes and Labels
types = 'Read Write Execute'.split( )
people = 'User Group Others'.split( )

# Create and place CheckBoxes and Labels
cbx = {}
x, y = 10, 0
for p in people:
    lbl = Label(text=p)
    lbl.geometry = x, y+10, 80, 15
    win.add(lbl)
    cbx[p] = {}
    for t in types:
        y += 35
        cbx[p][t] = CheckBox(text=t)
        cbx[p][t].geometry = x, y, 80, 25
        win.add(cbx[p][t])
    x += 90; y = 0

# Set the CheckBoxes' values
def refresh( ):
```

```
        mode, mask = os.stat(filename)[0], 256
        for p in people:
            for t in types:
                cbx[p][t].on = mode & mask
                mask = mask >> 1

    # initial setting of checkbox values
    refresh( )

    # callbacks for button clicks
    def chmod( ):
        mode, mask = 0, 256
        for p in people:
            for t in types:
                if cbx[p][t].on:
                    mode = mode | mask
                mask = mask >> 1
        os.chmod(filename, mode)
        # reset checkbox values
        refresh( )

    def chmod_and_exit( ):
        chmod( )
        sys.exit( )

    # Make and add the buttons
    opt = Options(y=140, width=80, height=25)
    apply = Button(opt, x=10, text='Apply', action=chmod)
    cancel = Button(opt, x=100, text='Cancel', action=sys.exit)
    ok = Button(opt, x=190, text='OK', action=chmod_and_exit)
    win.add(apply, cancel, ok)

    # and finally...let 'er rip!
    app.run( )
```

Discussion

Don't you like how the anydbm standard module lets you access any of several different DBM implementations? Or how xml.sax lets you access any of several XML parsers? Welcome to anygui, a new project designed to be a similar solution for simple
GUIs, especially GUI applications that need to be deployable in a wide variety of settings. anygui is absolutely not meant to replace any of the many, wonderful GUI toolkits Python is blessed with, any more than anydbm was ever intended to replace dbm,
ndbm, and so on. Rather, anygui is implemented as a frontend that sits on top of any
of several backends (which in turn are coded in terms of Tkinter, wxPython, Swing
for Jython, and so on) and provides a uniform application-programming interface to
a reasonable subset of the toolkits' power. There's even a curses-based, text-oriented
GUI simulation backend for emergency cases in which you cannot run a real GUI but
still want to deploy an anygui-based application.

At the time of writing, anygui is in early beta stage; you can download it and play with it (with several backends more or less in a running state), but it's not yet stable and solid enough for production work. However, things often change quickly in open source projects with many enthusiastic contributors. You should visit *http:// www.anygui.org/*, download the latest release of anygui and your favorite backends, and see if it is already what you are looking for.

The example in this recipe uses functionality that is small and basic enough to keep running on whatever level of anygui is available at the time you read this, although I tested it only with the newest release at the time of this writing (fresh from the CSV repository) and several backends. Although I suspect a GUI-based *chmod* is hardly the killer application for anygui, it might prove to be useful for you.

See Also

anygui is available and described at *http://www.anygui.org/*.

9.10 Creating Color Scales

Credit: Alexander Pletzer

Problem

You need to represent numbers in a given range as colors on a pseudocolor scale, typically for data-visualization purposes.

Solution

Given a magnitude mag between given limits cmin and cmax, the basic idea is to return a color (R,G,B) tuple: light blue for cold (low magnitude) all the way to yellow for hot (high magnitude). For generality, each of R, G, and B can be returned as a float between 0.0 and 1.0:

```
import math

def floatRgb(mag, cmin, cmax):
    """ Return a tuple of floats between 0 and 1 for R, G, and B. """
    # Normalize to 0-1
    try: x = float(mag-cmin)/(cmax-cmin)
    except ZeroDivisionError: x = 0.5 # cmax == cmin
    blue  = min((max((4*(0.75-x), 0.)), 1.))
    red   = min((max((4*(x-0.25), 0.)), 1.))
    green = min((max((4*math.fabs(x-0.5)-1., 0.)), 1.))
    return red, green, blue
```

Discussion

In practical applications, R, G, and B will usually need to be integers between 0 and 255, and the color will be a tuple of three integers or a hex string representing them:

```
def rgb(mag, cmin, cmax):
    """ Return a tuple of integers, as used in AWT/Java plots. """
    red, green, blue = floatRgb(mag, cmin, cmax)
    return int(red*255), int(green*255), int(blue*255)

def strRgb(mag, cmin, cmax):
    """ Return a hex string, as used in Tk plots. """
    return "#%02x%02x%02x" % rgb(mag, cmin, cmax)
```

When given a magnitude mag between cmin and cmax, these two functions return a color tuple (red, green, blue) with each component on a 0–255 scale. The tuple can be represented as a hex string (strRgb), as required in Tk calls, or as integers (rgb), as required in Java (AWT) applications.

I often use these utility functions in my programs to create simple pseudo-color graphics under Python-Tkinter and Jython-AWT. The color maps are linear functions of the three colors (red, green, blue) with saturation. Low magnitudes are associated with a light, cold blue, high magnitudes with a warm yellow.

9.11 Using Publish/Subscribe Broadcasting to Loosen the Coupling Between GUI and Business Logic Systems

Credit: Jimmy Retzlaff

Problem

You need to loosen the coupling between two subsystems, since each is often changed independently. Typically, the two subsystems are the GUI and business-logic subsystems of an application.

Solution

Tightly coupling application-logic and presentation subsystems is a bad idea. Publish/subscribe is a good pattern to use for loosening the degree of coupling between such subsystems. The following broadcaster module (*broadcaster.py*) essentially implements a multiplexed function call in which the caller does not need to know the interface of the called functions:

```
# broadcaster.py

__all__ = ['Register', 'Broadcast', 'CurrentSource', 'CurrentTitle', 'CurrentData']
```

```python
listeners = {}
currentSources = []
currentTitles = []
currentData = []

def Register(listener, arguments=(), source=None, title=None):
    if not listeners.has_key((source, title)):
        listeners[(source, title)] = []
    listeners[(source, title)].append((listener, arguments))

def Broadcast(source, title, data={}):
    currentSources.append(source)
    currentTitles.append(title)
    currentData.append(data)

    listenerList = listeners.get((source, title), [])[:]
    if source != None:
        listenerList += listeners.get((None, title), [])
    if title != None:
        listenerList += listeners.get((source, None), [])

    for listener, arguments in listenerList:
        apply(listener, arguments)

    currentSources.pop()
    currentTitles.pop()
    currentData.pop()

def CurrentSource():
    return currentSources[-1]

def CurrentTitle():
    return currentTitles[-1]

def CurrentData():
    return currentData[-1]
```

The broker module (*broker.py*) enables the retrieval of named data even when the source of the data is not known:

```python
# broker.py

__all__ = ['Register', 'Request', 'CurrentTitle', 'CurrentData']

providers = {}
currentTitles = []
currentData = []

def Register(title, provider, arguments=()):
    assert not providers.has_key(title)
    providers[title] = (provider, arguments)

def Request(title, data={}):
    currentTitles.append(title)
    currentData.append(data)
```

```
        result = apply(apply, providers.get(title))

        currentTitles.pop( )
        currentData.pop( )

        return result

    def CurrentTitle( ):
        return currentTitles[-1]

    def CurrentData( ):
        return currentData[-1]
```

Discussion

In a running application, the broadcaster and broker modules enable loose coupling between objects in a publish/subscribe fashion. This recipe is particularly useful in GUI applications, where it helps to shield application logic from user-interface changes, although the field of application is more general.

Essentially, broadcasting is equivalent to a multiplexed function call in which the caller does not need to know the interface of the called functions. broadcaster can optionally supply data for the subscribers to consume. For example, if an application is about to exit, it can broadcast a message to that effect, and any interested objects can perform whatever finalization tasks they need to do. Another example is a user-interface control that can broadcast a message whenever its state changes so that other objects (both within the GUI, for immediate feedback, and outside of the GUI, typically in a business-logic subsystem of the application) can respond appropriately.

broker enables the retrieval of named data even when the source of the data is not known. For example, a user-interface control (such as an edit box) can register itself as a data provider with broker, and any code in the application can retrieve the control's value with no knowledge of how or where the value is stored. This avoids two potential pitfalls:

1. Storing data in multiple locations, thereby requiring extra logic to keep those locations in sync
2. Proliferating the dependency upon the control's API

broker and broadcaster work together nicely. For example, consider an edit box used for entering a date. Whenever its value changes, it can broadcast a message indicating that the entered date has changed. Anything depending on that date can respond to that message by asking broker for the current value. Later, the edit box can be replaced by a calendar control. As long as the new control broadcasts the same messages and provides the same data through broker, no other code should need to be changed. Such are the advantages of loose coupling.

The following *sample.py* script shows an example of using broadcaster and broker:

```python
# sample.py

from __future__ import nested_scopes

import broadcaster
import broker

class UserSettings:
    def __init__(self):
        self.preferredLanguage = 'English'
        # The use of lambda here provides a simple wrapper around
        # the value being provided. Every time the value is requested,
        # the variable will be reevaluated by the lambda function.
        # Note the dependence on nested scopes, thus Python 2.1 or later is required.
        broker.Register('Preferred Language', lambda: self.preferredLanguage)

        self.preferredSkin = 'Cool Blue Skin'
        broker.Register('Preferred Skin', lambda: self.preferredSkin)

    def ChangePreferredSkinTo(self, preferredSkin):
        self.preferredSkin = preferredSkin
        broadcaster.Broadcast('Preferred Skin', 'Changed')

    def ChangePreferredLanguageTo(self, preferredLanguage):
        self.preferredLanguage = preferredLanguage
        broadcaster.Broadcast('Preferred Language', 'Changed')

def ChangeSkin():
    print 'Changing to', broker.Request('Preferred Skin')

def ChangeLanguage():
    print 'Changing to', broker.Request('Preferred Language')

broadcaster.Register(ChangeSkin, source='Preferred Skin', title='Changed')
broadcaster.Register(ChangeLanguage, source='Preferred Language',
    title='Changed')

userSettings = UserSettings()
userSettings.ChangePreferredSkinTo('Bright Green Skin')
userSettings.ChangePreferredSkinTo('French')
```

Note that the idiom in this recipe is thread-hostile: even if access to the module-level variables was properly controlled, this style of programming is tailor-made for deadlocks and race conditions. Consider the impact carefully before using this approach from multiple threads. In a multithreaded setting, it is probably preferable to use Queue instances to store messages for other threads to consume and architect a different kind of broadcast (multiplexing) by having broker post to appropriate registered Queues.

See Also

Recipe 9.6 for one approach to multithreading in a GUI setting; Recipe 13.7 to see publish/subscribe used in a distributed processing setting.

9.12 Module: Building GTK GUIs Interactively

Credit: Brian McErlean

One of Python's greatest strengths is that it allows you to try things interactively at the interpreter. Tkinter shares this strength, since you can create buttons, windows, and other widgets, and see them instantly on screen. You can click on buttons to activate callbacks and still be able to edit and add to the widgets from the Python command line.

While the Python GTK bindings are generally excellent, one of their flaws is that interactive development is not possible. Before anything is actually displayed, the gtk. mainloop function must be called, ending the possibility of interactive manipulation.

Example 9-1 simulates a Python interpreter while transparently letting the user use GTK widgets without requiring a call to mainloop, which is similar to how Tk widgets work. This version contains enhancements added by Christian Robottom Reis to add readline-completion support.

This program works by running the GTK main loop in a separate thread. The main thread is responsible only for reading lines input by the user and for passing these to the GTK thread, which deals with pending lines by activating a timeout. The resulting program is virtually identical to the Python interpreter, except that there is now no need to call gtk.mainloop for GTK event handling to occur.

Example 9-1. Building GTK GUIs interactively

```
import __builtin__, __main__
import codeop, keyword, gtk, os, re, readline, threading, traceback, signal, sys

def walk_class(klass):
    list = []
    for item in dir(klass):
        if item[0] != "_":
            list.append(item)

    for base in klass.__bases__:
        for item in walk_class(base):
            if item not in list: list.append(item)

    return list

class Completer:
    def __init__(self, lokals):
        self.locals = lokals
```

Example 9-1. Building GTK GUIs interactively (continued)

```python
        self.completions = keyword.kwlist + \
                           __builtins__.__dict__.keys() + \
                           __main__.__dict__.keys()

    def complete(self, text, state):
        if state == 0:
            if "." in text:
                self.matches = self.attr_matches(text)
            else:
                self.matches = self.global_matches(text)
        try:
            return self.matches[state]
        except IndexError:
            return None

    def update(self, locs):
        self.locals = locs

        for key in self.locals.keys():
            if not key in self.completions:
                self.completions.append(key)

    def global_matches(self, text):
        matches = []
        n = len(text)
        for word in self.completions:
            if word[:n] == text:
                matches.append(word)
        return matches

    def attr_matches(self, text):
        m = re.match(r"(\w+(\.\w+)*)\.(\w*)", text)
        if not m:
            return
        expr, attr = m.group(1, 3)

        obj = eval(expr, self.locals)
        if str(obj)[1:4] == "gtk":
            words = walk_class(obj.__class__)
        else:
            words = dir(eval(expr, self.locals))

        matches = []
        n = len(attr)
        for word in words:
            if word[:n] == attr:
                matches.append("%s.%s" % (expr, word))
        return matches

class GtkInterpreter(threading.Thread):
```

Example 9-1. Building GTK GUIs interactively (continued)

```
""" Run a GTK mainloop() in a separate thread. Python commands can be passed to the
thread, where they will be executed. This is implemented by periodically checking for
passed code using a GTK timeout callback. """
TIMEOUT = 100 # interval in milliseconds between timeouts

def __init__(self):
    threading.Thread.__init__ (self)
    self.ready = threading.Condition ()
    self.globs = globals ()
    self.locs = locals ()
    self._kill = 0
    self.cmd = ''          # current code block
    self.new_cmd = None # waiting line of code, or None if none waiting

    self.completer = Completer(self.locs)
    readline.set_completer(self.completer.complete)
    readline.parse_and_bind('tab: complete')

def run(self):
    gtk.timeout_add(self.TIMEOUT, self.code_exec)
    gtk.mainloop()

def code_exec(self):
    """ Execute waiting code. Called every timeout period. """
    self.ready.acquire()
    if self._kill: gtk.mainquit()
    if self.new_cmd != None:
        self.ready.notify()
        self.cmd = self.cmd + self.new_cmd
        self.new_cmd = None
        try:
            code = codeop.compile_command(self.cmd[:-1])
            if code:
                self.cmd = ''
                exec code, self.globs, self.locs
                self.completer.update(self.locs)
        except:
            traceback.print_exc()
            self.cmd = ''

    self.ready.release()
    return 1

def feed(self, code):
    """ Feed a line of code to the thread. This function will block until the code is
    checked by the GTK thread. Returns true if the thread has executed the code.
    Returns false if deferring execution until complete block is available. """
    if code[-1:]!='\n': code = code +'\n' # raw_input strips newline
    self.completer.update(self.locs)
    self.ready.acquire()
    self.new_cmd = code
```

Example 9-1. Building GTK GUIs interactively (continued)

```
        self.ready.wait()  # Wait until processed in timeout interval
        self.ready.release()

        return not self.cmd

    def kill(self):
        """ Kill the thread, returning when it has been shut down. """
        self.ready.acquire()
        self._kill=1
        self.ready.release()
        self.join()

# Read user input in a loop and send each line to the interpreter thread

def signal_handler(*args):
    print "SIGNAL:", args
    sys.exit()

if __name__=="__main__":
    signal.signal(signal.SIGINT, signal_handler)
    signal.signal(signal.SIGSEGV, signal_handler)

    prompt = '>>> '
    interpreter = GtkInterpreter()
    interpreter.start()
    interpreter.feed("from gtk import *")
    interpreter.feed("sys.path.append('.')")
    if len (sys.argv) > 1:
        for file in open(sys.argv[1]).readlines():
            interpreter.feed(file)
    print 'Interactive GTK Shell'

    try:
        while 1:
            command = raw_input(prompt) + '\n' # raw_input strips newlines
            prompt = interpreter.feed(command) and '>>> ' or '... '
    except (EOFError, KeyboardInterrupt): pass

    interpreter.kill()
    print
```

See Also

PyGTK is described and available at *http://www.daa.com.au/~james/pygtk*.

CHAPTER 10

Network Programming

10.0 Introduction

Credit: Guido van Rossum, creator of Python

Network programming is one of my favorite Python applications. I wrote or started most of the network modules in the Python standard library, including the socket and select extension modules and most of the protocol client modules (such as ftplib), which set an example. I also wrote a popular server framework module, SocketServer, and two web browsers in Python, the first predating Mosaic. Need I say more?

Python's roots lie in a distributed operating system, Amoeba, which I helped design and implement in the late '80s. Python was originally intended to be the scripting language for Amoeba, since it turned out that the Unix shell, while ported to Amoeba, wasn't very useful for writing Amoeba system-administration scripts. Of course, I designed Python to be platform-independent from the start. Once Python was ported from Amoeba to Unix, I taught myself BSD socket programming by wrapping the socket primitives in a Python extension module and then experimenting with them using Python; this was one of the first extension modules.

This approach proved to be a great early testimony of Python's strengths. Writing socket code in C is tedious: the code necessary to do error checking on every call quickly overtakes the logic of the program. Quick: in which order should a server call accept, bind, connect, and listen? This is remarkably difficult to find out if all you have is a set of Unix manpages. In Python, you don't have to write separate error-handling code for each call, making the logic of the code stand out much clearer. You can also learn about sockets by experimenting in an interactive Python shell, where misconceptions about the proper order of calls and the argument values that each call requires are cleared up quickly through Python's immediate error messages.

Python has come a long way since those first days, and now few applications use the socket module directly; most use much higher-level modules such as urllib or smtplib. The examples in this chapter are a varied bunch: there are some that construct and send complex email messages, while others dig in the low-level bowels of the network implementation on a specific platform. My favorite is Recipe 10.12, which discusses PyHeartBeat: it's useful, it uses the socket module, and it's simple enough to be a good educational example.

The socket module itself is still the foundation of all network operations in Python. It's a plain transliteration of the socket APIs—first introduced in BSD Unix and now widespread on all platforms—into the object-oriented paradigm. You create socket objects by calling the socket.socket factory function, then calling methods on these objects to perform typical low-level network operations. Of course, you don't have to worry about allocating and freeing memory for buffers and the like—Python handles that for you automatically. You express IP addresses as (host,port) pairs, in which host is a string in either dotted-quad ('1.2.3.4') or domain-name ('www.python.org') notation. As you can see, even low-level modules in Python aren't as low-level as all that.

But despite the various conveniences, the socket module still exposes the actual underlying functionality of your operating system's network sockets. If you're at all familiar with them, you'll quickly get the hang of Python's socket module, using Python's own *Library Reference*. You'll then be able to play with sockets interactively in Python to become a socket expert, if that is what you need. The classic work on this subject is *UNIX Network Programming, Volume 1: Networking APIs - Sockets and XTI, Second Edition*, by W. Richard Stevens (Prentice-Hall), and it is highly recommended. For many practical uses, however, higher-level modules will serve you better.

The Internet uses a sometimes dazzling variety of protocols and formats, and Python's standard library supports many of them. In Python's standard library, you will find dozens of modules dedicated to supporting specific Internet protocols (such as smtplib to support the SMTP protocol to send mail, nntplib to support the NNTP protocol to send and receive Network News, and so on). In addition, you'll find about as many modules that support specific Internet formats (such as htmllib to parse HTML data, the email package to parse and compose various formats related to email—including attachments and encoding—and so on).

Clearly, I cannot even come close to doing justice to the powerful array of tools mentioned in this introduction, nor will you find all of these modules and packages used in this chapter, nor in this book, nor in most programming shops. You may never need to write any program that deals with Network News, for example, so you will not need to study nntplib. But it is reassuring to know it's there (part of the "batteries included" approach of the Python standard library).

Two higher-level modules that stand out from the crowd, however, are urllib and urllib2. Each can deal with several protocols through the magic of URLs—those now-familiar strings, such as *http://www.python.org/index.html*, that identify a protocol (such as *http*), a host and port (such as *www.python.org*, port 80 being the default here), and a specific resource at that address (such as *index.html*). urllib is rather simple to use, but urllib2 is more powerful and extensible. HTTP is the most popular protocol for URLs, but these modules also support several others, such as FTP and Gopher. In many cases, you'll be able to use these modules to write typical client-side scripts that interact with any of the supported protocols much quicker and with less effort than it might take with the various protocol-specific modules.

To illustrate, I'd like to conclude with a cookbook example of my own. It's similar to Recipe 10.6, but rather than a program fragment, it's a little script. I call it *wget.py* because it does everything for which I've ever needed *wget*. (In fact, I wrote it on a system where *wget* wasn't installed but Python was; writing *wget.py* was a more effective use of my time than downloading and installing the real thing.)

```
import sys, urllib
def reporthook(*a): print a
for url in sys.argv[1:]:
    i = url.rfind('/')
    file = url[i+1:]
    print url, "->", file
    urllib.urlretrieve(url, file, reporthook)
```

Pass it one or more URLs as command-line arguments; it retrieves those into local files whose names match the last components of the URLs. It also prints progress information of the form:

```
(block number, block size, total size)
```

Obviously, it's easy to improve on this; but it's only seven lines, it's readable, and it works—and that's what's so cool about Python.

Another cool thing about Python is that you can incrementally improve a program like this, and after it's grown by two or three orders of magnitude, it's still readable, and it still works! To see what this particular example might evolve into, check out *Tools/webchecker/websucker.py* in the Python source distribution. Enjoy!

10.1 Writing a TCP Client

Credit: Luther Blissett

Problem

You want to connect to a socket on a remote machine.

Solution

Assuming you're using the Internet to communicate:

```
import socket

# Create a socket
sock = socket.socket(socket.AF_INET, socket.SOCK_STREAM)
```

```
# Connect to the remote host and port
sock.connect((remote_host, remote_port))

# Send a request to the host
sock.send("Why don't you call me any more?\r\n")

# Get the host's response, no more than, say, 1,024 bytes
response_data = sock.recv(1024)

# Terminate
sock.close( )
```

Discussion

The remote_host string can be either a domain name, such as 'www.python.org', or a dotted quad, such as '194.109.137.226'. The remote_port variable is an integer, such as 80 (the default HTTP port). If an error occurs, the failing operation raises an exception of the socket.error class. The socket module does not give you the ability to control a timeout for the operations you attempt; if you need such functionality, download the timeoutsocket module from *http://www.timo-tasi.org/python/timeoutsocket.py*, place it anywhere on your Python sys.path, and follow the instructions in the module itself.

If you want file-like objects for your network I/O, you can build one or more with the makefile method of the socket object, rather than using the latter's send and receive methods directly. You can independently close the socket object and each file obtained from it, without affecting any other (or you can let garbage collection close them for you). For example, if sock is a connected socket object, you could write:

```
sockOut = sock.makefile('wb')
sockIn = sock.makefile('r')
sock.close( )
print >> sockOut, "Why don't you call me any more?\r"
sockOut.close( )
for line in sockIn:        # Python 2.2 only; 'in sockin.xreadlines( )' in 2.1
    print 'received:', line,
```

See Also

Recipe 10.2; documentation for the standard library module socket in the *Library Reference*; the timeout modifications at *http://www.timo-tasi.org/python/timeoutsocket.py*, although these will likely be incorporated into Python 2.3; *Perl Cookbook* Recipe 17.1.

10.2 Writing a TCP Server

Credit: Luther Blissett

Problem

You want to write a server that waits for clients to connect over the network to a particular port.

Solution

Assuming you're using the Internet to communicate:

```
import socket

# Create a socket
sock = socket.socket(socket.AF_INET, socket.SOCK_STREAM)

# Ensure that you can restart your server quickly when it terminates
sock.setsockopt(socket.SOL_SOCKET, socket.SO_REUSEADDR, 1)

# Set the client socket's TCP "well-known port" number
well_known_port = 8881
sock.bind(('', well_known_port))

# Set the number of clients waiting for connection that can be queued
sock.listen(5)

# loop waiting for connections (terminate with Ctrl-C)
try:
    while 1:
        newSocket, address = sock.accept( )
        print "Connected from", address
        # loop serving the new client
        while 1:
            receivedData = newSocket.recv(1024)
            if not receivedData: break
            # Echo back the same data you just received
            newSocket.send(receivedData)
        newSocket.close( )
        print "Disconnected from", address
finally:
    sock.close( )
```

Discussion

Setting up a server takes a bit more work than setting up a client. We need to bind to a well-known port that clients will use to connect to us. Optionally, as we do in this recipe, we can set SO_REUSEADDR so we can restart the server when it terminates without waiting for a few minutes, which is quite nice during development and testing.

We can also optionally call listen to control the number of clients waiting for connections that can be queued.

After this preparation, we just need to loop, waiting for the accept method to return; it returns a new socket object already connected to the client and the client's address. We use the new socket to hold a session with a client, then go back to our waiting loop. In this recipe, we just echo back the same data we receive from the client.

The SocketServer module lets us perform the same task in an object-oriented way. Using it, the recipe becomes:

```
import SocketServer

class MyHandler(SocketServer.BaseRequestHandler):
    def handle(self):
        while 1:
            dataReceived = self.request.recv(1024)
            if not dataReceived: break
            self.request.send(dataReceived)

myServer = SocketServer.TCPServer(('',8881), MyHandler)
myServer.serve_forever( )
```

One handler object is instantiated to serve each connection, and the new socket for that connection is available to its handle method (which the server calls) as self.request.

Using the SocketServer module instead of the lower-level socket module is particularly advisable when we want more functionality. For example, to spawn a new and separate thread for each request we serve, we would need to change only one line of code in this higher-level solution:

```
myServer = SocketServer.ThreadingTCPServer(('',8881), MyHandler)
```

while the socket-level recipe would need substantially more recoding to be transformed into a similarly multithreaded server.

See Also

Recipe 10.1; documentation for the standard library module socket in the *Library Reference*; *Perl Cookbook* Recipe 17.2.

10.3   Passing Messages with Socket Datagrams

Credit: Jeff Bauer

Problem

You need to communicate small messages between machines on a TCP/IP network in a lightweight fashion, without needing absolute assurance of reliability.

Solution

This is what the UDP protocol is for, and Python makes it easy for you to access it, via datagram sockets. You can write a server (*server.py*) as follows:

```
import socket
port = 8081
s = socket.socket(socket.AF_INET, socket.SOCK_DGRAM)
# Accept UDP datagrams, on the given port, from any sender
s.bind(("", port))
print "waiting on port:", port
while 1:
    # Receive up to 1,024 bytes in a datagram
    data, addr = s.recvfrom(1024)
    print "Received:", data, "from", addr
```

And you can write a client (*client.py*) as follows:

```
import socket
port = 8081
host = "localhost"
s = socket.socket(socket.AF_INET, socket.SOCK_DGRAM)
s.sendto("Holy Guido! It's working.", (host, port))
```

Discussion

Sending short text messages with socket datagrams is simple to implement and provides a lightweight message-passing idiom. Socket datagrams should not be used, however, when reliable delivery of data must be guaranteed. If the server isn't available, your message is lost. However, there are many situations in which you won't care whether the message gets lost, or, at least, you won't want to abort a program just because the message can't be delivered.

Note that the sender of a UDP datagram (the client in this example) does not need to bind the socket before calling the sendto method. On the other hand, to receive UDP datagrams, the socket does need to be bound before calling the recvfrom method.

Don't use this recipe's simple code to send very large datagram messages, especially under Windows, which may not respect the buffer limit. To send larger messages, you will probably want to do something like this:

```
BUFSIZE = 1024
while msg:
    bytes_sent = s.sendto(msg[:BUFSIZE], (host, port))
    msg = msg[bytes_sent:]
```

The sendto method returns the number of bytes it has actually managed to send, so each time, you retry from the point where you left off, while ensuring that no more than BUFSIZE octets are sent in each datagram.

Note that with datagrams (UDP) you have no guarantee that all or none of the pieces that you send as separate datagrams arrive to the destination, nor that the pieces that do arrive are in the same order that they were sent. If you need to worry about any of these reliability issues, you may be better off with a TCP connection, which gives you all of these assurances and handles many delicate behind-the-scenes aspects nicely on your behalf. Still, I often use socket datagrams for debugging, especially (but not exclusively) where the application spans more than one machine on the same, reliable local area network.

See Also

Recipe 10.12 for a typical, useful application of UDP datagrams in network operations; documentation for the standard library module socket in the *Library Reference*.

10.4 Finding Your Own Name and Address

Credit: Luther Blissett

Problem

You want to find your own fully qualified hostname and IP address.

Solution

The socket module has functions that help with this task:

```
import socket

myname = socket.getfqdn(socket.gethostname())
myaddr = socket.gethostbyname(myname)
```

This gives you your primary, fully qualified domain name and IP address. You might have other names and addresses, and if you want to find out about them, you can do the following:

```
thename, aliases, addresses = socket.gethostbyaddr(myaddr)
print 'Primary name for %s (%s): %s' % (myname, myaddr, thename)
for alias in aliases: print "AKA", alias
for address in addresses: print "address:", address
```

Discussion

gethostname is specifically useful only to find out your hostname, but the other functions used in this recipe are for more general use. getfqdn takes a domain name that may or may not be fully qualified and normalizes it into the corresponding fully qualified domain name (FQDN) for a hostname. gethostbyname can accept any valid hostname and look up the corresponding IP address (if name resolution is working correctly, the network is up, and so on), which it returns as a string in dotted-quad form (such as '1.2.3.4').

gethostbyaddr accepts a valid IP address as a string in dotted-quad form (again, if reverse DNS lookup is working correctly on your machine, the network is up, and so on) and returns a tuple of three items. The first item is a string, the primary name by which the host at that IP address would like to be known. The second item is a list of other names (aliases) by which that host is known—note that it can be an empty list. The third item is the list of IP addresses for that host (it will never be empty because it contains at least the address you passed when calling gethostbyaddr).

If an error occurs during the execution of any of these functions, the failing operation raises an exception of the socket.error class.

See Also

Documentation for the standard library module socket in the *Library Reference*; *Perl Cookbook* Recipe 17.8.

10.5 Converting IP Addresses

Credit: Alex Martelli, Greg Jorgensen

Problem

You need to convert IP addresses from dotted quads to long integers and back, and extract network and host portions of such addresses.

Solution

The socket and struct modules let you easily convert long integers to dotted quads and back:

```
import socket, struct

def dottedQuadToNum(ip):
    "convert decimal dotted quad string to long integer"
    return struct.unpack('>L',socket.inet_aton(ip))[0]

def numToDottedQuad(n):
    "convert long int to dotted quad string"
    return socket.inet_ntoa(struct.pack('>L',n))
```

To split an IP address into network and host portions, we just need to apply a suitable binary mask to the long integer form of the IP address:

```
def makeMask(n):
    "return a mask of n bits as a long integer"
    return (2L<<n-1)-1

def ipToNetAndHost(ip, maskbits):
    "return tuple (network, host) dotted-quad addresses given IP and mask size"
    # by Greg Jorgensen
```

```
n = dottedQuadToNum(ip)
m = makeMask(maskbits)

host = n & m
net = n - host

return numToDottedQuad(net), numToDottedQuad(host)
```

Discussion

The format we use for the struct.pack and struct.unpack calls must start with a '>', which specifies big-endian byte order. This is the network byte order used by the socket.inet_aton and socket.inet_ntoa functions. If you omit the '>', struct instead uses the native byte order of the machine the code is running on, while the socket module still uses big-endian byte order.

The network part of an IP address used to be expressed as an explicit bit mask (generally also in dotted-quad form) such as:

```
'192.168.23.0/255.255.255.0'
```

However, the bit mask invariably had a certain number (N) bits that were 1 followed by $32–N$ bits that were 0. The current form, which is much more compact and readable, is therefore structured like:

```
'192.168.23.0/24'
```

The part after the / is just N: the number of bits that must be 1 in the mask. If you know about a network that is expressed in this form, you can use the functions in this recipe to check if a host is within that network:

```
def isHostInNet(host_ip, net_ip_with_slash):
    net_ip, mask_length = net_ip_with_slash.split('/')
    mask_length = int(mask_length)
    net_net, net_host = ipToNetAndHost(net_ip, 32-mask_length)
    assert net_host == '0.0.0.0'
    host_net, host_host = ipToNetAndHost(host_ip, 32-mask_length)
    return host_net == net_net
```

Note that the slash format of network addresses gives the number of bits in the mask for the network, although we wrote the ipToNetAndHost function to take the number of bits in the mask for the host. Therefore, we pass 32-mask_length in the two calls that isHostInNet makes to the ipToNetAndHost function. The assert statement is not strictly necessary, but it does assure us that the argument passed as net_ip_with_slash is correct, and (as assert statements usually do) serves as a general sanity check for the proceedings.

See Also

Documentation for the standard library modules socket and struct in the *Library Reference*.

10.6 Grabbing a Document from the Web

Credit: Gisle Aas

Problem

You need to grab a document from a URL on the Web.

Solution

urllib.urlopen returns a file-like object, and you can call read on it:

```
from urllib import urlopen

doc = urlopen("http://www.python.org").read( )
print doc
```

Discussion

Once you obtain a file-like object from urlopen, you can read it all at once into one big string by calling its read method, as I do in this recipe. Alternatively, you can read it as a list of lines by calling its readlines method or, for special purposes, just get one line at a time by calling its readline method in a loop. In addition to these file-like operations, the object that urlopen returns offers a few other useful features. For example, the following snippet gives you the headers of the document:

```
doc = urlopen("http://www.python.org")
print doc.info( )
```

such as the Content-Type: header (text/html in this case) that defines the MIME type of the document. doc.info returns a mimetools.Message instance, so you can access it in various ways without printing it or otherwise transforming it into a string. For example, doc.info( ).getheader('Content-Type') returns the 'text/html' string. The maintype attribute of the mimetools.Message object is the 'text' string, subtype is the 'html' string, and type is also the 'text/html' string. If you need to perform sophisticated analysis and processing, all the tools you need are right there. At the same time, if your needs are simpler, you can meet them in very simple ways, as this recipe shows.

See Also

Documentation for the standard library modules urllib and mimetools in the *Library Reference*.

10.7 Being an FTP Client

Credit: Luther Blissett

Problem

You want to connect to an FTP server and upload or retrieve files. You might want to automate the one-time transfer of many files or automatically mirror an entire section of an FTP server.

Solution

The `ftplib` module makes this reasonably easy:

```
import ftplib

ftp = ftplib.FTP("ftp.host.com")
ftp.login(username, password)
ftp.cwd(directory)
# Retrieve a binary file to save on your disk
ftp.retrbinary('RETR '+filename, open(filename,'wb').write)
# Upload a binary file from your disk
ftp.storbinary('STOR '+filename, open(filename,'rb'))
```

Discussion

`urllib` may be sufficient for getting documents via FTP, but the `ftplib` module offers more functionality (including the ability to use FTP to upload files, assuming, of course, that you have the needed permission on the server in question) and finer-grained control for this specific task.

`login` defaults to an anonymous login attempt if you call it without arguments, but you normally pass username and password arguments. `cwd` changes the current directory on the server. `retrbinary` retrieves binary data from the server and repeatedly calls its second argument with the data. Thus, you will usually pass a file object's `write` bound method as the second argument. `storbinary` stores binary data on the server, taking the data from its second argument, which must be a file-like object (the method calls `read(N)` on it). There are also the `retrlines` and `storlines` methods, which work similarly but on text data, line by line.

Functions and methods in the `ftplib` module may raise exceptions of many classes to diagnose possible errors. To catch them all, you can use `ftplib.all_errors`, which is the tuple of all possible exception classes:

```
try: ftp = ftplib.FTP("ftp.host.com")
except ftp.all_errors, error:
    print "Cannot connect:", error
else:
    try: ftp.login(username, password)
    except ftp.all_errors, error:
```

```
              print "Cannot login:", error
        else:
              ...
```

See Also

Documentation for the standard library module ftplib in the *Library Reference*.

10.8 Sending HTML Mail

Credit: Art Gillespie

Problem

You need to send HTML mail and embed a message version in plain text, so that the message is also readable by MUAs that are not HTML-capable.

Solution

The key functionality is supplied by the MimeWriter and mimetools modules:

```
def createhtmlmail(subjectl, html, text=None):
    "Create a mime-message that will render as HTML or text, as appropriate"
    import MimeWriter
    import mimetools
    import cStringIO

    if text is None:
        # Produce an approximate textual rendering of the HTML string,
        # unless you have been given a better version as an argument
        import htmllib, formatter
        textout = cStringIO.StringIO( )
        formtext = formatter.AbstractFormatter(formatter.DumbWriter(textout))
        parser = htmllib.HTMLParser(formtext)
        parser.feed(html)
        parser.close( )
        text = textout.getvalue( )
        del textout, formtext, parser

    out = cStringIO.StringIO( ) # output buffer for our message
    htmlin = cStringIO.StringIO(html)
    txtin = cStringIO.StringIO(text)

    writer = MimeWriter.MimeWriter(out)

    # Set up some basic headers. Place subject here
    # because smtplib.sendmail expects it to be in the
    # message body, as relevant RFCs prescribe.
    writer.addheader("Subject", subject)
    writer.addheader("MIME-Version", "1.0")
```

```
# Start the multipart section of the message.
# Multipart/alternative seems to work better
# on some MUAs than multipart/mixed.
writer.startmultipartbody("alternative")
writer.flushheaders()

# the plain-text section: just copied through, assuming iso-8859-1
subpart = writer.nextpart()
pout = subpart.startbody("text/plain", [("charset", 'iso-8859-1')])
pout.write(txtin.read())
txtin.close()

# the HTML subpart of the message: quoted-printable, just in case
subpart = writer.nextpart()
subpart.addheader("Content-Transfer-Encoding", "quoted-printable")
pout = subpart.startbody("text/html", [("charset", 'us-ascii')])
mimetools.encode(htmlin, pout, 'quoted-printable')
htmlin.close()

# You're done; close your writer and return the message body
writer.lastpart()
msg = out.getvalue()
out.close()
return msg
```

Discussion

This module is completed in the usual style with a few lines to ensure that, when run as a script, it runs a self-test by composing and sending a sample HTML mail:

```
if __name__=="__main__":
    import smtplib
    f = open("newsletter.html", 'r')
    html = f.read()
    f.close()
    try:
        f = open("newsletter.txt", 'r')
        text = f.read()
    except IOError:
        text = None
    subject = "Today's Newsletter!"
    message = createhtmlmail(subject, html, text)
    server = smtplib.SMTP("localhost")
    server.sendmail('agillesp@i-noSPAMSUCKS.com',
        'agillesp@i-noSPAMSUCKS.com', message)
    server.quit()
```

Sending HTML mail is a popular concept, and as long as you avoid sending it to newsgroups and open mailing lists, there's no reason your Python scripts shouldn't do it. When they do, don't forget to embed two alternative versions of your message: the HTML version and a text-only version. Lots of folks still prefer character-mode mail readers (technically known as a mail user agent, or MUA), and it makes no sense to alienate them by sending mail that they can't conveniently read. This recipe shows how easy Python makes this.

Ideally, your input will be a properly formatted text version of the message, as well as the HTML version. But if you don't have this input, you can still prepare a text version on the fly; one way to do this is shown in the recipe. Remember that htmllib has some limitations, so you may want to use alternative approaches, such as saving the HTML string to disk and using:

```
text=os.popen('lynx -dump %s'%tempfile).read( )
```

or whatever works best for you. Alternatively, if all you have as input is plain text (following some specific conventions, such as empty lines to mark paragraphs and underlines for emphasis), you can parse the text and throw together some HTML markup on the fly. See Recipe 12.7 for some ideas on how to synthesize structured-text markup from plain text following these rather common conventions.

The emails generated by this code have been successfully tested on Outlook 2000, Eudora 4.2, Hotmail, and Netscape Mail. It's likely that they will work in other HTML-capable MUAs as well. MUTT has been used to test the acceptance of messages generated by this recipe in text-only MUAs. Again, others would be expected to work just as acceptably.

See Also

Recipe 10.10 shows how Python 2.2's email package can be used to compose a MIME multipart message; Recipe 12.7 for other text synthesis options; documentation for the standard module email for a Python 2.2 alternative to classic Python modules such as mimetools and MimeWriter; Henry Minsky's article on MIME (*http://www.arsdigita.com/asj/mime/*) for information on the issues of how to send HTML mail.

10.9   Sending Multipart MIME Email

Credit: Richard Jones, Michael Strasser

Problem

You need to put together a multipart MIME email message to be sent with smtplib (or by other means).

Solution

Multipart messages can be composed with the MimeWriter module:

```
import sys, smtplib, MimeWriter, base64, StringIO

message = StringIO.StringIO( )
writer = MimeWriter.MimeWriter(message)
```

```
writer.addheader('Subject', 'The kitten picture')
writer.startmultipartbody('mixed')

# Start off with a text/plain part
part = writer.nextpart( )
body = part.startbody('text/plain')
body.write('This is a picture of a kitten, enjoy :)')

# Now add an image part
part = writer.nextpart( )
part.addheader('Content-Transfer-Encoding', 'base64')
body = part.startbody('image/jpeg; name=kitten.jpg')
base64.encode(open('kitten.jpg', 'rb'), body)

# Finish it off
writer.lastpart( )
```

Once you have composed a suitable message, you can send it with the `smtplib` module:

```
smtp = smtplib.SMTP('smtp.server.address')
smtp.sendmail('from@from.address', 'to@to.address', message.getvalue( ))
smtp.quit( )
```

Discussion

The order of the calls to the writer is important. Note that headers are always added before body content. The top-level body is added with a subtype of 'mixed', which is appropriate for mixed content, such as that of this recipe. Other subtypes can be found in RFC 1521 (e.g., 'mixed', 'alternative', 'digest', and 'parallel'), RFC 1847 (e.g., 'signed' and 'encrypted'), and RFC 2387 ('related'). Each RFC is available at *http://www.ietf.org/rfc*.

Of course, you could wrap this kind of functionality up in a class, which is what Dirk Holtwick has done. (See his solution at *http://sourceforge.net/snippet/detail. php?type=snippet&id=100444*.) In Python 2.2, the new email package in the standard library offers an excellent alternative for handling email messages, such as documents compatible with RFC 2822 (which superseded the earlier RFC 822) that include MIME functionality. Recipe 10.10 shows how the email package can be used to compose a MIME multipart message.

See Also

Recipes 10.8 and 10.10; documentation for the standard library modules email, smtplib, MimeWriter, base64, and StringIO in the *Library Reference*; the IETF RFC archive (*http://www.ietf.org/rfc/rfcNNNN.txt*); the MimeMail snippet (*http://sourceforge.net/snippet/detail.php?type=snippet&id=100444*).

10.10 Bundling Files in a MIME Message

Credit: Matthew Dixon Cowles

Problem

You want to create a multipart MIME message that includes all files in the current directory.

Solution

If you often deal with composing or parsing mail messages, or mail-like messages such as Usenet news posts, the new email module gives you sparkling new opportunities:

```python
#!/usr/bin/env python

import base64, quopri
import mimetypes, email.Generator, email.Message
import cStringIO, os

# sample addresses
toAddr="example@example.com"
fromAddr="example@example.com"
outputFile="dirContentsMail"

def main():
    mainMsg = email.Message.Message()
    mainMsg["To"] = toAddr
    mainMsg["From"] = fromAddr
    mainMsg["Subject"] = "Directory contents"
    mainMsg["Mime-version"] = "1.0"
    mainMsg["Content-type"] = "Multipart/mixed"
    mainMsg.preamble = "Mime message\n"
    mainMsg.epilogue = "" # to ensure that message ends with newline
    # Get names of plain files (not subdirectories or special files)
    fileNames = [f for f in os.listdir(os.curdir) if os.path.isfile(f)]
    for fileName in fileNames:
        contentType,ignored = mimetypes.guess_type(fileName)
        if contentType==None: # If no guess, use generic opaque type
            contentType = "application/octet-stream"
        contentsEncoded = cStringIO.StringIO()
        f = open(fileName, "rb")
        mainType = contentType[:contentType.find("/")]
        if mainType=="text":
            cte = "quoted-printable"
            quopri.encode(f, contentsEncoded, 1) # 1 to encode tabs
        else:
            cte = "base64"
            base64.encode(f, contentsEncoded)
        f.close()
        subMsg = email.Message.Message()
        subMsg.add_header("Content-type", contentType, name=fileName)
        subMsg.add_header("Content-transfer-encoding", cte)
```

```
            subMsg.add_payload(contentsEncoded.getvalue())
            contentsEncoded.close()
            mainMsg.add_payload(subMsg)

        f = open(outputFile,"wb")
        g = email.Generator.Generator(f)
        g(mainMsg)
        f.close()
        return None

    if __name__=="__main__":
        main()
```

Discussion

The email module, new in Python 2.2, makes manipulating MIME messages easier than it used to be (with the standard Python library modules already present in Python 2.1 and earlier). This is not a trivial point, so this recipe's example may be useful. See the standard *Library Reference* for detailed documentation about the email module.

MIME (Multipurpose Internet Mail Extensions) is the Internet standard for sending files and non-ASCII data by email. The standard is specified in RFCs 2045-2049. There are a few points that are especially worth keeping in mind:

- The original specification for the format of an email (RFC 822) didn't allow for non-ASCII characters and had no provision for attaching or enclosing a file along with a text message. Therefore, not surprisingly, MIME messages are very common these days.

- Messages that follow the MIME standard are backward-compatible with ordinary RFC 822 (now RFC 2822) messages. A mail reader that doesn't understand the MIME specification will probably not be able to display a MIME message in a way that's useful to the user, but the message will be legal and therefore shouldn't cause unexpected behavior.

- An RFC 2822 message consists of a set of headers, a blank line, and a body. MIME handles attachments and other multipart documents by specifying a format for the message's body. In multipart MIME messages, the body is divided into submessages, each of which has a set of headers, a blank line, and a body. Generally, each submessage is referred to a MIME part, and parts may nest recursively.

- MIME parts (whether in a multipart message or not) that contain characters outside of the strict US-ASCII range are encoded as either base-64 or quoted-printable data, so that the resulting mail message contains only ordinary ASCII characters. Data can be encoded with either method, but generally, only data that has few non-ASCII characters (basically text, possibly with a few extra characters outside of the ASCII range, such as national characters in Latin-1 and similar codes) is worth encoding as quoted-printable, because even without decoding it may be readable. If the data is essentially binary, with all bytes being equally likely, base-64 encoding is more compact.

Not surprisingly, given all that, manipulating MIME messages is often considered to be a nuisance. Before Python 2.2, the standard library's modules for dealing with MIME messages were quite useful but rather miscellaneous. In particular, putting MIME messages together and taking them apart required two distinct approaches. The email module, new in Python 2.2, unifies and simplifies these two related jobs.

See Also

Recipe 10.11 shows how the email module can be used to unpack a MIME message; documentation for the standard library modules email, smtplib, mimetypes, base64, quopri, and cStringIO in the *Library Reference*. attachments.

10.11 Unpacking a Multipart MIME Message

Credit: Matthew Dixon Cowles

Problem

You have a multipart MIME message and want to unpack it.

Solution

The walk method of message objects generated by the email module (new as of Python 2.2) makes this task really easy:

```
import email.Parser
import os, sys

def main( ):
    if len(sys.argv)==1:
        print "Usage: %s filename" % os.path.basename(sys.argv[0])
        sys.exit(1)

    mailFile = open(sys.argv[1], "rb")
    p = email.Parser.Parser( )
    msg = p.parse(mailFile)
    mailFile.close( )

    partCounter = 1
    for part in msg.walk( ):
        if part.get_main_type( )=="multipart":
            continue
        name = part.get_param("name")
        if name==None:
            name = "part-%i" % partCounter
        partCounter+=1
```

```
        # In real life, make sure that name is a reasonable filename
        # for your OS; otherwise, mangle it until it is!
        f = open(name,"wb")
        f.write(part.get_payload(decode=1))
        f.close( )
        print name

if __name__=="__main__":
    main( )
```

Discussion

The email module, new in Python 2.2, makes parsing MIME messages reasonably easy. (See the *Library Reference* for detailed documentation about the email module.) This recipe shows how to recursively unbundle a MIME message with the email module in the easiest way, using the walk method of message objects.

You can create a message object in several ways. For example, you can instantiate the email.Message.Message class and build the message object's contents with calls to its add_payload method. In this recipe, I need to read and analyze an existing message, so I worked the other way around, calling the parse method of an email.Parser.Parser instance. The parse method takes as its only argument a file-like object (in the recipe, I pass it a real file object that I just opened for binary reading with the built-in open function) and returns a message object, on which you can call message object methods.

The walk method is a generator, i.e., it returns an iterator object on which you can loop with a for statement. Usually, you will use this method exactly as I use it in this recipe:

```
    for part in msg.walk( ):
```

The iterator sequentially returns (depth-first, in case of nesting) the parts that comprise the message. If the message is not a container of parts (has no attachments or alternates, i.e., message.is_multipart( ) is false), no problem: the walk method will return an iterator with a single element: the message itself. In any case, each element of the iterator is also a message object (an instance of email.Message.Message), so you can call on it any of the methods a message object supplies.

In a multipart message, parts with a type of 'multipart/something' (i.e., a main type of 'multipart') may be present. In this recipe, I skip them explicitly since they're just glue holding the true parts together. I use the get_main_type method to obtain the main type and check it for equality with 'multipart'; if equality holds, I skip this part and move to the next one with a continue statement. When I know I have a real part in hand, I locate its name (or synthesize one if it has no name), open that name as a file, and write the message's contents (also known as the message's payload), which I get by calling the get_payload method, into the file. I use the decode=1 argument to ensure that the payload is decoded back to a binary content (e.g., an image, a sound file, a movie, etc.) if needed, rather than remaining in text form. If the payload is not encoded, decode=1 is innocuous, so I don't have to check before I pass it.

See Also

Recipe 10.10; documentation for the standard library modules email, smtplib, mimetypes, base64, quopri, and cStringIO in the *Library Reference*.

10.12 Module: PyHeartBeat—Detecting Inactive Computers

Credit: Nicola Larosa

When we have a number of computers connected by a TCP/IP network, we are often interested in monitoring their working state. The pair of programs presented in Examples 10-1 and 10-2 help you detect when a computer stops working, while having minimal impact on network traffic and requiring very little setup. Note that this does not monitor the working state of single, specific services running on a machine, just that of the TCP/IP stack and the underlying operating system and hardware components.

PyHeartBeat is made up of two files: *PyHBClient.py* sends UDP packets, while *PyHBServer.py* listens for such packets and detects inactive clients. The client program, running on any number of computers, periodically sends an UDP packet to the server program that runs on one central computer. In the server program, one thread dynamically builds and updates a dictionary that stores the IP numbers of the client computers and the timestamp of the last packet received from each. At the same time, the main thread of the server program periodically checks the dictionary, noting whether any of the timestamps is older than a defined timeout.

In this kind of application, there is no need to use reliable TCP connections, since the loss of a packet now and then does not produce false alarms, given that the server-checking timeout is kept suitably larger than the client-sending period. On the other hand, if we have hundreds of computers to monitor, it is best to keep the bandwidth used and the load on the server at a minimum. We do this by periodically sending a small UDP packet, instead of setting up a relatively expensive TCP connection per client.

The packets are sent from each client every 10 seconds, while the server checks the dictionary every 30 seconds, and its timeout defaults to the same interval. These parameters, along with the server IP number and port used, can be adapted to one's needs.

Also note that the debug printouts can be turned off by using the -O option of the Python interpreter, as that option sets the __debug__ variable to 0. However, some would consider this usage overcute and prefer a more straightforward and obvious approach: have the scripts accept either a -q flag (to keep the script quiet, with verbosity as the default) or a -v flag (to make it verbose, with quiet as the default). The getopt standard module makes it easy for a Python script to accept optional flags of this kind.

Example 10-1 shows the *PyHBClient.py* heartbeat client program, which should be run on every computer on the network, while Example 10-2 shows the heartbeat server program, *PyHBServer.py*, which should be run on the server computer only.

Example 10-1. PyHeartBeat client

```
""" PyHeartBeat client: sends an UDP packet to a given server every 10 seconds.

Adjust the constant parameters as needed, or call as:
    PyHBClient.py serverip [udpport]
"""

from socket import socket, AF_INET, SOCK_DGRAM
from time import time, ctime, sleep
import sys

SERVERIP = '127.0.0.1'      # local host, just for testing
HBPORT = 43278              # an arbitrary UDP port
BEATWAIT = 10               # number of seconds between heartbeats

if len(sys.argv)>1:
    SERVERIP=sys.argv[1]
if len(sys.argv)>2:
    HBPORT=sys.argv[2]

hbsocket = socket(AF_INET, SOCK_DGRAM)
print "PyHeartBeat client sending to IP %s , port %d"%(SERVERIP, HBPORT)
print "\n*** Press Ctrl-C to terminate ***\n"
while 1:
    hbsocket.sendto('Thump!', (SERVERIP, HBPORT))
    if __debug__:
        print "Time: %s" % ctime(time())
    sleep(BEATWAIT)
```

Example 10-2. PyHeartBeat server

```
""" PyHeartBeat server: receives and tracks UDP packets from all clients.

While the BeatLog thread logs each UDP packet in a dictionary, the main
thread periodically scans the dictionary and prints the IP addresses of the
clients that sent at least one packet during the run, but have
not sent any packet since a time longer than the definition of the timeout.

Adjust the constant parameters as needed, or call as:
    PyHBServer.py [timeout [udpport]]
"""

HBPORT = 43278
CHECKWAIT = 30
```

Example 10-2. PyHeartBeat server (continued)

```python
from socket import socket, gethostbyname, AF_INET, SOCK_DGRAM
from threading import Lock, Thread, Event
from time import time, ctime, sleep
import sys

class BeatDict:
    "Manage heartbeat dictionary"

    def __init__(self):
        self.beatDict = {}
        if __debug__:
            self.beatDict['127.0.0.1'] = time()
        self.dictLock = Lock()

    def __repr__(self):
        list = ''
        self.dictLock.acquire()
        for key in self.beatDict.keys():
            list = "%sIP address: %s - Last time: %s\n" % (
                list, key, ctime(self.beatDict[key]))
        self.dictLock.release()
        return list

    def update(self, entry):
        "Create or update a dictionary entry"
        self.dictLock.acquire()
        self.beatDict[entry] = time()
        self.dictLock.release()

    def extractSilent(self, howPast):
        "Returns a list of entries older than howPast"
        silent = []
        when = time() - howPast
        self.dictLock.acquire()
        for key in self.beatDict.keys():
            if self.beatDict[key] < when:
                silent.append(key)
        self.dictLock.release()
        return silent

class BeatRec(Thread):
    "Receive UDP packets, log them in heartbeat dictionary"

    def __init__(self, goOnEvent, updateDictFunc, port):
        Thread.__init__(self)
        self.goOnEvent = goOnEvent
        self.updateDictFunc = updateDictFunc
        self.port = port
        self.recSocket = socket(AF_INET, SOCK_DGRAM)
        self.recSocket.bind(('', port))

    def __repr__(self):
        return "Heartbeat Server on port: %d\n" % self.port
```

Example 10-2. PyHeartBeat server (continued)

```
    def run(self):
        while self.goOnEvent.isSet():
            if __debug__:
                print "Waiting to receive..."
            data, addr = self.recSocket.recvfrom(6)
            if __debug__:
                print "Received packet from " + `addr`
            self.updateDictFunc(addr[0])

def main():
    "Listen to the heartbeats and detect inactive clients"
    global HBPORT, CHECKWAIT
    if len(sys.argv)>1:
        HBPORT=sys.argv[1]
    if len(sys.argv)>2:
        CHECKWAIT=sys.argv[2]

    beatRecGoOnEvent = Event()
    beatRecGoOnEvent.set()
    beatDictObject = BeatDict()
    beatRecThread = BeatRec(beatRecGoOnEvent, beatDictObject.update, HBPORT)
    if __debug__:
        print beatRecThread
    beatRecThread.start()
    print "PyHeartBeat server listening on port %d" % HBPORT
    print "\n*** Press Ctrl-C to stop ***\n"
    while 1:
        try:
            if __debug__:
                print "Beat Dictionary"
                print `beatDictObject`
            silent = beatDictObject.extractSilent(CHECKWAIT)
            if silent:
                print "Silent clients"
                print `silent`
            sleep(CHECKWAIT)
        except KeyboardInterrupt:
            print "Exiting."
            beatRecGoOnEvent.clear()
            beatRecThread.join()

if __name__ == '__main__':
    main()
```

See Also

Documentation for the standard library modules socket, threading, and time in the *Library Reference*; Jeff Bauer has a related program using UDP for logging information known as Mr. Creosote (*http://starship.python.net/crew/jbauer/creosote/*); UDP is described in *UNIX Network Programming, Volume 1: Networking APIs - Sockets and*

XTI, Second Edition, by W. Richard Stevens (Prentice-Hall, 1998); for the truly curious, the UDP protocol is described in the two-page RFC 768 (*http://www.ietf.org/rfc/rfc768.txt*), which, when compared with current RFCs, shows how much the Internet infrastructure has evolved in 20 years.

10.13 Module: Interactive POP3 Mailbox Inspector

Credit: Xavier Defrang

Suppose you have a POP3 mailbox somewhere, perhaps on a slow connection, and need to examine messages, and perhaps mark them for deletion, in an interactive way. Perhaps you're behind a slow Internet link and don't want to wait for that funny 10-MB MPEG movie that you already received twice yesterday to be fully downloaded before you can read your mail. Or maybe there's a peculiar malformed message that is hanging your MUA. This issue is best tackled interactively, but you need a helping script to let you examine some data about each message and determine which messages should be removed.

Instead of telneting to your POP server and trying to remember the POP3 protocol commands (or hoping that the server implements help), you can use the small script shown in Example 10-3 to inspect your mailbox and do some cleaning. Basically, Python's standard POP3 module, poplib, remembers the protocol commands on your behalf, and this script helps you use them appropriately.

Example 10-3 uses the poplib module to connect to your mailbox. It then prompts you about what to do with each undelivered message. You can view the top of the message, leave it on the server, or mark it for deletion. No particular tricks or hacks are used in this piece of code: it's a simple example of poplib usage. In addition to being practically useful in emergencies, it can show how poplib works. The poplib.POP3 call returns an object that is ready for connection to a POP3 server specified as its argument. We complete the connection by calling the user and pass_ methods to specify a user ID and password. Note the trailing underscore in pass_: this method could not be called pass because that is a Python keyword (the do-nothing statement), and by convention, such issues are always solved by appending an underscore to the identifier.

After connection, we keep working with methods of the pop object. The stat method returns the number of messages and the total size of the mailbox in bytes. The top method takes a message-number argument and returns information about that message, as well as the message itself as a list of lines (you can specify a second argument *N* to ensure that no more than *N* lines are returned). The dele method also takes a message-number argument and deletes that message from the mailbox (without renumbering all other messages). When we're done, we call the quit method. If you're familiar with the POP3 protocol, you'll notice the close correspondence between these methods and the POP3 commands.

Example 10-3. Interactive POP3 mailbox inspector

```
# Helper interactive script to clean POP3 mailboxes from malformed mails that
# hangs MUA's, messages that are too large, etc.
#
# Iterates over nonretrieved mails, prints selected elements from the headers,
# and prompts interactively about whether each message should be deleted

import sys, getpass, poplib, re

# Change according to your needs
POPHOST = "pop.domain.com"
POPUSER = "jdoe"
POPPASS = ""
# The number of message body lines to retrieve
MAXLINES = 10
HEADERS = "From To Subject".split()

args = len(sys.argv)
if args>1: POPHOST = sys.argv[1]
if args>2: POPUSER = sys.argv[2]
if args>3: POPPASS = sys.argv[3]
if args>4: MAXLINES= int(sys.argv[4])
if args>5: HEADERS = sys.argv[5:]

# Headers you're actually interested in
rx_headers  = re.compile('|'.join(headers), re.IGNORECASE)

try:
    # Connect to the POPer and identify user
    pop = poplib.POP3(POPHOST)
    pop.user(POPUSER)

    if not POPPASS or POPPASS=='=':
        # If no password was supplied, ask for it
        POPPASS = getpass.getpass("Password for %s@%s:" % (POPUSER, POPHOST))

    # Authenticate user
    pop.pass_(POPPASS)

    # Get some general information (msg_count, box_size)
    stat = pop.stat()

    # Print some useless information
    print "Logged in as %s@%s" % (POPUSER, POPHOST)
    print "Status: %d message(s), %d bytes" % stat

    bye = 0
    count_del = 0
    for n in range(stat[0]):
```

Example 10-3. Interactive POP3 mailbox inspector (continued)

```
        msgnum = n+1

        # Retrieve headers
        response, lines, bytes = pop.top(msgnum, MAXLINES)

        # Print message info and headers you're interested in
        print "Message %d (%d bytes)" % (msgnum, bytes)
        print "-" * 30
        print "\n".join(filter(rx_headers.match, lines))
        print "-" * 30

        # Input loop
        while 1:
            k = raw_input("(d=delete, s=skip, v=view, q=quit) What?")
            k = k[:1].lower()
            if k == 'd':
                # Mark message for deletion
                k = raw_input("Delete message %d? (y/n)" % msgnum)
                if k in "yY":
                    pop.dele(msgnum)
                    print "Message %d marked for deletion" % msgnum
                    count_del += 1
                    break
            elif k == 's':
                print "Message %d left on server" % msgnum
                break
            elif k == 'v':
                print "-" * 30
                print "\n".join(lines)
                print "-" * 30
            elif k == 'q':
                bye = 1
                break

        # Time to say goodbye?
        if bye:
            print "Bye"
            break

    # Summary
    print "Deleting %d message(s) in mailbox %s@%s" % (
        count_del, POPUSER, POPHOST)

    # Commit operations and disconnect from server
    print "Closing POP3 session"
    pop.quit()

except poplib.error_proto, detail:

    # Fancy error handling
    print "POP3 Protocol Error:", detail
```

See Also

Documentation for the standard library modules poplib and getpass in the *Library Reference*; the POP protocol is described in RFC 1939 (*http://www.ietf.org/rfc/rfc1939.txt*).

10.14 Module: Watching for New IMAP Mail Using a GUI

Credit: Brent Burley

Suppose you need to poll an IMAP inbox for unread messages and display the sender and subject in a scrollable window using Tkinter. The key functionality you need is in the standard Python module imaplib, with some help from the rfc822 module. Example 10-4 reads the server name, user, and password from the ~/.imap file. They must be all on one line, separated by spaces.

The hard (and interesting) part of developing this program was figuring out how to get the IMAP part working, which took a fair bit of investigating. The most productive approach to understanding the IMAP protocol proved to be talking to the IMAP server directly from a Python interactive session to see what it returned:

```
>>> import imaplib
>>> M = imaplib.IMAP4(imap_server)
>>> M.login(imap_user, imap_password)
('OK', ['LOGIN complete'])
>>> M.select(readonly=1)
('OK', ['8'])
>>> M.search(None, '(UNSEEN UNDELETED)')
('OK', ['8'])
>>> M.fetch(8, '(BODY[HEADER.FIELDS (SUBJECT FROM)])')
('OK', [('8 (BODY[HEADER.FIELDS (SUBJECT FROM)] {71}', 'From: John Doe
<John.Doe@nowhere.com>
Subject: test
message

'), ')'])
```

Interactive exploration is so simple with Python because of excellent interactive environments such as the standard interactive session (with readline and completion) or IDEs such as IDLE. As such, it is often the best way to clarify one's doubts or any ambiguities one may find in the documentation.

Example 10-4. Watching for new IMAP mail with a GUI

```
import imaplib, string, sys, os, re, rfc822
from Tkinter import *

PollInterval = 60 # seconds
```

Example 10-4. Watching for new IMAP mail with a GUI (continued)

```
def getimapaccount():
    try:
        f = open(os.path.expanduser('~/.imap'))
    except IOError, e:
        print 'Unable to open ~/.imap: ', e
        sys.exit(1)
    global imap_server, imap_user, imap_password
    try:
        imap_server, imap_user, imap_password = string.split(f.readline())
    except ValueError:
        print 'Invalid data in ~/.imap'
        sys.exit(1)
    f.close()

class msg: # a file-like object for passing a string to rfc822.Message
    def __init__(self, text):
        self.lines = string.split(text, '\015\012')
        self.lines.reverse()
    def readline(self):
        try: return self.lines.pop() + '\n'
        except: return ''

class Mailwatcher(Frame):
    def __init__(self, master=None):
        Frame.__init__(self, master)
        self.pack(side=TOP, expand=YES, fill=BOTH)
        self.scroll = Scrollbar(self)
        self.list = Listbox(self, font='7x13',
                             yscrollcommand=self.scroll.set,
                             setgrid=1, height=6, width=80)
        self.scroll.configure(command=self.list.yview)
        self.scroll.pack(side=LEFT, fill=BOTH)
        self.list.pack(side=LEFT, expand=YES, fill=BOTH)

    def getmail(self):
        self.after(1000*PollInterval, self.getmail)
        self.list.delete(0,END)
        try:
            M = imaplib.IMAP4(imap_server)
            M.login(imap_user, imap_password)
        except Exception, e:
            self.list.insert(END, 'IMAP login error: ', e)
            return

        try:
            result, message = M.select(readonly=1)
            if result != 'OK':
                raise Exception, message
            typ, data = M.search(None, '(UNSEEN UNDELETED)')
            for num in string.split(data[0]):
                try:
                    f = M.fetch(num, '(BODY[HEADER.FIELDS (SUBJECT FROM)])')
```

Example 10-4. Watching for new IMAP mail with a GUI (continued)

```
                    m = rfc822.Message(msg(f[1][0][1]), 0)
                    subject = m['subject']
                except KeyError:
                    f = M.fetch(num, '(BODY[HEADER.FIELDS (FROM)])')
                    m = rfc822.Message(msg(f[1][0][1]), 0)
                    subject = '(no subject)'
                fromaddr = m.getaddr('from')
                if fromaddr[0] == "": n = fromaddr[1]
                else: n = fromaddr[0]
                text = '%-20.20s  %s' % (n, subject)
                self.list.insert(END, text)
            len = self.list.size()
            if len > 0: self.list.see(len-1)
        except Exception, e:
            self.list.delete(0,END)
            print sys.exc_info()
            self.list.insert(END, 'IMAP read error: ', e)
        M.logout()

if __name__=='__main__':
    getimapaccount()
    root = Tk(className='mailwatcher')
    root.title('mailwatcher')
    mw = Mailwatcher(root)
    mw.getmail()
    mw.mainloop()
```

See Also

Documentation for the standard library modules imaplib and rfc822 in the *Library Reference*; information about Tkinter can be obtained from a variety of sources, such as Pythonware's *An Introduction to Tkinter*, by Fredrik Lundh (*http://www. pythonware.com/library*), New Mexico Tech's *Tkinter reference* (*http://www.nmt.edu/ tcc/help/lang/python/docs.html*), and various books; the IMAP protocol is described in RFC 2060 (*http://www.ietf.org/rfc/rfc1939.txt*).

## CHAPTER 11

Web Programming

11.0 Introduction

Credit: Andy McKay

The Web has been a key technology for many years now, and it has become unusual to develop an application that doesn't involve some aspects of the Web. From showing a help file in a browser to using web services, the Web has become an integral part of most applications.

I came to Python through a rather tortuous path of ASP, then Perl, some Zope, and then Python. Looking back, it seems strange that I didn't find Python earlier, but the dominance of Perl and ASP in this area makes it hard for new developers to see the advantages of Python shining through all the other languages.

Unsurprisingly, Python is an excellent language for web development, and, as a "batteries included" language, Python comes with most of the modules you will need. The inclusion of xmlrpclib in Python 2.2 has made the standard libraries even more useful. One of the modules I often use is urllib, which demonstrates the power of a simple, well-designed module—saving a file from the Web in two lines (using urlretrieve) is easy. The cgi module is another example of a module that has enough to work with, but not too much to make the script too slow and bloated.

Compared to other languages, Python seems to have an unusually large number of application servers and templating languages. While it's easy to develop anything for the Web in Python, it would be peculiar to do so without first looking at the application servers available. Rather than continually recreating dynamic pages and scripts, the community has taken on the task of building these application servers to allow other users to create the content in easy-to-use templating systems.

Zope is the most well-known product in the space and provides an object-oriented interface to web publishing. With features too numerous to mention, it allows a robust and powerful object-publishing environment. Quixote and WebWare are two other application servers with similar, highly modular designs. These can be a real help to the overworked web developer who needs to reuse components and give other users the ability to create web sites.

There are times when an application server is just too much and a simple CGI script is all you need. The first recipe in this chapter, Recipe 11.1, is all you need to make sure your web server and Python CGI scripting setup are working correctly. Writing a CGI script doesn't get much simpler than this, although, as the recipe's discussion points out, you could use the cgi.test function to make it even shorter.

Another common task is the parsing of HTML, either on your own site or on other web sites. Parsing HTML tags correctly is not as simple as many developers first think, as they optimistically assume a few regular expressions or string searches will see them through. While such approaches will work for parsing data from other sites, they don't provide enough security to ensure that incoming HTML contains no malicious tags. Recipe 11.6 is a good example of using sgmllib to parse incoming data and strip any offending JavaScript. Most web developers create more than just dynamic web pages, and there are many relevant, useful recipes in other chapters that describe parsing XML, reading network resources and systems administration, for example.

11.1 Testing Whether CGI Is Working

Credit: Jeff Bauer

Problem

You want a simple CGI program to use as a starting point for your own CGI programming or to test if your setup is functioning properly.

Solution

The cgi module is normally used in Python CGI programming, but here we use only its escape function to ensure that the value of an environment variable doesn't accidentally look to the browser as HTML markup. We do all of the real work ourselves:

```
#!/usr/local/bin/python
print "Content-type: text/html"
print
print "<html><head><title>Situation snapshot</title></head><body><pre>"

import sys
sys.stderr = sys.stdout

import os
from cgi import escape
print "<strong>Python %s</strong>" % sys.version
keys = os.environ.keys()
keys.sort()
for k in keys:
```

```
    print "%s\t%s" % (escape(k), escape(os.environ[k]))
print "</pre></body></html>"
```

Discussion

The Common Gateway Interface (CGI) is a protocol that specifies how a web server runs a separate program (often known as a CGI script) that generates a web page dynamically. The protocol specifies how the server provides input and environment data to the script and how the script generates output in return. You can use any language to write your CGI scripts, and Python is well-suited for the task.

This recipe is a simple CGI program that displays the current version of Python and the environment values. CGI programmers should always have some simple code handy to drop into their *cgi-bin* directories. You should run this script before wasting time slogging through your Apache configuration files (or whatever other web server you want to use for CGI work). Of course, cgi.test does all this and more, but it may, in fact, do too much. It does so much, and so much is hidden inside cgi's innards, that it's hard to tweak it to reproduce whatever specific problems you may be encountering in true scripts. Tweaking the program in this recipe, on the other hand, is very easy, since it's such a simple program, and all the parts are exposed.

Besides, this little script is already quite instructive in its own way. The starting line, #!/usr/local/bin/python, must give the absolute path to the Python interpreter with which you want to run your CGI scripts, so you may need to edit it accordingly. A popular solution for non-CGI scripts is to have a first line (the so-called "shebang line") that looks something like this:

```
#!/usr/bin/env python
```

However, this puts you at the mercy of the PATH environment setting, since it runs the first program named python it finds on the PATH, and that probably is not what you want under CGI, where you don't fully control the environment. Incidentally, many web servers implement the shebang line even when you run them under non-Unix systems, so that, for CGI use specifically, it's not unusual to see Python scripts on Windows start with a first line such as:

```
#!c:/python22/python.exe
```

Another issue you may be contemplating is why the import statements are not right at the start of the script, as is the usual Python style, but are preceded by a few print statements. The reason is that import could fail if the Python installation is terribly misconfigured. In case of failure, Python will emit diagnostics to standard error (which is typically directed to your web server logs, depending, of course, on how you set up and configured your web server), and nothing will go to standard output. The CGI standard demands that all output be on standard output, so, we first ensure that a minimal quantity of output will display a result to a visiting browser. Then, assuming that import sys succeeds (if it fails, the whole installation and configuration is so badly broken that there's very little you can do about it!), you immediately make the following assignment:

```
sys.stderr = sys.stdout
```

This ensures that error output will also go to standard output, and you'll have a chance to see it in the visiting browser. You can perform other import operations or do further work in the script only when this is done. In Python 2.2, getting useful tracebacks for errors in CGI scripts is much simpler. Simply add the following at the start of your script:

```
import cgitb; cgitb.enable()
```

and the new standard module cgitb takes care of the rest

Just about all known browsers let you get away with skipping most of the HTML tags that this script outputs, but why skimp on correctness, relying on the browser to patch your holes? It costs little to emit correct HMTL, so you should get into the habit of doing things right, when the cost is so modest.

See Also

Documentation of the standard library module cgi in the *Library Reference*; a basic introduction to the CGI protocol is available at *http://hoohoo.ncsa.uiuc.edu/cgi/overview.html*.

11.2 Writing a CGI Script

Credit: Luther Blissett

Problem

You want to write a CGI script to process the contents of an HTML form. In particular, you want to access the form contents and produce valid output in return.

Solution

A CGI script is a server-side program that a web server launches to generate a web page dynamically based on remote client requests (typically, the user filled in an HTML form on his web browser and submitted it). The script receives its input information from the client through its standard input stream and its environment and generates HTTP headers and body on its standard output stream. Python's standard cgi module handles input tasks on the script's behalf, and your script directly generates output as needed:

```
#!/usr/bin/python

# Get the cgi module and the values of all fields in the form
import cgi
formStorage = cgi.FieldStorage()
```

```
# Get a parameter string from the form
theValue = formStorage['PARAM_NAME'].value

# Output an HTML document
outputTemplate = """Content-Type: text/plain

<html><head><title>%(title)s</title></head><body>
%(body)s
</body></html>
"""
print outputTemplate % {'title': "Howdy there!",
    'body': '<p>You typed: <tt>%s</tt></p>'%cgi.escape(theValue)
    }
```

Discussion

A CGI script needs to decode the input to a web page according to a well-defined format. This task is performed by Python's standard cgi module. You simply call cgi.FieldStorage and obtain a mapping from each name of a form's field to the field's contents. You can index it directly, as is done in this recipe. You can also use the get method to supply a default if a field is absent, and the keys method to get a list of keys. While this is all typical dictionary functionality, the mapping is not actually a dictionary (so it can handle repeated field names in a form and the cases in which the user is uploading large files), so you need to use the value attribute, as shown in the recipe, to actually get at each field's contents. See Recipe 11.3 for a simple way to turn a field storage object into a plain dictionary in cases in which you don't need the extra functionality it supplies.

To generate the resulting web page, you have many more choices, so the cgi module does not handle this part. Python embodies many other string-processing facilities to let you generate the strings you want to output, and you can simply use print statements to emit them once they're ready. What cgi does supply for this part of the task is a function, cgi.escape, which takes any string and escapes special characters it might contain. In other words, it turns each occurrence of the characters &, <, and > into the equivalent HTML entity, to ensure that the data you're emitting does not disturb the user's browser's ability to parse the actual HTML structure of your output document.

In this recipe, I use Python's % string format operator to generate the web page. I use it once with a mapping as the righthand side and with the named items title for the page's title and body for its body. I use it a second time to generate the body itself, in the simpler positional way that takes a tuple on the righthand side. When the tuple would have just one item (as it does here), you can also use just the item itself as further simplification, and this is what I do in the recipe.

See Also

Recipe 11.1 for a quick way to test your CGI setup; Recipe 11.3 for a simple way to turn a field storage object into a plain dictionary; documentation of the standard library module cgi in the *Library Reference*; a basic introduction to the CGI protocol is available at *http://hoohoo.ncsa.uiuc.edu/cgi/overview.html*.

11.3 Using a Simple Dictionary for CGI Parameters

Credit: Richie Hindle

Problem

You want to lead a simpler life when writing simple CGI scripts, accessing form fields from a simple dictionary rather than from a cgi.FieldStorage instance.

Solution

The cgi module offers sophisticated functionality in its FieldStorage class, but for most web pages, you can access the form's data as a normal dictionary. It's not hard to build the dictionary from the FieldStorage object:

```
#!/usr/bin/python

import cgi

def cgiFieldStorageToDict(fieldStorage):
    """ Get a plain dictionary rather than the '.value' system used by the
    cgi module's native fieldStorage class. """
    params = {}
    for key in fieldStorage.keys():
        params[key] = fieldStorage[key].value
    return params

if __name__ == "__main__":
    dict = cgiFieldStorageToDict(cgi.FieldStorage())
    print "Content-Type: text/plain"
    print
    print dict
```

Discussion

Rather than using Python's cgi.FieldStorage class, a simple dictionary is enough for 90% of CGI scripts. This recipe shows you how to convert a FieldStorage object into a simple dictionary.

Install the above script into your *cgi-bin* directory as *cgitest.py*, then visit the script with some parameters. For example:

```
http://your-server/cgi-bin/cgitest.py?x=y
```

You should see a simple dictionary printed in response:

```
{'x': 'y'}
```

Note that the first line of the script must give the complete path to the Python interpreter with which you want to run your CGI script, so you may have to edit it, depending on your configuration and setup.

The FieldStorage system is necessary when your HTML form contains multiple fields with the same name, or when users upload large files to your script, but if all you have is a simple set of uniquely named controls, a plain dictionary is easier (and more Pythonic!) to work with. Since the point of the recipe is simplicity, we of course do not want to do anything complicated, such as subclassing FieldStorage or anything similar; getting a simple dictionary is the whole point, and this recipe is a simple way to satisfy this simple requirement.

See Also

Recipe 11.1 for a quick way to test your CGI setup; documentation of the standard library module cgi in the *Library Reference*; a basic introduction to the CGI protocol is available at *http://hoohoo.ncsa.uiuc.edu/cgi/overview.html*.

11.4   Handling URLs Within a CGI Script

Credit: Jürgen Hermann

Problem

You need to build URLs within a CGI script—for example, to send an HTTP redirection header.

Solution

To build a URL within a script, you need information such as the hostname and script name. According to the CGI standard, the web server sets up a lot of useful information in the process environment of a script before it runs the script itself. In a Python script, we can access the process environment as os.environ, an attribute of the os module:

```
import os, string

def isSSL():
    """ Return true if we are on an SSL (https) connection. """
    return os.environ.get('SSL_PROTOCOL', '') != ''
```

```python
    def getScriptname():
        """ Return the scriptname part of the URL ("/path/to/my.cgi"). """
        return os.environ.get('SCRIPT_NAME', '')

    def getPathinfo():
        """ Return the remaining part of the URL. """
        pathinfo = os.environ.get('PATH_INFO', '')

        # Fix for a well-known bug in IIS/4.0
        if os.name == 'nt':
            scriptname = getScriptname()
            if string.find(pathinfo, scriptname) == 0:
                pathinfo = pathinfo[len(scriptname):]

        return pathinfo

    def getQualifiedURL(uri = None):
        """ Return a full URL starting with schema, servername, and port.
            Specifying uri causes it to be appended to the server root URL (uri must
            start with a slash).
        """
        schema, stdport = (('http', '80'), ('https', '443'))[isSSL()]
        host = os.environ.get('HTTP_HOST', '')
        if not host:
            host = os.environ.get('SERVER_NAME', 'localhost')
            port = os.environ.get('SERVER_PORT', '80')
            if port != stdport: host = host + ":" + port

        result = "%s://%s" % (schema, host)
        if uri: result = result + uri

        return result

    def getBaseURL():
        """ Return a fully qualified URL to this script. """
        return getQualifiedURL(getScriptname())
```

Discussion

There are, of course, many ways to manipulate URLs, but many CGI scripts have common needs. This recipe collects a few typical high-level functional needs for URL synthesis from within CGI scripts. You should never hardcode hostnames or absolute paths in your scripts, of course, because that would make it difficult to port the scripts elsewhere or rename a virtual host. The CGI environment has sufficient information available to avoid such hardcoding, and, by importing this recipe's code as a module, you can avoid duplicating code in your scripts to collect and use that information in typical ways.

The recipe works by accessing information in os.environ, the attribute of Python's standard os module that collects the process environment of the current process and lets your script access it as if it was a normal Python dictionary. In particular, os.environ has a get method, just like a normal dictionary does, that returns either the mapping for a given key or, if that key is missing, a default value that you supply in the call to get. This recipe performs all accesses through os.environ.get, thus ensuring sensible behavior even if the relevant environment variables have been left undefined by your web server (this should never happen, but, of course, not all web servers are bug-free).

Among the functions presented in this recipe, getQualifiedURL is the one you'll use most often. It transforms a URI into a URL on the same host (and with the same schema) used by the CGI script that calls it. It gets the information from the environment variables HTTP_HOST, SERVER_NAME, and SERVER_PORT. Furthermore, it can handle secure (https) as well as normal (http) connections, and it selects between the two by using the isSSL function, which is also part of this recipe.

Suppose you need to redirect a visiting browser to another location on this same host. Here's how you can use the functions in this recipe, hardcoding only the redirect location on the host itself, but not the hostname, port, and normal or secure schema:

```
# an example redirect header:
print "Location:", getQualifiedURL("/go/here")
```

See Also

Documentation of the standard library module os in the *Library Reference*; a basic introduction to the CGI protocol is available at *http://hoohoo.ncsa.uiuc.edu/cgi/overview.html*.

11.5 Resuming the HTTP Download of a File

Credit: Chris Moffitt

Problem

You need to resume an HTTP download of a file that has been partially transferred.

Solution

Large downloads are sometimes interrupted. However, a good HTTP server that supports the Range header lets you resume the download from where it was interrupted. The standard Python module urllib lets you access this functionality almost seamlessly. You need to add only the needed header and intercept the error code the server sends to confirm that it will respond with a partial file:

```
import urllib, os

class myURLOpener(urllib.FancyURLopener):
    """ Subclass to override error 206 (partial file being sent); okay for us """
    def http_error_206(self, url, fp, errcode, errmsg, headers, data=None):
        pass    # Ignore the expected "non-error" code
```

```
def getrest(dlFile, fromUrl, verbose=0):
    loop = 1
    existSize = 0
    myUrlclass = myURLOpener()
    if os.path.exists(dlFile):
        outputFile = open(dlFile,"ab")
        existSize = os.path.getsize(dlFile)
        # If the file exists, then download only the remainder
        myUrlclass.addheader("Range","bytes=%s-" % (existSize))
    else:
        outputFile = open(dlFile,"wb")

    webPage = myUrlclass.open(fromUrl)
    if verbose:
        for k, v in webPage.headers.items():
            print k, "=", v

    # If we already have the whole file, there is no need to download it again
    numBytes = 0
    webSize = int(webPage.headers['Content-Length'])
    if webSize == existSize:
        if verbose: print "File (%s) was already downloaded from URL (%s)"%(
            dlFile, fromUrl)
    else:
        if verbose: print "Downloading %d more bytes" % (webSize-existSize)
        while 1:
            data = webPage.read(8192)
            if not data:
                break
            outputFile.write(data)
            numBytes = numBytes + len(data)

    webPage.close()
    outputFile.close()

    if verbose:
        print "downloaded", numBytes, "bytes from", webPage.url
    return numbytes
```

Discussion

The HTTP Range header lets the web server know that you want only a certain range of data to be downloaded, and this recipe takes advantage of this header. Of course, the server needs to support the Range header, but since the header is part of the HTTP 1.1 specification, it's widely supported. This recipe has been tested with Apache 1.3 as the server, but I expect no problems with other reasonably modern servers.

The recipe lets urllib.FancyURLopener to do all the hard work of adding a new header, as well as the normal handshaking. I had to subclass it to make it known that the error 206 is not really an error in this case—so you can proceed normally. I also do some extra checks to quit the download if I've already downloaded the whole file.

Check out the HTTP 1.1 RFC (2616) to learn more about what all of the headers mean. You may find a header that is very useful, and Python's urllib lets you send any header you want. This recipe should probably do a check to make sure that the web server accepts Range, but this is pretty simple to do.

See Also

Documentation of the standard library module urllib in the *Library Reference*; the HTTP 1.1 RFC (*http://www.ietf.org/rfc/rfc2616.txt*).

11.6   Stripping Dangerous Tags and Javascript from HTML

Credit: Itamar Shtull-Trauring

Problem

You have received some HTML input from a user and need to make sure that the HTML is clean. You want to allow only safe tags, to ensure that tags needing closure are indeed closed, and, ideally, to strip out any Javascript that might be part of the page.

Solution

The sgmllib module helps with cleaning up the HTML tags, but we still have to fight against the Javascript:

```
import sgmllib, string

class StrippingParser(sgmllib.SGMLParser):
    # These are the HTML tags that we will leave intact
    valid_tags = ('b', 'a', 'i', 'br', 'p')
    tolerate_missing_closing_tags = ('br', 'p')
    from htmlentitydefs import entitydefs # replace entitydefs from sgmllib

    def __init__(self):
        sgmllib.SGMLParser.__init__(self)
        self.result = []
        self.endTagList = []

    def handle_data(self, data):
        self.result.append(data)

    def handle_charref(self, name):
        self.result.append("&#%s;" % name)
```

```
        def handle_entityref(self, name):
            x = ';' * self.entitydefs.has_key(name)
            self.result.append("&%s%s" % (name, x))

        def unknown_starttag(self, tag, attrs):
            """ Delete all tags except for legal ones. """
            if tag in self.valid_tags:
                self.result.append('<' + tag)
                for k, v in attrs:
                    if string.lower(k[0:2]) != 'on' and string.lower(
                            v[0:10]) != 'javascript':
                        self.result.append(' %s="%s"' % (k, v))
                self.result.append('>')
                if tag not in self.tolerate_missing_closing_tags:
                    endTag = '</%s>' % tag
                    self.endTagList.insert(0,endTag)

        def unknown_endtag(self, tag):
            if tag in self.valid_tags:
                # We don't ensure proper nesting of opening/closing tags
                endTag = '</%s>' % tag
                self.result.append(endTag)
                self.endTagList.remove(endTag)

        def cleanup(self):
            """ Append missing closing tags. """
            self.result.extend(self.endTagList)

    def strip(s):
        """ Strip unsafe HTML tags and Javascript from string s. """
        parser = StrippingParser( )
        parser.feed(s)
        parser.close( )
        parser.cleanup( )
        return ''.join(parser.result)
```

Discussion

This recipe uses sgmllib to get rid of any HTML tags, except for those specified in
the valid_tags list. It also tolerates missing closing tags only for those tags specified
in tolerate_missing_closing_tags.

Getting rid of Javascript is much harder. This recipe's code handles only URLs that
start with javascript: or onClick and similar handlers. The contents of <script> tags
will be printed as part of the text, and vbscript:, jscript:, and other weird URLs
may be legal in some versions of IE. We could do a better job on both scores, but
only at the price of substantial additional complications.

There is one Pythonic good habit worth noticing in the code. When you need to put
together a large string result out of many small pieces, don't keep the string as a string
during the composition. All the += or equivalent operations will kill your performance

(which would be $O(N^2)$—terrible for large enough values of N). Instead, keep the result as a list of strings, growing it with calls to append or extend, and make the result a string only when you're done accumulating all the pieces with a single invocation of ''.join on the result list. This is a much faster approach (specifically, it's roughly $O(N)$ when amortized over large-enough N). If you get into the habit of building strings out of pieces the Python way, you'll never have to worry about this aspect of your program's performance.

See Also

Recipe 3.5; documentation for the standard library module sgmllib in the *Library Reference*; the W3C page on HTML (*http://www.w3.org/MarkUp/*).

11.7   Running a Servlet with Jython

Credit: Brian Zhou

Problem

You need to code a servlet using Jython.

Solution

Java (and Jython) is most often deployed server-side, and thus servlets are a typical way of deploying your code. Jython makes them easy to use:

```
import java, javax, sys

class hello(javax.servlet.http.HttpServlet):

    def doGet(self, request, response):
        response.setContentType("text/html")
        out = response.getOutputStream( )
        print >>out, """<html>
<head><title>Hello World</title></head>
<body>Hello World from Jython Servlet at %s!
</body>
</html>
""" % (java.util.Date( ),)
        out.close( )
        return
```

Discussion

This is no worse than a typical JSP! (See *http://jywiki.sourceforge.net/index. php?JythonServlet* for setup instructions.) Compare this recipe to the equivalent Java code; with Python, you're finished coding in the same time it takes to set up the framework in Java. Note that most of your setup work will be strictly related to

Tomcat or whatever servlet container you use; the Jython-specific work is limited to copying *jython.jar* to the *WEB-INF/lib* subdirectory of your chosen servlet context and editing *WEB-INF/web.xml* to add `<servlet>` and `<servlet-mapping>` tags so that `org.python.util.PyServlet` serves the **.py* `<url-pattern>`.

The key to this recipe (like most other Jython uses) is that your Jython scripts and modules can import and use Java packages and classes as if the latter were Python code or extensions. In other words, all of the Java libraries that you could use with Java code are similarly usable with Python (Jython) code. This example servlet needs to use the standard Java servlet response object to set the resulting page's content type (to text/html) and to get the output stream. Afterwards, it can just print to the output stream, since the latter is a Python file-like object. To further show off your seamless access to the Java libraries, you can also use the Date class of the java.util package, incidentally demonstrating how it can be printed as a string from Jython.

See Also

Information on Java servlets at *http://java.sun.com/products/servlet/*; information on JythonServlet at *http://jywiki.sourceforge.net/index.php?JythonServlet*.

11.8 Accessing Netscape Cookie Information

Credit: Mark Nenadov

Problem

You need to access cookie information, which Netscape stores in a *cookie.txt* file, in an easily usable way, optionally transforming it into XML or SQL.

Solution

Classes are always good candidates for grouping data with the code that handles it:

```
class Cookie:
    "Models a single cookie"
    def __init__(self, cookieInfo):
        self.allInfo = tuple(cookieInfo)

    def getUrl(self):    return self.allInfo[0]
    def getInfo(self, n): return self.allInfo[n]

    def generateSQL(self):
        sql = "INSERT INTO Cookie(Url,Data1,Data2,Data3,Data4,Data5) "
        sql += "VALUES('%s','%s','%s','%s','%s','%s');" % self.allInfo
        return sql

    def generateXML(self):
        xml = "<cookie url='%s' data1='%s' data2='%s' data3='%s'" \
```

```
            " data4='%s' data5='%s' />" % self.allInfo
        return xml

class CookieInfo:
    "models all cookies from a cookie.txt file"
    cookieSeparator = "        "

    def __init__(self, cookiePathName):
        cookieFile = open(cookiePathName, "r")
        self.rawCookieContent = cookieFile.readlines()
        cookieFile.close()

        self.cookies = []
        for line in self.rawCookieContent:
            if line[:1] == '#': pass
            elif line[:1] == '\n': pass
            else: self.cookies.append(
                Cookie(line.split(self.cookieSeparator)))

    def count(self):
        return len(self.cookies)
    __len__ = count

    # Find a cookie by URL and return a Cookie object, or None if not found
    def findCookieByURL(self, url):
        for cookie in self.cookies:
            if cookie.getUrl() == url: return cookie
        return None

    # Return list of Cookie objects containing the given string
    def findCookiesByString(self, str):
        results = []
        for c in self.cookies:
            if " ".join(c.allInfo).find(str) != -1:
                results.append(c)
        return results

    # Return SQL for all the cookies
    def returnAllCookiesInSQL(self):
        return '\n'.join([c.generateSQL() for c in self.cookies]) + '\n'

    # Return XML for all the cookies
    def returnAllCookiesInXML(self):
        return "<?xml version='1.0' ?>\n\n<cookies>\n" + \
            '\n'.join([c.generateXML() for x in self.cookies]) + \
            "\n\n</cookies>"
```

Discussion

The CookieInfo and Cookie classes provide developers with a read-only interface to
the *cookies.txt* file in which Netscape stores cookies received from web servers. The
CookieInfo class represents the whole set of cookies from the file, and the Cookie

class represents one of the cookies. CookieInfo provides methods to search for cookies and to operate on all cookies. Cookie provides methods to output XML and SQL equivalent to the cookie.

Here is some test/sample code for this recipe, which you can modify to fit your specific cookies file:

```
if __name__=='__main__':
    c = CookieInfo("cookies.txt")
    print "You have:", len(c), "cookies"

    # prints third data element from www.chapters.ca's cookie
    cookie = c.findCookieByURL("www.chapters.ca")

    if cookie is not None:
        print "3rd piece of data from the cookie from www.chapters.ca:", \
            cookie.getData(3)
    else:
        print "No cookie from www.chapters.ca is in your cookies file"

    # prints the URLs of all cookies with "mail" in them
    print "url's of all cookies with 'mail' somewhere in their content:"
    for cookie in c.findCookiesByString("mail"):
        print cookie.getUrl( )

    # prints the SQL and XML for the www.chapters.ca cookie
    cookie = c.findCookieByURL("www.chapters.ca")
    if cookie is not None:
        print "SQL for the www.chapters.ca cookie:", cookie.generateSQL( )
        print "XML for the www.chapters.ca cookie:", cookie.generateXML( )
```

These classes let you forget about parsing cookies that your browser has received from various web servers so you can start using them as objects. The Cookie class's generateSQL and generateXML methods may have to be modified, depending on your preferences and data schema.

A large potential benefit of this recipe's approach is that you can write classes with a similar interface to model cookies, and sets of cookies, in other browsers, and use their instances polymorphically (interchangeably), so that your system-administration scripts that need to handle cookies (e.g., to exchange them between browsers or machines, or remove some of them) do not need to depend directly on the details of how a given browser stores cookies.

See Also

Recipe 11.9; the Unofficial Cookie FAQ (*http://www.cookiecentral.com/faq/*) is chock-full of information on cookies.

11.9 Finding an Internet Explorer Cookie

Credit: Andy McKay

Problem

You need to find a specific IE cookie.

Solution

Cookies that your browser has downloaded contain potentially useful information, so it's important to know how to get at them. With IE, you need to access the registry to find where the cookies are, then read them as files:

```
from string import lower, find
import re, os, glob
import win32api, win32con

def _getLocation():
    """ Examines the registry to find the cookie folder IE uses """
    key = r'Software\Microsoft\Windows\CurrentVersion\Explorer\Shell Folders'
    regkey = win32api.RegOpenKey(win32con.HKEY_CURRENT_USER, key, 0,
        win32con.KEY_ALL_ACCESS)
    num = win32api.RegQueryInfoKey(regkey)[1]
    for x in range(num):
        k = win32api.RegEnumValue(regkey, x)
        if k[0] == 'Cookies':
            return k[1]

def _getCookieFiles(location, name):
    """ Rummages through all the filenames in the cookie folder and returns
    only the filenames that include the substring 'name'. name can be the domain;
    for example 'activestate' will return all cookies for activestate.
    Unfortunately, it will also return cookies for domains such as
    activestate.foo.com, but that's unlikely to happen, and you can
    double-check later to see if it has occurred. """
    filemask = os.path.join(location, '*%s*' % name)
    filenames = glob.glob(filemask)
    return filenames

def _findCookie(files, cookie_re):
    """ Look through a group of files for a cookie that satisfies a
    given compiled RE, returning the first such cookie found. """
    for file in files:
        data = open(file, 'r').read()
        m = cookie_re.search(data)
        if m: return m.group(1)

def findIECookie(domain, cookie):
    """ Finds the cookie for a given domain from IE cookie files """
    try:
        l = _getLocation()
    except:
```

```
        # Print a debug message
        print "Error pulling registry key"
        return None

    # Found the key; now find the files and look through them
    f = _getCookieFiles(l, domain)
    if f:
        cookie_re = re.compile('%s\n(.*?)\n' % cookie)
        return _findCookie(f, cookie_re)
    else:
        print "No cookies for domain (%s) found" % domain
        return None


if __name__=='__main__':
    print findIECookie(domain='kuro5hin', cookie='k5-new_session')
```

Discussion

While Netscape cookies are in a text file, which you can access as shown in Recipe 11.8, IE keeps cookies as files in a directory, and you need to access the registry to find which directory that is. This recipe uses the win32all Windows-specific extensions to Python for registry access; as an alternative, the _winreg module that is part of Python's standard distribution for Windows can be used. The code has been tested and works on IE 5 and 6.

In the recipe, the _getLocation function accesses the registry and finds and returns the directory IE is using for cookies files. The _getCookieFiles function receives the directory as an argument and uses standard module glob to return all filenames in the directory whose names include a particular requested domain name. The _findCookie function opens and reads all such files in turn, until it finds one that satisfies a compiled regular expression which the function receives as an argument. It then returns the substring of the file's contents corresponding to the first parenthesized group in the RE, or None if no satisfactory file is found. As the leading underscore in each of these functions' names indicates, these are all internal functions, meant only as implementation details of the only function this module is meant to expose, namely findIECookie, which appropriately uses the other functions to locate and return a specific cookie's value for a given domain.

An alternative to this recipe could be to write a Python extension, or use calldll, to access the InternetGetCookie API function in *Wininet.DLL*, as documented on MSDN. However, the added value of the alternative seems to be not worth the effort of dropping down from a pure Python module to a C-coded extension.

See Also

Recipe 11.8; the Unofficial Cookie FAQ (*http://www.cookiecentral.com/faq/*) is chock-full of information on cookies; Documentation for win32api and win32con in win32all (*http://starship.python.net/crew/mhammond/win32/Downloads.html*) or ActivePython (*http://www.activestate.com/ActivePython/*); Windows API documentation available from Microsoft (*http://msdn.microsoft.com*); *Python Programming on Win32*, by Mark Hammond and Andy Robinson (O'Reilly); calldll is available at Sam Rushing's page (*http://www.nightmare.com/~rushing/dynwin/*).

11.10 Module: Fetching Latitude/Longitude Data from the Web

Credit: Will Ware

Given a list of cities, Example 11-1 fetches their latitudes and longitudes from one web site (*http://www.astro.ch*, a database used for astrology, of all things) and uses them to dynamically build a URL for another web site (*http://pubweb.parc.xerox.com*), which, in turn, creates a map highlighting the cities against the outlines of continents. Maybe someday a program will be clever enough to load the latitudes and longitudes as waypoints into your GPS receiver.

The code can be vastly improved in several ways. The main fragility of the recipe comes from relying on the exact format of the HTML page returned by the *www.astro.com* site, particularly in the rather clumsy for x in inf.readlines() loop in the findcity function. If this format ever changes, the recipe will break. You could change the recipe to use htmllib.HTMLParser instead, and be a tad more immune to modest format changes. This helps only a little, however. After all, HTML is meant for human viewers, not for automated parsing and extraction of information. A better approach would be to find a site serving similar information in XML (including, quite possibly, XHTML, the XML/HTML hybrid that combines the strengths of both of its parents) and parse the information with Python's powerful XML tools (covered in Chapter 12).

However, despite this defect, this recipe still stands as an example of the kind of opportunity already afforded today by existing services on the Web, without having to wait for the emergence of commercialized web services.

Example 11-1. Fetching latitude/longitude data from the Web

```
import string, urllib, re, os, exceptions, webbrowser

JUST_THE_US = 0

class CityNotFound(exceptions.Exception): pass

def xerox_parc_url(marklist):
    """ Prepare a URL for the xerox.com map-drawing service, with marks
    at the latitudes and longitudes listed in list-of-pairs marklist. """
    avg_lat, avg_lon = max_lat, max_lon = marklist[0]
    marks = ["%f,%f" % marklist[0]]
    for lat, lon in marklist[1:]:
        marks.append(";%f,%f" % (lat, lon))
```

Example 11-1. Fetching latitude/longitude data from the Web (continued)

```python
            avg_lat = avg_lat + lat
            avg_lon = avg_lon + lon
            if lat > max_lat: max_lat = lat
            if lon > max_lon: max_lon = lon
        avg_lat = avg_lat / len(marklist)
        avg_lon = avg_lon / len(marklist)
        if len(marklist) == 1:
            max_lat, max_lon = avg_lat + 1, avg_lon + 1
        diff = max(max_lat - avg_lat, max_lon - avg_lon)
        D = {'height': 4 * diff, 'width': 4 * diff,
             'lat': avg_lat, 'lon': avg_lon,
             'marks': ''.join(marks)}
        if JUST_THE_US:
            url = ("http://pubweb.parc.xerox.com/map/db=usa/ht=%(height)f" +
                   "/wd=%(width)f/color=1/mark=%(marks)s/lat=%(lat)f/" +
                   "lon=%(lon)f/") % D
        else:
            url = ("http://pubweb.parc.xerox.com/map/color=1/ht=%(height)f" +
                   "/wd=%(width)f/color=1/mark=%(marks)s/lat=%(lat)f/" +
                   "lon=%(lon)f/") % D
        return url

def findcity(city, state):
    Please_click = re.compile("Please click")
    city_re = re.compile(city)
    state_re = re.compile(state)
    url = ("""http://www.astro.ch/cgi-bin/atlw3/aq.cgi?expr=%s&lang=e"""
           % (string.replace(city, " ", "+") + "%2C+" + state))
    lst = [ ]
    found_please_click = 0
    inf = urllib.FancyURLopener( ).open(url)
    for x in inf.readlines( ):
        x = x[:-1]
        if Please_click.search(x) != None:
            # Here is one assumption about unchanging structure
            found_please_click = 1
        if (city_re.search(x) != None and
            state_re.search(x) != None and
            found_please_click):
            # Pick apart the HTML pieces
            L = [ ]
            for y in string.split(x, '<'):
                L = L + string.split(y, '>')
            # Discard any pieces of zero length
            lst.append(filter(None, L))
    inf.close( )
    try:
        # Here's a few more assumptions
        x = lst[0]
        lat, lon = x[6], x[10]
    except IndexError:
        raise CityNotFound("not found: %s, %s"%(city, state))
```

Example 11-1. Fetching latitude/longitude data from the Web (continued)

```
    def getdegrees(x, dividers):
        if string.count(x, dividers[0]):
            x = map(int, string.split(x, dividers[0]))
            return x[0] + (x[1] / 60.)
        elif string.count(x, dividers[1]):
            x = map(int, string.split(x, dividers[1]))
            return -(x[0] + (x[1] / 60.))
        else:
            raise CityNotFound("Bogus result (%s)" % x)
    return getdegrees(lat, "ns"), getdegrees(lon, "ew")

def showcities(citylist):
    marklist = [ ]
    for city, state in citylist:
        try:
            lat, lon = findcity(city, state)
            print ("%s, %s:" % (city, state)), lat, lon
            marklist.append((lat, lon))
        except CityNotFound, message:
            print "%s, %s: not in database? (%s)" % (city, state, message)
    url = xerox_parc_url(marklist)
    # Print URL
    # os.system('netscape "%s"' % url)
    webbrowser.open(url)

# Export a few lists for test purposes

citylist = (("Natick", "MA"),
            ("Rhinebeck", "NY"),
            ("New Haven", "CT"),
            ("King of Prussia", "PA"))

citylist1 = (("Mexico City", "Mexico"),
             ("Acapulco", "Mexico"),
             ("Abilene", "Texas"),
             ("Tulum", "Mexico"))

citylist2 = (("Munich", "Germany"),
             ("London", "England"),
             ("Madrid", "Spain"),
             ("Paris", "France"))

if __name__=='__main__':
    showcities(citylist1)
```

See Also

Documentation for the standard library module htmllib in the *Library Reference*;
information about the Xerox PARC map viewer is at *http://www.parc.xerox.com/istl/
projects/mapdocs/*; *AstroDienst* hosts a worldwide server of latitude/longitude data
(*http://www.astro.com/cgi-bin/atlw3/aq.cgi*).

## CHAPTER 12

Processing XML

12.0 Introduction

Credit: Paul Prescod, co-author of XML Handbook (Prentice Hall)

XML has become a central technology for all kinds of information exchange. Today, most new file formats that are invented are based on XML. Most new protocols are based upon XML. It simply isn't possible to work with the emerging Internet infrastructure without supporting XML. Luckily, Python has had XML support since Version 2.0.

Python and XML are perfect complements for each other. XML is an open-standards way of exchanging information. Python is an open source language that processes the information. Python is strong at text processing and at handling complicated data structures. XML is text-based and is a way of exchanging complicated data structures.

That said, working with XML is not so seamless that it takes no effort. There is always somewhat of a mismatch between the needs of a particular programming language and a language-independent information representation. So there is often a requirement to write code that reads (deserializes or parses) and writes (serializes) XML.

Parsing XML can be done with code written purely in Python or with a module that is a C/Python mix. Python comes with the fast Expat parser written in C. This is what most XML applications use. Recipe 12.6 shows how to use Expat directly with its native API.

Although Expat is ubiquitous in the XML world, it is not the only parser available. There is an API called SAX that allows any XML parser to be plugged into a Python program, as anydbm allows any database to be plugged in. This API is demonstrated in recipes that check that an XML document is well-formed, extract text from a document, count the tags in a document, and do some minor tweaking of an XML document. These recipes should give you a good understanding of how SAX works.

Recipe 12.12 shows the generation of XML from lists. Those of you new to XML (and some with more experience) will think that the technique used is a little primitive. It just builds up strings using standard Python mechanisms instead of using a special XML-generation API. This is nothing to be ashamed of, however. For the vast majority of XML applications, no more sophisticated technique is required. Reading XML is much harder than writing it. Therefore, it makes sense to use specialized software (such as the Expat parser) for reading XML, but nothing special for writing it.

XML-RPC is a protocol built on top of XML for sending data structures from one program to another, typically across the Internet. XML-RPC allows programmers to completely hide the implementation languages of the two communicating components. Two components running on different operating systems, written in different languages, can communicate easily. XML-RPC is built into Python 2.2. This chapter does not deal with XML-RPC because, together with its alternatives (which include SOAP, another distributed-processing protocol that also relies on XML), XML-RPC is covered in Chapter 13.

The other recipes are a little bit more eclectic. For example, one shows how to extract information from an XML document in environments where performance is more important than correctness (e.g., an interactive editor). Another shows how to auto-detect the Unicode encoding that an XML document uses without parsing the document. Unicode is central to the definition of XML, so it helps to understand Python's Unicode objects if you will be doing sophisticated work with XML.

The PyXML extension package has a variety of useful tools for working with XML in more advanced ways. It has a full implementation of the Document Object Model (DOM)—as opposed to the subset bundled with Python itself—and a validating XML parser written entirely in Python. The DOM is an API that loads an entire XML document into memory. This can make XML processing easier for complicated structures in which there are many references from one part of the document to another, or when you need to correlate (e.g., compare) more than one XML document. There is only one really simple recipe that shows how to normalize an XML document with the DOM (Recipe 12.8), but you'll find many other examples in the PyXML package (*http://pyxml.sourceforge.net/*).

There are also two recipes that focus on XSLT: Recipe 12.4 shows how to drive two different XSLT engines, and Recipe 12.9 shows how to control XSLT stylesheet loading when using the XSLT engine that comes with the FourThought 4Suite package (*http://www.4suite.org/*). This package provides a sophisticated set of open source XML tools above and beyond those provided in core Python or in the PyXML package. In particular, this package has implementations of a variety of standards, such as XPath, XSLT, XLink, XPointer, and RDF. This is an excellent resource for XML power users.

For more information on using Python and XML together, see *Python and XML* by Christopher A. Jones and Fred L. Drake, Jr. (O'Reilly).

12.1 Checking XML Well-Formedness

Credit: Paul Prescod

Problem

You need to check if an XML document is well-formed (not if it conforms to a DTD or schema), and you need to do this quickly.

Solution

SAX (presumably using a fast parser such as Expat underneath) is the fastest and simplest way to perform this task:

```
from xml.sax.handler import ContentHandler
from xml.sax import make_parser
from glob import glob
import sys

def parsefile(file):
    parser = make_parser( )
    parser.setContentHandler(ContentHandler( ))
    parser.parse(file)

for arg in sys.argv[1:]:
    for filename in glob(arg):
        try:
            parsefile(filename)
            print "%s is well-formed" % filename
        except Exception, e:
            print "%s is NOT well-formed! %s" % (filename, e)
```

Discussion

A text is a well-formed XML document if it adheres to all the basic syntax rules for XML documents. In other words, it has a correct XML declaration and a single root element, all tags are properly nested, tag attributes are quoted, and so on.

This recipe uses the SAX API with a dummy `ContentHandler` that does nothing. Generally, when we parse an XML document with SAX, we use a `ContentHandler` instance to process the document's contents. But in this case, we only want to know if the document meets the most fundamental syntax constraints of XML; therefore, there is no processing that we need to do, and the do-nothing handler suffices.

The parsefile function parses the whole document and throws an exception if there is an error. The recipe's main code catches any such exception and prints it out like this:

```
$ python wellformed.py test.xml
test.xml is NOT well-formed! test.xml:1002:2: mismatched tag
```

This means that character 2 on line 1,002 has a mismatched tag.

This recipe does not check adherence to a DTD or schema. That is a separate procedure called *validation*. The performance of the script should be quite good, precisely because it focuses on performing a minimal irreducible core task.

See Also

Recipes 12.2, 12.3, and 12.5 for other uses of the SAX API; the PyXML package (*http://pyxml.sourceforge.net/*) includes the pure-Python validating parser xmlproc, which checks the conformance of XML documents to specific DTDs; the PyRXP package from ReportLab is a wrapper around the faster validating parser RXP (*http://www.reportlab.com/xml/pyrxp.html*), which is available under the GPL license.

12.2 Counting Tags in a Document

Credit: Paul Prescod

Problem

You want to get a sense of how often particular elements occur in an XML document, and the relevant counts must be extracted rapidly.

Solution

You can subclass SAX's ContentHandler to make your own specialized classes for any kind of task, including the collection of such statistics:

```
from xml.sax.handler import ContentHandler
import xml.sax

class countHandler(ContentHandler):
    def __init__(self):
        self.tags={}

    def startElement(self, name, attr):
        if not self.tags.has_key(name):
            self.tags[name] = 0
        self.tags[name] += 1

parser = xml.sax.make_parser( )
handler = countHandler( )
parser.setContentHandler(handler)
parser.parse("test.xml")
```

```
tags = handler.tags.keys()
tags.sort()
for tag in tags:
print tag, handler.tags[tag]
```

Discussion

When I start with a new XML content set, I like to get a sense of which elements are in it and how often they occur. I use variants of this recipe. I can also collect attributes just as easily, as you can see. If you add a stack, you can keep track of which elements occur within other elements (for this, of course, you also have to override the endElement method so you can pop the stack).

This recipe also works well as a simple example of a SAX application, usable as the basis for any SAX application. Alternatives to SAX include pulldom and minidom. These would be overkill for this simple job, though. For any simple processing, this is generally the case, particularly if the document you are processing is very large. DOM approaches are generally justified only when you need to perform complicated editing and alteration on an XML document, when the document itself is complicated by references that go back and forth inside it, or when you need to correlate (e.g., compare) multiple documents with each other.

ContentHandler subclasses offer many other options, and the online Python documentation does a good job of explaining them. This recipe's countHandler class overrides ContentHandler's startElement method, which the parser calls at the start of each element, passing as arguments the element's tag name as a Unicode string and the collection of attributes. Our override of this method counts the number of times each tag name occurs. In the end, we extract the dictionary used for counting and emit it (in alphabetical order, which we easily obtain by sorting the keys).

In the implementation of this recipe, an alternative to testing the tags dictionary with has_key might offer a slightly more concise way to code the startElement method:

```
def startElement(self, name, attr):
    self.tags[name] = 1 + self.tags.get(name,0)
```

This counting idiom for dictionaries is so frequent that it's probably worth encapsulating in its own function despite its utter simplicity:

```
def count(adict, key, delta=1, default=0):
    adict[key] = delta + adict.get(key, default)
```

Using this, you could code the startElement method in the recipe as:

```
def startElement(self, name, attr): count(self.tags, name)
```

See Also

Recipes 12.1, 12.3, and 12.5 for other uses of the SAX API.

12.3 Extracting Text from an XML Document

Credit: Paul Prescod

Problem

You need to extract only the text from an XML document, not the tags.

Solution

Once again, subclassing SAX's ContentHandler makes this extremely easy:

```
from xml.sax.handler import ContentHandler
import xml.sax
import sys

class textHandler(ContentHandler):
    def characters(self, ch):
        sys.stdout.write(ch.encode("Latin-1"))

parser = xml.sax.make_parser( )
handler = textHandler( )
parser.setContentHandler(handler)
parser.parse("test.xml")
```

Discussion

Sometimes you want to get rid of XML tags—for example, to rekey a document or to spellcheck it. This recipe performs this task and will work with any well-formed XML document. It is quite efficient. If the document isn't well-formed, you could try a solution based on the XML lexer (shallow parser) shown in Recipe 12.11.

In this recipe's textHandler class, we subclass ContentHander's characters method, which the parser calls for each string of text in the XML document (excluding tags, XML comments, and processing instructions), passing as the only argument the piece of text as a Unicode string. We have to encode this Unicode before we can emit it to standard output. In this recipe, we're using the Latin-1 (also known as ISO-8859-1) encoding, which covers all Western-European alphabets and is supported by many popular output devices (e.g., printers and terminal-emulation windows). However, you should use whatever encoding is most appropriate for the documents you're handling and is supported by the devices you use. The configuration of your devices may depend on your operating system's concepts of locale and code page. Unfortunately, these vary too much between operating systems for me to go into further detail.

See Also

Recipes 12.1, 12.2, and 12.5 for other uses of the SAX API; see Recipe 12.11 for a very different approach to XML lexing that works on XML fragments.

12.4 Transforming an XML Document Using XSLT

Credit: David Ascher

Problem

You have an XSLT transform that you wish to programmatically run through XML documents.

Solution

The solution depends on the XSLT processor you're using. If you're using Microsoft's XSLT engine (part of its XML Core Services package), you can drive the XSLT engine through its COM interface:

```
def process_with_msxslt(xsltfname, xmlfname, targetfname):
    import win32com.client.dynamic
    xslt = win32com.client.dynamic.Dispatch("Msxml2.DOMDocument.4.0")
    xslt.async = 0
    xslt.load(xsltfname)
    xml = win32com.client.dynamic.Dispatch("Msxml2.DOMDocument.4.0")
    xml.async = 0
    xml.load(xmlfname)
    output = xml.transformNode(xslt)
    open(targetfname, 'wb').write(output)
```

If you'd rather use Xalan's XSLT engine, it's as simple as using the right module:

```
import Pyana
output = Pyana.transform2String(source=open(xmlfname).read( ),
                                style=open(xsltfname).read( ))
open(targetfname, 'wb').write(output)
```

Discussion

There are many different ways that XML documents need to be processed. Extensible Stylesheet Language Transformations (XSLT) is a language that was developed specifically for transforming XML documents. Using XSLT, you define a stylesheet, which is a set of templates and rules that defines how to transform specific parts of an XML document into arbitrary outputs.

The XSLT specification is a World Wide Web Consortium Recommendation (*http://www.w3.org/TR/xslt*) that has been implemented by many different organizations. The two most commonly used XSLT processors are Microsoft's XLST engine, part of its XML Core Services, and the Apache group's Xalan engines (C++ and Java versions are available).

If you have an existing XSLT transform, running it from Python is easy with this recipe. The first variant uses the COM interface (provided automatically by the win32com package, part of win32all) to Microsoft's engine, while the second uses

Brian Quinlan's convenient wrapper around Xalan, Pyana (*http://pyana.sourceforge.net/*). While this recipe shows only the easiest way of using Xalan through Pyana, there's a lot more to the package. You can easily extend XSLT and XPath with Python code, something which can save you a lot of time if you know Python well.

XSLT is definitely trendy, partially because it seems at first well-suited to processing XML documents. If you're comfortable with XSLT and want to use Python to help you work with your existing stylesheets, these recipes will start you on your way. If, however, you're quite comfortable with Python and are just starting with XSLT, you may find that it's easier to forget about these newfangled technologies and use good old Python code to do the job. See Recipe 12.5 for a very different approach.

See Also

Recipe 12.5 for a pure Python approach to the same problem; Recipe 12.9; Pyana is available and documented at *http://pyana.sourceforge.net*; Apache's Xalan is available and documented at *http://xml.apache.org*; Microsoft's XML technologies are available from Microsoft's developer site (*http://msdn.microsoft.com*).

12.5   Transforming an XML Document Using Python

Credit: David Ascher

Problem

You have an XML document that you want to tweak.

Solution

Suppose that you want to convert element attributes into child elements. A simple subclass of the XMLGenerator object gives you complete freedom in such XML-to-XML transformation tasks:

```
from xml.sax import saxutils, make_parser
import sys

class Tweak(saxutils.XMLGenerator):
    def startElement(self, name, attrs):
        saxutils.XMLGenerator.startElement(self, name, {})
        attributes = attrs.keys()
        attributes.sort()
        for attribute in attributes:
            self._out.write("<%s>%s</%s>" % (attribute,
                            attrs[attribute], attribute))
```

```
parser = make_parser()
dh = Tweak(sys.stdout)
parser.setContentHandler(dh)
parser.parse(sys.argv[1])
```

Discussion

This particular recipe defines a Tweak subclass of the XMLGenerator class provided by the xml.sax.saxutils module. The only purpose of the subclass is to perform special handling of element starts while relying on its base class to do everything else. SAX is a nice and simple (after all, that's what the S stands for) API for processing XML documents. It defines various kinds of events that occur when an XML document is being processed, such as startElement and endElement.

The key to understanding this recipe is to understand that Python's XML library provides a base class, XMLGenerator, which performs an identity transform. If you feed it an XML document, it will output an equivalent XML document. Using standard Python object-oriented techniques of subclassing and method override, you are free to specialize how the generated XML document differs from the source. The code above simply takes each element (attributes and their values are passed in as a dictionary on startElement calls), relies on the base class to output the proper XML for the element (but omitting the attributes), and then writes an element for each attribute.

Subclassing the XMLGenerator class is a nice place to start when you need to tweak some XML, especially if your tweaks don't require you to change the existing parent-child relationships. For more complex jobs, you may want to explore some other ways of processing XML, such as minidom or pulldom. Or, if you're really into that sort of thing, you could use XSLT (see Recipe 12.4).

See Also

Recipe 12.4 for various ways of driving XSLT from Python; Recipes 12.1, 12.2, and 12.3 for other uses of the SAX API.

12.6 Parsing an XML File with xml.parsers.expat

Credit: Mark Nenadov

Problem

The expat parser is normally used through the SAX interface, but sometimes you may want to use expat directly to extract the best possible performance.

Solution

Python is very explicit about the lower-level mechanisms that its higher-level modules' packages use. You're normally better off accessing the higher levels, but sometimes, in the last few stages of an optimization quest, or just to gain better understanding of what, exactly, is going on, you may want to access the lower levels directly from your code. For example, here is how you can use Expat directly, rather than through SAX:

```
import xml.parsers.expat, sys

class MyXML:
    Parser = ""

    # Prepare for parsing
    def __init__(self, xml_filename):
        assert xml_filename != ""
        self.xml_filename = xml_filename
        self.Parser = xml.parsers.expat.ParserCreate()

        self.Parser.CharacterDataHandler = self.handleCharData
        self.Parser.StartElementHandler = self.handleStartElement
        self.Parser.EndElementHandler = self.handleEndElement

    # Parse the XML file
    def parse(self):
        try:
            xml_file = open(self.xml_filename, "r")
        except:
            print "ERROR: Can't open XML file %s"%self.xml_filename
            raise
        else:
            try: self.Parser.ParseFile(xml_file)
            finally: xml_file.close()

    # to be overridden by implementation-specific methods
    def handleCharData(self, data): pass
    def handleStartElement(self, name, attrs): pass
    def handleEndElement(self, name): pass
```

Discussion

This recipe presents a reusable way to use xml.parsers.expat directly to parse an XML file. SAX is more standardized and rich in functionality, but expat is also usable, and sometimes it can be even lighter than the already lightweight SAX approach. To reuse the MyXML class, all you need to do is define a new class, inheriting from MyXML. Inside your new class, override the inherited XML handler methods, and you're ready to go.

Specifically, the MyXML class creates a parser object that does callbacks to the callables that are its attributes. The StartElementHandler callable is called at the start of each element, with the tag name and the attributes as arguments. EndElementHandler is called at the end of each element, with the tag name as the only argument. Finally, CharacterDataHandler is called for each text string the parser encounters, with the string as the only argument. The MyXML class uses the handleStartElement, `handleEndElement`, and `handleCharData` methods as such callbacks. Therefore, these are the methods you should override when you subclass `MyXML` to perform whatever application-specific processing you require.

See Also

Recipes 12.1, 12.2, 12.3, and 12.5 for uses of the higher-level SAX API; while Expat was the brainchild of James Clark, Expat 2.0 is a group project, with a home page at *http://expat.sourceforge.net/*.

12.7 Converting Ad-Hoc Text into XML Markup

Credit: Luther Blissett

Problem

You have plain text that follows certain common conventions (e.g., paragraphs are separated by empty lines, text meant to be highlighted is marked up _like this_), and you need to mark it up automatically as XML.

Solution

Producing XML markup from data that is otherwise structured, including plain text that rigorously follows certain conventions, is really quite easy:

```
def markup(text, paragraph_tag='paragraph', inline_tags={'_':'highlight'}):
    # First we must escape special characters, which have special meaning in XML
    text = text.replace('&', "&amp;")\
               .replace('<', "&lt;")\
               .replace("'", "&quot;")\
               .replace('>', "&gt;")

    # paragraph markup; pass any false value as the paragraph_tag argument to disable
    if paragraph_tag:
        # Get list of lines, removing leading and trailing empty lines:
        lines = text.splitlines(1)
        while lines and lines[-1].isspace(): lines.pop()
        while lines and lines[0].isspace(): lines.pop(0)

        # Insert paragraph tags on empty lines:
        marker = '</%s>\n\n<%s>' % (paragraph_tag, paragraph_tag)
        for i in range(len(lines)):
            if lines[i].isspace():
                lines[i] = marker
                # remove 'empty paragraphs':
                if i!=0 and lines[i-1] == marker:
                    lines[i-1] = ''

        # Join text again
        lines.insert(0, '<%s>'%paragraph_tag)
```

```python
            lines.append('</%s>\n'%paragraph_tag)
        text = ''.join(lines)

        # inline-tags markup; pass any false value as the inline_tags argument to disable
        if inline_tags:
            for ch, tag in inline_tags.items():
                pieces = text.split(ch)
                # Text should have an even count of ch, so pieces should have
                # odd length. But just in case there's an extra unmatched ch:
                if len(pieces)%2 == 0: pieces.append('')
                for i in range(1, len(pieces), 2):
                    pieces[i] = '<%s>%s</%s>'%(tag, pieces[i], tag)
                # Join text again
                text = ''.join(pieces)

        return text

if __name__ == '__main__':
    sample = """
Just some _important_ text,
with inlike "_markup_" by convention.

Oh, and paragraphs separated by
empty (or all-whitespace) lines.
Sometimes more than one, wantonly.


I've got _lots_ of old text like that
around -- don't you?
"""
    print markup(sample)
```

Discussion

Sometimes you have a lot of plain text that needs to be automatically marked up in a structured way—usually, these days, as XML. If the plain text you start with follows certain typical conventions, you can use them heuristically to get each text snippet into marked-up form with reasonably little effort.

In my case, the two conventions I had to work with were: paragraphs are separated by blank lines (empty or with some spaces, and sometimes several redundant blank lines for just one paragraph separation), and underlines (one before, one after) are used to indicate important text that should be highlighted. This seems to be quite far from the brave new world of:

```
<paragraph>blah blah</paragraph>
```

But in reality, it isn't as far as all that, thanks, of course, to Python! While you could use regular expressions for this task, I prefer the simplicity of the split and splitlines methods, with join to put the strings back together again.

See Also

StructuredText, the latest incarnation of which, ReStructuredText, is part of the docutils package (*http://docutils.sourceforge.net/*).

12.8 Normalizing an XML Document

Credit: David Ascher, Paul Prescod

Problem

You want to compare two different XML documents using standard tools such as diff.

Solution

Normalize each XML document using the following recipe, then use a whitespace-insensitive *diff* tool:

```
from xml.dom import minidom
dom = minidom.parse(input)
dom.writexml(open(outputfname, "w"))
```

Discussion

Different editing tools munge XML differently. Some, like text editors, make no modification that is not explicitly done by the user. Others, such as XML-specific editors, sometimes change the order of attributes or automatically indent elements to facilitate the reading of raw XML. There are reasons for each approach, but unfortunately, the two approaches can lead to confusing differences—for example, if one author uses a plain editor while another uses a fancy XML editor, and a third person is in charge of merging the two sets of changes. In such cases, one should use an XML-difference engine. Typically, however, such tools are not easy to come by. Most are written in Java and don't deal well with large XML documents (performing tree-diffs efficiently is a hard problem!).

Luckily, combinations of small steps can solve the problem nicely. First, normalize each XML document, then use a standard line-oriented *diff* tool to compare the normalized outputs. This recipe is a simple XML normalizer. All it does is parse the XML into a Document Object Model (DOM) and write it out. In the process, elements with no children are written in the more compact form (<foo/> rather than <foo></foo>), and attributes are sorted lexicographically.

The second stage is easily done by using some options to the standard *diff*, such as the -w option, which ignores whitespace differences. Or you might want to use

Python's standard module `difflib`, which by default also ignores spaces and tabs, and has the advantage of being available on all platforms since Python 2.1.

There's a slight problem that shows up if you use this recipe unaltered. The standard way in which `minidom` outputs XML escapes quotation marks results in all " inside of elements appearing as ". This won't make a difference to smart XML editors, but it's not a nice thing to do for people reading the output with *vi* or *emacs*. Luckily, fixing `minidom` from the outside isn't hard:

```
def _write_data(writer, data):
    "Writes datachars to writer."
    replace = _string.replace
    data = replace(data, "&", "&amp;")
    data = replace(data, "<", "&lt;")
    data = replace(data, ">", "&gt;")
    writer.write(data)

def my_writexml(self, writer, indent="", addindent="", newl=""):
    _write_data(writer, "%s%s%s" % (indent, self.data, newl))

minidom.Text.writexml = my_writexml
```

Here, we substitute the `writexml` method for `Text` nodes with a version that calls a new `_write_data` function identical to the one in `minidom`, except that the escaping of quotation marks is skipped. Naturally, the preceding should be done before the call to `minidom.parse` to be effective.

See Also

Documentation for `minidom` is part of the XML documentation in the *Standard Library* reference.

12.9   Controlling XSLT Stylesheet Loading

Credit: Jürgen Hermann

Problem

You need to process XML documents and access external documents (e.g., stylesheets), but you can't use filesystem paths (to keep documents portable) or Internet-accessible URLs (for performance and security).

Solution

4Suite's `xml.xslt` package (*http://www.4suite.org/*) gives you all the power you need to handle XML stylesheets, including the hooks for sophisticated needs such as those met by this recipe:

```python
# uses 4Suite Version 0.10.2 or later
from xml.xslt.Processor import Processor
from xml.xslt.StylesheetReader import StylesheetReader

class StylesheetFromDict(StylesheetReader):
    "A stylesheet reader that loads XSLT stylesheets from a python dictionary"

    def __init__(self, styles, *args):
        "Remember the dict we want to load the stylesheets from"
        StylesheetReader.__init__(self, *args)
        self.styles = styles
        self.__myargs = args

    def __getinitargs__(self):
        "Return init args for clone()"
        return (self.styles,) + self.__myargs

    def fromUri(self, uri, baseUri='', ownerDoc=None, stripElements=None):
        "Load stylesheet from a dict"
        parts = uri.split(':', 1)
        if parts[0] == 'internal' and self.styles.has_key(parts[1]):
            # Load the stylesheet from the internal repository (your dictionary)
            return StylesheetReader.fromString(self, self.styles[parts[1]],
                baseUri, ownerDoc, stripElements)
        else:
            # Revert to normal behavior
            return StylesheetReader.fromUri(self, uri,
                baseUri, ownerDoc, stripElements)

if __name__ == "__main__":
    # test and example of this stylesheet's loading approach

    # the sample stylesheet repository
    internal_stylesheets = {
        'second-author.xsl': """
            <person xmlns:xsl="http://www.w3.org/1999/XSL/Transform"
                xsl:version="1.0">
            <xsl:value-of select="books/book/author[2]"/>
            </person>
        """
    }

    # the sample document, referring to an "internal" stylesheet
    xmldoc = """
        <?xml-stylesheet href="internal:second-author.xsl"
            type="text/xml"?>
        <books>
          <book title="Python Essential Reference">
            <author>David M. Beazley</author>
            <author>Guido van Rossum</author>
          </book>
        </books>
    """
```

```
# Create XSLT processor and run it
processor = Processor( )
processor.setStylesheetReader(StylesheetFromDict(internal_stylesheets))
print processor.runString(xmldoc)
```

Discussion

If you get a lot of XML documents from third parties (via FTP, HTTP, or other means), problems could arise because the documents were created in their environments, and now you must process them in your environment. If a document refers to external files (such as stylesheets) in the filesystem of the remote host, these paths often do not make sense on your local host. One common solution is to refer to external documents through public URLs accessible via the Internet, but this, of course, incurs substantial overhead (you need to fetch the stylesheet from the remote server) and poses some risks. (What if the remote server is down? What about privacy and security?)

Another approach is to use private URL schemes, such as stylesheet:layout.xsl. These need to be resolved to real, existing URLs, which this recipe's code does for XSLT processing. We show how to use a hook offered by 4Suite, a Python XSLT engine, to refer to stylesheets in an XML-Stylesheet processing instruction (see *http://www.w3.org/TR/xml-stylesheet/*).

A completely analogous approach can be used to load the stylesheet from a database or return a locally cached stylesheet previously fetched from a remote URL. The essence of this recipe is that you can subclass StylesheetReader and customize the fromUri method to perform whatever resolution of private URL schemes you require. The recipe specifically looks at the URL's protocol. If it's internal: followed by a name that is a known key in an internal dictionary that maps names to stylesheets, it returns the stylesheet by delegating the parsing of the dictionary entry's value to the fromString method of StylesheetReader. In all other cases, it leaves the URI alone and delegates to the parent class's method.

The output of the test code is:

```
<?xml version='1.0' encoding='UTF-8'?>
<person>Guido van Rossum</person>
```

This recipe requires at least Python 2.0 and 4Suite Version 0.10.2.

See Also

The XML-Stylesheet processing instruction is described in a W3C recommendation (*http://www.w3.org/TR/xml-stylesheet/*); the 4Suite tools from FourThought are available at *http://www.4suite.org/*.

12.10 Autodetecting XML Encoding

Credit: Paul Prescod

Problem

You have XML documents that may use a large variety of Unicode encodings, and you need to find out which encoding each document is using.

Solution

This is a task that we need to code ourselves, rather than getting an existing package to perform it, if we want complete generality:

```python
import codecs, encodings

""" Caller will hand this library a buffer and ask it to convert
it or autodetect the type. """

# None represents a potentially variable byte. "##" in the XML spec...
autodetect_dict={ # bytepattern      : ("name",
                (0x00, 0x00, 0xFE, 0xFF) : ("ucs4_be"),
                (0xFF, 0xFE, 0x00, 0x00) : ("ucs4_le"),
                (0xFE, 0xFF, None, None) : ("utf_16_be"),
                (0xFF, 0xFE, None, None) : ("utf_16_le"),
                (0x00, 0x3C, 0x00, 0x3F) : ("utf_16_be"),
                (0x3C, 0x00, 0x3F, 0x00) : ("utf_16_le"),
                (0x3C, 0x3F, 0x78, 0x6D): ("utf_8"),
                (0x4C, 0x6F, 0xA7, 0x94): ("EBCDIC")
                }

def autoDetectXMLEncoding(buffer):
    """ buffer -> encoding_name
    The buffer should be at least four bytes long.
        Returns None if encoding cannot be detected.
        Note that encoding_name might not have an installed
        decoder (e.g., EBCDIC).
    """
    # A more efficient implementation would not decode the whole
    # buffer at once, but then we'd have to decode a character at
    # a time looking for the quote character, and that's a pain

    encoding = "utf_8" # According to the XML spec, this is the default
                       # This code successively tries to refine the default:
                       # Whenever it fails to refine, it falls back to
                       # the last place encoding was set
    bytes = byte1, byte2, byte3, byte4 = tuple(map(ord, buffer[0:4]))
    enc_info = autodetect_dict.get(bytes, None)

    if not enc_info: # Try autodetection again, removing potentially
                     # variable bytes
        bytes = byte1, byte2, None, None
        enc_info = autodetect_dict.get(bytes)
```

```
    if enc_info:
        encoding = enc_info # We have a guess...these are
                            # the new defaults

        # Try to find a more precise encoding using XML declaration
        secret_decoder_ring = codecs.lookup(encoding)[1]
        decoded, length = secret_decoder_ring(buffer)
        first_line = decoded.split("\n", 1)[0]
        if first_line and first_line.startswith(u"<?xml"):
            encoding_pos = first_line.find(u"encoding")
            if encoding_pos!=-1:
                # Look for double quotes
                quote_pos = first_line.find('"', encoding_pos)

                if quote_pos==-1:                  # Look for single quote
                    quote_pos = first_line.find("'", encoding_pos)

                if quote_pos>-1:
                    quote_char = first_line[quote_pos]
                    rest = first_line[quote_pos+1:]
                    encoding = rest[:rest.find(quote_char)]

    return encoding
```

Discussion

The XML specification describes the outlines of an algorithm for detecting the Unicode encoding that an XML document uses. This recipe implements this algorithm and helps your XML processing programs find out which encoding is being used by a specific document.

The default encoding (unless we can determine another one specifically) must be UTF-8, as this is part of the specifications that define XML. Certain byte patterns in the first four, or sometimes even just the first two, bytes of the text, can let us identify a different encoding. For example, if the text starts with the 2 bytes 0xFF, 0xFE we can be certain this is a byte-order mark that identifies the encoding type as little-endian (low byte before high byte in each character) and the encoding itself as UTF-16 (or the 32-bits-per-character UCS-4 if the next 2 bytes in the text are 0, 0).

If we get as far as this, we must also examine the first line of the text by decoding the text from a byte string into Unicode with the encoding determined so far, and detecting the first line-end '\n' character. If the first line begins with u'<?xml', it's an XML declaration and may explicitly specify an encoding by using the keyword encoding as an attribute. The nested if statements in the recipe check for that, and, if they find an encoding thus specified, the recipe returns it as the encoding it has determined. This step is absolutely crucial, since any text starting with the single-byte ASCII-like representation of the XML declaration, <?xml, would be otherwise erroneously identified as encoded in UTF-8, while its explicit encoding attribute may specify it as being, for example, one of the ISO-8859 standard encodings.

This code detects a variety of encodings, including some that are not yet supported by Python's Unicode decoders. So the fact that you can decipher the encoding does not guarantee that you can decipher the document itself!

See Also

Recipes 3.17 and 3.18; Unicode is a huge topic, but a recommended book is *Unicode: A Primer*, by Tony Graham (Hungry Minds, Inc.)—details are available at *http://www.menteith.com/unicode/primer/*.

12.11 Module: XML Lexing (Shallow Parsing)

Credit: Paul Prescod

It's not uncommon to want to work with the form of an XML document rather than with the structural information it contains (e.g., to change a bunch of entity references or element names). The XML may be slightly incorrect, enough to choke a traditional parser. In such cases, you need an XML lexer, also known as a shallow parser.

You might be tempted to hack together a regular expression or two to do some simple parsing of XML (or other structured text format), rather than using the appropriate library module. Don't—it's not a trivial task to get the regular expressions right! However, the hard work has already been done for you in Example 12-1, which contains already-debugged regular expressions and supporting functions that you can use for shallow-parsing tasks on XML data (or, more importantly, on data that is almost, but not quite, correct XML, so that a real XML parser seizes up with error diagnostics when you try to parse your data with it).

A traditional XML parser does a few tasks:

- It breaks up the stream of text into logical components (tags, text, processing instructions, etc.).
- It ensures that these components comply with the XML specification.
- It throws away extra characters and reports the significant data. For instance, it would report tag names but not the less-than and greater-than signs around them.

The shallow parser in Example 12-1 performs only the first task. It breaks up the document and presumes that you know how to deal with the fragments yourself. That makes it efficient and forgiving of errors in the document.

The lexxml function is the code's entry point. Call lexxml(data) to get back a list of tokens (strings that are bits of the document). This lexer also makes it easy to get back the exact original content of the document. Unless there is a bug in the recipe, the following code should always succeed:

```
tokens = lexxml(data)
data2 = "".join(tokens)
assert data == data2
```

If you find any bugs that disallow this, please report them! There is a second, optional argument to lexxml that allows you to get back only markup and ignore the text of the document. This is useful as a performance optimization when you care only about tags. The walktokens function in the recipe shows how to walk over the tokens and work with them.

Example 12-1. XML lexing

```
import re

class recollector:
    def __init__(self):
        self.res={}
    def add(self, name, reg ):
        re.compile(reg) # Check that it is valid
        self.res[name] = reg % self.res

collector = recollector()
a = collector.add

a("TextSE" , "[^<]+")
a("UntilHyphen" , "[^-]*-")
a("Until2Hyphens" , "%(UntilHyphen)s(?:[^-]%(UntilHyphen)s)*-")
a("CommentCE" , "%(Until2Hyphens)s>?")
a("UntilRSBs" , "[^\\]]*](?:[^\\]]+])*]+")
a("CDATA_CE" , "%(UntilRSBs)s(?:[^\\]>]%(UntilRSBs)s)*>" )
a("S" , "[ \\n\\t\\r]+")
a("NameStrt" , "[A-Za-z_:]|[^\\x00-\\x7F]")
a("NameChar" , "[A-Za-z0-9_:.-]|[^\\x00-\\x7F]")
a("Name" , "(?:%(NameStrt)s)(?:%(NameChar)s)*")
a("QuoteSE" , "\"[^\"]*\"|'[^']*'")
a("DT_IdentSE" , "%(S)s%(Name)s(?:%(S)s(?:%(Name)s|%(QuoteSE)s))*" )
a("MarkupDeclCE" , "(?:[^\\]\"'><]+|%(QuoteSE)s)*>" )
a("S1" , "[\\n\\r\\t ]")
a("UntilQMs" , "[^?]*\\?+")
a("PI_Tail" , "\\?>|%(S1)s%(UntilQMs)s(?:[^>?]%(UntilQMs)s)*>" )
a("DT_ItemSE" ,
    "<(?:!(?:--%(Until2Hyphens)s>|[^-]%(MarkupDeclCE)s)|\\?%(Name)s"
    "(?:%(PI_Tail)s))|%%%(Name)s;|%(S)s"
)
a("DocTypeCE" ,
"%(DT_IdentSE)s(?:%(S)s)?(?:\\[(?:%(DT_ItemSE)s)*](?:%(S)s)?)?>?" )
a("DeclCE" ,
    "--(?:%(CommentCE)s)?|\\[CDATA\\[(?:%(CDATA_CE)s)?|DOCTYPE"
    "(?:%(DocTypeCE)s)?")
a("PI_CE" , "%(Name)s(?:%(PI_Tail)s)?")
```

Example 12-1. XML lexing (continued)

```
a("EndTagCE" , "%(Name)s(?:%(S)s)?>?")
a("AttValSE" , "\"[^<\"]*\"|'[^<']*'")
a("ElemTagCE" ,
    "%(Name)s(?:%(S)s%(Name)s(?:%(S)s)?=(?:%(S)s)?(?:%(AttValSE)s))*"
    "(?:%(S)s)?/?>?")

a("MarkupSPE" ,
    "<(?:!(?:%(DeclCE)s)?|\\?(?:%(PI_CE)s)?|/(?:%(EndTagCE)s)?|"
    "(?:%(ElemTagCE)s)?)")
a("XML_SPE" , "%(TextSE)s|%(MarkupSPE)s")
a("XML_MARKUP_ONLY_SPE" , "%(MarkupSPE)s")


def lexxml(data, markuponly=0):
    if markuponly:
        reg = "XML_MARKUP_ONLY_SPE"
    else:
        reg = "XML_SPE"
    regex = re.compile(collector.res[reg])
    return regex.findall(data)

def assertlex(data, numtokens, markuponly=0):
    tokens = lexxml(data, markuponly)
    if len(tokens)!=numtokens:
        assert len(lexxml(data))==numtokens, \
            "data = '%s', numtokens = '%s'" %(data, numtokens)
    if not markuponly:
        assert "".join(tokens)==data
    walktokens(tokens)

def walktokens(tokens):
    print
    for token in tokens:
        if token.startswith("<"):
            if token.startswith("<!"):
                print "declaration:", token
            elif token.startswith("<?xml"):
                print "xml declaration:", token
            elif token.startswith("<?"):
                print "processing instruction:", token
            elif token.startswith("</"):
                print "end-tag:", token
            elif token.endswith("/>"):
                print "empty-tag:", token
            elif token.endswith(">"):
                print "start-tag:", token
            else:
                print "error:", token
        else:
            print "text:", token

def testlexer():
    # This test suite could be larger!
```

Example 12-1. XML lexing (continued)

```
    assertlex("<abc/>", 1)
    assertlex("<abc><def/></abc>", 3)
    assertlex("<abc>Blah</abc>", 3)
    assertlex("<abc>Blah</abc>", 2, markuponly=1)
    assertlex("<?xml version='1.0'?><abc>Blah</abc>", 3,
        markuponly=1)
    assertlex("<abc>Blah&foo;Blah</abc>", 3)
    assertlex("<abc>Blah&foo;Blah</abc>", 2, markuponly=1)
    assertlex("<abc><abc>", 2)
    assertlex("</abc></abc>", 2)
    assertlex("<abc></def></abc>", 3)

if __name__=="__main__":
    testlexer()
```

See Also

This recipe is based on the following article, with regular expressions translated from Perl into Python: "REX: XML Shallow Parsing with Regular Expressions", Robert D. Cameron, *Markup Languages: Theory and Applications*, Summer 1999, pp. 61–88, *http://www.cs.sfu.ca/~cameron/REX.html*.

12.12 Module: Converting a List of Equal-Length Lists into XML

Credit: Julius Welby

Parsers of tabular data or comma-separated values (CSV) files usually output a list of lists. Converting these into XML allows them to be manipulated with XSLT and other XML tools. Example 12-2 takes a list of equal-length lists and converts it into XML (or, optionally, into an HTML table).

Example 12-2. Converting a list of equal-length lists into XML

```
# LL2XML.py -- Version 0.3 -- 15 July 2001
# http://www.outwardlynormal.com/python/ll2XML.htm for the full docs
import string

# Set up exceptions
class Error(Exception):
    def __init__(self, errcode,  heading_num = 0, sublist_length = 0):
        self.errcode = errcode
        if self.errcode == "Length Error - Sublists":
            self.message = ["All the sublists must be of uniform length."]
        elif self.errcode == "Heading Error - heading/sublist mismatch":
            self.message = ["There is at least one empty heading item.\n",
                        "Please supply non-empty headings."]
        elif self.errcode == "Length Error: heading/sublist mismatch":
            self.message = ["Number of headings =", 'heading_num', "\n",
```

Example 12-2. Converting a list of equal-length lists into XML (continued)

```
                        "Number of elements in sublists =",
                        'sublist_length', "\n",
                        "These numbers must be equal."]
        else: self.message = [""]
        self.errmsg = string.join(self.message)

    def __str__(self):
        return self.errmsg

def escape(s):
    """ Replace special characters '&', "'", '<', '>', and '"'
      with XML entities. """
    s = s.replace("&", "&amp;") # Must be done first!
    s = s.replace("'", "&apos;")
    s = s.replace("<", "&lt;")
    s = s.replace(">", "&gt;")
    s = s.replace('"', "&quot;")
    return s

def cleanTag(s):
    if type(s) != type(""):
        s = 's'
    s = string.lower(s)
    s = string.replace(s," ", "_")
    s = escape(s)
    return s

def LL2XML(LL, headings_tuple = (), root_element = "rows",
        row_element = "row", xml_declared = "yes"):

    if headings_tuple == "table":
        headings_tuple = ("td",) * len(LL[0])
        root_element = "table"
        row_element = "tr"
        xml_declared = "no"

    root_element = cleanTag(root_element)
    row_element = cleanTag(row_element)
    if not headings_tuple:
        headings =  LL[0]
        firstRow = "headings"
    else:
        headings = headings_tuple
        firstRow = "data"

    # Sublists all of the same length?
    sublist_length = len(LL[0])
    for sublist in LL:
        if len(sublist) != sublist_length:
            raise Error("Length Error - Sublists")

    # Check headings
    heading_num = len(headings)
```

Example 12-2. Converting a list of equal-length lists into XML (continued)

```
        if heading_num != sublist_length:
            raise Error("Heading Error - heading/sublist mismatch",
                        heading_num, sublist_length)

        for item in headings:
            if not item:
                raise Error("Heading Error - Empty Item")

        # Do the conversion
        bits = []
        def add_bits(*somebits):
            bits.extend(list(somebits))
        if xml_declared == "yes":
            xml_declaration = '<?xml version="1.0" encoding="iso-8859-1"?>\n'
        else:
            xml_declaration = ""
        add_bits(xml_declaration, '<', root_element, '>')
        if firstRow == "headings":
            LL = LL[1:]              # Remove redundant heading row, if present
        for sublist in LL:
            add_bits("\n  <", row_element, ">\n")
            i = 0
            for item in sublist:
                tag = headings[i]
                tag = cleanTag(tag)
                if type(item) != type(""):
                    item = `item`
                item = escape(item)
                add_bits("    <", tag, ">", item, "</", tag, ">\n")
                i = i+1
            add_bits("  </", row_element, ">")
        add_bits("\n</", root_element, ">")
        return string.join(bits, "")

def test():
    LL = [
    ['Login', 'First Name', 'Last Name', 'Job', 'Group', 'Office', 'Permission'],
    ['auser', 'Arnold', 'Atkins', 'Partner', 'Tax', 'London', 'read'],
    ['buser', 'Bill', 'Brown', 'Partner', 'Tax', 'New York', 'read'],
    ['cuser', 'Clive', 'Cutler', 'Partner', 'Management', 'Brussels', 'read'],
    ['duser', 'Denis', 'Davis', 'Developer', 'ISS', 'London', 'admin'],
    ['euser', 'Eric', 'Ericsson', 'Analyst', 'Analysis', 'London', 'admin'],
    ['fuser', 'Fabian', 'Fowles', 'Partner', 'IP', 'London', 'read']
        ]

    LL_no_heads = LL[1:]

    # Example 1
    print "Example 1: Simple case, using defaults.\n"
    print LL2XML(LL)
    print
```

Example 12-2. Converting a list of equal-length lists into XML (continued)

```
    # Example 2
    print """Example 2: LL has its headings in the first line,
and we define our root and row element names.\n"""
    print LL2XML(LL,(),"people","person")
    print

    # Example 3
    print """Example 3: headings supplied using the headings argument(tuple),
using default root and row element names.\n"""
    print LL2XML(LL_no_heads,
        ("Login","First Name","Last Name","Job","Group","Office","Permission"))
    print

    #Example 4
    print """Example 4: The special case where we ask for an HTML table as
    output by just giving the string "table" as the second argument.\n"""
    print LL2XML(LL,"table")
    print

if __name__ == '__main__':
    test()
```

If the first sublist is a list of headings, these are used to form the element names of the rest of the data, or else the element names can be defined in the function call. Root and row elements can be named if required.

This recipe is coded for compatibility with all versions of Python, including extremely old versions, to the point of reimplementing the escape functionality rather than relying on those supplied by Python's standard library.

See Also

For the specific job of parsing CSV you should probably use one of the existing Python modules available at the Vaults of Parnassus (*http://www.vex.net/parnassus/apyllo.py?find=csv*); two such parsers are at *http://tratt.net/laurie/python/asv/* and *http://www.object-craft.com.au/projects/csv/*; the permanent home of this module is *http://www.outwardlynormal.com/python/ll2XML.htm*.

CHAPTER 13
Distributed Programming

13.0 Introduction

Credit: Jeremy Hylton, PythonLabs

The recipes in this chapter describe some simple techniques for using Python in distributed systems. Programming distributed systems is hard, and recipes alone won't even come close to solving all your problems. What the recipes do is help you get programs on different computers talking to each other so you can start writing applications.

Remote procedure call (RPC) is an attractive approach to structuring a distributed system. The details of network communication are exposed through an interface that looks like normal procedure calls. When you call a function on a remote server, the RPC system is responsible for all the communication details. It encodes the arguments so they can be passed over the network to the server, which might use different internal representations for the data. It invokes the right function on the remote machine and waits for a response.

The recipes here use three different systems that provide RPC interfaces: CORBA, SOAP, and XML-RPC. These systems are attractive because they make it easy to connect programs, whether they are running on different computers or are written in different languages.

You can find Fredrik Lundh's XML-RPC library for Python in the standard library, starting with the 2.2 release. For earlier versions of Python, and for CORBA and SOAP, you'll need to install more software before you can get started. The recipes include pointers to the software you need.

The Python standard library also provides a good set of modules for doing the lower-level work of network programming: socket, select, asyncore, and asynchat. It also has modules for marshaling data and sending it across sockets: struct, pickle, and xdrlib. These modules, in turn, provide the plumbing for many other modules. Jeff Bauer offers a recipe using the telnetlib module to send commands to remote machines.

Four of the recipes focus on XML-RPC, a new protocol that uses XML and HTTP to exchange simple data structures between programs. Rael Dornfest demonstrates how to write an XML-RPC client program that retrieves data from O'Reilly's Meerkat service. It's a three-line recipe, including the `import` statement, which is its chief appeal.

Brian Quinlan and Jeff Bauer contribute two recipes for constructing XML-RPC servers. Quinlan shows how to use the `SimpleXMLRPCServer` module from the Python 2.2 standard library to handle incoming requests in Recipe 13.2. Bauer's Recipe 13.3 uses Medusa, a framework for writing asynchronous network servers. In both cases, the libraries do most of the work. Other than a few lines of initialization and registration, the server looks like normal Python code.

SOAP is an XML-based protocol that shares its origins with XML-RPC. Graham Dumpleton explains how to create a server that can talk to clients with either protocol in Recipe 13.4, one of three recipes that use his OSE framework. The two protocols are similar enough that a single HTTP server and service implementation can support both protocols. There are gotchas, of course. Dumpleton mentions several. For starters, XML-RPC does not support `None`, and SOAP does not support empty dictionaries.

An alternative to the XML-based protocols is CORBA, an object-based RPC mechanism that uses its own protocol, IIOP. Compared to XML-RPC and SOAP, CORBA is a mature technology; it was introduced in 1991. The Python language binding was officially approved in February 2000, and several ORBs (roughly, CORBA servers) support Python. Duncan Grisby lays out the basics of getting a CORBA client and server running in Recipe 13.5, which uses omniORB, a free ORB, and the Python binding he wrote for it.

CORBA has a reputation for complexity, but Grisby's recipe makes it look straightforward. There are more steps involved in the CORBA client example than in the XML-RPC client example, but they aren't hard to follow. To connect an XML-RPC client to a server, you just need a URL. To connect a CORBA client to a server, you need a special corbaloc URL, and you need to know the server's interface. Of course, you need to know the interface regardless of protocol, but CORBA uses it explicitly. Generally, CORBA offers more features—such as interfaces, type checking, passing references to objects, and more (and it supports both `None` and empty dictionaries).

Regardless of the protocols or systems you choose, the recipes here can help get you started. Interprogram communication is an important part of building a distributed system, but it's just one part. Once you have a client and server working, you'll find you have to deal with other interesting, hard problems, such as error detection, concurrency, and security, to name a few. The recipes here won't solve these problems, but they will prevent you from getting caught up in unimportant details of the communication protocols.

13.1 Making an XML-RPC Method Call

Credit: Rael Dornfest, Jeremy Hylton

Problem

You need to make a method call to an XML-RPC server.

Solution

The `xmlrpclib` package makes writing XML-RPC clients very easy. For example, we can use XML-RPC to access O'Reilly's Meerkat server and get the five most recent items about Python:

```
# needs Python 2.2 or xmlrpclib from http://www.pythonware.com/products/xmlrpc/
from xmlrpclib import Server

server = Server("http://www.oreillynet.com/meerkat/xml-rpc/server.php")

print server.meerkat.getItems(
    {'search': '[Pp]ython', 'num_items': 5, 'descriptions': 0}
)
```

Discussion

XML-RPC is a simple and lightweight approach to distributed processing. `xmlrpclib`, which makes it easy to write XML-RPC clients and servers in Python, has been part of the core Python library since Python 2.2, but you can also get it for older releases of Python from *http://www.pythonware.com/products/xmlrpc/*.

To use `xmlrpclib`, instantiate a proxy to the server (the `ServerProxy` class, also known as the `Server` class for backward compatibility) by passing in the URL to which you want to connect. Then, on that instance, access whatever methods the remote XML-RPC server supplies. In this case, you know that Meerkat supplies a `getItems` method, so if you call the method of the same name on the server-proxy instance, the instance relays the call to the server and returns the results.

This recipe uses O'Reilly's Meerkat service, intended for the syndication of contents such as news and product announcements. Specifically, the recipe queries Meerkat for the five most recent items mentioning either "Python" or "python". If you try this, be warned that, depending on the quality of your Internet connection, the time of day, and the level of traffic on the Internet, response times from Meerkat are variable. If the script takes a long time to answer, it doesn't mean you did something wrong, it just means you have to be patient!

Using `xmlrpclib` by passing raw dictionaries is quite workable, but rather unPythonic. Here's an easy alternative that looks quite a bit nicer:

```
from xmlrpclib import Server
server = Server("http://www.oreillynet.com/meerkat/xml-rpc/server.php")
```

```
class MeerkatQuery:
    def __init__(self, search, num_items=5, descriptions=0):
        self.search = search
        self.num_items = num_items
        self.descriptions = descriptions

q = MeerkatQuery("[Pp]ython")
print server.meerkat.getItems(q)
```

Of course, you can package the instance attributes and their default values in several different ways, but the point of this variation is that, as the argument to the getItems method, an instance object with the right attributes works just as well as a dictionary object with the same information packaged as dictionary items.

See Also

The XML-RPC library ships with recent versions of Python; if it isn't in your version of Python, you can get it from *http://www.pythonware.com/products/xmlrpc/*; Meerkat is at *http://www.oreillynet.com/meerkat/*.

13.2 Serving XML-RPC Requests

Credit: Brian Quinlan

Problem

You need to implement an XML-RPC server.

Solution

The xmlrpclib package also makes writing XML-RPC servers pretty easy. Here's how you can write an XML-RPC server:

```
# server coder sxr_server.py
# needs Python 2.2 or the XML-RPC package from PythonWare

import SimpleXMLRPCServer

class StringFunctions:
    def __init__(self):
        # Make all of the Python string functions available through
        # python_string.func_name
        import string
        self.python_string = string

    def _privateFunction(self):
        # This function cannot be called directly through XML-RPC because
        # it starts with an underscore character '_', i.e., it's "private"
        pass
```

```
        def chop_in_half(self, astr):
            return astr[:len(astr)/2]

        def repeat(self, astr, times):
            return astr * times

    if __name__=='__main__':
        server = SimpleXMLRPCServer.SimpleXMLRPCServer(("localhost", 8000))
        server.register_instance(StringFunctions())
        server.register_function(lambda astr: '_' + astr, '_string')
        server.serve_forever()
```

And here is a client that accesses the server you just wrote:

```
# server coder sxr_client.py
# needs Python 2.2 or the XML-RPC package from PythonWare

import xmlrpclib

server = xmlrpclib.Server('http://localhost:8000')
print server.chop_in_half('I am a confidant guy')
print server.repeat('Repetition is the key to learning!\n', 5)
print server._string('<= underscore')
print server.python_string.join(['I', 'like it!'], " don't ")
print server._privateFunction()    # will throw an exception
```

Discussion

This recipe demonstrates the creation of a simple XML-RPC server using the SimpleXMLRPCServer class. It requires Python 2.2 or later or the XML-RPC package from PythonWare (*http://www.pythonware.com/products/xmlrpc/index.htm*).

SimpleXMLRPCServer is a simple class that listens for HTTP requests on a specified port and dispatches any XML-RPC calls to a registered instance or a registered function. This recipe demonstrates both usages. To create a server, we instantiate SimpleXMLRPCServer, supplying the hostname and port for the server. Then, on that instance, we can call register_instance as many times as needed to make other instances available as services. Alternately, we can call register_function to make functions similarly available as services. Once we have registered all the instances and functions we want to expose, we call serve_forever on the server instance, and our XML-RPC server is active. Yes, it is really that simple.

Registering a function (as opposed to an instance) is necessary if your function's name begins with an underscore (_) or contains characters not allowed in Python identifiers (e.g., Unicode characters, plus signs, etc.) Note that dotted names (e.g., python_string.join) are correctly resolved for registered instances.

See Also

The XML-RPC library ships with recent versions of Python; if it isn't in your version of Python, you can get it from *http://www.pythonware.com/products/xmlrpc/*.

13.3 Using XML-RPC with Medusa

Credit: Jeff Bauer

Problem

You need to establish a distributed processing system and want to use the XML-RPC protocol.

Solution

The `medusa` package lets you implement lightweight, highly scalable servers, even with old versions of Python. An XML-RPC handler is included in the Medusa distribution. Here is how you code a server with Medusa:

```
# xmlrpc_server.py
from socket import gethostname
from medusa.xmlrpc_handler import xmlrpc_handler
from medusa.http_server import http_server
from medusa import asyncore

class xmlrpc_server(xmlrpc_handler):
    # initializes and runs the server
    def __init__(self, host=None, port=8182):
        if host is None:
            host = gethostname()
        hs = http_server(host, port)
        hs.install_handler(self)
        asyncore.loop()

    # an example of a method to be exposed via the XML-RPC protocol
    def add(self, op1, op2):
        return op1 + op2

    # the infrastructure ("plumbing") to expose methods
    def call(self, method, params):
        print "call method: %s, params: %s" % (method, str(params))
        if method == 'add':
            return apply(self.add, params)
        return "method not found: %s" % method

if __name__ == '__main__':
    server = xmlrpc_server()
```

And here is an `xmlrpclib`-based client of this server:

```
# xmlrpc_client.py
from socket import gethostname
from xmlrpclib import Transport, dumps

class xmlrpc_connection:
    def __init__(self, host=None, port=8182):
        if host is None:
            host = gethostname( )
        self.host = "%s:%s" % (host, port)
        self.transport = Transport( )

    def remote(self, method, params=( )):
        """ remote invokes the server with the method name and an optional set
        of parameters. The return value is always a tuple. """

        response = self.transport.request(self.host, '/RPC2',
                                          dumps(params, method))

        return response

if __name__ == '__main__':
    connection = xmlrpc_connection( )
    (answer,) = connection.remote("add", (40, 2))
    print "The answer is:", answer
```

Discussion

This recipe demonstrates remote method calls between two machines (or two pro-cesses, even on the same machine) using the XML-RPC protocol. A complete example of working client/server code is provided. XML-RPC is one of the easiest ways to han-dle distributed processing tasks. There's no messing around with the low-level socket details, nor is it necessary to write an interface definition. The protocol is platform- and language-neutral. The XML-RPC specification can be found at *http://www.xml-rpc.com* and is well worth studying.

With Medusa (*http://www.nightmare.com*), you implement an XML-RPC server by subclassing the `xmlrpc_handler` class and passing an instance of your class to the `install_handler` method of an instance of `http_server`. HTTP is the transport-level protocol, and `http_server` handles all transport-level issues on your behalf. You need to provide only the handler part by customizing `xmlrpc_handler` through subclassing and method overriding. Specifically, you must override the `call` method, which the Medusa framework calls on your instance with the name of the XML-RPC method being called, along with its parameters, as arguments. This is exactly what we do in this recipe, in which we expose a single XML-RPC method named `add` which accepts two numeric parameters and returns their sum as the method's result.

The sample XML-RPC client uses `xmlrpclib` in a more sophisticated way than Recipe 13.1 by using the `Transport` class explicitly. This lets you see what happens under the covers of an XML-RPC method call a bit more transparently and also lets you control things in a finer-grained way, although we don't use that fine-grained–control potential in this recipe (and you will need it only rarely in XML-RPC clients that you actually deploy, anyway).

xmlrpclib can also be used on its own, without separately downloading and installing Medusa, and comes with similar client and server program examples. However, the asynchronous operation of Medusa can significantly enhance performance, particularly scalability. Medusa (and asyncore and asynchat) are applicable to client- and server-side programming, but this recipe does not use the asynchronous approach in its example client, only in its example server. Of course, the benefits of the asynchronous approach come when a program does several network operations at once (in such cases, asynchronous Medusa operations can give you substantial performance benefits when compared to alternatives such as multiprocessing and multithreading). This is almost always the case for servers, which need to be able to field several requests arriving simultaneously from different clients. It's certainly not unheard of for clients, too, if the client needs to make several requests at once.

See Also

The XML-RPC (xmlrpclib) library ships with recent versions of Python; if it isn't in your version of Python, you can get it from *http://www.pythonware.com/products/xmlrpc/*; the Medusa library at *http://www.nightmare.com*; recent Python releases include the asyncore and asynchat modules from Medusa as parts of the Python standard library (not, however, other parts of Medusa, such as xmlprc_handler).

13.4   Writing a Web Service That Supports Both XML-RPC and SOAP

Credit: Graham Dumpleton

Problem

You need to expose a service on the Web in a way that makes the service accessible to both XML-RPC and SOAP clients.

Solution

The OSE package offers a lot of extra flexibility for Python distributed processing, both server-side and client-side. Here is how we can code the actual web service:

```
# the actual web service, dbwebser.py
# needs the OSE package from http://ose.sourceforge.net

import netsvc
import netsvc.xmlrpc
```

```
import netsvc.soap
import signal
import dbm

class Database(netsvc.Service):

  def __init__(self, name):
      netsvc.Service.__init__(self, name)
      self._db = dbm.open(name,'c')
      self.exportMethod(self.get)
      self.exportMethod(self.put)
      self.exportMethod(self.keys)
      self.joinGroup("web-services")

  def get(self, key):
      return self._db[key]

  def put(self, key, value):
      self._db[key] = value

  def keys(self):
      return self._db.keys()

dispatcher = netsvc.Dispatcher()
dispatcher.monitor(signal.SIGINT)
httpd = netsvc.HttpDaemon(8000)

database = Database("test")

rpcgw1 = netsvc.xmlrpc.RpcGateway("web-services")
httpd.attach("/xmlrpc/database", rpcgw1)

rpcgw2 = netsvc.soap.RpcGateway("web-services")
httpd.attach("/soap/database", rpcgw2)

httpd.start()
dispatcher.run()
```

Here's a client that accesses the service via XML-RPC:

```
# dbclient.py
# an XML-RPC client using the PythonWare xmlrpclib module (also
# included in the standard library with Python 2.2 and later)

import xmlrpclib

url = "http://localhost:8000/xmlrpc/database/test"
service = xmlrpclib.Server(url)

for i in range(10):
    service.put('X'+str(i), str(i*i))

for key in service.keys():
    print key, service.get(key)
```

And here's a SOAP client that uses the `pywebsvcs` SOAP module:

```
import SOAP

url = "http://localhost:8000/soap/database/test"
service = SOAP.SOAPProxy(url)

for i in range(10):
    service.put('S'+str(i), str(i*i))

for key in service.keys( ):
    print key, service.get(key)
```

Discussion

This recipe gives yet another example of an XML-RPC–capable web service. But this recipe is different in that the service can be accessed at the same time using the SOAP protocol. Confusion is avoided by having clients for each protocol use different URLs to access the service.

The ability to support both XML-RPC and SOAP at the same time avoids the question of which to use. Only a single implementation of the service needs to be written. If one protocol wins out over the other, you haven't wasted any time; you simply don't deploy the gateway for the protocol you don't want to support anymore. Deploying both also gives users a wider choice of client implementations.

Issues that arise in going down this road are that, since XML-RPC supports only positional parameters and not named parameters, you are reduced to using only positional parameters through the SOAP interface. There is also the problem that XML-RPC doesn't support the Python `None` type, nor various other scalar data types that can be used with SOAP (e.g., extended date and time values). XML-RPC restricts you to using strings as key values in dictionaries that you wish to pass around using the protocol. What's worse is that SOAP further constrains what those key values can be, and SOAP cannot handle an empty dictionary.

Thus, although it may be good to support both protocols, you are forced to use a set of data types and values that will work with both, which is a typical least-common-denominator syndrome similar to other cross-platform development efforts. In this case, the issue can be further complicated since some SOAP implementations may not preserve type information through to the server side, whereas in XML-RPC this is not a problem. Therefore, any server-side code may have to deal with values of specific types arriving in different forms. You need to run tests against a wide variety of clients to ensure that you've covered this ground.

The `netsvc` module used by this example comes with OSE, which can be found at *http://ose.sourceforge.net*. The recipe's server script instantiates a `Dispatcher`, an `HttpDaemon` serving on port 8000, and two `RpcGateway` instances, one from the `soap` and one from the `xmlrpc` module of OSE's `netsvc` package. Both gateways expose the services from a group named web-services, and we instantiate a single instance of our Database class, a subclass of netsvc's Service class, which joins that group. Thus, the Database instance implements all services that this server offers. Specifically, it does so by calling the exportMethod method (which it gets from its base class) on each of its own bound methods it wants to expose as part of its initialization. Both SOAP and XML-RPC servers expose the same Database instance via different URLs, and thus, both SOAP and XML-RPC clients end up accessing (and thus sharing) the same data structure.

Note that the OSE package provides a framework for building distributed applications, of which this recipe represents only a small portion. The OSE package comes with its own XML-RPC protocol implementation, but for SOAP, it currently relies upon the SOAP module from the pywebsvcs package, which can be found at *http://sourceforge.net/projects/pywebsvcs*, along with an alternate set of modules worth exploring called the Zolera SOAP Infrastructure (ZSI).

See Also

Recipes 13.7 and 13.8 for different uses of OSE; the OSE package (*http://ose.sourceforge.net*); the SOAP module from the pywebsvcs package (*http://sourceforge.net/projects/pywebsvcs*).

13.5   Implementing a CORBA Client and Server

Credit: Duncan Grisby

Problem

You need to implement a CORBA server and client to distribute a processing task, such as the all-important network-centralized, fortune-cookie distribution.

Solution

CORBA is a mature object-oriented RPC protocol, and several CORBA ORBs offer excellent Python support. This recipe requires multiple files. Here is the interface definition file, *fortune.idl*:

```
module Fortune {
  interface CookieServer {
    string get_cookie( );
  };
};
```

The server script is a simple Python program:

```
import sys, os
import CORBA, Fortune, Fortune__POA

FORTUNE_PATH = "/usr/games/fortune"
```

```
class CookieServer_i(Fortune__POA.CookieServer):
    def get_cookie(self):
        pipe   = os.popen(FORTUNE_PATH)
        cookie = pipe.read( )
        if pipe.close( ):
            # An error occurred with the pipe
            cookie = "Oh dear, couldn't get a fortune\n"
        return cookie

orb = CORBA.ORB_init(sys.argv)
poa = orb.resolve_initial_references("RootPOA")

servant = CookieServer_i( )
poa.activate_object(servant)

print orb.object_to_string(servant._this( ))

poa._get_the_POAManager().activate( )
orb.run( )
```

And here's a demonstration of the client code, using the Python interactive command line:

```
>>> import CORBA, Fortune
>>> orb = CORBA.ORB_init( )
>>> o = orb.string_to_object(
...     "corbaloc::host.example.com/fortune")
>>> o = o._narrow(Fortune.CookieServer)
>>> print o.get_cookie( )
```

Discussion

CORBA has a reputation for being hard to use, but it is really very easy, especially if you use Python. This example shows the complete CORBA implementation of a fortune-cookie server and its client. To run this example, you need a Python CORBA implementation (or two, as you can use two different CORBA implementations, one for the client and one for the server, and let them interoperate with the IIOP inter-ORB protocol). There are several free ones you can download.

With most ORBs, you must convert the IDL interface definition into Python declarations with an IDL compiler. For example, with omniORBpy:

```
$ omniidl -bpython fortune.idl
```

This creates Python modules named Fortune and Fortune__POA to be used by clients and servers, respectively.

In the server, we implement the CookieServer CORBA interface by importing Fortune__POA and subclassing the CookieServer class that the module exposes. Specifically, in our own subclass, we need to override the get_cookie method (i.e., implement the methods that the interface asserts we're implementing). Then, we start CORBA to get an orb instance, ask the ORB for a POA, instantiate our own interface-implementing object, and pass it to the POA instance's activate_object method. Finally, we call the activate method on the POA manager and the run method on the ORB to start our service.

When you run the server, it prints out a long hex string, such as:

```
IOR:010000001d00000049444c3a466f7274756e652f436f6f6b69655365727665723
a312e30000000000100000000000005c000000010102000d0000003135382e313234
2e36342e330000f90a07000000666f7274756e6500020000000000000008000000010
00000005454441010000001c0000000100000001000100010000000100010509010100
0100000009010100
```

Printing this is the purpose of the object_to_string call that our recipe's server performs just before it activates and runs.

You have to give this value to the client's orb.string_to_object call to contact your server. Of course, such long hex strings may not be very convenient to communicate to clients. To remedy this, it's easy to make your server support a simple corbaloc URL string, like the one used in the client example, but this involves omniORB-specific code. (See the omniORBpy manual for details of corbaloc URL support.)

See Also

omniORBpy at *http://www.omniorb.org/omniORBpy/*.

13.6 Performing Remote Logins Using telnetlib
Credit: Jeff Bauer

Problem

You need to send commands to one or more logins that can be on the local machine or on a remote machine, and the Telnet protocol is acceptable.

Solution

Telnet is one of the oldest protocols in the TCP/IP stack, but it may still be serviceable (at least within an intranet that is well-protected against sniffing and spoofing attacks). In any case, Python's standard module telnetlib supports Telnet quite well:

```
# auto_telnet.py - remote control via telnet
import os, sys, string, telnetlib
from getpass import getpass

class AutoTelnet:
    def __init__(self, user_list, cmd_list, **kw):
        self.host = kw.get('host', 'localhost')
        self.timeout = kw.get('timeout', 600)
        self.command_prompt = kw.get('command_prompt', "$ ")
```

```python
        self.passwd = {}
        for user in user_list:
            self.passwd[user] = getpass("Enter user '%s' password: " % user)
        self.telnet = telnetlib.Telnet()
        for user in user_list:
            self.telnet.open(self.host)
            ok = self.action(user, cmd_list)
            if not ok:
                print "Unable to process:", user
            self.telnet.close()

    def action(self, user, cmd_list):
        t = self.telnet
        t.write("\n")
        login_prompt = "login: "
        response = t.read_until(login_prompt, 5)
        if string.count(response, login_prompt):
            print response
        else:
            return 0
        t.write("%s\n" % user)
        password_prompt = "Password:"
        response = t.read_until(password_prompt, 3)
        if string.count(response, password_prompt):
            print response
        else:
            return 0
        t.write("%s\n" % self.passwd[user])
        response = t.read_until(self.command_prompt, 5)
        if not string.count(response, self.command_prompt):
            return 0
        for cmd in cmd_list:
            t.write("%s\n" % cmd)
            response = t.read_until(self.command_prompt, self.timeout)
            if not string.count(response, self.command_prompt):
                return 0
            print response
        return 1

if __name__ == '__main__':
    basename = os.path.splitext(os.path.basename(sys.argv[0]))[0]
    logname = os.environ.get("LOGNAME", os.environ.get("USERNAME"))
    host = 'localhost'
    import getopt
    optlist, user_list = getopt.getopt(sys.argv[1:], 'c:f:h:')
    usage = """
usage: %s [-h host] [-f cmdfile] [-c "command"] user1 user2 ...
    -c  command
    -f  command file
    -h  host  (default: '%s')

Example:  %s -c "echo $HOME" %s
""" % (basename, host, basename, logname)
    if len(sys.argv) < 2:
```

```
            print usage
            sys.exit(1)
    cmd_list = []
    for opt, optarg in optlist:
        if opt == '-f':
            for r in open(optarg).readlines():
                if string.rstrip(r):
                    cmd_list.append(r)
        elif opt == '-c':
            command = optarg
            if command[0] == '"' and command[-1] == '"':
                command = command[1:-1]
            cmd_list.append(command)
        elif opt == '-h':
            host = optarg
    autoTelnet = AutoTelnet(user_list, cmd_list, host=host)
```

Discussion

Python's `telnetlib` lets you easily automate access to Telnet servers, even from non-Unix machines. As a flexible alternative to the popen functions, `telnetlib` is a handy technique to have in your system-administration toolbox.

Generally, production code will be more robust, but this recipe should be enough to get you started in the right direction. The recipe's `AutoTelnet` class instantiates a single `telnetlib.Telnet` object that it uses in a loop over a list of users. For each user, it calls the open method of the `Telnet` instance to open the connection to the specified host, runs a series of commands in `AutoTelnet`'s action method, and finally calls the close method of the `Telnet` instance to terminate the connection.

`AutoTelnet`'s action method is where the action is. All operations depend on two methods of the `Telnet` instance. The `write` method takes a single string argument and writes it to the connection. The `t.read_until` method takes two arguments, a string to wait for and a timeout in seconds, and returns a string with all the characters received from the connection until the timeout elapsed or the waited-for string occurred. action's code uses these two methods to wait for a login prompt and send the username; wait for a password prompt and send the password; and, repeatedly, wait for a command prompt (typically from a Unix shell at the other end of the connection) and send the commands in the list sequentially.

One warning (which applies to Telnet and other old protocols): except, perhaps, for the transmission of completely public data not protected by a password that might be of interest to intruders of ill will, do not run Telnet (or nonanonymous FTP) on networks on which you are not completely sure that nobody is packet-sniffing, since these protocols date from an older, more trusting age. They let passwords, and everything else, travel in the clear, open to any snooper. This is not Python-specific. Whether you use Python or not, be advised: if there is any risk that somebody might be packet-sniffing, use *ssh* instead, so no password travels on the network in the clear, and the connection stream itself is encrypted.

See Also

Documentation on the standard library module `telnetlib` in the *Library Reference*.

13.7 Using Publish/Subscribe in a Distributed Middleware Architecture

Credit: Graham Dumpleton

Problem

You need to allow distributed services to set themselves up as publishers of information and/or subscribers to that information by writing a suitable central exchange (middleware) server.

Solution

The OSE package supports a publisher/subscriber programming model through its `netsvc` module. To exploit it, we first need a central middleware process to which all others connect:

```
# The central.py script -- needs the OSE package from http://ose.sourceforge.net

import netsvc
import signal

dispatcher = netsvc.Dispatcher()
dispatcher.monitor(signal.SIGINT)

exchange = netsvc.Exchange(netsvc.EXCHANGE_SERVER)
exchange.listen(11111)

dispatcher.run()
```

Then, we need service processes that periodically publish information to the central middleware process, such as:

```
# The publish.py script -- needs the OSE package from http://ose.sourceforge.net

import netsvc
import signal
import random

class Publisher(netsvc.Service):

    def __init__(self):
        netsvc.Service.__init__(self,"SEED")
```

```
            self._count = 0
            time = netsvc.DateTime()
            data = { "time": time }
            self.publishReport("init", data, -1)
            self.startTimer(self.publish, 1, "1")

        def publish(self,name):
            self._count = self._count + 1
            time = netsvc.DateTime()
            value = int(0xFFFF*random.random())
            data = { "time": time, "count": self._count, "value": value }
            self.publishReport("next", data)
            self.startTimer(self.publish, 1, "1")

dispatcher = netsvc.Dispatcher()
dispatcher.monitor(signal.SIGINT)

exchange = netsvc.Exchange(netsvc.EXCHANGE_CLIENT)
exchange.connect("localhost", 11111, 5)

publisher = Publisher()

dispatcher.run()
```

Finally, we need services that subscribe to the published information, such as:

```
# The subscribe.py script -- needs the OSE package from http://ose.sourceforge.net

import netsvc
import signal

class Subscriber(netsvc.Service):

    def __init__(self):
        netsvc.Service.__init__(self)
        self.monitorReports(self.seed, "SEED", "next")

    def seed(self, service, subjectName, content):
        print "%s - %s" % (content["time"], content["value"])

dispatcher = netsvc.Dispatcher()
dispatcher.monitor(signal.SIGINT)

exchange = netsvc.Exchange(netsvc.EXCHANGE_CLIENT)
exchange.connect("localhost", 11111, 5)

subscriber = Subscriber()

dispatcher.run()
```

Discussion

This recipe is a simple example of how to set up a distributed publish/subscribe system. It shows the creation of a central exchange service that all participating processes connect to. Services can then set themselves up as publishers, and other services can subscribe to what is being published. This recipe can form the basis of many different types of applications, ranging from instant messaging to alarm systems for monitoring network equipment and stock market data feeds. (Partly because Python is used at various levels, but also because of how the underlying architecture is designed, you shouldn't expect to be able to pass the huge amount of data updates that make up a complete stock market feed through applications built in this manner. Generally, such applications deal only with a subset of this data anyway.)

The netsvc module comes as part of the OSE package, which is available from *http:// ose.sourceforge.net*. This recipe shows only a small subset of the actual functionality available in OSE. Other middleware-like functionality, such as a system for message-oriented request/reply, is also available (see Recipe 13.8).

The first script in the recipe, *central.py*, implements the middleware process to which all others subscribe. Like all OSE processes, it instantiates a Dispatcher, instantiates an Exchange in the role of an exchange server, tells it to listen on port 11111, and runs the dispatcher.

The second script, *publish.py*, implements an example of a publisher service. It, too, instantiates a Dispatcher and then an Exchange, but the latter is an exchange client and, therefore, rather than listening for connections, it connects to port 11111 where the middleware must be running. Before running the dispatcher, its next crucial step is instantiating a Publisher, its own custom subclass of Service. This in turn calls Service's publishReport method, at first with an 'init' message, then through the startTimer method, which is told to run the publish method with a 'next' message every second. Each published message is accompanied by an arbitrary dictionary, which, in this recipe, carries just a few demonstration entries.

The third script, *subscribe.py*, implements an example of a subscriber for the publisher service in *publish.py*. Like the latter, it instantiates a Dispatcher and an Exchange, which connects as an exchange client to port 11111 where the middleware must be running. It implements Subscriber, the Service subclass, which calls Service's monitorReports method for the 'next' message, registering its own seed method to be called back for each such message that is published. The latter method then prints out a couple of the entries from the content dictionary argument so we can check if the whole arrangement is functioning correctly.

To try this recipe, after downloading and installing the OSE package, run python central.py from one terminal. Then, from one or more other terminals, run an arbitrary mix of python publish.py and python subscribe.py. You will see that all subscribers are regularly notified of all the messages published by every publisher.

In a somewhat different sense, publish/subscribe is also a popular approach to loosening coupling in GUI architectures (see Recipe 9.11).

See Also

Recipe 13.8 describes another feature of the OSE package, while Recipe 9.11 shows a different approach to publish/subscribe in a GUI context; the OSE package (*http://ose.sourceforge.net*).

13.8 Using Request/Reply in a Distributed Middleware Architecture

Credit: Graham Dumpleton

Problem

You need to allow some distributed services to supply methods, and other distributed services to access and use those methods, in a location-independent way by writing a suitable central exchange (middleware) server.

Solution

The OSE package also supports the request/reply architecture. First, we need a central middleware process to which all others connect:

```
# The central.py script -- needs the OSE package from http://ose.sourceforge.net

import netsvc
import signal

dispatcher = netsvc.Dispatcher( )
dispatcher.monitor(signal.SIGINT)

exchange = netsvc.Exchange(netsvc.EXCHANGE_SERVER)
exchange.listen(11111)

dispatcher.run( )
```

Next, we need a server that supplies methods through the middleware:

```
# The server.py script -- needs the OSE package from http://ose.sourceforge.net

import netsvc
import signal

class Service(netsvc.Service):

    def __init__(self):
        netsvc.Service.__init__(self, "math")
        self.joinGroup("web-services")
        self.exportMethod(self.multiply)

    def multiply(self, x, y):
        return x*y
```

```
    dispatcher = netsvc.Dispatcher()
    dispatcher.monitor(signal.SIGINT)

    exchange = netsvc.Exchange(netsvc.EXCHANGE_CLIENT)
    exchange.connect("localhost",11111,5)

    service = Service()

    dispatcher.run()
```

Then, we need a client that consumes methods through the middleware:

```
# The client.py script -- needs the OSE package from http://ose.sourceforge.net

import netsvc
import signal
import random

class Client(netsvc.Service):

    def __init__(self):
        netsvc.Service.__init__(self, "")
        self.startTimer(self.call, 1, "1")

    def call(self,name):
        service = self.serviceEndPoint("math")
        if service != None:
            x = int(random.random()*1000)
            id = service.multiply(x, x)
            self.monitorResponse(self.result, id)
        self.startTimer(self.call, 1, "1")

    def result(self,square):
        print square

dispatcher = netsvc.Dispatcher()
dispatcher.monitor(signal.SIGINT)

exchange = netsvc.Exchange(netsvc.EXCHANGE_CLIENT)
exchange.connect("localhost", 11111, 5)

client = Client()

dispatcher.run()
```

We can also write a gateway exposing an XML-RPC service for the same methods:

```
# The gateway.py script -- needs the OSE package from http://ose.sourceforge.net

import signal
import netsvc
import netsvc.xmlrpc

dispatcher = netsvc.Dispatcher()
dispatcher.monitor(signal.SIGINT)
```

```
httpd = netsvc.HttpDaemon(8000)
rpcgw = netsvc.xmlrpc.RpcGateway("web-services")
httpd.attach("/xmlrpc/service", rpcgw)
httpd.start()

exchange = netsvc.Exchange(netsvc.EXCHANGE_CLIENT)
exchange.connect("localhost", 11111, 5)

dispatcher.run()
```

Discussion

This recipe is a simple example of setting up a distributed message–oriented request/reply architecture. It shows the creation of a central exchange service that all participating processes connect to. Services assign themselves a name and export the methods that are remotely accessible. Client services can then make calls against the exported methods.

This recipe provides an alternative to systems dependent on XML-RPC and SOAP, which only create connections to other processes when required. In this architecture, the processes are always connected through the central exchange process, avoiding the cost of setting up and ripping down the socket connections for each request. That said, an XML-RPC or SOAP gateway can also be connected to the system to allow similar remote access using the HTTP protocol. Although each service is shown in a separate process, they could just as well be in the same process, as the means of communication is the same. The services shown may also publish data, which other services can subscribe to if required, as shown in Recipe 13.7.

The *central.py* script is the same as in Recipe 13.7, which highlights how the central middleware in OSE architectures is independent from the contents of the application and can offer both publish/subscribe and request/reply mediation. The *server.py* script defines a subclass of Service and calls the joinGroup and exportMethod methods, which we already examined in Recipe 13.4. The *client.py* script uses Service's startTimer method for periodic invocation of its own call method. This method in turn uses serviceEndPoint to access the specific service named 'math', calls the multiply method on the latter, and calls monitorResponse to get its own method result called back when the server responds with a result.

The *gateway.py* script shows how OSE lets you use the same infrastructure to expose the same services via the Web, as we already illustrated in Recipe 13.4.

See Also

Recipe 13.4; Recipe 13.7 describes a different feature of the OSE package; the OSE package (*http://ose.sourceforge.net*).

## CHAPTER 14

Debugging and Testing

14.0 Introduction

Credit: Mark Hammond, co-author of Python Programming on Win32 (O'Reilly)

The first computer I had in my home was a 64-KB Z80 CP/M machine. Having the machine available at home meant I had much more time to deeply explore this exciting toy. Turbo Pascal had just been released, and it seemed the obvious progression from the various BASIC dialects and assemblers I had been using. Even then, I was somehow drawn towards developing reusable libraries for my programs, and as my skills and employment progressed, I remained drawn to building tools that assist developers as much as building end-user applications.

Building tools for developers means that debugging and testing are often in the foreground. Although images of an interactive debugger may pop into your head, the concepts of debugging and testing are much broader than you may initially think. Debugging and testing are sometimes an inseparable cycle. Your testing will often lead you to discover bugs. You debug until you believe you understand the cause of the error and make the necessary changes. Rinse and repeat as required.

Often, debugging and testing are more insidious. I am a big fan of Python's assert statement, and every time I use it, I am debugging and testing my program. Large projects will often develop strategies to build debugging and testing capabilities directly into the application itself, such as centralized logging and error handling. In larger projects, it could be argued that this style of debugging and testing is more critical than the post mortem activities I just described.

Python, in particular, supports a variety of techniques to help developers in their endeavors. The introspective and dynamic nature of Python (the result of Guido's "we are all consenting adults" philosophy of programming) means that your opportunities for debugging techniques are limited only by your imagination. You can replace functions at runtime, add methods to classes, and extract everything about your program that there is to know. All at runtime, and all quite simple and Pythonic.

In this chapter, you will find a nice collection of recipes from which even the most hardened critic will take gastronomic delight. Whether you want customized error logging, deep diagnostic information in Python tracebacks, or even help with your garbage, you have come to the right place. So tuck in your napkin; your next course has arrived!

14.1 Reloading All Loaded Modules

Credit: Sébastien Keim

Problem

When you repeatedly run a test script during an interactive session, it always uses the first version of the modules you are developing, even if you made changes to the code. You need to ensure that modules are reloaded.

Solution

There are a few ways to accomplish this goal. Here's a solution that is simple and drastic, but it may not work with integrated development environments (IDEs):

```
import sys
sys.modules.clear()
```

And here is a solution that is a bit more careful and is compatible with IDEs:

```
import sys
if globals().has_key('init_modules'):
    # second or subsequent run: remove all but initially loaded modules
    for m in sys.modules.keys():
        if x not in init_modules:
            del(sys.modules[m])
else:
    # first run: find out which modules were initially loaded
    init_modules = sys.modules.keys()
```

Discussion

When you create a Python module, you can use a test script that imports your module. But you have probably noticed that when you repeatedly run the test script inside a given interactive session, it always uses the first version of your module, even if you made changes in the code. This is because the import statement checks if the module is already in memory and does the actual importing only if this is the first time the module is used. This is an important optimization that lets you use the import statement freely, but it does get in the way in such development situations.

You can use the reload function, but this is difficult if you perform changes in a module that isn't directly imported by your test script. One simple solution is to remove all modules from memory before running the test script. For this, two lines at the start of your test script, as shown in the first solution, suffice.

If you work with a framework that executes user code in the same interpreter as the IDE itself (such as IDLE), however, you will notice that this technique fails. This is because sys.modules.clear removes IDLE from memory, so you will have to use the second solution in that case. On the first run, the solution determines which modules are initial modules for the system (all those that are loaded at this point). On all other runs, the solution cleans up all modules whose names are not in this initial list. This, of course, relies on globals (i.e., the dictionary of this test script, seen as a module) being unchanged when this test script is run again.

See Also

Documentation on the sys standard library module, along with the reload and globals built-ins, in the *Library Reference*; the section on the import statement in the *Language Reference*.

14.2   Tracing Expressions and Comments in Debug Mode

Credit: Olivier Dagenais

Problem

You are coding a program that cannot use an interactive, step-by-step debugger, so you need detailed logging of state and control flow to perform debugging effectively despite this.

Solution

The extract_stack function from the traceback module is the key here, as it lets our code easily perform runtime introspection to find out about the code that called it:

```
import types, string, sys
from traceback import *

traceOutput = sys.stdout
watchOutput = sys.stdout
rawOutput = sys.stdout

""" Should print out something like:
File "trace.py", line 57, in __testTrace
  secretOfUniverse <int> = 42
"""
def watch(variableName):
    if __debug__:
        stack = extract_stack()[-2:][0]
```

```
            actualCall = stack[3]
            if actualCall is None:
                actualCall = "watch([unknown])"
            left = string.find(actualCall, '(')
            right = string.rfind(actualCall, ')')
            paramDict = {}
            paramDict["varName"]    = string.strip(
                actualCall[left+1:right]) # all from '(' to ')'
            paramDict["varType"]    = str(type(variableName))[7:-2]
            paramDict["value"]      = repr(variableName)
            paramDict["methodName"] = stack[2]
            paramDict["lineNumber"] = stack[1]
            paramDict["fileName"]   = stack[0]
            outStr = 'File "%(fileName)s", line %(lineNumber)d, in' \
                    ' %(methodName)s\n    %(varName)s <%(varType)s>' \
                    ' = %(value)s\n\n'
            watchOutput.write(outStr % paramDict)

""" Should print out something like:
File "trace.py", line 64, in ?
  This line was executed!
"""
def trace(text):
    if __debug__:
        stack = extract_stack()[-2:][0]
        paramDict = {}
        paramDict["methodName"] = stack[2]
        paramDict["lineNumber"] = stack[1]
        paramDict["fileName"]   = stack[0]
        paramDict["text"]       = text
        outStr = 'File "%(fileName)s", line %(lineNumber)d, in' \
                ' %(methodName)s\n  %(text)s\n\n'
        traceOutput.write(outStr%paramDict)

""" Should print out something like:
  Just some raw text
"""
def raw(text):
    if __debug__:
        rawOutput.write(text)
```

Discussion

Many different programs don't make it easy to use traditional, interactive step-by-step debuggers. Examples include CGI programs; servers intended to be accessed from the Web and/or via protocols such as sockets, XML-RPC, and SOAP; and Windows services and Unix daemons.

Of course, you can remedy this by sprinkling a bunch of print statements all through the program, but this is unsystematic and needs clean-up when a given problem is fixed. This recipe shows that a better-organized approach is quite feasible, by supplying a few functions that allow you to output the value of an expression, a variable, or a function call, with scope information, trace statements, and general comments.

The key is the extract_stack function from the traceback module. traceback. extract_stack returns a list of tuples with four items—giving the filename, line number, function name, and source code of the calling statement—for each call in the stack. Item [-2] (the penultimate item) of this list is the tuple of information about our direct caller, and that's the one we use in this recipe to prepare the information to emit on file-like objects bound to the traceOutput and watchOutput variables.

If you bind the traceOutput, watchOutput, or rawOutput variables to an appropriate file-like object, each kind of output is redirected appropriately. When __debug__ is false (i.e., when you run the Python interpreter with the -O or -OO switch), all the debugging-related code is automatically eliminated. And this doesn't even make your byte-code any larger, because the compiler knows about the __debug__ variable.

Here is a usage example, leaving all output streams on standard output, in the form we'd generally use to make such a module self-testing, by appending the example at the end of the module:

```
def __testTrace():
    secretOfUniverse = 42
    watch(secretOfUniverse)

if __name__ == "__main__":
    a = "something else"
    watch(a)
    __testTrace()

    trace("This line was executed!")
    raw("Just some raw text...")
```

When run with just python (no -O switch), this emits:

```
File "trace.py", line 61, in ?
  a <str> = 'something else'
File "trace.py", line 57, in __testTrace
  secretOfUniverse <int> = 42
File "trace.py", line 64, in ?
  This line was executed!
Just some raw text...
```

This recipe is meant to look very much like the traceback information printed by good old Python 1.5.2 and to be compatible with any version of Python. It's easy to modify the formats to your liking, of course.

See Also

Recipes 14.3 and 14.4; documentation on the traceback standard library module in the *Library Reference*; the section on the __debug__ flag in the *Language Reference*.

14.3   Wrapping Tracebacks in HTML

Credit: Dirk Holtwick

Problem

In a CGI (or other web-based) program, you want to display tracebacks in the result-ing HTML pages (not on sys.stderr, where tracebacks normally go), using HTML-compatible markup.

Solution

The format_tb and format_exception functions from the traceback module give us traceback information in string form, so we can return it to our caller, optionally escaped so it is printable within an HTML document:

```
def ErrorMsg(escape=1):
    """
    returns: string

    simulates a traceback output, and, if argument escape is set to 1 (true),
    the string is converted to fit into HTML documents without problems.
    """
    import traceback, sys, string

    limit = None
    type, value, tb = sys.exc_info( )
    list = traceback.format_tb(tb, limit
        ) + traceback.format_exception_only(type, value)
    body = "Traceback (innermost last):\n" + "%-20s %s" % (
        string.join(list[:-1], ""), list[-1] )
    if escape:
        import cgi
        body = '\n<PRE>'+cgi.escape(body)+'</PRE>\n'
    return body

if __name__=="__main__":
    try:
        1/0
    except:
        print ErrorMsg( )
```

Discussion

Well-structured CGI scripts and other web programs first write their output into something like a StringIO instance and then write it out. Therefore, this recipe may be helpful, as it returns error information as a multiline string that you can add to the appropriate StringIO instance in such cases. Normally, you would want some HTML markup to ensure that the error information is correctly displayed, and, by default, the ErrorMsg function in this recipe supplies this useful service as well (delegating it to the cgi.escape function, save for the wrapping of the whole escaped string into an HTML pre tag).

The recipe uses the sys.exc_info function to obtain information about the exception currently being handled (type, value, and a traceback object). The assumption is that this function is called from an exception handler (the except clause in a try/except statement). Then, the recipe calls the format_tb and format_exception functions from the traceback module to build the whole traceback information as a string to return to the caller, after optionally escaping it for HTML use.

This recipe can also be useful in other circumstances in which stderr may not be going to useful places, such as programs with GUIs—for example, you may want to dump error-trace information to a file for later examination. Of course, you would typically remove the HTML markup part of the recipe for such cases (or call the recipe's ErrorMsg function with a parameter of 0).

See Also

Recipe 14.2 for another way of tracing calls that could be combined with this recipe; Recipe 14.4; the cgitb module, part of recent Python standard libraries, provides an extended version of this recipe with colorful formatting of tracebacks, links to the source code, etc.

14.4 Getting More Information from Tracebacks

Credit: Bryn Keller

Problem

You want to display all of the available information when an uncaught exception is raised.

Solution

A traceback object is basically a linked list of nodes, in which each node refers to a frame object. Frame objects, in turn, form their own linked list opposite the linked list of traceback nodes, so we can walk back and forth if needed. This recipe exploits this structure and the rich amount of information held by frame objects, including the dictionary of local variables for the function corresponding to each frame, in particular:

```
import sys, traceback

def print_exc_plus( ):
    """
    Print the usual traceback information, followed by a listing of all the
```

```
        local variables in each frame.
        """
        tb = sys.exc_info( )[2]
        while 1:
            if not tb.tb_next:
                break
            tb = tb.tb_next
        stack = []
        f = tb.tb_frame
        while f:
            stack.append(f)
            f = f.f_back
        stack.reverse( )
        traceback.print_exc( )
        print "Locals by frame, innermost last"
        for frame in stack:
            print
            print "Frame %s in %s at line %s" % (frame.f_code.co_name,
                                                 frame.f_code.co_filename,
                                                 frame.f_lineno)
            for key, value in frame.f_locals.items( ):
                print "\t%20s = " % key,
                # We have to be VERY careful not to cause a new error in our error
                # printer! Calling str( ) on an unknown object could cause an
                # error we don't want, so we must use try/except to catch it --
                # we can't stop it from happening, but we can and should
                # stop it from propagating if it does happen!
                try:
                    print value
                except:
                    print "<ERROR WHILE PRINTING VALUE>"
```

Discussion

The standard Python traceback module provides useful functions to produce lots of information about where and why an error occurred. However, traceback objects actually contain a great deal more information than the traceback module displays (indirectly, via the frame objects they refer to). This extra information can greatly assist in detecting the cause of some errors you encounter. This recipe gives an example of an extended traceback printer you might use.

Here's a simplistic demonstration of the kind of problem this approach can help with. Basically, we have a simple function that manipulates all the strings in a list. The function doesn't do any error checking, so when we pass a list that contains something other than strings, we get an error. Figuring out which bad data caused the error is easier with our new print_exc_plus function to help us:

```
data = ["1", "2", 3, "4"]      # Typo: we 'forget' the quotes on data[2]
def pad4(seq):
    """
    Pad each string in seq with zeros up to four places. Note that there
```

```
        is no reason to actually write this function; Python already
        does this sort of thing much better. It's just an example!
        """
    return_value = []
    for thing in seq:
        return_value.append("0" * (4 - len(thing)) + thing)
    return return_value
```

Here's the (limited) information we get from a normal traceback.print_exc:

```
>>> try:
...     pad4(data)
... except:
...     traceback.print_exc()
...
Traceback (most recent call last):
  File "<stdin>", line 2, in ?
  File "<stdin>", line 9, in pad4
TypeError: len() of unsized object
```

Now here's how it looks with our new function:

```
>>> try:
...     pad4(data)
... except:
...     print_exc_plus()
...
Traceback (most recent call last):
  File "<stdin>", line 2, in ?
  File "<stdin>", line 9, in pad4
TypeError: len() of unsized object
Locals by frame, innermost last

Frame ? in <stdin> at line 4
                    sys = <module 'sys' (built-in)>
                   pad4 = <function pad4 at 0x007C6210>
             __builtins__ = <module '__builtin__' (built-in)>
                 __name__ = __main__
              traceback = <module 'traceback' from 'C:\Python22\lib\traceback.py'>
                   data = ['1', '2', 3, '4']
                  __doc__ = None
           print_exc_plus = <function print_exc_plus at 0x00802038>

Frame pad4 in <stdin> at line 9
                  thing = 3
           return_value = ['0001', '0002']
                    seq = ['1', '2', 3, '4']
```

Note how easy it is to see the bad data that caused the problem. The thing variable
has a value of 3, so we know that the TypeError we got was because of this. A quick
look at the value for data shows that we simply forgot the quotes on that item.

So we can either fix the data or decide to make pad4 a bit more tolerant (e.g., by
changing the loop to for thing in map(str,seq):). This kind of thing is an important

design choice, but the point of this recipe is to save you time in understanding what's going on, so you can make your design choices with all the available information.

The recipe relies on the fact that each traceback object refers to the next traceback object in the stack through the tb_next field, forming a linked list. Each traceback object also refers to a corresponding frame object through the tb_frame field, and each frame refers to the previous frame through the f_back field (a linked list going the other way around from that of the traceback objects).

For simplicity, the recipe accumulates references to all the frame objects in a local list called stack, then loops over the list, emitting information about each frame. For each frame, it first emits some basic information (function name, filename, line number, and so on) then turns to the dictionary representing the local variables of the frame, to which the f_locals field refers. Just like for the dictionaries built and returned by the locals and globals built-in functions, each key is a variable name, and the corresponding value is the variable's value. The only point of note here is that while printing the name is safe (it's just a string), printing the value might fail, because it could invoke an arbitrary and buggy __str__ method of a user-defined object. So the value is printed within a try/except statement to prevent raising an uncaught exception while handling another exception.

I use a technique very similar to this in the applications I develop. Unexpected errors are logged in a format like this, which makes it a lot easier to figure out what's gone wrong.

See Also

Recipes 14.2 and 14.3; documentation on the traceback module and the exc_info function in the sys module in the *Library Reference*.

14.5 Starting the Debugger Automatically After an Uncaught Exception

Credit: Thomas Heller

Problem

When running a script, Python normally responds to uncaught exceptions by printing a traceback and terminating execution, but you would prefer to automatically enter an interactive debugger in such cases when feasible.

Solution

By setting sys.excepthook, you can control what happens after uncaught exceptions:

```
# code snippet to be included in sitecustomize.py
# Needs Python 2.1 or later!
import sys

def info(type, value, tb):
    if hasattr(sys, 'ps1') or not sys.stderr.isatty():
        # You are in interactive mode or don't have a tty-like
        # device, so call the default hook
        sys.__excepthook__(type, value, tb)
    else:
        import traceback, pdb
        # You are NOT in interactive mode; print the exception...
        traceback.print_exception(type, value, tb)
        print
        # ...then start the debugger in post-mortem mode
        pdb.pm()

sys.excepthook = info
```

Discussion

When Python runs a script and an uncaught exception is raised, a traceback is printed to standard error, and the script is terminated. Python 2.1 has introduced sys.excepthook, which can be used to override the handling of uncaught exceptions. This lets you automatically start the debugger on an unexpected exception when Python is not running in interactive mode but a tty-like device is available.

The code in this recipe is meant to be included in *sitecustomize.py*, which is automatically imported by Python at startup. The debugger is started only when Python is run in noninteractive mode, and only when a tty-like device is available for interactive debugging. (Thus, it is not started for CGI scripts, daemons, and so on; to handle such cases, see Recipe 14.2.) If you do not have a *sizecustomize.py* file, create one and place it somewhere on your Python path (normally in the *site-packages* directory).

A nice further extension to this recipe would be to detect if a GUI IDE is in use, and in this case, trigger the IDE's appropriate debugging environment rather than Python's own core *pdb*, which is appropriate only for text-interactive use. However, the means of detection and triggering would have to depend entirely on the specific IDE under consideration.

See Also

Recipe 14.2; documentation on the __excepthook__ function in the sys module and the traceback, sitecustomize, and pdb modules in the *Library Reference*.

14.6   Logging and Tracing Across Platforms

Credit: Luther Blissett

Problem

You have a program that needs to run on both Windows and Unix, and you want to trace and/or log output (typically for debugging) simply and flexibly.

Solution

You can rebind `sys.stdout` so that `print` statements will be logged and use a sophisticated class for the rebinding to ensure that auxiliary functionality such as automatic timestamping is done in a platform-independent way:

```
# tweakable timestamper callable
import time
class Timestamper:
    msg_format = "%y%m%d %H%M%S", time.localtime, "%s: %s"
    def __call__(self, msg):
        tfmt, tfun, gfmt = self.msg_format
        return gfmt%(time.strftime(tfmt,tfun()), msg)

# Bind name 'syslogger' to an output-to-system-log function (if any)
try: import syslog
except ImportError:
    try: import servicemanager
    except ImportError:
        # no logging available -- maybe OutputDebugString?
        try: import win32api
        except ImportError: # none, give up and use a dummy function
            def syslogger(msg): pass
        else:
            timestamp = Timestamper()
            def syslogger(msg): win32api.OutputDebugString(timestamp(msg))
    else: syslogger = servicemanager.LogInfoMsg
else: syslogger = syslog.syslog

class FunctionFilelikeWrapper:
    def __init__(self, func):
        self.func = func
    def write(self, msg):
        self.func(msg)

syslogfile = FunctionFilelikeWrapper(syslogger)

class TeeFilelikeWrapper:
    def __init__(self, *files):
        self.files = files
    def write(self, msg):
        for f in self.files: f.write(msg)
```

```
class FlushingWrapper:
    def __init__(self, *files):
        self.files = files
    def write(self, msg):
        for f in self.files:
            f.write(msg)
            f.flush( )

def logto(*files):
    sys.stdout = TeeFilelikeWrapper(*files)
```

Discussion

When you write a Windows NT service, you can log information to the system log with calls to functions in the servicemanager module. But servicemanager is a peculiar module that lives only in the special *PythonService.Exe* interpreter, so it's not even available to nonservice programs on Windows, let alone non-Windows platforms. On Unix-like platforms, any Python program can do logging with the syslog module, but there is no such thing on Windows.

Another Windows possibility is OutputDebugString. For this, you need to have a system debugger running, but it can get debug strings from multiple sources and serialize them to a log display window and/or file. Of course, on any platform, you can also write to a file, as long as you make sure the file is unbuffered. According to the Python documentation, this works only if the underlying C library has setvbuf, or if you ensure that flush is called with each write (to avoid wondering if setvbuf is there).

Besides, I really like to use print statements, because they're good for debugging. And sometimes, I like to see the tracing information that I'm logging for debugging purposes also appear on a terminal window or console (when my program has one of those, of course) in real time. I also like to send the information to a more permanent log (or file) for later analysis (and I want it timestamped, unless it's going to a logging service, such as syslog, which will timestamp it for me).

This might seem like a tall order, but not with Python. The module in this recipe gives you all the bricks you need to build the debug-oriented output you need. Most of the time, I import logger, then call:

```
logger.logto(sys.stderr, logger.syslogfile, open("/tmp/mylog.txt","w"))
```

(Maybe I should be more punctilious and use the tempfile module to get the temporary file's directory instead.) But the logger module also gives me all the tools for fine-tuning when I want them. Now, whenever I print something, it goes to the terminal (standard error) if one exists; to the syslog, if one exists (possibly OutputDebugString); and to a text file in the temporary directory, just in case.

When I want to call another function automatically to display something I print, I wrap it in a logger.FunctionFilelikeWrapper. And, of course, it's easy to tweak and customize this recipe, since it is so utterly simple, adding whatever other bricks I frequently use.

The recipe shows how to use quite a few important Pythonic idioms:

- Using try/except around an import for conditional import purposes
- Using a do-nothing function that is callable without harm, rather than using None, which you have to test for before each call
- A Timestamper class that offers usable default class attributes (for such things as format strings) but accesses them via self, so they're tweakable per instance, if needed
- File-like objects that wrap other objects, such as a function or a collection of other file-like objects.

Some of the idioms used in this recipe are generalized or explained further in other recipes in this book. For example, the do-nothing function is vastly generalized and extended in the Null Object design pattern (see Recipe 5.23). But seeing the various Pythonic pieces work together like this, albeit in a more restricted setting, can help understand them better. Besides, this recipe does make logging and tracing much easier and more pleasant.

This discussion concludes with a few principles of operation. Starting from the end, the logto function accepts any number of arguments, passes them to the constructor of a new instance of the TeeFilelikeWrapper class, and assigns that instance as the new value of the sys.stdout system variable, which is the standard output of any Python program. The print statement emits what you are printing to whatever object is referenced by sys.stdout, and all it asks of that object is that it expose a callable attribute (method) named write, which takes a string argument. (It also requires that an attribute named softspace be settable and gettable for print's own internal purposes, but that's no problem as long as you use normal instance objects, since arbitrary attributes can be set and retrieved from such instances).

The TeeFilelikeWrapper class has an instance constructor that accepts an arbitrary sequence of files (arbitrary objects with a write method, as above) and saves the sequence as the self.files instance member. The write method loops on self.files, making identical write calls on each. We could use an amusing variation on this theme by extracting the write methods at initialization and calling them in write. This has two advantages: earlier failure if we pass an object to __init__ without a write method by mistake, and better performance by avoiding the method extraction on each write call. Neither is a huge advantage, and a beginner might find the approach confusing, so I've stuck with the obvious approach in the recipe, but for completeness, here is the alternative:

```
class TeeFilelikeWrapper:
    def __init__(self, *files):
        self.write_methods = [ f.write for f in files ]
```

```
def write(self, msg):
    for w in self.write_methods: w(msg)
```

The FlushingWrapper class is just like TeeFilelikeWrapper, but after write, it also calls flush on each of the file objects it's wrapping to ensure that output has actually occurred.

The FunctionFilelikeWrapper class wraps a function (actually any callable object), which it receives in the instance constructor, as a file-like object, translating each call to write into a call to the function it wraps. The code in the recipe just before the definition of this class tries to determine the best function to use as syslogger. The try/except statements around import statements ensure that we use syslog.syslog on a Unix-like platform that supplies it, servicemanager.LogInfoMsg if the current program is a Python-coded Win32 service, OutputDebugString for other Win32 programs, or nothing at all (a do-nothing function, to be precise) if none of these conditions is satisfied.

With OutputDebugString, a timestamp object is also used, specifically to ensure that a timestamp accompanies each message being logged (not needed if we're using a real logging system, be it syslog or one of Win32's, since the timestamping will be done by the system). For this purpose, we also have a Timestamper class that we instantiate. Alternatively, a simple timestamp function might be defined and used, but a class has the added value of being tweakable. If elsewhere we need other timestamping but with a different format, or a different way to obtain the time, we can still use Timestamper by setting an instance's value for msg_format appropriately.

See Also

Recipe 5.23 for a much more generalized version of the do-nothing function; documentation for the syslog module in the *Library Reference*; the manpages for syslog on your system; documentation for servicemanager and win32api in win32all (*http://starship.python.net/crew/mhammond/win32/Downloads.html*) or ActivePython (*http://www.activestate.com/ActivePython/*); Windows API documentation available from Microsoft (*http://msdn.microsoft.com*).

14.7 Determining the Name of the Current Function

Credit: Alex Martelli

Problem

You have error messages that include the name of the function emitting them. To copy such messages to other functions, you have to edit them each time, unless you can automatically find the name of the current function.

Solution

This introspective task is easily performed with sys._getframe. This function returns a frame object whose attribute f_code is a code object and the co_name attribute of that object is the function name:

```
import sys
this_function_name = sys._getframe().f_code.co_name
```

The frame and code objects also offer other useful information:

```
this_line_number = sys._getframe().f_lineno
this_filename = sys._getframe().f_code.co_filename
```

By calling sys._getframe(1), you can get this information for the caller of the current function. So you can package this functionality into your own handy functions:

```
def whoami():
    import sys
    return sys._getframe(1).f_code.co_name

me = whoami()
```

This calls sys._getframe with argument 1, because the call to whoami is now frame 0. Similarly:

```
def callersname():
    import sys
    return sys._getframe(2).f_code.co_name

him = callersname()
```

Discussion

You want to determine the name of the currently running function—for example, to create error messages that don't need to be changed when copied to other functions. The function _getframe function of the sys module does this and much more. This recipe is inspired by Recipe 10.4 in the *Perl Cookbook*. Python's sys._getframe, new in 2.1, offers information equivalent to (but richer than) Perl's built-in caller, __LINE__, and __FILE__. If you need this functionality for older Python releases, see Recipe 14.8.

See Also

Recipe 14.8 for a version that works with older Python versions; documentation on the _getframe method of the sys module in the *Library Reference*; *Perl Cookbook* Recipe 10.4.

14.8 Introspecting the Call Stack with Older Versions of Python

Credit: Richard Philips, Christian Tismer

Problem

You need to introspect information about a function on the call stack, but you also need to maintain compatibility with older Python versions.

Solution

For debugging purposes, you often want to know where a function was called from or other call-stack information. The _getframe function helps. Just ensure that the following code is executed during your program's startup:

```
import sys
try: sys._getframe
except AttributeError:    # We must be using some old version of Python, so:
    def _getframe(level=0):
        try: 1/0
        except: tb = sys.exc_info( )[-1]
        frame = tb.tb_frame
        while level >= 0:
            frame = frame.f_back
            level = level - 1
        return frame
    sys._getframe = _getframe
    del _getframe
```

Now you can use sys._getframe regardless of which version of Python you are using.

Discussion

The sys._getframe function, which is invaluable for introspection anywhere in the call stack, was introduced in Python 2.1. If you need to introspect the call stack but maintain compatibility with older Python versions, this recipe shows how to simulate sys._getframe and inject the function's implementation in the sys module, so that you can use it freely regardless of which version of Python you use.

See Also

Recipe 14.7; documentation on the _getframe method of the sys module in the *Library Reference*.

14.9   Debugging the Garbage-Collection Process

Credit: Dirk Holtwick

Problem

You know that memory is leaking from your program, but you have no indication of what exactly is being leaked. You need more information to help you figure out where the leaks are coming from, so you can remove them and lighten the garbage-collection work periodically performed by the standard gc module.

Solution

The gc module lets you dig into garbage-collection issues:

```
import gc

def dump_garbage():
    """
    show us what the garbage is about
    """
    # Force collection
    print "\nGARBAGE:"
    gc.collect()

    print "\nGARBAGE OBJECTS:"
    for x in gc.garbage:
        s = str(x)
        if len(s) > 80: s = s[:77]+'...'
        print type(x),"\n  ", s

if __name__=="__main__":
    gc.enable()
    gc.set_debug(gc.DEBUG_LEAK)

    # Make a leak
    l = []
    l.append(l)
    del l

    # show the dirt ;-)
    dump_garbage()
```

Discussion

In addition to the normal debugging output of gc, this recipe shows the garbage objects to help you get an idea of where the leak may be. Situations that could lead to garbage collection should be avoided. Most of the time, they're caused by objects that refer to themselves, or similar reference loops (also known as cycles).

Once you've found where the reference loops are coming from, Python offers all the needed tools to remove them, particularly weak references (in the weakref standard library module). But especially in big programs, you first have to get an idea of where to find the leak before you can remove it and enhance your program's performance. For this, it's good to know what the objects being leaked contain, so the dump_garbage function in this recipe can come in quite handy on such occasions.

This recipe works by first calling gc.set_debug to tell the gc module to keep the leaked objects in its gc.garbage list rather than recycling them. Then, this recipe's dump_garbage function calls gc.collect to force a garbage-collection process to run, even if there is still ample free memory, so it can examine each item in gc.garbage and print out its type and contents (limiting the printout to no more than 80 characters to avoid flooding the screen with huge chunks of information).

See Also

Documentation for the gc module in the *Library Reference*.

14.10 Tracking Instances of Particular Classes

Credit: David Ascher, Mark Hammond

Problem

You're trying to track down memory usage of specific classes in a large system, and Recipe 14.9 either gives too much data to be useful or fails to recognize cycles.

Solution

You can design the constructors of suspect classes to keep a list of weak references to the instances in a global cache:

```
tracked_classes = {}
import weakref
def logInstanceCreation(instance):
    name = instance.__class__.__name__
    if not tracked_classes.has_key(name):
        tracked_classes[name] = []
    tracked_classes[name].append(weakref.ref(instance))

def reportLoggedInstances(classes): # "*" means all known instances
    if classes == '*':
        classes = tracked_classes.keys()
    else:
        classes = classes.split()
    classes.sort()
    for classname in classes:
        for ref in tracked_classes[classname]:
            ob = ref()
```

```
        if ob is not None:
            print ref( )
```

To use this code, add a call to `logInstanceCreation(self)` to the `__init__` calls of the classes whose instances you want to track. When you want to find out which instances are currently alive, call `reportLoggedInstances( )` with the name of the classes in question (e.g., `MyClass.__name__`).

Discussion

Tracking memory problems is a key skill for developers of large systems. The above code was dreamed up to deal with memory allocations in a system that involved three different garbage collectors; Python was only one of them. Due to the references between Python objects and non-Python objects, none of the individual garbage collectors could be expected to detect cycles between objects managed in different memory-management systems. Furthermore, being able to ask a class which of its instances are alive can be useful even in the absence of cycles (e.g., when making sure that the right numbers of instances are created following a particular user action in a GUI program).

The recipe hinges on a global dictionary called `tracking_classes`, which uses class names as keys, and a list of weak references to instances of that class in correspondence with each key. The `logInstanceCreation` function updates the dictionary (adding a new empty list if the name of specific class whose instance is being tracked is not a key in the dictionary, then appending the new weak reference in any case). The `reportLoggedInstances` function accepts a string argument that is either `'*'`, meaning all classes, or all the names of the pertinent classes separated by whitespace. The function checks the dictionary entry for each of these class names, examining the list and printing out those instances of the class that still exist. It checks whether an instance still exists by calling the weak reference that was put in the list to it. When called, a weak reference returns `None` if the object it referred to does not exist; otherwise, it returns a normal (strong) reference to the object in question.

Something you may want to do when using this kind of code is make sure that the possibly expensive debugging calls are wrapped in a `if __debug__:` test, as in:

```
    class TrackedClass:
        def __init__(self):
            if __debug__: logInstanceCreation(self)
            ...
```

The pattern `if __debug__:` is detected by the Python parser in Python 2.0 and later. The body of any such marked block is ignored in the byte code–generation phase if the -O command-line switch is specified. Consequently, you may write inefficient debug-time code, while not impacting the production code. In this case, this even avoids some unimportant byte-code generation. These byte-code savings can't amount to much, but the feature is worth noting.

Also note that the ignominiously named setdefault dictionary method can be used to compact the logInstanceCreation function into a logical one-liner:

```
def logInstanceCreation(instance):
    tracked_classes.setdefault(instance.__class__.__name__, []
                              ).append(weakref.ref(instance))
```

But such space savings are hardly worth the obfuscation cost, at least in the eyes of these authors.

See Also

Documentation on the weakref standard library module in the *Library Reference*.

## CHAPTER 15

Programs About Programs

15.0 Introduction

Credit: Paul F. Dubois, Ph.D., Program for Climate Model Diagnosis
and Intercomparison, Lawrence Livermore National Laboratory

This chapter covers topics such as lexing, parsing, and program introspection. Python has extensive facilities related to lexing and parsing, and the large number of user-contributed modules related to parsing standard languages reduces the need for doing your own programming. This introduction contains a general guide to solving some common problems in these categories.

Lexing and parsing are among the most common of programming tasks, and as a result, both are the subject of much theory and much prior development. Therefore, in these areas more than most, you will often profit if you take the time to search for solutions before resorting to writing your own. The recipes in this chapter concern accomplishing certain tasks in Python. The most important of these is currying, in which functions are created that are really other functions with predetermined arguments.

Lexing

Lexing is the process of dividing an input stream into meaningful units, or tokens, which are then processed. Lexing occurs in tasks such as data processing and creating tools for inspecting and modifying text.

The regular-expression facilities in Python are extensive and highly evolved, so your first consideration for a lexing task is to see if it can be formulated using regular expressions. Also, see the next section about parsers for common languages and how to lex them.

The tokenize module splits an input stream into Python-language tokens. Since Python's tokenization rules are similar to those of many other languages, this module may be suitable for other tasks.

The built-in string method `split` can also be used for many simple cases. For example, consider a file consisting of colon-separated text fields, with one record per line. You can read a line from the file as follows:

```
fields = line.split(':')
```

This produces a list of the fields. If at this point you fear spurious whitespace at the beginning and ends of the fields, you can remove it with:

```
fields = map(lambda x: x.strip(), fields)
```

For example:

```
>>> x = "abc :def:ghi    : klm\n"
>>> fields = x.split(':')
>>> print fields
['abc ', 'def', 'ghi    ', ' klm\n']
>>> print map(lambda x: x.strip(), fields)
['abc', 'def', 'ghi', 'klm']
```

Do not elaborate on this example. There are existing packages that have been written for tab, comma, or colon-separated values. There is a module in the ScientificPython package for reading and writing with Fortran-like formats. (See *http://starship.python.net/crew/hinsen/scientific.html*. For other links related to numeric data processing, see *http://www.pfdubois.com/numpy/*.)

A common "gotcha" for beginners is that, while this technique can be used to read numerical data from a file, at the end of this stage, the entries are text strings, not numbers. The `string` module methods `atoi` and `atof`, or the `int` and `float` built-in functions, are frequently needed here:

```
>>> x = "1.2, 2.3, 4, 5.6"
>>> import string
>>> print map(lambda f: string.atof(f.strip()), x.split(','))
[1.2, 2.2999999999999998, 4.0, 5.5999999999999996]
```

Parsing

Parsing refers to discovering semantic meaning out of a series of tokens according to the rules of a grammar. Parsing tasks are quite ubiquitous. Programming tools may attempt to discover information about program texts or modify them to fit a task. (Python's introspection capabilities come into play here, which we will discuss later.) "Little languages" is a name given to application-specific languages that serve as human-readable forms of computer input. These can vary from simple lists of commands and arguments to full-blown languages.

In the previous lexing example, there was a grammar, but it was implicit: the data you need is organized as one line per record with the fields separated by a special character. The "parser" in that case was supplied by the programmer reading the lines from the file and applying the simple `split` function to obtain the information. This sort of input file can easily lead to requests for a more elaborate form. For example, users may wish to use comments, blank lines, conditional statements, or alternate forms. While most of this can be handled with simple logic, at some point, it becomes so complicated that it is much more reliable to use a real grammar.

There is no hard and fast way to decide which part of the job is a lexing task and which belongs to the grammar. For example, comments can often be discarded in the lexing, but this is not wise in a program-transformation tool that needs to produce output that must contain the original comments.

Your strategy for parsing tasks can include:

- Using a parser for that language from the standard library.
- Using a parser from the user community. You can find one by visiting the Vaults of Parnassus or by searching *http://www.python.org*.
- Generating a parser using a parser generator.
- Using Python itself as your input language.

A combination of approaches is often fruitful. For example, a simple parser can turn input into Python-language statements, which Python executes in concert with a supporting package that you supply.

A number of parsers for specific languages exist in the standard library and in the user community. In particular, there are parsing packages for XML, HTML, SGML, command-line arguments, configuration files, and for Python itself.

You do not need to parse C to connect C routines to Python. Use SWIG (*http://www.swig.org*). Likewise, you do not need a Fortran parser to connect Fortran and Python. See the Numerical Python web page at *http://www.pfdubois.com/numpy/* for further information.

PLY and SPARK

PLY and SPARK are Python-based parser generators. That is, they take as input statements that describe the grammar to be parsed and generate the parser for you. To make a useful tool, you must then add the semantic actions to be taken when a certain statement is recognized.

PLY (*http://systems.cs.uchicago.edu/ply*) is a Python implementation of the popular Unix tool *yacc*. SPARK (*http://www.cpsc.ucalgary.ca/~aycock/spark*) is a cleverly introspective method that parses a more general set of grammars than *yacc*.

The chief problem in using both these tools is that you need to educate yourself about grammars and learn to write them. Except for very simple grammars, a novice will encounter some difficulty. There is a lot of literature out there to teach you how to use *yacc*, and most of this knowledge will help you use SPARK as well.

If you are interested in this area, the ultimate reference is Aho, Sethi, and Ullman's *Compilers* (Addison-Wesley), affectionately known as "The Dragon Book" to generations of computer-science majors.

Using Python Itself as a Little Language

Python itself can be used to create many application-specific languages. By writing suitable classes, you can rapidly make something that is easy to get running yet is extensible later. Suppose I want a language to describe graphs. There are nodes that have names and edges that connect the nodes. I want a way to input such graphs so that after reading the input, I will have the data structures in Python that I need. So, for example:

```
nodes = {}

def getnode(name):
    "Return the node with the given name, creating it if necessary."
    if not nodes.has_key(name):
        nodes[name] = node(name)
    return nodes[name]

class node:
    "A node has a name and a list of edges emanating from it."
    def __init__(self, name):
        self.name = name
        self.edgelist = []

class edge:
    "An edge connects two nodes."
    def __init__(self, name1, name2):
        self.nodes = (getnode(name1), getnode(name2))
        for n in self.nodes:
            n.edgelist.append(self)

    def __repr__(self):
        return self.nodes[0].name + self.nodes[1].name
```

Using just these simple statements, I can now parse a list of edges that describe a graph, and afterwards have data structures that contain all my information. Here, I enter a graph with four edges and print the list of edges emanating from node 'A':

```
>>> edge('A', 'B')
>>> edge('B', 'C')
>>> edge('C', 'D')
>>> edge('C', 'A')
>>> print getnode('A').edgelist
[AB, CA]
```

Suppose that I now want a weighted graph. I could easily add a weight=1.0 argument to the edge constructor, and the old input would still work. Also, I could easily add error-checking logic to ensure that edge lists have no duplicates. Furthermore, I already have my node class and can start adding logic to it. I can easily turn the entries in the dictionary nodes into similarly named variables that are bound to the node objects. After adding a few more classes corresponding to other input I need, I am well on my way.

The advantage to this approach is clear. For example, the following is already handled correctly:

```
edge('A', 'B')

if not nodes.has_key('X'):
    edge('X', 'A')

def triangle(n1, n2, n3):
    edge(n1, n2)
    edge(n2, n3)
    edge(n3, n1)
triangle('A','W','K')

execfile('mygraph.txt')      # Read graph from a datafile
```

So I already have syntactic sugar, user-defined language extensions, and input from other files. Usually, the definitions will go into a module, and the user will simply import them. Had I written my own language, such accomplishments might be months away.

Introspection

Python programs have the ability to examine themselves; this set of facilities comes under the general title of introspection. For example, a Python function object knows the names of its arguments and the docstring comment that was given when it was defined:

```
>>> def f(a, b):
        "Return the difference of a and b"
        return a-b

>>> dir(f)
['__dict__', '__doc__', '__name__', 'func_closure', 'func_code',
'func_defaults', 'func_dict', 'func_doc', 'func_globals', 'func_name']
>>> f.func_name
'f'
>>> f.func_doc
'Return the difference of a and b'
>>> f.func_code
<code object f at 0175DDF0, file "<pyshell#18>", line 1>
>>> dir (f.func_code)
['co_argcount', 'co_cellvars', 'co_code', 'co_consts', 'co_filename',
'co_firstlineno', 'co_flags', 'co_freevars', 'co_lnotab', 'co_name',
'co_names', 'co_nlocals', 'co_stacksize', 'co_varnames']
>>> f.func_code.co_names
('a', 'b')
```

SPARK makes an interesting use of introspection. The grammar is entered as doc strings in the routines that take the semantic actions when those grammar constructs are recognized. (Hey, don't turn your head all the way around like that! Introspection has its limits.)

Python is the most powerful language that you can still read. The kinds of tasks discussed in this chapter show just how versatile and powerful it really is.

15.1 Colorizing Python Source Using the Built-in Tokenizer

Credit: Jürgen Hermann

Problem

You need to convert Python source code into HTML markup, rendering comments, keywords, operators, and numeric and string literals in different colors.

Solution

`tokenize.tokenize` does most of the work and calls us back for each token found, so we can output it with appropriate colorization:

```python
""" MoinMoin - Python Source Parser """
import cgi, string, sys, cStringIO
import keyword, token, tokenize

# Python Source Parser (does highlighting into HTML)

_KEYWORD = token.NT_OFFSET + 1
_TEXT    = token.NT_OFFSET + 2
_colors = {
    token.NUMBER:       '#0080C0',
    token.OP:           '#0000C0',
    token.STRING:       '#004080',
    tokenize.COMMENT:   '#008000',
    token.NAME:         '#000000',
    token.ERRORTOKEN:   '#FF8080',
    _KEYWORD:           '#C00000',
    _TEXT:              '#000000',
}

class Parser:
    """ Send colorized Python source as HTML to an output file (normally stdout).
    """

    def __init__(self, raw, out = sys.stdout):
        """ Store the source text. """
        self.raw = string.strip(string.expandtabs(raw))
        self.out = out
```

```python
    def format(self):
        """ Parse and send the colorized source to output. """
        # Store line offsets in self.lines
        self.lines = [0, 0]
        pos = 0
        while 1:
            pos = string.find(self.raw, '\n', pos) + 1
            if not pos: break
            self.lines.append(pos)
        self.lines.append(len(self.raw))

        # Parse the source and write it
        self.pos = 0
        text = cStringIO.StringIO(self.raw)
        self.out.write('<pre><font face="Lucida,Courier New">')
        try:
            tokenize.tokenize(text.readline, self) # self as handler callable
        except tokenize.TokenError, ex:
            msg = ex[0]
            line = ex[1][0]
            self.out.write("<h3>ERROR: %s</h3>%s\n" % (
                    msg, self.raw[self.lines[line]:]))
        self.out.write('</font></pre>')

    def __call__(self, toktype, toktext, (srow,scol), (erow,ecol), line):
        """ Token handler """
        if 0:  # You may enable this for debugging purposes only
            print "type", toktype, token.tok_name[toktype], "text", toktext,
            print "start", srow,scol, "end", erow,ecol, "<br>"

        # Calculate new positions
        oldpos = self.pos
        newpos = self.lines[srow] + scol
        self.pos = newpos + len(toktext)

        # Handle newlines
        if toktype in [token.NEWLINE, tokenize.NL]:
            self.out.write('\n')
            return

        # Send the original whitespace, if needed
        if newpos > oldpos:
            self.out.write(self.raw[oldpos:newpos])

        # Skip indenting tokens
        if toktype in [token.INDENT, token.DEDENT]:
            self.pos = newpos
            return

        # Map token type to a color group
        if token.LPAR <= toktype <= token.OP:
            toktype = token.OP
        elif toktype == token.NAME and keyword.iskeyword(toktext):
```

```
            toktype = _KEYWORD
        color = _colors.get(toktype, _colors[_TEXT])

        style = ''
        if toktype == token.ERRORTOKEN:
            style = ' style="border: solid 1.5pt #FF0000;"'

        # Send text
        self.out.write('<font color="%s"%s>' % (color, style))
        self.out.write(cgi.escape(toktext))
        self.out.write('</font>')

if __name__ == "__main__":
    import os, sys
    print "Formatting..."

    # Open own source
    source = open('python.py').read()

    # Write colorized version to "python.html"
    Parser(source, open('python.html', 'wt')).format()

    # Load HTML page into browser
    if os.name == "nt":
        os.system("explorer python.html")
    else:
        os.system("netscape python.html &")
```

Discussion

This code is part of MoinMoin (see *http://moin.sourceforge.net/*) and shows how to use the built-in keyword, token, and tokenize modules to scan Python source code and re-emit it with appropriate color markup but no changes to its original formatting ("no changes" is the hard part!).

The Parser class's constructor saves the multiline string that is the Python source to colorize and the file object, which is open for writing, where you want to output the colorized results. Then, the format method prepares a self.lines list that holds the offset (the index into the source string, self.raw) of each line's start.

format then calls tokenize.tokenize, passing self as the callback. Thus, the __call__ method is invoked for each token, with arguments specifying the token type and starting and ending positions in the source (each expressed as line number and offset within the line). The body of the __call__ method reconstructs the exact position within the original source code string self.raw, so it can emit exactly the same whitespace that was present in the original source. It then picks a color code from the _colors dictionary (which uses HTML color coding), with help from the keyword standard module to determine if a NAME token is actually a Python keyword (to be emitted in a different color than that used for ordinary identifiers).

The test code at the bottom of the module formats the module itself and launches a browser with the result. It does not use the standard Python module webbrowser to ensure compatibility with stone-age versions of Python. If you have no such worries, you can change the last few lines of the recipe to:

```
# Load HTML page into browser
import webbrowser
webbrowser.open("python.html", 0, 1)
```

and enjoy the result in your favorite browser.

See Also

Documentation for the webbrowser, token, tokenize, and keyword modules in the *Library Reference*; the colorizer is available at *http://purl.net/wiki/python/ MoinMoinColorizer*, part of MoinMoin (*http://moin.sourceforge.net*).

15.2 Importing a Dynamically Generated Module

Credit: Anders Hammarquist

Problem

You have code in either compiled or source form and need to wrap it in a module, possibly adding it to sys.modules as well.

Solution

We build a new module object, optionally add it to sys.modules, and populate it with an exec statement:

```
def importCode(code, name, add_to_sys_modules=0):
    """ code can be any object containing code -- string, file object, or
        compiled code object. Returns a new module object initialized
        by dynamically importing the given code and optionally adds it
        to sys.modules under the given name.
    """
    import imp
    module = imp.new_module(name)

    if add_to_sys_modules:
        import sys
        sys.modules[name] = module
    exec code in module.__dict__

    return module
```

Discussion

This recipe lets you import a module from code that is dynamically generated or obtained. My original intent for it was to import a module stored in a database, but it will work for modules from any source. Thanks to the flexibility of the exec statement, the `importCode` function can accept code in many forms: a string of source (implicitly compiled), a file object (ditto), or a previously compiled code object, for example.

The addition of the newly generated module to `sys.modules` is optional. You shouldn't normally do this for such dynamically obtained code, but there are exceptions—for example, when `import` statements for the module's name are later executed, and it's important that they're retrieved from `sys.modules`. Note that if you want the `sys.modules` addition, it's best to perform it before the module's code body executes, just as normal import statements do, in case the code body relies on that normal behavior (which it normally doesn't, but it can't hurt to prepare for this).

Note that the normal Python statement:

```
import foo
```

is basically equivalent to:

```
if 'foo' in sys.modules:
    foo = sys.modules['foo']
else:
    foofile = open("/path/to/foo.py")
    foo = importCode(foofile, "foo", 1)
```

An example of using this recipe:

```
code = """
def testFunc( ):
    print "spam!"

class testClass:
    def testMethod(self):
        print "eggs!"
"""

m = importCode(code,"test")
m.testFunc( )
o = m.testClass( )
o.testMethod( )
```

See Also

Sections on the `import` and `exec` statements in the *Language Reference*; documentation on the `modules` attribute of the `sys` standard library module and the `imp` module in the *Library Reference*.

15.3 Importing from a Module Whose Name Is Determined at Runtime

Credit: Jürgen Hermann

Problem

You need to import a name from a module, such as `from module import name`, but *module* and *name* are runtime-computed expressions. This need often arises, for example when you want to support user-written plug-ins.

Solution

The `__import__` built-in function allows this:

```
def importName(modulename, name):
    """ Import a named object from a module in the context of this function.
    """
    try:
        module = __import__(modulename, globals(), locals(), [name])
    except ImportError:
        return None
    return vars(module)[name]
```

Discussion

This recipe's function lets you perform the equivalent of `from module import name`, in which either or both *module* and *name* are dynamic values (i.e., expressions or variables) rather than constant strings. For example, this can be used to implement a plug-in mechanism to extend an application with external modules that adhere to a common interface. Some programmers' instinctive reaction to this task would be to use exec, but this instinct would be a pretty bad one. The exec statement is a last-ditch measure, to be used only when nothing else is available (which is basically never). It's just too easy to have horrid bugs and/or security weaknesses where exec is used. In almost all cases, there are better ways. This recipe shows one such way for an important problem.

For example, suppose you have in the *MyApp/extensions/spam.py* file:

```
class Handler:
    def handleSomething(self):
        print "spam!"
```

and in the *MyApp/extensions/eggs.py* file:

```
class Handler:
    def handleSomething(self):
        print "eggs!"
```

then as long as the *MyApp* directory is on sys.path, and both it and the *extensions* directory are identified as packages by containing a file named *__init__.py*, we can get and call both implementations with this code:

```
for extname in 'spam', 'eggs':
    HandlerClass = importName("MyApp.extensions." + extname, "Handler")
    handler = HandlerClass( )
    handler.handleSomething( )
```

It's possible to remove the constraints about sys.path and *__init__.py*, and dynamically import from anywhere, with the imp standard module. However, this is substantially harder to use than the __import__ built-in function, and you can generally arrange things to avoid imp's generality and difficulty.

This pattern is used in MoinMoin (*http://moin.sourceforge.net/*) to load extensions implementing variations of a common interface, such as "action", "macro", and "formatter".

See Also

Documentation on the __import__ and vars built-ins in the *Library Reference*; Moin-Moin is available at *http://moin.sourceforge.net*.

15.4   Importing Modules with Automatic End-of-Line Conversions

Credit: David Goodger

Problem

You need to move (or share, via a network-shared filesystem) *.py* modules between different platforms without worrying about the different ways the platforms represent end-of-line.

Solution

Python's import hooks are mostly used for advanced, complicated tasks, but can sometimes come in handy for a simple system-administration task, such as dealing with this recipe's problem. Put this code in your *sitecustomize.py*, which can be located anywhere on sys.path, and you'll be able to import Python modules with any Unix, Mac, or Windows line endings:

```
import ihooks, imp, py_compile

class MyHooks(ihooks.Hooks):
    def load_source(self, name, filename, file=None):
```

```
        """ Compile source files with any line ending. """
        if file:
            file.close()
        py_compile.compile(filename)      # Line-ending conversion is in here
        cfile = open(filename + (__debug__ and 'c' or 'o'), 'rb')
        try:
            return self.load_compiled(name, filename, cfile)
        finally:
            cfile.close()

class MyModuleLoader(ihooks.ModuleLoader):
    def load_module(self, name, stuff):
        """ Special-case package directory imports """
        file, filename, (suff, mode, type) = stuff
        path = None
        if type == imp.PKG_DIRECTORY:
            stuff = self.find_module_in_dir("__init__", filename, 0)
            file = stuff[0]              # package/__init__.py
            path = [filename]
        try:                            # Let superclass handle the rest
            module = ihooks.ModuleLoader.load_module(self, name, stuff)
        finally:
            if file:
                file.close()
        if path:
            module.__path__ = path      # necessary for pkg.module imports
        return module

    ihooks.ModuleImporter(MyModuleLoader(MyHooks())).install()
```

Discussion

This recipe's code eliminates the need to convert line endings when moving Python source modules between operating systems (or sharing sources via a network-shared filesystem, which is even harder for those who need to do conversions). Put this recipe's code in your *sitecustomize.py* file, which can be placed anywhere on Python's initial sys.path, and you'll be able to import Python modules with any Unix, Mac, or Windows line endings, on any operating system.

I develop code on a Mac and test it on Windows and Unix-like operating systems. Converting line endings used to be a pain. Delving deep into the innards of the import mechanism and *ihooks.py*, I was finally able to get this import hook working. No more line-ending conversion needed!

This hard work is performed in Python's standard library module py_compile in the compile function. It normalizes all line endings in the source before arranging for the rest of the compilation process. This recipe exploits the import hooks scheme to ensure that all the importing of sources goes through this function, and thus provides the benefits of normalized handling of line endings, rather than relying on

Python's automatic compilation, which requires line endings that are compatible with the platform in use.

See Also

Documentation on the `ihooks`, `imp`, and `py_compile` standard library modules in the *Library Reference*.

15.5 Simulating Enumerations in Python

Credit: Will Ware

Problem

You want to define an enumeration in the spirit of C's enum type.

Solution

Python's introspection facilities let you add a version of enum, even though Python, as a language, does not support this construct:

```
import types, string, pprint, exceptions

class EnumException(exceptions.Exception):
    pass

class Enumeration:
    def __init__(self, name, enumList, valuesAreUnique=1):
        self.__doc__ = name
        lookup = { }
        reverseLookup = { }
        i = 0
        uniqueNames = {}
        uniqueValues = {}
        for x in enumList:
            if type(x) == types.TupleType:
                x, i = x
            if type(x) != types.StringType:
                raise EnumException, "enum name is not a string: " + x
            if type(i) != types.IntType:
                raise EnumException, "enum value is not an integer: " + i
            if uniqueNames.has_key(x):
                raise EnumException, "enum name is not unique: " + x
            if valuesAreUnique and uniqueValues.has_key(i):
                raise EnumException, "enum value is not unique for " + x
            uniqueNames[x] = 1
            uniqueValues[i] = 1
            lookup[x] = i
            reverseLookup[i] = x
```

```
            i = i + 1
        self.lookup = lookup
        self.reverseLookup = reverseLookup
    def __getattr__(self, attr):
        try: return self.lookup[attr]
        except KeyError: raise AttributeError
    def whatis(self, value):
        return self.reverseLookup[value]
```

Discussion

In C, enum lets you declare several constants, typically with unique values (although you can also explicitly arrange for a value to be duplicated under two different names), without necessarily specifying the actual values (except when you want it to).

Python has an accepted idiom that's fine for small numbers of constants:

```
A, B, C, D = range(4)
```

But this idiom doesn't scale well to large numbers and doesn't allow you to specify values for some constants while leaving others to be determined automatically. This recipe provides for all these niceties, while optionally verifying that all values (specified and unspecified) are unique. Enum values are attributes of an Enumeration class (Volkswagen.BEETLE, Volkswagen.PASSAT, etc.). A further feature, missing in C but really quite useful, is the ability to go from the value to the corresponding name inside the enumeration (of course, the name you get is somewhat arbitrary for those enumerations in which you don't constrain values to be unique).

This recipe's Enumeration class has an instance constructor that accepts a string argument to specify the enumeration's name and a list argument to specify the names of all values for the enumeration. Each item of the list argument can be a string (to specify that the value named is one more than the last value used), or else a tuple with two items (the string that is the value's name and the value itself, which must be an integer). The code in this recipe relies heavily on strict type-checking to find out which case applies, but the recipe's essence would not change by much if the checking was performed in a more lenient way (e.g., with the isinstance built-in function).

Therefore, each instance is equipped with two dictionaries: self.lookup to map names to values and self.reverselookup to map values back to the corresponding names. The special method __getattr__ lets names be used with attribute syntax (e.x is mapped to e.lookup['x']), and the whatis method allows reverse lookups (i.e., finds a name, given a value) with comparable syntactic ease.

Here's an example of how you can use this Enumeration class:

```
if __name__ == '__main__':

    Volkswagen = Enumeration("Volkswagen",
        ["JETTA", "RABBIT", "BEETLE", ("THING", 400), "PASSAT", "GOLF",
```

```
        ("CABRIO", 700), "EURO_VAN", "CLASSIC_BEETLE", "CLASSIC_VAN"
        ])

    Insect = Enumeration("Insect",
        ["ANT", "APHID", "BEE", "BEETLE", "BUTTERFLY", "MOTH", "HOUSEFLY",
         "WASP", "CICADA", "GRASSHOPPER", "COCKROACH", "DRAGONFLY"
         ])

    def demo(lines):
        previousLineEmpty = 0
        for x in string.split(lines, "\n"):
            if x:
                if x[0] != '#':
                    print ">>>", x; exec x; print
                    previousLineEmpty = 1
                else:
                    print x
                    previousLineEmpty = 0
            elif not previousLineEmpty:
                print x
                previousLineEmpty = 1

    def whatkind(value, enum):
        return enum.__doc__ + "." + enum.whatis(value)

    class ThingWithType:
        def __init__(self, type):
            self.type = type

    demo("""
car = ThingWithType(Volkswagen.BEETLE)
print whatkind(car.type, Volkswagen)
bug = ThingWithType(Insect.BEETLE)
print whatkind(bug.type, Insect)
print car.__dict__
print bug.__dict__
pprint.pprint(Volkswagen.__dict__)
pprint.pprint(Insect.__dict__)
""")
```

Note that attributes of car and bug don't include any of the enum machinery, because that machinery is held as class attributes, not as instance attributes. This means you can generate thousands of car and bug objects with reckless abandon, never worrying about wasting time or memory on redundant copies of the enum stuff.

See Also

Recipe 5.15, which shows how to define constants in Python; documentation on __getattr__ in the *Language Reference*.

15.6 Modifying Methods in Place

Credit: Ken Seehof

Problem

You need to globally change the behavior of existing classes in a third-party library—for example, by wrapping existing __init__ methods.

Solution

Avoid the antipattern of modifying library code, even though you have source for it, or you'll be forever chasing upgrades to the library and reapplying your changes to each release. Python's introspection lets you noninvasively obtain the same desired effect without changing the library's source code:

```python
# needs Python 2.1 or later
from __future__ import nested_scopes
import new

def enhance__init__(klass, f):
    try: ki = klass.__init__
    except AttributeError:
        def ki(self, *args, **kwds): pass
    klass.__init__ = new.instancemethod(
        lambda *args, **kwds: f(ki, *args, **kwds), None, klass)

def demo():
    class X:
        def __init__(self, v):
            self.v = v

    def g(__init__, self, v):
        __init__(self, v)
        self.parrot='dead'

    enhance__init__(X, g)

    x = X(2)
    print x.parrot

demo()
```

Discussion

Once in a while it becomes necessary to globally change the behavior of classes in a third-party library, ideally without modifying the source code for that library. This recipe demonstrates the ability to modify the __init__ method of an arbitrary class in place at runtime by wrapping the method in any given metafunction. In my experience, this approach is also good for making functional programmers wince, which can be entertaining.

Of course, many other forms of currying besides the lambda used in this recipe could be used to build the underlying function for the enhanced method.

See Also

Recipe 15.7 for currying in general; Recipes 5.13 and 15.9 for other examples of modifying the methods of an instance; antipatterns (patterns that tell how to go from a problem to a bad solution) are discussed in detail on the Portland Pattern Wiki-Wiki (*http://c2.com/cgi/wiki?AntiPatterns*).

15.7 Associating Parameters with a Function (Currying)

Credit: Scott David Daniels, Ben Wolfson, Nick Perkins, and Alex Martelli

Problem

You need to tweak a function (or other callable) to get another callable with fewer formal arguments, keeping the original arguments' given values fixed (i.e., you need to *curry* a callable to make another).

Solution

Curry is not just a spice used in Asian cuisine; it's also an important technique in Python and other programming languages:

```
class curry:
    def __init__(self, fun, *args, **kwargs):
        self.fun = fun
        self.pending = args[:]
        self.kwargs = kwargs.copy( )

    def __call__(self, *args, **kwargs):
        if kwargs and self.kwargs:
            kw = self.kwargs.copy( )
            kw.update(kwargs)
        else:
            kw = kwargs or self.kwargs

        return self.fun(*(self.pending + args), **kw)
```

Discussion

Popular in functional programming, currying is a way to bind some of the function's arguments and wait for the rest of the arguments to show up later. Currying is named in honor of Haskell Curry, a mathematician who laid some of the corner-stones in the theory of formal systems and processes. The curry function defined in this recipe is called with a callable and some or all of the arguments to the callable. The curry function returns a function that takes subsequent parameters as arguments, and curry calls the original with all of those parameters. This recipe uses a class instance to hold the curried parameters until they're needed. For example:

```
double = curry(operator.mul, 2)
triple = curry(operator.mul, 3)
```

Currying is often implemented with lambda forms, but a dedicated class such as the one provided in this recipe is clearer and more readable. However, lambda does have the advantage that the arguments can be given in any order. If you have such needs and prefer to use explicit currying classes (or functions) rather than lambda, you may have to code other dedicated adapters for the purpose of renaming or reordering arguments.

A typical use of curry is to construct callback functions for GUI operations. When the operation does not merit a new function name, curry can be useful in creating these little functions. For example, this can be the case with commands for Tkinter buttons:

```
self.button = Button(frame, text='A', command=curry(transcript.append, 'A'))
```

Recipe 9.1 shows a specialized subset of curry functionality intended to produce callables that require no arguments, which are often needed for such GUI-callback usage. However, the recipe shown here is vastly more flexible, without substantial extra cost in complexity or performance.

Currying can also be used interactively to make versions of your functions with debugging-appropriate defaults or initial parameters filled in for your current case. For example, database debugging work might begin by setting:

```
Connect = curry(ODBC.Connect, dsn='MyDataSet')
```

Another example of the use of curry in debugging is wrapping methods:

```
def report(originalFunction, name, *args, **kw):
    print "%s(%s)"%(name, ', '.join(map(repr, args) +
        [k+'='+repr(kw[k]) for k in kw.keys()])
    result = originalFunction(*args, **kw)
    if result: print name, '==>', result
    return result

class Sink:
    def write(self, text): pass

dest = Sink()
dest.write = curry(report, dest.write, 'write')
print >>dest, 'this', 'is', 1, 'test'
```

If you are creating a function for regular use, and there is a good choice for a name, the def fun form of function definition is usually more readable and more easily extended. As you can see from the implementation, no magic happens to specialize the function with the provided parameters. curry should be used when you feel the code is clearer with its use than without. Typically, this will emphasize that you are only providing parameters to a commonly used function, not providing separate processing.

Currying also works well in creating a lightweight subclass. You can curry the constructor of a class to give the illusion of a subclass:

```
BlueWindow = curry(Window, background="blue")
```

Of course, BlueWindow.__class__ is still Window, not a subclass. But if you're changing only default parameters, not behavior, currying is arguably more appropriate than subclassing anyway. And you can still pass additional parameters to the curried constructor.

An alternative implementation of currying uses lexically nested scopes, available in Python 2.2 (or 2.1 with from __future__ import nested_scopes). The most general way to use nested scopes for currying is something like:

```
def curry(*args, **kwds):
    def callit(*moreargs, **morekwds):
        kw = kwds.copy()
        kw.update(morekwds)
        return args[0](*(args[1:]+moreargs), **kw)
    return callit
```

This curries positional arguments from the left and gives named arguments specified at call time precedence over those specified at currying time, but these policies are clearly easy to alter. This version using nested scopes rather than a class is more general, because it avoids unintentionally capturing certain argument names, which is inevitable with the class approach. For example, in the class-based solution in the recipe, imagine needing to curry callable with a keyword argument fun=23.

See Also

Recipe 9.1 shows a specialized subset of the curry functionality that is specifically for GUI callbacks.

15.8 Composing Functions

Credit: Scott David Daniels

Problem

You need to construct a new function by composing existing functions (i.e., each call of the new function must call one existing function on its arguments, then another on the result of the first one).

Solution

Composition is a fundamental operation between functions that yields a new function as a result—the new function must call one existing function on its arguments, then another on the result of the first one. For example, a function that, given a string, returns a copy that is lowercase and does not have leading and trailing blanks, is the composition of the existing `string.lower` and `string.trim` functions (in this case, it does not matter in which order the two existing functions are applied, but generally, it could be important). A class defining the special method `__call__` is often the best Pythonic approach to constructing new functions:

```python
class compose:
    '''compose functions. compose(f,g,x...)(y...) = f(g(y...),x...))'''
    def __init__(self, f, g, *args, **kwargs):
        self.f = f
        self.g = g
        self.pending = args[:]
        self.kwargs = kwargs.copy()

    def __call__(self, *args, **kwargs):
        return self.f(self.g(*args, **kwargs), *self.pending, **self.kwargs)

class mcompose(compose):
    '''compose functions. mcompose(f,g,x...)(y...) = f(*g(y...),x...))'''
    TupleType = type(())

    def __call__(self, *args, **kwargs):
        mid = self.g(*args, **kwargs)
        if isinstance(mid, self.TupleType):
            return self.f(*(mid + self.pending), **self.kwargs)
        return self.f(mid, *self.pending, **self.kwargs)
```

Discussion

The two classes in this recipe show two styles of function composition. The only difference is when the second function, g, returns a tuple. compose passes the results of g as f's first argument anyway, while mcompose treats them as a tuple of arguments to pass along. Note that the extra arguments provided for compose or mcompose are treated as extra arguments for f (as there is no standard functional behavior to follow here):

```
compose(f,g, x...)(y...) = f(g(y...), x...)
mcompose(f,g, x...)(y...) = f(*g(y...), x...)
```

As in currying (see Recipe 15.7), this recipe's functions are for constructing functions from other functions. Your goal should be clarity, since there is no efficiency gained by using the functional forms.

Here's a quick example for interactive use:

```python
parts = compose(' '.join, dir)
```

When applied to a module, the callable we just bound to `parts` gives you an easy-to-view string that lists the module's contents.

I separated `mcompose` and `compose` because I think of the two possible forms of function composition as being quite different. However, inheritance comes in handy for sharing the `__init__` method, which is identical in both cases. Class inheritance, in Python, should not be thought of as mystical. Basically, it's just a lightweight, speedy way to reuse code (code reuse is good, code duplication is bad).

In Python 2.2 (or 2.1 with `from __future__ import nested_scopes`), there is a better and more concise alternative that uses closures in lieu of class instances. For example:

```
def compose(f, g, *orig_args, **orig_kwds):
    def nested_function(*more_args, **more_kwds):
        return f(g(*more_args, **more_kwds), *orig_args, **orig_kwds)
    return nested_function
```

This `compose` function is substantially equivalent to, and roughly interchangeable with, the `compose` class presented in the solution.

See Also

Recipe 15.7 for an example of currying (i.e., associating parameters with partially evaluated functions).

15.9 Adding Functionality to a Class
Credit: Ken Seehof

Problem

You need to add functionality to an existing class without changing the source code for that class, and inheritance is not applicable (since it would make a new class, not change the old one).

Solution

Again, this is a case for introspection and dynamic change. The `enhance_method` function alters a `klass` class object to substitute a named method with an enhanced version, decorated by the `replacement` function argument. The `method_logger` method exemplifies a typical case of `replacement` by decorating any method with `print` statements tracing its calls and returns:

```
# requires Python 2.1, or 2.2 with classic classes only

from __future__ import nested_scopes
import new
```

```
    def enhance_method(klass, method_name, replacement):
        'replace a method with an enhanced version'
        method = getattr(klass, method_name)
        def enhanced(*args, **kwds): return replacement(method, *args, **kwds)
        setattr(klass, method_name, new.instancemethod(enhanced, None, klass))

    def method_logger(old_method, self, *args, **kwds):
        'example of enhancement: log all calls to a method'
        print '*** calling: %s%s, kwds=%s' % (old_method.__name__, args, kwds)
        return_value = old_method(self, *args, **kwds) # call the original method
        print '*** %s returns: %r' % (old_method.__name__, return_value)
        return return_value

    def demo():
        class Deli:
            def order_cheese(self, cheese_type):
                print 'Sorry, we are completely out of %s' % cheese_type

        d = Deli()
        d.order_cheese('Gouda')

        enhance_method(Deli, 'order_cheese', method_logger)
        d.order_cheese('Cheddar')
```

Discussion

This recipe is useful when you need to modify the behavior of a standard or third-party Python module, but changing the module itself is undesirable. In particular, this recipe can be handy for debugging, since you can use it to log all calls to a library method that you want to watch without changing the library code or needing interactive access to the session. The method_logger function in the recipe shows this specific logging usage, and the demo function shows typical usage.

Here's another, perhaps more impressive, use for this kind of approach. Sometimes you need to globally change the behavior of an entire third-party Python library. For example, say a Python library that you downloaded has 50 different methods that all return error codes, but you want these methods to raise exceptions instead (again, you don't want to change their code). After importing the offending module, you repeatedly call this recipe's enhance_method function to hook a replacement version that checks the return value and issues an exception if an error occurred around each method, wrapping each of the 50 methods in question with the same enhancement metafunction.

The heart of the recipe is the enhance_method function, which takes the class object, method name string, and replacement decorator function as arguments. It extracts the method with the getattr built-in function and replaces the method with the reciprocal setattr built-in function. The replacement is a new instance method (actually, an unbound method, as specified by the second None argument to new.instancemethod) that wraps an enhanced function, which is built with a local def. This relies on lexically nested scopes, since the local (nested) enhanced function must be able to see the method and replacement names that are local variables of the enclosing (outer) enhance_method function. The reliance on nested scopes is the reason this recipe specifies Python 2.1 or 2.2 (to work in 2.1, it needs the from __future__ import nested_scopes statement at the start of the module).

See Also

Recipe 15.6; Recipes 5.13 and 15.10 for other approaches to modifying the methods of an instance; documentation on the new standard library module in the *Library Reference*.

15.10 Adding a Method to a Class Instance at Runtime

Credit: an anonymous contributor, Moshe Zadka

Problem

During debugging, you want to identify certain specific instance objects so that print statements display more information when applied to those objects.

Solution

The print statement implicitly calls an object's __str__ special method, so we can rebind the __str__ attribute of the object to a suitable new bound method, which the new module lets us build:

```python
import string
import new

def rich_str(self):
    classStr = ''
    for name, value in self.__class__.__dict__.items(
            ) + self.__dict__.items( ):
        classStr += string.ljust(name, 15) + '\t' + str(value) + '\n'
    return classStr

def addStr(anInstance):
    anInstance.__str__ = new.instancemethod(rich_str,
        anInstance, anInstance.__class__)

# Test it
class TestClass:
    classSig = 'My Sig'
```

```
    def __init__(self, a = 1, b = 2, c = 3):
        self.a = a
        self.b = b
        self.c = c

test = TestClass()
addStr(test)
print test
```

Discussion

This recipe demonstrates the runtime addition of a __str__ special method to a class
instance. Python calls obj.__str__ when you ask for str(obj) or when you print
obj. Changing the __str__ special method of obj lets you display more information
for the specific instance object in question when the instance is printed during
debugging.

The recipe as shown is very simple and demonstrates the use of the special attributes
__dict__ and __class__. A serious defect of this approach is that it creates a reference cycle in the object. Reference cycles are no longer killers in Python 2.0 and later,
particularly because we're focusing on debugging-oriented rather than production
code. Still, avoiding reference cycles, when feasible, makes your code faster and more
responsive, because it avoids overloading the garbage-collection task with useless
work. The following function will add any function to an instance in a cycle-free way
by creating a specially modified class object and changing the instance's class to it:

```
def add_method(object, method, name=None):
    if name is None: name = method.func_name
    class newclass(object.__class__):
        pass
    setattr(newclass, name, method)
    object.__class__ = newclass
```

We could also use the new module to generate the new class object, but there is no
particular reason to do so, as the class statement nested inside the add_method function suits our purposes just as well.

With this auxiliary function, the addStr function of the recipe can, for example, be
more effectively (and productively) coded as:

```
def addStr(anInstance):
    add_method(anInstance, rich_str, '__str__')
```

The second approach also works for new-style classes in Python 2.2. The __class__
attribute of such an instance object is assignable only within certain constraints, but
because newclass extends the object's existing class, those constraints are met (unless
some strange metaclass is in use). In Python 2.2, operations on instances of new-style
classes don't use special methods bound in the instance, but only special methods

bound in the class (in all other cases, per-instance binding still override per-class bindings).

See Also

Recipe 15.6; Recipes 5.13 and 15.9 for other approaches to modifying the methods of an instance; documentation on the new standard library module in the *Library Reference*.

15.11 Defining a Custom Metaclass to Control Class Behavior

Credit: Luther Blissett

Problem

You want to control the behavior of a class object and all of its instance objects, paying minimal runtime costs.

Solution

Python 2.2 lets you easily define your own custom metaclasses so you can build class objects whose behavior is entirely under your control, without runtime overhead except when the classes are created. For example, if you want to ensure that all methods a class defines (but not those it inherits and doesn't override) are traced, a custom metaclass that wraps the methods at class-creation time is easy to write:

```python
# requires Python 2.2 or later
import types

def tracing(f, name):
    def traced_f(*a, **k):
        print '%s(%s,%s) ->'%(name,a,k),
        result = f(*a, **k)
        print result
        return result
    return traced_f

class meta_tracer(type):
    def __new__(self, classname, bases, classdict):
        for f in classdict:
            m = classdict[f]
            if isinstance(m, types.FunctionType):
                classdict[f] = tracing(m, '%s.%s'%(classname,f))
        return type.__new__(self, classname, bases, classdict)

class tracer:
    __metaclass__ = meta_tracer
```

Discussion

This recipe's tracing function is nothing special—it's just a tracing wrapper closure that makes good use of the lexically nested scopes supported in Python 2.2 (or 2.1 with from __future__ import nested_scopes). We could use such a wrapper explicitly in each class that needs to be traced. For example:

```
class prova:
    def a(self):
        print 'body: prova.a'
    a = tracing(a, 'prova.a')
    def b(self):
        print 'body: prova.b'
    b = tracing(b, 'prova.a')
```

This is okay, but it does require the explicit boilerplate insertion of the decoration (wrapper) around each method we want traced. Boilerplate is boring and therefore error-prone.

Custom metaclasses let us perform such metaprogramming at class-definition time without paying substantial overhead at each instance creation or, worse, at each attribute access. The custom metaclass meta_tracer in this recipe, like most, inherits from type. In our metaclasses, we typically want to tweak just one or a few aspects of behavior, not recode every other aspect, so we delegate all that we don't explicitly override to type, which is the common metaclass of all built-in types and new-style classes in Python 2.2. meta_tracer overrides just one method, the special method __new__, which is used to create new instances of the metaclass (i.e., new classes that have meta_tracer as their metaclass). __new__ receives as arguments the name of the new class, the tuple of its bases, and the dict produced by executing the body of the class statement. In meta_tracer.__new__, we go through this dictionary, ensuring that each function in it is wrapped by our tracing wrapper closure. We then call type.__new__ to do the rest.

That's all! Every aspect of a class that uses meta_tracer as its metaclass is the same as if it used type instead, except that every method has automagically been wrapped as desired. For example:

```
class prova(tracer):
    def a(self):
        print 'body: prova.a'
    def b(self):
        print 'body: prova.b'
```

This is the same as the prova class of the previous snippet, which explicitly wrapped each of its methods. However, the wrapping is done automatically because this prova inherits from tracer and thus gets tracer's metaclass (i.e., meta_tracer). Instead of using class inheritance, we could control metaclass assignment more explicitly by placing the following statement in the class body:

```
__metaclass__ = meta_tracer
```

Or, more globally, we could place the following statement at the start of the module (thus defining a module-wide global variable named __metaclass__, which in turn defines the default metaclass for every class that doesn't inherit or explicitly set a metaclass):

```
__metaclass__ = meta_tracer
```

Each approach has its place in terms of explicitness (always a good trait) versus convenience (sometimes not to be sneered at).

Custom metaclasses also existed in Python Versions 2.1 and earlier, but they were hard to use. (Guido's essay introducing them is titled "The Killer Joke", the implication being that those older metaclasses could explode your mind if you thought too hard about them!). Now they're much simpler thanks to the ability to subclass type and do a few selective overrides, and to the high regularity and uniformity of Python 2.2's new object model. So there's no reason to be afraid of them anymore!

See Also

Currently, metaclasses are poorly documented; the most up-to-date documentation is in PEP 253 (*http://www.python.org/peps/pep-0253.html*).

15.12 Module: Allowing the Python Profiler to Profile C Modules

Credit: Richie Hindle

Profiling is the most crucial part of optimization. What you can't measure, you cannot control. This definitely applies to your program's running time. To make sure that Python's standard profile module can also measure the time spent in C-coded extensions, you need to wrap those extensions with the module shown in Example 15-1. An alternative to the approach in this module is to use the new Hotshot profiler that ships with Python 2.2 and later.

This module lets you take into account time spent in C modules when profiling your Python code. Normally, the profiler profiles only Python code, so it's difficult to find out how much time is spent accessing a database, running encryption code, sleeping, and so on. This module makes it easy to profile C code as well as Python code, giving you a clearer picture of how your application is spending its time.

This module also demonstrates how to create proxy objects at runtime that intercept calls between preexisting pieces of code. Furthermore, it shows how to use the new module to create new functions on the fly. We could do many of these things in a somewhat lightweight fashion, but systematically using the new module is a good way to demystify its reputation for difficulty.

Here's a small piece of code using the rotor encryption module:

```
import rotor, profile
r = rotor.newrotor('key')
profile.run("r.encrypt('Plaintext')")
```

This won't produce any profiler output for the encrypt method, because the method is implemented in C. The profilewrap module presented in this recipe can wrap the rotor object in dynamically generated Python code that is accessible to the profiler, like this:

```
import rotor, profile, profilewrap
r = rotor.newrotor('key')
r = profilewrap.wrap(r)  # profilewrap in action, replacing
                         # 'r' with a profilable wrapper
profile.run("r.encrypt('Plaintext')")
```

You can now see an entry in the profiler output that is something like:

```
1 0.003 0.003 0.003 0.003 PW_rotor.py:1(encrypt)
```

The filename *PW_rotor.py* is derived from the name of the object or module to which the method belongs. *PW_rotor.py* doesn't actually exist, but that little detail does not disturb the profiler.

In addition to objects, you can wrap individual functions (e.g., sleep=profilewrap.wrap(time.sleep)) and whole modules (e.g., os=profilewrap.wrap(os)). Note that wrapping a module wraps only the functions that the module exports; it doesn't automatically wrap objects created by those functions. See _profileMe in Example 15-1.

Example 15-1. Allowing the Python profiler to profile C modules

```
""" profilewrap.py:
Wraps C functions, objects and modules in dynamically generated Python code
so you can profile them. Here's an example using the rotor module:
>>> import profilewrap, rotor, profile
>>> r = profilewrap.wrap(rotor.newrotor('key'))
>>> profile.run("r.encrypt('Plaintext')")
This will produce output including something like this:
    1    0.003    0.003    0.003    0.003 PW_rotor.py:1(encrypt)

See the _profileMe function for examples of wrapping C functions, objects, and
modules. Run profilewrap.py to see the output from profiling _profileMe. """

import new, types

def _functionProxy(f, *args, **kwargs):
    """ The prototype for the dynamic Python code wrapping each C function """
    return apply(f, args, kwargs)

class _ProfileWrapFunction:
    """ A callable object that wraps each C function we want to profile. """
    def __init__(self, wrappedFunction, parentName="unnamed"):
```

Example 15-1. Allowing the Python profiler to profile C modules (continued)

```
        # Build the code for a new wrapper function, based on _functionProxy
        filename = "PW_%s.py" % parentName
        name = wrappedFunction.__name__
        c = _functionProxy.func_code
        newcode = new.code(c.co_argcount, c.co_nlocals, c.co_stacksize,
                           c.co_flags, c.co_code, c.co_consts, c.co_names,
                           c.co_varnames, filename, name, 1, c.co_lnotab)

        # Create a proxy function using the new code
        self._wrapper = new.function(newcode, globals())
        self._wrappedFunction = wrappedFunction

    def __call__(self, *args, **kwargs):
        return apply(self._wrapper, (self._wrappedFunction,) + args, kwargs)

class _ProfileWrapObject:
    """ A class that wraps an object or a module and dynamically creates a
    _ProfileWrapFunction for each method. Wrappers are cached for speed. """
    def __init__(self, wrappedObject):
        self._wrappedObject = wrappedObject
        self._cache = {}

    def __getattr__(self, attrName):
        # Look for a cached reference to the attribute. If it isn't there,
        # fetch it from the wrapped object.
        notThere = 'Not there'
        returnAttr = self._cache.get(attrName, notThere)
        if returnAttr is notThere:
            attr = getattr(self._wrappedObject, attrName, notThere)
            if attr is notThere:
                # The attribute is missing - let it raise an AttributeError
                getattr(self._wrappedObject, attrName)

            # We wrap only C functions, which have the BuiltinMethodType type
            elif isinstance(attr, types.BuiltinMethodType):
                # Base the fictitious filename on the module or class name
                if isinstance(self._wrappedObject, types.ModuleType):
                    objectName = self._wrappedObject.__name__
                else:
                    objectName = type(self._wrappedObject).__name__
                returnAttr = _ProfileWrapFunction(attr, objectName)
                self._cache[ attrName ] = returnAttr

            # All non-C-function attributes are returned directly
            else:
                returnAttr = attr

        return returnAttr

def wrap(wrappee):
    """ Wrap the given object, module, or function in a Python wrapper. """
    if isinstance(wrappee, types.BuiltinFunctionType):
```

```
        return _ProfileWrapFunction(wrappee)
    else:
        return _ProfileWrapObject(wrappee)

def _profileMe( ):
    # Wrap a built-in C function
    wrappedEval = wrap(eval)
    print wrappedEval('1+2*3')

    # Replace a C module with its wrapped equivalent
    import os
    os = wrap(os)
    print os.getcwd( )

    # Wrap a C object
    import rotor
    r = wrap(rotor.newrotor('key'))
    print repr(r.encrypt('Plaintext'))

if __name__ == '__main__':
    import profile
    profile.run('_profileMe( )')
```

See Also

No discussion of Python profiling is complete without mentioning the new Python profiler, *HotShot*, which, as of this writing, is not documented in the standard documentation; see Fred Drake's talk about HotShot, available from his home page (*http://starship.python.net/crew/fdrake/*).

CHAPTER 16
Extending and Embedding

16.0 Introduction

Credit: David Beazley, University of Chicago

One of Python's most powerful features is its ability to hook to libraries and programs written in compiled languages, such as C, C++, and Fortran. In fact, a large number of Python's built-in library modules are written as extension modules in C, so that operating-system services, networking functions, databases, and other features can be easily accessed from the interpreter. In addition, a number of application programmers are writing extensions, which can use Python as a framework for controlling large software packages written in compiled languages.

The gory details of how Python interfaces with other languages can be found in various Python programming books and at *http://www.python.org*. However, the general approach revolves around the creation of special wrapper functions that hook into the interpreter. For example, say you have a C function such as this:

```
int gcd(int x, int y) {
    int g = y;
    while (x > 0) {
        g = x;
        x = y % x;
        y = g;
    }
    return g;
}
```

If you want to access it from Python in a spam module, you'd have to write a special wrapper code like this:

```
#include "Python.h"
extern int gcd(int, int);

PyObject *wrap_gcd(PyObject *self, PyObject *args) {
    int x,y,g;
```

```
        if(!PyArg_ParseTuple(args, "ii", &x, &y))
            return NULL;
        g = gcd(x, y);
        return Py_BuildValue("i", g);
    }

    /* List of all functions in the module */
    static PyMethodDef spammethods[] = {
        {"gcd", wrap_gcd, METH_VARARGS },
        { NULL, NULL }
    };

    /* Module initialization function */
    void initspam(void) {
        Py_InitModule("spam", spammethods);
    }
```

Once this code is compiled into an extension module, the gcd function is used as you would expect. For example:

```
>>> import spam
>>> spam.gcd(63,56)
7
>>> spam.gcd(71,89)
1
```

This short example extends in a natural way to larger programming libraries—each function that you want to access from Python simply gets its own wrapper.

Although writing simple extension functions is fairly straightforward, the process of writing wrappers quickly becomes tedious and prone to error if you are building anything of reasonable complexity. Therefore, a lot programmers rely on automatic module-building tools to simplify the process. Python is fortunate to have a variety of such tools:

bgen

A module-building tool found in the *Tools* directory of a standard Python distribution. Maintained by Jack Jansen, it is used to generate many of the extension modules available in the Macintosh version of Python.

pyfort

A tool developed by Paul Dubois that can be used to build extension modules for Fortran code. Details are available at *http://pyfortran.sourceforge.net*.

CXX

Also developed by Paul Dubois, CXX is a library that provides a C++ friendly API for writing Python extensions. An interesting feature of CXX is that it allows Python objects such as lists and tuples to be used naturally with algorithms in the STL. The library also provides support for converting C++ exceptions into Python exceptions. Information about CXX is available at *http://cxx.sourceforge.net*.

f2py

> A wrapper generator for creating extensions in Fortran 90/95 developed by Pearu Peterson. Details are available at *http://cens.ioc.ee/projects/f2py2e/*.

SIP

> A C++ module builder developed by Phil Thompson that creates wrappers for C++ classes. The system has most notably been used to create the PyQt and PyKDE extension modules. More information can be found at *http://www.thekompany.com/projects/pykde*.

WrapPy

> Another C++ module builder that produces extension modules by reading C++ header files. It was developed by Greg Couch and is available at *http://www.cgl.ucsf.edu/home/gregc/wrappy/index.html*.

Boost Python Library

> Developed by David Abrahams, the Boost Python Library provides one of the more unusual C++ wrapping techniques. Classes are automatically wrapped into Python extensions by simply writing a few additional C++ classes that specify information about the extension module. More information is available at *http://www.boost.org/libs/python/doc/*.

SWIG

> An automatic extension-building tool that reads annotated C and C++ header files and produces extension modules for Python, Tcl, Perl, and a variety of other scripting languages. SWIG can wrap a large subset of C++ language features into an Python extension module. However, since I developed SWIG, I may be a little biased. In any event, further details are available at *http://www.swig.org*.

Regardless of the approach used to build Python extension modules, certain topics remain somewhat mysterious to many extension programmers. Therefore, the recipes in this chapter describe some of the common problems and extension-building tricks that are rarely covered in the standard documentation or other Python books. Topics include interacting with threads, returning NULL values, defining classes from C, implementing C/C++ functions in Python, creating extension types, and debugging.

16.1 Implementing a Simple Extension Type

Credit: Alex Martelli

Problem

You want to code and build a C extension type for Python with a minimal amount of hard work.

Solution

First of all, we need to create a *setup.py* using the distutils package (in Python 2.0 and later) to build and install our module:

```python
from distutils.core import setup, Extension

setup(name = "elemlist",
      version = "1.0",
      maintainer = "Alex Martelli",
      maintainer_email = "amcx@aleax.it",
      description = "Sample, simple Python extension module",

      ext_modules = [Extension('elemlist',sources=['elemlist.c'])]
)
```

Then we need an *elemlist.c* file with our module's source code:

```c
#include "Python.h"

/* type-definition and utility-macros */
typedef struct {
    PyObject_HEAD
    PyObject *car, *cdr;
} cons_cell;
staticforward PyTypeObject cons_type;
/* a type-testing macro (we don't actually use it here) */
#define is_cons(v) ((v)->ob_type == &cons_type)
/* utility macros to access car and cdr, both as lvalues and rvalues */
#define carof(v) (((cons_cell*)(v))->car)
#define cdrof(v) (((cons_cell*)(v))->cdr)

/* ctor ("internal" factory function) and dtor */
static cons_cell*
cons_new(PyObject *car, PyObject *cdr)
{
    cons_cell *cons = PyObject_NEW(cons_cell, &cons_type);
    if(cons) {
        cons->car = car; Py_INCREF(car); /* INCREF when holding a PyObject */
        cons->cdr = cdr; Py_INCREF(cdr); /* ditto */
    }
    return cons;
}
static void
cons_dealloc(cons_cell* cons)
{
    /* DECREF when releasing previously held PyObject*'s */
    Py_DECREF(carof(cons)); Py_DECREF(cdrof(cons));
    PyObject_DEL(cons);
}

/* The Python type-object */
statichere PyTypeObject cons_type = {
    PyObject_HEAD_INIT(0)    /* initialize to 0 to ensure Win32 portability */
```

```
    0,                 /*ob_size*/
    "cons",            /*tp_name*/
    sizeof(cons_cell), /*tp_basicsize*/
    0,                 /*tp_itemsize*/
    /* methods */
    (destructor)cons_dealloc, /*tp_dealloc*/
    /* implied by ISO C: all zeros thereafter, i.e., no other method */
};

/* module functions */
static PyObject*
cons(PyObject *self, PyObject *args)    /* the exposed factory function */
{
    PyObject *car, *cdr;
    if(!PyArg_ParseTuple(args, "OO", &car, &cdr))
        return 0;
    return (PyObject*)cons_new(car, cdr);
}
static PyObject*
car(PyObject *self, PyObject *args)     /* car accessor */
{
    PyObject *cons;
    if(!PyArg_ParseTuple(args, "O!", &cons_type, &cons)) /* type-checked */
        return 0;
    return Py_BuildValue("O", carof(cons));
}
static PyObject*
cdr(PyObject *self, PyObject *args)     /* cdr accessor */
{
    PyObject *cons;
    if(!PyArg_ParseTuple(args, "O!", &cons_type, &cons)) /* type-checked */
        return 0;
    return Py_BuildValue("O", cdrof(cons));
}
static PyMethodDef elemlist_module_functions[] = {
    {"cons",   cons,   METH_VARARGS},
    {"car",    car,    METH_VARARGS},
    {"cdr",    cdr,    METH_VARARGS},
    {0, 0}
};

/* module entry point (module initialization) function */
void
initelemlist(void)
{
    /* Create the module with its functions */
    PyObject *m = Py_InitModule("elemlist", elemlist_module_functions);
    /* Finish initializing the type objects */
    cons_type.ob_type = &PyType_Type;
}
```

Discussion

C-coded Python extension types have an undeserved aura of mystery and difficulty. Sure, it's a lot of work to implement every possible nicety, but a fundamental, useful type doesn't take all that much effort.

This module is roughly equivalent to the Python-coded module:

```
def cons(car, cdr): return car, cdr
def car(conscell): return conscell[0]
def cdr(conscell): return conscell[1]
```

except that the C version contains about 25 times more lines of code, even excluding comments and empty lines (and it is not much faster than the Python-coded version, either).

However, the point of this recipe is to demonstrate a minimal C-coded extension type. I'm not even supplying object methods (except the necessary destructor) but, rather, module-level functions for car and cdr access. This also shows the utter simplicity of building a C-coded extension module on any platform, thanks to the distutils package, which does all of the hard work.

Because this is meant as an introduction to writing extension modules in C for Python, here are the instructions on how to build this extension module, assuming you have a Windows machine with Python 2.0 or later, and Microsoft Visual C++ 6 (or the free command-line equivalent that you can download from Microsoft's site as a part of their .NET Framework SDK). You can presumably translate mentally to other platforms such as Linux with gcc, for example. On the other hand, using non-Microsoft compilers on Windows takes more work, and I'm not going to cover that here (see *http://www.python.org/doc/current/inst/non-ms-compilers.html*). The steps are:

1. Make a new directory, *C:\Temp\EL*, for example.

2. Open a command prompt (MS-DOS box) and go to the new directory.

3. In the new directory, create the files *setup.py* and *elemlist.c* with the contents of the recipe's text.

4. Run the following at the DOS prompt (assuming you've done a standard Python install, *C:\Python22* is where your *python.exe* lives):

   ```
   C:\Temp\EL> C:\Python22\python setup.py install
   ```

   This will give lots of output, but presumably, all goes well and the new extension has been built and installed.

5. Now test it by running the following at the DOS prompt:

   ```
   C:\Temp\EL> C:\Python22\python
   snipped -- various greeting messages from Python
   >>> from elemlist import cons
   >>> a=cons(1,cons(2,cons(3,())))
   >>> from elemlist import car, cdr
   ```

```
>>> car(cdr(a))
2
```

Now your new extension module is installed and ready!

See Also

The *Extending and Embedding* manual is available as part of the standard Python documentation set at *http://www.python.org/doc/current/ext/ext.html*; the *Distributing Python Modules* section of the standard Python documentation set is still incomplete, but it is the best source of information on the distutils package.

16.2 Translating a Python Sequence into a C Array with the PySequence_Fast Protocol

Credit: Luther Blissett

Problem

You have an existing C function that takes as an argument a C array of C-level values (e.g., doubles), and want to wrap it into a Python callable C extension that takes as an argument a Python sequence (or iterator).

Solution

The easiest way to accept an arbitrary Python sequence in the Python C API is with the PySequence_Fast function, which builds and returns a tuple when needed, but returns only its argument (with the reference count incremented) if the argument is already a list:

```
#include <Python.h>

/* a preexisting C-level function you want to expose -- e.g: */
static double total(double* data, int len)
{
    double total = 0.0;
    int i;
    for(i=0; i<len; ++i)
        total += data[i];
    return total;
}

/* here is how you expose it to Python code: */
static PyObject *totalDoubles(PyObject *self, PyObject *args)
{
    PyObject* seq;
    double *dbar;
    double result;
    int seqlen;
    int i;
```

```
    /* get one argument as a sequence */
    if(!PyArg_ParseTuple(args, "O", &seq))
        return 0;
    seq = PySequence_Fast(seq, "argument must be iterable");
    if(!seq)
        return 0;

    /* prepare data as an array of doubles */
    seqlen = PySequence_Fast_GET_SIZE(seq);
    dbar = malloc(seqlen*sizeof(double));
    if(!dbar) {
        Py_DECREF(seq);
        return PyErr_NoMemory();
    }
    for(i=0; i < seqlen; i++) {
        PyObject *fitem;
        PyObject *item = PySequence_Fast_GET_ITEM(seq, i);
        if(!item) {
            Py_DECREF(seq);
            free(dbar);
            return 0;
        }
        fitem = PyNumber_Float(item);
        if(!fitem) {
            Py_DECREF(seq);
            free(dbar);
            PyErr_SetString(PyExc_TypeError, "all items must be numbers");
            return 0;
        }
        dbar[i] = PyFloat_AS_DOUBLE(fitem);
        Py_DECREF(fitem);
    }

    /* clean up, compute, and return result */
    Py_DECREF(seq);
    result = total(dbar, seqlen);
    free(dbar);
    return Py_BuildValue("d", result);
}

static PyMethodDef totalMethods[] = {
    {"total", totalDoubles, METH_VARARGS, "Sum a sequence of numbers."},
    {0} /* sentinel */
};

void
inittotal(void)
{
    (void) Py_InitModule("total", totalMethods);
}
```

Discussion

The two best ways for your C-coded, Python-callable extension functions to accept generic Python sequences as arguments are `PySequence_Fast` and `PyObject_GetIter` (in Python 2.2 only). The latter can often save memory, but it is appropriate only when it's okay for the rest of your C code to get the items one at a time without knowing beforehand how many items there will be in total. Often, you have preexisting C functions from an existing library that you want to expose to Python code, and those most often require that their input sequences are C arrays. Thus, this recipe shows how to build a C array (in this case, an array of `double`) from a generic Python sequence argument, so you can pass the array (and the integer that gives the array's length) to your existing C function (represented here, as an example, by the `total` function at the start of the recipe).

`PySequence_Fast` takes two arguments: a Python object to be presented as a sequence and a string to use as the error message in case the Python object cannot be presented as a sequence, in which case it returns 0 (the null pointer, an error indicator). If the Python object is already a list or tuple, `PySequence_Fast` returns the same object with the reference count increased by one. If the Python object is any other kind of sequence (or, in Python 2.2, any iterator or iterable), `PySequence_Fast` builds and returns a new tuple with all items already in place. In any case, `PySequence_fast` returns an object on which you can call `PySequence_Fast_GET_SIZE` to learn the sequence length (as we do in the recipe to `malloc` the appropriate amount of storage for the C array) and `PySequence_Fast_GET_ITEM` to get an item given a valid index (between 0, included, and the sequence length, excluded).

The recipe requires quite a bit of care, which is typical of all C-coded Python extensions (and, more generally, any C code), to deal with memory and error conditions properly. For C-coded Python extensions, it's imperative that you know which functions return new references (which you must `Py_DECREF` when you are done with them) and which return borrowed references (which you must not `Py_DECREF`, but on the contrary, `Py_INCREF` if you want to keep a copy for a longer time). In this specific case, you have to know the following (by reading the Python documentation):

- `PyArg_ParseTuple` always gives you borrowed references.
- `PySequence_Fast` returns a new reference.
- `PySequence_Fast_GET_ITEM` returns a borrowed reference.
- `PyNumber_Float` returns a new reference.

There is method to this madness: even though as you start your career as a coder of C API Python extensions, you'll no doubt have to double-check each case. Python's C API strives to return borrowed references for performance when it knows it can always do so safely (i.e., it knows that the reference it is returning necessarily refers to an already existing object). It has to return a new reference when it's possible (or certain) that a new object may have to be created.

For example, in the above list, PyNumber_Float and PySequence_Fast may be able to return the same object they were given as an argument, but it's also quite possible that they may have to create a new object for this purpose to ensure that the returned object has the correct type. Therefore, these two functions are specified as always returning new references. PyArg_ParseTuple and PySequence_Fast_GET_ITEM, on the other hand, will always return references to objects that already exist elsewhere (as items in the arguments' tuple or items in the fast-sequence container, respectively), and therefore, these two functions can afford to return borrowed references and are thus specified as doing so.

One last note: when we have an item from the fast-sequence container, we immediately try to transform it into a Python float object and deal with the possibility that the transformation will fail (e.g., if we're passed a sequence containing a string, a complex number, etc.). It is often quite futile to first attempt a check (with PyNumber_Check), because the check might succeed, and the later transformation attempt might fail anyway (e.g., with a complex-number item).

As usual, the best way to build this extension (assuming you've saved it to a *total.py* file) is with the distutils package. Place a file named *setup.py* such as:

```
from distutils.core import setup, Extension

setup(name = "total", maintainer = "Luther Blissett", maintainer_email =
    "situ@tioni.st", ext_modules = [Extension('total',sources=['total.c'])]
)
```

in the same directory as the C source, then build and install by running:

```
$ python setup.py install
```

The nice thing about this is that it works on any platform (assuming you have Python 2.0 or later and have access to the same C compiler used to build your version of Python).

See Also

The *Extending and Embedding* manual is available as part of the standard Python documentation set at *http://www.python.org/doc/current/ext/ext.html*; documentation on Python C API at *http://www.python.org/doc/current/api/api.html*; the *Distributing Python Modules* section of the standard Python documentation set is still incomplete, but it is the best source of information on the distutils package.

16.3 Accessing a Python Sequence Item-by-Item with the Iterator Protocol

Credit: Luther Blissett

Problem

You want to write a Python callable C extension that takes as an argument a Python sequence (or iterator) and accesses it sequentially, requiring no extra storage.

Solution

If you can afford to access the sequence item by item without knowing in advance the number of items it has, and you are running Python 2.2 or better, you can sometimes save memory by using PyObject_GetIter instead of PySequence_Fast:

```c
#include <Python.h>

static PyObject *totalIter(PyObject *self, PyObject *args)
{
    PyObject* seq;
    PyObject* item;
    double result;

    /* get one argument as an iterator */
    if(!PyArg_ParseTuple(args, "O", &seq))
        return 0;
    seq = PyObject_GetIter(seq);
    if(!seq)
        return 0;

    /* process data sequentially */
    result = 0.0;
    while((item=PyIter_Next(seq))) {
        PyObject *fitem;
        fitem = PyNumber_Float(item);
        if(!fitem) {
            Py_DECREF(seq);
            Py_DECREF(item);
            PyErr_SetString(PyExc_TypeError, "all items must be numbers");
            return 0;
        }
        result += PyFloat_AS_DOUBLE(fitem);
        Py_DECREF(fitem);
        Py_DECREF(item);
    }

    /* clean up and return result */
    Py_DECREF(seq);
    return Py_BuildValue("d", result);
}
```

```
static PyMethodDef totitMethods[] = {
    {"totit", totalIter, METH_VARARGS, "Sum a sequence of numbers."},
    {0} /* sentinel */
};

void
inittotit(void)
{
    (void) Py_InitModule("totit", totitMethods);
}
```

Discussion

PyObject_GetIter is available only in Python 2.2, and it is appropriate only when it's okay for the rest of your C code to get the items one at a time without knowing beforehand how many items there will be in total. When these conditions are met, PyObject_GetIter gives you roughly the same performance as PySequence_Fast if the input argument is a list or tuple, but it can save memory allocation, and therefore running time, if the input argument is an iterator or another kind of sequence or iterable.

PyObject_GetIter takes one argument: a Python object from which an iterator is desired (much like Python's iter built-in function). It either returns 0, indicating an error, or an iterator object, on which you can call PyIter_Next to get the next item (or 0, which is not an error at the end of the iteration). Both PyObject_GetIter and PyIter_Next return new references, so we must Py_DECREF when we're done with the respective objects.

As usual, the best way to build this extension (assuming you've saved it in a *totit.c* file) is with the distutils package. Place a file named *setup.py* such as:

```
from distutils.core import setup, Extension

setup(name = "totit", maintainer = "Luther Blissett", maintainer_email =
    "situ@tioni.st", ext_modules = [Extension('total',sources=['totit.c'])]
)
```

in the same directory as the C source, then build and install by running:

```
$ python setup.py install
```

The nice thing about this is that it works on any platform (assuming, of course, you have Python 2.0 or later and have access to the same C compiler used to build your version of Python).

Since Python extensions are often coded in C to maximize performance, it's interesting to measure performance compared to that of pure Python code dealing with the same task. A typical measurement setup might be a script such as:

```
import time, operator, total, totit

def timo(f, xs):
    start = time.clock()
```

```
        for x in xs: res = f(x)
        stend = time.clock( )
        print f.__name__, stend-start

    def totpy(x):
        result = 0.0
        for item in x: result += item
        return result

    def totre(x):
        return reduce(operator.add, x)

seq = range(200000)
print 'on lists:'
timo(totre, 10*[seq])
timo(totpy, 10*[seq])
timo(total.total, 10*[seq])
timo(totit.totit, 10*[seq])
print 'on iters:'
timo(totre, [iter(seq) for i in range(10)])
timo(totpy, [iter(seq) for i in range(10)])
timo(total.total, [iter(seq) for i in range(10)])
timo(totit.totit, [iter(seq) for i in range(10)])
```

On my machine, running with the command-line switch -0 so that Python can optimize operations, the timing results are:

```
on lists:
totre 2.88
totpy 0.91
total 0.31
totit 0.32
on iters:
totre 3.02
totpy 0.91
total 0.64
totit 0.32
```

As you can see, the most important optimization is to avoid the attractive nuisance of the reduce built-in function. We can be about three times as fast with a simple Python-coded function! But the C-coded extension total, which we saw in Recipe 16.2, is three times faster yet when run on lists, as is the totit extension in this recipe. The advantage of totit over total is seen when they are run on iterators rather than lists. In that case, totit can be roughly twice as fast as total, because it saves the overhead of memory allocation in PySequence_Fast.

See Also

The *Extending and Embedding* manual is available as part of the standard Python documentation set at *http://www.python.org/doc/current/ext/ext.html*; documentation on the Python C API at *http://www.python.org/doc/current/api/api.html*; the *Distributing*

Python Modules section of the standard Python documentation set is still incomplete, but it is the best source of information on the distutils package.

16.4 Returning None from a Python-Callable C Function

Credit: Alex Martelli

Problem

Your C-coded, Python-callable function in an extension module needs to return nothing in particular (i.e., a Python None), but it must, of course, do so without messing up reference counts.

Solution

Suppose we need an empty, C-coded function equivalent to Python:

```
def empty1(*args):
    pass
```

or, identically:

```
def empty2(*args):
    return None
```

there is still a right and a wrong way to solve the problem. The wrong way messes up reference counts:

```
static PyObject*
empty3(PyObject* self, PyObject* args)
{
    return Py_None;
}
```

But it's not hard to do it right. Here is the simplest way:

```
static PyObject*
empty4(PyObject* self, PyObject* args)
{
    return Py_BuildValue("");
}
```

And here is the canonical way:

```
static PyObject*
empty5(PyObject* self, PyObject* args)
{
    Py_INCREF(Py_None);
    return Py_None;
}
```

Discussion

Often, a function written in C for Python needs to return nothing in particular. In other words, it should return None in Python terms, but you can't return Py_None from C, because that will mess up reference counts. None—the Python object we must explicitly return from a Python-callable, C-coded function—is a perfectly normal Python object, still subject to all normal reference-count rules. One of these rules is that each function must Py_INCREF the Python object it returns.

So a bare return Py_None; is a nasty lurking bug. Either explicitly Py_INCREF the None object you're returning, or delegate the work to handy function Py_BuildValue (simpler, but costs a few machine cycles), which can be used to handle just about all cases of returning values from C to Python, offering potential uniformity advantages. To have Py_BuildValue build a properly incremented None on your behalf, call it with an empty format string.

See Also

The *Extending and Embedding* manual is available as part of the standard Python documentation set at *http://www.python.org/doc/current/ext/ext.html*; documentation on the Python C API at *http://www.python.org/doc/current/api/api.html*.

16.5 Coding the Methods of a Python Class in C

Credit: Brent Burley

Problem

You have a Python class and want to recode it as a C extension for speed while keeping all client-code unchanged, so it must remain a class.

Solution

One hardly ever sees Python class objects built in C extensions. And yet it's anything but difficult, and, in fact, it's quite handy:

```
#include <Python.h>

static PyObject* Foo_init(PyObject *self, PyObject *args)
{
    printf("Foo.__init__ called\n");
    Py_INCREF(Py_None);
    return Py_None;
}

static PyObject* Foo_doSomething(PyObject *self, PyObject *args)
{
    printf("Foo.doSomething called\n");
```

```
        Py_INCREF(Py_None);
        return Py_None;
    }

    static PyMethodDef FooMethods[] =
    {
        {"__init__", Foo_init, METH_VARARGS, "doc string"},
        {"doSomething", Foo_doSomething, METH_VARARGS, "doc string"},
        {0, 0},
    };

    static PyMethodDef ModuleMethods[] = { {0, 0} };

    #ifdef __cplusplus
    extern "C"
    #endif
    void initFoo()
    {
        PyMethodDef *def;

        /* create new module and class objects */
        PyObject *module = Py_InitModule("Foo", ModuleMethods);
        PyObject *moduleDict = PyModule_GetDict(module);
        PyObject *classDict = PyDict_New();
        PyObject *className = PyString_FromString("Foo");
        PyObject *fooClass = PyClass_New(NULL, classDict, className);
        PyDict_SetItemString(moduleDict, "Foo", fooClass);
        Py_DECREF(classDict);
        Py_DECREF(className);
        Py_DECREF(fooClass);

        /* add methods to class */
        for (def = FooMethods; def->ml_name != NULL; def++) {
            PyObject *func = PyCFunction_New(def, NULL);
            PyObject *method = PyMethod_New(func, NULL, fooClass);
            PyDict_SetItemString(classDict, def->ml_name, method);
            Py_DECREF(func);
            Py_DECREF(method);
        }
    }
```

Discussion

This recipe shows how to define a new Python class from a C extension module. The class's methods are implemented in C, but the class can still be instantiated, extended, and subclassed from Python. The same technique can also be used with inheritance to extend an existing Python class with methods written in C. In this recipe, the first argument to PyClass_New is passed as NULL, indicating that the new class has no base classes. Pass the tuple of base classes in this spot, and you'll get normal

Python inheritance behavior, even though your new class is being built in a C extension rather than in Python source code.

The usual method of creating new types in an extension module is to define a new instance of PyTypeObject and provide callbacks to the various C functions that implement the type. However, it may be better to define the new type as a Python class, so that the type can be instantiated and subclassed from Python. In some cases, when defining a custom exception type, for example, it is required that the new type be a Python class.

The methods in this recipe are coded as C functions and are described by a table of PyMethodDef statements in the same way that a module's methods (functions) are described. The key fact that allows these functions to become unbound methods is that each of them is first wrapped in a PyCFunction object and then in a PyMethod object. The PyCFunction turns the C function into a Python object, and the PyMethod associates the function with a particular class as an unbound method. Finally, the methods are added to the class's dictionary, which makes them callable on instances of the class.

Note that base classes can be specified for the new class by passing a tuple of class objects as the first argument to PyClass_New. These can be existing Python classes. The second argument passed to PyCFunction_New becomes the self argument passed to the C function. This can be any Python object, but it's not very useful in most cases since you can just as easily keep a static C variable. However, it can be very handy when you want to use the same C function, associated with different data, to implement more than one Python function or method. Also note that the class instance is passed to the C functions as the first argument in the args tuple.

See Also

The *Extending and Embedding* manual is available as part of the standard Python documentation set at *http://www.python.org/doc/current/ext/ext.html*; documentation on the Python C API at *http://www.python.org/doc/current/api/api.html*.

16.6   Implementing C Function Callbacks to a Python Function

Credit: Swaminathan Narayanan

Problem

You must call a C function that takes a function callback as an argument, and you want to pass a Python function as the callback.

Solution

For this, we must wrap the Python function in a C function to be passed as the actual C-level callback. For example:

```
#include "python.h"

/* the C standard library qsort function, just as an example! */
extern void qsort(void *, size_t, size_t, int (*)(const void *, const void *));

/* static data (sigh), as we have no callback data in this (nasty) case */
static PyObject *py_compare_func = NULL;

static int
stub_compare_func(const void *cva, const void *cvb)
{
    int retvalue = 0;
    const PyObject **a = (const PyObject**)cva;
    const PyObject **b = (const PyObject**)cvb;

    // Build up the argument list...
    PyObject *arglist = Py_BuildValue("(OO)", *a, *b);

    // ...for calling the Python compare function
    PyObject *result = PyEval_CallObject(py_compare_func, arglist);

    if (result && PyInt_Check(result)) {
        retvalue = PyInt_AsLong(result);
    }

    Py_XDECREF(result);
    Py_DECREF(arglist);

    return retvalue;
}

static PyObject *pyqsort(PyObject *obj, PyObject *args)
{
    PyObject *pycompobj;
    PyObject *list;
    if (!PyArg_ParseTuple(args, "OO", &list, &pycompobj))
        return NULL;

    // Make sure second argument is a function
    if (!PyCallable_Check(pycompobj)) {
        PyErr_SetString(PyExc_TypeError, "Need a callable object!");
    } else {
        // Save the compare function. This obviously won't work for multithreaded
        // programs and is not even a reentrant, alas -- qsort's fault!
        py_compare_func = pycompobj;
        if (PyList_Check(list)) {
```

```
        int size = PyList_Size(list);
        int i;

        // Make an array of (PyObject *), because qsort does not know about
        // the PyList object
        PyObject **v = (PyObject **) malloc( sizeof(PyObject *) * size );
        for (i=0; i<size; ++i) {
            v[i] = PyList_GetItem(list, i);
            // Increment the reference count, because setting the list
            // items below will decrement the reference count
            Py_INCREF(v[i]);
        }
        qsort(v, size, sizeof(PyObject*), stub_compare_func);
        for (i=0; i<size; ++i) {
            PyList_SetItem(list, i, v[i]);
            // need not do Py_DECREF - see above
        }
        free(v);
    }
  }
  Py_INCREF(Py_None);
  return Py_None;
}

static PyMethodDef qsortMethods[] = {
    { "qsort", pyqsort, METH_VARARGS },
    { NULL, NULL }
};

__declspec(dllexport) void initqsort(void) {
    PyObject *m;
    m = Py_InitModule("qsort", qsortMethods);
}
```

Discussion

Let's say you have a function in C or C++ that takes a function callback as an argument. You want to call this function and pass a Python function as the callback. For example, you want to call the standard C library function qsort on a suitably arrayized Python list and pass a Python function as the comparison function:

```
>>> import qsort
>>> a = [9, 3, 5, 4, 1]
>>> def revcmp(a, b): return cmp(b, a)
...
>>> qsort.qsort(a, revcmp)
>>> a
[9, 5, 4, 3, 1]
```

Of course, this is strictly for demonstration purposes, since Python's own sort list method is far better!

When extending Python, you may come across existing C functions that take a function callback. It makes sense to pass Python a function as the callback function. The trick is to have a C function callback call the Python function by suitably marshaling the arguments. This is done by `stub_compare_func` in the recipe. `Py_BuildValue` is used to pass the two Python objects being compared back to the Python function.

In the case of `qsort`, there is no user data that can be passed, which is usually the callback convention. This means that we have to store the Python function in a static variable and use it to call in the C callback. This is not an ideal situation, given that it would not work in a multithreaded, or otherwise reentrant, program). While there is no solution for this particular case (as far as I know), the usual trick is to pass the Python function as user data to the function callback, an approach that is reentrant and thread-safe. But the possibility of using this better approach depends on whether the C-level callback architecture is well-designed.

This recipe's wrapper of `qsort` copies the `PyObject` pointers to a separate array that is sorted using the C library's `qsort`. The pointers are then put back in the original list. The reference counts of the items in the list that are being replaced are decreased behind the scenes. However, this is okay, because we increased them beforehand. Consequently, we do not need to do a `Py_DECREF` after setting the item in the list. Thus, this recipe also serves nicely as an example of a reference count handling quirk.

See Also

The *Extending and Embedding* manual is available as part of the standard Python documentation set at *http://www.python.org/doc/current/ext/ext.html*; documentation on the Python C API at *http://www.python.org/doc/current/api/api.html*; documentation on `qsort` for your standard C library.

16.7   Debugging Dynamically Loaded C Extensions with gdb

Credit: Joseph VanAndel, Michael Aivazis

Problem

A dynamically loaded C/C++ Python extension is giving you trouble on Unix or a Unix-like platform, and you would like to use the interactive debugger *gdb* to find out more about what's wrong.

Solution

One way to find the cause of core dumps or other serious trouble with a C Python extension is to compile the extension source with -g and then follow these steps (you may also want to recompile any other extensions you use, such as Numeric, with -g):

```
% gdb /usr/bin/python2.1
(gdb) br _PyImport_LoadDynamicModule
(gdb) cont    # Repeat until your extension is loaded
(gdb) finish # to load your extension
(gdb) br wrap_myfunction  # the entry point in your code
(gdb) disable 1    # don't want to break for more modules being loaded
(gdb) continue
```

Discussion

If a dynamically loaded C/C++ extension is causing Python to core dump, or causing some other kind of serious trouble, this recipe can help you find out the root cause by showing a technique to debug your extension using *gdb* (if you use Unix or a Unix-like platform, and *gdb* is your debugger of choice). Note that the overall concept generalizes to other debuggers with abilities similar to *gdb*'s. You cannot set a break on your function all at once, because your function lives in a dynamic library (shared object) that isn't initially loaded. However, you can break in the PyImport_LoadDynamicModule function and eventually (when your module is at long last loaded) get control at the debugger prompt after your module is in memory. You will be able, at last, to set the breakpoint you need.

This technique works. However, if you often do this kind of thing, the process of stepping through all the modules, as Python loads them at startup, can easily become tedious. There's a handier alternative, although it's more invasive, because it requires you to modify your Python sources and rebuild Python from them.

The key idea of this handier alternative is to add a do-nothing function somewhere in the body of code that Python loads immediately. Specifically, you can edit the *Modules/main.c* file to include one new function:

```
void Py_DebugTrap(void) { }
```

In whatever extension you're debugging, add a call to Py_DebugTrap right where you want to break into the code. The Py_DebugTrap symbol is immediately available when you start *gdb*, because the symbol lives in *main.c*. So you can immediately set a breakpoint there when you are at the *gdb* prompt, then continue. This even works in parallel under MPI.

See Also

The *gdb* online documentation (just type help at the interactive prompt), manpages, and online manual (*http://www.gnu.org/manual/gdb-4.17/gdb.html*).

16.8 Debugging Memory Problems

Credit: Will Ware

Problem

You're developing C extensions, and you experience memory problems. You suspect mismanagement of reference counts and want to check whether your C extension code is managing reference counts correctly.

Solution

To chase these problems optimally, you need to alter Python's sources and rebuild Python. Specifically, add this function in *Objects/object.c* immediately before the _Py_PrintReferences function:

```
void
_Py_CountReferences(FILE *fp)
{
    int n;
    PyObject *op;
    for (n = 0, op = refchain._ob_next;
        op != &refchain;
        op = op->_ob_next, n += op->ob_refcnt)
    { }
    fprintf(fp, "%d refs\n", n);
}
```

I place in the following macros in my C extension:

```
#if defined(Py_DEBUG) || defined(DEBUG)
extern void _Py_CountReferences(FILE*);
#define CURIOUS(x) { fprintf(stderr, __FILE__ ":%d ", __LINE__); x; }
#else
#define CURIOUS(x)
#endif
#define MARKER()          CURIOUS(fprintf(stderr, "\n"))
#define DESCRIBE(x)       CURIOUS(fprintf(stderr, "  " #x "=%d\n", x))
#define DESCRIBE_HEX(x)   CURIOUS(fprintf(stderr, "  " #x "=%08x\n", x))
#define COUNTREFS()       CURIOUS(_Py_CountReferences(stderr))
```

To debug, I rebuild Python using make OPT="-DPy_DEBUG", which causes the code under Py_TRACE_REFS to be built. My own makefile for my extensions does the same trick by including these lines:

```
debug:
        make clean; make OPT="-g -DPy_DEBUG" all
CFLAGS = $(OPT) -fpic -O2 -I/usr/local/include -I/usr/include/python1.5
```

Discussion

If I'm developing C extensions and I run into memory problems, I find that the typical cause is mismanagement of reference counts, particularly abuses of `Py_INCREF` and `Py_DECREF`, as well as forgetfulness of the reference-count effects of functions such as `Py_BuildValue`, `PyArg_ParseTuple`, `PyTuple/List_SetItem/GetItem`, etc. The 1.5.2 source code base offers some help with this (search for `Py_TRACE_REFS`), but I found it useful to add this recipe's function in *Objects/object.c* just before `_Py_PrintReferences`.

Unlike `_Py_PrintReferences`, this recipe's function will print only the total of all the reference counts in the system, so it can be used safely in loops that will repeat millions of times, whereas `_Py_PrintReferences` would print out way too many counts to be useful. This can help you identify errantly wandering `Py_INCREF`s and `Py_DECREF`s.

So when I suspect that one of my functions is responsible for memory problems, I liberally sprinkle the suspect function with calls to the `COUNTREFS` macro. This allows me to keep track of exactly how many references are being created or destroyed as I go through my function. This is particularly useful in tight loops, in which dumb mistakes can cause reference counts to grow ridiculously fast. Also, reference counts that shrink too fast (overzealous use of `Py_DECREF`) can cause core dumps because the memory for objects that should still exist has been reallocated to new objects.

See Also

The only documentation in this case is the source code ("Use the source, Luke!").

16.9 Using SWIG-Generated Modules in a Multithreaded Environment

Credit: Joseph VanAndel, Mark Hammond

Problem

You want to use SWIG-generated modules in a multithreaded environment; therefore, the C code in these modules must release the Python global interpreter lock.

Solution

Use a typemap for SWIG (written by Mark Hammond) as posted on *comp.lang.python*. It maps Win32 API functions that return `BOOL` to Python functions that return `None`, but may raise exceptions. The wrapped function must set the standard Windows global `LastError` if it returns false (indicating that it has detected an error). The wrapping

function must also automatically release the Python global interpreter lock for the
duration of the function, and thus allow free multithreading.

```
%typedef BOOL BOOLAPI

%typemap(python,except) BOOLAPI {
        Py_BEGIN_ALLOW_THREADS
        $function
        Py_END_ALLOW_THREADS
        if (!$source) {
                $cleanup
                 return PyWin_SetAPIError("$name");
        }
}
```

Discussion

To use multiple threads effectively, you must release the Python global interpreter
lock from your extension C code whenever feasible. The simplest way to do this with
SWIG is to use an except directive, as shown in the recipe's typemap. Another interesting effect of this typemap is that it turns the C-oriented error-return convention
(returning a 0 value and setting a global error indicator code) into a highly Pythonic
convention (raising an exception).

See Also

SWIG and its typemaps are documented at *http://www.swig.org*; Windows API documentation on LastError available from Microsoft (*http://msdn.microsoft.com*).

## CHAPTER 17

Algorithms

17.0 Introduction

Credit: Tim Peters, PythonLabs

Algorithm research is what drew me to Python—and I fell in love. It wasn't love at first sight, but it was an attraction that grew into infatuation, which grew steadily into love. And that love shows no signs of fading. Why? I've worked in fields pushing the state of the art, and, in a paradoxical nutshell, Python code is easy to throw away!

When you're trying to solve a problem that may not have been solved before, you may have some intuitions about how to proceed, but you rarely know in advance exactly what needs to be done. The only way to proceed is to try things, many things, everything you can think of, just to see what happens. Python eases this by minimizing the time and pain from conception to code: if your colleagues are using, for example, C or Java, it's not unusual for you to try and discard six different approaches in Python while they're still getting the bugs out of their first attempt.

In addition, you will have naturally grown classes and modules that capture key parts of the problem domain, simply because you find the need to keep reinventing them when starting over from scratch. A true C++ expert can give you a good run, but C++ is so complex that true experts are very rare. Moderate skill with Python is much easier to obtain, yet much more productive for research and prototyping than merely moderate C++ skill.

So if you're in the research business—and every programmer who doesn't know everything occasionally is—you've got a nearly perfect language in Python. How then do you develop the intuitions that can generate a myriad of plausible approaches to try? Experience is the final answer, as we all get better at what we do often, but studying the myriad approaches other people have tried develops a firm base from which to explore. Toward that end, here are the most inspiring algorithm books I've read—they'll teach you possibilities you may never have discovered on your own:

Jon Bentley's Programming Pearls and More Programming Pearls (Addison-Wesley)
Every programmer should read these books from cover to cover for sheer joy. The chapters are extended versions of a popular column Bentley wrote for the Communications of the Association for Computing Machinery (CACM). Each chapter is generally self-contained, covering one or two lovely (and often surprising, in the "Aha! why didn't I think of that?!" sense) techniques of real practical value.

Robert Sedgewick's Algorithms in C++ or Algorithms in C (Addison-Wesley)
These books cover the most important general algorithms, organized by problem domain, and provide brief but cogent explanations, along with working code. The books cover the same material; the difference is in which computer language is used for the code. I recommend the C++ book for Python programmers, because idiomatic Python is closer to C++ than to C, and Sedgewick's use of C++ is generally simple and easily translated to equivalent Python. This is the first book to reach for if you need to tackle a new area quickly.

Donald Knuth's The Art of Computer Programming series (Addison-Wesley)
For experts (and those who aspire to expertise), this massive series in progress is the finest in-depth exposition of the state of the art. Nothing compares to its unique combination of breadth and depth, rigor, and historical perspective. Note that these books aren't meant to be read, they have to be actively studied, and many valuable insights are scattered in answers to the extensive exercises. While there's detailed analysis, there's virtually no working code, except for programs written in assembly language for a hypothetical machine of archaic design (yes, this can be maddeningly obscure). It can be hard going at times, but few books reward time invested so richly.

After consorting with the algorithm gods, a nasty practical problem arises back on Earth. When you have two approaches available, how do you measure which is faster? It turns out this is hard to do in a platform-independent way (even in Python) when one approach isn't obviously much faster than the other. One of the nastiest problems is that the resolution of timing facilities varies widely across platforms, and even the meaning of time varies. Your two primary choices for time measurement in Python are time.time and time.clock.

time.time shouldn't be used for algorithm timing on Windows, because the timer updates only 18.2 times per second. Therefore, timing differences up to about 0.055 seconds are lost to quantization error (over a span of time briefer than that, time.time may return exactly the same number at each end). On the other hand, time.time typically has the best resolution on Unix-like systems. However, time.time measures wall-clock time. So, for example, it includes time consumed by the operating system when a burst of network activity demands attention. For this reason (among others), it's important to close all nonessential programs when running delicate timing tests and, if you can, shut down your network daemons.

time.clock is a much better choice on Windows and often on Unix-like systems. The Windows time.clock uses the Win32 QueryPerformanceCounter facility, and the timer updates more than a million times per second. This virtually eliminates quantization error but also measures wall-clock time, so it is still important to close other programs while timing. time.clock has good and bad aspects on most Unix-like systems. The good side is that it generally measures user time, an account of how much time the CPU spent in the process that calls time.clock, excluding time consumed by other processes. The bad side is that this timer typically updates no more than 100 times per second, so a quantization error can still give misleading results. The best approach to this is to do many repetitions of the basic thing you're timing, so that the time delta you compute is large compared to the timer's updating frequency. You can then divide the time delta by the number of repetitions to get the average time.

Overall, there's no compelling best answer here! One useful approach is to start your timing code with a block such as:

```
if 1:
    from time import clock as now
else:
    from time import time as now
```

Then use now in your timing code and run your timing tests twice, switching the underlying timing function between runs by changing 1 to 0 (or vice versa).

Another pitfall is that a Python-level function call is expensive. Suppose you want to time how long it takes to add 1 to 2 in Python. Here's a poor approach that illustrates several pitfalls:

```
def add(i, j):
    i + j

def timer(n):
    start = now( )
    for i in range(n):
        add(1, 2)
    finish = now( )
    # Return average elapsed time per call
    return (finish - start) / n
```

Mostly, this program measures the time to call add, which should be obvious. What's less obvious is that it's also timing how long it takes to build a list of n integers, including the time Python takes to allocate memory for each of n integer objects, fiddle with each integer object's reference count, and free the memory again for each.

All of this is more expensive than what add's body does. In other words, the thing you're trying to time is lost in the timing approach's overhead.

It helps to build the list of timing loop indexes outside the range of the bracketing now calls, which you'll often see done. It helps even more to build the list in a different way, reusing the same object n times. This helps because the reference-count manipulations hit the same piece of memory each time instead of leaping all over memory because the i index variable is bound and unbound as the for loop proceeds:

```
def add(i, j, indices):
    for k in indices: i + j

def timer(n):
    indices = [None] * n  # may be more convenient as a module global
    start = now()
    add(1, 2, indices)
    finish = now()
    return (finish - start) / n
```

Putting i+j on the same line as the for clause is another subtle trick. Because they're on the same line, we avoid measuring time consumed by the Python SET_LINENO opcode that the Python compiler would generate (if run without the -0 switch) if the two pieces of code were on different lines.

There's one more twist I recommend here. No matter how quiet you try to make your machine, modern operating systems and modern CPUs are so complex that it's almost impossible to get the same result from one run to the next. If you find that hard to believe, it's especially valuable to run the timer body inside another loop to accumulate the results from several runs of add:

```
def timer(n_per_call, n_calls):
    indices = [None] * n_per_call
    results = []
    for i in range(n_calls):
        start = now()
        add(1, 2, indices)
        finish = now()
        results.append((finish - start) / n_per_call)
    results.sort()
    return results

print "microseconds per add:"
for t in timer(100000, 10):
    print "%.3f" % (t * 1e6),
print
```

Here's output from a typical run on an 866-MHz Windows 98SE box using time.clock:

```
microseconds per add:
0.520 0.549 0.932 0.987 1.037 1.073 1.126 1.133 1.138 1.313
```

Note that the range between the fastest and slowest computed average times spans a factor of 2.5! If I had run the test only once, I might have gotten any of these values and put too much faith in them.

If you try this, your results should be less frightening. Getting repeatable timings is more difficult under Windows 98SE than under any other operating system I've tried, so the wild results above should be viewed as an extreme. More likely (if you're not running Windows 98), you'll see a bimodal distribution with most values clustered around the fast end and a few at the slow end. The slowest result is often computed on the first try, because your machine's caches take extra time to adjust to the new task.

As befits a chapter on algorithms, the recipes here have nothing in common. Rather, it's a grab-bag of sundry interesting techniques, ranging from two-dimensional geometry to parsing date strings. Let your natural interests guide you. I have a special fondness for Recipe 17.15: it's a near-trivial wrapper around the standard `bisect.insert` function. Why is that so cool? On three occasions I've recommended using the same trick to coworkers in need of a priority queue. Each time, when I explained that `bisect` maintains the queue as a sorted list, they were worried that this would be too inefficient to bear. The attraction of getting a priority queue with no work on their part overcame their reluctance, though, and, when I asked a month later, they were still using it—performance was not a real problem. So if the previous discussion of timing difficulties discouraged you, here's cause for optimism: as noted innumerable times by innumerable authors, the speed of most of your code doesn't matter at all. Find the 10% that consumes most of the time before worrying about any of it.

17.1   Testing if a Variable Is Defined

Credit: Hamish Lawson

Problem

You want to take different courses of action based on whether a variable is defined.

Solution

In Python, all variables are expected to be defined before use. The `None` object is a value you often assign to signify that you have no real value for a variable, as in:

```
try: x
except NameError: x = None
```

Then it's easy to test whether a variable is bound to `None`:

```
if x is None:
    some_fallback_operation( )
```

```
    else:
        some_operation(x)
```

Discussion

Python doesn't have a specific function to test whether a variable is defined, since all variables are expected to have been defined before use, even if initially assigned the None object. Attempting to access a variable that hasn't previously been defined raises a NameError exception (which you can handle with a try/except statement, as you can for any other Python exception).

It is considered unusual in Python not to know whether a variable has already been defined. But if you are nevertheless in this situation, you can make sure that a given variable is in fact defined (as None, if nothing else) by attempting to access it inside a try clause and assigning it the None object if the access raises a NameError exception. Note that None is really nothing magical, just a built-in object used by convention (and returned by functions that exit without returning anything specific). You can use any other value suitable for your purposes to initialize undefined variables; for a powerful and interesting example, see Recipe 5.23.

Instead of ensuring that a variable is initialized, you may prefer to test whether it's defined where you want to use it:

```
try: x
except NameError: some_fallback_operation( )
else: some_operation(x)
```

This is a perfectly acceptable alternative to the code in the recipe, and some would say it's more Pythonic. Note, however, that if you choose this alternative, you have to code things in this order: the anomalous, error case first, then the normal, no-error case. With the recipe's approach, you may want to invert the guard condition to if x is not None and code the normal case first. These points are minutiae, to be sure, but sometimes clarity can be improved this way. Furthermore, you must be careful to avoid the variation in this alternative:

```
try:
    x
    some_operation(x)
except NameError:
    some_fallback_operation( )
```

In this variation, the call to some_operation is also covered by the exception handler, so if there is a bug in the some_operation function, or in any function called from it, this code would mask the bug and apparently proceed to operate normally when it should fail with an error message. You should always be careful that your try clauses (in try/except statements) do not accidentally cover more code than you actually intend to cover, which might easily mask bugs. The else clause in the try/except statement is for code that should execute only if no exception was raised but should not itself be covered by the exception handler, because you do not expect exceptions from it and want to diagnose the problem immediately if exceptions do occur.

Many situations that you might think would naturally give rise to undefined variables, such as processing configuration files or web forms, are handled better by employing a dictionary and testing for the presence of a key (with the has_key method, a try/except, or the get or setdefault methods of dictionary objects). For example, instead of dealing with a user configuration file this way:

```
execfile('userconfig')
try: background_color
except NameError: background_color = 'black'
try: foreground_color
except NameError: foreground_color = 'white'
...
```

do it this way:

```
config = dict(globals())
execfile('userconfig', config)
background_color = config.get('background_color', 'black')
foreground_color = config.get('foreground_color', 'white')
...
```

dict requires Python 2.2, but you can get a similar effect in earlier versions of Python by using config = globals().copy() instead. Using an explicitly specified dictionary for exec, eval, and execfile is advisable anyway, to keep your namespace under control. One of the many benefits of using such an explicitly specified dictionary is, as shown here, that you don't need to worry about undefined variables but can simply use the dictionary's get method to fetch each key with an explicitly specified default value to be used if the key is not present in the dictionary.

If you know for sure which namespace the variable is in (i.e., specifically locals or specifically globals), you can also use methods such as has_key or get on the relevant dictionary. However, variables that are in neither locals nor globals may exist (thanks to the nested scopes feature that is optional in Python 2.1, but is always on in Python 2.2 and later). Also, the special namespace directories returned by locals and globals are not suitable for mutating methods such as setdefault, so you're still better off arranging to use your own explicit dictionary rather than the local or global namespaces, whenever that's feasible.

See Also

Recipe 5.23.

17.2 Evaluating Predicate Tests Across Sequences

Credit: Jon Dyte

Problem

You need to know whether all items in a sequence satisfy a certain predicate or if only some of them do.

Solution

The simplest approach for either problem is to loop on the sequence and return a result as soon as it's known, just as the and and or Python operators short-circuit logical evaluation:

```
def every (pred, seq):
    """ true if pred(x) is true for all x in seq, else false """
    for x in seq:
        if not pred(x): return 0
    return 1

def any (pred, seq):
    """ false if pred(x) is false for all x in seq, else true """
    for x in seq:
        if pred(x): return 1
    return 0
```

Discussion

Often, it is useful to know whether all elements of a sequence meet certain criteria or if only some do. The two functions every and any do just that, with the simplest, and thus clearest, approach:

```
>>> every(lambda c: c > 5, (6, 7, 8, 9))
1
>>> every(lambda c: c > 5, (6, 4, 8, 9))
0
>>> any(lambda c: c > 5, (6, 7, 8, 9))
1
>>> any(lambda c: c < 5, (6, 7, 8, 9))
0
```

If you want to get fancy, here are two more techniques (perhaps with some performance gain, though you shouldn't take my word for it—always measure performance for the specific cases you need):

```
def every(pred, seq): return len(seq) == len(filter(pred, seq))
def any(pred, seq): return len(filter(pred, seq))
```

or:

```
import operator
def every(pred, seq):
    return reduce(operator.and_, map(pred, seq))
def any(pred, seq):
    return reduce(operator.or_, map(pred, seq))
```

Functional forms are elegant and often fast, as long as they do not involve a `lambda`.

17.3 Removing Duplicates from a Sequence

Credit: Tim Peters

Problem

You have a sequence that may include duplicates, and you need to remove the duplicates in the fastest possible way without knowing much about the properties of the items in the sequence. You do not care about the order of items in the resulting sequence.

Solution

The key is to try several approaches, fastest first, and use try/except to handle the failing cases of the fastest approaches:

```
def unique(s):
    """ Return a list of the elements in s in arbitrary order, but without
    duplicates. """

    # Get the special case of an empty s out of the way very rapidly
    n = len(s)
    if n == 0:
        return []

    # Try using a dict first, because it's the fastest and will usually work
    u = {}
    try:
        for x in s:
            u[x] = 1
    except TypeError:
        del u  # Move on to the next method
    else:
        return u.keys()

    # Since you can't hash all elements, try sorting, to bring equal items
    # together and weed them out in a single pass
    try:
        t = list(s)
        t.sort()
    except TypeError:
        del t  # Move on to the next method
```

```
        else:
            assert n > 0
            last = t[0]
            lasti = i = 1
            while i < n:
                if t[i] != last:
                    t[lasti] = last = t[i]
                    lasti += 1
                i += 1
            return t[:lasti]

        # Brute force is all that's left
        u = []
        for x in s:
            if x not in u:
                u.append(x)
        return u
```

Discussion

The purpose of this recipe's unique function is to take a sequence s as an argument
and return a list of the items in s in arbitrary order, but without duplicates. For example, calling unique([1, 2, 3, 1, 2, 3]) returns an arbitrary permutation of [1, 2, 3],
calling unique("abcabc") returns an arbitrary permutation of ["a", "b", "c"], and
calling unique(([1, 2], [2, 3], [1, 2])) returns an arbitrary permutation of [[2, 3],
[1, 2]].

The fastest way to remove duplicates from a sequence depends on some pretty subtle properties of the sequence elements, such as whether they're hashable and
whether they support full comparisons. The unique function shown in this recipe
tries three methods, from fastest to slowest, letting runtime exceptions pick the best
method available for the sequence at hand.

For best speed, all sequence elements should be hashable. When they are, the unique
function will usually work in linear time (i.e., O(N), or directly proportional to the
number of elements in the input, which is a good and highly scalable performance
characteristic).

If it turns out that hashing the elements (using them as dictionary keys) is not possible, the next best thing is that the elements enjoy a total ordering. If list(s).sort()
doesn't raise a TypeError, we can assume that s's elements do enjoy a total ordering.
Then unique will usually work in O(N×log(N)) time. Note that Python lists' sort
method was specially designed to be highly efficient in the presence of many duplicate
elements, so the sorting approach may be more effective in Python than elsewhere.

If sorting also turns out to be impossible, the sequence elements must at least support equality testing, or else the very concept of duplicates can't really be meaningful
for them. In this case, unique works in quadratic time (i.e., O(N^2), or proportional to
the square of the number of elements in the input, which is not very scalable, but is

the least of all evils, given the sequence item's obviously peculiar nature if we get all the way to this subcase).

This is a pure example of how algorithm efficiency depends on the strength of the assumptions you can make about the data. Of course, you could split this into three distinct functions and directly call the one that best meets your needs. In practice, however, the brute-force method is so slow for large sequences that nothing measurable is lost by simply letting the function as written try the faster methods first.

If you need to preserve the same order of items in the output sequence as in the input sequence, see Recipe 17.4.

See Also

Recipe 17.4.

17.4 Removing Duplicates from a Sequence While Maintaining Sequence Order

Credit: Alex Martelli

Problem

You have a sequence that may include duplicates, and you need to remove the duplicates in the fastest possible way. Also, the output sequence must respect the item ordering of the input sequence.

Solution

The need to respect the item ordering of the input sequence means that picking unique items will be a very different problem than that explored in Recipe 17.3. This kind of need often arises in conjunction with a function f that defines an equivalence relation among items (i.e., x is equivalent to y if and only if f(x)==f(y)), in which case the need to remove duplicates may be better described as picking the first representative of each occurring equivalence class:

```
# f defines an equivalence relation among items of sequence seq, and
# f(x) must be hashable for each item x of seq (e.g., cPickle.dumps)
def uniquer(seq, f=None):
    """ Keeps earliest occurring item of each f-defined equivalence class """
    if f is None:    # f's default is the identity function
        def f(x): return x
    already_seen = {}
    result = []
    for item in seq:
        marker = f(item)
        # Python 2.2-ism; in older Pythons, use not already_seen.get(marker, 0)
        if marker not in already_seen:
```

```
                    already_seen[marker] = 1
                    result.append(item)
        return result
```

Picking the most recent (last occurring) representative of each equivalence class is a bit harder:

```
    def uniquest(seq, f=None):
        """ Keeps last occurring item of each f-defined equivalence class.
        However, it's O(N+N1*log(N1)), in which N1 is the count of "unique" items. """
        import sys
        if f is None:
            def f(x): return x
        already_seen = {}
        for item, index in zip(seq, xrange(sys.maxint)):
            marker = f(item)
            already_seen[marker] = index, item
        auxlist = already_seen.values()
        auxlist.sort()     # the O(N1*log(N1)) step
        return [item for index, item in auxlist]


    def uniquique(seq, f=None):
        """ Keeps last occurring item of each f-defined equivalence class.
        O(N), but slower than uniquest in many practical cases. """
        if f is None:
            def f(x): return x
        already_seen = {}
        result = []
        seq = list(seq)
        seq.reverse()
        for item in seq:
            marker = f(item)
            # Python 2.2-ism; in older Pythons, use not already_seen.get(marker, 0)
            if marker not in already_seen:
                already_seen[marker] = 1
                result.append(item)
        result.reverse()
        return result


    def uniquoque(seq, f=None):
        """ Keeps last occurring item of each f-defined equivalence class.
        Also O(N). """
        import sys
        if f is None:
            def f(x): return x
        where_seen = {}
        output_this_item = [0]*len(seq)
        for item, index in zip(seq, xrange(sys.maxint)):
            marker = f(item)
            previously_seen = where_seen.get(marker)
            if previously_seen is not None:
                output_this_item[previously_seen] = 0
            output_this_item[index] = 1
            where_seen[marker] = index
```

```
    return [item for item, output_this in zip(seq, output_this_item)
            if output_this]
```

These functions can be made more general (without adding substantial complication) by adding another argument p, which is a function that picks the most suitable item of each equivalence class, either when presented with a pair of candidates (index and item) or with a list of indexes and items for each whole equivalence class:

```
def fancy_unique(seq, f, p):
    """ Keeps "most-appropriate" item of each f-defined equivalence class,
    with precedence function p doing pairwise choice of (index, item) """
    already_seen = {}
    for item, index in zip(seq, xrange(sys.maxint)):
        marker = f(item)
        if already_seen.has_key(marker):  # or, "if marker in already_seen"
            # It's NOT a problem to rebind index and item within the
            # for loop: the next leg of the loop does not use their binding
            index, item = p((index, item), already_seen[marker])
        already_seen[marker] = index, item
    auxlist = already_seen.values()
    auxlist.sort()
    return [item for index, item in auxlist]

def fancier_uniquer(seq, f, p):
    """ Keeps "most-appropriate" item of each f-defined equivalence class,
    with precedence function p choosing appropriate (index, item) for each
    equivalence class from the list of candidates passed to it """
    already_seen = {}
    for item, index in zip(seq, xrange(sys.maxint)):
        marker = f(item)
        already_seen.setdefault(marker, []).append((index, item))
    auxlist = [p(candidates) for candidates in already_seen.values()]
    auxlist.sort()
    return [item for index, item in auxlist]
```

Discussion

Recipe 17.3 is applicable only if you do not care about item ordering or, in other words, if the sequences involved are meaningful only as sets of items, which is often the case. When sequential order is significant, a different approach is needed.

If the items are hashable, it's not hard to maintain sequence order, keeping only the first occurrence of each value. If the items are not hashable, but are of types supported by cPickle.dumps, it might be worth using this function for long-enough sequences. Another possibility suggested by this approach is to handle uniqueness within equivalence classes. In other words, have the uniqueness function accept as an argument a function f that must return hashable objects, such that f(x)==f(y) if and only if items x and y are equivalent. Identity (in the mathematical sense, not in the Python sense) is used as the default if no argument f is supplied, but the caller can pass cPickle.dumps or whatever other equivalence-defining function is appropriate. This approach is shown in the uniquer function in the solution.

If you need to keep the last occurring rather than the earliest occurrence of an item in each equivalence class, a different approach may be appropriate, as shown in the uniquest function in the solution. In this case, we do one pass through the input sequence, associating the latest index in it to each equivalence class, then sort those indexes to reconstruct the ordering for the output sequence.

However, the sort degrades performance to $O(N1 \times \log(N1))$, in which $N1$ is the number of unique items. To keep the last occurring with $O(N)$ performance, it's simplest to reverse the input sequence (or a copy thereof into a local list, since the input sequence might be immutable) and reverse the result, as shown in uniquique. An alternative approach, shown in uniquoque, is to build and maintain a list of flags parallel to seq, in which each flag is true if and only if the corresponding item must be part of the output sequence. Then we can use a list comprehension (or a loop) to build the output in a separate second pass. Each of these general idioms has many uses and is worth keeping in mind as a worthwhile sequence-processing technique.

But coming back to uniquest, it's interesting to notice that it easily generalizes to cases in which the choice among multiple items in the same equivalence class depends on an arbitrary precedence function p that considers both the actual items and their indexes of occurrence. As long as function p can operate pairwise, you only need to replace the simple assignment used in uniquest:

```
already_seen[marker] = index, item
```

with a call to the precedence function, which returns the (index, item) pair for the chosen occurrence among the two. Precedence functions that need to examine the whole set of equivalent items to make their choice can also be accommodated, of course, but you need to build the set in one pass and perform only the selections when that pass is finished. These fancy approaches are clearly only useful for substantial equivalence functions (not for identity, nor for functions meant to act as proxies for identity, such as cPickle.dumps), so f defaulting to the identity function has been removed from the fancy_unique and fancier_uniquer functions, which show these (perhaps overgeneralized) approaches.

An example of fancy_unique may help. Say we're given a list of words, and we need to get a sublist from it, respecting order, such that no two words on the sublist begin with the same letter. Out of all the words in the original list that begin with each given letter, we need to keep the longest word and, in case of equal lengths, the word appearing later on the list. This sounds complicated, but with fancy_unique to help us, it's really not that bad:

```
def complicated_choice(words):
    def first_letter(aword): return aword[0].lower()
    def prefer((indx1, word1), (indx2, word2)):
        if len(word2) > len(word1): return indx2, word2
```

```
    else: return indx1, word1
  return fancy_unique(words, first_letter, prefer)
```

The prefer function is simplified, because it knows fancy_unique always calls it with indx2<indx1. So the older indx2, word2 pair must be returned only when word2 is longer than word1; otherwise, indx1, word1 is always the proper result. The automatic tuple unpacking in prefer's signature is debatable, stylewise, but I personally like it (it reminds me of Haskell).

Out of all the general programming techniques presented in the various functions of this recipe, that of writing higher-order functions, which organize a computation and appropriately call back to functions they receive as arguments, is easily the most precious. This is well worth keeping in mind in several circumstances, and not just for old Haskell-heads, as it often works great in Python.

See Also

Recipe 17.3.

17.5 Simulating the Ternary Operator in Python

Credit: Jürgen Hermann, Alex Martelli, Oliver Steele, Lloyd Goldwasser, Chris Perkins, and Brent Burley

Problem

You want to express in Python the equivalent of C's so-called ternary operator ?: (as in, *condition?iftrue:iffalse*).

Solution

There are many ways to skin a ternary operator. An explicit if/else is most Pythonic, but somewhat verbose:

```
for i in range(1, 3):
    if i == 1:
        plural = ''
    else:
        plural = 's'
    print "The loop ran %d time%s" % (i, plural)
```

Indexing is compact if there are no side effects in the *iftrue* and *iffalse* expressions:

```
for i in range(1, 3):
    print "The loop ran %d time%s" % (i, ('', 's')[i != 1])
```

For the specific case of plurals, there's also a neat variant using slicing:

```
for i in range(1, 3):
    print "The loop ran %d time%s" % (i, "s"[i==1:])
```

Short-circuited logical expressions can deal correctly with side effects:

```
for i in range(1, 3):
    print "The loop ran %d time%s" % (i, i != 1 and 's' or '')
```

The output of each of these loops is:

```
The loop ran 1 time
The loop ran 2 times
```

However, the short circuit (which is necessary when either or both of *iftrue* and *iffalse* have side effects) fails if turned around:

```
for i in range(1, 3):
    print "The loop ran %d time%s" % (i, i == 1 and '' or 's')
```

Since `''` evaluates as false, this snippet outputs:

```
The loop ran 1 times
The loop ran 2 times
```

So generally, when *iftrue* and *iffalse* are unknown at coding time (either could have side effects or be false), we need:

```
for i in range(1, 3):
    print "The loop ran %d time%s" % (i, (i == 1 and [''] or ['s'])[0])
```

or:

```
for i in range(1, 3):
    print "The loop ran %d time%s" % (i, (lambda:'', lambda:'s')[i!=1]())
```

or even weirder variations:

```
for i in range(1, 3):
    print "The loop ran %d time%s" % (i, [i==1 and '', i!=1 and 's'][i!=1])
for i in range(1, 3):
    print "The loop ran %d time%s" % (
        i, (i==1 and (lambda:'') or (lambda:'s'))())
```

And now for something completely different (for plurals only, again):

```
for i in range(1, 3):
    print "The loop ran %d time%s" % (i, 's'*(i!=1))
```

Discussion

Programmers coming to Python from C, C++, or Perl sometimes miss the so-called ternary operator ?:. It's most often used for avoiding a few lines of code and a temporary variable for simple decisions, such as printing the plural form of words after a counter, as in this recipe's examples. In most cases, Python's preference for making things clear and explicit at the cost of some conciseness is an acceptable tradeoff, but one can sympathize with the withdrawal symptoms of ternary-operator addicts.

99.44 times out of 100, you will be better off using a plain if/else statement (perhaps in a named local function if you wanted an if/else that fits in an expression to fit that expression inside a lambda form). But for the remaining 56 cases out of 10,000, the idioms in this recipe can be useful. A typical case would be if you're transliterating from another language into Python and need to keep program structure as close as possible to the original, as mentioned in Recipe 1.9.

There are several ways to get the ternary operator effect in Python, and this recipe tries to display a fair selection of the wide range of possibilities. One can always, after all, use a good old if/else statement. Indexing can help, and, for the specific case of plurals, there's a neat variant of it based on slicing. However, neither indexing nor slicing apply to cases in which either or both of the *iftrue* and *iffalse* expressions may have side effects. If such side effects are an issue, the short-circuiting effect of and/or can be used, but care may be needed if we don't know (at coding time) if *iftrue* and *iffalse* have side effects; they might also be Python values evaluated as false. To meet both the side-effect issue and the might-be-false risk, two variants in this recipe mix indexing and function calling or a lambda form, but this starts to verge on an excess of subtlety! Just to dispell any doubt, even weirder mixtures of lambda and indexing or short-circuiting are shown at the end of this recipe.

See Also

Recipe 1.9.

17.6 Counting Items and Sorting by Incidence (Histograms)

Credit: John Jensen, Fred Bremmer

Problem

You need to produce ascending- or descending-count histograms, such as the most or least common words in a file, popular pages on a web site, etc.

Solution

Histogramming is basically an issue of counting item occurrences (a Python dictionary makes this quite easy) and sorting by the counts. In Python, the two actions, and the dictionary that holds the counts, are easily wrapped into a class:

```
class Counter:
    def __init__(self):
        self.dict = {}
    def add(self, item):
        count = self.dict.get(item, 0)
        self.dict[item] = count + 1
    def counts(self, desc=None):
        """ Returns list of keys sorted by values.
        Pass desc as 1 if you want a descending sort. """
```

```
result = map(None, self.dict.values(), self.dict.keys())
result.sort()
if desc: result.reverse()
return result
```

Discussion

The add method shows the normal Python idiom for counting occurrences of arbitrary (but hashable) items, using a dictionary to hold the counts. The counts method is where all the action is. It takes the dictionary and produces an ascending or descending sort of keys by values, returning a list of pairs representing the desired histogram. The map call takes advantage of an interesting but little-known tidbit of documented Python behavior. While the values and keys methods of a dictionary return their results in an arbitrary order, the ordering is compatible when the two methods are called without any intervening modification to the dictionary object. In other words, d[d.keys()[x]] is d.values(x) for any valid index x. This lets us elegantly zip values and keys with the value as the first item and the key as the second item in each pair, so the sort method will work right (by using map with a first argument of None rather than zip, we keep compatibility with 1.5.2).

Here is an example:

```
sentence = "Hello there this is a test.  Hello there this was a test, " \
           "but now it is not."
words = sentence.split()
c = Counter()
for word in words:
    c.add(word)
print "Ascending count:"
print c.counts()
print "Descending count:"
print c.counts(1)
```

This produces:

```
Ascending count:
[(1, 'but'), (1, 'it'), (1, 'not.'), (1, 'now'), (1, 'test,'), (1, 'test.'),
(1, 'was'), (2, 'Hello'), (2, 'a'), (2, 'is'), (2, 'there'), (2, 'this')]
Descending count:
[(2, 'this'), (2, 'there'), (2, 'is'), (2, 'a'), (2, 'Hello'), (1, 'was'),
(1, 'test.'), (1, 'test,'), (1, 'now'), (1, 'not.'), (1, 'it'), (1, 'but')]
```

If you give up on 1.5.2 compatibility and use a list comprehension instead of the map call, the code arguably becomes a little easier to read:

```
def counts(self, desc=None):
    result = [(val, key) for key, val in self.dict.items()]
    result.sort()
    if desc: result.reverse()
    return result
```

However, if this issue ever arises in a spot of your program that is a critical speed bottleneck, you should measure performance accurately for each version of counts. Often (but not always), map displays surprisingly good performance characteristics when compared to list comprehensions (at least when no lambda is involved in the use of map).

17.7 Memoizing (Caching) the Return Values of Functions

Credit: Paul Moore

Problem

You have a pure function that is often called with the same arguments (particularly a recursive function) and is slow to compute its results, and you are looking for a simple way to gain substantial performance.

Solution

The key idea behind memoizing is to store a function's results in a dictionary, keyed by the arguments that produce each result. Of course, this makes sense only for a pure function (i.e., one that yields the same result when called repeatedly with given arguments). It's easy to memoize a function by hand. For example, using the recursive Fibonacci function:

```
fib_memo = {}
def fib(n):
    if n < 2: return 1
    if not fib_memo.has_key(n):
        fib_memo[n] = fib(n-1) + fib(n-2)
    return fib_memo[n]
```

Having to code the memoization inside each function to be memoized, however, is repetitive and interferes with the function's readability. A good alternative is to encapsulate the memoization mechanics into a class:

```
class Memoize:
    def __init__(self, fn):
        self.fn = fn
        self.memo = {}
        self.cacheable = self.misses = self.noncacheable = 0L
    def __call__(self, *args, **kwds):
        if not kwds:
            self.cacheable += 1
            try: return self.memo[args]
            except KeyError:
                self.misses += 1
                self.memo[args] = self.fn(*args)
                return self.memo[args]
```

```
        except TypeError: self.cacheable -= 1
    self.noncacheable += 1
    return self.fn(*args, **kwds)
```

Using this class to memoize fib, the function definition becomes obvious without caching boilerplate to obscure the algorithm. However, you must assign the Memoize instance to the same name, fib, as the recursive function. Otherwise, the recursive calls bypass the memoizing:

```
def fib(n):
    if n < 2: return 1
    return fib(n-1) + fib(n-2)
fib = Memoize(fib)
```

For functions that take mutable arguments, you can sometimes use the cPickle module to memoize them anyway:

```
class MemoizeMutable:
    def __init__(self, fn):
        self.fn = fn
        self.memo = {}
    def __call__(self, *args, **kwds):
        import cPickle
        str = cPickle.dumps(args, 1)+cPickle.dumps(kwds, 1)
        if not self.memo.has_key(str):
            self.memo[str] = self.fn(*args, **kwds)
        return self.memo[str]
```

Discussion

The Memoize class is instantiated with one argument, a function f, and returns an instance that acts like f but memoizes its arguments and result if the actual arguments to a call are hashable (nonmutable) and positional. Calls with mutable or keyword arguments are counted in the x.noncacheable instance attribute, cacheable calls are counted in the x.cacheable instance attribute, and cache misses in cacheable calls are counted in the x.misses attribute. Unless x.misses and x.noncacheable are low compared to x.cacheable, you're better off not memoizing the function. So do a few dry runs that are representative of your intended production usage to examine these statistics and decide if memoization is worth using for your specific application.

As we've already noted in the recipe's example of the Memoize class, it is important that the value of fib is replaced by the memoized version. Storing the memoized version elsewhere, as in memoized_fib = Memoize(fib), will not work, because the recursive calls will then call fib directly, bypassing the cache. This is an issue only for recursive functions, but since recursive functions are prime candidates for memoizing, it's worth keeping in mind.

Obviously, functions to be memoized must be pure (i.e., they must have no side effects and must always return the same value whenever they are called with the same set of arguments). More significantly, the Memoize class (and the inline version above) does not memoize calls that receive mutable arguments, such as `len` on a list. (Note that you cannot memoize functions that change their mutable arguments because they are not pure functions). `MemoizeMutable` weakens this constraint a bit and also accepts named arguments, as long as all arguments can be handled by the `cPickle` module (most types can, but by no means all).

`Memoize` and friends cannot really check the semantics of the functions you wrap in them. In other words, the notions of "same value" and "same set of arguments" are somewhat vaguely defined in many cases, so take care. `Memoize` does try to field occasional calls with keyword and mutable arguments (with an interesting mix of checking and try/except), but performance will suffer unless such cases are occasional. As we already noted, `Memoize` also keeps counts of cacheable calls, noncacheable calls, and misses. This is a bit of overhead, so you may want to rip the count-keeping out for a lighter, faster, simpler version of `Memoize` once you've taken all the measurements you need to convince yourself that memoizing is a good choice for a given function. `MemoizeMutable`, just to highlight the contrast, does not try to field nonpicklable arguments and uses checking instead of try/except to detect cache misses (but if you have many hits and few misses, try/except can be a bit faster).

One possible enhancement, like for all caching approaches, would be to use weak references (from the `weakref` standard module), rather than normal references, for the `self.memo` cache. This may weaken the cache by reducing its hit rate, but as a plus, it avoids keeping objects alive just because the cache is holding on to them. The trade-off crucially depends on the specifics of your application, so be sure to consider it carefully. For details on weak references, see *http://python.sourceforge.net/ peps/pep-0205.html*.

A similar approach could be used to cache results from external processes (i.e., commands). However, in this case it becomes less feasible to ensure that the crucial characteristics of no side effects and the same results for a given set of arguments are in place, so issues naturally arise about more complex procedures, such as time-based cache expiration, LRU disciplines, and so on. All in all, including such extras in this recipe would complicate it enormously without offering substantial benefits for typical cases. The possibilities mentioned here should, however, be kept in mind for those complicated cases in which they might come in handy.

17.8 Looking Up Words by Sound Similarity

Credit: Greg Jorgensen, Scott David Daniels

Problem

You need to look up words (most often people's surnames) by sound, rather than by spelling, so that likely spelling mistakes don't spoil the search.

Solution

The Soundex algorithm (by Odell and Russell, made popular by Knuth) transforms each surname into a signature that is more representative of how that surname is likely to sound when pronounced than of how it's spelled:

```python
def soundex(name, len=4):
    """ soundex module conforming to Odell-Russell algorithm """

    # digits holds the soundex values for the alphabet
    soundex_digits = '01230120022455012623010202'
    sndx = ''
    fc = ''

    # Translate letters in name to soundex digits
    for c in name.upper():
        if c.isalpha():
            if not fc: fc = c    # Remember first letter
            d = soundex_digits[ord(c)-ord('A')]
            # Duplicate consecutive soundex digits are skipped
            if not sndx or (d != sndx[-1]):
                sndx += d

    # Replace first digit with first letter
    sndx = fc + sndx[1:]

    # Remove all 0s from the soundex code
    sndx = sndx.replace('0', '')

    # Return soundex code truncated or 0-padded to len characters
    return (sndx + (len * '0'))[:len]
```

Discussion

The common approach to avoiding confusion when a name's spelling induces lookup errors is the Soundex algorithm, by Odell and Russell, as reported by Knuth. The algorithm is designed for English-language surnames. If you have a significant number of non-English surnames, you might want to alter the values in digits to improve your matches. For example, to accommodate a large number of Spanish surnames, you might count "J" and "L" ("L" because of how "ll" is used) as vowels, setting their positions in digits to 0.

The basic assumptions of Soundex are that the consonants are more important than the vowels, and they are placed in groups of letters that can be confused with each other. Coming up with a set of such groups for a language is not horribly tough if you know that language's typical pronunciation issues. Just remember that each group should contain all letters that can be confused with any of those in the group.

For example, a slightly better code for both English and Spanish names has the digits "01230120002055012623010202".

In languages such as Italian, which has strong and very distinct vowels, the basic assumptions of Soundex break down. There, vowels should probably play a contrary role, that of anchors that cannot be confused with each other. However, Italian phonetics teaches us that this is true to a varying degree, depending in part on where the phonic accent falls in the surname—semivowels in destressed syllables are not good anchors—and these complications are somewhat difficult to handle in a simple-minded, speedy algorithm.

See Also

Soundex is described in Donald Knuth's *The Art of Computer Programming* (Addison-Wesley), which is discussed at *http://www-cs-staff.stanford.edu/~knuth/taocp.html*.

17.9 Computing Factorials with lambda

Credit: Anurag Uniyal

Problem

You want to write a recursive function, such as a factorial, using `lambda` (you probably made a bet about whether it could be done).

Solution

Use a short-circuiting, ternary-operator idiom and, crucially, bind the `lambda` form to a name, so it can recurse:

```
f = lambda n: n-1 + abs(n-1) and f(n-1)*n or 1
```

Discussion

This recipe implements the recursive definition of the factorial function as a `lambda` form. Since `lambda` forms can only be expressions, this is slightly tricky, since `if`/`else` is a statement, and therefore not allowed inside an expression. Still, a short-circuiting form of a Python idiom for a conditional (ternary) operator takes care of that (see Recipe 17.5 for other ways to simulate the ternary operator, both with and without short-circuiting).

The real issue, of course, is that since `lambda`'s forte is making anonymous functions, how then do we recurse? This question is what makes this recipe's subject a good bet to win a drink from your Python-using friends and acquaintances who are misguided enough that they have not yet read this book cover to cover.

Just make sure the terms of the bet mention only `lambda` and do *not* specify that the resulting function will be left unnamed. Some might consider this cheating, but we Python programmers are a bunch of pragmatists. Thus, we simply bind a name to the `lambda` form with an assignment statement, and in the body of the `lambda` itself, we use the name to which we will assign the `lambda`. Since the body executes only when the `lambda` is called (not at the time it's created), the name will be bound by the time we use it. And the bet is won!

See Also

Recipe 17.5 for other ways to simulate the ternary operator.

17.10 Generating the Fibonacci Sequence

Credit: Tom Good

Problem

You need to implement a Python 2.2 generator for an infinite sequence, for example, the Fibonacci sequence.

Solution

Python 2.2's generators provide a wonderful way to implement infinite sequences, given their intrinsically lazy-evaluation semantics:

```
from __future__ import generators

def fib():
    "unbounded generator, creates Fibonacci sequence"
    x = 0
    y = 1
    while 1:
        x, y = y, x + y
        yield x

if __name__ == "__main__":
    g = fib()
    for i in range(9):
        print g.next(),
    print
```

Discussion

Python 2.2 generators let you work with infinite (unbounded) sets. As shown in this recipe, it is easy to create a generator that produces the Fibonacci sequence. Running the recipe's script produces the following result:

```
c:\python22> python fib.py
 1 1 2 3 5 8 13 21 34
```

In Python 2.2, if you start your module with the statement from __future__ import generators, yield becomes a keyword. (In 2.3 and later versions of Python, yield will always be a keyword; the "import from the future" statement lets you use it in 2.2, but only when you specifically request it.)

A generator is a function containing the keyword yield. When you call a generator, the function body does not execute. Rather, calling the generator gives you a special iterator object that wraps the function's body, the set of its local variables (including the arguments, which are local variables that happen to be initialized by the caller), and the current point of execution, which is initially the start of the function.

When you call this iterator object's next method, the function body executes up to the next yield statement. Then yield's argument is returned as the result of the iterator's next method, and the function is frozen with its execution state intact. When you call next again on the same iterator object, execution of the function body continues from where it left off, again up to the next yield statement to execute.

If the function body falls off the end or executes a return statement, the iterator object raises a StopIteration to indicate the end of the sequence. But, of course, if the sequence that the generator is producing is not bounded, the iterator will never raise a StopIteration. That's okay, as long as you don't rely on this as the only way to terminate a loop. In this recipe, for example, the loop's termination is controlled by an independent counter i, so the fact that g would never terminate is not a problem.

The main point to keep in mind is that it's all right to have infinite sequences represented by generators, since generators are computed lazily (in which each item is computed just in time), as long as a control structure ensures that only a finite number of items are required from the generator.

Leonardo Pisano (meaning "from Pisa"), most often called Leonardo Bigollo ("the traveler" or "the good for nothing") during his lifetime in the 12th and 13th centuries, and occasionally Leonardo Fibonacci (for his connection to the Bonacci family), must look down with considerable pride from his place in the mathematicians' Empyreon. The third problem in his Liber Abaci, which he originally expressed in terms of a rabbit-raising farm, still provides interesting applications for the distant successors of the abacus, modern computers.

See Also

Recipe 17.11 shows one approach to restriction (filtering) of potentially unbounded iterators (and thus, as a special case, generators).

17.11 Wrapping an Unbounded Iterator to Restrict Its Output

Credit: Tom Good

Problem

You need to filter the sequence produced by a potentially unbounded Python 2.2 iterator or limit the sequence length by a condition.

Solution

Python 2.2 generators are suitable for wrapping other generators (or other kinds of iterators) and tweaking their output—for example, by limiting the output's length:

```python
from __future__ import generators

def genWhile(g, condition):
    """ Run generator g, stopping when condition(g.next()) is false. condition
    can be any callable. genWhile returns an iterator. """
    g = iter(g)
    while 1:
        next = g.next()
        if condition(next):
            yield next
        else:
            return

def take(n, g):
    """ A subiterator limited to the first n items of g's sequence """
    g = iter(g)
    for i in range(n): yield g.next()

def drop(n, g):
    """ A subiterator removing the first n items from g's sequence """
    g = iter(g)
    for i in range(n): g.next()
    while 1: yield g.next()

# an example of an unbounded sequence generator
def genEven():
    x = 0
    while 1:
        x += 2
        yield x

def main():
    print [x for x in genWhile(genEven(), lambda x: x<12)]
    print [x for x in take(5, genEven())]
    print [x for x in take(5, drop(5, genEven()))]
```

Discussion

With Python 2.2 and later, you can make iterators that return unbounded output (for example, see Recipe 17.10). By creating a wrapper generator that runs another iterator, you can restrict the resulting sequence to a defined subset. The g=iter(g) idiom at the start of each wrapper in this recipe ensures that you can polymorphically wrap sequences as well as iterators (remember, all generators return iterators, but not all iterators come from generators). The iter built-in function, new in Python 2.2, can be applied to any sequence (in which case, it yields an iterator on that sequence), to any iterator (in which it yields the same iterator on which it was called), or to user-defined objects whose classes define a special method __iter__ (in this case, iter(x) is the same as x.__iter__).

The genEven generator, given in the recipe as an example, generates all positive even numbers. To see the positive even numbers less than 12, it would be tempting to write something like:

```
[x for x in genEven( ) if x < 12]
```

But this approach does not work. A list-comprehension construct cannot know that in this specific case, once x becomes greater than 12, it will never become less than 12 again. So the list comprehension would keep looking, in case an item less than 12 appears, until genEven terminates (i.e., it would keep looking, and looping, forever). Instead, we can use the genWhile wrapper to get a similar effect, as shown in the main function of the recipe.

The take and drop wrappers are also quite useful, and are patterned on the homonymous functions of Haskell, a language whose semantics are all defined in terms of lazy evaluation. Iterators are Python's systematic foray into the lazy evaluation field. Previous releases of Python had some ad hoc lazy-evaluation cases, such as xrange and xreadlines, but no systematic conceptual framework for them. Note that take limits sequence length, but drop doesn't, and drop(n, g) is also an unlimited-sequence iterator, if g is.

Also, each of these wrappers can be freely used on unbounded iterators (such as those iter(s) gives from any sequence s). If any call to g.next from inside a wrapper raises a StopIteration, the exception simply propagates and thus stops the iteration of the wrapper without fuss. So, for example, take(n, g) does not ensure that it yields exactly n items but, rather, at most n.

See Also

Recipe 17.10 shows how to make unbounded iterators; Recipe 17.12 for a more systematic approach to wrapping generators and other iterators.

17.12 Operating on Iterators

Credit: Sami Hangaslammi

Problem

You need to operate on iterators (including normal sequences) with the same semantics as normal sequence operations, except that lazy evaluation is a must, because some of the iterators involved could represent unbounded sequences.

Solution

Python 2.2 iterators are easy to handle via higher-order functions, and lazy evaluation (such as that performed by the xrange built-in function) can be generalized. Here are some elementary operations that include concatenating several iterators, terminating iteration when a function becomes false, terminating iteration after the first *n* values, and returning every nth result of an iterator:

```python
from __future__ import generators

def itercat(*iterators):
    """ Concatenate several iterators into one. """
    for i in iterators:
        i = iter(i)
        for x in i:
            yield x

def iterwhile(func, iterator):
    """ Iterate for as long as func(value) returns true. """
    iterator = iter(iterator)
    while 1:
        next = iterator.next()
        if not func(next):
            raise StopIteration      # or: return
        yield next

def iterfirst(iterator, count=1):
    """ Iterate through 'count' first values. """
    iterator = iter(iterator)
    for i in xrange(count):
        yield iterator.next()

def iterstep(iterator, n):
    """ Iterate every nth value. """
    iterator = iter(iterator)
    while 1:
        yield iterator.next()
        # Skip n-1 values
        for dummy in range(n-1):
            iterator.next()
```

A bit less elementary, but still generally useful, are functions that transform an iterator's output, not just selecting which values to return and which to skip, but actually changing the structure. For example, here is a function that bunches up an iterator's results into a sequence of tuples, each of length count:

```
from __future__ import generators

def itergroup(iterator, count, keep_partial=1):
    """ Iterate in groups of 'count' values. If there aren't enough values for
    the last group, it's padded with None's, or discarded if keep_partial is
    passed as false. """
    iterator = iter(iterator)
    while 1:
        result = [None]*count
        for x in range(count):
            try: result[x] - iterator.next()
            except StopIteration:
                if x and keep_partial: break
                else: raise
        yield tuple(result)
```

And here are generalizations to lazy evaluation of the non-lazy existing built-in Python functions zip, map, filter, and reduce:

```
from __future__ import generators

def xzip(*iterators):
    """ Iterative (lazy) version of built-in 'zip' """
    iterators = map(iter, iterators)
    while 1:
        yield tuple([x.next() for x in iterators])

def xmap(func, *iterators):
    """ Iterative (lazy) version of built-in 'map'. """
    iterators = map(iter, iterators)
    count = len(iterators)
    def values():
        # map pads shorter sequences with None when they run out of values
        result = [None]*count
        some_ok = 0
        for i in range(count):
            if iterators[i] is not None:
                try: result[i] = iterators[i].next()
                except StopIteration: iterators[i] = None
                else: some_ok = 1
        if some_ok: return tuple(result)
        else: raise StopIteration
    while 1:
        args = values()
        if func is None: yield args
        else: yield func(*args)

def xfilter(func, iterator):
    """ Iterative version of built-in 'filter' """
```

```
            iterator = iter(iterator)
            while 1:
                next = iterator.next()
                if func(next):
                    yield next

        def xreduce(func, iterator, default=None):
            """ Iterative version of built-in 'reduce' """
            iterator = iter(iterator)
            try: prev = iterator.next()
            except StopIteration: return default
            single = 1
            for next in iterator:
                single = 0
                prev = func(prev, next)
            if single:
                return func(prev, default)
            return prev
```

Discussion

This recipe is a collection of small utility functions for iterators (all functions can also be used with normal sequences). Among other things, the module presented in this recipe provides generator (lazy) versions of the built-in sequence-manipulation functions. The generators can be combined to produce a more specialized iterator. This recipe requires Python 2.2 or later, of course.

The built-in sequence-manipulation functions zip, map, and filter are specified to return sequences (and the specifications cannot be changed for backward compatibility with versions of Python before 2.2, which lacked iterators); therefore, they cannot become lazy. However, it's easy to write lazy iterator–based versions of these useful functions, as well as other iterator-manipulation functions, as exemplified in this recipe.

Of course, lazy evaluation is not terribly useful in certain cases. The semantics of reduce, for example, require that all of the sequence is evaluated anyway. While in some cases one could save some memory by looping through the sequence that the iterator yields, rather than expanding it, most often it will be more practical to use reduce(func, iterator) instead of the xreduce function presented in this recipe.

Lazy evaluation is most useful when the resulting iterator-represented sequence is used in contexts that may be able to use just a reasonably short prefix of the sequence, such as the zip function and the iterwhile and iterfirst functions in this recipe. In such cases, lazy evaluation enables free use of unbounded sequences (of course, the resulting program will terminate only if each unbounded sequence is used only in a context in which only a finite prefix of it is taken) and sequences of potentially humungous length.

See Also

Recipes 17.10 and 17.11 for other uses of iterators.

17.13 Rolling Dice

Credit: Tim Keating

Problem

You need to generate pseudo-random numbers simulating the roll of several dice, in which the number of dice and number of sides on each die are parameters.

Solution

An implicit loop performed by the reduce built-in function turns out to be the fastest solution, although this is not immediately obvious:

```
import random

def dice(num, sides):
    return reduce(lambda x, y, s=sides: x + random.randrange(s),
        range(num+1)) + num
```

If you prefer to avoid lambda in favor of a named nested function, here is an equivalent but somewhat more readable alternative:

```
def dice(num, sides):
    def accumulate(x, y, s=sides): return x + random.randrange(s)
    return reduce(accumulate, range(num+1)) + num
```

Discussion

This recipe presents a simple but subtle function that permits you to generate random numbers by emulating a dice roll. The number of dice and the number of sides on each die are the parameters of the function. For example, to roll four six-sided dice, you would call dice(4, 6). Simulating a dice roll is a good way to generate a random number with an expected binomial profile. For example, rolling three six-sided dice will generate a bell-shaped (but discrete) probability curve with an average of 10.5.

After trying a more manual approach (a for loop with an accumulator), I found that using reduce is generally faster. It's possible that this implementation could be faster still, as I haven't profiled it very aggressively. But it's fast enough for my purposes.

This recipe's use of reduce is peculiar, since the function used for the reduction actually ignores its second argument, y, which comes from the range(num+1) sequence that is being reduced. The only purpose of reduce here is to call the accumulate function (or its lambda equivalent) num times (the first time with an x of 0, since that's the first item in the range, then every other time with the previous result as argument x). Each time, the accumulate function adds a new random integer in the range from 0 included to sides excluded, which is returned from the randrange function of the random standard module. In the end, we just need to add num because each of the num random numbers was in the range 0 to sides-1 rather than from 1 to sides.

This peculiar way to use reduce does, according to measurement, appear to be marginally faster than, or at the very least equal to, some clearer and more obvious alternatives, such as:

```
def dice(num, sides):
    return reduce(operator.add,
        [random.randrange(sides) for i in range(num)]) + num
```

and:

```
def dice(num, sides):
    return reduce(operator.add, map(random.randrange, num*[sides])) + num
```

See Also

Documentation for the random standard library module the *Library Reference*.

17.14 Implementing a First-In First-Out Container

Credit: Sébastien Keim

Problem

You need a container that allows element insertion and removal, in which the first element inserted is also the first to be removed (i.e., a first-in first-out, FIFO, queue).

Solution

We can use a class to wrap a Pythonic implementation of a linked list:

```
class Fifo:
    def __init__(self):
        self.first = None
        self.last = None
    def append(self, data):
        node = [data, None]  # [payload, 'pointer'] "pair"
        if self.first is None:
            self.first = node
        else:
            self.last[1] = node
        self.last = node
    def pop(self):
        if self.first is None :
            raise IndexError
        node = self.first
```

```
            self.first = node[1]
        return node[0]

    if __name__=='__main__':  # Run a test/example when run as a script:
        a = Fifo( )
        a.append(10)
        a.append(20)
        print a.pop(0)
        a.append(5)
        print a.pop(0)
        print a.pop(0)
```

Discussion

Most likely, the best way to do a FIFO in Python is to use standard lists with append and pop(0) methods. Since lists are built-ins, they are usually far more efficient than this recipe, despite theoretical considerations of O(1) versus O(N) performance. If you want to try this, it's easy:

```
class FifoList:
    def __init__(self):
        self.data = []
    def append(self, data):
        self.data.append(data)
    def pop(self):
        return self.data.pop(0)
```

A quirky variation that ensures O(1) performance can be built on top of a dictionary:

```
class FifoList:
    def __init__(self):
        self.data = {}
        self.nextin = 0
        self.nextout = 0
    def append(self, data):
        self.nextin += 1
        self.data[self.nextin] = data
    def pop(self):
        self.nextout += 1
        result = self.data[self.nextout]
        del self.data[self.nextout]
        return result
```

I developed this recipe after I read an academic paper that said that double-linked lists were the natural way to create this kind of container (in contrast with stacks). I convinced myself that it was possible and quite natural to create a FIFO container with single-linked lists, instead. It suffices to have two references to first and last in the Fifo class itself. The class in the recipe's solution shows one way to build a single-linked list in Python via pairs that reference the actual data (also known as the payload) as their first item and use the second item to refer to another such pair (None being used as a null pointer here).

The append method builds such a pair (actually a two-item list) and threads it onto the list, altering the `first` and `last` attributes of `self` appropriately. The popmethod unthreads the node at the head of the list in a similar but mirrored way.

17.15 Modeling a Priority Queue

Credit: *Sébastien Keim*

Problem

You need a container that lets you specify the relative order of the data by priority (i.e., a priority queue).

Solution

The `bisect` module, from the standard Python library, is very handy for maintaining a sorted list:

```
import bisect

class PriorityQueue:
    def __init__(self):
        self.queue = []
    def insert(self, data, priority):
        """ Insert a new element in the queue according to its priority. """
        bisect.insert(self.queue, (priority, data))
    def pop(self):
        """ Pop the highest-priority element of the queue. """
        return self.queue.pop( )[1]

if __name__=='__main__':     # Run a test/example when run as a script:
    a=PriorityQueue( )
    a.append('L',5)
    a.append('E',4)
    a.append('L',5)
    a.append('O',8)
    a.append('H',1)

    for i in range(5):
        print a.pop(0),
    print
```

Discussion

This kind of container is generally implemented with binary trees. Since Python does not support binary trees in its standard library, I've used an ordered list instead, which the `bisect` standard module supports. If you have a great need for performance, you should have a look at the Vaults of Parnassus (*http://www.vex.net/parnassus/apyllo.py?find=tree*). The Vaults, always a good place to start searching for

Pythonic stuff, contain several Python modules and C extensions that define binary trees and similar data structures.

The key to the recipe's functioning is the insert function of the bisect standard module. insert must be called with a first argument that is a currently sorted list and an arbitrary second argument. The function inserts the second argument in the list so that the list remains sorted, and does so in logarithmic ($O(\log(N))$) time. Here, we insert the pair (priority, data). Since pairs (and other tuples, lists, and sequences in general) are compared lexicographically, this means that data will be placed in increasing order of priority. Therefore, the pop function, by getting (and removing, via the lists' pop method) the last item in list self.queue, is assured to get the item with the highest priority among those currently in the queue. It then applies indexing [1] to throw the priority away and return only the data.

See Also

Documentation on the bisect module in the *Library Reference*.

17.16 Converting Numbers to Rationals via Farey Fractions

Credit: Scott David Daniels

Problem

You have a number v (of almost any type) and need to find a rational number (in reduced form) that is as close to v as possible but with a denominator no larger than a prescribed value.

Solution

Farey fractions, whose crucial properties were studied by Cauchy, are an excellent way to find rational approximations of floating-point values:

```
def farey(v, lim):
    """ No error checking on args. lim = maximum denominator.
    Results are (numerator, denominator); (1, 0) is "infinity".
    """
    if v < 0:
        n, d = farey(-v, lim)
        return -n, d
    z = lim - lim    # Get a "0 of right type" for denominator
    lower, upper = (z, z+1), (z+1, z)
    while 1:
        mediant = (lower[0] + upper[0]), (lower[1] + upper[1])
        if v * mediant[1] > mediant[0]:
            if lim < mediant[1]: return upper
            lower = mediant
```

```
        elif v * mediant[1] == mediant[0]:
            if lim >= mediant[1]: return mediant
            if lower[1] < upper[1]: return lower
            return upper
        else:
            if lim < mediant[1]: return lower
            upper = mediant
```

For example, farey(math.pi, 100) == (22, 7).

Discussion

The rationals resulting from this algorithm are in reduced form (numerator and denominator mutually prime), but the proof, which was given by Cauchy, is rather subtle (see *http://www.cut-the-knot.com/blue/Farey.html*).

Note the trickiness with z. It is a zero of the same type as the lim argument. This lets you use longs as the limit if necessary, without paying a performance price (not even a test) when there's no such need.

To print odds, you can use:

```
n, d = farey(probability, lim)
print "Odds are %d : %d" % (n, d-n)
```

This algorithm is ideally suited for reimplementation in a lower-level language (e.g., C or assembly) if you use it heavily. Since the code uses only multiplication and addition, it can play to hardware strengths.

If you are using this in an environment where you call it with a lot of values near 0.0, 1.0, or 0.5 (or simple fractions), you may find that its convergence is too slow. You can improve its convergence in a continued fraction style by appending to the first if in the farey function:

```
if v < 0:
...
elif v < 0.5:
    n, d = farey((v-v+1)/v, lim) # lim is wrong; decide what you want
    return d, n
elif v > 1:
    intpart = floor(v)
    n, d = farey(v-intpart)
    return n+intpart*d, d
...
```

James Farey was an English surveyor who wrote a letter to the *Journal of Science* around the end of the 18th century. In that letter he observed that, while reading a privately published list of the decimal equivalents of fractions, he noticed the following: for any three consecutive fractions in the simplest terms (e.g., A/B, C/D, E/F), the middle one (C/D), called the mediant, is equal to the ratio (A + E)/(B + F). I enjoy envisioning Mr. Farey sitting up late on a rainy English night, reading tables of decimal expansions of fractions by an oil lamp. Calculation has come a long way since his day, and I'm pleased to be able to benefit from his work.

See Also

Recipe 17.17 for another mathematical evaluation recipe.

17.17 Evaluating a Polynomial

Credit: Luther Blissett

Problem

You need to evaluate a polynomial function, and you know that the obvious way to evaluate a polynomial wastes effort; therefore, Horner's well-known formula should always be used instead.

Solution

We often need to evaluate a polynomial $f(x)$, defined by its coefficients ($c[0]+c[1] \times x+c[2] \times x^2+...$), at a given point x. There is an obvious (naive) approach to this, applying the polynomial's definition directly:

```
def poly_naive(x, coeff):
    result = coeff[0]
    for i in range(1, len(coeff)):
        result = result + coeff[i] * x**i
    return result
```

However, this is a substantial waste of computational effort, since raising to a power is a time-consuming operation. Here, we're wantonly raising x to successive powers. It's better to use Horner's well-known formula, based on the observation that the polynomial formula can also be indifferently written as $c[0]+x \times (c[1]+x \times (c[2]+....$ In other words, it can be written with nested parentheses, but without raise-to-power operations, only additions and multiplications. Coding a loop for it gives us:

```
def poly_horner(x, coeff):
    result = coeff[-1]
    for i in range(-2, -len(coeff)-1, -1):
        result = result*x + coeff[i]
    return result
```

Discussion

Python programmers generally emphasize simplicity, not speed. However, when equally simple solutions exist, and one is always faster (even by a little), it seems sensible to use the faster solution. Polynomial evaluation is a case in point. The naive approach takes an addition, a multiplication, and an exponentiation for each degree of the polynomial. Horner's formula takes just a multiplication and an addition for each degree. On my system, evaluating 10,000 integer (long) polynomials of order 40 takes 3.37 seconds the naive way and 1.07 seconds the Horner way. With float arithmetic, it takes 0.53 seconds the naive way and 0.30 seconds the Horner way. Waste not, want not, I say.

See Also

Recipe 17.16 for another mathematical evaluation recipe.

17.18 Module: Finding the Convex Hull of a Set of 2D Points

Credit: Dinu C. Gherman

Convex hulls of point sets are an important building block in many computational-geometry applications. Example 17-1 calculates the convex hull of a set of 2D points and generates an Encapsulated PostScript (EPS) file to visualize it. Finding convex hulls is a fundamental problem in computational geometry and is a basic building block for solving many problems. The algorithm used here can be found in any good textbook on computational geometry, such as *Computational Geometry: Algorithms and Applications, 2nd edition* (Springer-Verlag). Note that the given implementation is not guaranteed to be numerically stable. It might benefit from using the Numeric package for gaining more performance for very large sets of points.

Example 17-1. Finding the convex hull of a set of 2D points

```
""" convexhull.py

Calculate the convex hull of a set of n 2D points in O(n log n) time.
Taken from Berg et al., Computational Geometry, Springer-Verlag, 1997.
Emits output as EPS file.

When run from the command line, it generates a random set of points
inside a square of given length and finds the convex hull for those,
emitting the result as an EPS file.
Usage:
    convexhull.py <numPoints> <squareLength> <outFile>

Dinu C. Gherman
"""
import sys, string, random

# helpers

def _myDet(p, q, r):
    """ Calculate determinant of a special matrix with three 2D points.
```

Example 17-1. Finding the convex hull of a set of 2D points (continued)

```
    The sign, - or +, determines the side (right or left, respectively) on which
    the point r lies when measured against a directed vector from p to q.
    """
    # We use Sarrus' Rule to calculate the determinant
    # (could also use the Numeric package...)
    sum1 = q[0]*r[1] + p[0]*q[1] + r[0]*p[1]
    sum2 = q[0]*p[1] + r[0]*q[1] + p[0]*r[1]
    return sum1 - sum2

def _isRightTurn((p, q, r)):
    "Do the vectors pq:qr form a right turn, or not?"
    assert p != q and q != r and p != r
    return _myDet(p, q, r) < 0

def _isPointInPolygon(r, P):
    "Is point r inside a given polygon P?"
    # We assume that the polygon is a list of points, listed clockwise
    for i in xrange(len(P)-1):
        p, q = P[i], P[i+1]
        if not _isRightTurn((p, q, r)):
            return 0 # Out!
    return 1 # It's within!

def _makeRandomData(numPoints=10, sqrLength=100, addCornerPoints=0):
    "Generate a list of random points within a square (for test/demo only)"
    # Fill a square with N random points
    min, max = 0, sqrLength
    P = []
    for i in xrange(numPoints):
        rand = random.randint
        x = rand(min+1, max-1)
        y = rand(min+1, max-1)
        P.append((x, y))
    # Add some "outmost" corner points
    if addCornerPoints:
        P = P + [(min, min), (max, max), (min, max), (max, min)]
    return P

# output

epsHeader = """%%!PS-Adobe-2.0 EPSF-2.0
%%%%BoundingBox: %d %d %d %d

/r 2 def                %% radius

/circle                 %% circle, x, y, r --> -
{
    0 360 arc           %% draw circle
} def

1 setlinewidth          %% thin line
newpath                 %% open page
```

Example 17-1. Finding the convex hull of a set of 2D points (continued)

```
0 setgray                %% black color
"""

def saveAsEps(P, H, boxSize, path):
    "Save some points and their convex hull into an EPS file."

    # Save header
    f = open(path, 'w')
    f.write(epsHeader % (0, 0, boxSize, boxSize))

    format = "%3d %3d"

    # Save the convex hull as a connected path
    if H:
        f.write("%s moveto\n" % format % H[0])
        for p in H:
            f.write("%s lineto\n" % format % p)
        f.write("%s lineto\n" % format % H[0])
        f.write("stroke\n\n")

    # Save the whole list of points as individual dots
    for p in P:
        f.write("%s r circle\n" % format % p)
        f.write("stroke\n")

    # Save footer
    f.write("\nshowpage\n")

# public interface

def convexHull(P):
    "Calculate the convex hull of a set of points."

    # Get a local list copy of the points and sort them lexically
    points = map(None, P)
    points.sort()

    # Build upper half of the hull
    upper = [points[0], points[1]]
    for p in points[2:]:
        upper.append(p)
        while len(upper) > 2 and not _isRightTurn(upper[-3:]):
            del upper[-2]

    # Build lower half of the hull
    points.reverse()
    lower = [points[0], points[1]]
    for p in points[2:]:
        lower.append(p)
        while len(lower) > 2 and not _isRightTurn(lower[-3:]):
            del lower[-2]
```

Example 17-1. Finding the convex hull of a set of 2D points (continued)

```
    # Remove duplicates
    del lower[0]
    del lower[-1]

    # Concatenate both halves and return
    return tuple(upper + lower)

# Test

def test():
    a = 200
    p = _makeRandomData(30, a, 0)
    c = convexHull(p)
    saveAsEps(p, c, a, file)

if __name__ == '__main__':
    try:
        numPoints = string.atoi(sys.argv[1])
        squareLength = string.atoi(sys.argv[2])
        path = sys.argv[3]
    except IndexError:
        numPoints = 30
        squareLength = 200
        path = "sample.eps"

    p = _makeRandomData(numPoints, squareLength, addCornerPoints=0)
    c = convexHull(p)
    saveAsEps(p, c, squareLength, path)
```

See Also

Computational Geometry: Algorithms and Applications, 2nd edition, by M. de Berg, M. van Kreveld, M. Overmars, and O. Schwarzkopf (Springer-Verlag).

17.19 Module: Parsing a String into a Date/Time Object Portably

Credit: Brett Cannon

Python's time module supplies the parsing function strptime only on some platforms, and not on Windows. Example 17-2 shows a strptime function that is a pure Python implementation of the time.strptime function that comes with Python. It is similar to how time.strptime is documented in the standard Python documentation. It accepts two more optional arguments, as shown in the following signature:

```
    strptime(string, format="%a %b %d %H:%M:%S %Y", option=AS_IS, locale_setting=ENGLISH)
```

option's default value of AS_IS gets time information from the string, without any checking or filling-in. You can pass option as CHECK, so that the function makes sure that whatever information it gets is within reasonable ranges (raising an exception otherwise), or FILL_IN (like CHECK, but also tries to fill in any missing information that can be computed). locale_setting accepts a locale tuple (as created by LocaleAssembly) to specify names of days, months, and so on. Currently, ENGLISH and SWEDISH locale tuples are built into this recipe's strptime module.

Although this recipe's strptime cannot be as fast as the version in the standard Python library, that's hardly ever a major consideration for typical strptime use. This recipe does offer two substantial advantages. It runs on any platform supporting Python and gives perfectly identical results on different platforms, while time.strptime exists only on some platforms and tends to have different quirks on each platform that supplies it. The optional checking and filling-in of information that this recipe provides is also quite handy.

The locale-setting support of this version of strptime was inspired by that in Andrew Markebo's own strptime, which you can find at *http://www.fukt.hk-r.se/~flognat/ hacks/strptime.py*. However, this recipe has a more complete implementation of strptime's specification that is based on regular expressions, rather than relying on whitespace and miscellaneous characters to split strings. For example, this recipe can correctly parse strings based on a format such as "%Y%m%d".

Example 17-2. Parsing a string into a date/time object portably

```
""" A pure-Python version of strptime.

As close as possible to time.strptime's specs in the official Python docs.
Locales supported via LocaleAssembly -- examples supplied for English and
Swedish, follow the examples to add your own locales.

Thanks to Andrew Markebo for his pure Python version of strptime, which
convinced me to improve locale support -- and, of course, to Guido van Rossum
and all other contributors to Python, the best language I've ever used!
"""
import re
from exceptions import Exception
__all__ = ['strptime', 'AS_IS', 'CHECK', 'FILL_IN',
           'LocaleAssembly', 'ENGLISH', 'SWEDISH']
# metadata module
__author__ = 'Brett Cannon'
__email__  = 'drifty@bigfoot.com'
__version__ = '1.5cb'
__url__ = 'http://www.drifty.org/'

# global settings and parameter constants
CENTURY = 2000
AS_IS = 'AS_IS'
CHECK = 'CHECK'
FILL_IN = 'FILL_IN'
```

Example 17-2. Parsing a string into a date/time object portably (continued)

```python
def LocaleAssembly(DirectiveDict, MonthDict, DayDict, am_pmTuple):
    """ Creates locale tuple for use by strptime.

    Accepts arguments dictionaries DirectiveDict (locale-specific regexes for
    extracting info from time strings), MonthDict (locale-specific full and
    abbreviated month names), DayDict (locale-specific full and abbreviated
    weekday names), and the am_pmTuple tuple (locale-specific valid
    representations of AM and PM, as a two-item tuple). Look at how the
    ENGLISH dictionary is created for an example; make sure your dictionary has values
    corresponding to each entry in the ENGLISH dictionary. You can override
    any value in the BasicDict with an entry in DirectiveDict.
    """
    BasicDict={'%d':r'(?P<d>[0-3]\d)', # Day of the month [01,31]
        '%H':r'(?P<H>[0-2]\d)', # Hour (24-h) [00,23]
        '%I':r'(?P<I>[01]\d)', # Hour (12-h) [01,12]
        '%j':r'(?P<j>[0-3]\d\d)', # Day of the year [001,366]
        '%m':r'(?P<m>[01]\d)', # Month [01,12]
        '%M':r'(?P<M>[0-5]\d)', # Minute [00,59]
        '%S':r'(?P<S>[0-6]\d)', # Second [00,61]
        '%U':r'(?P<U>[0-5]\d)', # Week in the year, Sunday first [00,53]
        '%w':r'(?P<w>[0-6])', # Weekday [0(Sunday),6]
        '%W':r'(?P<W>[0-5]\d)', # Week in the year, Monday first [00,53]
        '%y':r'(?P<y>\d\d)', # Year without century [00,99]
        '%Y':r'(?P<Y>\d\d\d\d)', # Year with century
        '%Z':r'(?P<Z>(\D+ Time)|([\S\D]{3,3}))', # Timezone name or empty
        '%%':r'(?P<percent>%)' # Literal "%" (ignored, in the end)
        }
    BasicDict.update(DirectiveDict)
    return BasicDict, MonthDict, DayDict, am_pmTuple

# helper function to build locales' month and day dictionaries
def _enum_with_abvs(start, *names):
    result = {}
    for i in range(len(names)):
        result[names[i]] = result[names[i][:3]] = i+start
    return result

""" Built-in locales """
ENGLISH_Lang = (
    {'%a':r'(?P<a>[^\s\d]{3,3})', # Abbreviated weekday name
     '%A':r'(?P<A>[^\s\d]{6,9})', # Full weekday name
     '%b':r'(?P<b>[^\s\d]{3,3})', # Abbreviated month name
     '%B':r'(?P<B>[^\s\d]{3,9})', # Full month name
     # Appropriate date and time representation.
     '%c':r'(?P<m>\d\d)/(?P<d>\d\d)/(?P<y>\d\d) '
          r'(?P<H>\d\d):(?P<M>\d\d):(?P<S>\d\d)',
     '%p':r'(?P<p>(a|A|p|P)(m|M))', # Equivalent of either AM or PM
     # Appropriate date representation
     '%x':r'(?P<m>\d\d)/(?P<d>\d\d)/(?P<y>\d\d)',
     # Appropriate time representation
     '%X':r'(?P<H>\d\d):(?P<M>\d\d):(?P<S>\d\d)'},
    _enum_with_abvs(1, 'January', 'February', 'March', 'April', 'May', 'June',
```

Example 17-2. Parsing a string into a date/time object portably (continued)

```
        'July', 'August', 'September', 'October', 'November', 'December'),
    _enum_with_abvs(0, 'Monday', 'Tuesday', 'Wednesday', 'Thursday',
        'Friday', 'Saturday', 'Sunday'),
    (('am','AM'),('pm','PM'))
    )
ENGLISH = LocaleAssembly(*ENGLISH_Lang)

SWEDISH_Lang = (
    {'%a':r'(?P<a>[^\s\d]{3,3})',
     '%A':r'(?P<A>[^\s\d]{6,7})',
     '%b':r'(?P<b>[^\s\d]{3,3})',
     '%B':r'(?P<B>[^\s\d]{3,8})',
     '%c':r'(?P<a>[^\s\d]{3,3}) (?P<d>[0-3]\d) '
         r'(?P<b>[^\s\d]{3,3}) (?P<Y>\d\d\d\d) '
         r'(?P<H>[0-2]\d):(?P<M>[0-5]\d):(?P<S>[0-6]\d)',
     '%p':r'(?P<p>(a|A|p|P)(m|M))',
     '%x':r'(?P<m>\d\d)/(?P<d>\d\d)/(?P<y>\d\d)',
     '%X':r'(?P<H>\d\d):(?P<M>\d\d):(?P<S>\d\d)'},
    _enum_with_abvs(1, 'Januari', 'Februari', 'Mars', 'April', 'Maj', 'Juni',
        'Juli', 'Augusti', 'September', 'Oktober', 'November', 'December'),
    _enum_with_abvs(0, 'Måndag', 'Tisdag', 'Onsdag', 'Torsdag',
        'Fredag', 'Lördag', 'Söndag'),
    (('am','AM'),('pm','PM'))
    )
SWEDISH = LocaleAssembly(*SWEDISH_Lang)


class StrptimeError(Exception):
    """ Exception class for the module """
    def __init__(self, args=None): self.args = args

def _g2j(y, m, d):
    """ Gregorian-to-Julian utility function, used by _StrpObj """
    a = (14-m)/12
    y = y+4800-a
    m = m+12*a-3
    return d+((153*m+2)/5)+365*y+y/4-y/100+y/400-32045

class _StrpObj:
    """ An object with basic time-manipulation methods """
    def __init__(self, year=None, month=None, day=None, hour=None, minute=None,
        second=None, day_week=None, julian_date=None, daylight=None):
        """ Sets up instances variables. All values can be set at
        initialization. Any info left out is automatically set to None. """
        def _set_vars(_adict, **kwds): _adict.update(kwds)
        _set_vars(self.__dict__, **vars())

    def julianFirst(self):
        """ Calculates the Julian date for the first day of year self.year """
        return _g2j(self.year, 1, 1)
```

Example 17-2. Parsing a string into a date/time object portably (continued)

```
    def gregToJulian(self):
    """ Converts the Gregorian date to day within year (Jan 1 == 1) """
        julian_day = _g2j(self.year, self.month, self.day)
        return julian_day-self.julianFirst()+1

    def julianToGreg(self):
        """ Converts the Julian date to the Gregorian date """
        julian_day = self.julian_date+self.julianFirst()-1
        a = julian_day+32044
        b = (4*a+3)/146097
        c = a-((146097*b)/4)
        d = (4*c+3)/1461
        e = c-((1461*d)/4)
        m = (5*e+2)/153
        day = e-((153*m+2)/5)+1
        month = m+3-12*(m/10)
        year = 100*b+d-4800+(m/10)
        return year, month, day

    def dayWeek(self):
        """ Figures out the day of the week using self.year, self.month, and
        self.day. Monday is 0. """
        a = (14-self.month)/12
        y = self.year-a
        m = self.month+12*a-2
        day_week = (self.day+y+(y/4)-(y/100)+(y/400)+((31*m)/12))%7
        if day_week==0: day_week = 6
        else: day_week = day_week-1
        return day_week

    def FillInInfo(self):
        """ Based on the current time information, it figures out what other
        info can be filled in. """
        if self.julian_date is None and self.year and self.month and self.day:
            julian_date = self.gregToJulian()
            self.julian_date = julian_date
        if (self.month is None or self.day is None
                ) and self.year and self.julian_date:
            gregorian = self.julianToGreg()
            self.month = gregorian[1] # year ignored, must already be okay
            self.day = gregorian[2]
        if self.day_week is None and self.year and self.month and self.day:
            self.dayWeek()

    def CheckIntegrity(self):
        """ Checks info integrity based on the range that a number can be.
        Any invalid info raises StrptimeError. """
        def _check(value, low, high, name):
            if value is not None and not low<value<high:
                raise StrptimeError, "%s incorrect"%name
        _check(self.month, 1, 12, 'Month')
        _check(self.day, 1, 31, 'Day')
```

```
        _check(self.hour, 0, 23, 'Hour')
        _check(self.minute, 0, 59, 'Minute')
        _check(self.second, 0, 61, 'Second')  # 61 covers leap seconds
        _check(self.day_week, 0, 6, 'Day of the Week')
        _check(self.julian_date, 0, 366, 'Julian Date')
        _check(self.daylight, -1, 1, 'Daylight Savings')

    def return_time(self):
        """ Returns a tuple of numbers in the format used by time.gmtime().
        All instances of None in the information are replaced with 0. """
        temp_time = (self.year, self.month, self.day, self.hour, self.minute,
            self.second, self.day_week, self.julian_date, self.daylight)
        return tuple([t or 0 for t in temp_time])

    def RECreation(self, format, DIRECTIVEDict):
        """ Creates re based on format string and DIRECTIVEDict """
        Directive = 0
        REString = []
        for char in format:
            if char=='%' and not Directive:
                Directive = 1
            elif Directive:
                try: REString.append(DIRECTIVEDict['%'+char])
                except KeyError: raise StrptimeError,"Invalid format %s"%char
                Directive = 0
            else:
                REString.append(char)
        return re.compile(''.join(REString), re.IGNORECASE)

    def convert(self, string, format, locale_setting):
        """ Gets time info from string based on format string and a locale
        created by LocaleAssembly() """
        DIRECTIVEDict, MONTHDict, DAYDict, AM_PM = locale_setting
        REComp = self.RECreation(format, DIRECTIVEDict)
        reobj = REComp.match(string)
        if reobj is None: raise StrptimeError,"Invalid string (%s)"%string
        for found in reobj.groupdict().keys():
            if found in 'y','Y': # year
                if found=='y': # without century
                    self.year = CENTURY+int(reobj.group('y'))
                else: # with century
                    self.year = int(reobj.group('Y'))
            elif found in 'b','B','m': # month
                if found=='m': # month number
                    self.month = int(reobj.group(found))
                else: # month name
                    try:
                        self.month = MONTHDict[reobj.group(found)]
                    except KeyError:
                        raise StrptimeError, 'Unrecognized month'
            elif found=='d': # day of the month
                self.day = int(reobj.group(found))
```

```
            elif found in 'H','I': # hour
                hour = int(reobj.group(found))
                if found=='H': # hour number
                    self.hour = hour
                else: # AM/PM format
                    try:
                        if reobj.group('p') in AM_PM[0]: AP = 0
                        else: AP = 1
                    except KeyError:
                        raise StrptimeError, 'Lacking needed AM/PM information'
                    if AP:
                        if hour==12: self.hour = 12
                        else: self.hour = 12+hour
                    else:
                        if hour==12: self.hour = 0
                        else: self.hour = hour
            elif found=='M': # minute
                self.minute = int(reobj.group(found))
            elif found=='S': # second
                self.second = int(reobj.group(found))
            elif found in 'a','A','w': # Day of the week
                if found=='w': # DOW number
                    day_value = int(reobj.group(found))
                    if day_value==0: self.day_week = 6
                    else: self.day_week = day_value-1
                else: # DOW name
                    try:
                        self.day_week = DAYDict[reobj.group(found)]
                    except KeyError:
                        raise StrptimeError, 'Unrecognized day'
            elif found=='j': # Julian date
                self.julian_date = int(reobj.group(found))
            elif found=='Z': # daylight savings
                TZ = reobj.group(found)
                if len(TZ)==3:
                    if TZ[1] in ('D','d'): self.daylight = 1
                    else: self.daylight = 0
                elif TZ.find('Daylight')!=-1: self.daylight = 1
                else: self.daylight = 0

def strptime(string, format='%a %b %d %H:%M:%S %Y',
        option=AS_IS, locale_setting=ENGLISH):
    """ Returns a tuple representing the time represented in 'string'.
    Valid values for 'options' are AS_IS, CHECK, and FILL_IN. 'locale_setting'
    accepts locale tuples created by LocaleAssembly(). """
    Obj = _StrpObj()
    Obj.convert(string, format, locale_setting)
    if option in FILL_IN,CHECK:
        Obj.CheckIntegrity()
    if option == FILL_IN:
        Obj.FillInInfo()
    return Obj.return_time()
```

See Also

The most up-to-date version of strptime is always available at *http://www.ocf.berkeley.edu/~bac/Askewed_Thoughts/HTML/code/index.php3#strptime*, where you will also find a test suite using PyUnit; Andrew Makebo's version of strptime is at *http://www.fukt.hk-r.se/~flognat/hacks/strptime.py*.

List of Contributors

A

Gisle Aas, 10.6
Michael Aivazis, 16.7
Kevin Altis, 7.15
David Ascher, Chapter 1 Introduction, 1.17,
     2.2, 3.17, 3.18, 4.16, 12.4, 12.5,
     12.8, 14.10

B

John E. Barham, 6.1
Jeff Bauer, 4.3, 10.3, 11.1, 13.3, 13.6
David Beazley, Chapter 16 Introduction
Bill Bell, 6.8, 7.16
André Bjärby, 6.5
Luther Blissett, 1.10, 1.12, 3.1, 3.2, 3.3, 3.4,
     3.5, 3.8, 3.16, 4.1, 4.2, 4.4, 4.6, 4.7,
     4.13, 4.14, 5.5, 7.3, 8.1, 8.2, 8.3,
     8.4, 8.6, 8.7, 9.2, 9.3, 10.1, 10.2,
     10.4, 10.7, 11.2, 12.7, 14.6, 15.11,
     16.2, 16.3, 17.17
Fred Bremmer, 17.6
Brent Burley, 1.2, 6.6, 9.4, 9.5, 10.14, 16.5,
     17.5

C

Brett Cannon, 2.10, 5.12, 17.19
Donn Cave, Chapter 7 Introduction
Mitch Chapman, 4.21, 4.26
Michael Chermside, 1.5
Matthew Dixon Cowles, 10.10, 10.11

D

Olivier Dagenais, 14.2
Scott David Daniels, 15.7, 15.8, 17.8, 17.16

Xavier Defrang, 3.14, 10.13
John B. Dell'Aquila, 8.11
Rael Dornfest, 13.1
Fred L. Drake, Jr., Chapter 3 Introduction
Paul F. Dubois, Chapter 15 Introduction
Graham Dumpleton, 13.4, 13.7, 13.8
Jon Dyte, 17.2

F

Jonathan Feinberg, 4.24
Frank Fejes, 4.23
Carel Fellinger, 5.6
Doug Fort, 6.2
Gyro Funch, 1.11

G

Dinu C. Gherman, 1.15, 5.23, 17.18
Art Gillespie, 10.8
Lloyd Goldwasser, 17.5
Tom Good, 3.11, 17.10, 17.11
David Goodger, 2.3, 15.4
Joel Gould, 3.21
Nathaniel Gray, 2.11
Duncan Grisby, 2.8, 13.5

H

Jacob Hallén, 9.6
Anders Hammarquist, 15.2
Mark Hammond, Chapter 14 Introduction,
     14.10, 16.9
Sami Hangaslammi, 1.8, 3.15, 6.3, 17.12
Horst Hansen, 3.6
Dave Haynes, 5.1
Thomas Heller, 5.7, 5.17, 14.5

Andrew M. Henshaw, 2.12
Jürgen Hermann, 3.6, 3.7, 5.2, 5.9, 5.21, 6.7,
        7.4, 11.4, 12.9, 15.1, 15.3, 17.5
Magnus Lie Hetland, 4.8, 9.9
Raymond Hettinger, 2.1
Richie Hindle, 11.3, 15.12
Eduard Hiti, 5.20
Steve Holden, 1.16, 2.8, 8.9, 8.10
Dirk Holtwick, 4.11, 14.3, 14.9
Jeremy Hylton, Chapter 13 Introduction,
        13.1

J

Tom Jenkins, 8.8
John Jensen, 17.6
Richard Jones, 10.9
Greg Jorgensen, 10.5, 17.8

K

Tim Keating, 17.13
Sébastien Keim, 5.16, 5.18, 14.1, 17.14,
        17.15
Bryn Keller, 14.4
Matt Keranen, 8.13
Daniel Kinnaer, 7.8
Joseph A. Knapka, 5.14

L

Nicola Larosa, 10.12
Hamish Lawson, 1.1, 4.12, 17.1
Devin Leung, 7.2, 7.14
Fredrik Lundh, Chapter 9 Introduction
Mark Lutz, Chapter 4 Introduction

M

Yakov Markovitch, 2.6
Alex Martelli, Chapter 5 Introduction, 1.4,
        1.7, 1.9, 1.13, 2.1, 2.2, 2.3, 2.5, 2.8,
        2.9, 3.9, 3.10, 3.13, 3.22, 4.8, 4.9,
        4.17, 4.18, 5.2, 5.3, 5.4, 5.6, 5.8,
        5.10, 5.11, 5.15, 5.22, 9.8, 9.9,
        10.5, 14.7, 15.7, 16.1, 16.4, 17.4,
        17.5
Brian McErlean, 9.12
Andy McKay, Chapter 11 Introduction, 1.3,
        1.8, 1.14, 7.11, 7.12, 11.9
Trent Mick, 4.15, 4.17
Chris Moffitt, 11.5

Skip Montanaro, 5.19
Paul Moore, 17.7

N

Swaminathan Narayanan, 16.6
Mark Nenadov, 7.5, 7.6, 8.5, 9.7, 11.8, 12.6
John Nielsen, 4.24, 7.13
Philip Nunez, 7.1

P

Joonas Paalasmaa, 3.20
Richard Papworth, 4.5
Robin Parmar, 3.12, 4.18, 4.22, 4.25
Chris Perkins, 1.8, 17.5
Nick Perkins, 2.6, 3.7, 15.7
David Perry, 6.4
Tim Peters, Chapter 2 Introduction, Chapter
        17 Introduction, 17.3
Richard Philips, 14.8
Alexander Pletzer, 9.10
Paul Prescod, Chapter 12 Introduction, 3.17,
        4.10, 12.1, 12.10, 12.11, 12.2, 12.3,
        12.8

Q

Brian Quinlan, 13.2

R

Jimmy Retzlaff, 9.11
Michael Robin, 3.19, 6.9

S

José Sebrosa, 2.4
Ken Seehof, 5.13, 15.6, 15.9
Itamar Shtull-Trauring, 11.6
Noah Spurrier, 2.5
Oliver Steele, 17.5
Michael Strasser, 10.9
Wolfgang Strobl, 7.7, 7.9, 7.10

T

Chui Tey, 4.20
Christian Tismer, 14.8

U

Anurag Uniyal, 17.9

V

Joseph VanAndel, 16.7, 16.9
Guido van Rossum, Chapter 10 Introduction

W

Dick Wall, 1.6
Will Ware, 11.11, 15.5, 16.8
Aaron Watters, Chapter 8 Introduction
Julius Welby, 4.19, 12.12
Iuri Wickert, 2.8
Greg Wilson, Chapter 6 Introduction
Paul M. Winkler, 1.15, 3.23
Ben Wolfson, 15.7
Matthew Wood, 2.7

Y

Danny Yoo, 9.1

Z

Moshe Zadka, 15.10
Brian Zhou, 8.12, 11.7

Index

Symbols

<< operator, 197
* and ** tokens, 3
[?? ??] and [!! !!] for embedded code
    blocks, 103
&quot and XML editors, 392
<?xml, 396
\ (backslash), 67, 113
    raw-string syntax and, 248
    Windows global IDs and, 232
, (comma), use in packing, 4
" (empty string) joiner, 80
/ (forward slash), 113
( ) (parentheses), tuples and, 4
+ (plus) operator, 72
" (quote, double), 67
' (quote, single), 67
'" or """" (quotes, triple), 67
> (right angle bracket), 337
; (semicolon), 145
#! (shebang), 360
' ' (space) joiner, 80
% (string-formatting operator), 69, 72, 362
    named-values variant, 99
?: (ternary operator), 516
    (see also ternary operator)
_ (underscore), 352
_findCookie, 375
_getCookieFiles, 375
_getframe, 440, 441
_getLocation, 375
_read_ready, 221
_winreg module, 236, 247

_write_data, 392
__call__, 189, 205, 453
    composing functions using, 466
__class_init__, 178
__contains__, 55
__copy__, 186
__debug__ variable, 429
__dict__, 470
    instance's state and, 273
__eq__, 209
__excepthook__, 435
__getattr__, 174, 460
__getstate__, 273
__hash__, 209
__import__, 456
__init__, 169
__setattr__, 174
__setstate__, 273
__slots__, 273
__str__, 469

Numbers

4Suite's xml.xslt package, 392

A

accept, 333
Access database application (see Microsoft)
accidental complexity, 214
accumulate, 532
acquire_read, 221
Active Directory Services Interface
    (ADSI), 259
adapter class, 131

We'd like to hear your suggestions for improving our indexes. Send email to *index@oreilly.com*.

bisect module, 46, 534
BLOBs (binary large objects)
    MySQL databases, storing in, 278
    PostgreSQL databases, storage in, 280
Boost Python Library, 479
Borg class, 208
Borg design nonpattern, 208–211
    alternatives to, 209
Borges, Jose Luis, 164
bound methods, 192
breakpoints, setting in dynamically loaded
        C/C++ extensions, 497
broadcaster module, 320
broker module, 321
buffers, implementing in ring form, 201
built-in methods, overriding, 165
built-in sequence-manipulation functions,
        generator versions, 530
byte offset, 138
byte-order issues, IP address conversion, 337
bytes, contrasted with characters, 94

C

C and C++
    breakpoints, setting in dynamically loaded
            extensions, 497
    C arrays, translating Python sequences
            into, 483–486
    C-coded Python extensions (see C-coded
            Python extensions)
    connecting C routines to Python, 448
    enum type, 460
        simulating in Python, 459
    performance, measuring compared to
            Python, 488
    Python extension module tools
            for, 478–479
    ternary operator, simulating in
            Python, 515–517, 523
caching the return values of
        functions, 519–521
__call__, 189, 205, 453
    composing functions using, 466
callables, currying, 463
callback functions, avoiding Lambda in
        writing, 302
canonicform, 78
"can't pickle file objects exception"
        TypeError, 272
Canvas widget, 301
capitalize (string function), 79
cascade entries, 304

case, conversions between upper and
        lower, 78
case statement, Python equivalent, 11
C-coded Python extensions, 482
    coding the methods of a Python
            class, 491–493
    compiler requirements, 488
    debugging with gdb, 496
    implementing C function callbacks to a
            Python function, 493–496
    memory problems, debugging, 498
    new and borrowed references, preventing
            problems with, 485
    Python sequence, accessing item by
            item, 487–490
    releasing the Python global interpreter
            lock, 499
    returning None from a callable C
            function, 490
        Py_None and reference counts, 491
    SWIG-generated modules in a
            multithreaded environment, 499
The Celestial Emporium of Benevolent
        Knowledge, 164
center (string object method), 71
central.py, 421–422, 424
CGI (Common Gateway Interface), 360
    cgi module, 359, 362
    CGI scripts, 361
        location of import statements, 360
        output of, 430
        writing a script, 361
    CGI testing, 359
        directing error output to standard
                output, 361
        handling URLs in a script, 364
        using a simple dictionary for CGI
                parameters, 363
cgi.escape, 431
cgitest.py, 364
character encodings, 95
    MIME parts, 345
character sets, 63
CharacterDataHandler, 388
characters
    contrasted with bytes, 94
    converting to values, 93
characters method, 384
checkbutton entries, 304
checkcache, 123
chmod, GUI implementation, 317
chr, 93

cursor's description attribute, using for
    display formatting, 286
custom metaclasses, 472
cwd, 339
CXX, 478

D

daemon processes, forking on Unix, 229
daemon threads, 216
DAO, Jet database migration using, 293
data, processing selected pairs of structured
    data efficiently, 40
database systems, 264–299
    accessing columns by field name, 282
    different types, 265
    field names, mapping to column
        numbers, 281
    JDBC access via Jython servlets, 290–292
    lazy connections to, 287–290
    Python programming for, 265
    relational databases, 265
    SQL implementations, 266
DatabaseTuple class, 284
datagram sockets, 334
    passing large messages, 334
dbutils.py, 282
__debug__ variable, 429
debugging and testing, 425–445
    C extensions, dynamically loaded,
        debugging with gdb, 496
    classes, adding functionality to, 468
    current function, determining the name
        of, 439
    currying, use in, 464
    debugging garbage collection, 442
    interactive debuggers, limitations of, 428
    introspecting the call stack with older
        Python versions, 441
    logging and tracing across
        platforms, 436–439
    memory problems associated with C
        extensions, 498
    modules, automating reloading, 426
    starting debugger automatically after
        uncaught exceptions, 434
    strategies, 425
    tracing a class's defined methods, 471
    tracing expressions and comments in
        debug mode, 427–429
    tracking instances of particular
        classes, 443
    wrapping tracebacks in HTML, 430

decorate-sort-undecorate (see DSU)
deep copies, 187
def statement, 162
dele (poplib module), 352
delegation, 163
    automatic, as an alternative to
        inheritance, 179
    of messages to multiple objects, 203
delete_thread_storage, 218
delSpaces, 84
design nonpatterns
    Borg class, 208
    Borg design nonpattern, 208–211
        alternatives to, 209
design patterns
    Letter/Envelope, 207
    Monostate pattern, 210
    Null Object design pattern, 211–213
    Singleton, 206–207
    Template-Method design pattern, 163
    (see also design nonpatterns)
dialog boxes, 305
    creating with Tkinter, 305
Dialog widget, 305
__dict__, 470
    instance's state, and, 273
dictionaries
    auxiliary, use in processing data pairs, 40
    classes, wrapping in, 13
    constructing without quoting keys, 4
    dispatch using, 11
    entries, adding, 7
    explicit specification, 507
    get, 6
    histograms, using for, 517
    intersections, finding between, 15
    keys, mapping multiple values to, 8
    setdefault, 7
    sorting of, 38–40
    storing function results in, 519
    threads, allocation of storage for, 217
    tracking_classes, 444
    type, hash table used for, 38
    values, obtaining from, 6
    wrapping into callable objects, 88
dictionary display, alternative to, 5
diff tool, 391
difflib module, 392
directories
    computing sizes across
        platforms, 150–152
    conditional addition to search path, 148

files, reading (*continued*)
  lines with continuation
      characters, 132
  text by paragraphs, 129
  retrieving a line at random, 123
  saving backups while writing, 156–159
  script portability and interface flexibility
      in Python, 115
  searching and replacing text, 121
  string substitution in, 121
  updating of random access files, 138
  versioning filenames, 154
  writing to, 114, 119
filter, 16
  alternative to, 20
  generalization to lazy evaluation, 529
_findCookie, 375
flatten, 23
floatRGB, 319
floats, spanning a range defined by, 28
flush, 437
FlushingWrapper class, 439
fork, 231
format_exception, 430
format_tb, 430
forName, 292
Fortran
  extension module tools for, 478, 479
  routines, connecting to Python, 448
fortune-cookie distribution over the
    network, 414
fortune.idl, 414
forward slash (/), 113
FourThought 4Suite package, 380
frame objects, 431
frange, 28
from __future__ import generators
    statement, 525
FTP (File Transfer Protocol) client
    script, 339
ftplib module, 339
function calls, pattern matches based on, 97
FunctionFilelikeWrapper class, 439
functions
  assigning to threads, 222
  associating parameters with
      (currying), 463–465
  composing, 465
  current function, finding the name for
      debugging, 439
  factory functions, 173
  generators, 525

in other languages, Python wrappers
    for, 478
making available as class attributes, 177
map, compared to list
    comprehensions, 48
memoization, requirements for, 520
memoizing (caching) return
    values, 519–521
funcToMethod, 188
functors, 76
Future class, 222

G

Gadfly, 266
garbage collection, debugging, 442
gateway.py, 424
gc module, 442
gc.collect, 443
gc.garbage, 443
gc.set_debug, 443
gdb, 497
generateSQL, 373
generateXML, 373
generators, 131, 525
  iterators, contrasted with, 527
  as wrappers for iterators, 526
genEven, 527
genWhile wrapper, 527
get, 6, 362
__getattr__, 174, 460
getCommandOutput(command), 229
getConnection (java.sql.DriverManager
    class), 292
_getCookieFiles, 375
getfqdn, 335
_getframe, 100, 440–441
gethostbyaddr, 336
gethostname, 335
getItems, 406
_getLocation, 375
get_main_type, 347
get_payload, 347
getQualifiedURL, 366
__getstate__, 273
get_thread_storage, 218
getting all members of a class hierarchy, 167
get_values_if_any, 9
GIFs, inline embedding using Tkinter, 309
GIL (Global Interpreter Lock), 215
g=iter(g) idiom, 527
global IDs and Windows, 232
Global Interpreter Lock (GIL), 215

globals, 427

graphical user interfaces (see GUIs)

graphs, application-specific language for, 449

Grayson, John E., 302

GTK GUIs, building interactively, 324–327

gtk.mainloop, running in a separate thread, 324

GUI toolkits, managing options, 194–198

GUIs (graphical user interfaces), 300
- anygui package, 317–319
  - current stage of development, 319
- anygui project, 302
- building toolkit-independent GUIs, 317
- constructing callback functions for (currying), 464
- creating, 300
- for polling an IMAP inbox, 355
- toolkits, 301

H

handleStartElement, handleEndElement, and handleCharData, 388

_ _hash_ _, 209

hash tables, Python dictionary type, 38

Haskell programming language, 59

has_key, 16

has_key_with_some_values, 9

HDC (Homogenize Different Cases), 171

helper, 58

histograms, 517–519

Homogenize Different Cases (HDC), 171

Horner's formula, 537

hostnames
- finding your own and your IP address, 335
- proper coding in CGI scripts, 365

hotkeys for Windows shortcuts, displaying, 262

HotShot, 476

HTML
- dangerous tags and Javascript, stripping out, 368
- dynamic creation of, 102
- email, sending, 340
- parsing, 359
- wrapping tracebacks in, 430

HTTP
- downloads, resumption after interruption, 366
- Range header, 367

I

IDEs (integrated development environments), compatible debugging and testing, 426

if _ _debug_ _: test, 444

IMAP inbox, polling and display of sender, subject, 355

imaplib module, 355

immutability of strings, 67

ImpersonateLoggedOnUser, 258

_ _import_ _, 456

import statements, 455
- CGI test script, 360
- memory checking by, 426

importCode, 455

in operator, 55

indentation of multiline strings, changing, 83

infinite sequences, generating, 524

inheritance, 163
- enabling code reuse, 196
- multiple inheritance, 163
- Python 2.2, 165
- single inheritance, 164

INI files, 135

_ _init_ _, 169

initOptions, 196

inner classes, 206

INSERT statement and binary data, 278, 280

insort, 535

instance objects, 161
- modifying the class hierarchies of, 189
- saving and restoring via cPickle module, 272–274
- state, 273

instancemethod, 189

integers and Roman numerals, conversion between, 109–112

integrated development environments (IDEs), compatible debugging and testing, 426

interactive debuggers, limitations of, 428

international standard encodings, 66

Internet, protocols and formats supported by Python, 329

intersections of dictionaries, finding, 15

intrinsic complexity, 214

introspection, 450

I/O (input/output)
- file objects, and, 114
- locking and unlocking, 215
- random access of files, 137

XSLT (Extensible Stylesheet Language
        Transformations), 380, 385
    processors, 385
    (see also XML)

Y

yacc, 448
YAPTU (Yet Another Python Templating
        Utility), 104–109
yield keyword, 525

Z

zip, 25
    generalization to lazy evaluation, 529
    looping through multiple lists, 28
    reversal of, 22
ZIP files, reading data from, 134
ZipFile, 134
zipfile module, 134
ZODB (Z-Object Database), 266
Zope, 358
    ExtensionClass class, 178

About the Editors

Alex Martelli spent eight years with IBM Research, winning three Outstanding Technical Achievement Awards. He then spent 13 years as a senior software consultant at think3 inc, developing libraries, network protocols, GUI engines, event frameworks, and web access frontends. He has also taught programming languages, development methods, and numerical computing at Ferrara University and other venues. He's a C++ MVP for Brainbench and a member of the Python Software Foundation. He currently works for AB Strakt (a Swedish Python-centered firm that develops new technologies for real-time workflow and groupware applications), mostly by telecommuting from his home in Bologna, Italy.

Alex's proudest achievement is the publication of two articles in *The Bridge World* (January/February 2000) that were hailed as giant steps toward solving issues that had haunted contract bridge theoreticians for decades.

David Ascher is the lead for Python projects at ActiveState, including Komodo, ActiveState's integrated development environment written mostly in Python. David has taught courses about Python to corporations, in universities, and at conferences. He also organized the Python track at the 1999 and 2000 O'Reilly Open Source Conventions, and was the program chair for the 10th International Python Conference. In addition, he co-wrote *Learning Python* and serves as a director of the Python Software Foundation. David holds a B.S. in physics and a Ph.D. in cognitive science, both from Brown University.

Colophon

Our look is the result of reader comments, our own experimentation, and feedback from distribution channels. Distinctive covers complement our distinctive approach to technical topics, breathing personality and life into potentially dry subjects.

The animal on the cover of *Python Cookbook* is a springhaas (*Pedetes capensis*), also known as a spring hare. Springhaas are not hares at all, but rather the only member of the family *Pedetidae* in the order *Rodentia*. They are not marsupials, but they are vaguely kangaroo-like, with small front legs, powerful hind legs designed for hopping, jumping, and leaping, and long, strong, bushy (but not prehensile) tails they use for balance and as a brace when sitting. They grow to be about 14–18 inches long, with tails as long as their bodies, and can weigh approximately 8 pounds. Springhaas have rich, glossy, tawny or golden-reddish coats with long, soft fur and white underbellies. Their heads are disproportionately large, and they have long ears (with a flap of skin at the base they can close to prevent sand from getting inside while they are digging) and large, dark brown eyes.

Springhaas mate throughout the year and have a gestation period of about 78–82 days. Females generally give birth to only one young (which stays with its mother until it is approximately seven weeks old) per litter but have three or four litters each year. Babies are born with teeth and fully furred, with their eyes closed and ears open.

Springhaas are terrestrial and well-adapted for digging, and they tend to spend their days in the small networks of their burrows and tunnels. They are nocturnal and primarily herbivorous, feeding on bulbs, roots, grains, and occasionally insects. While they are foraging, they move about on all fours, but they are able to move 10–25 feet in a single horizontal leap and are capable of quick getaways when frightened. Although they are often seen foraging in groups in the wild, they do not form an organized social unit and usually nest alone or in breeding pairs. Springhaas can live up to 15 years in captivity. They are found in Zaire, Kenya, and South Africa, in dry, desert, or semiarid areas, and they are a favorite and important food source in South Africa.

Matt Hutchinson was the production editor for *Python Cookbook*. Matt Hutchinson and Rachel Wheeler copyedited the book. Colleen Gorman and Mary Anne Weeks Mayo provided quality control. John Bickelhaupt wrote the index.

Pam Spremulli designed the cover of this book, based on a series design by Edie Freedman. The cover image is from *Animal Creation: Mammalia*. Emma Colby produced the cover layout with QuarkXPress 4.1 using Adobe's ITC Garamond font.

David Futato designed the interior layout. This book was converted to FrameMaker 5.5.6 with a format conversion tool created by Erik Ray, Jason McIntosh, Neil Walls, and Mike Sierra that uses Perl and XML technologies. The text font is Linotype Birka; the heading font is Adobe Myriad Condensed; and the code font is Lucas-Font's TheSans Mono Condensed. This colophon was written by Rachel Wheeler.

Other Titles Available from O'Reilly

Scripting Languages

Programming Python, 2nd Edition

By Mark Lutz
2nd Edition March 2001
1256 pages, Includes CD-ROM
ISBN 0-596-00085-5

Programming Python, 2nd Edition, focuses on advanced applications of Python, an increasingly popular object-oriented scripting language. Endorsed by Python creator Guido van Rossum, it demonstrates advanced Python programming techniques, and addresses software design issues such as reusability and object-oriented programming. The enclosed platform-neutral CD-ROM has book examples and various Python-related packages, including the full Python Version 2.0 source code distribution.

Learning Python

By Mark Lutz & David Ascher
1st Edition April 1999
384 pages, ISBN 1-56592-464-9

Learning Python is an introduction to the increasingly popular Python programming language—an interpreted, interactive, object-oriented, and portable scripting language. This book thoroughly introduces the elements of Python: types, operators, statements, classes, functions, modules, and exceptions. It also demonstrates how to perform common programming tasks and write real applications.

Python in a Nutshell

By Alex Martelli
1st Edition November 2002 (est.)
400 pages (est.), ISBN 0-596-00188-6

This book offers Python programmers one place to look when you need help remembering or deciphering the most important tools and modules of this open source language. The book deals with the most frequently used parts of the standard library, and the most popular and important third party extensions. Python is an easy scripting language with a huge library that is enormously rich. *Python in a Nutshell* presents the highlights of all modules and functions, which cover well over 90% of a programmer's practical needs.

Exploring Expect

By Don Libes
1st Edition December 1994
602 pages, ISBN 1-56592-090-2

Written by the author of Expect, this is the first book to explain how this part of the Unix toolbox can be used to automate Telnet, FTP, passwd, rlogin, and hundreds of other interactive applications. Based on Tcl (Tool Command Language), Expect lets you automate interactive applications that have previously been extremely difficult to handle with any scripting language.

Jython Essentials

By Noel Rappin & Samuele Pedroni
1st Edition March 2002
300 pages, ISBN 0-596-00247-5

Jython is an implementation of the Python programming language written in Java, allowing Python programs to integrate seamlessly with any Java code. The secret to Jython's popularity lies in the combination of Java's libraries and tools with Python's rapid development capabilities. *Jython Essentials* provides a solid introduction to the language, numerous examples of Jython/Java interaction, and valuable reference material on modules and libraries of use to Jython programmers.

Ruby in a Nutshell

By Yukihiro Matsumoto
With translated text by
David L. Reynolds Jr.
1st Edition November 2001
218 pages, ISBN 0-59600-214-9

Written by Yukihiro Matsumoto ("Matz"), creator of the language, *Ruby in a Nutshell* is a practical reference guide covering everything from Ruby syntax to the specifications of its standard class libraries. The book is based on Ruby 1.6, and is applicable to development versions 1.7 and the next planned stable version 1.8. As part of the successful "in a Nutshell" series *Ruby in a Nutshell* is for readers who want a single desktop reference for all their needs.

O'REILLY®

To order: *800-998-9938* • *order@oreilly.com* • *www.oreilly.com*
Online editions of most O'Reilly titles are available by subscription at *safari.oreilly.com*
Also available at most retail and online bookstores.

How to stay in touch with O'Reilly

1. Visit our award-winning web site

http://www.oreilly.com/

★ "Top 100 Sites on the Web"—PC Magazine
★ CIO Magazine's Web Business 50 Awards

Our web site contains a library of comprehensive product information (including book excerpts and tables of contents), downloadable software, background articles, interviews with technology leaders, links to relevant sites, book cover art, and more. File us in your bookmarks or favorites!

2. Join our email mailing lists

Sign up to get email announcements of new books and conferences, special offers, and O'Reilly Network technology newsletters at:

http://www.elists.oreilly.com

It's easy to customize your free elists subscription so you'll get exactly the O'Reilly news you want.

3. Get examples from our books

To find example files for a book, go to:

http://www.oreilly.com/catalog

select the book, and follow the "Examples" link.

4. Work with us

Check out our web site for current employment opportunities:

http://jobs.oreilly.com/

5. Register your book

Register your book at:
http://register.oreilly.com

6. Contact us

O'Reilly & Associates, Inc.
1005 Gravenstein Hwy North
Sebastopol, CA 95472 USA
TEL: 707-827-7000 or 800-998-9938
        (6am to 5pm PST)
FAX: 707-829-0104

order@oreilly.com
For answers to problems regarding your order or our products. To place a book order online visit:

http://www.oreilly.com/order_new/

catalog@oreilly.com
To request a copy of our latest catalog.

booktech@oreilly.com
For book content technical questions or corrections.

corporate@oreilly.com
For educational, library, and corporate sales.

proposals@oreilly.com
To submit new book proposals to our editors and product managers.

international@oreilly.com
For information about our international distributors or translation queries. For a list of our distributors outside of North America check out:

http://international.oreilly.com/distributors.html

O'REILLY®

To order: *800-998-9938* • *order@oreilly.com* • *www.oreilly.com*
Online editions of most O'Reilly titles are available by subscription at *safari.oreilly.com*
Also available at most retail and online bookstores.